D1548831

From The
Library Of
Barb
Weston

What Did They Mean By That?

A Dictionary of Historical and Genealogical Terms Old and New

Paul Drake, J.D.

HERITAGE BOOKS
2003

HERITAGE BOOKS
AN IMPRINT OF HERITAGE BOOKS, INC.

Books, CDs, and more – Worldwide

For our listing of thousands of titles see our website
at
www.HeritageBooks.com

Published 2003 by
HERITAGE BOOKS, INC.
Publishing Division
1540 Pointer Ridge Place #E
Bowie, Maryland 20716

Other Heritage Books by Paul Drake:

You Ought To Write All That Down: A Guide to Organizing and Writing Genealogical Narrative

Genealogy: How To Find Your Ancestors (with Margaret Grove Driskill)

Now In Our Fourth Century: Some American Families. A Documentary And Pictorial History Of Some Twenty-Five Families Who Were Settled In The American Colonies Before The Year 1750, More Than Fifteen Of Whom Arrived Before 1700, And Of More Than 4000 Of Their Ancestors, Kin, And Descendants.

ISBN 0-7884-2500-5
52550
9 780788 425004

International Standard Book Number: **0-7884-2500-5**

To dearest Brittany, Bethany, Evan, Diane, Allison, Mikaila, Drake and those who are destined to follow them as our descendants.

ACKNOWLEDGEMENTS

As originally, I remain always grateful to Jo White Linn, C.G., for her encouragement in the very first edition of this effort; without her early suggestions, this work would not have been carried to completion. Equally, only Roxanne Carlson at Heritage Books would have had the patience to wade through my many, many changes, errors, and poor handwriting over now a half dozen years. I also am very much indebted to the members of the Genealogical Support Group of Crossville, Tennessee, for their many contributions, to Deane Ferguson Mills for her contributions of many early Virginia and North Carolina expressions, to Colleen Green Sims, Tacy A. Arledge Lewis and my wonderful children, Paul, Diane and Cheryl, for their encouragement in my efforts, to my adorable grandchildren for the inspiration needed to continue with this and all other of the works of my life and, last but surely not least, to the ancestors now so long gone who wrote of their times and my students who insisted upon knowing what their words meant. Thank you ever, ever so much, all.

P.D.
2000

INTRODUCTION

Since but few of the great mass of ordinary colonial men (and even fewer women) could read and write, paper was very expensive, writing instruments were crude, and postal service was either non-existent or in its infancy, messages over long distances by other than merchants and representatives of government were but few and far between. Moreover, those businessmen and traders who did require knowledge and evidence of transactions from afar had long before developed business forms of sorts—negotiable instruments—and a jargon or vernacular of their trades that required only minimal use of additional written language. For those reasons, one could wander through the streets of colonial America and, save for those in commerce, find virtually no one engaged in writing anything.

Upon entering the courthouses however, all would be different. Virtually every office of government had people working, quill pens in hand; they, the scribes, the scriveners. For a full millennium, the common law, by which all life, business, and—most importantly to those who thought in English—inheritances and real estate transactions were based and determined, had required that decisions affecting rights and duties of rich and poor alike should be memorialized, accessible, and remembered, thus necessitating courts minutes, orders, and records.

Then too, the taxing authorities, without whom there would be no income to support the government and institutions of the day, had to record identity, ownership, and exchanges of monies and credits. Finally, those legislators, who in the name of peace, the public good, and prosperity determined what actions were proper and what were not, were constrained to set forth their mandates with particularity and give notice of those requirements to the whole of society. Otherwise, those governed could not know what was expected of them.

There was yet one more institution where those learned in the "art and mystery" of writing were to be found—the church. Indeed, in the earliest of times it was only the clerics and the lawmakers who were literate as we know that term today, and, in fact, it may be argued that throughout the long, long "dark ages" only the church had clinged to, preserved, and sent forward to us what we now call archives.

The language that those myriad now gone used in creating records—that device we call American English—was and remains an incredibly rich and powerful tool. But we must remember that it is not and never has been a static language, and its many variations are not carved in stone somewhere such that we may seek out what is correct or incorrect. Mr. Justice Holmes said it best: "A word is not a crystal, transparent and unchanging. It is, rather, the skin of a living thought, and its meaning may vary greatly with the time and the context in which it is found."

So, while but minimal effort is required to read and understand even the earliest writings of our colonial ancestors, some components have varied over these centuries, and many words—like our ancestors who wrote those—have come upon the stage of the great play of history and then, as quietly as they arrived, disappeared into the soft black of the past.

The family historian must seek out the records of the merchants, the courts, the legislators, and the churches, all the while striving to remain aware that just as we have created words like television, computer, space station and gigabyte, and set aside words and expressions such as ticking and ice box, our ancestors had to do the same. While they took up German words like hex, sauerkraut, fresh, hoodlum, and kindergarten; Spanish words such as barbecue, chocolate, and tornado; French sounds like bayou, levee, depot, and chowder; and Indian words such as hickory, pecan, hominy, moccasin, and raccoon. Though they invented the likes of popcorn, sweet potato, eggplant, bullfrog, and backwoodsman, they left behind them terms and sounds no longer needed in their daily lives, such were improlificate, peel, horse tree and the long "a" sounds of England, such as "fahst" for fast, "dahnce" for dance, and "hoff" for half.

Then too, whether the words be new or of remote origin, spelling and punctuation were not terribly important to our forebears; if the message was a simple one—as most were—a detailed and precise management of words was not called for. To the merchants and scribes of 1725, the esoteric pronouncements of the grammarians of today would have been viewed as but a waste of time, paper and talent.

Just as good researchers never make judgements concerning the conduct, attitudes, and institutions of ancestors, likewise we must make no evaluations of their spelling, punctuation, and grammar. They got along very well without our rules of grammatical propriety, and used, adopted, or invented those words they found necessary. Here are a few of those myriad sounds and expressions.

ABBREVIATIONS

An entry in the early Surry County, Virginia, court records states that a jury

> "...returned for virdt. we find no caus: of accon upon ye defdts. motn: the juryes verdt is confirm. the suit dismist and the sd Hines ordrd to pay all Costs als exo."

That order meant, simply, that the jury's verdict was that the plaintiff had no cause of action against the defendant. After the verdict the plaintiff moved that the jury confirm (probably by voice) that indeed they had so decided, which they did, whereupon the court dismissed the lawsuit. Hines - the loser - was ordered to pay all court costs, and an execution was ordered in case he failed to pay those sums."

In early times, the difficulty of writing with a quill pen, coupled with the tedium arising from the many repetitive phrases, especially in legal writings, court reports, and in the daily entries of merchants and bookkeepers, considerably more so than today, made it convenient to abbreviate many names, words, and phrases. Such abbreviations were limited only by the imagination of the writer, hence the following are but a few of the more common ones. Notice too, that many given names were written by setting forth a few of the first letters, often followed by a period, colon, or the last letter, e.g, Richard often was Richd, William was Wm. or Wm:, James was Ja: or Jas, Henry was Hen., Elizabeth was Eliz., Catherine was Cath., Edward was Ed:, Law: was Lawrence, Xtoph: and Xor were Christopher, and so on.

Commas and other punctuation marks often were not used by some writers, while others did so with great consistency. Further, there were two (2) symbols commonly used in early days that we no longer employ, namely, the crossed p (ꝑ or ꝑ) and the thorn (þ) or (y).

As to those, the crossed p was used particularly for the prefixes per, pre, pro, and pur, and generally for any word commencing with a p where the following letters obviously revealed the meaning, e.g, Pish for parish, phaps for perhaps, psnt or psent for present, ppcon for proportion, pservation for preservation, psonal for personal, pbate for probate, ptest for protest, pduce for produce, pticular for particular, and pill meaning peril, etc. The thorn represented the sound th, and commonly appeared as "ye" for "the" (our ancestors were not saying "ye"), yt for it, yat for that, yis or ys for this, yose for those, yer or yere for there, etc. Some of the more common abbreviations follow.

Common Abbreviations

& caske = with cask, container
&c = and so forth, etc.
= a hyphen (-)
@, a) = at, as "at @ 10 cents lb."
10br, Xbr = December
7br:, 7ber = September
8br:, 8ber = October
9br:, 9ber = November
Ab:, Abrhm = Abraham
accot., acct., acompt, accon = account, or action at law
Admr., admr., admr = administrator
Admrx., Admx: = administratrix
aforsd, aforesd: = aforesaid
agt. = against or agent
als., als, alsoe, als. = alius, the second, also
Ano., An. = year, as in "Ano 1683"
appls, applls = appeals, as in law
Apr., Aprill, Abrill = April
att, att. = at or attorney
attachmt, attachm: = attachment, as in law
Augst., Aug., Augs. = August
bal., ball, ball: = an account balance
bbl= barrel
B.L.M.= U.S. Bureau of Land Management
Capt. = Captain
Clke., Clk., Cl., Cl Ct., Cl CT., ClCt: = Clerk (of a court or county)
cold., col.: = abbreviation for negro or black person, often found in legal documents and censuses.
Coll., Colln., Col. = Colonel
complt. = complaint
confest = confessed, as in confession of a judgement
Cort, Crte. = court
Cr or cr. = as now, a credit
cwt. = a hundredweight; one hundred and twelve pounds, e.g., "The inventory revealed three cwt. of bronze."
deced., decd., dcd. = deceased
Decmb., Decmbr., Dec. = December
defendt., defend. defdt. = defendant
demi, demi-, dem.: abbreviation for one half or smaller than.
dep., depty = deputy
D.O.W. = died of wounds
dol, $: abbreviation for U.S. dollar and Spanish milled dollar, and occasionally an early Peso.
dischd, discd. = discharged
Dr., dr. = as now, a debtor, debt, or indebted to, especially in account ledgers
drest = dressed (as in meat)
dyet = food, meals, as in a prisoner's dyet
Esq., esqur = esquire
Ex:, ex., Exx, exx: = executor, executrix
Excelly = Excellancy
exit. atta: = attachment was signed and issued by the court
exit: it goes forth, the issuance of a process, writ, ètc., by a court
exon, excn., exec., execn: = execution, as in law suits
F.A.S.G.: a Fellow Of The American Society Of Genealogists, an honor society limited to 50 members.
F.I.G.R.S.: a Fellow Of The Irish Genealogical Research Society (Ireland), an honor awarded those who have made outstanding contributions to Irish research.
F.N.G.S.: a Fellow Of The National Genealogical Society, an honor awarded for outstanding contributions to American or British genealogical research.
F.S.G: a Fellow Of The Society Of Genealogists, an honor awarded for outstanding contributions to British genealogy (London).
Febr., FebR., Feb. = February

fi. fa. = a writ of fieri facias
fiveteen = fifteen
fower = four (4)
gal., gall.: abbreviation for gallon.
Genll. = General, an officer
Govr., Gov:, Govr: = Governor, Royal Governor
grand jur, grnd jur = grand jury
handks, hk, hhk = handkerchief or handkerchiefs
hhd., hd. = *hogshead*, see definition.
Honble = Honorable
importacon = importation
imps.= *imprimis*, see definition.
inqst = inquest, as in coroner's inquest
Janry., JanRy., Jan., Jan = January
Joyne = in litigation, an assertion or claim by one and the response thereto by another
Ju, Ju. = June
judgmt, judgmnt, etc., = judgement, as at law
Jul. = July
Junr., Jr. = junior
K.I.A. = killed in action
lb.= *pound*, see definition.
Lt. = Lieutenant
Lt. Coll., Lt. Col. = Lt. Colonel
m., M = thousand
M.I.A. = missing in action
Madm., Mdm, mdm = Madam
Maj:, Majr. = Major
Mar., Mar, mRch = March
Matys., Mats:, majt. = Majesty's, as in his Majesty's horse
mrkd, mrked = marked, branded, as in cattle
M.T., MT = early, the Michaelmas term of court, November 2 - November 25
N.A. = non allocatur, not allowed
n.o.v., judgment n.o.v. = notwithstanding the verdict of a jury
non est invent, non est inv, non est inventus, N.E.I.: = notation by an officer of court that a person sought was not found; usually meant recently deceased
no. vo. = nolens volens, with or without consent
Novmbr., Novm, Novmb = November
O.C. = Orphan's Court
o.c. = ope consilio, an accessory, usually criminal
Oct. Oct = October
ordrd, ordr = ordered, order
orpht, Orpht, orpns. = orphan, orphans
O.S. = old style calendar (Julian)
o.s.p. = died without issue
P.O.W. = prisoner of war
p: = per, as in an amount chargeable to a purchase
p:pole, p:poll = per person
p:cells = parcels, usually of land (with or without a crossed p)
pds., #, Pounds = pounds of weight
Pish (crossed p), Parsh = parish
plt. = plaintiff
plu., plur., plur: = pluries, a 3rd or subsequent writ, warrant, or court order
powr. = any power to act for another, as in power of attorney
P.P. propria persona, in propria persona = a litigant who represents himself
pr, pr., prs. = two (2) or a pair; a number of pairs
psentmt = a presentment - charge - made by a grand jury
pte. = part
pymt, pymnt = payment
q.e.n. = wherefore *execution* (q.v.) should not issue
qrtr, qtr, qr. = quarter
recd. = received

reffrd = referred
reqt. = request
R. = king or queen
Rt., Rt. Honab: = Right Honorable, a title
rt:, rt. = right, as in a right of dower
rudimnts, rudmnts = rudiments
sd. = said
Senr:, Senr., Sen: = senior
Sept. = September
servt., serv. = servant, indentured or otherwise
sm, sm., sma = small
Sterl. = Sterling
sub- , sub/ = as in sub-Sheriff, a deputy or chief assistant
suffi., sufftly = sufficient, sufficiently
suite = suit, as at law
T = township
to., to-w = to-wit, e.g., "He addressed the petition to the richest residents of the precinct, to., the Parkeses, the Harrisons, and others."
tobo., tob. = tobacco
v., vs., = versus, as in a law suit
virdt:, Virdt., verd:, verdt = verdict, usually of a jury
Virga:, Virga. = Virginia
W.I.A. = wounded in action
warrt. = warrant
wch. = which
wido:, wido. = widow
wth., wt. = with
xt = next, as in next friend
xt. court, xt. crt. = next term of court
Xtian, xtian = Christian
yds = yards
yre = year

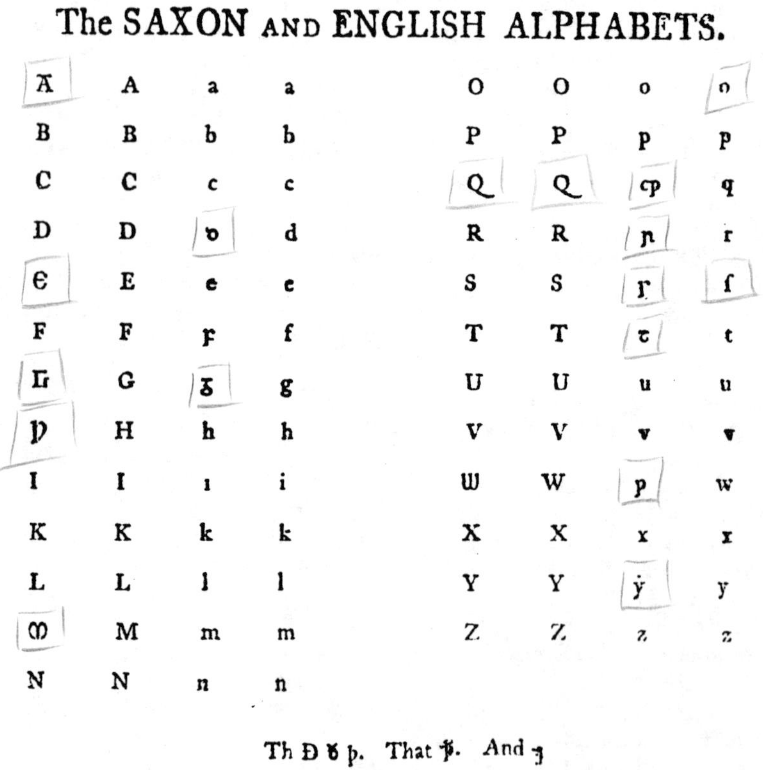

The SAXON AND ENGLISH ALPHABETS.

Ꭺ	A	a	a	O	O	o	o
B	B	b	b	P	P	p	p
C	C	c	c	Q	Q	cp	q
D	D	ꝺ	d	R	R	ꞃ	r
Є	E	e	e	S	S	ꞅ	ſ
F	F	ꝼ	f	T	T	ꞇ	t
Ᵹ	G	ᵹ	g	U	U	u	u
Ꮒ	H	h	h	V	V	v	v
I	I	ı	i	Ꮃ	W	ƿ	w
K	K	k	k	X	X	x	x
L	L	l	l	Y	Y	ẏ	y
ꟽ	M	m	m	Z	Z	z	z
N	N	n	n				

Th Ð ð þ. That ꝥ. And ⁊

The alphabet as illustrated in Samuel Johnson's famous 1802 *Dictionary of the English Language.*

1st Marines: See ***military combat units, famous.***
7th U.S. Cavalry: See ***military combat units, famous.***
8th Air Force: See ***military combat units, famous.***
14th Ohio: See ***military combat units, famous.***
14th Virginia Infantry: See ***military combat units, famous.***
23rd Royal Welsh Fusilier: See ***military combat units, famous.***
38th Infantry: See ***military combat units, famous.***
40 et 8: See ***forty and eight.***
43rd North Carolina: See ***military combat units, famous.***
82nd Airborne: See ***military combat units, famous.***
94th Pursuit Squadron: See ***military combat units, famous.***

A

a- (a prefix): from the language of Scotland, common in the ***Scotch-Irish*** (q.v.) settlements of the Southern Appalachians even now, e.g., "Tennessee expressions, such as a-goin', a-coming, a-doing, a-washin', and goin' a-fishing, are typical of the Scots-Irish influence."

a consilius, a cons.: of counsel, e.g., "A name appearing at the end of a legal document or writing, followed by the words 'a consilius' reveals that person to have been an attorney in that matter."

a la daub: food suspended in flavored gelatin; in ***jelly*** (q.v.), e.g., "Mrs. Mills served pheasants, partridges, quail, and fish a la daub."

a mensa et thoro: a separation—not a divorce—of husband and wife, literally, from table and bed, e.g., "Early separations a mensa et thoro revealed marital differences not legally sufficient for or resulting in divorces." Also see ***divorce*** and see ***a vinculo matrimonii.***

a posteriori: from or by reason of what follows; where the effect reveals the cause, e.g., "Jean could not legally convey the land away, a posteriori the ***entailment*** (q.v.)."

a sight of, seen a: See ***seen a sight of.***

a vinculo matrimonii: a divorce, as we know the term today; a dissolution of a marriage, to be distinguished from a divorce ***a mensa et thoro*** (q.v.), e.g., "Their Pennsylvania divorce a vinculo matrimonii left both parties free to remarry."

A.E.F.: See ***World War I.***

A.G.: an Accredited Genealogist; one who has passed the rigorous test administered by Family History Library (FHL) of Salt Lake City.

a'waltzing: See ***go a'waltzing.***

ab initio: from the beginning, e.g., "The court ordered the trespasser to pay the fair rental value of the property ab initio, that is, since the first day of his having been there without authority or right."

ab intestato: ownership through the death of another without a will (***intestate***, q.v.), e.g., "The court order related that Mikaila owned the land ab intestato."

abaft: nautical term meaning at or toward the stern of a ship, e.g., "Jones directed that the men arming the cannon abaft come forward for the time being."

abandon: a voluntary giving up or relinquishment with intent to not again take up the property, e.g., "Since Drake was said to have 'abandoned' the grant, the researcher knew that he almost surely was alive at the date of that abandonment."

abate, plea in abatement: a reduction in amount or of rights; a request for reduction or diminution of an amount or quantum of ownership, e.g., "The court abated as excessive the damages awarded by the lower court"; "Having newly learned of an additional child who went 'West', the lawyer made a plea in abatement that the legacies be reduced proportionately."

abatis: an impediment, defense, or other work of war made of trees felled in the path of an enemy, e.g., "In the vast American forest, abatis was a common and easily constructed military means of temporary defense."

abettor: one who aids and encourages another, e.g., "In 1676, William West was one of the abettors of Bacon."

abode: a place of dwelling, residence, "domicile," e.g., "His statement that his abode was in Smith County reveals that he likely was legally required to vote there."

abolition, Abolitionists: those of the ***Civil War*** (q.v.) period and the years preceding who actively spoke out for the freedom of slaves and the end of the institution of slavery, e.g., "***Uncle Tom's Cabin*** (q.v.) brought the abolitionists to new heights of activity."

abscess: early, the site of any infection or undue tenderness, whether within or without the body, e.g., "Asa Sherwood was said to have died in 1852 of an 'abscess in the side', probably acute appendicitis."

absolution: a remission of sins or penance, e.g., "At the point of death, he requested absolution."

abstract: those pertinent or principal portions of documents that tend to prove title to real estate; in genealogy, a statement or setting forth of pertinent portions of a writing or document; the act of selecting pertinent portions of a writing, e.g., "Jo did a scholarly abstract of the Rowan County personal property tax records"; "She abstracted the recorded deeds of Rowan County." See also ***extract***.

abuse: early, to seduce or attempt to seduce; an unwarranted censure; an ill use of anything, e.g., "In 1703 John Drake abused Ann West and so was required to apologize for his actions in open court"; "She abused the privileges given her as an ***apprentice*** (q.v.)."

abut: reveals a jointure of two or more tracts of land, e.g., "In early descriptions, the ends of property abutted and sides were said to ***adjoin*** (q.v.)."

accomplice: one of two or more people who, with knowledge, intentionally and voluntarily undertake a crime, e.g., "The old entry, having recited that he was an accomplice, revealed their common plan and execution of the crime."

accompt: early, an account or accretion of debt, e.g., "To his accompt with Wren, he charged 3 ***ells*** (q.v.) of ***serge*** (q.v.)."

accomptant: book keeper or keeper of accounts; an accountant, e.g., "The Bater accomptant had served as an apprentice to the accounts keeper at Mt. Vernon."

accord and satisfaction: a settlement made by one against whom a claim or right of action exists, e.g., "His accord and satisfaction was not considered to be an admission of the debt."

account, to go on the: to receive wares, goods or merchandise to be paid for at a later time, e.g., "Mikaila wrote that Ferguson's Mill had allowed her to go on the account for her flour and meal."

accountant: See ***accomptant***.

acknowledge, acknowledgment: affirming the truth or validity of an act or words of oneself or of another; that portion of a writing wherein the validity or truth of the document is confirmed, e.g., "At their request, she acknowledged that the deed bore their signatures"; "The acknowledgment in the lease bore the signature of a neighbor."

acquittance: a deliverance or release from an offense; a determination that one did not act as alleged, e.g., "His acquittance of the charges was noted in the Loose Papers."

acre right: in New England, a varying right to the use and enjoyment of the common land of the town, e.g., "A five-acre right in the town was equal to at least fifty acres of upland and five acres of meadow."

acre: a common measure of area; a parcel of land equal to 440 square yards, or 160 perches; 43,560 sq. ft., e.g., "A square mile is 640 acres, a ***section*** (q.v.) also is a square mile, and 36 square miles—36 sections—are a ***township*** (q.v.)."

acta publica: matters well-known to the public or transacted before officers or officials, e.g., "Her acknowledgment before the justice of the peace was said to be acta publica."

actio quod jusso: suit against an owner for a wrongful act of his ***slave*** (q.v.), e.g., "He sued Harrison actio quod jusso by reason of damage done by the slave, Kitt."

action: now, in genealogy and law, a lawsuit or claim at law or in equity; early, an action personal was a right of one person against another, an action real was by one person against another who possessed some real estate sued for, and an action mixt was one that sought the recovery of some property from the person who held it, e.g., "His action was against the administrator and sought a division of the cattle"; "His action mixt was for the return of the three cows and for the profit lost because the defendant refused to return them."

actionable: punishable, redressible, or that which admits of an action at law or in equity, e.g., "His use of the Ferguson land at Malvern Hill without permission was actionable."

ad litem: having to do with this suit or proceeding, e.g., "Since the person suing was under age, Jones was appointed guardian ad litem." See also ***next friend***.

adjoined: reveals a jointure of tracts of land, e.g., "In early descriptions, the ends of property were said to ***abut*** (q.v.) and sides were said to adjoin."

adjudge: to judge or decree; to declare that one position or contention prevails over another, e.g., "In light of the evidence, she was adjudged insane."

adjudicate: to adjudge, to decide a case or matter involving the law or equity, e.g., "As the one hearing the case, it was his task to adjudicate as to her sanity."

administrator with will annexed, administratrix w.w.a.: a person, male or female, appointed by the court to administer an estate where the will does not control or is legally defective, e.g., "The will was not witnessed properly, so the court was required to appoint an administrator with the will annexed."

administrator, administratrix: a person, male or female, appointed by a court to administer the estate of one who has died a) without a will, or b) with a will wherein no executor was named, or where he who was named in the will was not legally qualified or chose not to serve, e.g., "The court appointed him and her as administrator and administratrix c.t.a. (***cum testamento annexo***, q.v.), respectively, of the estate of John Smith." See also ***administrator with will annexed***.

administrators' bonds: See ***bonds***.

adoption: A legal process whereby one makes someone else's child legally his or her own, where adoptive parents undertake the duties of natural parents to a child and the adopted child gains the rights, privileges, and duties of a natural child; the judicial or political recognition of an assumption of the duties of parenthood by a person or persons who are not natural parents. e.g., "They sought a decree of adoption when they assumed parental duties over little Allison."

adult, adulthood: at ***civil law*** (q.v.), a male of fourteen or more or a female of twelve or more years; at ***common law*** (q.v.), twenty-one or more years old, however in some jurisdictions eighteen was viewed as adulthood; sometimes early, that age at which one's peers presumed him or her to be able to manage his or her own affairs; not necessarily synonymous with "of age" which term carries legal connotations, e.g., "The neighbors considered him to be at adulthood, even though he was but fifteen." Also see ***of age***.

adverse possession: an intentional holding of and claiming real property as against all the world and the rightful owner, e.g., "Even though Drake claimed to own it and lived on the land for three years, his rights to the land were denied, since the Tennessee State Code required eight years of occupancy before one could claim ownership by adverse possession."

adze, adz: a tool for different uses with blades of various shapes placed at right angles to the handle, used to shape wood, e.g., "Since the inventory revealed a ***cooper's*** (q.v.) adze, the researcher had some evidence of the occupation of the ancestor."

AE, ae, a.e.: as found on headstones, meaning "age" or "aged," e.g., "The headstone of Martha Midlam states that she had 'died October 17, 1890 ae 92 yrs'."

affair of honor: a duel with weapons capable of bringing death or great injury, e.g., "In April of 1826, Henry Clay challenged John Randolph to an affair of honor with pistols, in which both missed with their first shots, Clay missed the second, and Randolph, sparing him, fired his second shot into the air, ending the matter."

affiance: an early term meaning to betroth or to bind another through a promise of marriage, e.g., "The court held that he was to pay £50 and costs by reason of the breach of his affiance."

affiant, affidavit: one who, before a person authorized to administer oaths, swears or affirms the truth of facts set forth in a writing, e.g., "The affiant signed the affidavit and then ***acknowledged*** (q.v.) the truth of it before a ***Notary Public*** (q.v.)."

affinity: the relationship between people whose kinship is by marriage, and not "by blood"; the relationship between a husband and his wife's relatives is by affinity, e.g., "The children of her sister-in-law are related to her by affinity." Also see ***consanguinity***.

affirmation: an open declaration, in lieu of an oath, as to the truth or validity of a fact, signature, or writing by one whose religious convictions prohibit oaths (Quakers and Mennonites were so prohibited), e.g., "Since

Ben Beeson affirmed the deed between John Jennings and Will Beeson, the researcher had a clue to his religious beliefs."

affix: to add to, to attach, usually at the end, e.g., "His seal was affixed after the parties executed the deed."

aforesaid, abovesaid, said: words used in legal documents that refer to a person, object, proposition, or premise previously set forth in the same document, e.g., "In the will, she wrote of the 'family farm' and then of several other tracts, and distinguished between them by referring to the former as the 'aforesaid family farm'."

Afrika Korps: See ***military combat units, famous.***

age of consent: early, that age at which one might marry without the permission of the parents; now, that age is determined by statute, usually eighteen or twenty-one, e.g., "In North Carolina, the age of consent for marriage is eighteen."

aggy: malaria, e.g., "The word aggy, meaning malaria, was common throughout the seventeenth and eighteenth centuries."

agitators: See ***paper making.***

agothy: thought to be a very expensive fabric, now unknown, "Revealing its quality, John Brown's account related the purchase of 1 ¾ yds of agothy at 10S/6p per ***ell*** (q.v.), while the finest ***lawn*** (q.v.) sold but for 3S an ell."

ague root: black snakeroot, e.g., "In early Virginia, ague root was the most common 'cure' administered for a shivering and shaking accompanied by chills, the ague."

ague: an early term meaning any intermittent fever and chills; a fever, early thought to be a disease rather than a symptom of one, e.g., "He suffered from agues over many years."

ahnentafel: (Ger., ancestor chart or table) a genealogical numbering system which traces the ancestry of an individual back in time, assigning that individual the number 1. The relationship and sex of any of that individual's ancestors may be determined, since the number of the father is always twice that of the child (thus, always even), and the number of the mother is always twice that of the child, plus one (thus, always odd). "In Evan's ahnentafel, since he is number 1, his father is number 2 and his mother is number 3. His paternal grandfather is 4 and his paternal grandmother is 5. His maternal grandfather is 6 and his maternal grandmother is 7. His paternal great-grandparents are therefore 8, 9, 10, and 11, and his maternal great-grandparents are 12, 13, 14, and 15.

aholt, take: See ***take aholt.***

Air Corps: the name given that organization of military aircraft and the crews and adjunct personnel necessary to maintain such prior to the organization of the U.S. Air Force, e.g., "After World War II, those pilots who flew for the Army Air Corps found themselves in the U.S. Air Force."

air rifle: See ***windgun.***

airs, putting on: a reference to those who pretended to an affluence or station above them, e.g., "Driving about in his doored carriage, he was considered to be putting on airs."

Akron, the: See ***lighter than air craft.***

Alabama, the, blockade runner: See ***warships, American.***

Alamo, siege of the: that siege, commencing 23 February, and battle of 6 March, 1836, in which Travis, Crockett, and 188 Texans were killed at the Alamo by General Santa Anna and some 3000 Mexicans, e.g., "Jim Bowie was one of those killed at the Alamo."

Alaska Gold Rush: See ***Klondike gold rush***.

Albany pony sleigh: See ***sleigh***.

Albemarle Colony: that settlement of the mid-1650s of Virginians and Marylanders across the Dismal Swamp in the area east of Chowan River and bordering Albemarle Sound in present day North Carolina, e.g., "Many of the names known to the Albemarle Colony may yet be found in Bertie and Chowan Counties of North Carolina."

alchemy, arkemy: the ancient investigation of chemistry; also, an alloy containing copper or brass, gold in color and often used in tableware or decorative housewares, e.g., "Early alchemists attempted to make gold by mixing chemicals and metals together"; "The decorative mortar and pestle found in the inventory were made of alchemy."

alcoholism: as recently, early thought to be a weakness of the body and treated as an ailment, e.g., "For her alcoholism, Dr. Drake prescribed cinchona, opium, zinc oxide, capsicum, and purges."

ale: an ancient intoxicating drink made by introducing malt to hot water, and then allowing fermentation and adding flavoring or sweeteners, e.g., "Barley was a favorite grain from which to make English ale."

alias, als., als, alias dictus: meaning, simply, another, but usually used to mean another or different name either assumed or by which a person is known; frequently early used to denote the maiden name of a married daughter, e.g., "The writ referred to her as Margaret Driskill, als. Grove, revealing to the researcher that the first was likely her married name and the latter her maiden name."

aliquot: any fraction, e.g., "He had an aliquot share of the estate."

alius capius: an order by a court, usually to a sheriff, issued when a prior similar or identical order has failed or not been fulfilled, e.g., "The old order read 'als. capius', so she knew that since a prior capius had gone unsatisfied perhaps the ancestor had not lived there."

All Saints Day: an ancient and religious holiday observed on November 1, e.g., "All Saints Day was celebrated widely in old England and the early American colonies."

All Souls Day: an ancient and religious holiday observed on November 2, the day following All Saints Day, e.g., "In the early colonies, All Saints Day and All Souls Day usually were celebrated together."

all square: See ***square, etc***.

allay: See ***alloy***.

allopathic medicine: as now, that practice of healing early taught by many physicians and schools; affecting healing and cures through the administration of remedies and medicines, e.g., "Being a practitioner of ***homeopathic*** (q.v.) medicine, those of the allopathic disciplines often disapproved of his methods."

allow as how: meaning one may do or permit an act or admit of some alternative solution or course of action, e.g., "Even though Evan thought that the Yankee army would win the battle, he did allow as how the Confederates had some fine generals and great spirit."

alloy: as now, a mixture of metals, e.g., "In early English and very early colonial law, any alloy containing silver could be and often was called lacus."

almoner: an officer of a church or an employee of the wealthy who had the responsibility of suggesting to whom charity should be extended, as in alms, e.g., "The Fitzhugh keeper of the accounts also served as the plantation almoner." Also see ***alms***.

alms: money or things of value given for the relief of the poor or disadvantaged, e.g., "As alms, he bequeathed ten shillings for the poor of the parish." Also see ***almoner***.

almshouse: a poorhouse; a residence for those who must rely upon charity, i.e., alms, e.g., "In the 1850 census Martha Drake was revealed to be residing in the almshouse."

alternative writ: an order of a court that a person either do as directed or show cause to the court why it should not be done, e.g., "The alternative writ provided that he return Kitt to his master or come before the court and show why he should not."

amanuensis: early, a stenographer; one who takes dictation, e.g., "Before literacy was commonplace, the calling of amanuensis was a worthwhile goal in life."

ambergris: a secretion from the innards of the sperm whale, long used in perfumery, e.g., "The pantries of many ***apothecaries*** (q.v.) and ***perfumers*** (q.v.) of the 17th, 18th, and early 19th centuries listed ambergris for the making of fine colognes, scented body lotions, etc."

ambrotype: a common, early ***picture*** (q.v.) created without printing, by placing the negative on a dark background, e.g., "Before the development of the process of printing a photo from a negative, ambrotypes were considered revolutionary advances."

amenorrhoea: absence of menstrual flow, e.g., "Black snakeroot was thought to have value in curing gout, rheumatism, and amenorrhoea."

American ax, ax: as now, e.g., "Unlike axes of the old countries, after 1700 American frontiersmen added the square poll and widened the handle, and after 1780 used steel and widened and added curves to the ***helve*** (q.v.), creating the American ax."

American Legion: that fraternal society, originally formed by World War I veterans, that now welcomes veterans of all American military services and is dedicated to the perpetuation of their works and memories, and to providing for their needs, governmental and otherwise, e.g., "The men of the Marion American Legion Post appear in virtually all local parades, and proudly display their mock ***40 et 8*** (q.v.) locomotive and cars."

American Revolution, The: See ***War of Independence***.

American War: See ***War of Independence***.

amicus curiae: literally, friend of the court, e.g., "In order to protect the interests of the community, the judge allowed testimony amicus curiae in the case between the two men."

amulet, periapt: early, an object hung around the neck, thought to affect cures or have medicinal value, e.g., "Her mother made an amulet of herbs thought to cure pleurisy."

anaphrodisia: diminished sexual desire, e.g., "When anaphrodisia was present, the old doctor administered phosphorus, musk, bayberry, and nutmeg."

ancestor: any person from whom one descends, or through whom lineage is traced, e.g., "His most interesting ancestor was his great-great grandfather."

ancestral memories: the term given what some believe to be the knowledge gained genetically from one's ancestors, e.g., "Sarah often discussed ancestral memories with her Grandmother Ferguson."

ancient deed: a deed made more than thirty years earlier and kept in a manner so as to reveal its importance to the owner; a deed that appears valid and unsuspicious, e.g., "Since he kept it in the safe, the court ruled it an ancient deed and ordered it recorded, even though the grantor and the witnesses were dead." Also see ***ancient writings***.

ancient writings: writings, at least thirty years old, that bear the marks or other evidence of age and were kept with care, thereby manifesting importance, e.g., "Of the two documents, one was a copy, and the other was admitted into evidence as an ancient writing." Also see ***ancient deed.***

ancillary administration: any administration of an estate in a state, county, or jurisdiction other than that in which the decedent resided or was domiciled at the time of death, e.g., "Even though he lived and died in Ohio, an ancillary administration was sought in Pennsylvania because he owned real estate there."

andirons, chimney dogs, dogs, dog irons, fire dogs: heavy iron supports placed on the floor of a fireplace in pairs, upon which logs were burned, e.g., "The **blacksmith** (q.v.) sold heavy chimney dogs, the price being 'two shillings (2S), the pair'"; "Evan made excellent andirons of old railroad rails."

andromania: nymphomania, e.g., "The entry set forth the cause of her insanity as andromania."

anemia: early often thought to be a disease, rather than a symptom, e.g., "Dr. Lockhart treated anemia with acid tonics, arsenic, iron, manganese, phosphites, and cold sponging."

anencephaly: See ***nodden-head.***

anesthetics: in the early colonies, only opium and alcoholic beverages were known, then morphine was introduced, and by the early nineteenth century laughing gas was available, e.g., "There being no morphine or opium at hand, Billy Drake underwent amputation of his leg with only whiskey as an anesthetic."

anil: an American term meaning a shrub or bush, the leaves of which yield the blue dye indigo, e.g., "Even though in Great Britain the plant and the blue dye derived from it were both known as ***indigo*** (q.v.), in the American colonies the plant often was known as anil."

animal batt: See ***batt, animal.***

animal dishes: any small covered bowl shaped like an animal or bird, e.g., "Mikaila had an animal dish shaped like a puppy."

animal lick: See ***lick.***

anise seed, aniseed: an ancient spice and seasoning, e.g., "She used the seeds of anise to flavor the brandy."

answer the contrary: or else; means that one will answer at law for a failure to do as ordered or be in contempt or suffer other sanctions of the court, e.g., "The Sussex court ordered that a certain list of people appear at the next court or answer the contrary."

antebellum, ante-bellum: usually, those years of the nineteenth century shortly prior to the American ***Civil War*** (q.v.); sometimes, any time period prior to that war and after the American Revolution, e.g., "Of the ante-bellum mansions, perhaps Lee's home at Arlington is the most typical."

anthrax: a common, early, and deadly disease of animals, particularly cattle, also including man, in whom it was excruciatingly painful, e.g., "Upon the appearance of a ***carbuncle*** (q.v.) -like swelling and lesion, Dr. Drake suspected that the patient had contracted the dreaded anthrax."

antichresis: a civil law device similar to a chattel mortgage; a pledge by which a debtor pledges income from property to a creditor, e.g., "The Louisiana researcher must be aware of the antichresis."

antimaccassar, macasser: coverings for the arms and backs of chairs to protect the upholstery; also a men's hairdressing, e.g., "The inventory revealed a '...quilted chair with macassars'."; "Well-groomed gentlemen 'slicked' their hair with maccassar."

antiseptics: See ***vinegar of the 4 thieves.***

anvil shoot: a contest for prizes: a pastime or source of entertainment where a specific quantity of gunpowder was placed beneath a large anvil and detonated so as to blow the anvil into the air, the purpose being to see who might gain the maximum height, e.g., "There was scarcely a single 19th-century fair or carnival in which there was not at least one anvil shoot."

anvil: a very heavy iron shaping device, usually mounted on a table or bench, and used by one who shapes metal, e.g., "The ***blacksmith*** (q.v.) had anvils of several sizes."

ap-: a Welsh prefix meaning son of or grandson of, e.g., "Owen, a son of John Griffith, was said to be ap-Griffith." Also see ***O'-***, ***Mc-***, and ***van-.***

Apache War: those armed conflicts with the Apaches that occurred between the 1871 Massacre at Camp Grant and the capture of Geronimo in 1886, "The U.S. Cavalry was engaged off and on with the Apaches throughout the fifteen year period known as the Apache War."

apartment: early, a portion of a house set aside for occupation by one person, while the remainder of the premises was occupied by others, e.g., "Having been said to have a sleeping apartment in the home, it is likely that he was not a member of the family."

aphonia: a loss of one's voice, usually temporarily, e.g., "Unless it was thought to be cancerous, Dr. Lockhart administered mustard ***plasters*** (q.v.) and electricity for aphonia."

apoplexy: "stroke"; cerebral hemorrhage; usually a break or rupture of a blood vessel in the brain, not produced by an external cause, e.g., "He suffered apoplexy ("stroke"), was given ***coriander*** (q.v.) and croton oil every hour, and soon died."

apothecary chest: a small, lidded, wooden chest with drawers used to store herbs, chemicals, etc., used by early apothecaries, e.g., "The appraisal listed the value of the apothecary chest as three shillings."

apothecary, pothecary: one who concocted, mixed, and sold medicines and drugs, e.g., "The apothecaries of the seventeenth century often enjoyed a greater respect than did the physicians."

appeals (courts of): See ***courts of appeals.***

appraisal, appraisement: an assessment of the value of property, real or personal; in genealogy, usually the evaluation of assets belonging to a ***decedent*** (q.v.) at the time of death, e.g., "The appraisal of the inventory was established at 3000 lbs. of tobacco."

appraiser: See ***prize.***

apprentice: commonly in genealogy, one who is bound to another for a set period of time, and who usually exchanged labor and time for sustenance, room, training in some discipline, and very often a measure of education, e.g., "At age twelve, Kersey was apprenticed to Parker to learn the ***art and mystery*** (q.v.) of the pewterer."

apprenticeships: See ***apprentice.***

apprizer: See ***prize.***

appurtenance: rights or assets contained upon, or associated or in conjunction with, real property and considered to be of value or worth, e.g., "In the deed for one half of the land, one of the appurtenances was a right to use the road across the other half."

apricots: See ***gages.***

aqua vitae: an intoxicant high in alcohol content; any spirituous liquor, e.g., "The aqua vitae listed in the inventory of the ***apothecary*** (q.v.) perhaps was medicinal brandy or liquor."

arbitrios: in Spanish and Mexican law, taxes imposed upon merchandise by cities and towns, e.g., "In early California and Texas, the researcher will find lists of arbitrios, which are tax lists."

architectural mirror, architectural wardrobe, etc.: any item of furniture built into the walls or basic structure of a house and complimentary to the styling and architecture of the whole, e.g. "Her architectural mirror was in the main hall."

archives, archive: a repository of those documents, writings, mementos, and artifacts that relate to the sponsor of or parental authority over that facility; also, the historic materials making up such a collection, e.g., "The state archives preserves those materials having to do with its formation and its people"; "That building contains the archives of the state."

ardent spirits: spirituous liquors, e.g., "Early records often speak of ardent spirits, meaning liquors, rums, and brandies, and not including wines." Also see ***aqua vitae.***

Arizona, U.S.S: See ***warships, American.***

armed men: men arrayed for battle, e.g., "During the Revolution, and particularly among the British troops, the armed men were divided into several categories, including artillerymen, cavalry, dragoons, guards, grenadiers, hussars, infantry and (by then, rarely) pikemen." Also see ***military combat units; famous;*** and ***musketry.***

armies, organization of: varied through the centuries, however in the U.S. from largest to smallest, the units of combat soldiers usually have been:

- **army**, the largest self-sustaining unit, usually commanded by a general or lieutenant general, and named for a region or given a number, e.g., (Patton's) Third Army, (Lee's) Army of Northern Virginia;
- **corps**, a unit of two or more army divisions, and usually given numbers (now Roman Numerals), e.g., First Corps, Fifth Corps, XVIII Corps;
- **division**, a unit of two or more brigades, usually numbered or named for the commander who often has been a major general, e.g., Second Division, Hancock's Division;
- **brigades**, units of two or more regiments usually numbered or named for the commander, who often was a brigadier general, e.g., Third Brigade, Texas Brigade;

♦ **regiment**, usually numbered, commanded by a colonel, and made up of a number of companies (8 to 10), e.g., 55th Ohio, 43rd North Carolina, 14th Virginia, sometimes given names, e.g., Edenton Blues, Coldstream Guards, 5th U.S. Sharpshooters, 4th Fusiliers;

♦ **battalions**, two or more companies, commanded by an officer less than a colonel, and usually numbered, e.g., 3rd Battalion;

♦ **companies**, usually lettered "A" et seq. (but no "J"), the letter being followed by the regimental name or number, and commanded by a junior officer (lieutenant, cornet, etc.), e.g., Co. K., 1st Infantry, Co. B, 7th Cavalry;

♦ **platoons**, usually numbered, commanded by noncommissioned officers, and consisting of two or more squads, e.g., 1st platoon, Co. K.;

♦ **squads**, the smallest organizational unit, usually assigned a letter, and consisting of 10 or so soldiers, e.g., B squad, 2nd Platoon.

armoire: (Fr.) a large cabinet used as a ***wardrobe*** (q.v.); sometimes, a large clothes press, usually of better wood and more or less ornate, e.g., "Since there was both a wardrobe and an armoire listed in the inventory, she might correctly guess that the armoire was more ornate, elaborate, and valuable."

armonica: See ***harmonica***.

armor: See ***coats of arms***.

armor: See ***mail*** and see ***corset***.

armorer: one who makes armor or weapons, or one who dresses another in armor, e.g., "In 1725, in Virginia, he was a metal worker and was called an armorer."

armorial bearings: See ***coats of arms***.

arms: generally, those emblements, insignia, and colors reserved to a person or family of nobility, usually by the Crown, e.g., "His arms were similar to those of the ancient Drakes of Devon." Also see ***heraldry***, and see ***coats of arms***.

army: See ***armies, organization of***.

arrack: an alcoholic drink made by fermenting coconut juice, e.g., "Arrack was a popular drink for the affluent of the late 18th century."

arraign: to bring an accused person before the court and read or state the criminal charge lodged against him, to which he then pleads, e.g., "On the first day of the May court he was brought in to be arraigned, during which he pleaded 'not guilty'."

arrow back chair: any of several styles, usually ***primitive*** (q.v.) and often plank bottom chairs having arrow shaped spindles, e.g., "Her primitive arrow back chair had a hickory seat and dated to 1820."

art and mystery: an early expression used to describe the knowledge needed to enter some calling, occupation, or profession, e.g., "Kersey was said to have learned the art and mystery of the pewterer."

artificer: Johnson (1802) says "a dexterous or artful fellow"; often a military category of men skilled in trades, usually ranked above ***private soldiers*** (q.v.) and below other ranks in importance, e.g., "Listed as an artificer among the Yankee artillerymen was the blacksmith, Richard Skeels."

ary, nary: mountain or country, probably Scotch-Irish pioneer terms used as synonyms for any and none, e.g., "Allison inquired if the storekeeper had '...ary a ***colander***' (q.v.), to which he replied, 'No, nary a one'."

asafetida, asafetida bags, asfetidy: (spelling varied) a gum or extract, originally from the East Indies, which had a strong taste and odor and was thought to have medicinal value; small bags of asafetida worn around the neck as an ***amulet*** (q.v.), e.g., "The mother insisted that her children wear asafetida bags during the winter to ward off diseases of the chest."

ascendants: our ancestors, e.g., "Ascendants are the opposite of descendants."

ascites: accumulation of fluid in the abdominal cavity; dropsy of the stomach, e.g., "An early medication for ascites, usually called dropsy, was a tea of cowslips."

Ash Wednesday: a day of religious significance celebrated on the first day (Wednesday) of Lent, e.g., "The county court was scheduled to meet on the first Monday after Ash Wednesday."

ashcake: See ***pone, etc.***

assault: a threat of harm to another coupled with an apparent ability and intention to carry it out, e.g., "His statement that, unless she stopped shouting, he would slap her did not constitute an assault." Also see ***battery***.

assessor: a person or board empowered to determine the value of some property or asset, usually for purposes of taxation, e.g., "The assessor determined that the land had a tax value of $6,000.00."

asset: any property, including ***real property*** (q.v.), and ***personalty*** (q.v.); among assets, personalty is all property other than real estate, and in addition to tangible property—cattle, refrigerators, tools, etc.—intangible property, such as stocks, bonds, negotiable writings, legal claims against others, and accounts receivable are also personalty, e.g., "As assets, he had real estate and personalty consisting of cattle, money, accounts receivable, and stock."

assignment of dower: the legal act by which a widow's share in her husband's assets is determined in amount and set aside for her, e.g., "Her assignment of dower was made within a few days after the ***inventory*** (q.v.) and ***appraisement*** (q.v.)."

assignment: a transfer to another of any interest in any asset or property, e.g., "Many early land warrants were transferred by assignment to another person, who then ***perfected*** (q.v.) the title."

Associators, associators: commonly refers to the mid-19th century efforts to bring together laboring people and their products in order to increase their bargaining power with consumers, business and industry, e.g., "The North American and the Sylvania Phalanxes were but two of the associator groups of the period 1845-1855."

assumpsit on quantum meruit: See ***quantum meruit***.

astringent bolus: See ***bolus***.

atamita: a third-great grandfather's sister, e.g., "In Louisiana, the term atamita occasionally appears, meaning one's fourth-great aunt."

atavia: one's third-great grandmother, e.g., "The term atavia occasionally appears in early Louisiana records."

atavunculus: the brother of one's third-great grandfather, e.g., "In Louisiana, the term atavunculus occasionally appears, meaning one's fourth-great uncle."

atavus: a third-great grandfather, e.g., "In Louisiana, the term atavus occasionally appears, meaning one's grandfather's great-grandfather."

attainder: virtually unknown now: early and during our Revolution, the forfeiture of most or all property and rights upon conviction of a felony or treason, e.g., "George III believed that all pro-revolutionary American colonists should be the subject of attainder for their treasonous conduct."

attest: to swear or affirm as to truth or genuineness, e.g., "He attested to the statement that the servant had accidentally drowned." Also see ***acknowledge***.

auction, licitation, outcry: a sale of property, usually public and most often the method chosen by courts, by orally offering it to the highest bidder, usually in early times, from the courthouse steps, e.g., "The sheriff was ordered to sell the goods on the courthouse steps by public auction and outcry."

auger: a hand-powered drill, usually of large diameter. Also see ***housewright's tools***.

aumbrey, ambry: a recess in a church wall where relics and items of religious significance are kept, e.g., "The ancient aumbry of the church was brought back into use in 1975 for the reservation of the Blessed Sacrament."

autogiro, autogyro: an airplane with a revolving wing; an early twentieth-century term nearly synonymous with helicopter, e.g., "The invention of the autogiro by Sikorsky and others led to the common helicopters of today."

avoirdupois ton: See ***long ton, short ton***.

avunculus: a maternal uncle; one's mother's brother, e.g., "In Louisiana research, one frequently finds the term avunculus."

awful: much unlike now, an awesome sight; a place of great reverence or vested with great dignity (Johnson; 1802), e.g., "When he wrote that the church sanctuary was awful, he meant it was most holy."

B

B.B. gun: See ***windgun***.

B.C.G.: See ***Board of Certification Of Genealogists***.

bachelors' ball: a party or dance for single men and women, e.g., "Being new in town, he was glad to receive the invitation to the bachelors' ball."

back stick: a log of sufficient size to last overnight placed in the back of a fireplace, e.g., "He said that the back stick in the ***mansion house*** (q.v.) was so large that a horse and log chain were required to bring it to the doorway."

backbar: other than as now, a lug in a chimney, e.g., "The ***blacksmith*** (q.v.) made the irons and backbars for their new cabin."

backbond: an indemnification bond assuring a ***surety*** (q.v.) that he or she would suffer no loss, e.g., "His sister posted a backbond guaranteeing the bondsman for the administrator that he would suffer no loss."

Bacon's Rebellion: those military actions against Eastern American Indians by Nathaniel Bacon and some 500 Virginia and Maryland colonials from May to October, 1676, that were declared treasonous by Governor Berkeley and resulted in 23 executions before forgiveness was granted the remainder, e.g., "Bacon's Rebellion collapsed after Bacon's sudden death on 18 October, 1676."

badge, to badge: as now and, early, to mark or brand any living thing, e.g., "It was said that Sagittarius was the badge of King George"; "Shakespeare spoke of badging someone."

badikins, whippletrees: iron holders or separators used to keep the chains of draft animals from entangling, e.g., "To find badikins in early estate inventories is common."

baggage car: that doored car making up part of a passenger train in which the baggage and luggage of passengers and others was carried, e.g., "Virtually every passenger train of the first half of the 20th century had a baggage car."

bail: a sum of money to be paid to gain freedom pending conclusion of the case of one charged with a crime, e.g., "The privilege of posting bail—a bond—to gain freedom in other than murder cases is an ancient one."

bailey: that place in an early London jail structure from which prisoners were let to bail for crimes, e.g., "The expression Old Bailey from London led to use in the colonies of the term bailey, the same derived from the words ***bail*** (q.v.), ***bailiwick*** (q.v.), and bail bond."

bailiff: an officer of court, early with considerably more authority than now, quite usually appointed and charged with keeping order and assisting the judge, e.g., "The bailiff was directed to bring the witnesses to the court room."

bailiwick: a specific area of jurisdiction or control, particularly of the early bailiffs; also, slang for an area frequented or controlled by someone, e.g., "If he found John Jones in his bailiwick, the Sheriff was ordered to bring him in"; "He looked upon the area of Jamestown as his own bailiwick."

bake oven: unlike now, a heavy, iron, lidded cooking pot with bails and short legs, usually ten or more inches in diameter, e.g., "The bake oven was placed over hot coals drawn from the fireplace with the ***stove rake*** (q.v.)."

bake-kettle: a Dutch oven, e.g., "There was a black iron bake-kettle in the inventory."

bakers: as now, and see ***sponge.***

bale: early, a small bucket; occasionally now, a handle for a bucket or pot; commonly now, drawer pulls, e.g., "There were two copper bales among his belongings"; "The drawer bales were missing."

baled hay house, fodder house: a common, usually temporary, structure of the Great Plains and used as a house with walls constructed of bales of hay, with a roof of thatch or sod, e.g., "To his new Ohio bride, the insect laden baled hay house the Nebraskan had built was almost more than she could bear."

baler: a machine for binding hay or other plants of long stalk, e.g., "The baler owned by Cornice in 1880 was appraised at $6.00."

ball: other than the common meaning, a round projectile fired in early rifles, e.g., "The ball was placed on a small swatch of cloth and forced down into the barrel with a ***ramrod*** (q.v.)." Also see ***muzzle loader*** and see ***cap and ball.***

balloon back chairs: any of a number of styles and designs of chairs with rounded and balloon shaped backs without splats, e.g., "Cheryl's twin balloon back chairs were Victorian and were of walnut."

bandog: See ***mastiff.***

Bang's disease: also called undulant fever or rock fever; a bacterial disease of cattle that infects the genitals and frequently brought spontaneous abortions, which bacteria also often brought the dreaded undulant fever (brucellosis) to humans e.g., "When the cow aborted, he considered it a sign that his family might contract Bang's disease."

banjer: a banjo, e.g., "Many of the folks of the Appalachian mountains speak of 'playin' a banjer'."

banjo clock: a hanging wall clock, so named by reason of its shape, e.g., "Ida's banjo clock was about 12 inches tall and made of walnut."

bank note table: published lists reflecting the true worth of notes—money—issued by banks and other financial institutions, e.g., "By 1844 the Findlay Courier carried a bank note table as a regular feature."

bank: to arrange burning fireplace logs so as to gain the maximum benefit and longevity of burning, especially during the night, e.g., "He always was careful to bank the fire before retiring."

banns (proclamation of): the requirement of the Church of England and the early Catholic Church that a marriage be announced publicly prior to its solemnization; a frequent term revealing an announcement in a church, on consecutive Sundays, that a marriage was intended, the purpose being to provide an opportunity for legitimate objections, e.g., "There having been no one speaking out against it after banns had been duly published, the priest was free to perform the marriage ceremony."

banquet table: a very long table for dining, usually having three sets of legs or three pedestals, and often with leaves, e.g., "Diane's mahogany, Duncan Phyffe, banquet table was on three pedestals."

banshee: interestingly, not mentioned by Johnson in 1755 or even in 1802, from Irish folklore, a wailing woman said to appear to a family when one of them is about to die, e.g., "Jean said that the children often screamed like banshees when told to go to bed."

baptism: an important, widespread religious service or action by which one (usually, the very young) is committed to religious service or thought; in genealogy, an excellent source of dates, names of witnesses, and of relatives, e.g., "His great aunt and uncle were witnesses at his baptism."

baptismal bowl: a small bowl, usually of better glass and decorated, in which holy water was placed for a baptism, after which the bowl was presented to the parents or sponsors as a memento, e.g., "She had a baptismal bowl for each of her children."

bar medals: See ***medals, etc.***

barbed wire, bobwire: invented in 1874, wire with twists of sharpened wire—barbs—placed at regular short intervals along its length, it was a boon to the cattle business and helped solve the enormous problem of fencing, e.g., "With the advent of barbed wire, for the first time in history domesticated animals could be effectively contained."

barber: as now and with additional duties, e.g., "Early barbers made, fitted, and dressed wigs, cut hair and shaved men, and performed what we would now call minor surgery, such as bloodletting, ***cupping***, (q.v.), draining of subcutaneous blood through the use of leeches, and removal of tonsils and blemishes such as pimples and boils."

barberry: a berry of sharp taste used in making pickles and thought to have medicinal value where an acid was called for, e.g., "During late summer, she gathered barberries for pickling"; "Dr. Lockhart administered barberry juice when he believed the stomach not to have sufficient acid."

barbers' bottles: See ***cologne bottles.***

barbers' itch: ringworm; a red, itchy, scaly fungi usually spread by the unsanitized tools of early barbers, e.g., "He caught the barber's itch and never returned to Greer's shop."

bark mill: an animal-drawn circular machine used to crush oak bark to produce tannin for tanning, e.g., "Bark mills often were driven or pulled by an ox." Also see ***tanners' tools.***

bark, barque: a common tub used to cure and tan skins; a sailing ship with three or more masts, e.g., "The barks and animal skins found in the inventory reveal that he was likely a tanner."

barkeep: an early term (later, bartender); one who tends the bar and dispenses beverages in an ***inn*** (q.v.), ***ordinary*** (q.v.), ***roadhouse*** (q.v.) or ***pub*** (q.v.), e.g., "Even though early barkeeps were entertainers, joke and tale tellers, and friends to their patrons, most importantly, they were bearers of the news of the day."

Barlow knife, charge hell with a: See ***charge hell with a Barlow knife.***

barm: See ***sponge.***

barn raisings: See ***raisings.***

baronage: refers to the entirety of British ***peerage*** (q.v.), e.g., "The baronage of Britain has its roots in Roman times."

baronet: a commoner, yet a member of Britain's hereditary order of honor and entitled to be addressed as "Sir," e.g., "A baronetcy is the rank or patent of a baronet." Also see ***knight.***

barouche: a sometimes very elegant, doored carriage with convertible top, opposing seats for four, with the driver situated on an elevated seat in front and outside the passenger compartment, e.g., "Barouches were carriages commonly used by families of wealth and often had both a driver and an assistant to him."

A CARD.

THE Citizens of Washington are particularly requested to call at M. DAVIDSON'S Carriage Factory, near Mr. Williamson's Mansion Hotel, and examine the most superb BAROUCHE that was ever built in the United States, which is offered for sale. For particulars inquire of Mr. D.

Jan 18—3t

From the "National Intelligencer," Washington (D.C.), Jan. 18, 1825.

barrel: 31 ½ gallons of other than wine or petroleum, e.g., "In early Pennsylvania, oil was stored in wooden casks of 42 gallons, a bit larger than a true barrel."

barrel, scrape the bottom of the: See ***scrape the bottom of the barrel.***

barrel swages: See ***gunsmiths' tools.***

base begotten, base born: usually, an illegitimate birth; a bastard child; sometimes, one born of very low station, yet not illegitimate, e.g., "The support for her base begotten child would be the county"; "Even though base born, he rose to a position of respect in the community."

base fee: a conditional or ***determinable fee*** (q.v.), e.g., "Since the property would revert if she died without male natural children, it was a base or conditional fee." Also see ***conditional fee.***

baseball with a knife: See ***mumblety-peg.***

basic training: See ***private, private soldier.***

basin stand: a small, usually well finished stand with a shelf and drawer below, splash boards at the sides and back, and the top cut out to permit the placing therein of a large basin or bowl, e.g., "Since indoor plumbing ended their value, most primitive basin stands ended up being kindling."

basset: a card game similar to ***faro*** (q.v.), played in the colonies and in Europe during the early years (1650-1750), e.g., "Maryland colonials liked to gamble, and basset and faro were two of their favorite games."

bat, batt, butter bat: wooden paddles used variously for stirring, e.g., "In addition to her butter bat, she had a laundry bat used to stir clothes while they were in boiling soap water."

bat, brick: See ***brick-bat.***

batavia: probably a fabric or cloth (***stuff***, q.v.) of higher quality, e.g., "In the late 18th century the fabric merchants Kuhn & Risberg advertised '***persian*** (q.v.) and batavias'."

bathes: See ***take the waters.***

bats in his (her, their) belfry: a friendly suggestion that someone might not be totally rational, e.g., "When the little girls suggested that they might wear their grandfather's work clothes and boots, with a smile Winnie told them they surely had bats in their belfry."

batt, animal: apparently a small, yet specific quantity of animal hair to be used for the making of hats, e.g., "He wrote of his pride in having 'needed 86 beaver batts' that day in his business."

batt, batting: raw, usually cotton or wool, and sometimes fiber or hair, sewn inside or beneath cloth or fabric to add body, thickness, or insulation, e.g., "She used cotton batting in her quilts."

battalion: See ***armies, organization of.***

battery: the striking of another, e.g., "He was charged with assault and battery, since he had threatened her (the assault) and then struck her (the battery)." Also see ***assault.***

batting: See ***batt.***

battle commission: See ***commissioned officers, etc.***

Bay Psalm Book: printed first in 1640, and running through 27 editions before 1750, doubtless the colonial bestseller of all time; a song book of lyrics without music, resulting in different melodies and timing by virtually every congregation, e.g., "While the words were from the Bay

Psalm Book in both cases, the New Jerseyites hardly recognized the hymns of Yorktown."

bay: in genealogy, a color; a brown or dark red-brown horse that is lighter brown and more red than the color chestnut, e.g., "He described the horse bequeathed to his second son as 'a bay named Libby'." Also see ***sorrel, chestnut, dun, roan, gray, black, buckskin, Appaloosa, and pinto (painted).***

beaker: early, a glass or cup used for drinking liquids; later and now, lipped glass containers of varying sizes used by chemists, e.g., "There were three beakers in the inventory."

beam: a large, strong piece of lumber; a balance or the bar of a balance ("beam and balance") from which scales are suspended, e.g., "The barn beams were 8 X 8 oak"; "The 'thin wooden beam' mentioned in the inventory likely was that of a scale, since beams of wood were seldom so described and inventoried."

bean, beaned, beanie: unknown to Johnson, one's head; any small, flat covering for the head, e.g., "He said that he had been beaned, meaning hit in the head"; "He smilingly referred to the skull cap—yarmulke—of his Jewish friend as a beanie."

bearbaiting, bear baiting: the early sport of inducing several dogs to attack a chained bear, e.g., "Gruesome as it now seems, bearbaiting was a popular pastime at early fairs and carnivals."

bearing tree: a mete; a land or property line tree monument, not usually a corner, from which the distance and direction of the next course was measured, e.g., "From the northwest bearing tree—a giant oak—the west line extended 120 poles south to an ash in the creek bank." Also see ***metes and bounds.***

beast: See ***work beasts.***

beasties: small animals, whether young or old; derived from the early practice of referring to all creatures other than fish, birds and insects as beasts, e.g., "Sarah's father referred to squirrels, chipmunks, and groundhogs as beasties."

beaten corn: corn that has been pounded, rather than ground, into fine granules, e.g., "In 1634 the Salem (MA) records revealed that Stephen Deane had beaten corn for the Plymouth Colony."

becker: a wooden dish for serving, e.g., "There were two beckers in the inventory."

bed: unlike now, usually a ***tick*** (q.v.), e.g., "The 1679 inventory listing of a flock bed referred to a rag (and scrapcloth) filled ticking bag—a tick—while the ***bedstead*** (q.v.) was the frame upon which the tick was placed."

bed and furniture: a common early expression meaning a specific bed (as we know it) and all that accompanied it, located in a certain room used as for sleeping, e.g., "The ***bequest*** (q.v.) of his bed and furniture meant that she was to receive the ***bedstead*** (and valance, if there was one), the ***tick***, a ***chest***, the ***curtains***, a ***rug***, and a ***comforter*** (all, q.v.)."

bed lounge: See ***sofa bed.***

bed warmer: a usually long-handled, metal pan with a lid into which were placed hot coals, the same rubbed over the sheets to warm the bed before retiring, and sometimes left within the bed to provide warmth for the feet, e.g., "To the pleasure of the elders of the family, through the use of the bed warmer the chill was taken from the bed."

Bedlam: originally, the hospital of St. Mary in London (Bethlehem), constructed c1250 and used as an insane asylum after about 1400; the anguish, screaming, and incoherent babbling heard there led to the term, e.g., "The anger vented by the crowd was almost bedlam."

Bedloe's Island: See ***Liberty Island.***

bedroom: early, usually the main sleeping room or rooms on the first floor, e.g., "The head of the household and his wife usually occupied the bedroom, and the children slept in ***chamber*** (q.v.) or chambers on a higher floor."

bedside table: now called a night stand; early, any of the many styles and designs of small, usually rectangular and single-drawered tables placed beside a bed for a lamp, medicines, pictures, etc., e.g., "Diane had a walnut bedside table for each of the rooms."

bedsores: (decubitis) those lesions—often causing deep scars—brought about by protracted stays in beds, early thought necessary to healing and recuperation, e.g., "Having lain in the bed for six weeks after the amputations, Billy Drake's bedsores were extensive and remained as deep scars for the rest of his life."

bedstead: See ***stead***, and also see ***bedstead and cord.***

bedstead and cord: now called a bed frame, or simply a bed; instead of slats, bedsteads (frames) often had rope strung horizontally and longitudinally within them, upon which a "bed" (ticking bag, later a mattress) was placed, e.g., "In her inventory were 2 bedsteads and cords, and 2 ***rugs*** (q.v.)."

bee hives: See ***scaps.***

Beecher's Bibles: name given to Sharp's rifles in 1856 by the Free States Party, the same to be used in the Kansas border wars, e.g., "Connor's pioneer relatives of Lawrence, Kansas were fortunate to avoid the wrath of Beecher's Bibles."

beehive hut: a common dwelling for the early poor, shaped like a beehive with a domed top and usually straight sides, usually made of sticks and thatch, e.g., "American Indians and early settlers often constructed beehive huts."

beer: as now, e.g., "In addition to those of today, fermented beers made of spruce oil or extract, molasses, ginger, and roots were common."

belfry: somewhat unlike now, the place from which bells, usually of a church, were rung, e.g., "While now we usually speak of bells being in a belfry, formerly they were considered to be above the belfry where those ringing them stood to do so."

Belgian: a breed of heavy, powerful, draft (draught) horses, popular in America, and originally bred in Belgium and northern Europe, e.g., "His team was made up of four fine Belgians." Also see ***draft animals.***

bell glass: a bell-shaped, glass dome used to display mementos; a domed glass used to protect young plants, e.g., "Her wedding shoes were placed in the bell glass and it, then, displayed on the mantle."

bell makers, bell casters: those who had knowledge of brass, alloys, and their working, and who manufactured—cast—bells, chimes, pipes for organs, etc., e.g., "Bells and bell makers were vitally important, especially to early churches, since bells often were tolled at births, marriages, deaths, when services were to begin, and often to inform the citizenry of emergencies or of the time of day, especially noon." Also see ***brasiers***, etc.

belladonna (deadly nightshade): an extract of belladonna roots and leaves were widely used as an antiseptic or as a heart and respiratory stimulant, e.g., "Dr. Drake regularly administered belladonna for heart palpitations."

bellman: a person who stood a night watch in early New England and was charged with the duty of tolling a bell at hours and sometimes half-hours, e.g., "In 1706 Sherwood was hired as the town bellman and was to serve between dusk and daylight every night except Thursday."

bellows: a hinged, sealed device, which, through opening and closing, forced air to a fire, e.g., "Through the use of his large bellows, the ***blacksmith*** (q.v.) was able to generate enough heat to make iron quite workable."

bellwether, belwether: early, the male sheep with a bell attached that is the leader of the flock; now, a person or place who or which has taken on a role of leadership or dominance in some field, e.g., "Maggie Carner's reference to the belwether being her son's pet would hardly be understood today"; "For years, Cambridge, Ohio, was the bellwether of the decorative pottery industry in the U.S."

belt loom, braid loom: a common small loom used to make belts, headbands, hairbands, straps, and decorative braiding, etc., e.g., "As an old lady, she enjoyed making items for her grandchildren on the belt loom."

bench shears: See ***coppersmiths' tools.***

bench warrant: a warrant issued from a judge during a session of court ordering the immediate seizure or arrest of a person, e.g., "The court, upon hearing the witnesses, immediately issued a bench warrant for Parker."

benefice: See ***rectory.***

beneficiary: one who benefits from an act of or provision made by another; one who inherits from another is said to be that person's beneficiary, e.g., "Sarah was one of the beneficiaries of his insurance."

benefit of clergy, pleaded their clergy: an ancient exemption from execution granted, first, to members of the clergy even of the lowest station, and later to all who could read (usually the Fifty First Psalm), e.g., "Having 'prayed his clergy'—claimed benefit of clergy—he was ordered transported to the Virginia colony."

bengal: a common, early striped muslin, e.g., "There was an ***ell*** (q.v.) of bengal charged to Anne's 1778 account."

benjamin: a popular, tailored man's coat of the Victorian and early Edwardian periods, said to be named for Prime Minister Benjamin Disraeli, e.g., "Among his belongings were bands, ***cravats*** (q.v.), knee stockings, and a fine ***worsted*** (q.v.) benjamin."

benzoin: a resin, often used as a stimulant and expectorant and as a base for perfumes and colognes, e.g., "Benzoin was a staple in the medicine chest of the country Doctor"; "As a ***perfumer*** (q.v.), Evan maintained a large supply of benzoin to be used as a base."

bequest, bequeath: a will provision directing that ownership in specific personal property is to be transferred to a named person or persons, e.g., "His bequest was a cow and a calf"; "She ***devised*** (q.v.) forty acres to her son, and bequeathed her favorite valance bed to her daughter."

beriberi, beri-beri: a disease caused by a lack of Vitamin B and common among early settlers and sailors, the symptoms being emaciation and swollen and painful, sometimes paralyzed, hands and feet, e.g., "Early

Virginia settlers frequently had no eggs, vegetables, nor citrus fruits in winter, hence some suffered from beriberi."

beryl: a semi-precious stone used as jewelry, frequently found in early inventories, e.g., "She had two beryls, an amber, and a gold ring."

Bess: See ***Good Queen Bess.***

best evidence (rule of): the best evidence of which a certain proposition is susceptible; original, as opposed to that which derives from some original source, e.g., "Rather than a newspaper account, a tombstone is the best evidence of the place of burial of that person."

betroth, betrothal, betrothed: an exchange of promises to marry, e.g., "As his intended wife, she was said to be betrothed to him."

betterment: an improvement (beyond a repair) to an estate that increases its value, e.g., "The court decided that the administrator was entitled to be compensated for the betterment of the structures."

betty lamp, phoebe lamp: betty lamps were pre-kerosene, shallow, open bowl-shaped lamps with a nipple through which a rag was drawn and lit, the other end resting in grease or ***tallow*** (q.v.); phoebe lamps were the same, but had a dish or small pan to catch the drippings, e.g., "With the advent of kerosene, housewives were glad to be rid of the smoking, dirty, and often stinking, betty and phoebe lamps."

bettys, Betties: See ***desserts, early.***

beyond a reasonable doubt: the highest and most exacting measure of proof in the law; that measure of proof considered beyond the requirements of genealogical research, e.g., "Where persons are charged with crimes, the law requires that if a conviction is to be had the proof against them be such as to convince the jurors or the judge of guilt beyond a reasonable doubt."

beyond sea, ouster le mer, over sea: beyond the control or jurisdiction—the 'legal reach'—of a colonial government, e.g., "The sheriff had learned that the accused criminal had boarded a sea-going vessel for parts unknown, so the warrant was returned to the court endorsed 'The defendant is beyond sea'."

bib and tucker, one's best bib and tucker: early, a cloth or blouse—bib—worn over a usually muslin or linen ***tucker*** (q.v.), both serving to cover the bosom of a lady; later and now, an expression meaning to dress well or for a special occasion, e.g., "Preparing for the wedding, Maggie told the girls to wear their very best bibs and tuckers."

Bible box, Bible stand: a small easel or box-shaped stand used for family devotions, usually made of better wood, strong and wide enough to hold a large opened Bible, often with a hinged top surface revealing a compartment to store the Bible for protection, and often kept in the parlor, better room, or near the dining table, e.g., "Cheryl's Bible stand was of walnut and her initials had been inlaid in the surface."

bickern: See ***coppersmiths' tools.***

bicycle: See ***high wheel cycle.***

big house: See ***plantation house.***

Big Red One: See ***military combat units, famous.***

bigamy: the act of entering into a marriage with one person while still legally married to another, where such a second marriage is illegal, e.g., "***Polygamy*** (q.v.) as practiced by Mormons was not bigamy, since in the latter there is criminal intent."

biggin: a cap or nightcap; a child's cap, e.g., "'...Ma in her kerchief and I in my cap....' equally could have been written '...kerchief and biggin'."; "Diane instructed her eldest daughter to see to it that her little sister wore her biggin when she went out to play."

big-wig, bigwig, big wig: derived form the larger size of the early wigs worn by the wealthy; slang and an often derisive reference to a person considered by himself or others to be important in life, e.g., "Jean said that Jerry acted like a big-wig, when in fact he was little more than a spoiled affluent man."

bile: a body fluid that aids in digestion, early thought to be a critical substance in diagnosing disease and affecting cures, e.g., "Black or yellow bile were thought to cause and be medical evidence of mental illness." Also see ***humours***.

bilge, bilge water, bilged: the deepest portion of the hold of a ship, above which all storage and activity takes place: a superlative used to compare taste or flavor of a liquid with the rancid water that results from small leaks and accumulates in the lowest part of a ship: to have a leak in the lower portion of a ship, e.g., "Measurements of the water in the bilge were evidence of leaks and of the seaworthiness of a vessel"; "He remarked that the beer served by the innkeeper tasted like bilge water"; "The records reveal that, in March of 1821, the 'ship *Argonaut* was bilged 1½ miles east of Portsmouth light'."

bilious fever: an inexact early description of any fever attended by yellow discoloration of the skin, usually thought to have been caused by an excess of bile and/or a liver dysfunction, e.g., "She was most concerned over her husband's health, since his bilious fever likely was a sign of serious illness or ensuing death."

bilious, biliousness: a condition now known to result from inadequate liver function, but early thought to result from an excess of ***bile*** (q.v.), hence the term, e.g., "The 'bilious plague' that appeared in Connecticut from 1794 through 1796 may have been yellow fever."

bill and crossbill: the means or complaint by which a legal action was commenced, the crossbill (cross petition, cross complaint) being a claim by the defendant against that person filing or bringing the bill (petition, complaint), e.g., "His bill was in ***assumpsit*** (q.v.), as was the crossbill."

bill of credit: a promissory note, usually issued by a government, intended to substitute for money, e.g., "The bills of credit issued by the Continental Congress were viewed with suspicion by virtually all merchants."

bill of exchange: an order or request by one person directing another to pay a certain sum to still a third person, often used in the American colonies as money, e.g., "Early planters often used bills of exchange in their trade and commerce with England."

bill of goods, sold a, bought a, etc.: meaning bested or being taken advantage of in a bargain as a result of buying merchandise from a list or an advertisement—a bill—without first examining the items to be purchased, e.g., "Mikaila admitted that she surely had bought a bill of goods when she bought from the salesman."

bill of lading: a writing given by a transporter, such as a ship's master, acknowledging his receipt of goods in a certain quantity and condition, often used as money in the early colonies, e.g., "There being a shortage of currency, he used bills of lading as a quite satisfactory substitute."

bill of sale: a written document evidencing the sale of personal property (sometimes including slaves) from one person to another, often recorded and indexed with early deeds, e.g., "I will need a bill of sale to confirm my purchase of the slaves, Kitt and Cloe."

billiard and pea: early, a gambling game similar to modern billiards, and played on a flat table with pockets, e.g., "Among the games, the 1679 Judith Parker inventory revealed a billiard and pea."

billious: See ***bilious fever.***

bills: early, a word of multiple meanings, e.g., "To the 18th-or 19th-century wife, a bill might mean a bird's beak, a hatchet with a hooked point, any written paper concerning debts, an account with a merchant, an act of a legislature, a physician's prescription, or an advertisement or handbill."

Billy Yank: a Union soldier or other Union serviceman during the Civil War, e.g., "Virtually all of the South referred to the Union men in arms as 'Billy Yanks'." Also see ***Rebels.***

billy: a cheap or often primitive pot or handled pan used to boil tea, coffee, soups, or other liquid sustenance at an open fire, e.g., "The tramps usually carried their billys in a sack over their shoulder or hanging from their waist."

bird gun: See ***shotgun.***

bird spit: a metal pan with feet used to roast small pieces of meat, birds, and animals, e.g., "There were three ***trivets*** (q.v.) and a bird spit in the inventory."

birding piece: See ***shotgun.***

birds eye: a common ***stuff*** (q.v.) with a small round pattern similar to the eye of a bird, e.g., "The inventory revealed that she had two summer dresses of birds eye."

birthing room: that room, having a fireplace or being near one or the kitchen, where prospective mothers were placed when their time was at hand, e.g., "Birthing rooms were always one of the warmer rooms of the house and usually had ready access to the kitchen by reason of the need for warm water."

biscuit ware, bisque ware: unglazed porcelain, very common through the Victorian era, and even down to now, e.g., "Her collection of high quality biscuit ware had been gathered over many years."

bishop: a favored intoxicating drink made of wine, oranges, and sugar, e.g., "When oranges were available, the innkeeper offered bishops to his customers."

bishopric: the totality of benefits, assets, duties, and jurisdiction of a bishop, e.g., "The bishopric of Winchester was formed in 1704."

bit: that implement (metal, rope, or leather) placed in the mouth of a horse and connected to the reins or harnessing by which commands are relayed to the animal; a metal drilling tool turned by a ***brace*** (q.v., early) or by a drill (now), e.g., "The horse took the bit in his teeth and ran wild"; "Braces and bits were indispensable to the wagonmaker."

bitch: a common term used to describe a female dog, early and now, e.g., "His Red Bone bitch had eight pups." Also see ***slut.***

bites (poisonous): animal poisons not being understood, unusual remedies were prescribed, e.g., "His scorpion bite was treated by applying silver nitrate and potassium hydroxide to the wound and by giving the patient alcohol and ammonia to drink."

bitters: early, a strong intoxicating drink, often taken and prescribed for their supposed (often, pretended) medicinal value; later, strong spices or seasoning made from leaves or roots, usually used in liquors and occasionally in foods, e.g., "After a long day, he always insisted on having his bitters"; "Cheryl's favorite fruitcake recipe called for a teaspoon of Angostura bitters."

bittlin: a milk bowl, usually of wood or glass, and occasionally of metal or pewter, e.g., "Listed among Diane's kitchen utensils was a pewter bittlin."

black betty: a spirituous liquor, given as a reward to participants in a wedding; a bottle of whiskey, e.g., "The guests raced on horseback from a point a mile or so away to the bride's house, the winner receiving a bottle of black betty as a prize"; "Many a Civil War soldier spoke of the appearance of black betty in the camp."

black book: See ***liber niger.***

Black Codes: those legislative enactments following the ***Civil War*** (q.v.) by which the Southern states sought to subvert the rights of the Negro, e.g., "One of the counteracting results of the Black Codes was the ***Freedman's Bureau*** (q.v.)."

Black Death: See ***bubonic plague.***

Black Dutch: Sephardic Jews who married Dutch Protestants to escape the Inquisition, many of their descendants later moving to the Americas, the "black" referring to their dark hair and complexions; perhaps rarely, German immigrants from the Black Forest region, e.g., "For the most part, the Black Dutch came after 1740."

black eyed peas: See ***cow peas.***

Black Hawk War: the name given the defeat of the upper Mississippi Sauk and Fox Indians under Chief Black Hawk in 1832, e.g., "At age 23, Lincoln was a Captain of Volunteers in the Black Hawk War."

black maria: a closed wagon used to move prisoners about; a "paddy wagon", e.g., "References to black marias are not uncommon in early New Jersey records."

black pudding, blood pudding: a common pudding made of corn meal, blood from swine or cattle, and seasoning, e.g., "Black pudding was a common dish in both the British Isles and the early American colonies."

Black Sheep Squadron: See ***military combat units, famous.***

black sheep: a reprobate or person thought to have a undesirable or reprehensible character, e.g., "Having been jailed twice, he was branded the family black sheep."

black snakeroot: See ***rattlesnake root.***

black strap molasses: See ***molasses.***

Black Thursday: See ***Roaring Twenties.***

Blackbeard: See ***pirates.***

blacking case, blacking cabinet: a small, usually decorated, wooden box seat, with a raisable top concealing a compartment for storage of materials used to clean and shine—"blacken"—shoes and boots, e.g., "Only the wealthy or near so had extravagances such as a blacking case."

blackleg: one who frequents places of gambling, and who gains every advantage that is not illegal; one whose conduct borders on being, yet is not quite, illegal, e.g., "Because of his incessant borderline conduct at the racetrack with touts and the unwary, he was commonly referred to as a blackleg."

blacksmith: one who works with iron, e.g., "The village blacksmith was a most vital and needed member of the community."

blacksmiths' tools: as now, e.g., "Forges, bellows, tongs of various sizes, and a quantity of iron appearing in an estate inventory likely reveal the work of a blacksmith." Also see ***blacksmith***.

blacktongue: pellagra; caused by a niacin deficiency, a disease causing severe diarrhea, nervous disorders, and blotches on and scaling of the skin, e.g., "The often fatal blacktongue ravaged the neighborhood of Tarboro in 1844 and 1845."

blain: very early, a "pustule"; an early term for any blister or seeping swelling in the skin, e.g., "Because she thought that the swelling had been caused by the cold and wet weather, Mikaila described it as a chillblain."

blanc mange: a sweet pudding, now largely unknown, made from the extract of almonds or vanilla, rum, cornstarch, and gelatin, e.g., "Before she died, Sarah's grandmother gave her a recipe for blanc mange."

blanket box: a common item of early furniture; a lidded chest without drawers used to store blankets and clothes and to protect the same against insects and moths, e.g., "As might have been expected, the inventory listed two blanket boxes."

blanket chest: usually, a short-legged chest with a top hinged upward, and often with a cedar lining, designed to store blankets safe from insects, mice, etc., e.g., "Allison's walnut blanket chest was lined with cedar."

blast, black stem rust: a fungus that often destroyed early Northeast and Midwest wheat crops, e.g., "Before learning that blast resulted from planting wheat near the fungus-bearing barberry, farmers thought the disease was caused by a 'vapors breaking out of the Earth'."

bleeding: the process of letting blood by opening a vein or artery, the same thought to have healing powers through the reduction of internal pressures, e.g., "The ***chirurgeons*** (q.v.) bled Washington many times before his death of pneumonia, which actions greatly weakened him." Also see ***cupping*** and see ***phlebotomy***.

blimp: See ***lighter than air craft.***

blind tiger: the house of a bootlegger who permitted drinking on the premises, e.g., "He was said to spend every evening with the blind tiger."

blinders: that part of animal harnessing that limits peripheral vision, and so causes their attention to be forward, e.g., "He used blinders on the team to prevent the animals from being distracted."

blister, metal: other than our common meaning, early, iron that has been fired in such a way to cause it to absorb carbon and become steel, e.g., "The need for better steel and the lack of uniformity in the hardness of blister caused the early founders to reheat and draw it under water."

blister: See ***poultice***.

blistering: one of the methods, along with bleeding, vomiting, and sweating, by which the bodily humours were thought to be purged, adjusted, or balanced, e.g., "Blistering was prescribed when it was thought that an excess of certain humours was the cause of some ailment."

block printers: those who printed wallpaper and cloth, e.g., "The ancient art of the block printers is alive yet today, especially in the business of supplying historical architects and restorers."

blockade runners: See ***warships, American.***

blocks, blocks and tackle, block and tackle: pulleys (blocks) and rope (tackle) so arranged as to gain mechanical advantage, common in early and recent rural and work settings, e.g., "With the blocks and tackle, one man could easily move a thousand pounds." Also see ***rigging.***

blood pudding: See ***black pudding.***

bloodletter, bloodlet: one who was knowledgeable in ***phlebotomy*** (q.v.); to take blood from a person e.g., "The old woman was the family bloodletter." See ***cupping***, and see ***bleeding.***

bloodstone: a deep green and blood-red semi-precious stone used as jewelry, often found in early inventories, e.g., "She had an amber necklace, a silver pin, and a bloodstone ring."

bloody flux, flux: See ***dysentery.***

bloom pin: See ***tanners' and curriers' tools.***

blow: as now, to strike; the act of a fly in depositing eggs in dead, putrid or rotting meat or fruit, e.g., "Upon seeing maggots in the veal, Anne commented that the flies had blown it."

blower: one engaged in the trade of ***glass making*** (q.v.), e.g., "The census revealed that he was engaged as a blower, meaning he was in the glass making trade."

blowing horn: See ***glass making.***

blubber: whale fat and fat flesh, which, upon rendering, yields whale oil, e.g., "Blubber had many uses, including the dressing of leather."

blue: other than the common meaning, a slate, dark gray, or dove colored horse, dog, or (occasionally) a cow, e.g., "His will described the gelding as a blue."

blue blood: as now, probably arising from the blue appearance of the blood vessels when viewed through the fair and untanned skin of those not engaged in physical labor or required to spend time in the bright sun and, as with the slang and derisive term "blue nose", anybody, man or woman, perceived to be of the upper class, e.g., "To the servants and even their wives, William Byrd, George Washington, and William Ferguson were blue blooded"; "When out of their hearing John often referred to the haughty Burgesses as blue noses."

blue john: skim milk, e.e., "Because of its very slight blue color when fresh, Betty and many others knew skim milk as blue john."

blue nose: See ***blue blood.***

bluer: one who was experienced in and worked with bluing; a dycr of cloth—***stuff*** (q.v.), e.g., "It was said in 1744 that New Englander John Prescott was a bluer."

bluing: (blue) indigo dissolved in water and used in dying cloth, e.g., "Indigo was the prime source of bluing available in the early days, and when not available, the juice of berries was used."

blunderbuss: an early firearm of large caliber or "gauge"; a firearm with a bell shaped muzzle, often depicted with early colonials, e.g., "The Pilgrims of New England often are depicted hunting with blunderbusses."

blur, blurpaper, blur paper: unlike now, blotting paper or stain paper, e.g., "Blur having meant stain, it is easy to understand why paper used to absorb it was called blurpaper."

bo'sun: See ***boatswain.***

boar: See ***swine.***

board cloth: a tablecloth; a cloth placed on the eating boards, e.g., "The Bater inventory listed a 'deble' (table) and 3 board cloths."

Board For Certification Of Genealogists (B.C.G.): a non-profit organization of genealogists, having as its principal purpose to insure a measure of quality and competence in both the hobby and the field of professional genealogy, e.g., "B.C.G. offers voluntary certification in six (6) categories, i.e., Certified Genealogical Record Searcher (C.G.R.S.); Certified American Lineage Specialist (C.A.L.S.); Certified American Indian Lineage Specialist (C.A.I.L.S.); Certified Genealogist (C.G.); Certified Genealogical Lecturer (C.G.L.); and Certified Genealogical Instructor (C.G.I.)."

board, boarding house, boarder, room and board: food, drink, and entertainment provided a guest at an inn, along with ***room*** (q.v.); that amount paid for food and drink in an inn or "boarding house"; any person, other than immediate family, residing within a household, e.g., "As room and board, Mark's sleeping room was $1.50 per week, and his two meals a day were an additional $1.75 for the same period"; "In the census of 1870, the farm hand was shown as a boarder."

boarders: See ***board, etc.***

boarding house: See ***board, etc.***

boards: a dance floor, e.g., "He spent most of the evening on the boards."

boats: See ***boatswain.***

boatswain, boatsman, bo'sun, boats: often abbreviated simply "boats," an ancient term referring to that enlisted member of a ship's company who has charge of all rigging, ropes, hardware for the sails, and anchors; later and since steam power, that enlisted member of a ship's company who has charge of repair and maintenance of the ship and of the ***captain's gig*** (q.v.), e.g., "Boatswain Richendollar was liked by all the seamen, even when he ordered them to paint and polish parts of the ship."

bob: a women's short hairstyle, dating from the ***Civil War*** (q.v.) and still fashionable from time to time; a small lot of flowers or ribbons worn as a corsage, e.g., "The bob was seen in fashion publications of the 1860s"; "Bethany wore a bob of pink roses and fern." Also see ***ear bobs.***

bobcherry: an early child's game played without the use of hands, wherein a cherry or piece of candy was dangled and moved about at mouth level, and children sought to seize it with their mouths, e.g., "They played ***gray wooley*** (q.v.) and bobcherry."

bobs, ear bobs: earrings, e.g., "In the early colonies, ear bobs were not commonly worn by other than women of some affluence."

bobtail driver: early, a co-venturer in hauling goods by wagon; one who drives a wagon partially at the direction and profit of the owner and partly on his own account; also, occasionally one who drove a laundry wagon, e.g., "He was described as a bobtail driver, and worked for Drake Bater and for himself."

boche, bosh, bok: slang and a disparaging term for a German, World War I foot soldier, e.g., "He wrote that he had seen many 'srenderd boshs', meaning German infantrymen (boches) who had given up the fight."

bodice: early, a quilted waistcoat, often with whalebone stays; a corset; a woman's undergarment extending from the neck to the waist, e.g., "There were two linen bodices listed in Anne's inventory."

bodkin: a small, sharp-pointed tool similar to an awl; sometimes, a dagger, e.g., "The shoemaker's belongings included two bodkins."

Bohea: a popular variety of tea from India, commonly consumed by the wealthy of the American colonies, e.g., "The ship *Lion* brought spices and Bohea on its return from Singapore."

bola, bolo: a neck tie that could be drawn tight, often made of leather or better, hard finish, durable fabric, and typically worn by men on horseback to keep dust from being inside the shirt, e.g., "Terry often wore bolas decorated with geodes or other pretty stones."

bole: a measure of grain equaling six bushels, e.g., "He sold eight boles of corn at 'one shilling (1S) the bole'."

bolster, boulster, bed and bolster: a thin pad for lounging or resting, often used as a pad under ***ticks*** (q.v.), and often used on ***daybeds*** (q.v.), e.g., "Virtually every inventory of the seventeenth century included at least one boulster."

bolt upright: from "bolt," meaning to quickly move away or aside, one who is startled or in fear and hurriedly arises or stands up, e.g., "Moore might have had his character bolt upright instead of leaping from his '...bed to see what was the matter'."

bolter: See ***searce.***

bolus: medicine, taken internally, made into a soft mass larger than a pill, as in a ***cordial*** (q.v.) (stimulative) or astringent (constrictive) boluses, e.g., "Allison made a cordial bolus of brandy, herbs, and honey, and an astringent bolus of zinc and copper sulfate."

bombard: a large wine barrel or large drinking utensil; a very large ***jack*** (q.v.), e.g., "The 1703 list of his belongings included a jack with gold, several ***flagons*** (q.v.), and a bombard, the last probably a large mug."

Bon Homme Richard, U.S.S: See ***warships, American.***

bona fides, mala fides: in good or bad faith, e.g., "In the eyes of the court, his actions, though illegal, were done bona fides."

bond: a sum of money, pledge of credit, insurance guaranty, or other thing of value deposited, usually with a court, as assurance that someone will faithfully perform certain duties or meet obligations, financial or otherwise, e.g., "As was to be expected, the administrator was required to post a bond equal to twice the value of the ***assets*** (q.v.)."

bondmaid, bondman: one who is bound to another, quite usually as a servant, e.g., "The bondmaid was fourteen and was bound to serve until her twenty-fifth birthday."

bondwoman: an early term often meaning a female slave, e.g., "Old Martha was a bondwoman, and was valued at but £8 Sterling."

bonesetter: early term meaning a surgeon (***chirurgeon,*** q.v.), e.g., "They went to the bonesetter for broken limbs and dislocations."

bone-shakers: high-wheel or other early bicycles, e.g., "Since early bicycles had no suspension springs, such provided a very rough ride, hence the name bone-shakers."

boniface: though very seldom seen, an innkeeper, e.g., "The early Cumberland County record speaks of Drake Bater as a boniface on the Calthrop Road."

bonnet box, bride's bonnet box, ladies' hat box: a small, lidded, wooden box in which to store a lady's hat (a bonnet), lined and often cloth-covered with decorative sewing as adornment, e.g., "Colleen had done the needlepoint work for the cover of her bonnet box."

Bonnet, Stede: See ***pirates.***

bookbinders and printers: as now, those who print for hire, and those who create and bind books for sale, e.g., "By 1860, virtually every sizable community had a printer who also worked as a bookbinder, or vice versa." Also see ***block printers.***

bookcase: any of the many styles and shapes of cabinets designed for the storage or display (or both) of books, the single common design feature being a writing surface, either flat or on a hinged leaf, e.g., "He had two bookcases, one a walnut cabinet with shelves above and below the writing surface, and the other, a drop front cabinet with three drawers below, and a single shelf above." Also see ***side by side*** and see ***stack bookcase.***

Boomers: name given those under Payne and Couch who sought to settle in Oklahoma in 1884 and were ousted by the U.S. Cavalry, e.g., "Some of the Boomers returned, participated in, and settled lands opened up by the ***Oklahoma Land Rush*** (q.v.) of 1890."

boot camp: See ***private, private soldier.***

boot hill: a burial place, typically in the West, for gunfighters, vagrants, ne'er-do-wells and those without family or friends desiring to bury them elsewhere, said to derive from the fact that those buried there usually died with their boots on and were taken there without ceremony other than a prayer, e.g., "Bill Hickok and Calamity Jane (Jane Canary) are buried in Boot Hill at Deadwood."

boot tree: a common wooden form, shaped like a leg and foot, over which boots were placed for drying, shaping, or stretching, e.g., "There were both small and large boot trees in the inventory."

bootjack: a wooden or metal device shaped like the letter "V", so designed as to permit removal of boots without bending over or dirtying one's hands, e.g., "A bootjack was usually placed near an outside door leading to the kitchen."

bootlegger, jointist: one who sells liquor or other intoxicating beverages without a license or contrary to law, e.g., "Every town in any ***dry state*** (q.v.) is sure to have a bootlegger or two."

boots: See ***shoes.***

Bordelais, Burdelais: wine made of grapes of the same name, popular since the seventeenth century, e.g., "Washington often served Bordelais and Madeira."

bordello, bordel: as now, a house of prostitution, e.g., "Every colony had its bordellos."

boree: an early dance, e.g., "At celebrations they often danced the ***reels*** (q.v.) and borees."

borough, -boro: a town or small city; a portion of a city or municipality; in Pennsylvania, New Jersey, and Connecticut, that portion of a township that has been chartered as a municipality, e.g., "In some states, boroughs were incorporated by definition"; "The borough of Queens is part of New York City."

borrow fire, carry fire: to gain coals or fire from another, e.g., "Before matches, if the household fires were allowed to go completely out and one had no flint, steel and tinder, it often was necessary to go to another house and borrow fire."

bosh: See ***boche.***

boss: usually a high quality and very large object even among such expected to be large, particularly a log or tree, e.g., "They came from the woods with a walnut boss log."

Boston Rocker: a typically American variation of the Windsor chair that first appeared in New England and consisted of a shaped seat, a tall back with usually seven or more upright spindles, curved arms, and medium-length rockers, e.g., "Her Boston Rocker had remained in the corner of the parlor for all the seventy years since she had died."

botcher: another name for cobbler, e.g., "While now, we sometimes say that poorly done work is botched up, formerly the word did not usually carry that negative connotation." Also see ***cobbler***, ***shoemaker***, and ***cordwainer***.

bots: small worms or parasites in the intestinal tracts or stomach of horses, mules, and donkeys, probably usually the larvae of bot-flies, e.g., "All horsemen and breeders of horses knew of the dangers likely to result from bots."

bottle: early, a container holding one quart of wine; now, a small glass container with a narrow neck, e.g., "He had four bottles of Madeira—one gallon."

bottom, bottoms: as now; and earlier, Johnson (1755) said a bundle of grass or hay; a ship, occasionally a ball of thread, e.g., "Shakespeare in 'Twelfth Night' said, 'My ventures are not in one bottom trusted....', a not uncommon use of the word to refer to a ship." See ***steeps.***

bound out, to bind out: that condition of young people whereby they were legally obligated to stay or live with and do the bidding of a person other than a family member, usually with the purpose of learning a trade, e.g., "The will of Jesse Drake required that his sons under the age of twelve be bound out to a tradesman, thereby assuring them a future livelihood."

bound servants: early, either indentured servants or Negroes, later, referred to indentured servants only, e.g., "The first Negroes likely came to the ***Virginia Colony*** (q.v.) in 1619 as 'bound servants'." Also see ***indentured servants.***

bounded tree, boundary tree: a tree marking a corner or sometimes a point in the boundary line of a tract of land, e.g., "The bounded tree marked the point at which the Fleming land joined the Meeting House Road." Also see ***bounders***.

bounders: marks or monuments (sometimes trees) at turns in or the ends of surveyed lines, e.g., "The bounders on the north and west lines were piles of stones, and that on the southwest corner was an oak tree." Also see ***bounded tree.***

bounty, animal: usually, money paid by a government for the capture or killing of ***varmints*** (q.v.) and pests, e.g., "Bounties were paid on crows' heads as late as 1960."

bounty jumpers: the name given those who, after accepting a bounty for enlistment during the Civil War and other early wars, would go to another town, often change their name, and again enlist and accept a bounty payment, e.g., "John Arnold was one of the many bounty jumpers in Civil War Ohio."

bounty lands: lands from the public domain given or granted, commencing in 1776 as a reward for desertion from the British Army, as compensation for military service or goods or equipment supplied to early governments or armies, e.g., "The bounty lands awarded by Connecticut after the Revolution, in part, were for horses, guns, clothing, and blankets supplied to the army units from that former colony."

Map of early reservations of Ohio land by Congress, for bounty and settlement purposes; by some states for similar purposes; and by the Ohio Company for profit.

bousy, boozy: an early term for drunkenness, e.g., "He was bousy most of the time, even at services."

bouwerye, bowery: in old Dutch New York, a farm occupied by the owner, e.g., "Old man In den Hoffen was proud of his bouwerye."

bowie knife: a long, heavy, single-edged working knife, named for wilderness scout Jim Bowie, who is said to have designed it, e.g., "The bowie knife was eminently practical for the woodsman and hunter."

bowls, bowling: a game of bowling played out of doors on grass, e.g., "Sir Francis Drake is said to have being playing at bowls when he learned of the approach of the Spanish Armada." See ***games***.

bowpin: See ***hatters' tools.***

box: apparently, a measure of now unknown quantity or weight of iron or metal, e.g., "Early store ledgers occasionally list 'boxes of iron'."

box iron: a smoothing iron with a closeable inner container for hot coals, e.g., "One of the most difficult tasks of the early housewife was the requirement that she spend hours over a heavy box iron or a ***sadiron*** (q.v.)."

box of tea: See ***tea chest.***

box wagon: a common, animal-drawn, farm wagon with a plain, unspringed board seat, e.g., "She regretted that while others went to church in ***spring wagons*** (q.v.) and even in surreys, she and her family had nothing better than a box wagon."

Boys in Blue: See ***Union Army.***

Boys in Gray: See ***Confederate Army.***

brace, brace and bit: that hand-operated device in which ***bits*** (q.v.) are fastened for boring holes, e.g., "Building barns would have been almost impossible without braces and bits."

brace: as now; also, a small number, usually two, of game birds that have been killed for use as food, e.g., "The expression he returned with a brace of grouse is ancient."

braced-back chair: a common, early, spindle-backed chair, with two or occasionally three additional vertical braces extending into a neck or protrusion at the back of the seat, e.g., "His braced-back chair was of ***American Windsor*** (q.v.) style, except for the extra braces."

bracer: early tincture or bandage, e.g., "To treat the wound, she made a bracer of iodine."

Braddock's Road: See ***roads, early.***

braid loom: See ***belt loom.***

brails: See ***rigging.***

brain tan: an early expression (and as now) of a tanner of hides, the meaning now likely lost, e.g., "Hines wrote that the goat had just the quantity of 'brains needed to brain tan' the hide."

brain, diseases of: The brain not being understood, drastic and sometimes even bizarre remedies were employed when the symptoms of "brain disease" appeared, e.g., "For anemia of the brain (meaning now lost), eucalyptus, phosphorus and camphor were popular remedies; for hyperaemia of the brain (excess blood in the brain), ***bleeding*** (q.v.), cold to the head, and anal injections were used; for inflammation of the brain, ***cupping*** (q.v.), bleeding, and ***blisters*** (q.v.) were used; for overtaxed brain, bromides and phosphorus served, and for softening of the brain, tincture of phosphorus was prescribed."

brain, softening of the: See ***brain, diseases of.***

braising pan: open, metal (usually iron) pan with short legs, used for braising, e.g., "In the list of ***personalty*** (q.v.) were three 'kittles' and a braising pan."

bramble: blackberry, raspberry, or dewberry bush, e.g., "The fruits of the many brambles growing on the Carlson property were used to make wines."

branch, brance: a creek or stream, a rivulet; "The Drake land was bordered on the southeast by Horsepen branch." Also see ***prong, etc.***

branch: a candle stand for more than one candle; also sometimes a part of a chandelier, e.g., "Whether the branch found in the inventory was a multiple candle stand or a part of a chandelier could not be ascertained."

brandlet: a common large trivet; a sturdy, legged, black iron stand placed over coals and embers, and upon which were placed kettles and large pots, e.g., "The kitchen inventory revealed two trivets and a brandlet."

brandy: a common, strong liquor distilled from any wine, e.g., "The brandy in the inventory may have been made on the property."

brasier, brassier, brazier: a metal pan designed to hold coals and embers over which cooking was done; one who worked with brass, bronze, and similar metals, e.g., "There were two small brasiers listed in the estate inventory"; "Parker was variously described as a pewterer and a brazier"

brass, brasses: in addition to the metal, an inscribed or decorated, usually small, marker or monument, especially those within a church, e.g., "The brasses of St. Andrew's are all of similar shape and size."

brazier: See ***brasier, etc.***

bread dough: See ***sponge.***

bread: any of many blended and baked mixtures of wheat or other ground grain, shortening, water and seasoning, whether leavened or not, e.g., "In 1859 'H. Rodriguez', New Orleans, among other items, advertised Pilot Bread, Navy Bread, and Wine Bread."

bread-stuffs, breadstuff: wheat or other grains suitable for grinding into flour for the making of breads, e.g., "He referred to his small stand of rye as a handsome crop of bread-stuffs."

break and scutch flax: to crush and separate flax to be made into linen thread or cloth, e.g., "Fridley was said to have a break and scutch mill."

break the Pope's neck: a game of adults or older children of both sexes, the rules apparently having been forgotten, e.g., "Virginians of the pre-Revolutionary period played break the Pope's neck." Also see ***games.***

break wind: to flatulate, e.g., "Heavy diets often caused indigestion and excessive gas in the stomach or intestines, then called wind, hence came the phrase 'to break wind'."

breakbone fever: See ***dengue.***

breakfront: any of the many designs and styles of large wooden cabinets with a center section that extends further forward than the two sides, or with a top section not extending equally to the front edge of the bottom section, e.g., "Cheryl's walnut breakfront, made in 1836, was valued at $4000.00."

breast knot: intertwined ribbons worn at the breast by women as dress decoration, e.g., "The old photo of her revealed a pretty breast knot."

breast plate: very common, early, sleeveless and backless armor made of metal or heavy leather; sometimes, a small decorative leather pad or disc attached to the harnessing and hung at the breast of a horse, e.g., "Probably the last armor to be found in the colonies and used in war was the breast plate."

breeches, britches: common early item of male clothing usually extending to just below the knee and tied there; now, any outer pants for men, e.g., "Breeches were found in most inventories of eighteenth-century gentlemen."

Brewster chair: a massive chair found throughout the seventeenth century, usually with turned spindles at the back and beneath the seat, almost indistinguishable from the Carver chair of the same period, e.g., "Adam Thorowgood's seventeenth-century Virginia home contains a beautiful example of a Brewster chair."

brewster: a maker of beer or other fermented ales and alcoholic beverages made from hops and grain, e.g., "When her husband died, Anne found it impossible to find a brewster equal to the task." (also a surname)

brickbat, brick-bat: usually a piece of broken brick used to strike or be thrown at another person with intent to injure, e.g., "Drake shouted that the next man to abuse the child would find a brick-bat in the side of his head."

bride's basket: thought to be an expensive, highly decorated or ornate, small, metal frame holding an ornate bowl, and used for sweetmeats or candies, e.g., "The inventory spoke of a ***chased silver*** (q.v.) bride's basket."

bridle: harnessing, including the bit, placed on the head of a horse, by which it is controlled, e.g., "Virtually every farm inventory before 1930 contained one or more bridles."

bridle path: early (and now) a path or way usually only wide enough for a horse and rider, e.g., "Most travel in early seventeenth-century Virginia was via bridle paths."

brig: a two-masted sailing ship; a lockable, secure compartment, usually in a ship, and used to house prisoners or "lunatics," e.g., "He wrote in 1864 that a seaman he knew had 'lost his mind and was throwed in the brig.'"

brigade: See ***armies, organization of.***

Bright's disease: nephritis or kidney disease; an extremely painful, dreaded, and common disease for which no cures were known, e.g., "There being no dialysis, old Dan Carner suffered terribly before dying of Bright's disease in 1908." Also see ***kidney disease.***

brimstone: sulfur, used for the burning of waste, in making gunpowder and explosives, and thought to have extensive medicinal value, e.g., "The armory might be expected always to have brimstone on hand"; "Flowers of sulfur, also called brimstone, was a mainstay of the apothecary trade."

brindle: a color of an animal, usually a dog or horse, dark over gray or buff, e.g., "Todd's brindle dog was his constant companion."

bristle: the coarse, stiff hair of swine, widely used for early brushes, e.g., "At the time of his death, there were several bristle brushes in his shop."

Bristol blue: a fine, dark blue, early, transparent or translucent glass used in better and usually decorative glassware, e.g., "Cheryl's Bristol blue candy dish was superb."

Bristol glass: an early, opaque, white glass similar to milk glass, popular for decorative glassware, e.g., "She had a butter dish of Bristol."

British Legion: See ***military combat units, famous.***

broadaxe, goosewing: a common axe with a broad, flat blade, chisel-shaped on one side only, and used widely for working logs into beams, e.g., "The beams had been hewn with a broad axe."

broadcasting: See ***sow.***

broadcloth: a closely woven fabric, usually of cotton, linen, or silk, and used for lighter clothes, e.g., "The tailor made Mr. Bater's shirts of silk and cotton broadcloth."

broadwife: a married, female slave whose husband was owned by a different master, e.g., "Where an estate or family record names a broadwife, the researcher is well advised to search for the husband in the records of neighboring slave holders."

brocade: a variegated cloth, usually of silk, e.g., "He had three brocade waistcoats."

broiler: unlike now, a long-handled, hinged, scissors-shaped kitchen utensil made of corrugated and perforated metal, usually iron, with a removable bottom, e.g., "Meat to be broiled was placed between the perforated jaws of the broiler and held in the fire until done."

broken to the plow: See ***new land.***

broken up ships, ships breakers: ships torn down or dismantled for salvage and those persons engaged in such breaking up, e.g., "Once the once proud and beautiful sister ship of *Lusitania, Mauretania* was broken up before World War II."

brother: as now, a sibling; a member of a religious order, particularly Catholic; the term often was used in the Biblical sense, e.g., "Care must be exercised, since the records of old churches often refer to unrelated members of the congregation as brothers and sisters." Also see ***sisters***, and see ***siblings***.

brougham, brome, broom: a closed carriage, usually seating four, with the driver high and in front outside, e.g., "Mr. Bater's wealth was reflected in his beautiful brougham with a ***liveried*** (q.v.) driver." Also see ***carriage***.

Brown Bess: flintlock muskets used by British forces in the eighteenth century, so called after Queen Elizabeth I and by reason of the metal being 'browned' and not 'blued', e.g., "During the ***French and Indian War*** (q.v.), a majority of the British soldiers carried Brown Besses ."

brownie: a copper penny, e.g., "She wrote that the little girl had saved 16 brownies during 1889."

brucellosis: See ***Bang's disease.***

brushes, scrub: See ***clamps***.

bub: very strong beer, ale, or other malt liquor, e.g., "The New England colonists very much enjoyed their bub."

bubo: any swelling of the lymph glands, especially in the groin and armpits, e.g., "Dr. Lockhart applied ice and ***poultices*** (q.v.) in his efforts to cure the bubo."

bubonic plague, Black Death: that disease, probably carried by fleas and rats, that killed perhaps one third of the populace of England and Europe during the middle ages, e.g., "The 'plague', reported by ***chirurgeon*** (q.v.) Stringer as the cause of death of Richard and Edward Newport, very likely was bubonic plague."

Buccaneer musket, Buckaneer gun: a common, long ***musket*** (q.v.) of the seventeenth and early eighteenth centuries, e.g., "In 1698, Owen

Griffith bequeathed his 'pistoll, houlster, and Buckaneer gun' to his eldest son."

buck: the chassis of a simple utility wagon, and when a plain wooden seat was added, the wagon was called a buckboard; lye, a buck tub was a tub in which cloth and yarn were cleaned and bleached with lye; a male animal; a now probably unknown game of children, e.g., "The buck deer dressed out at 165 pounds"; "The note revealed that the Haskins children had played buck all morning." Also see ***games (of children).***

buck and wing: See ***buck dancing.***

buck dancing, buck and wing: an informal dance of rapid movements, turns, and heel clicking and typically found in early Black society, especially in the South, e.g., "Anne wrote that on Sunday evening the slaves and been '...busy with their buck and wing'."

buck gloves: deerskin gloves, e.g., "Nineteenth-century ads for gloves usually offered kid gloves (goat skin) or buck gloves (deerskin)."

buck, buck naked: to have intercourse; a superlative concerning being naked; as in how one would usually be dressed during intercourse, e.g., "When he wrote that his friend was buck naked, he was relating that the person was wearing no clothes."

buck, buckbasket: to wash clothes, a basket in which newly washed and wet clothes were placed before drying, e.g., "Diane wrote that Monday was the day she bucked clothes, and Tuesday was the day for ***smoothing*** (q.v.)." Also see ***iron (to).***

buckbasket: See ***buck.***

bucket bench: a cupboard of much utility, usually with doors below and a rimmed, shallow shelf and work surface above, e.g., "As were many, the bucket bench was made of ash and maple."

buckles: common types in inventories were 'shoe', 'belt', 'hat', and 'spur', e.g., "The pilgrims often mistakenly are depicted with shiny, silver shoe buckles." See also ***desserts, early.***

buckram: formerly, a strong, coarse, stiffened linen cloth, widely used for book binding, e.g., "Books not bound in leather usually were done in buckram."

buckskin: deer skin; a very light brown, cream colored, or tan equine, e.g., "He wore a buckskin coat"; "Diane was very proud of her buckskin mare."

Bucktails, Pennsylvania: See ***military combat units, famous.***

buff: coarse leather prepared from buffalo skin and often used for belts or harnessing, e.g., "Buff belts and moccasins were very common in the early west."

buffalo robe, robe: a hide or animal skin with the hair yet in place and used as a rug or blanket for warmth, e.g., "Dr. Drake had an old buffalo robe that he placed over his legs and feet when in the buggy on cold nights."

buffet: curiously, sometimes the name given a ***side by side*** (q.v.); a long, rather narrow, waist-high serving piece, usually made of better-quality, highly-finished wood, with several drawers and one or two doored compartments below the top on either end of the drawers, used to serve a variety of foods "buffet style," e.g., "Sarah's Victorian walnut buffet had belonged to her grandmother."

bugbear: from the Welsh, a frightening apparition or specter, e.g., "Early mothers often threatened unruly children with the possibility that they might be captured by a bugbear."

bugger, booger: an expression of the 19th century, unknown to Johnson, sometimes profane and meaning a male sodomite; strangely, sometimes a term of affection for children, e.g., "He sure was a cute little bugger."

buggy: a light, four-wheeled carriage having one seat and often a removable top, e.g., "Dr. Drake's buggy and his old dog 'Watch' were well known in old Arlington." Also see ***road wagon***, and see ***carriage.***

bull pen: See ***games (of children).***

bullet mold, pincer mold: a hinged metal mold into which melted lead was poured to form bullets; a mold was needed for each caliber of weapon, e.g., "His grandfather's 59-caliber bullet mold was a prized memento."

bullseye lamp: a wicked, oil lamp with directional reflectors; a lamp that reflected light in a certain direction, e.g., "In his close work as a clock maker, his bullseye lamp was invaluable."

bum: quite unlike now, early, our posterior, e.g., "While today a bum is a person of little worth or ambition, Johnson cites Shakespeare's definition of the term as 'the part (of our bodies) on which we sit.'"

bumper: unlike now, a large metal or glass drinking utensil; any filled cup, e.g., "The tavern keeper kept his patron's bumpers displayed on the backbar"; "They raised their bumpers in a toast."

bumping hammer: See ***coppersmiths' tools.***

bumpkin, country bumpkin: countrified; illiterate, or but little educated; of crude manner and bearing, e.g., "Though he spoke like a country bumpkin, he had an extraordinary musical talent."

bundle, bundling: the little-understood eighteenth-century practice of young lovers sleeping or being in bed together with their clothes on, usually separated by a low board, e.g., "English and Southern ladies and gentlemen were shocked by the widespread New England practice of bundling."

bung: the stopper for a drain of a cask or barrel, e.g., "Bungs were placed in wooden barrels and wine casks after those containers were drained, cleaned and thoroughly rinsed for the next use."

Bureau Of Indian Affairs, U.S.: established in 1836 and thereafter modified by numerous acts and reforms, this legislative branch of the federal government assumed responsibility for all matters pertaining to American Indians and their lands within the U.S., e.g., "One of the many responsibilities assumed by the Bureau Of Indian Affairs was the administration of the western lands ceded to the Chickasaw Indians in 1818 in exchange for the sale to the U.S. by that tribe of their lands in Tennessee." Also see ***Compact of 1806.***

Bureau of Vital Statistics: See ***vital statistics.***

bureau: See ***chiffonier.***

burgess: as in Pennsylvania, the chief executive officer of a borough, having generally the same duties as a mayor of a city; in Connecticut, comparable to trustees or commissioners in other states; in early Virginia, freemen elected to the House of Burgesses (legislature) commencing in 1619, e.g., "Allison learned that her ancestor was the burgess of the borough of Coxetown."

burglary: originally, breaking into and entering the home of another at night with felonious intentions; later, any breaking and entering with felonious intent, day or night, e.g., "He was found guilty of burglary and was ordered transported to the colonies."

Burgundy: as now, a dark red, sweet wine, very popular in the eighteenth and nineteenth centuries, and named for the province of Burgundy in France, e.g., "There was a hogshead of Burgundy shown on his ***accompt*** (q.v.)."

burial: See ***church yard.***

burins: See ***silversmiths' tools.***

burl grain: now, increasingly rare, speckled, beautiful graining created in a burl (growth) on the side of a tree, e.g., "Almost all burls were and are cut into veneer in order that the most use might be made of the beautiful wood there contained."

burlap sack, burlap bag: See ***gunny sack*** and see ***croaker sack.***

burn a wet mule, enough money to: a superlative, meaning one who has great wealth, i.e., paper money to burn sufficient in quantity to set ablaze a wet, dead mule, e.g., "In describing the assets of a local industrialist, Evan said, 'Lord, he has enough enough money to burn a wet mule'."

burning glass: a magnifying glass; a piece of finely ground glass so shaped as to concentrate sunlight to a degree sufficient to bring ignition and, before matches, often used to start fires, e.g., "Early inventories occasionally reveal burning glasses."

burr-mill, raccoon burr mill, raccoon mill: a small grist mill, the word raccoon referring to the minimal size of an animal required to power it, e.g., "His little mill could grind only four (4) to six (6) bushels of grain a day, hence was branded a burr mill by the neighbors."

bushel: a measure of volume of weight (four pecks, eight gallons, or thirty-two quarts); a measure of weight of grain, 50 lbs.; a large basket, e.g., "A favored way of telling one that his or her talents or knowledge should be used and openly displayed was 'Don't hide your light under a bushel'"; "His harvest consisted of two hundred bushels of wheat and sixty of barley"; "His cart load, having weighed 350 pounds, was said to be seven (7) bushels."

business wagon: any wagon for hauling, but usually a ***buckboard*** (q.v.) for hire, e.g., "The livery stable advertised ***hacks*** (q.v.) and business wagons for hire."

busk: the steel or whalebone braces used to strengthen a woman's ***stays*** (q.v.), as in a corset, e.g., "Fashions of the 19th century often required the wearing of busks."

buskins: See ***shoes.***

bussened: probably meant ruptured, or a male made incapable of sexual activity by reason of injury to the genitalia, e.g., "In 1867, Diane wrote that 'Terry had returned bussened from the War'."

bustard: a Wild Turkey, e.g., "Even Audubon referred to the present-day American Wild Turkey as a bustard."

busted: as now; to lose military rank or rating as a result of some disciplinary action, usually a court-martial, e.g., "Stevens was busted from Petty Officer to Seaman after wrecking the ***captain's gig*** (q.v.)."

bustle: a very common framework, usually of wire or whalebone, placed under the back of a woman's dress or gown, intended to spread and display more of the dress being worn, e.g., "Miss Margaret regularly wore her bustle, however she found it rather uncomfortable." Also see ***hoop, hoop skirt.***

butler: as now; early, a man servant who furnished a dining table, e.g., "While today we think of butlers as those who perform many domestic functions, originally the term meant those who served food and supplied a dining table."

butler's desk: a large three- or four-drawered cabinet, with a flat top, appearing like a chest of drawers, with what appears to be the top drawer front hinged so as to drop down and reveal ***pigeon holes*** (q.v.), small drawers, and a writing surface of felt, leather or buckram, e.g., "The elegant Empire butler's desk was ***flame grain*** (q.v.) mahogany."

butler's sideboard, butler sideboard: a common item of furniture among the more affluent; a sideboard, usually with a two-doored china or glass compartment above, two or three drawers below, with a fall-front revealing ***pigeon holes*** (q.v.) for linens and a serving surface, e.g., "His walnut butler's sideboard had belonged to his great-grandfather."

butt, butts, half-butt, quarter-butt: container designed to hold 125 gallons of wine or divisions thereof, e.g., "Mikaila's 1798 ledger reveals that she sent a servant to merchant Evan Haskins for a half-butt of newly arrived ***Malaga*** (q.v.)."

butter bat: a small, flat, wooden utensil used to work butter, e.g., "Her inventory listed a butter bat and a ***butter churn*** (q.v.)." Also see ***bat.***

butter churn, churn (and dasher): a cylindrical container of 2 to 5 or more gallons, usually earthen ware early and glass later, in which was placed fresh whole milk, the same then churned (dashed) by rapidly moving the dasher up and down, thereby separating butter from the non-fat liquids (buttermilk), e.g., "While churns are often yet to be found in antique shops, very few original dashers have survived."

butter mold: a wooden mold, usually with a decorative design in the head of the plunger, into which bulk butter was placed and then pressed out with a plunger, thereby measuring and shaping it, e.g., "Helen's favorite butter mold pressed her initials into the butter."

buttermilk paint: See ***milk paint.***

buttery: a pantry; a cool place of storage for cheese, butter, sauces, etc.; e.g., "Her buttery was in the coolest part of the winter kitchen." Also see ***fruitery.***

button: a child's game, perhaps now unknown, yet maybe a box of buttons which children placed on a string, e.g., "Early Appalachian records reveal children playing button."

butts and bounds: See ***metes and bounds.***

by blood: See ***consanguinity.***

by the board: See ***gone by the board.***

byroad: a neighborhood road or lane of early New Jersey, legally recognized, yet not public and not private in that the public was authorized to use it irregularly only, e.g., "His land was traversed by a byroad, and the county helped maintain it by requiring road work."

C

C.G.: See ***Certified Genealogist.***

cabbage chopper, cabbage cutter, kraut cutter: a common wooden kitchen utensil, usually from 18 to 36 inches long and 6 to 9 inches wide, having a sliding platform that moved to and fro across a sharp blade, thereby shredding cabbage (and other fruits and vegetables), e.g., "Virtually every early housewife had a cabbage chopper—a kraut cutter."

cabin: a small, often windowless structure with no plumbing and often with no fireplace, used as a crude residence, e.g., "In 1856, Arnold moved Rebecca and her children into a cabin valued at $20.00 at Little Sandusky."

cabinetmaker, cabinet making: as distinguished from a carpenter, a cabinetmaker was one who made fine, small, wooden cabinets, chests, and boxes; later, one who made fine wooden furniture and cabinets of any size, e.g., "Cheryl's elegant Empire ***chest on chest*** (q.v.) was made by the local cabinetmaker."

caboose: no longer used; formerly, a stove-heated simple, railroad car at the end of a freight train with benches, in which often rode the conductor and other of the train crew; a free-standing bake ***oven*** (q.v.), e.g., "The use of cabooses on freight trains ended in the 1980s"; "The caboose in the inventory was an oven, and had nothing to do with trains."

cabriolet: early, a one-horse, single-seated, two-wheeled carriage; later, a one-horse, four-passenger carriage with a canopy, e.g., "In the 1846 sale of Cole's ***personalty*** (q.v.) his cabriolet brought $40.00."

cachet: usually, an envelope upon which a seal had been placed or a stamp or design was printed, e.g., "Her remark that the money came in a cachet likely meant that the envelope in which it had been placed was sealed after closure."

cachexes, cachexia: chronic ill health, accompanied with emaciation, e.g., "Dr. Lockhart administered ***tonics*** (q.v.), usually with a high alcohol content, for cachexia, especially if the complaint was the result of a cancer."

cag: See ***keg.***

cairn: a pile of rocks used to cover and mark a burial place; a pile of rocks designating a corner or turning point in a survey, e.g., "The cairn of the commanding officer may yet be seen at King's Mountain battlefield"; "The northwest corner was marked by a tree and the northeast corner was marked by a cairn."

caisson: a wheeled box or chest used to haul powder, ***shot*** (q.v.), and supplies needed for a cannon, e.g., "Traditionally, the body of an army officer is transported to the cemetery on a caisson."

Cajuns: the name given those descendants of the French settlers of Acadia and New Brunswick who were transported to Louisiana by the British government before the French and Indian War; the name probably was corrupted from "Acadians" to "Cadians" to "Cadyans", and finally to "Cajuns"; e.g., "The Cajuns brought great food and the civil law to Louisiana."

calabash: a gourd; a drinking or eating utensil made from a dried gourd, e.g., "Every summer she dried gourds to be used as calabashes."

calamine, calamine brass: as now, a lotion for insect bites and burns made from oxides of zinc and iron; an ***alloy*** (q.v.), e.g., "Calamine lotion was in use before 1880"; "Calamine brass, used as an imitation for gold, was an alloy of zinc carbonate and copper."

calash: a light, 2-horse carriage, with low wheels and a seat for the driver outside the passenger compartment, e.g., "Except at ***livery*** (q.v.)

rental facilities, calashes were only for the wealthy since such vehicles required 2 horses and a driver.

calculi, calculus: as with pebbles; the formation of stones within the bladder or kidneys, e.g., "Stewart's Pocket Therapeutics suggests that the treatment for calculi—'the stone'—should be alkalis, 'mineral acids', narcotics, and nitric acid if renal and anesthetics if biliary, ice bags, morphine, and a mixture of ***turpentine*** (q.v.) and ether."

caldron: See ***cauldron.***

calenture: yellow fever; the violent and delirious fever that attacked people on shipboard, especially sailors in the tropics. Early epidemics of calenture occurred in New York in 1668, Boston in 1691, and Charleston in 1699, e.g., "In the early colonies, calenture quite usually resulted in death."

calf, don't lick my: See ***lick my calf, don't.***

caliber: the diameter of the projectile for, or the bore of, a firearm, usually given in percentages of inches, e.g., "The muskets carried in the Civil War were of several calibers, including .45, .57, and .69."

calico, callaco: a common cotton cloth (***stuff,*** q.v.), originally from India; a yellow, black and red-brown, large-spotted cat, e.g., "She made their aprons of calico"; "The famous poem described the dog as ***gingham*** (q.v.) and the cat as calico."

California gold rush: See ***Forty-niners.***

calimanco, calamancoes: a cloth or fabric (***stuff,*** q.v.) popular in the 17th and 18th centuries and probably no longer used; an expensive fabric made of wool and so woven and treated that the pattern is visible on one side only, that side also being glossy, e.g., "Before 1850 Kuhn & Risberg of Philadelphia advertised goods of calimanco, including ladies' shoes."

calivar: See ***caliver.***

caliver, calivar: an early, hand-held firearm, e.g., "The militia was armed with only ***blunderbusses*** (q.v.) and a few calivers."

calling, feel the calling, being called: an urge, strong inclination or emotional attraction to a trade or profession or to the ministry, e.g., "When but a small girl, she told her parents that she felt a calling to be a nurse."

callosity: early word for any hardened, thickened, or (sometimes) swollen portion of the body that was not accompanied by pain, e.g., "He had a large red callosity on his abdomen."

calomel: mercuric chloride; a widely used purge (laxative), also thought to have medicinal value in curing syphilis, yellow fever, and many other ailments e.g., "The old country doctors were sure to have calomel in their medicine satchels."

calotype: perhaps no longer known, e.g., "In 1877, Judith wrote that her husband's calotype was completely destroyed."

caltrop, crowfoot: a small and deadly instrument of war, being a piece of metal with four very sharp points and so designed that, no matter how dropped, at least one of the points will extend upward, e.g., "During the French and Indian War and at many other times of conflict, caltrops were dipped in excrement and dropped along Indian paths, thereby causing painful and highly infected injuries to those walking or running along such ways."

camblet: probably ***camlet*** (q.v.); a fabric (***stuff,*** q.v.) made originally of camel hair and silk and later of wool and silk, e.g., "Camblets were commonly advertised for sale in America during the late 18th century."

cambric, cambrick: a fine linen fabric, "In April of 1862, A. R. Wiggin, a New Hampshire merchant, advertised '***Thibet*** (q.v.), Muslin, and Cambric Robes'."

camel back trunk: so called by reason of the rounded appearance of the hinged top, such trunks having been very sturdy, made of wood, leather, and metal, with hasps and locks, and with compartments and removable trays within, e.g., "He had two camel back trunks that dated from 1870."

camlet: See ***camblet.***

camp fever, flux, bloody flux: that ailment common to military installations, thought usually to have been dysentery, e.g., "Men serving in the Civil War suffered terribly from camp fever."

camphor, camphire: that sap or material extruded by the tree of the same name and widely thought to have medicinal value, e.g., "In early times, camphor was used by nearly all physicians."

camus: a thin dress, e.g., "She had several camuses for warm weather wear."

can: originally, a cup made of tin or copper, e.g., "The cans listed in the inventory probably were drinking cups."

Canadian Regiment ("Congress' Own"): See ***military combat units, famous.***

canal boat: a wide, shallow-draft barge, pulled by mules driven along a path on the causeway or bank, e.g., "Many of the young men of old Holidaysburg gained employment as drivers of the mules used to pull canal boats."

canal horn: a brass horn used to call attention to the presence of canal and river boats, e.g., "The inventory of property of the old captain revealed a brass canal horn."

canals, well known: commencing in 1817 with the authorization of the Erie Canal linking Albany with Buffalo and continuing in wide use through the coming of the railroad, e.g., "Some of the better known canals were the Morris Co. Canal across New Jersey; the Delaware and Hudson connecting Homesdale, Pennsylvania, with Kingston, New York; James River and Kanawha from Richmond to Buchanan, Virginia; Chesapeake and Ohio, and Pennsylvania Portage and Canal System from Philadelphia to Pittsburgh; Welland connecting Lakes Erie and Ontario; Wabash and Erie between Toledo and Evansville, Indiana; and the Illinois and Michigan between Lake Michigan and the Illinois River."

Canary, Tenerife: sweet wines from the Canary Islands, and very popular in the colonies, e.g., "The Boston Rocker served Madeira, ***Burgundy*** (q.v.), and Canary."

cancer: as now, but early not at all understood, e.g., "For 'a cancer' of the stomach, Dr. Drake administered arsenic and carbon disulfide, and for other internal cancers he often prescribed carbolic acid, chromic acid, zinc sulfide or zinc chloride."

candle arm: a small holder for one, two, or three candles, usually suspended against the wall; a ***sconce*** (q.v.), e.g., "There were two candle arms and two ***chandeliers*** (q.v.) in the inventory."

candle beam: a crude, roughly made, candle ***chandelier*** (q.v.), e.g., "Being a ***blacksmith*** (q.v.), he made the candle beam from black iron."

candle mold: metal (usually tin) tubes, open at the top and having a string hole at the bottom, several of which were mounted in a holder or rack. A string wick was placed through the hole and the length of the tube, then the tube was filled with molten wax or ***tallow*** (q.v.), e.g., "Before lamp oil, nearly all homes had one or more candle molds."

candle stand: any of the many shapes and styles of small, lightweight, easily movable stands for two or more candles, usually of wood, and designed to stand on the floor and provide illumination, e.g., "The wealth of Mrs. Haskins made it possible for her to have candle stands made variously of walnut, cherry, and mahogany."

candlebox: a container, widely varying in size and usually wooden, used to store 6 to 20 candles and ***tapers*** (q.v.), e.g., "Sarah's candlebox was about fourteen inches long, eight inches wide and six inches deep, and held about sixteen candles."

candlelight: the end of the day; near dark, e.g., "He came to call at candlelight."

Candlemas: an ancient English holiday held on February 2; the feast of the purification of the Virgin Mary celebrated in the church with many candles, e.g., "Wherever the Church of England was to be found, Candlemas was celebrated regularly."

candlestick: See **stick**.

candler: See chandler.

candles: as now, e.g., "Her recipe for candles was '...cut tallow into small pieces, put into a tin vessel with a spout, and set it in boiling water, stir until ***tallow*** (q.v.) is melted but do not boil as it will flake, pour into molds'." Also see ***tapers***.

candy: as now, confections were known and enjoyed, e.g., "Of the many candies, rock candy was sugar crystallized on a string, suckets were hard candies to be dissolved in the mouth, toffee (taffy) was as now, sweetmeats were candied fruits, often eaten with the hands, and sugar plums often were lumps of crystallized sugar dipped in fruit juices."

candy pull, candy stew, candy boil, toffee pull, taffy pull: a social gathering of folks, usually young, for the purpose of enjoying the company of each other and making candy, e.g., "Being new in town, Drake was happy to gain an invitation to the candy pull."

candy stew: See ***candy pull.***

canister: very early, a small basket; in the 17th, 18th, and 19th centuries, artillery projectiles shaped like a basket and containing numerous smaller projectiles, the same designed to burst apart upon impact, e.g., "Through the use of canister the Union artillery is said to have devastated the ranks of men in Pickett's Assault."

cannabis: usually hashish, sometimes marijuana, e.g., "The flower parts of Indian hemp, now called hashish, were early known to be hallucinating and were called cannabis."

cannonball bed: a ***bedstead*** (q.v.), common after the Civil War, with posts, the tops of which were decorated with cannonball-shaped carvings, e.g., "The walnut cannonball bed was beautiful."

canoe: a common boat, pointed at both ends, considerably larger than those in use today, and often used on shallow rivers to haul freight, e.g., "By 1750, there were many small boats and canoes plying the Blackwater, Meharrin, and Chowan rivers."

canon, canon law: law enacted and promulgated by ecclesiastical councils or bodies, e.g., "The canon law provided rules of religious conduct for the early settlers."

canopy bed: See ***poster bed.***

cantatrice: a professional female singer, e.g., "New York newspapers of the day referred to Jenny Lind as a 'magnificent cantatrice'."

canter: See ***gaits, horse.***

Canterbury gallop: an early word meaning canter. See ***gaits, horse.***

cap and ball: an ignition cap and a projectile, however the term described those rifles, pistols, and ***shot guns*** (q.v.) that succeeded ***flintlocks*** (q.v.), preceded breech-loaded arms, and were fired by a springed hammer striking a small explosive ignition "cap" placed over a small tube (nipple) leading to the powder propellant, the ignition of which propelled the "ball", e.g., "The cap and ball rifles were vastly more reliable than the old flintlocks, especially in damp weather."

caparison: a cover for a horse, e.g., "There was substantial ***harnessing*** (q.v.) and three caparisons in the inventory."

caparisoned, caparisoned horse: sometimes the harnessing, often expensive and elaborate tack and trappings of a horse, e.g., "When General Marion mentioned that Washington's mount was finely caparisoned, he was referring to the quality and beauty of the tack and harnessing."

capitation tax: See ***poll tax.***

capius: literally, "take that"; a term used variously for writs or orders to an officer of a court directing arrest, notification, confiscation, attachment, etc.; should the first capius fail in its purpose, an alias capius would issue, and should it fail, a third, it known as a pluries capius was issued, e.g., "A capius and then an alius capius was issued to Sheriff Massenburg ordering the gathering and sale of the ***assets*** (q.v.) of Jones."

capon: early and now, a rooster, castrated when young, e.g., "Allison wrote that her husband regularly had all roosters '...made capons when very young, as he thought the meat greatly improved thereby'."

caps: See ***cap and ball.***

capuchin: a woman's hooded cloak made in the style of the Capuchin monks, e.g., "On chilly days Mikaila wore a fine wool capuchin."

caraco: a short woman's jacket, e.g., "In Jean's inventory were two dresses, three gowns, and a caraco.

carat, caract: a measure of weight, quite usually of gemstones, equaling four grains; also, a measure of the fineness of gold, whereby the whole is divided into twenty-four parts and the number of those parts which are pure gold are the caratage, e.g., "His wife's diamond weighed six grains, thus was one and one half carats"; "The base metal made up six parts and the gold, eighteen, so the alloy was eighteen carat gold."

caraway seeds: as now, used for gas, flatulence, ***colic*** (q.v.), ***hiccups*** (q.v.), and, interestingly, for a loss of hair, e.g., "The housewife of the early years always planted caraway in the ***kitchen garden*** (q.v.)."

carbine: a short-barreled firearm, designed to be easily carried on horseback or through a heavily wooded area, and usually having a rifled barrel, e.g., "Cavalrymen usually were armed with carbines."

carboy: a large glass container around which a wooden framework was built, e.g., "By the year 1825 many acids and embalming and tanning fluids were being transported in carboys."

carbuncle: a painful inflammation and swelling under the skin, more serious than a boil, e.g., "The carbuncle was lanced and ***cupped*** (q.v.) and ***turpentine*** (q.v.) was applied."

card (wool), cards, carding mill, carding machine, to card: a small, handled, wooden or leather tool with fine wire teeth, used to separate the fibers of wool and other animal hair, flax, or cotton; to vigorously comb wool, thereby separating the fibers and removing the dirt and extraneous matter preparatory to making woolen thread and cloth, e.g., "Few were the 18th- or early 19th-century households that did not possess two or more cards"; "There was a water-driven carding mill one block off the main street in Cardington, Ohio, from whence the community derived its name." Also see ***card.***

card catalog: now computerized, formerly, a listing of books and materials arranged alphabetically on small cards by title, name, category, subject, and author, and a "must" for the researcher, e.g., "The maps listed in the card catalog were valuable research tools for her."

card table: unlike now, a small table with a drop leaf, usually supported by a hinged leg, e.g., "There was a card table and a ***center table*** (q.v.) in the inventory."

card: often unlike now, a short notice, as in the classified advertising section of early papers, e.g., "Davidson placed a card in the Intelligencer advertising a ***barouche*** (q.v.) for sale." Also see ***card (wool), etc.***

cardinal: a woman's hooded cloak, named after the garb of a Roman Catholic Cardinal, e.g., "Helen wore her wool and cotton cardinal on chilly days."

caries: early, a decay of teeth or bones; now usually a decay of teeth, e.g., "Dr. Lockhart viewed the withering and loss of bone in Evan's arm as a caries."

carmine: a color, crimson or bright red, e.g., "She made carmine by adding powdered insects called ***cochineal*** (q.v.) to vinegar and hot water."

Carolina Parakeets, Carolina Parrots: yellow, orange, with green and white, small, gregarious, the only native parrot of what now is the southern United States; now extinct, but common and popular as pets in the 17th, 18th and first half of the 19th centuries, e.g., "The Carolina Parakeet went the way of the Passenger Pigeon, likely by reason of its propensity to eat fresh fruit from colonial orchards." Also see ***pigeon.***

carpenter: one who does construction with wood, usually houses, barns, other buildings, porches, shelves, etc., e.g., "While he was a knowledgeable carpenter, he did not have the skills of a ***cabinetmaker*** (q.v.)."

carpet: early, any colored covering for floors or other medium to large surfaces, e.g., "He had a hand woven carpet to cover the carriage seats."

carpetbaggers: so-called by reason of their belongings often being placed in a bag made of old carpeting, when they went South during ***Reconstruction*** (q.v.) hoping to gain office or otherwise take advantage of the disrupted institutions, e.g., "Those who seek ancestors who emigrated to the South during the period 1867-1885 often will find that they are hunting for carpetbaggers."

carriage: a general term for any of many styles and sizes of horse-drawn vehicles for business and pleasure, with or without tops and, unlike ***wagons*** (q.v.), with but limited space for luggage or light hauling, i.e., cart, gig, chaise, etc., e.g., "Ida was quite conscious of the fact that her father could afford a carriage, while the fathers of most of her friends could not." "Some of the many horse drawn vehicles were omnibus, wagonette, ***surrey***

(q.v.), ***cutter*** (q.v.), ***sleigh*** (q.v.), top buggy, ***runabout*** (q.v.), ***road wagon*** (q.v.), and ***chaise*** (q.v.)."

carriage horses: light horses used to pull carriages, gigs, and other light vehicles, e.g., "Her pair of chestnut carriage horses were her pride and joy." Also see ***draft horses.***

carriage, salt: See ***salt carriage.***

carry: to take someone someplace, e.g., "He asked if the neighbor might carry his son to school."

carsey: See ***kersey.***

cart: a two-wheeled, animal-drawn vehicle used to haul all manner of materials, very common in the 17th and 18th centuries because of the yet undeveloped roads on this continent, e.g., "In early Virginia, there were myriad carts, yet only a few four-wheeled vehicles."

carte de visite: (French; cards of or for the visit or call—calling cards); in the U.S., photographs small enough to be carried on the person; small ***pictures*** (q.v.) widely made and sold during and for 30 years after the Civil War and, as today, given as remembrances, e.g., "Cartes de visite of General Sherman were being advertised within a few weeks after the March To The Sea."

cartouche: variously, a box for cartridges or individual small thin paper containers holding the ball and powder necessary to load one round in a firearm, e.g., "The '200 cartouches' in his 1861 list doubtless were individually wrapped rounds of powder and ball for his musket."

cartridge box: a small, closeable, heavy waterproofed cloth or leather box, usually hung from the waist by a belt loop, the same holding ***cartouches*** (q.v.) and, later, metal cartridges, e.g., "The cartridge box usually issued to Union soldiers was made of heavy black leather."

Carver chair: now, virtually indistinguishable from the ***Brewster chair*** (q.v.).

carvers: usually, one who shapes or creates architectural, utilitarian, or decorative wood products, e.g., "Accomplished carvers were eagerly sought by the Victorian mansion builders."

case drink, English: unknown, apparently an intoxicating liquor, e.g., "An early Isle of Wight record reveals a debt for a shipment of 'English Case Drink'."

case knife: early, a large kitchen knife; later, any small knife with a folding blade; presently, any small pocket knife, e.g., "There were three ***slicers*** (q.v.) and two case knives in the inventory."

case: early, a box of nearly any size; later, a trunk, or a medium to large chest with drawers (***chest of drawers,*** q.v.); a common early abbreviation for trespass on the case, a legal action providing a remedy where injury arose through the acts of another, even though there was no force applied nor intended against the injured, e.g., "There were two (2) 'old cases' listed in the inventory."; e.g., "His action on the case arose out of his injuries sustained when the neighbor's rickety barn collapsed upon him."

casement cloth: a light, loosely woven cloth used to make curtains for windows and beds, e.g., Her account revealed '3 ***ells*** (q.v.) of casement'."

cashmere, cassimere, cashmaretts: the woolen cloth or "stuff" made from the very fine under-fur from the Indian Kasimir goat, e.g., "The merchant inventory listing cassimere in association with other ***stuffs*** (q.v.) reveal his trade with people of affluence."

casing: pipe of substantial size; the thin membrane from the intestines of hogs and sheep, stuffed with bulk sausage creating "link sausages", e.g., "He ordered 1000 feet of 6.5" casing for the oil well"; "Casing was much in demand at ***killing time*** (q.v.) as sausages of several varieties were universally made."

cask: a medium to large barrel of any measure, e.g., "There were several casks of tobacco in the inventory."

casket supports: sturdy, well finished, splayed leg, supports for caskets, e.g., "In early times when the dead were shown in the home, casket supports were common and shared among neighbors."

cassia: a rather uncommon sweet cooking spice, occasionally made into a liqueur, e.g., "Her purchase of a small amount of cassia was revealed in the account ledger."

caster, caster set: a small wheel or roller, such as used on the legs of chests, cabinets, commodes, washstands, and bedsteads; a small, usually metal holder for cruets of condiments and spices, placed at the table while eating; a stand to hold four to seven ***cruets*** (q.v.), e.g., "The casters of the walnut ***commode*** (q.v.) were of white porcelain"; "The cruets were of cut glass and the caster was of silver plate." Also see ***founder.***

castine: perhaps a New England ***sachem*** (q.v.) or Indian village, e.g., "The records of Salem reveal that Samuel Trask was 'redeemed from castine' in 1725."

castor set: See ***caster.***

casualty, casualties: very early, any loss of military personnel that decreased the numbers of those present for duty, including loses by death, wounds, capture, disease, desertion, and sometimes even discharge; through the last half of the 19th century and to now, one who has been killed, wounded or injured even slightly, while engaged in armed military service, whether through battle or otherwise, e.g., "During the Civil War, the 1st Maine Heavy Artillery suffered the highest casualties of all units in the Federal Army."

cat ball: See ***games (of children).***

cataplasm: See ***poultice.***

catarrh, coryza: almost any inflammation or disease of the respiratory tract, e.g., "Hot spirituous ***cordials*** (q.v.) at bedtime and the inhalation of ammonia and ***camphor*** (q.v.) were often administered for catarrh."

catch-penny ways: methods of eliciting tips or gratuities for petty services, e.g., "Early traveling Southerners often complained about the catch-penny ways of waiters, doormen, etc., working in Northern hotels."

cathartics: See ***purge, purgatives, cathartics.***

catheads and sop: biscuits and gravy, e.g., "He ordered sausage, catheads and sop every morning for years."

cathedral: the head church of a diocese; containing the ***fee*** (q.v.) of an Episcopal bishop (Johnson, 1802), e.g., "There may be numerous churches within a diocese, but quite usually only one cathedral."

Catholic school records: See ***Orders of Nuns.***

Cato conspiracy: the most serious (Sept. 9, 1739) of slave uprisings in and near Charleston, SC, resulting in 30 white and 44 black deaths, and the hanging of some 50 blacks thought to be participants, e.g., "Genealogists have uncovered the names of many of those involved, both black and white, in the Stono Cato conspiracy." Also see ***Nat Turner Uprising,*** and see ***Slave insurrections.***

catsup: unlike now, a condiment with a walnut or mushroom base, e.g., "Until the mid-19th century catsup found in recipes contained no tomatoes."

cattail: a tall plant that grows in moist soil, the leaves of which were used in basketry and the tops as ***ticking*** (q.v.), e.g., "The cattails that grew in the marsh below the house provided material for her basket making and their bedding, as well."

catted chimney, catted chimnees: perhaps, chimney caulking to which has been added animal hair as a strengthening agent, e.g., "In 1656, in Salem, George Norton entered into a lease for land upon which he was to construct a house with 'sufficient catted chimnees.'"

catwhipper: a traveling or itinerant ***cobbler*** (q.v.) or ***botcher*** (q.v.), e.g., "The catwhipper always was welcome for the news he carried."

caudle: a warm mixture for the sick, and usually containing food and wine, beer, or other intoxicant; the root for our word "coddle", e.g., "When her children had the chills she gave them a caudle of warm wine and cooked oatmeal"; "Sarah coddled her aged mother, just as she had so treated her children."

caul: an elaborate hat worn by ladies, e.g., "Cheryl wrote that she was awed by the various beautiful cauls worn by the ladies at Easter."

cauldron, caldron: any large boiling pot or kettle, usually with three legs, e.g., "The inventory revealed a number of kettles and a caldron."

cauterization, cauterizing: bringing about a cessation of bleeding through searing or burning of the exposed open blood vessels, e.g., "After amputation of Billy Drake's arm the bleeding was stopped by cauterization."

Cavaliers: whether of high station or common tenant farmers, those followers of Charles I in his differences with Parliament (as opposed to the "Roundheads" who were pro-Parliament) who, when that king was beheaded in 1649, sought refuge in the American colonies, particularly pro-Royalist Virginia, e.g., "The erroneous notion that most or all Cavaliers were of high station and wealth arose in the 19th century."

caveat, caveat to a will: literally, "beware"; the filing of a document stating a claim of rights in land, the purpose being to prevent the issuance of a patent or grant for the same tract to another person; a legal attack upon the validity of a will; a demand upon an administrator or apparent heirs that a will be produced and probated; e.g., "His caveat stated that his survey showed part of the tract about to be patented to Smith"; "Her caveat to the will stated that the heirs believed the will to not be the last one written."

celice: See ***horsehair upholstery.***

cellar: a cool space, usually under the house or below ground, where vegetables, fruits, and other perishable foods were kept, as in "cold cellar"; a small container for salt, etc., as in salt cellar (salt shaker); a large container, box, or storage space used for any number of commodities, as in oil cellar, wine cellar, or tool cellar, e.g., "The salt cellars were of cut glass."

cellaret, cellarette: a small rack or case, usually kept near the place of taking meals and designed to hold several bottles of wine, e.g., "Diane's cellaret was on the floor at the end of the ***sideboard*** (q.v.).

cemetery: See ***church yard.***

cenotaph: a monument to one who is buried elsewhere or whose burial place is undetermined or does not exist, e.g., "Colonel Wilson's cenotaph is in Bowling Green; his burial place is unknown."

censer: a container or dish in which incense is burned, e.g., "Anna had a silver plated censer that had belonged to her grandmother."

census, census taker: usually, a listing of all persons within a political subdivision (precinct, city, county, state, nation); formerly, a census was taken solely by census-takers who went from door to door listing the names, ages, occupations, etc., of the occupants of each dwelling; most commonly, the Decennial Censuses taken by the U.S. Government every ten years commencing in 1790; often imprecisely used interchangeably with ***enumeration*** (q.v.) e.g., "The Eighth Decennial Census of the U.S. was taken in 1860"; "The censuses taken before 1850 are more properly called enumerations, since not all persons within a household were named." Also see ***enumerations.***

center table: See ***parlor table.***

century, centuries: 100-year periods, the 1800s being the 19th century, the 1700s being the 18th century, etc., e.g., "Miss Ferguson was born in 1701, the beginning of the 18th century."

cephalgy: early, a severe headache, perhaps the modern "migraine", e.g., "The diary stated that he often suffered from cephalgy."

cephalic, cephalick: any medicine used to relieve a headache, e.g., "Maggie often administered sassafras tea and honey as a cephalick."

cepi: (I have taken or done) a common return written on a ***capius*** (q.v.) by the officer serving the same, e.g., "The capius in the loose papers was endorsed 'cepi corpus', meaning he had physically taken the defendant into custody."

cerecloth: a bandage or cloth smeared with ointment or salve, the same to be applied to a wound or open sore, e.g., "Her comment that she had prepared 'many cerecloths' for the wound revealed that it likely was a severe and long-healing injury."

certificate land: usually, land granted anew to a different owner through a certification by a clerk of the court that a prior owner had abandoned the premises, had failed to ***seat*** (q.v.) the property, or otherwise had lost rights of ownership; Pennsylvania land owned pursuant to certificates issued to veterans in lieu of payment for service in the American Revolution, e.g., "The are many examples of certifications in the early Virginia patent lists"; "Carner had sixty acres of certificate land." Also see ***land grants.***

certificate: in legal records, any written evidence that the any political subdivision, business, or person owes the holder money, services or property, e.g., "He had a 'certificate for a bear's head', meaning that he was entitled to be paid a ***bounty*** (q.v.) upon presentation of that writing to the officer responsible." Also see ***exit certificate.***

Certified American Indian Lineage Specialist (C.A.I.L.S.): See ***Board of Certification Of Genealogists.***

Certified American Lineage Specialist (C.A.L.S.): See ***Board of Certification Of Genealogists.***

Certified Genealogical Instructor (C.G.I.): See ***Board of Certification Of Genealogists.***

Certified Genealogical Lecturer (C.G.L.): See ***Board of Certification Of Genealogists.***

Certified Genealogical Record Searcher (C.G.R.S.): See ***Board of Certification Of Genealogists.***

Certified Genealogist (C.G.): See ***Board of Certification Of Genealogists.***

certiorari, writ of: an ancient writ from one court to a lower court ordering that some record of that lower court be certified and sent to the upper court, e.g., "The Supreme Court issued a writ of certiorari for the records in the case of *Plessey vs. Ferguson*."

cerulean: blue, the color of the sky; a very popular early color for ladies' clothing, e.g., "She wore a cerulean shawl of fine linen."

cesset executio: a term often endorsed on early court orders, meaning cease or stay the execution of that order, e.g., "The capius bore the words cesset executio, so she knew the court had withdrawn the order of arrest of the ancestor."

chafe, chafing dish, chaffern: to warm or sear food, e.g., "When she said she had chafed it, she meant that she had seared the meat."

chaff bed: a ***ticking bag*** (q.v.) stuffed with chaff and used as a mattress, e.g., "While many ***ticks*** (q.v.) contained chaff, straw, or even dry grass, the better ones were of feathers."

chaffern: See ***chafe, chafing dish.***

chain bearer, chainbearer: See ***chain, chain carrier, etc.***

chain mail: See ***mail.***

chain of title: documents or writings showing the chronological sequence of ownership of land through which present title has devolved, e.g., "With the deed came a statement showing the chain of title from the original land grant down to the new owner."

chain, chain carrier, Chain Carrier, Surveyor's Chain Carrier, chain bearer: a measure of length, 66 (or early, sometimes 100) feet long; one who literally carries the chain forward as a surveyor progresses along a line being established; a responsible surveyor's assistant, of age, and trained in the activities and needs of the surveyor and (early) sworn to be honest in his measurements, e.g., "Unlike today, in early times the responsibility of the chain carrier was highly significant."

chair table: a table with a top hinged so as to raise to an upright position and thereby serve as the back for a seat hidden when the table is in the horizontal position, e.g., "Chair tables saved much needed space in small homes of past centuries."

chair wheel: a spinning wheel with a seat facilitating the use of double or divided treadles, e.g., "Divided treadles required a chair wheel."

chaise, shay: a two-wheeled carriage, pulled by one horse and seating two people, usually with a top that opened and closed, e.g., "The famous 19th-century poem 'The One Horse Shay' spoke of the construction of a fine chaise." Also see ***carriage***.

chaisemaker: See ***carriage***.

chalice: any cup used for religious purposes (Johnson, 1755), e.g., "The church chalice was beaten gold and thought to have dated to 1709."

chalk-line: See ***housewright's tools.***

Chamber of Commerce: a non-profit organization of those who work to further the welfare of a community, state and nation, e.g., "Jean located the ancestral property with the help of ***U.S.G.S.*** (q.v.) maps she procured from the local Chamber of Commerce."

chamber: a sleeping room, usually on the second floor and named according to the room over which it was situated, e.g., "She slept in the parlor chamber, and the two youngest children were placed in the kitchen chamber."

chamber pot, thundermug, night jar, commode jar, commode pot: a usually lidded pot used for relieving oneself, ordinarily of a capacity of a gallon or more, and stored in a ***commode*** (q.v.) in a sleeping room or chamber, e.g., "Fine 18th-century chamber pots were made of metal and porcelain."

chambray: a two-colored fabric made of any material, e.g., "The cotton chambray dress was pink and violet."

chancel: early, the eastern end of a church; the end of a church building where is found the alter or communion table, e.g., "Early Episcopal churches almost always had the chancel on the east side or end of the building."

chancellor(s): early, those judges with the authority to moderate or temper the law when conscience or fairness required it, e.g., "In some states, such as Tennessee, a distinction between chancellors and judges at law was maintained down to the middle years of the 20th century."

chancery, courts of: except in a very few states, no longer distinguished from courts of law; a court having general equity powers as distinguished from those "at law", e.g., "In early times, courts of chancery universally were separate and distinct from law courts."

chancre, chancroid: a sore arising from a sexually transmitted disease, e.g., "The chancres described in early medical records were caused by the '***secret diseases***' (q.v.)."

chandelier: from the word candle and **chandler** (q.v.); early, any hanging fixture designed to hold candles or lamps, e.g., "Only better homes had other than the crudest of chandeliers."

chandler: the occupation of one who makes and sells candles, that gave rise to the surname Chandler; occasionally one who sells trinkets, ***curios*** (q.v.), gewgaws, etc., e.g., "Knowledge of the many waxes and

tallows (q.v.), their sources, methods of molding, and the several additives used to vary burning time or to add colors gave rise to the ancient calling of the chandler"; "The local chandler also sold toys."

charbon: See ***anthrax***.

charcoal irons: smoothing tools (now, "irons") into which coals were placed to maintain heat for a long period, e.g., "Her charcoal irons were very heavy and exhausting to use." Also see ***iron (to)***.

charge hell with a Barlow knife: a superlative concerning bravery; "A Barlow knife being but a small, non-working knife carried in the pocket or vest by gentlemen, it would be extraordinarily brave (or foolish) to undertake an assault with only that as a weapon."

charger: a large, flat, shallow metal or wooden dish used for serving meats and poultry, e.g., "Chargers were very common items in early inventories."

charter: in genealogy, any writing by which any governmental body bestows rights or privileges usually having to do with land or business, e.g., "The charter of the Ohio Company granted extensive rights to the use of land in the Northwest Territory."

charwoman: a woman hired for menial housework, e.g., "The record of Betty working as a charwoman reveals her low station in the community at that time."

chase, animal: a hunt on horseback with dogs, usually for fox, very common early and even to now in the Southern States, and always attended by pomp, tradition, and ancient custom, with many of the participants in riding habit, e.g., "Old Zeke, even with a bit of a hangover, told Isabel to hurry along, that the 'chase was on'." Also see ***cut to the chase***.

chase, chaser, chased: usually, to engrave metal, or to decorate one metal with another; one who is skilled in chasing metals; a metal object that has been decorated or embossed with another metal or gemstones, e.g., "The ***caster*** (q.v.) was brass chased with silver"; "The brooch belonging to Miss Haskins was silver plate chased with a ***beryl*** (q.v.)."

chase, cut to the: See ***cut to the chase***.

chatelaine: a pin or brooch-like clasp, worn at the waist by women, e.g., "Her chatelaine was of red gold with seed pearls."

chattel: any tangible, movable personal property; rarely, "chattels personal" referring to intangibles that are negotiable instruments or evidence of debt, or "chattels real" referring to an interest in realty less than a ***freehold*** (q.v.), e.g., "Among his chattels were farm implements and tools."

chaunt, chaunted: to chant, e.g., "He noted in his diary that he had attended a church youth meeting and they had chaunted and celebrated for hours."

cheap: unlike now, inexpensive, e.g., "Currier and Ives advertised that their prints were fine and cheap."

cheapskate: derived from the fact that ice skates sometimes were made from sharpened sticks tied beneath and parallel to the shoes, a person who to a fault uses the least expensive of materials in any project, e.g., "His recurring gifts to his wife of very inexpensive perfumes despite his wealth caused the family to consider him a cheapskate." Also see ***tightwad***.

chebobbin: a "drag sled"; a large, sturdy, usually animal drawn sled used to haul logs and other heavy loads, e.g., "With an axe, a mule, an old chebobbin, and a lot of work, he cut and sold enough logs to feed his family."

checked linen: See ***chect linen.***

checkers: As now, and see ***pool checkers.***

checks, a game played with peach seeds, and see ***games (of children).***

chect linen, checked linen: a common early linen fabric made with various colors woven in the shape of a checkerboard, e.g., "William Parham's store stocked chect linen."

cheese press: used in making cheese by pressing liquids (whey) from milk curds, e.g., "The housewife put the cheese press to good use each autumn."

cheesemonger: a merchant or one who deals in cheeses, e.g., "There were several cheesemongers listed in early New York City."

chemise, chemmy: a long, straight, loose undergarment or night gown; a long, straight, plain dress with sleeves, e.g., "At her death, Susannah had two chemises." Also see ***mother hubbard.***

chemisette: cloth or scarf worn by women around the neck and usually of sufficient length to cover the breasts, very similar to a bib or ***tucker*** (q.v.), "The inventory listed several dresses and a linen chemisette."

cherriderry: rather rough, calico-like cotton fabric (***stuff,*** q.v.) cloth used to make clothes for work and for children, e.g., "Because of the hard use that his work clothes had to bear, she made his cool-weather shirts of cherriderry."

Cherry Valley and Wyoming Valley Massacres: July 3, and Nov. 11, 1778, the name given those murders of New York and Pennsylvania settlers by Loyalists and Indians under Butler and Johnson, e.g., "The Pennsylvania county histories contain many tales of the Cherry Valley and Wyoming Valley Massacres."

Chesapeake, U.S.S: See ***warships, American.***

chessart: a vat used for making cheese, e.g., "The 'large chessart' listed in the inventory likely revealed that the family made cheese enough for the family and for sale to the townspeople."

chest: early, any medium to large wooden box without drawers, but usually with a hinged lid, sometimes made of sassafras, redwood, or cedar in order to discourage insects, e.g., "Two 'old chests' appeared in the 1691 list of furniture."

chest of drawers: any of several designs and shapes, with and without legs, of chests containing drawers, e.g., "Most country folks spoke only of chests of drawers, having never owned ***highboys*** (q.v.), ***chests on chests*** (q.v.), ***chests on frames*** (q.v.), etc." Also see ***chiffonier.***

chest of tea: See ***tea chest.***

chest on chest: appearing to be two "chests" of drawers, one atop the other, with the upper usually being narrower with slightly smaller drawers, and usually on short legs, e.g., "The chest on chest was made of bird's-eye maple, as was common in the early days."

chest on frame: a chest of two or three drawers having the appearance of a chest of drawers placed on a legged frame, e.g., "Her Chippendale chest on frame was truly elegant."

chest over drawers: a seldom-used term to describe a chest of drawers with a hinged lid over a box-shaped compartment atop these drawers, e.g., "Chests over drawers were not common in the colonies or states."

chestnut: as now, a nut-bearing tree; in genealogy, a color; a horse of deep, rich chocolate brown color, e.g., "She had a bay mare and a chestnut colt."

chew the fat: probably from the early practice by hunters, marching soldiers, and walking travelers of chatting and chewing a piece of animal fat, especially ***suet*** (q.v.), just as we now chew gum, e.g., "Any 18th-century ***'Over the Mountain Man'*** (q.v.) would know whereof you spoke if you accused him of chewing the fat."

chew the rag: from the time when newspapers were made of rags and cloth and the news therein was discussed—"mouthed about"—at coffee shops, courthouses, etc.; to chat about current or interesting matters, e.g., "His wife accused him of spending his mornings at the courthouse, telling lies, and chewing the rag with his friends."

Chicago Police Assoc.: See ***slaves, fugitive.***

chicken pox: a disease, now principally of children, that lasted for six to eight days, brought a fever and a red rash, which rash, if disturbed, left minor scarring, e.g., "Before the advent of inoculations for the disease, virtually all children contracted chicken pox."

chicken, fighting: See ***dominicker.***

chickens, dungle fowl: early, young hens, as distinguished from roosters; chickens were called dungle fowl, meaning dung-hill fowl, after their habit of gleaning seeds from animal dung, e.g., "She had several capons, a rooster, and ten dunglefowl."

chiffonier, bureau: a short-legged chest, usually of four drawers, with a mirror mounted in the bonnet, and of many styles, e.g., "She had purchased the oak chiffonier from the local ***cabinetmaker*** (q.v.).

chigger, harvest mite: a common mite causing severe itching, particularly aggravating at harvest season when men were required to handle grain crops extensively, e.g., "The chiggers were very annoying, especially at ***haying time*** (q.v.)."

chilblains: a temporary red rash usually occurring during cold weather, probably resulting from parasites or allergic reaction to wool against the skin, e.g., "Diane thought that colds almost always followed chilblains."

child's part, child's portion: that portion to which a widow is entitled in lieu of either ***dower*** (q.v.) or of a provision of a ***will*** (q.v.), and equal to the intestate interest of any child of the decedent, but subject to its prorata share of expenses down to final distribution, e.g., "She having objected to the provisions made for her by her dead husband, the court set off her child's part of the estate."

chills and fevers: a common expression meaning any chilling and feverish condition early thought to be diseases rather than symptoms, e.g., "For chills and fevers, pioneer mothers often made a tea of redbud bark."

chimney board, fire fender, fender: a low shield placed before the fire, especially at night, to prevent hot coals from being ejected into the room, e.g., "Because of Maggie's fear of fire, she always had the chimney board in place."

chimney corner: a place by the fire; often used as a description of the place where would be found loafers or the indolent, e.g., "Byrd referred to early North Carolina men as likely to be found in the chimney corner while their wives did the work."

chimney hooks: iron hooks, attached to the sides of the fireplace, from which stew pots and kettles were hung, e.g., "The ***blacksmith*** (q.v.) made the fireplace tools for the village, including ***lugs*** (q.v.) and chimney hooks."

chimney jack: See ***smoke jack.***

china cabinet, china closet, curio, china: often called simply a "china," a medium sized, usually well-finished, doored cabinet with glass on the sides or in the doors or both, and often designed as a corner cabinet, and used to display and store glassware, china, and curios, e.g., "Her walnut china cabinet had a small mirror mounted on the bonnet."

china closet: See ***china cabinet.***

china root: a root thought to have medicinal value, originally imported from China, e.g., "The ***apothecary*** (q.v.) maintained a supply of china root."

chinkey, chinky: an unevenly rounded stone used to fill a hole in a masonry wall or surface or used as a hammer or pounding and driving force, e.g., "His elder brother grabbed a chinkey and threw it at the snake."

chinks: See ***daub his cabin.***

chintz, chints, chintzy: a simple, inexpensive, printed cotton cloth, from which came the term "chincy" meaning very inexpensively made; the wares of or a person who uses, provides, or deals in very inexpensively made goods, e.g., "Mrs. Bater made the children's everyday shirts and blouses from chintz"; "He was known as a chintzy old man by all in the community." Also see ***shoddy.***

chintzy: See ***chintz.***

chip hat: a straw hat; a warm weather hat for men or women, made of woven straw, hemp, etc., "They wore chip hats to keep the hot sun off their faces and heads."

chippy, chippies: a prostitute, e.g., "Sarah's husband well knew the chippies of Yorktown."

chirurgeon: a surgeon; one who through manual dexterity and training set bones, extracted teeth, and performed the limited surgery of early days, always distinguished from the physicians, who sought to heal others through the use of concoctions, herbs, and medications, e.g., "The ship's chirurgeon set his broken arm." Also see ***physicians.***

chisel, cold chisel, wood chisel, bricklayers' chisel, etc.: a wedge-shaped tool used to shape, cut, and size brick (bricklayer's chisel), wood (wood chisel) or metal (cold chisel), e.g., "The inventory reference to several cold chisels revealed that he had worked with metal other than that hot from a forge such as used by a blacksmith."

chittlings, chittlins: muscles surrounding the intestines of hogs, deep fried and salted, e.g., "Chitlins were but seldom eaten by upper class Southerners."

chitterling: See ***chittlings.***

chivalry, chivalrous: early, having to do only with knights, and not used to refer to matters pertaining to inheritable nobility; later and now, any noble or gentlemanly conduct; e.g., "As a knight, he was expected to display the traits of chivalry."

chlorosis: anemia resulting from iron deficiency, the symptoms being dull yellow-green skin and complexion, e.g., "Arsenic mistakenly was thought to assist in curing chlorosis."

chocolate: other than as now, a pan used to melt chocolate, e.g., "There was 'a chocolate' listed in the appraisal, meaning a small pan."

choir vestry: the space, often in a ***transept*** (q.v.), dedicated to use by the choir, e.g., "The north transept of St. Paul's was used as a choir vestry."

choke, full choke, modified choke, cylinder bore, full bore, open choke, etc.: the measure of the extent of constriction at the end of a shotgun barrel, such constriction being determinative of the degree to which the shot charge spreads after leaving the barrel, e.g., "For maximum killing power at the outer limits of range of a shotgun, a full choke is desirable."

cholera, hog cholera: an acute, very painful and, in early days, usually fatal disease, symptoms of which were severe vomiting, diarrhea, and horrendous cramps, e.g., "An epidemic of cholera ravaged central Ohio in the early 1850s, for which physicians administered ***calomel*** (q.v.), silver nitrate, chloroform, ice, tea and coffee, and even strychnine and arsenic."

chologogues: those concoctions used to purge one of "bile", e.g., "In early Virginia, chologogues were used along with blistering and bleeding."

cholor: bile; the bodily liquid formerly thought to cause irascibility, e.g., "The doctor thought his frequent anger revealed an excess of cholor."

cholramaubs: an imaginary ailment, illness or effect told of by women to induce a change in some eating habit of children, e.g., "Nannie Crockett told the boys that if they continued to swallow their food whole, they would surely have cholramaubs."

chop house: a low class house of entertainment, e.g., "The chop house was never attended by the upper class Charlestonians."

chop: as now; early, sometimes unknown, but apparently a narrow, shallow passage to a cove or backwater, e.g., "The records of Salem reveal that in 1820 the sloop Leader went aground 'on the west chop of Holmes Hole'." Also see ***hole***.

chordee: a downward bending of the penis, congenital or more often resulting from gonorrhea, e.g., "For chordee, Dr. Lockhart administered aconite, ***belladonna*** (q.v.) and ***camphor*** (q.v.)."

chore: early and now, those daily or regular tasks assigned to some member of the family, e.g., "The little girls' daily chores included feeding the chickens and gathering eggs."

chorea, St. Vitus Dance: early, a usually fatal disease of the central nervous system, the principle symptom of which is twitching, shaking, and involuntary movements, e.g., "Aconite and arsenic both were thought to assist in treating the deadly chorea."

christening: a religious ceremony by which the life (and name) of a person (usually a child) is recognized by and dedicated or pledged to the church or a higher power; the naming of a son or daughter for a church official; quite usually, such ceremonies include ***dedications*** (q.v.), e.g., "In 1807, he was christened "Johannes George Schnyder, Jr."

chronological: a listing or ordering of events by date, e.g., "She set forth the births of her nieces and nephews in chronological order."

chum: unlike now, one who shared a room or bedroom with another, particularly at a university, e.g., "His reference to Parker as a chum may not have meant that they were close friends."

church yard, churchyard, cemetery, burials: a cemetery; early, the cemetery adjoining a church, quite usually reserved for members and immediate families of members of that congregation; now, environs of a church with or without a burial ground, e.g., "Very early all but criminals and the excommunicated were buried in a church, church yard, or on private property, and criminals were buried out of the sight of God, in a "cemetery", e.g., "Since the preferred place of burial was near the church-in the church yard-until the twentieth century that term often was preferred over cemetery because of the history of the latter term."

churches, Revolutionary period: religion was widespread and varied, even very early, e.g., "Paulin and Wright in Atlas of Historical Geography of the U.S. (Greenwood Press, 1975) found that of the faiths represented in 1775, Congregational churches numbered 668; Presbyterian numbered 558; Episcopal, 495; Baptist, 494; Friends, 310; German Reformed, 159; Lutheran, 150; Dutch Reformed, 120; Methodist, 65; Catholic, 56; and all others totaled 120 churches."

churchwardens' pipes: a clay pipe with a long stem, e.g., "One's churchwarden pipe might be loaned to a guest, who would break off a piece of the long stem before smoking it."

chymical: common, early form of "chemical", e.g., "The medication was made of a mixture of chymicals."

ciborium: any container used to house consecrated bread or sacred waters to be used in religious services, e.g., "The ancient ciborium of the Church of St. Peter and St. Paul is of coin silver and bears a crucifix on the cover."

cicatrix, cicatrice, cicatrize: a scar left from a wound; the actions of a body in healing a wound, e.g., "The cicatrix from the musket ball was very large."

cigar cases, cigar poke: small, closeable, usually well or finely decorated wooden boxes for the storage of cigars by gentlemen; leather or fabric containers usually holding 4 to 8 cigars and small enough to fit in a man's pocket, e.g., "His teak cigar case was inlaid with ivory"; "The leather cigar poke of Thomas Roberts remains in the family collection."

cinchona, Peruvian bark: the medically prized bark of the cinchona tree, from which was made quinine, tonics, salves, etc., e.g., "In his inventory, the old doctor had several pounds of cinchona bark."

Cincinnati, Order of: See ***Order of the Cincinnati.***

Cincinnatus: See ***Order of the Cincinnati.***

cinnabar: mercuric sulfide, that mineral from which is extracted mercury, e.g., "The earliest physicians thought the medicinal value of cinnabar and of the mercury extracted from it to be very great."

cinnamon, spirits of, oil of: a spice dissolved in water or alcohol, thought to have medicinal value, e.g., "Dr. Knight prescribed ***cordial*** (q.v.) waters and ***spirits*** (q.v.) of cinnamon."

cipher, ciphered, cypher: to do arithmetical calculations; initials or letters embroidered on cloth, e.g., "He was not good at his ciphers"; "She had three ciphered handkerchiefs." Also see ***rule of three.***

circa, ca., c., c: approximately; chronologically near to; in genealogy, a term used when a precise date or year is unknown, yet the date given is thought to be nearly accurate, e.g., "He knew she was born after 1820 yet before 1824, so he listed her birth year as circa 1822 (c1822)."

circuit courts: See ***courts (circuit).***

cista: See ***deed box.***

cistern: a large, usually stone or concrete lined and lidded hole in the ground in which rainwater was caught and stored for household use; any large container for liquids, e.g., "The Midlam cistern was at the corner of the house and was about six feet deep."

citation: in genealogy, those words that state the source from which cited information was gained, e.g., "The citation set forth for the treaty date was, Richard L. Morton, Colonial Virginia, 2 Vols. (Univ. of N.C. Press, 1960), p. 216."

citrine: an early known and popular semi-precious stone; amber or yellow/orange in color, e.g., "She had a ring of citrine and two of opal."

city: in the U.S., usually a municipality, larger than a town or village, which governs itself under a charter granted by a state, e.g., "A city is not part of a county, yet is governed in much the same the way."

civil law: in genealogy, a system of laws not arising out of the common and ecclesiastical law and adopted in early Louisiana by reason of the French citizenry and influence, e.g., "The use of the civil law makes Louisiana research in courts' records different from Virginia research."

Civil War (American): that armed conflict that took place between the South and the North during the years 1861-1865; sometimes called the War between the States or, by the North, the "War of the Rebellion" and, by the South, the "War for Southern Independence", and in which there were some 625,000 casualties, e.g., "The bloodiest single day of the Civil War, and of the U.S. was September 17, 1862, the Battle of Antietam or Sharpsburg."

clabbered: interestingly, apparently unknown to Johnson (1755 and 1802); soured, curdled as in sour milk, e.g., "Allison often referred to milk that had soured as having clabbered." Also see ***curds.***

clabbord: See ***clapboard.***

clamps: thought to be large brushes such as were used to scrub floors, e.g., "References to clamps sometimes appear in association with containers such as large buckets, wash pails or kettles."

clap: See ***gonorrhea.***

clapboard, clabbord: wooden siding placed over studding or other covering; from the very early meaning of clap, i.e., to add one thing to another (Johnson 1802), e.g., "Clapboard siding has been known, particularly in New England, since the earliest settlements"; "Evan wrote that as a very young boy he had helped 'cunstruck the clabbord sides' of his father's house."

claret: a red wine, originally French; the color red, e.g., "It was considered appropriate, then and now, to serve claret with lamb," "He stained the table claret."

claricord: a stringed instrument built in the shape of a spinet, e.g., "The claricord in the inventory probably revealed a measure of appreciation of music."

claspknife: early, any knife in which the blade folded into the handle, e.g., "His large claspknife was unusual for the 17th century."

clean as a plow board: derived from the scraping of the soil across the ***moldboard*** (q.v.) behind a plow point, resulting in the "board" being very smooth or shiny immediately after use, e.g., "It was truly a compliment when Martha said that Bethany's pans were as clean as a plow board."

clear and convincing: a measure of proof beyond and more certain than that called ***"preponderance of the evidence"*** (q.v.), but not as legally convincing as ***"beyond a reasonable doubt"*** (q.v.); in genealogy, that quantum of evidence that leaves the researcher satisfied that one hypothesis is almost certainly correct as against all others, or that no other solution is likely to be found, e.g., "Clear and convincing usually is the measure of proof required by courts in matters akin to genealogy, such as dealing with wills, deeds, and explaining words used in other than ordinary ways."

cleaver: a large, heavy-bladed, handled knife, used to chop small bones within meat, e.g., "The expression 'pork chops' and 'veal chops' arose from the need to use a cleaver to chop the rib bones in those cuts of meat."

clerk: in genealogy, that person acting as the keeper of records (and early, the scribe) of a political subdivision, business or court, usually the last named, e.g., "Mr. Gary Williams has been the Clerk of and to the Circuit Court of Sussex County for more than twenty years."

clerk's desk: See ***schoolmaster's desk.***

clevis, clovis: a common tool of many uses; a heavy wooden or iron "U" with holes in both ends through which an iron or heavy wooden pin was placed in order to secure ropes, hitches, etc., "In the inventory were several clevises."

clews: See ***rigging.***

clicker: a low paid employee who stood outside or at the door of a business and beckoned in customers, e.g., "As a young man, he earned extra money as a clicker for the Drake Bater Dry Goods Store."

clicket: a door knocker, e.g., "Jean's brass clicket was shaped like a frog, and was most unusual."

clicking wheel: a game played with a ***wagon tire*** (q.v.) and a stick, e.g., "The little boys spent hours rolling or spinning their wagon tire and enjoying the noise made by a stick placed against the spokes."

clipper ships: the fast, beautiful, and usually three-masted ships designed for speed and in common use from 1845 or so until the 1870s and later, e.g., "After the magnificent clipper ships came the unwieldy appearing, steam-driven vessels."

clocks: as now; early, unlike now, small woven decorations, usually on stockings of gentlemen and sometimes ladies, found at or near the ankle, e.g., "Evan's worsted stockings were said to have had decorative clocks."

clogs: See ***shoes.***

cloisonné: colorful oil based decoration and painting where the colors are separated by metal or metallic paint, e.g., "Miss Haskins had both jewelry and vases of cloisonné."

close: early, the entirety of the inside of a dwelling house; later, a small, fenced field, e.g., "To enter the close without permission was a trespass"; "There was a close just outside the door to the kitchen."

closestool: a potty chair; a box, chair, or stool with a circular hole in the seat and a shelf below the hole, designed to hold a ***chamber pot*** (q.v.), e.g., "The closestool was of cherry and very well made."

closet: early, a small room; now, a cabinet or recessed, doored storage space, e.g., "Her jelly closet was kept in a corner of the ***cold cellar*** (q.v.)."

clothes press, press, linen press: a doored chest of drawers in which clothes could be stored flat-'pressed'; occasionally, a wardrobe or ***armoire*** (q.v.), e.g., "Her clothes press was of cherry and had four drawers."

clothes smoothers: See ***iron (to), etc.***

clothes squeezer: See ***wringer.***

clouting diaper(s): quite unlike what we might imagine, probably a sturdy cotton fabric sold for use as mending patches, e.g., "In the late 18th century Kuhn & Risberg of Philadelphia advertised clouting diaper for sale."

clove: a frequently used spice; a bud from which oil of cloves is pressed, the same used to flavor foods and medicines, e.g., "Mrs Ferguson mixed clove oil with chloroform and applied it to the child's sore tooth."

clustergrape: a black currant, e.g., "What Maggie called clustergrape jelly was made from black currants, sugar, lemon juice, and gelatin."

Clydesdales: a breed of heavy, powerful draft horses, popular in America early and now, and originally bred in Scotland, noted for long hair (feathers) on the backs of the legs and just above the hooves, e.g., "Budweiser Brewery re-introduced the long-popular Clydesdales to the modern business and entertainment world."

clyster, glyster: an enema; any injection through the anus; a very common curative procedure until well into the twentieth century, e.g., "During the 17th century, clyster syringes often were listed in inventories."

coach: a common term for any closed, animal powered, four-wheeled vehicle with seats facing each other, used for pleasure or ceremonies of state, e.g., "The coaches offered for hire usually were well-kept and clean."

coachmaker: one knowledgeable in the materials needed for and the construction of passenger vehicles of fine quality, e.g., "The ***wagonmaker*** (q.v.) created more massive vehicles for moving grain and heavy materials, while the coachmaker made vehicles to move people."

coal box sleigh: See ***sleigh.***

coal oil lamps: See ***lamps.***

coal oil, lamp oil: a common term, usually meaning the petroleum distillate kerosene; the term coal oil derived from the erroneous notion that kerosene was a by-product of or found in conjunction with coal; early, "lamp oil" often referred to whale oil, e.g., "The ready availability of coal oil after the 1860s brought the demise of illumination by candles and whale oil."

coaster: a small to medium size ship moving and trading between coastal ports, e.g., "Coasters were active early in such as James River and Albemarle Sound."

coasting vessels: See ***coasters.***

COAL OIL LAMPS.

WM. P. FOGG,

COR. OF SUPERIOR AND SENECA-STS.,

Wholesale and Retail Dealer in

COAL OIL LAMPS.

—ALSO—

Wicks, Chimneys, Shades, Brushes, &c.

A GOOD COAL OIL LAMP,
Complete with Chimney and Wick, for Fifty Cents.

A MARBLE STAND COAL OIL LAMP,
With best Patent Burner, Chimney and Wick, for Seventy-Five Cents.

COAL OIL CHANDELIERS,
For Churches and Halls, with 2, 3 and 4 Lights.

COAL OIL,
Of the best quality, by the Barrel or Gallon.

PULPIT, STAND AND HANGING LAMPS,
Altered to Burn Coal Oil.

LAMPS FOR CHURCHES.

A Large Assortment of Coal Oil Lamps and Chandeliers, with 1, 2, 3 and 4 burners, can be found at the lowest prices, at

W. P. FOGG'S,
Corner of Superior and Seneca-Sts.

☞ Lard Oil, Fluid and Camphene Lamps altered to burn Coal Oil at a small expense.

Country Merchants are Invited to Call.
july28

An 1864 ad for coal oil lamps.

coats of arms, coat armor, armor: heraldic ensigns and emblems, originally painted on shields, e.g., "His coat armor bore lions rampant." Also see ***heraldry***.

cobbler: one who repairs shoes, boots, harnessing, and leather goods, e.g., "Even though the distinction was often clouded, a ***shoemaker*** (q.v.) or ***cordwainer*** (q.v.) made shoes, and the less-skilled cobblers and sometimes ***botchers*** (q.v.) repaired them."

cochineal: early, a color; a dye made from the ground bodies of cochineal bugs, e.g., "The red dye in common cloth usually was made of cochineal."

cock, rooster: a male of any species of large birds; a decorative weathervane in the shape of a rooster, as in weathercock; an iron projection from a plow blade; the hammer, spring, and latchback in the ***lock*** (q.v.) of a firearm, e.g., "She had several cocks and three dozen hens"; "The blacksmith made Evan a new plow blade as he had broken the cock from the old one"; "The gunsmith made a new cock for the old man's gun."

cock, to cock a gun: derived from the fact that hammers of early firearms appeared like the head and neck of a rooster; to move the hammer of a firearm into a position from which the spring will snap the hammer forward and backwards, either by ***cap*** (q.v.) or ***powder pan*** (q.v.), the weapon will be discharged, e.g., "While we yet universally say that a firearm is cocked, the reason for the expression is now quite forgotten." And see ***cock, rooster***.

cocked hat: a man's jaunty, pointed hat with a large, stiff brim turned up, e.g., "He was the town dandy and was said to 'wear a cocked hat'."

cocklestairs: an early term for a spiral staircase, e.g., "Cocklestairs were common in the homes of the wealthy of early Virginia."

cockloft: derives from a high place where might be found roosters or birds crowing or roosting; a room in the ***garret*** (q.v.), e.g., "She had placed two old chairs and an old ***chest*** (q.v.) in the cockloft."

cockney: early, a citizen of the East End of London; now, the English dialect of those people characterized by rhymes or limericks, e.g., "He spoke cockney and was proud of it." See also ***King's English***.

coddle: See ***caudle***.

codicil: usually, an amendment to a provision or term of a will, dated, signed and witnessed, and added thereto subsequent to the signing of the original will, e.g., "The codicil added Margaret's youngest granddaughter to the list of beneficiaries."

codpiece: very early, a man's penis; by the mid-seventeenth century, a let-down, button flap on the front of a man's pants, e.g., "Until 1952, regulations required that U.S. Navy enlisted dress uniform pants have a 13 button codpiece, button or zipper flys having been prohibited."

coffee mill: any of the small household coffee grinders, used to grind coffee beans before modern sealed canning permitted the purchase of previously ground coffee; a large coffee grinder such as was used in stores, e.g., "By not grinding the beans in the coffee mill until time for its use, Helen kept her coffee much fresher and more flavorful."

coffer: early, a chest, usually lined with cloth, for keeping money and other valuables; later and now, a savings account or bookkeeping place, e.g., "In *Richard II*, Shakespeare spoke of using the lining of the coffers to make coats for soldiers engaged in the Irish wars."

coffin clock: a ***grandfather clock*** (q.v.), e.g., "By reason of its shape, Mikaila always referred to the big, hall clock as a coffin clock."

cognac: originally, a brandy from the region of Cognac in France; later and now, any high quality brandy, e.g., "The cognac listed in the 1757 inventory probably was imported from France."

cognation: in ***civil law*** (q.v.), any relationship, whether by blood or family, e.g., "The relationship between brothers may be called cognation in Louisiana records."

cohabitation: literally, living together; in genealogy, a man and woman, either or both unmarried, conducting themselves as a family unit, e.g., "They had cohabited on the frontier for many years and were married as soon as the church was established there."

cohabitation bond: official records created after the Civil War that legitimized marriages and the children of slaves who had previously lived together, e.g., "Jerry and Betty were happy to sign the cohabitation bond and so be married in the eyes of the church and the state."

cohorts: anciently and early, a military unit within a Roman Legion, usually 1/10th of the number of men in the Legion; now, associates—often friends—in a plan, scheme, or activity, e.g., "He labeled as cohorts the three boys who had helped him with the prank."

coif, coif of mail: now, usually the style of a woman's hair; early, a headdress or head wear of any sort; the armor covering for the head, usually of metal or ***mail*** (q.v.), e.g., "Even though remarkable for the colonies, the pulled back coif of Griffith's effigy revealed long hair."

coin silver: silver of coin quality; fine alloy, very high in silver content, e.g., "Evan has the coin silver watch that Tom Roberts bought in 1878."

colander: as now, a sieve-like pan or bowl with small holes in the bottom, used to drain and strain food, e.g., "Her colander was necessary in preparing meals for the very young or the very old." Also see ***riddle***, and see ***tea strainer***.

cold chisel: See ***chisel, cold, etc.***

cold., col.: abbreviation for person of "colored" skin, usually meaning Negro or black, but also used to describe mulatto or Native American people; often found in legal documents and censuses.

cole: Saxon for cabbage, from whence comes "cole slaw", slaw meaning salad, e.g., "She bought cabbage at the weekly market and made cole slaw." Also see ***cabbage chopper***.

coleslaw: See ***slaw***.

colic, colick, colicky: as now, any discomfort of the stomach, usually in the very young, e.g., "Very early, it was thought that wolf dung carried about would aid one suffering from colic, and pioneer remedies for the colic included vinegar and water, Crawley root tea, nitroglycerin, ***calomel*** (q.v.), and ***asafetida*** (q.v.)."

collar: as now; that padded portion of ***harness*** (q.v.) attached to the ***hames*** (q.v.) and against which the horse pushes to move a load, e.g., "The collar and hames are under great stress when a draft horse is moving a heavy load."

collateral lines, collateral branches: all relatives who are not directly (lineally) related; those families and persons related to the subject person through brothers or sisters of ancestors, or through marriages to such brothers or sisters, e.g., "The children of his great-grandfather's brother were collateral lines in which he had genealogical interest."

collier: early, anyone who digs coal; later and now, one who digs, processes, or sells coal, e.g., "Thomas Baynham was a collier in Leicestershire and continued in that occupation in early Ohio." Also see ***iron master.***

collop: a small piece of meat broiled over open coals, e.g., "Diane wrote that she had served veal collops."

collyrium: an ointment for the eyes, e.g., "Dr. Drake made up a boric acid collyrium for his patients suffering from ***redeye*** (q.v.)."

cologne, cologne water: unlike now, often made at home, e.g., "Loreda's recipe for 'cologne water' was '3 qts. spirits of wine, 6 ***drachms*** (q.v.) oil of lavender, 1 drachm of rosemary, 3 drachms lemon oil, 10 drops cinnamon oil, mix well'." Also see ***foo-foo.***

cologne bottles, barbers' bottles: any of the many small, necked, ornate or decorated glass or ceramic bottles, often with a glass stopper, in which were stored colognes and perfumes, e.g., "Some of the early cologne bottles truly are works of art."

Cologneware: now, any stoneware or crockery, so-called by reason of the early high quality of such wares made in Cologne, Germany, e.g., "Being Pennsylvania Dutch, she called her best crockery Cologneware even though it had been made locally."

colonial churches: See ***churches, Revolutionary period.***

colonial: those years before the American Revolution during which the American states-to-be were colonies of England, France, Spain, etc., e.g., "By the 1750s, many colonials had begun to refer to themselves as Americans."

colors: the flag or pennant bearing those symbols and colors chosen to represent a specific military unit, usually a regiment, originally carried into battle by a junior officer known as a ***cornet*** (q.v.), e.g., "The loss of their colors in the Cornfield at Antietam caused great consternation and regret among the brave Texans."

colporteur: (from the French) usually an itinerant Bible or book seller; occasionally one who distributes or delivers books or tracts, etc., for another, e.g., "Boniol was a colporteur for Drake and Evan Press of New Orleans."

colt: See ***horse.***

colter: See ***coulter.***

coma: as now, a state of unconsciousness from which one seems incapable of awakening, e.g., "Dr. Lockhart administered blisters and mustard plasters, croton oil, and cathartics for coma."

comb vise: a common tool of the ***horn smith*** (q.v.), used to hold slices of horn while teeth were being cut, e.g., "The inventory listing of a comb vise and 'a large box of steer horn' revealed that the decedent probably had worked as a horn smith."

combat units, famous: See ***military combat units, famous.***

comb-back chair: a variation of the ***Windsor chair*** (q.v.); a chair with thin vertical back slats set nearly parallel to each other and resembling a large comb, e.g., "Margaret had a beautiful walnut comb-back chair."

combing jackets: a lacy or sheer, full ladies' cape worn about the home or while dressing the hair, e.g., "Only wealthy ladies owned or thought it necessary to wear a combing jacket."

comfit: See ***confiture.***

comfortable drinks: intoxicating liquors or beverages, drinks containing grain alcohol, e.g., "The early distrust in native water led to an increased consumption of comfortable drinks."

comforter: a quilt; a heavy cover, usually quilted or of wool; occasionally, a woolen scarf, e.g., "She made a big comforter for use on cold nights."

coming up: growing up, usually the period from infancy through the early teens, e.g., "Anne mentioned that when she was coming up in old Virginia, adolescent boys were expected to be gentlemanly."

commission of administration: See ***letters of administration.***

commissioned officers, commissioned, officers' training, field commission, battle commission: those members of the military services who have completed training for and have been promoted to ranks of leadership as officers, e.g., "Except for those who in wartime received battle (or 'field') commissions by reason of an imminent need for men to take command of enlisted men, all commissioned officers have undergone officers' training and by reason of their character and competence have been commissioned."

commitment: early, incarceration; later incarceration in a penal or lunatic asylum, e.g., "The sheriff was ordered to enforce the order of commitment for lunacy."

Committees of Safety: those citizens locally appointed in Revolutionary times and having the authority to call out the ***militia*** (q.v.) if and as danger approached, e.g., "When Cornwallis neared Tarboro, the Committee of Safety alerted the militia and the citizenry."

commode jar: See ***chamber pot.***

commode pot: See ***chamber pot.***

commode: in England early, a headdress of women; in the American colonies, a small cabinet with one or more small drawers for towels, etc., and a small doored compartment in which to place a ***chamber pot*** (q.v.), e.g., "Most 19th-century commodes were made of oak or poplar, and only a few were of walnut or mahogany."

common lands: those usually adjacent lands granted to or later purchased or otherwise gained by New England towns particularly, and other colonial settlements generally, the same used in common for pasturage and planting, sold or otherwise transferred to citizenry (often as a reward for coming to the settlement or for staying), or held in reserve for future expansion, e.g., "In 1635 1000 acres was jointly sought from Massachusetts common lands by Balch, Conant, Trask, Palfrey and Woodberry, presumably for speculative purposes."

common law: those customs and mores assimilated into court decisions, which through long use and recognition have gained the strength of law; as opposed to statutory law which derives its authority from the legislative and executive branches of government, e.g., "***Primogeniture*** (q.v.) had its roots in the common law." Also see ***civil law.***

common pleas (courts of): early, the name given the lowest court of general jurisdiction in some states, while other names have come into use elsewhere, e.g., "While in Ohio and South Carolina the first court of general jurisdiction is Common Pleas, in North Carolina it is called Pleas and Quarter Sessions, and in Virginia is known as Circuit Court."

Common Prayer, Book Of: the printed liturgy and approved public form of prayer prescribed by the Church of England; widely circulated, used and read throughout the early colonies, e.g., "The Book of Common Prayer was in virtually every colonial household that had a literate master."

common scold: See ***scold***.

common: of low class, e.g., "She often referred to those of low station and manners as common"; "Indeed, those people are common."

common-law marriage: an agreement to marry, followed by cohabitation, which arrangement has not been formalized in any legally accepted manner, and as to which relationship there was required a continued, not occasional, recognition by the parties, e. g, "By reason of their common-law marriage, she asserted a claim to a widow's share of his estate."

Commonwealth, The Interregnum (between sovereigns) : ruled Great Britain from January 30, 1649 through May 28, 1660

community property: property owned in common by husband and wife; property gained by a husband or wife during marriage, not intended by the couple to be owned singly, e.g., "Their furniture was viewed by the court as community property, even though she had purchased and paid for it when he was not present."

Compact of 1806: an agreement between the states of North Carolina and Tennessee as a result of their separation in 1796; a compact by which unoccupied land in Tennessee was transferred to that state, a) reserving to North Carolina lands previously granted by reason of military service of its veterans, b) requiring Tennessee to maintain land for school use, and c) reserving to the U.S. the ***Congressional Reservation Land*** (q.v.), e.g., "As a result of the Compact of 1806, the federal government and North Carolina continued to meet their land obligations to veterans, as could Tennessee thereafter, and land was secured to Tennessee for future settlement and educational purposes."

company: See ***armies, organization of.***

compass plane: See ***wainwrights and coachmakers, tools of.***

compass: See ***cooper's tools***, and see ***joiner's tools.***

compeer: to be equal with, usually in social or socio-economic standing, e.g., "The Virginian, Mrs. Parker felt that Mrs. Thorogood was a compeer, however she felt that the wives of the ***chirurgeon*** (q.v.) and the blacksmith surely were not."

compilation: a literary writing or recording formed by the collection and assembling of "...preexisting materials...that are selected, coordinated, or arranged in such a way that the resulting work constitutes an original work of authorship." 17 U.S.C. 101, e.g., "Waynette's compilation of 17th-century records required that she be very selective."

complainant: one who brings suit; a ***plaintiff*** (q.v.) in an action at law or in equity, e.g., "The plaintiff is called a complainant in many jurisdictions."

compote, compotier: occasionally, a cooked, sweetened, fruit dessert; usually, a stemmed, lidded glass bowl in which to serve nuts, candies, or small confections, e.g., "Mrs. Haskins and Mrs. Bater have nearly identical, beautiful, pressed glass compotes, both made about 1875."

Compromise of 1850: those five acts of Congress designed to quell unrest over slavery and territorial admissions, either imminent or projected. These brought together for the last time the oratory of Clay,

Calhoun and Webster and resulted in the admission of California as free States, permitted Texas, Utah, and New Mexico to choose, continued the several Fugitive Slave acts, and abolished slavery in the District of Columbia, e.g., "The legislation called the Compromise of 1850 would not last much beyond the deaths of the great orators who in no small measure brought it about."

compt, accompt: early term for an account or computation, e.g., "He kept compts for most of his customers."

compurge, compurgation, compurgators: the act of attesting to the credibility, veracity, or truthfulness of another person, e.g., "In early courts records of trials, character witnesses often were called compurgators."

conceits: fancy desserts or confections, e.g., "Mrs. Randolph wrote of a conceit called a 'Hens' Nest', made of sweetened lemon and ***blanc mange*** (q.v.)."

concoction: an early term, usually for any mixture thought to have medicinal value, e.g., "Physicians and ***apothecaries*** (q.v.) kept ***receipts*** (q.v.) for many concoctions thought to have curative value."

condemnation: a taking of private property by government where the owner is not compensated, e.g., "His tavern was declared a public nuisance and was condemned and closed by the colony." Also see ***eminent domain.***

condiment: as now, seasoning or sauce used with other food, e.g., "Sally kept condiments at the table in her cruet ***caster*** (q.v.)."

condyloma, condylomata: a wart-like growth in the area of the genitals, e.g., "He suffered greatly from a condyloma, and treated it with ***calomel*** (q.v.) and weak nitric acid."

Conestoga: a large wagon, ribbed and canvas covered, with huge wheels, designed for transportation of freight, heavy goods, and large loads, first made in Conestoga, Lancaster County, Pennsylvania, and thereafter in many places; a large, heavy and powerful breed of draft horses, so named by reason of their use with large wagons, such as the Conestoga, e.g., "He rented Conestogas and wagons in Lancaster"; "By 1840, there were many hundreds of Conestoga wagons travelling the Philadelphia Wagon Road."

confections: See ***desserts, and candy.***

Confederate Army, Boys in Gray, Rebels, Johnnies, Johnny Rebs: the armed forces and servicemen of the Southern states during the Civil War, e.g., "The last surviving Confederate Army soldier was John Salling."

Confederacy, Confederate States Of America, Southern Confederacy: See ***secession.***

confess: to consent to a legal remedy sought or to admit the truth of an allegation or charge, e.g., "He confessed judgment in favor of Hunt."

confirmation: in genealogy, a religious service by which one who is of the age of discretion is established (confirmed) as a member or participant in a chosen faith, e.g., "Sarah's confirmation took place on 26 January, 1900." Also see ***baptism and christening.***

confiture, comfit: a ***sweetmeat*** (q.v.), confection or candy, usually of fruit preserved in sugar, e.g., "She had confitures of both raspberries and strawberries"; "The comfits she made were fit for the King."

Congress' Own (Canadian Regiment): See ***military combat units, famous.***

Congressional Reservation Land: land reserved by Congress to be used as rewards or compensation for services to the U.S. by veterans and others, similar to lands reserved by the states (previously colonies) such as the Connecticut Military Reservation or District in Ohio and elsewhere, e.g., "The Congressional Reservation Lands provided compensation for services rendered, especially in the Revolution and the War of 1812, new opportunities for prospective settlers and, ultimately, an increased tax base for government at all levels."

conjugal rights: the right of a husband or wife to the companionship and affection of the other; often used to describe the rights of a spouse to sexual relations, e.g., "He was deprived of his conjugal rights by reason of her protracted mental illness."

conniption, conniption fit: hysteria, involuntary shaking or jerking; often used as a humorous and exaggerated description of the effect one's actions would have upon another, e.g., "Margaret told the children, 'If you dirty your Sunday clothes, your mother will have a conniption fit'."

connubial: matrimonial, e.g., "The newspaper account revealing Ida and Drue's marriage spoke of their entering into a state of connubial bliss."

consanguinity: of the same blood; relationship to another through birth or 'blood'; the relationship between one and those related to him or her through ancestry or descendency, e.g., "His great aunt's grandchildren were his second cousins through consanguinity." Also see ***affinity***, and see ***collateral lines.***

conscription, conscripts: an enrollment of persons, usually into a military unit, e.g., "The Civil War was the first war to utilize conscripts."

conservator: a protector of assets or property, e.g., "She was no longer able to care for her interests, so a conservator was appointed."

consideration: in law and genealogy, the reason or motivation by which a sale, bargain, or contract are entered upon; that asset or thing considered by the parties to be of value and given over in exchange for something else, e.g., "In his deed to Martha, the consideration for 300 acres was 200 dollars Proclamation money (q.v.) and 'love and affection'." See also ***deed of gift.***

console table, half-table: a small side or ***lamp table*** (q.v.), or a table with a half-round top, e.g., "She had a mahogany console table that she kept against the wall in the main hall."

consort: a non-specific term designating a husband or wife when the other spouse is still living, e.g., "The consort of Queen Elizabeth II is Prince Philip."

constable: a public officer of a town or section of a county, whose duties include matters of the peace, the service of **writs** (q.v.), and the custody of jurors, and whose powers vary and are less than those of a sheriff; early, a more important officer of the law than now, hence the title and office were actively sought, e.g., "Constables of the 18th century usually had the same duties as today, however their positions then carried a greater measure of respect."

Constitution, U.S.S: See ***warships, American.***

consumption, quick consumption, phthisis: often, any disease accompanied by great weight loss or loss of muscular tissue and associated with racking coughs, ***pleurisy*** (q.v.), fever, and cancers, e.g., "***Tuberculosis*** (q.v.) caused a rapid and severe deterioration of the body of its victim, hence was one of the diseases known as quick consumption."

contemplation of death: See ***in contemplation of death.***

contemporary: at the same time or of the same period; a record created at the time of the event memorialized, e.g., "Pepys' Diary is a classic example of a contemporary record, it having been kept by him throughout the 1660s."

contiguous: in quite close proximity, yet, and unlike now, usually not connecting or touching, e.g., "While the tracts of his sons were said to be contiguous, they may not have adjoined his."

Continental Line: soldiers of the Revolutionary War who served at least two years and were of the so-called ***regular army*** (q.v.), that is, other than ***State militia*** (q.v.) and ***conscripts*** (q.v.), e.g., "Cornice served in the Continental Line from October of 1778 until February of 1781, and then in the Virginia State Militia until the surrender at Yorktown."

Continental, not worth a: almost valueless; an early reference to the very much reduced value of the currency authorized by the Continental Congress soon after it was issued, e.g., "While the outcome of the Revolutionary War was yet undetermined, any currency that would not be freely accepted in trade was sometimes said to not be worth a Continental."

contrat: (Fr.) contract, e.g., "The Louisiana records revealed that the matter was in the nature of contrat."

conversation, conversacon: to keep the company of another, usually of the opposite sex and for illicit or immoral purposes, e.g., "He was said to have been 'of lewd life and conversacon'."

convey, conveyance: to transfer certain rights or a measure of title or ownership to another, e.g., "Wayne conveyed 640 acres and a cow to his son, Tim."

cook stove: See ***cookstove***.

cookie: apparently unknown to Johnson and other lexicographers of the 18th century. See ***crackers***.

cookstove: usually a cast iron stove that burned wood or coal, and was generally used in a kitchen. Also see ***four-plated stove,*** e.g., "Bethany's cookstove was huge and weighed more than 400 lbs."

cooley can: a ten- to twenty-quart metal container for cold water, having an insert into which whole milk was poured for cooling and so causing the cream to rise to the top for removal, sometimes with a spigot at the bottom to draw off the milk, e.g., "Most poor farmers did not spend the money for a cooley can."

coop, coop up: a cage for small animals, especially fowl and rabbits; to be closed in, e.g., "There were several coops revealed by the appraisal"; "He felt very cooped up in the small office space he was provided."

cooper: a maker of barrels and other round wooden containers; e.g., "He worked both as a slack cooper, making barrels for liquids, and as a dry cooper, making containers for dry substances."

cooper's tools: as now, e.g., "Inventories of estates which reveal sun planes, hand adzes, kerfing saws, crozes, compasses, pod augers, temses, and sheepskins may reveal the deceased to have been a cooper or ***whitesmith*** (q.v.)." Also see ***cooper***.

cooperage: a term of trade meaning the cost of the barrels or containers required to deliver a product being bought or sold, e.g., "In 1700, the flour was priced at nine Shillings (9S) per hundredweight and the cooperage was agreed to be two pence (2p).

coparcenary, coparceners: joint inheritance; those who jointly inherit some property, e.g., "The property of the intestate went to his brothers and sisters as coparceners."

copper: early, a very large pot or kettle; later, a copper, brass or bronze coin of small denomination, usually a penny, e.g., "The little child was proud of the three coppers he had saved."

copperas: iron sulfate; a common yellow dye, e.g., "Margaret kept copperas in order that she might dye cloth yellow."

coppersmith: one who manufactures or works with copper, e.g., "Paul Revere was one of the most famous of American coppersmiths."

coppersmiths' tools: as now, e.g., "The appearance in inventories of heads (large anvils), bickerns, bench shears, hatchet stakes, bumping and planishing hammers, and horses reveal the work of the ***coppersmith*** (q.v.)."

coppicer: unknown; perhaps one who cuts trees to be used as fuel, e.g., "The early family records of the Driskills of North Carolina reveal that a coppicer in their employ had 'cut the neck of woods'."

copyright: the title for that U.S. government recognition accorded an author of a literary product; refers to that Constitutionally based statutory right to gain protection for writings and other products of the intellect. See Harper and Row, etc. vs. Nation Enterprises (1985) 471 U.S. 539; 85 L. Ed. 2nd 588; 105 S. Ct. 2218. Time limits 17 U.S.C. Sections 301, 3021, e.g., "Jo Linn was granted a copyright for her Rowan County record abstracts"; "Martha Ann knew that she could copyright her work if it was an original and unique product of her own efforts."

coracle: a small, usually round fishing boat early made of leather or skins stretched over a wooden framework, e.g., "Early Welsh fishermen made their own coracles."

coram nobis: literally, before us; a finding of error by a court of equal authority; refers to a writ setting forth an error of another court of the same jurisdiction, e.g., "The writ of coram nobis was directed from the full court to the court at ***nisi prius*** (q.v.)."

coram non judice: refers to a matter heard by a court that had no jurisdiction in the matter, e.g., "Despite its lack of jurisdiction, the Ohio county court found him guilty of a felony, so a writ of coram non judice was issued."

coram vobis: an order from a higher court to a lower, ordering a correction of a prior error by the lower court; refers to a review by a higher court of a decision of a lower court, e.g., "The writ of coram vobis from the ***court of appeals*** (q.v.) ordered the ***circuit court*** (q.v.) to correct its error."

coram, coram me: meaning in the presence of, or in my presence, e.g., "The indenture was executed by the parties and the witnesses signed their names followed by the words coram me."

cord: usually, a measure of firewood equaling 128 cu. ft. (8' X 4' X 4'); two (2) ***ricks*** (q.v.) of wood, e.g., "In 1850, the price in Ohio for a cord of good fireplace oak was less than $1.00."

cordial bolus: See ***bolus.***

cordial: early, a stimulant, especially for the heart, and containing alcohol; sometimes in ***bolus*** (q.v.) form and made from common compounds, including mace, nutmeg, licorice, rhubarb, barley and oil of roses, e.g., "The early physician mixed a powerful cordial of iodides and alcohol."

cordiner: See ***cordwainer.***

cordovan, cordwain: soft, fine-grained, highly finished leather, usually of brown or red-brown color, e.g., "His best boots were of cordovan." See also ***cordwainer, cordiner.***

corduroy bridge: See ***turnpike.***

corduroy fabric: See ***duroy.***

corduroy road: See ***turnpike.***

cordwainer, cordiner: one who makes shoes, boots, wallets, etc., from fine leather, e.g., "Being a cordwainer, Evan was quick to distinguish himself from a mere ***cobbler*** (q.v.) or ***botcher*** (q.v.)."

cordwinder: See ***cordwainer.***

coriander: as now, a seasoning; a popular early medication for palsy and ***apoplexy*** (q.v.), e.g., "She kept coriander both for cooking and for making medicines."

corn dodgers: See ***pone.***

corn hills: those small mounds of dirt which resulted from covering grains of corn and other plants after planting, rather than sowing, which hills settled with the coming of a few rains, e.g., "A newly planted field of grain would be spotted over with many little corn hills."

corn husking bee: a game of harvest season in which the winner was he who husked the most corn in a given time period or finished a given row or section in the least time, e.g., "Autumn was made enjoyable, despite the very hard work, by pastimes such as corn husking bees."

corn meal mush: See ***mush.***

corn soup and fat back: a soup very common to the Great Plains and corn producing states with pork scraps, salt port, ***fat back*** (q.v.), or bacon added for flavoring, e.g., "Pam fondly remembered her grandmother's corn soup and bacon."

corn whiskey, corn liquor, "corn likker", corn, moonshine, hooch, white lightning, white mule: whiskey made from fermented corn, e.g., "Corn whiskey, often called moonshine after it became illegal, was (and is) illegally manufactured throughout the Appalachian Mountains."

corn, beaten: See ***beaten corn.***

corn, maize: early, maize was known to the American Indians but not in England; any grain that did not grow in pods; any unharvested feed grain, such as wheat, barley, oats, and rye, e.g. "The 1666 Joyner 'corn mill' probably saw many other grains—barley, rye, oats, etc.—than what we now call corn (maize)."

corner ball: See ***games (of children).***

corner chair: a free-standing chair, wherein the back is on two sides, divided and at right angles permitting the same to be used in a corner, thus saving space, e.g., "There was a padded corner chair in the small library."

corner seat: benches of varying sizes that were placed on each side of a chimney during the cold months, the same serving to warm the family even when cooking was being done in front of the fireplace, e.g., "Tom Drake accused his North Carolina cousins of letting their wives work while they spent most mornings in the corner seats."

Cornet, cornet, cornett, cornette: an honor; a wind musical instrument with usually 3 keys now, but as many as 6 keys during mediaeval times; that person, usually commissioned to do so, who carried the colors or guidon of a troop of cavalry; a usually elaborate decoration or hat for a lady, e.g., "Matheny was a Cornet in the ***horse*** (q.v.) of Charles I"; "The cornet has been with us since at least the early 15th century"; "Allison's beautiful cornet purchased in England appeared very much out of place in the austere Williamsburg of 1704."

cornice: a shield or cover, so hung as to cover the rods, hooks, and hangers upon which drapes and curtains were suspended, e.g., "Sarah's bed cornices were painted with blue buttermilk paint."

coroner: an ancient office; a county officer whose duty it is to inquire into any violent, unexplained, or sudden death; in some jurisdictions the coroner still assumes the duties of the sheriff upon any disability of that officer, e.g., "After causing the suspected persons to ***'stroke the body'*** (q.v.), coroner Bater determined that the death was accidental."

coroner's inquest: an examination or investigation by a coroner and a jury summoned for the purpose of investigating the cause of a death which occurred under suspicious or unknown circumstances, e.g., "There are many Colonial records of coroner's inquests." Also see ***coroner***.

corporeal property: material objects, usually ***personal property*** (q.v.), e.g., "While the building was corporeal property, the income from it was incorporeal."

corps: See ***armies, organization of.***

corpse: See ***stroking of a corps(e).***

corroborating evidence: in genealogy, that evidence which confirms or strengthens prior proof or other evidentiary material, e.g., "The entry in the Bible corroborated the facts stated in the newspaper column."

corsair: a privateer, e.g., "During the 16th and 17th centuries the ***Spanish Main*** (q.v.) abounded in corsairs. Also see ***pirate***.

corset, corselet, corselette: unlike now, light armor, usually of metal plate or ***mail*** (q.v.), designed to protect the front of the body, e.g., "Griffith's 17th century inventory revealed a 'corset with arms.'"

corting, cort, corted: early Appalachian Mountain spelling of courting, e.g., "Evan Haskins wrote, 'I nurly corted her to high heaven before she sed yes.'"

cosmopathic: healing by appeal to some supernormal or extraordinary power or force, e.g., "In our early days, some folks believed that comets had cosmopathic powers." See also ***homeopathic***.

cosset, to: a common expression, particularly of the Tidewater South and meaning to pamper one, particularly a child; Johnson (1802) says, a lamb raised without its dam, e.g., "Judith mentioned that she was accustomed to and enjoyed cosseting her aged mother." Also see ***dotage***.

costermonger: one who peddles fruit and vegetables, as at a public or farmers' market, e.g., "As a boy, Charles Drake often worked weekends as a costermonger at the Yorktown market." Also see ***monger***.

costrel: a drinking bag or container, made of skin or leather, with handles, e.g., "Costrels were seldom used in the colonies, except on the frontier." See also ***jack***.

co-tenancy, co-tenants: a tenancy of owners having distinct and varying titles, yet sharing enjoyment of the premises either physically or in income, e.g., "Judith had an interest by ***devise*** (q.v.) and Drake a lesser one through purchase, so, even though unequal in the means by which each came to ownership, they were co-tenants."

cot: now, a simple cloth and frame bed or resting device, usually collapsible; until the late 18th century, a small house, shelter or hut without plumbing; a cabin or cottage, e.g., "Evan wrote that the weather was so cold that each night he was required to construct a cot of pine bows." Also see ***cottage.***

cotillion, cotillion party: unknown to Johnson, the name of a dance thought to have been 18th-century French in origin; a ball for debutantes or others, or a formal party where dancing took place, e.g., "Jean and Eli danced three ***quadrilles*** (q.v.) and two cotillions that evening"; "The spring cotillion was a much anticipated event in pre-Civil War Richmond, especially by well bred young women, such as Martha."

cottage: unlike now, Johnson (1802) says "a hut, a mean habitation", e.g., "***Oiled paper*** (q.v.) served the purposes of glass panes in early New England cottages."

cotter pole: an iron bar in the fireplace over which pots and kettles are hung, e.g., "The ***blacksmith*** (q.v.) made the cotter poles for most everybody."

cotton batting: See ***batting.***

cotton notes: warehouse receipts given for bales or otherwise packaged quantities of cotton stored in public warehouses, often used as early currency, e.g., "Mark's estate contained cotton notes of substantial worth."

cotton snobs: from the ante-bellum North, an expression used to describe the Southern upper class whose wealth came from cotton, e.g., "While they were glad to have the business of the cotton snobs, many Northern businessman resented their great wealth."

couch: unlike now, an upholstered, long couch without a back, and having an elevated end designed for and used as a headrest; sometimes early, a large bed for but one person, e.g., "The couch was of tufted wool and Victorian in styling"; "A couch and two ***bedsteads*** (q.v.) were listed with other ***chamber furniture*** (q.v.)." Also see ***lounge.***

coucher: a person trained in the art of ***paper making*** (q.v.), e.g., "The ledger revealed that in Burbank's shop there were three couchers employed."

coulter: a knife-like piece of iron (early) or steel (later), 8 to 10 inches long, mounted ahead of and in the path of a plow point, so designed as to cut roots while breaking new land, e.g., "The two coulters in the inventory revealed that Mark may have broken ***new land*** (q.v.)."

count coup: See ***coup, etc.***

count, countess: ancient terms; now, in Britain, an earl and his lady, e.g., "Of the ***nobility*** (q.v.) present, the count—earl—and his lady, the countess, enjoyed the greatest wealth." Also see ***peerage.***

countermark, counter mark: a mark, hole, or other alteration of the teeth of a horse or mule, the same serving to identify its owner, e.g., "Drake preferred to countermark his animals, since brands in the skin marred the appearance of the fine animals."

counterpane: a bed ***coverlet*** (q.v.), formerly sewn in squares resembling window panes, now of any pattern, e.g., "Miss Anne Lindsey proudly displayed her hand-made counterpanes at the county fair." Also see ***rug.***

carry provender: See ***provender.***

counterpoison: an antidote, e.g., "Dr. Drake's Day Book referred to a vial of counterpoison for snakebite."

counting house, counting room: a very early term meaning those facilities used for bookkeeping and accounting records and procedures; a department of a business wherein the keeping of accounts and records takes place or are kept, e.g., "Allison knew that her father might be found in the counting room whenever his laborers were due to be paid."

country furniture: refers, not to quality, but to any early furniture made by other than the well-known and recognized cabinetmakers, e.g., "Even though country furniture, the walnut table and chairs made by the early Vermont ***cabinetmaker*** (q.v.) were exquisite."

country linen: rough, sturdy, homespun fabric, made of flax and used in clothes of heaviest wear, e.g., "Their station in life was apparent by their use of country linen clothes for church wear."

country, trial by the: See ***pais, per.***

county courts: courts of record having jurisdiction at ***nisi prius*** (q.v.), guardianships, limited criminal jurisdiction, and usually hearing appeals from the justices of the peace, e. g, "Judge Richeson was a very able Ohio county court judge, even though he had no legal education."

county history: refers to those many late 19th- and early 20th-century publications of varying quality that told of specific counties, their people, politics and happenings, subscriptions for which usually were gained prior to publication, the subscribers submitting information of genealogical interest, e.g., "In the York County History, Anne found a map and an early tax list, both of which revealed the presence of her Dawe Revolutionary ancestor."

county home, county house, poorhouse, infirmary, county infirmary: early facilities, usually barracks-like, for the care and housing of the aged, weak, sick, poor, and others who were public charges, usually having extensive fruit and vegetable gardens in order to supply a portion of the sustenance of the residents, e.g., "The first Marion County Home, often called the 'county infirmary', supplied not only its own fruits, vegetables, and medicinal herbs and roots, but had enough extra of those items of produce to engage in barter and truck farming."

county house: See ***county home.***

county infirmary: See ***county home.***

county seat: that designated community or place within a county where court regularly was and is held, estates were administered, deeds recorded, and taxes paid; the term is very old, and referred to the place where the judges literally sat and dispensed justice and where ***court days*** (q.v.) were held as needed, e.g., "Diane and Evan went over to Findlay, the county seat, where she shopped and he paid their taxes."

county town: the ***county seat*** (q.v.) of a county or ***shire*** (q.v.), e.g., "County seats are quite usually known as county towns in the United Kingdom."

county: next to colonial governments and later the governments of the States of the Union, the most important subdivisions of early America and the principal political subdivision within a state, each county maintaining courts of general and special jurisdiction, the taxing authority, a repository for documents, law enforcement officers, and a treasurer, e.g., "Our pioneer ancestors looked mostly to the county for both the benefits of and the restrictions issuing from government." See also ***precinct, town,*** and ***manor.***

coup, coup sticks, touch coup, count coup: those polished or decorated sticks or poles having religious significance but of no value as weapons, early carried by Native Americans and often used to demonstrate bravery by touching such sticks to an enemy during mortal combat, e.g., "It was said that no less than three Sioux Indians touched coup on General Custer."

courses and distances: land boundaries set forth in compass points and measured distances, e.g., "Beginning at the southwest corner, the course and distance of the west line was 'north 10 degrees east, a distance of 310 feet'." Also see ***metes and bounds.***

coursing bees: See ***lining bees.***

court cupboard: a usually elaborate and large, high cupboard with an open bottom, one or more a shelves, and hinged doors concealing shelves at the top, e.g., "Her old court cupboard was made of tulip poplar."

court days: those predetermined dates during which regularly scheduled court sessions were held, usually quarterly, and during which celebration and games, shopping, trading, meetings, and elections were held, e.g., "The horse races were held in May during court days."

court of chancery: See ***chancery (court of).***

court of common pleas: See ***common pleas (courts of).***

court of oyer and terminer: See ***oyer and terminer (courts of).***

court of pleas and quarter sessions: See ***pleas and quarter sessions (courts of).***

court of probate: See ***probate courts.***

court of quarter sessions of the peace: See ***quarter sessions of the peace (courts of).***

court: in genealogy, either a judge or the judicial office of judges; an officer appointed or elected to make decisions "at law" or "in equity"; early, a judge of cases at law, as opposed to those in equity, which latter were decided "in chancery" by ***chancellors*** (q.v.), e.g., "The court decided that the case was one of ***assault*** (q.v.) and ***battery*** (q.v.)"; "The summer session of the court of pleas and quarter sessions commenced in early June."

courtesy: See ***curtesy.***

courting chair: See ***love seat.***

courts of appeals: in the courts of the United States, those courts of seven judges each, established for each of the nine U.S. circuits; in D.C., Kentucky, Maryland and New York, meaning the court of last resort; the next highest court in all other states, as well as in Connecticut, Virginia and West Virginia, however in Connecticut the highest court is the Supreme Court of Errors, and in the Virginia the highest is known as the Supreme Court of Appeals, e.g., "Drake's appeal was heard in the Court of Appeals for the Third Circuit"; "During her research, Brittany was careful to note the precise name given the court of appeals in states with which she was not familiar."

courts, circuit: those courts called common pleas in Ohio and South Carolina are the equivalent of the circuit courts in Virginia, "Sterritt, a Clerk of Courts in Ohio, and Williams, a Clerk to the Circuit Court in Virginia, hold virtually identical positions."

cousins, once removed, twice removed, etc.: the descendants of one's cousins, e.g., "His second cousin's son was his second cousin, once removed"; "His third cousin's grandson was his third cousin, twice removed."

cousins: early, any person related by blood who was not an ancestor, aunt or uncle, or a brother or sister; later and now, those blood relatives who descend from siblings of an ancestor, e.g., "His third cousins were descended from the siblings of his great-great grandfather."

cove: See ***hollow, etc.***

covenant: early, a formal enforceable pledge to do something or pay over money or other thing of value; in common parlance, an agreement or compact, written or unwritten, e.g., "In a deed, the covenant of seisin provides guaranties of the grantee's rights to possession."

cover, roger, cut: vulgar terms, meaning to have intercourse; breeding stallions were said to "cover" a mare, hence the application of the term to humans, e.g., "In confidence, she told her friend that he had covered her the night before"; "Samuel Pepys wrote of rogering his female acquaintances."

coverlet: as now, a bedspread; the outermost covering of a bed, e.g., "There were but two coverlets in the inventory, even though there were five beds."

coverture: the state and legal condition of a married woman, e.g., "During early coverture, without his written and formal permission she had no right of sale in her own real estate."

cow doctors: a veterinarian; physicians also often acted as veterinarians during early times, e.g., "William Carter was a cow doctor who lived in Jamestown in 1625."

cow peas: usually, black-eyed peas, e.g., "While cow peas was the term often applied to any inexpensive, podded vegetable used as cattle feed or otherwise, more often than not the term meant black-eyed peas, then and now a popular food in the deep South."

cowcatcher: the steel scoop or V-shaped ram placed a few inches above the track on the front of all early locomotives, designed to push animals, trees, and other debris from the tracks, e.g., "With the coming of the twentieth century, the cowcatcher was doomed."

cowl, cowle: a large vessel or kettle on a pole held between two persons, and in which liquids are carried; a large tub; also, a thick, heavy linen fabric, such as used in the garb of a monk, e.g., "The two men carried the cowl of water to the slaughter area"; "Early records occasionally reveal the presence of cowle for use as outerwear."

cowle: See ***cowl.***

cozy: a padded cover to maintain the warmth of a chocolate, tea, or other drink pot, e.g., "She had several cozies for use on the ***huntboard*** (q.v.) during cool morning chases." See ***chase, animal.***

cracker, crackers, corn cracker, firecrackers: originally in England, a noisy, boisterous person; in the early states and still sometimes in the south and west, illiterate country people; also meaning the drovers or drivers of cattle or animals by reason of their use of long whips which were snapped—cracked—over the heads of the animals to cause the beasts to move here or there as desired; celebratory firecrackers, e.g., "Townspeople referred to uneducated farmers as crackers, and many often so spoke of all Georgians"; "Bill Williams told that the popping noise in the air caused by their whips led early Georgian drovers to be known as crackers"; "For the children at the 4th of July celebration, he always made a few crackers from gunpowder."

crackers as food: probably as now, and also the baked pastries we call cookies, e.g., "Even though he advertised that he had a broad inventory, Rodriguez mentioned only his breads and crackers, of which 'Boston crackers' and 'Sugar crackers' were what we now call cookies."

cracklins: apparently never pronounced "cracklings"; those small pieces of meat, skin, etc., that rise surface as lard is rendered, e.g., "She always skimmed off, cooled, and gave the cracklins to the children as treats." Also see ***render***.

cracks, trotting cracks: slang for a sleek, fast horse, whether a running horse or a trotter, e.g., "Currier and Ives print 'Trotting Cracks At The Forge' is one of the most popular of their 19th century lithographs."

cradle: a bed for an infant; a narrow, slatted, platform attached to the foot of a ***scythe*** (q.v.), the same used to catch the stalks or stems of grain, e.g., "Without the cradle, the harvesting would have been much more time consuming and difficult."

crambo: a very early game for folks of all ages, in which, by turns, one person selected a word, whereupon others attempted to speak a rhyming word, "Bethany wrote that at the holiday all the adults had played crambo and had very much enjoyed that time spent."

crane: a crooked pipe or siphon for drawing liquors from a cask or barrel; the iron rod from which were hung kettles on pot hooks in a fireplace, e.g., "The innkeeper used a crane to take wine from the big casks"; "The crane was of black iron and often held the stew pot." Also see ***crook,*** and see ***pot hook.***

crank: See ***cranky.***

cranked horse: See ***coppersmiths' tools.***

cranky: irritable, upset, e.g., "The word cranky likely derives from the ancient nautical term, 'likely to crank', which meant that a ship was loaded to the point that it might overturn."

cranny, crannies: See ***nook and cranny.***

crap: See ***crapper***.

crapper, crap: a toilet; excrement; a term of scorn concerning something said or written, e.g., "It is supposed that the words crapper and crap derive from the name of the inventor of a flushable toilet, one Thomas Crapper"; "He said that the explanation of the thief was a 'bunch of crap.'"

cravat: early called a neckcloth, cravats were both decorative and provided warmth, e.g., "The cravats of the early days became the neckties of today."

craze: to cause the appearance of myriad cracks in the glazing of pottery or glassware, e.g., "Crazed vases were very popular at the turn of the twentieth century."

crazy quilt: a quilt made of many different patterns and fabrics placed in random order, e.g., "Brittany has a crazy quilt made from the clothes of her ancestors." Also see ***linsey-woolsey.***

cream-faced: a coward; one of very pale or delicate complexion, e.g., "When she wrote that her husband '...was a cream-face back then', she meant that he had been cowardly during the Civil War"; "His comment that she had a cream face was complimentary of her complexion."

creamware: any buff, oyster, or cream colored pottery, crockery or earthenware, e.g., "Bethany had a creamware bowl that had belonged to her grandmother."

Creek War: that series of conflicts in Alabama and present Mississippi between the Creek Indians and the frontiersmen and Tennessee militiamen under Andrew Jackson, which small war ended at the Battle of Horseshoe Bend, and resulted in the cession to the U.S. of most of the Creek lands, e.g., "James Findlay was a Captain of Volunteers in the Creek War."

creepers: unlike now, small, low, black iron racks to hold burning logs, e.g., "The creepers were used in the parlor fireplace." Also see ***andirons.***

Creole: a person born in Louisiana or the West Indies (usually the latter), having mixed French or Spanish ancestry, e.g., "Ante-bellum Creole women were said to be particularly beautiful."

cresset, cressets, crussie: large lamps or lights on metal poles or high pedestals, used as beacons; a black iron basket in which were burned oil, ***pitch*** (q.v.), ***faggots*** (q.v.), small logs, or other combustibles, the same used for outdoor illumination, e.g., "Cressets are yet used as street lamps in Colonial Williamsburg."

crest: a term of ***heraldry*** (q.v.); the devices or designs granted to and designating a certain person or family, set over a coat of arms and often mounted on helmets, etc., e.g., "Evan's crest, in part bearing two falcons, was known to all."

cricket: See ***footstool.***

crisps: See ***desserts, early.***

critters: very commonly used generally in the South, particularly in the stead of the words "bugs", "pests", or "varmints" and derives from the word "creatures" (precisely pronounced, kree-ah-tyers), e.g., "Referring to the many insects present, Sally said that she had sprayed castor oil on the flowers and thus had gotten 'rid of those critters'."

Croatan inscription: the letters "CRO" on a rock and the word "Croatan" on a post were the sole evidence remaining of Raleigh's Colony that disappeared between mid summer of 1586 and 22 July 1587, e.g., "The Croatan inscriptions perhaps revealed the island called Croatan as the destination of the settlers when the Indian difficulties forced them to abandon Raleigh's Colony."

crock, crockery, crock jug: any container or dish made of clay; earthenware; a handled clay container for liquids, e.g., "Diane had several crocks, including one for butter"; "Cheryl referred to her clay water pitcher as a crock jug."

croker sack: a large sack or bag made of burlap, e.g., "In the South, large sacks and bags made of burlap were universally called croker sacks." Also see ***gunny sack.***

crome: a pitchfork with down-turned tines used to unload a manure cart or wagon, e.g., "The crome was used to pull the manure along the bed and off the wagon."

crony: an acquaintance and friend over a long period of time, e.g., "Evan and Drake had been cronies for 30 years."

crook: a pot hook, quite usually of iron, e.g., "Every home had several crooks." Also see ***chimney hook and crane.***

cropper, share cropper: one who, though having no ownership in the land, farms it in exchange for a share of the crops produced, e.g., "In the post-Civil War South, many who previously had owned land worked as croppers."

crossbill: See ***bill and crossbill.***

crossed "p" (ꝑ or ꝓ***):*** that character or symbol universally found in early writings in the English language which appears like an ornate letter "p"; usually meaning "per-" or "pre-" or "pro-", "pai-" e.g., "As was typical, in the 1679 inventory of Judith Parker, the word 'pair' is several times written with a crossed p and the letter r, and the verification is in the words '***Vera record*** (q.v.) ꝑ W. E. ClCt', meaning 'this record verified per W. E., Clerk of the Court."

crotch grain: See ***flame grain.***

croup: early and now, a severe infection of the larynx or throat, usually accompanied with congestion, and in early times often fatal to children, e.g., "The early writings reveal that croup and ***whooping cough*** (q.v.) brought death to many children."

crow, crow bar: a metal door knocker, usually of brass or iron; a pry bar; a steel or iron bar with a bent, pointed tip, used to shift, raise or move heavy items, e.g., "She had a pretty brass crow at the parlor door"; "Without the crow bar, the task of the wagonmaker would have been much more difficult." Also see ***clicket.***

crowfoot: See ***caltrop.***

crown: early, often called a dollar; a British silver or gold coin worth 5 shillings or one quarter ***pound*** (£), (q.v.), e.g., "The crown was probably the most common coin in colonial America." Also see ***half-crown.***

crownglass: meaning glass fit for the Crown—the king or queen—the finest of window glass, e.g., "The homes of some of the wealthiest of colonials had windows of crownglass."

croze: See ***cooper's tools.***

cruciform: in the shape of a cross; a crucifix, e.g., "In keeping with the faith, many churches of our ancestors were cruciform in shape."

cruet, cruets, cruet holder, cruet rack: small stoppered or lidded glass bottles used for ***condiments*** (q.v.), and placed at the dining table; a ***caster*** (q.v.) of decorative metal (often silver or brass) usually placed on the table, into which were placed individual cruets, e.g., "Her cut-glass cruets were kept in a solid silver cruet holder." Also see ***caster.***

crumbcloth: a tablecloth; a cloth placed upon the table to facilitate removal of crumbs and to protect the wooden surface of the table, etc., "Her everyday crumbcloths were made of pink cotton."

crummy: in addition to the present meaning, a caboose of a freight train, e.g., "When Paul told precious little Brittany that he had ridden all the way from Fredericksburg on a crummy, she knew he meant a caboose."

cruse, cruskin: in England, a small cup; in the colonies, a large kettle or pot with a handle and a spout for pouring, e.g., "Martha boiled the soap in a cruse and carried it to the yard for the laundry."

cruset: the melting pot of a goldsmith, e.g., "The appearance of a cruset in the inventory made Diane suspect that the ancestor worked with gold."

cryer: an auctioneer, e.g., "The court ordered the sheriff to contract with a cryer for the sale of Bethany's jewelry and fine clothing."

crystal: glass of the finest quality, without blemish or discoloration, and usually containing lead, e.g., "The crystal wine glasses in the inventory probably were made in England." Also see ***leaded glass.***

cubbies: See ***pigeon holes.***

cubby holes: See ***pigeon holes.***

cubs: in the Americas, the young of bears and foxes, e.g., "There were six fox cubs in the den."

cuck: very early, to defecate, e.g., "The word cuck has been found but once in Virginia colonial records." But See ***cucking, cucking stool.***

cucking, cucking stool: seemingly not derived from the word "***cuck***" (q.v.), much like a ducking stool; Johnson (1802) says "an engine designed for the punishment of scolds and unquiet women", meaning a chair to which women (usually, and occasionally men) were strapped for specified periods of time in order that the public might know of and scorn their offensive words or actions, e.g., "In cases of particularly offensive words or gossip, women were sentenced to being tied to cucking stools for stoning and then dunked into water." Also see ***ducking stool.***

cullion, cullions: Johnson (1802) says a "vile fellow or scoundrel"; more recently, testicles or the scrotum, e.g., "Sarah wrote that, as had been his father, he was an '...unabashed cullion'."

cultivator: an implement used to work soil after plowing and before harrowing, e.g., "After the plow had opened the ground, the cultivator was the next step in the preparation of the soil for planting."

cum testamento annexo: literally, "with the will annexed"; an administration of an estate where one dies with a will, yet no executor was named in that will or the executor named was not qualified or otherwise could not serve, e.g., "The will named Evan as the executor, however the bond named Drake as executor cum testamento annexo." Also see ***administrator.***

cumber: early, a commonly used word meaning to embarrass, entangle in social problems, or to distract, e.g., "It was said by some New Englanders that the rules of gentlemanly conduct sometimes cumbered Southern businessmen."

Cumberland Gap: that pass in the mountains between what is now northeast Tennessee and southeast Kentucky, through which passed myriad of our ancestors on their migrations west, after the passage of which the immigrants went west and south to Tennessee and beyond, or north and west to Danville, Harrodsburg, Louisville and the ***Ohio Country*** (q.v.), e.g., "Many of the settlers on the Ohio River at Evansville had their roots in the Carolinas south and east of Cumberland Gap."

cup, cupping: in addition to the common meaning, the act of bleeding someone through an incision by placing a warmed glass cup over the wound and then cooling the glass and so creating a partial vacuum; ***phlebotomy*** (q.v.), e.g., "Most planters cupped themselves and their families, rather than call a physician or ***chirurgeon*** (q.v.)." Also see ***cupping glass.***

cupboard, step back cupboard: any of many cabinets, usually having set-back, open shelves above creating a shallow work space at waist level and having doored compartments below, e.g., "The word cupboard originally meant a board for hanging cups."

cupping glass: a small glass vessel with a smooth top used to ***cup*** (q.v.) e.g., "Seventeenth-century inventories often reveal cupping glasses." Also see ***cup, cupping.***

cupplate: a small flat plate or saucer upon which a cup was placed after some of its liquid contents were poured into a larger saucer to be used for drinking, e.g., "Only in the finest of early homes was a cupplate placed next to the cup and saucer in which tea, coffee, or hot chocolate were served."

curate: sometimes unlike now, a clergyman hired to perform the duties of another and, occasionally, a parish priest, e.g., "The curate of St. Stephen's held his office under another appointee during the long illness of the latter."

curator, curatrix: In civil law, a guardian, male or female; one who is appointed by a court to attend to the affairs of another, e.g., "In Texas and Louisiana, curators were appointed, yet one should notice that in Tennessee, Virginia and Ohio such persons were called guardians."

curds: as now, as in 'curds and whey', the solids in sour milk, e.g., "Curds and cream was a favorite Southern dish, made of curds 'carefully spooned to remove the whey, laid in a shallow dish, surrounded with thick cream, and eaten with powdered sugar'."

curio: any small memento or ***pretty*** (q.v.); any curiosity or ***heirloom*** (q.v.), especially if made of glass or fabric; frequently, a paned, doored cabinet designed to hold mementos, e.g., "Diane kept a dozen or so curios in her grandmother's ***side by side*** (q.v.)." Also see ***china cabinet.***

curricle: an uncommon, light, two-wheeled carriage or ***chaise*** (q.v.) drawn by two horses side by side, e.g., "He used the curricle for business trips of some distance."

Currier and Ives: that very well known, mid to late 19th-century manufacturer of colored prints and etchings, often idyllic, and usually of stylized home settings, but also of horses, transportation, trains, farms, and scenery, e.g., "Currier and Ives brought color and pleasure to millions of otherwise drab and somber rooms."

currier: one who prepares and dresses leather for use by other trades, e.g., "The currier's task well done resulted in beautiful shoes, boots, and fine harnessing." Also see ***tanner***.

curry: a brush or scratcher used to smooth the coat of a horse or mule, e.g., "Mrs. Bater directed the stable hands to carefully curry her mare every day, in order that it be free of parasites and dirt."

curtain top desk: See ***roll-type desk.***

curtains, curtins: early, usually the filmy or gauze-like hangings that surrounded a ***bed*** (q.v.), used in summer to keep insects from sleepers and, when more heavily textured, used in winter to prevent drafts or provide a measure of warmth and privacy, e.g., "The inventory of Helen's estate revealed 2 ***valance beds*** (q.v.) and the curtains and ***rugs*** (q.v.) to go with those beds."

curtesy: early, the life estate in the real property of a deceased wife to which a husband was entitled if the couple had lawful children born alive, e.g., "Through the law of curtesy, at the death of his wife, Mr. Haskins became a life tenant in the forty acres his wife had inherited from her father."

curtins: See ***curtains***.

curved horse: See ***coppersmiths' tools.***

cuss: unknown to Johnson, the word apparently arose in 19th century America; as now, to curse or use profane language, e.g., "He cussed too much, his mother said."

customhouse: that facility at which taxes were collected on goods being imported or exported, e.g., "The first customhouse for the Virginia Colony was located at Jamestown."

custrel: a wine glass, e.g., "There were several custrels in the inventory."

cut a fat hog in the rear (or, in the ass): a superlative, arising from the fact that a ham (hind leg) from a fattened hog was considered the choicest meat of the animal; to take advantage of an opportunity and benefit substantially; to succeed economically rather quickly, before it was anticipated, or to a greater degree than expected, e.g., "When his invention sold better than anyone had anticipated, it was said that he truly had cut a fat hog in the rear."

cut in, cut out: as now, to interrupt a dancing couple and take one of the partners as one's own, e.g., "When Drake cut in, Sarah was delighted."

cut to the chase: a directive or expression of urging that some person or persons hasten to the business at hand, or spend no more time with preliminaries, e.g., "After the participants of the chase spent more time with breakfast, conversation and brandy than Sarah thought was appropriate, she asked old Zeke to please tell them to cut to the chase before the morning was gone."

cut: a unit of length equal to 900 feet or 300 yards, e.g., "The factory made one half cut of ***serge*** (q.v.) per day."

cutgut: the linings of animal intestines prepared for early use in bookbinding and as strings for musical instruments, fishing lines and tennis rackets, e.g., "In the 1790s Philadelphia merchants Kuhn & Risberg advertised for sale 'black and brown buckrams and cutgut'."

cutlass, cutlace, cutlash, cutilax, kutlass: a broad, usually short, single-edged sword, generally thought of as the weapon of gentlemen, e.g., "In 1698 Owen Griffith, a former ***Cavalier*** (q.v.), bequeathed his kutlass to his youngest son."

cutler: early and now, one who makes or sells knives, or sometimes swords, sabers, etc., e.g., "Mark was a cutler by trade."

cuts, spin her cuts: apparently, a small or indeterminate quantity of flax or wool to be spun into thread, e.g., "In the letter, Todd described Diane as being '...busy spinning her cuts.'"

cutteau, couteau: a type of pocket knife carried by soldiers and hunters. "In the 1790s Philadelphia merchants Kuhn & Risberg advertised for sale 'cutteau and pistol capt pocket knives and razors'."

cutter: a small, light, usually one-horsed sleigh, seating two persons; a fast, light sailing ship used for near-shore and coastal waters, e.g., "During the long Vermont winters, the old doctor used the cutter to be about Benson"; "By reason of its handling qualities, the cutter *Phoenix* was a favorite of the old sailors."

cutting horse: an agile horse of great endurance used by cattlemen to work within a herd, e.g., "He preferred his black cutting horse when cattle were to be rounded up and moved."

cycle: See ***high wheel cycle.***

cylinder top desk, cylinder desk, cylinder front desk: usually a good to very fine quality, medium to large desk, with a recessing top for the writing surface that was shaped like a quarter circle or quarter barrel, e.g., "His magnificent cylinder desk was of solid walnut."

cynanthropy: mental illness; madness, e.g., "It was said that a person who suffered from any of the many mental illnesses had or suffered cynanthropy."

cypher: See ***cipher.***

D

d (preceded by a number): abbreviation for pence or penny; a designator of the size of nails, e.g., "In early times, there were twelve pence (12d) in a shilling (later 10)"; "There were '1500 9d nails' in the 1679 Judith Parker inventory."

d.s.p.: (Lat.) decessit sine prole, meaning that a person died without having had children, and often seen in genealogies or genealogical charts, e.g., "Elizabeth Carner, 1831-1917, d.s.p., meant that she had not ever given birth to children." Also see ***obit sin prole.***

daguerreotype: named for Louis Daguerre in 1839, a process by which a picture was made through exposure of a silver surface (made sensitive by iodine) to the vapors of mercury, e.g., "Many old daguerreotypes still exist in museums and in private collections, as well." Also see ***ambrotype***.

dale, vale: a valley, e.g., "The expression across 'hill and dale' means simply across hills and valleys."

dam: usually, a female equine parent; a term of breeders and owners of horses, e.g., "The Belgian dam and sire both were of the finest bloodlines."

damages: in the law, that money or thing of value ordered paid to compensate one who, through action, inaction or negligence of another, has suffered loss, detriment or injury to person, estate, family, or property, e.g., "To compensate Bater for the injury to his person and reputation, the court awarded and ordered paid to him damages in the amount of £5."

damask: linen or silk woven with a texture, e.g., "Todd's ***weskit*** (q.v.) of linen damask was most elegant."

damnified: to be damaged, as at law, e.g., "Many early court records make references to plaintiffs being damnified."

damps, damp: it was early thought that noxious vapors arose from lowlands and swamps, especially at night, and that the same were infectious or otherwise caused health problems; also defined by Johnson as a "noxious vapor exhaled from the earth", e.g., "All mothers were careful to see that their children avoided the damps"; "Milton wrote '...but with black air accompanyd, with damps and dreadful gloom....'." Also see ***drafts***.

dance a jig: See ***giggs***

dances: as now, e.g., "Some early popular dances, other than dances traditional to specific nations, included ***Virginia reels*** (q.v.), polkas, minuets, jigs (***giggs***, q.v.), square dances and ***borees*** (q.v.)."

dandy: slang, sometimes meaning splendid; a less than complimentary manner of referring to a young man known for overly stylish dress and partying, e.g., "Kenneth was the town dandy, and preferred the company of young women to his children or wife."

Danzik, Danzig: an early, better brandy, e.g., "The innkeeper listed two quarts of Danzig and a barrel of apple jack."

dapple gray: a color, gray with spots or splotches of lighter gray or white, usually of a horse, e.g., "His dapple gray ***Percherons*** (q.v.) were the largest in the show."

Dark Day, the: May 19, 1780; that day when it was widely observed that the sun did not rise, and that darkness prevailed over all the American colonies, e.g., "The Dark Day, if it truly did occur, is credited by most meteorologists to have resulted from an enormous and very widespread dust cloud of unknown origin."

dark of the moon: See ***waxing and waning.***

dasher (a person): a young person known for partying and revelry, e.g., "She wrote of encountering a handsome dasher."

dasher (a utensil): See **butter churn.**

daub, to, daub his cabin: to fill open spaces—chinks—such as between logs and in cracks, usually with clay or with mud mixed with straw, and so insulate and keep out the weather, e.g., "Daubing the cabin was an annual chore of all pioneers who had concern for the comfort and health of their families."

Daughters of the American Revolution, (Society of The, D. A. R.): a patriotic, hereditary, and charitable organization of women descended from men and women who performed patriotic or military service during the American Revolution, e.g., "Since Sarah's fourth-great grandfather had served in the ***Continental Line*** (q.v.) of Pennsylvania, she was eligible for membership in The Daughters of the American Revolution."

Daughters of the Confederacy (The United, U. D. C): a patriotic, hereditary, and non-profit society of women descended lineally or collaterally from persons who served honorably in either Confederate government service or in the armed forces of the Confederacy, e.g., "Since Allison's third-great grandfather was an Asst. Adjutant General under President Davis, she was eligible for membership in The United Daughters of the Confederacy."

daybed: a narrow single bed, usually used for daytime naps; a ***chaise lounge*** (q.v.); rarely, a long, padded seat, usually with a low back, the same for lounging or napping, e.g., "Except when guests were expected, Maggie kept the daybed in the corner of the parlor."

de bonis asportatis: an early action at law in trespass seeking the return of personal property taken away unlawfully, e.g., "The early records reveal many cases in trespass de bonis asportatis."

de bonis non (administratis): a successor or subsequent administrator of assets not previously administered, e.g., "When a previously unknown or undiscovered asset was uncovered after an estate had been closed, it was necessary for the courts to appoint administrators or administratrixes de bonis non." See ***administrator*** and see ***administratrix.***

de jure: legitimate; of right and legal title; the true legal state of a title, state of being, or relationship, even though contrary to the matter ***de facto*** (q.v.), e.g., "Though Larry and Sarah were married de jure, he was de facto married to Darren because he had never gained a divorce from Sarah, had lived with Darren for several years, had publicly acted as though she was his wife, and they had a child together."

de novo: of new; again; a second time, e.g., "The court issued a venire de novo summoning a jury for a new trial of the case."

dead beat: as in the sound that comes from a drum when the head (skin) is not tight; a person of little worth or who repeatedly fails to pay his debts or meet his obligations, e.g., "When it was learned widely that his word was not to be relied upon, he was known about town as a dead beat."

dead man's hand: the poker hand held by Hickok when he was shot dead, at Deadwood, SD, e.g., "Aces and eights with a nine has been the 'dead man's hand' since 1876."

dead pan: origin is perhaps lost, but see ***pan, pan powder.***

dead run: top running speed of an animal, usually a horse, and derived from some beliefs that a horse often will continue at its fastest pace until it collapses and dies, e.g., "Even at a dead run, his horse was no match for that of his opponent."

deadened timber: trees yet standing that have been killed, usually through girdling or by fire, e.g., "He had let the deadened timber stand so long that it was rotten."

deal, standard deal, slit deal, whole deal and deal ends: early units of measurement of unfinished lumber, a standard deal was 3" ('12/4') X 9" X 12', from which term and from card playing came the expression "good deal," "fine deal," "fast deal," etc., e.g., "There were forty deals of poplar in that load."

Dean, Deanery: as now; also, the next highest office of a diocese (q.v.); a priest appointed by a bishop to handle affairs in some certain division of a diocese; the assets and jurisdiction of a Dean, e.g., "Except in institutions of learning, the title of Dean is not now commonly used in the United States."

death, contemplation of: See ***in contemplation of death.***

debility: many early ailments were thought to be diseases rather than series of symptoms of other diseases, and were so called, e.g., "For many debilities, Dr. Drake prescribed cinchona, eucalyptus, quinine, ***bitters*** (q.v.), and alcoholic stimulants."

debt, bondage for: See ***peonage.***

debt, imprisonment for: See ***debtors' prisons.***

debtors' prisons: early, imprisonment often was ordered where one failed to pay debts without legal justification for that failure, the records of which are valuable research tools, e.g., "Debtors' prisons were eliminated commencing in 1817, some of the last to do so having been Kentucky in 1821, Ohio in 1828, Vermont and New Jersey in 1830, New York in 1832, Connecticut in 1837, Louisiana in 1840, Missouri in 1845, and Alabama in 1848. Also see ***peonage.***

decedent: usually, one who has lately died, either with or without a will, e.g., "Since her ancestor was described in the record as a decedent, she knew that he probably had died not long before that entry was written."

decessit sine prole: See ***d.s.p.***

deckles: See ***paper making.***

decoct, decoction: to boil or dissolve in hot water, e.g., "Early physicians often wrote of their decoctions."

decoy: as now, and see ***shawfowl***.

dedication: similar to ***baptism*** (q.v.), but without the use of water; a "conscious" proclamation or devotion; a usually Baptist service having as its objective a commitment of thought and action to religious purposes, e.g., "At his dedication, Drake pledged his life to good works."

dedimus potestatum: a commission, usually temporary, granted to take testimony or to perform acts in behalf of a court, usually at some distance, e.g. "The court record stated that a dedimus potestatum had issued to Mr. Haskins to gain the testimony of Mrs. Bater."

deed box, cista: a small box with a lid and usually a lock in which were kept valuable papers, wills, documents, deeds, etc., e.g., "His deed box was made of mahogany." Also see ***strong box.***

deed of gift: a document by which something thought to be of value is transferred to another with the intention that nothing of monetary value be given in return, e.g., "The deed of gift transferred a horse and ***buggy*** (q.v.) to her and mentioned his fatherly love."

deed: a formal, written document that memorializes a transfer of ownership of property (quite usually real estate) from one person or persons to another one or more people; when imprecisely used as a verb, the act of transferring interests in land, e.g., "Todd executed a deed to Allison for the 100 acres"; "Mark deeded the property to his daughter, Mikaila."

deef: See ***dumb.***

defendant: as in the law, any person against whom an indictment, information, charge, complaint, or claim has been filed in a court, e.g., "As a defendant charged with a crime, Evan had the ages-old right to confront his accusers."

defensives: an early general term referring to medicines and ***concoctions*** (q.v.) thought to prevent various ailments, e.g., "Ben Franklin advised hot bathes as defensives against many ailments."

defluxion: early, a description of what was thought to be the flow of bodily ***humours*** (q.v.) downward, e.g., "The swelling of Brittany's legs and feet was said by Bethany to result from a defluxion."

dehairing knife: See ***tanners' and curriers' tools.***

delftware, Delftware, Delfware, Holland china: better quality, glazed earthenware, usually from Holland and often glazed with tin, e.g., "Dr. Bater had a beautiful and large delftware bowl."

delirium: mental illness not having been understood, fevers associated with hysteria, lack of consciousness as to surroundings or actions, or nonsensical babbling were treated as ailments, e.g., "For delirium, Dr. Drake prescribed ***belladonna*** (q.v.), ***digitalis*** (q.v.), opiates, quinine and several different herbs."

dellain: high grade woolen ***stuff*** (q.v.), fabrics, e.g., "Clothing made of dellain was widely advertised and often purchased by those of affluence who desired to dress in more expensive clothing."

demand note: a promissory note that the holder, at his election, may declare due and payable at anytime after its execution, e.g., "Early extensions of credit, as now, very often were in the form of demand notes."

dementia praecox: (also known as adolescent insanity) an ill-defined term used to describe any of several varieties of mental illness, e.g., "Dr. Lockhart treated her dementia praecox with hot and cold compresses."

demi-boots: See ***shoes***.

demijohn: a large, small-necked glass container, usually protected by an open wooden encasement or a wicker jacket, e.g., "President Washington kept demijohns of favorite wines."

demi-sangue: (Fr.) of half blood, e.g., "Louisiana records sometimes speak of mulattos as being demi-sangue."

demise: death, or occasionally an end of some action, e.g., "Shortly before Paul's demise in 1672, he leased the tract for twenty years."

Democrats: See ***Whigs***.

dengue: breakbone fever; a severe and painful disease of the joints and muscles, peculiar to the South and not appearing in the records until after the beginning of the eighteenth century, e.g., "The dengue was similar to severe arthritis, however after a few weeks the mysterious disease subsided, apparently with no after effects."

denomination: a worth or value stated and set forth on the surface of coin or paper currency; a faith or religious discipline claiming allegiance by a group of persons, e.g., "The bills were in two, three, five, and ten dollar denominations"; "The old church was attended by those of the Baptist denomination."

deodand: an ancient term meaning something given to the church in the name of God to pacify wrath, e.g., "Some early colonials offered deodands, hoping thereby to prevent epidemics or ill fortune."

deponent: See ***depose***.

depose, deponent, deposition: the taking of a statement of facts from one who is under oath, usually in response to questions; one who gives testimony under oath in other than open court concerning the truth of some matter, which testimony is reduced to a writing called a deposition; the word ***affiant*** (q.v.) is often imprecisely used when referring to a deponent, e.g., "The deposition consisted of the statements of three deponents, all sworn and deposed together." Also see ***affidavit***.

deposition: See ***depose***.

depressions: See ***panics***.

deputy: a person usually empowered to act in behalf of another, usually refers to an officer of government, e.g., "In the absence of the ***coroner*** (q.v.), the deputy coroner exercised the duties of the former."

derringer: named for 1850s ***gunsmith*** (q.v.) Henry Derringer, a common short-barreled pistol carried in a purse, pocket, or hidden on the person, e.g., "It was a bullet from a derringer that killed Abraham Lincoln." Also see ***revolver***.

descend: real property (real estate) passing by operation of law at the moment of death, e.g., "The land descended to Todd in accordance with the statutes of ***descent and distribution*** (q.v.)."

descendant: one who lineally descends from another, no matter through how many generations; occasionally, those to whom property descends at a death, no matter of what kinship, e.g., "Drake was a descendent of a *Mayflower* passenger"; "There being no other known heirs, the land descended to his aunt's grandson."

descent: hereditary succession of real estate; that land received by virtue of being an heir at law of another, e.g., "Being the only child, upon the death of his parents ***intestate*** (q.v.), Evan became the owner of the land by descent."

descent and distribution: the effect of statutory and case law directing the disposition of property upon ***intestate*** (q.v.) death, e.g., "Since, at death, ***realty*** (q.v.) is said to descend and ***personalty*** (q.v.) is said to be distributed, laws controlling such activity are said to be 'laws of descent and distribution'."

descry: Johnson (1802) says to make known something newly discovered; to enthusiastically and quickly announce a discovery or unearthment, e.g., "With great pleasure, Bethany descried the arrow heads and burial place she had located."

deshabille, dishabille: a negligee, e.g., "Only the most stylish and affluent colonial women could rightly speak of their nightgowns as deshabilles."

desiccants, desiccatives: concoctions (q.v.) made to dry up sores and wounds, e.g., "The American Indians used various plants as desiccants."

desk box, lap desk, escritoire: a lap-size, wooden box with a liftable, hinged lid exposing a writing surface, and having space inside for storage of the supplies for writing, e.g., "As a planter who took long coach trips, Mr. Bater used his desk box frequently"; "While some called her writing box an escritoir, Bethany felt that to do so was to ***'put on airs'*** (q.v.)."

desk, slant-top desk, drop-leaf desk, drop-front desk, fall-front desk: a ***chest*** (q.v.) with a writing surface; early, any of several designs and styles, usually with a drop-leaf writing surface, behind which were ***pigeon holes*** (q.v.), a small drawer or two, having 2 or 3 drawers below the writing surface, and often with glass-paned, doored shelves above; later, any ***furniture*** (q.v.) designed for working on a writing surface and having drawers, e.g., "Her desk was mahogany, with ball-and-claw feet and brass typical of the period." Also see ***knee-hole desk, cylinder-top desk,*** and ***fall-front desk.***

desserts, early: as now, fruit was a popular ingredient for sweet dishes of many varieties, e.g., "In addition to ***sweetmeats*** (q.v.) and ***suckets*** (q.v.), patties were little sweet cakes; fried pies were spiced and sugared fruit in a fold of crust fried in a skillet; chess pie was a single crust pie of molasses, eggs, and flour, and henrietta pudding was similar, with brandy added but without a crust; bettys were sweetened fruit between crumb, shortening, and sugar crusts, while dowdies (pan dowdies) were bettys with a cream and fruit filling; if the top was of spices, sugar and flour, and it had no bottom or the bottom was of crumb, shortening, and sugar crust, it was a crisp; if fruit was covered with a layer of cake and then topped with flour, sugar, and spices before baking, it was a buckle; a cobbler was spiced fruit with a baked biscuit dough or other pastry top; if steamed, cobblers were called grunts, and if turned upside down for serving they became slumps; others were cheese cake, jumbals, flummeries, transparents, and pumpkin puddings."

detainer: usually, a legal action taken when one who was legally in possession has refused to give over possession of the land at the end of the term; where one assumes an appearance of ownership or undertakes a possessory interest to which he or she has no legal right, "When Mills refused to give up the land at the end of his lease, Bater filed an ***action*** (q.v.) in detainer." Also see ***forcible entry and detainer***.

detective, railroad: See ***dick, railroad.***

determinable fee: See ***fee determinable.***

detinue, writ of, or action in or of: an ancient ***common law*** (q.v.) action by which one sought to recover personal property lawfully obtained in the first instance, yet unlawfully later withheld from the rightful owner, e.g., "When Miller would not surrender the merchandise that Evan had paid him to store, Evan filed an action in detinue."

Deutsch: as in "Pennsylvania Dutch," See ***Dutch***.

Deutschland, the: See ***Pennsylvania Dutch*** and see ***lighter than air craft.***

Devil's Fruit: See ***tomato.***

Devil's grip: See ***pleurodynia.***

deviner: See ***dowser, etc.***

devise, devisor, devisee: to give or grant land (real estate) to another by will, e.g., "Paul devised 100 acres to Brittany"; "Evan was the devisor of the tract"; "As one of Drake's devisees, Bethany received forty acres." Also see ***bequest***.

dewberry: raspberries, e.g., "Some early cookbooks spoke of dewberries when referring to raspberries."

diabolic: See ***diabolism.***

diabolism, diabolic: devil, evil spirits, or fallen Angel worship, from which root we derive diabolic, e.g., "Some not thought to be witches still were believed to be involved in diabolism."

diacodium: the oil from poppies and poppy seeds; an opiate, e.g., "Old Dr. Cheryl gave diacodium for most nervous disorders."

diamond stack woodburner: See ***woodburner***.

diaper: very early, linen woven into floral patterns; later, a napkin, e.g., "The mention of diaper in early inventories has nothing to do with infants."

diaphoretic, diarrhoetick: as now, a ***purge*** (q.v.); a ***concoction*** (q.v.) that promoted perspiring, vomiting, or passage of body waste was thought useful in balancing the ***humours*** (q.v.), e.g., "Dr. Drake prescribed hot, bitter, diaphoretic ***cordials*** (q.v.)."

diarrhea: as now, e.g., "Early remedies for common stomach complaints accompanied by diarrhea included teas made of combinations of whole geraniums, black raspberry bark, and the bark of the roots of red oak." Also see ***dysentery, flux***.

dibble, dibbele: a small spade, e.g., "The inventory revealed a ***mattock*** (q.v.), a ***dung fork*** (q.v.), and a dibble."

dice box: a small box from which dice were shaken and then rolled during games, usually of chance, e.g., "The presence of a dice box revealed leisure time dedicated to games and gambling by adults." Also see ***billiard and pea.***

dick, railroad dick: now, vulgar; formerly, a detective, particularly for the railroads, whose task it was to learn the causes of accidents, identify illegalities and mischief makers, determine losses from such as thievery and other losses to the railroad and to its customers, e.g., "Bill Ferguson was a railroad dick for the R.F. & P. for more than 20 years."

diet-drink: as now; yet early, a medicated liquor, usually prescribed to promote general well-being, e.g., "His prescription of diet-drinks had nothing to do with obesity."

digit: a measure of length equaling .75 inches, and supposedly the breadth of a man's thumb, e.g., "The musket was bored a bit less than a digit."

digitalis: used since early times, a widely used and effective stimulant for the heart made from the dried leaves of the purple foxglove plant, e.g., "The 18th- and 19th-century physicians always carried digitalis for use by their heart patients."

digs, dugs, old digs, old dug: a place of habitation; a prior and usually humbler residence or abode of a person, e.g., "He wrote that they had three '...lights, but in the old digs, we had but one'." Also see ***light***.

dimity: early, common, fine cotton cloth, e.g., "Laura carried handkerchiefs of beautiful laced dimity."

dinner: early and occasionally now, that usually heavy meal eaten at mid-day, now often called lunch; later and often now, that meal, formerly called supper, eaten in the evening after the work-day was over, e.g., "By reason of the hard work and long hours required of rural families, the main meal of the day was that known as dinner and taken at mid-day."

dinner bell, dinner horn, dinner chime: a bell or horn rung or blown and used to summon to a meal those workers in the fields or at a distance, e.g., "Virtually every American farm of the 19th century had a dinner bell or horn." Also see ***dinner***.

dinner pot: that large, often 2 to 10 gallon kettle, usually hung in the fireplace on a ***crane*** (q.v.), and in which meat and vegetables were cooked into a stew, e.g., "In order that family members coming in from the cold might be warmed and nourished, the dinner pot usually was kept warm throughout the winter."

diocese: the entirety of the jurisdiction of a bishop, e.g., "Being within his diocese, the Bishop consecrated the church at Yorktown."

dip, dipping, dipping snuff: early, as now, the practice of placing small amounts—a dip—of chopped, smokeless tobacco (***snuff***, q.v.) between the teeth and cheek, e.g., "The practice by both men and women of dipping snuff was widespread, particularly in the early South."

diphtheria: a dreaded, acute, and usually fatal bacterial disease, for which there was no inoculation until 1895, the symptoms of which were a raging fever, extreme sore throat, and severe congestion, e.g. "During the 1860s, as a cure for diphtheria, Dr. Drake administered a gargle of honey, vinegar and alum, and stimulants, such as alum and sulfur, lactic acid, and ice, none of which effected a cure."

direct indexes, reverse indexes: indexes to deeds and mortgages compiled in alphabetical order by surnames of grantors or mortgagors and grantees or mortgagees; often called grantor or grantee indexes, e.g., "Mikaila knew that the direct indices found in Tennessee registers' offices served the same purpose as the grantor indices of Ohio." Also see ***grantor indexes***.

dirigibles: See ***lighter than air craft***.

dirk: a dagger; a common, small, knife-like weapon, usually carried hidden on the person, e.g., "The inventory included a dirk and a ***case knife*** (q.v.)."

dirt devil: See ***dust devil.***

disc: See ***harrow.***

discharge: as now; a release of a person from military obligation which may be "honorable", "dishonorable" "special" or other; that written document intended to provide proof of the release of someone from a military unit, e.g., "Bethany found the Civil War discharge of her 3rd-great grandfather among her own grandfather's papers."

discutient: any early application of medication thought to have preventative qualities, e.g., "For a discutient, she prepared a garlic ***amulet*** (q.v.)."

disentailment: the legal result of those statutes of and after William IV by which ***entailments*** (q.v.) were extinguished, e.g., "Even though the deed to Brittany was in ***fee tail*** (q.v.), the statute disentailed the land." Also see ***dock.***

dish: unlike now, a broad, wide container or platter from which solid food was served; sometimes, a rather deep, hollow container from which liquid food was served, e.g., "While the inventory listed only two dishes, the reason was that the word then had a quite different meaning."

dish-top table: any of several popular styles of small tables, including ***tilt tops*** (q.v.) that have a slightly depressed top or a rim around the top creating an appearance of a depression, e.g., "Her tilt dish-top table was mahogany and of Victorian styling."

disinherited, disherison, disinherison: the state of being deliberately excluded from an estate inheritance in which one would expect and otherwise legally be entitled to share; e.g., "In his will, the father mentioned the son's supposed transgressions and then specifically disinherited him"; "Early Oregon and Louisiana records sometimes speak of the disherison of children."

dismission: early, Milton used the word to mean an honorable discharge from public office; later and now, to be discharged under any circumstances, e.g., "Skeels received his dismission as ***fence viewer*** (q.v.) on Dec. 1, 1699."

dissent: when the provisions of a will gave a widow less than she would have received by law had there been no will, she could dissent from the will and the courts would award her that portion she would have otherwise gained. "Having given her but the income from one fourth of his estate, upon her dissent the court raised the income to that received from one third of the total assets." Also see ***take against a will.***

distemper: a common term used until the mid-nineteenth century to describe almost any disease or sickness; nervous disorders, usually thought to emanate from the brain or central nervous system, e.g., "The mother would describe as a distemper almost any ailment that she did not understand"; "For distempers, Todd often administered oils of plants such as of cloves, cinnamon, and cassia, or penny royal, wintergreen, and even ***turpentine*** (q.v.)."

distress, make distress: a court-ordered seizure and assumption of ownership of assets to pay some debt or obligation, e.g., "The court ordered the sheriff to 'make distress' of and seize the property of any person who failed to pay the new tax levy."

dittany: a plant with purple flowers, common to the eastern U.S., thought to have great medicinal value, and used widely by early physicians and healers, e.g., "For snakebites, Dr. Lockhart often prescribed a ***decoction*** (q.v.) of dittany."

divers: early expression, not synonymous with "diverse" (Johnson, 1755); widely used, especially in the King James Bible meaning an indeterminate yet considerable number of the subject items, e.g., "Mikaila noted that there were divers wild animals on her father's land."

divination: a telling of future events, e.g., "What we now call fortune tellers would have been said to be involved 'in divination'."

divining rod: See ***dowser, etc.***

division: See ***armies, organization of.***

divorce: formerly, either the dissolution of marriage by a divorce ***"a vinculo matromonii"*** (q.v.) (from the bonds of matrimony) or through a separation by divorce ***"a mensa et thoro"*** (q.v., from table and bed or bed and board), the latter being a suspension of duties that usually left the marriage in full force and effect; now, the word applies to all forms, e.g., "A divorce a vinculo matromonii left the parties free to remarry, while divorces a mensa et thoro were similar to modern legal separations and forbade cohabitation, yet left the marriage and property rights arising therefrom intact."

do you have fishhooks in your pocket?: See ***fishhooks in your pocket, have you.***

dobe, dobes: not mentioned by Johnson (1755 & 1802); quite probably a prepared or cooked delicacy containing meat, yet now unknown, e.g., "In 1859, R. A. Howard of New Orleans advertised for sale ' boned turkeys, French pates, boiled hams, dobes, (and) gallatines...'." Also see ***gallatines.***

Dobra, double johannes, Johannes, double joe, etc.: a Portuguese coin equaling to about four pounds Sterling (£3/18S/5p), e.g., "There being very little currency available in the colonies, the merchants accepted the coin of many countries, including the sailors' gold Dobras, often called double joes."

dock, dock an entailment: e.g., "When an entailment was extinguished by action of law or by a court, that entailment usually was said to have been docked." Also see ***entailment.***

dock, docking: the stump that remains after an animal's tail has been removed; to cut an animals tail, e.g., "She thought her ***filly*** (q.v.) would be a prettier ***mare*** (q.v.) if her tail was docked."

dodger, corn dodger: See ***pone.***

dog, to dog, dogging: to hunt indefatigably, as a hunting dog might do, e.g., "When Worrell wrote 'May God dog you', he was expressing a desire that his friend always be mindful of the Almighty."

dog dollar, lion dollar: an early Dutch coin, so called by reason of a lion imprinted thereon which had the appearance of a dog, e.g., "By reason of the lack of currency, New York and Philadelphia merchants were happy to accept dog dollars from immigrating Hollanders and seamen."

dog fox: a male fox, e.g., "There were 2 ***vixens*** (q.v.), 6 ***cubs*** (q.v.), and a dog fox in the group."

dog in that fight, no: See ***no dog in that fight.***

dog irons: See ***andirons.***

dog lock: a flintlock with a hammer of a design appearing like a dog's shoulders and head, e.g., "A few mentions of dog locks appeared in early New England writings."

dog, bench dog: a simple device tapped down into a work surface, designed to hold material being shaped or worked, e.g., "Mark had several bench dogs in his workshop."

dogdays: July 3 until August 11; those days during which Sirius, the "Dog Star", rises and sets with the sun, e.g., "Dogdays were thought to bring ***distempers*** (q.v.), especially of a mental sort."

dogie, dogey, dogy: apparently unknown in England, in the American colonies, especially in the 19th-century West, an orphaned calf, e.g., "The lyrics in the old cowboy song, "...get along little dogey..." had nothing to do with dogs."

dogs: See ***andirons, etc.***

dogtrot: a walkway; a hallway, openable or opened at both ends and usually extending from one end or side of a house to the other, the same providing air circulation, e.g., "On rainy days, the dogtrot provided a safe, dry place of play for children."

dog-watch, lobster shift, lobster watch: a seaman's term, early meaning that lookout duty time from 1600 hours to 1800 hours (4:00 PM to 6:00 PM), and later and now, probably from 1800 hours to 2000 hours (6:00 PM to 8:00 PM), e.g., "While in port all sailors preferred the dog watch, since there was ample time thereafter to go ashore for the evening."

doily: early, thin cotton or woolen cloth or ***napkin*** (q.v.); later, as now, a small piece of usually loosely woven cloth used as a shlef or table pad or decoration under some small object, e.g., "The ***ell*** (q.v.) of doily listed in the ledger revealed that napkins, as we now know that term, likely would be made from that material."

doldrums: unlike now, that band of intermittent and non-directional winds lying between the Northern and the Southern Trade Winds, e.g., "When blown into the doldrums sailing ships had great difficulty regaining their schedules." Also see ***trade winds.***

dollar: at the turn of the nineteenth century, a Dutch or German coin, e.g., "If an early reference to a dollar is found in a neighborhood of Hollanders or Pennsylvania Dutch, the meaning may have been different from now." Also see ***milled dollar*** and ***Spanish dollar.***

dolly stick, dolly tub: a narrow, wooden paddle or wide stick used to agitate clothes during laundering in a large kettle called the dolly tub, e.g., "One of the chores of the little girls was to help by working the dolly stick."

dolly tub: See ***dolly stick.***

Domesday Book: that most revealing and incredibly detailed and accurate effort commissioned by William I—"the Conqueror"—and undertaken by five justices within each county in England commencing in 1081 and ending in 1086, e.g., "The Domesday Book consisted of two volumes, and in all of English history is probably the most valuable series of extant writings touching upon early life."

domestic, a: a female doing work or performing services about the house, often in exchange for pay or room and board, e.g., "The 1870 census listed Sarah next after the children and revealed that she was a domestic in the home."

dome-top trunk: See ***camel-back trunk.***

domicile: that place which one considers "home," and to which one might choose to return over any other residences; that place where one has chosen to live and vote, e.g., "During the work week, Allison lived in New York City, however her home in Alabama was her true domicile."

dominicker: a fighting rooster (fighting chicken), e.g., "He noted in the diary that he had sold '3 dominickers' that day and had gotten the best of the deal." Also see ***deal.***

don't lick my calf: a common expression, particularly in the South, derived from the fact that a cow may sometimes lick the calf of another cow, thus drawing its attentions from its true mother; meaning do not so treat someone as to draw away the affection of that person from another to whom affection or duty is owed, e.g., "Jean angrily told her meddling sister-in-law, 'You stop licking my calf—NOW!'"

don't wing him, if you shoot the king: words of precaution that if one undertakes acts that are potentially dangerous to that actor's future well-being, economically or physically, those acts must be thorough, well thought out, and very effective, e.g., "When she learned that he intended to expose the philandering of his well-known and powerful political opponent, Miss Ferguson advised, 'Believe me, if you intend to shoot that king, don't wing him'."

donatio causa mortis: a gift of personal property in anticipation or apprehension of death, with the understanding that should the giver survive, the gift will be null and void and that property again will become that of the giver, e.g., "His gift to the child of two steers was donatio causa mortis." Also see ***in contemplation of death.***

door shutter: an outside door, as in our storm doors, e.g., "While window shutters were inside the house and sash, door shutters were not."

dornick: Scottish linen cloth used on a table or as ***napkins*** (q.v.), e.g., "The inventory listing of dornick revealed a genteel lifestyle or background."

dorser: leather or cloth carriage bags that hang across, usually one on each side, of an animal, e.g., "Drake used leather dorsers across his donkey to carry the raw opals to town for sale."

dorseteen, dorsetine: a cloth or fabric, probably now unknown, e.g., "In 1798 Kuhn & Risberg of Philadelphia advertised 'assorted silk ***camblets*** (q.v.), hairbines and dorseteens' for sale."

dory: early and now, a flat-bottomed rowboat with high sides, popular as a fishing boat, e.g., "In early times there were many dories in and about Chesapeake Bay and James River."

dotage, dotard, to dote: a loss of understanding upon attaining old age; childlike actions sometimes seen in the very old, e.g., "In the 1844 lawsuit Jacob Kistler was said to be a dotard; that is, he was in his dotage."

dotard: See ***dotage.***

dote, to: See ***dotage.***

double action, double action revolver: See ***single action,*** and see ***handgun.***

Double Eagle: See ***Eagle.***

double time, double: a military term meaning at a pace twice or more than that of a walk or march; from "on the double", at a fast pace, at a run, very quickly, e.g., "The sergeant announced that the exercise would be at double time"; "The drill instructor shouted that he expected the men out of the barracks on the double."

doublet: a close-fitting, vest-like garment, having a tail around like a very short skirt, usually without sleeves, e.g., "Both men and women regularly wore doublets during early colonial times." Also see ***jerkin.***

doubletree: See ***swingletree.***

doubloon, doublon: a Spanish coin equaling two pistoles, e.g., "It is common to find mention of doubloons in early southern and southwestern records."

dough table, dough box: a small table or bin of women's waist height, "V"-shaped, usually with a shallow-lidded top; a dough box has a compartment under the hinged top surface, the same used to knead and work dough which then is placed beneath the top for rising, e.g., "Jean's dough table was kept in the corner of the winter kitchen near the stove."

Dough-boy Brigade: See ***military combat units, famous.***

Dough-Boys: American infantrymen serving in Europe, especially during World War I, e.g., "Dough Boy, Howard Carner, lost his left hand and the use of his left arm in 1918 during the battles in the Argonne Forest."

Dover's Powder: a widely known mixture said to have curative powers for many ailments and concocted by of Dr. Thomas Dover, it was a mixture of opium and ipecac, and after 400 years is yet used as a ***diaphoretic*** (q.v.), e.g., "The inventor of Dover's Powder had been a ***pirate*** (q.v.)."

dovetail: a widely used method to join corners of ***furniture*** (q.v.) or drawers, the cuts being shaped like the tail of a dove and then interlocked, hence the name, e.g., "The drawers were hand dovetailed both front and back, thereby revealing the high quality of the early workmanship."

dowager: early, a title of respect given to older ladies (as distinguished from women) who survived their husbands, e.g., "Her husband having been a gentleman, she was referred to as a dowager."

dowdies: See ***desserts, early.***

dower: that portion of the estate of a decedent that is reserved by law for the maintenance and support of the surviving spouse and their children; originally a portion cut from those funds derived or produced from any real estate gained by the deceased during marriage which his children might have inherited; rights of a widow in real property of her deceased husband that varied from state to state, e.g., "At his death, the court ordered her dower to be set aside in cash."

dower chest: a decorated, usually well made ***chest of drawers*** (q.v.), e.g., "In many families, each daughter was given a dower chest."

down you, down someone, (to) put someone down: to belittle another person, e.g., "He advised his son that no one in the family would permit another to down him."

dowry: that property brought to the marriage by the bride, which, in early years, became the property of the husband, e.g., "As her dowry, Bethany brought sixteen head of ***neat cattle*** (q.v.)."

dowser, deviner, water witch, divining rod: one who is thought able to detect underground water, minerals, oil, etc., by use of a divining rod, usually a small fork of wood from peach, apple, cherry, plum, or witch hazel (particularly) trees, those thought to have mystical powers to reveal water, oil, or treasure when used by one who had knowledge of such matters, e.g., "Haskins was widely known for his powers as a deviner or water witch"; "Many was the early dowser who, hazel fork in hand, selected the spot to drill for water."

drab: thick, usually coarse woolen cloth, generally dyed or naturally appearing yellow-brown, from which our current word 'drab' derives, e.g., "Evan's overcoat was made of drab."

drachm: See ***dram.***

draft: ***conscription*** (q.v.) into military service, common in the U.S. during all wars after the Mexican War, e.g., "The locals failed to volunteer, hence were placed among the first in the local draft rolls."

draft, the: See ***private, private soldier.***

draft age: See ***military age.***

draft animals, draught horses: heavy, powerful horses widely used for work, plowing, pulling heavy loads, turning stiles, etc., e.g., "Drake's team of ***Belgian*** (q.v.) draft horses weighed 4300 pounds." Also see ***Clydesdale, Conestoga, Percheron.***

drafts, draughts: slight, cool or cold breezes or movements of air, early thought to be a cause of many and various maladies; also, the game of checkers, e.g., "She sought to keep drafts from sleeping children"; "Draughts was a popular pub game in England." Also see ***damps.***

drag: a simple conveyance, usually a platform on two poles, pulled—dragged—behind a man or animal, e.g., "Hines wrote of making a drag to bring the wounded man back from the forest."

drag sled, drag sledge: a wide-runnered, heavy, flat-bedded wooden sled, usually pulled by 1 or 2 horses and used for heavy hauling about a farm, e.g., "In the winter, Mr. Keener would hitch the mare to the drag sled, spread straw on it, and permit the young folks to take it to the fields for play."

dragoon, dragoons: a soldier taught, equipped, and prepared to fight, usually on horseback but sometimes on foot, e.g., "The English Dragoons were dismounted during the Battle at Bunker Hill." Also see ***armed men.***

drain, dreen, drean: as now, and a gully or natural drainage course, e.g., "Early land descriptions sometimes mention drains as landmarks or boundaries."

dram or drachm: a measure of dry weight equaling 3 ***scruples*** (q.v.); an eighth of an ounce; 3.89 grams; a small drink of any intoxicating liquor, e.g., "He took his drams with great pleasure"; "Early apothecaries and physicians very often referred to and wrote of drachms of medications"

dram shop: occasionally, a drinking shop; a place where liquor was sold for consumption on the premises, e.g., "There was a dram shop near the Governor's Palace at Williamsburg."

draper: a seller or merchant of usually better quality fabric (stuff, q.v.), e.g., "In the seventeenth century one of the drapers of Cheapside, London was named Drake." Also see ***occupations as surnames.***

draught animals: See ***draft animals.***

draughts: See ***drafts.***

draw a bead, drawed a bead: meaning to aim carefully while preparing to shoot a firearm, and derived from early firearms which had a metallic button at the end of the barrel over which one sighted the weapon, e.g., "Old Tennessee mountaineer John Nye told that he had 'drawed a bead, ***touched her off*** (q.v.) and down went the wolf'."

draw block: See ***silversmiths' tools.***

draw knife, drawknife: a bladed tool with handles on both ends, so designed as to cut when the tool is drawn toward the body, e.g., "Every early carpenter and ***cabinetmaker*** (q.v.) had drawknives of varying sizes."

draw machine: See ***silversmiths' tools.***

drawers, long johns: as now, warm undergarments, whether covering the legs and lower part of the body or only the lower body, e.g., "His drawers were of cotton."

draws: an early word meaning drawers of a box, cabinet or ***chest*** (q.v.), e.g., "Brittany had a ***chest on chest*** (q.v.) with three draws above and two below."

dray, dray cart: very early, a two-wheeled cart used to haul beer; later, any sturdily built cart or wagon used for the transport of goods, especially for hire, e.g., "The Capitol City Line had 8 drays and 14 draymen in its employ."

drean: See ***drain.***

Dred Scott Case, Dred Scott vs. Sandford: that classic and much studied Supreme Court decision of 1857 that deeply angered the North by determining generally that Scott, a slave, by residing for a period in a "free" State, was not himself thereby free, and that the ***Missouri Compromise*** (q.v.), insofar as it declared him free, was unconstitutional on the grounds that it deprived persons of property in the form of slaves without due process and so was contrary to the 14th Amendment, e.g., "For the first time since Marbury vs. Madison (1803), the Dred Scott decision found an act of Congress unconstitutional."

dredger, drudger: a shallow box in which meat, etc., is floured or from which, at the fireplace, flour is placed on cooking foods, e.g., "Her dredger was large enough for a whole loin of pork."

dreen: See ***drain.***

dress makers: See ***mantua, mantua maker.***

dressed out, dressed: refers to a food animal carcass from which the head, entrails, and skin have been removed, e.g., "The steer weighed 900 lbs. before being dressed out and 575 lbs. afterwards"; "Evan's turkey, dressed, weighed eleven pounds."

dresser: one who serves a surgeon as an assistant or otherwise, often as an apprentice while learning that ***'art and mistery'*** (q.v.); a table upon which meat was ***dressed*** (q.v.), cut or trimmed, e.g., "Dr. Evan provided training and room and board and paid $1.75 per week so long as she acted as a dresser for him"; "Diane Frances's dresser and knives in the early inventory had nothing to do with 'making up' by women, even though the dressing room mentioned surely did."

dressing glass: a free standing, framed mirror of many sizes, e.g., "Being poor, Mrs. Haskins had but one small dressing glass which was carried from room to room as the family needed it."

dressing table (ladies): a small table, with one or two drawers beneath and sometimes one or two small drawers at the rear or sides of the top, often with a backboard or mirror, e.g., "In her bedchamber, she had a mahogany dressing table."

drill, seed drill, corn drill: as now, a device for boring holes; a manually operated device that inserted a pre-selected quantity of seed into a hole in the ground made by the lower end of the device, e g., "The drill was a great labor-saver in spring planting." Also see ***sow.***

dripping pan: a utensil for cooking meat, with a perforated tray positioned above the bottom through which the melted grease and oil could drip, the same sometimes saved for later use in illumination and soap making, e.g., "Hunt gained a dripping pan and several other kitchen items from the estate."

droit: (Fr.) in French law, a legal right, e.g., "In Louisiana and Canada, the researcher encounters droits of many sorts; droit d'accession, droit d'execution, droit de detraction, droit de suite, etc."

drop-front desk: See ***fall-front desk.***

drop-leaf desk: See ***fall-front desk.***

drop-leaf table: usually, a well-finished dining table, having one or two leaves that fold downward for economy of space when not in use, and often with a small drawer on one or both ends used for knives, utensils, etc., "Diane's Sheraton drop-leaf table was of beautiful cherry and walnut and was made about 1840."

dropsical: See ***dropsy.***

dropsy: any unneeded collection of water in the body; retention of water, e.g., "During his last years General Winfield Scott suffered so from dropsy that he had to be lifted to the saddle." Also see ***defluxion*** and see ***gout.***

drover: sometimes, one who fattened cattle; usually, one who herded or drove livestock to market, e.g., "In the 1860s Richard Roberts and his sons were farmers and drovers."

drownder, goose drownder, frog drownder: superlatives; very heavy rain, e.g., "Brittany said, 'Talk of rain, that was a real goose drownder'."

druggist: early, a wholesale merchant or purveyor of chemicals, drugs, herbs, etc., for medicinal use, e.g., "As a druggist was a wholesaler of medicinal products and the makings therefor, the ***apothecary*** (q.v.), later called a pharmacist, was a mixer and retailer of those products."

drugster: an early druggist, e.g., "The references to him as a drugster and as an ***apothecary*** (q.v.) both had the same meaning."

drummer: early, a travelling salesman; later, and sometimes now, commercial agents who supply retailers, e.g., "As a drummer of farm machinery, he had many occasions to travel by stagecoach."

drums, beat up the: to draw attention by loud playing of drums, e.g., "The records of old Boston refer to a day when the 'drums (were) beat up and proclamations made'."

dry, dry states, dry county, dry area: a political ***subdivision*** (q.v.) that prohibits the sale of alcoholic beverages, e.g., "For many years it was dry across Tennessee and Kentucky from the north Chattanooga city limits to the south limits of Cincinnati."

dry county: See ***dry, dry states.*** etc.

dry dock: the facility and premises used for ship repair when the vessel must be out of the water to accommodate the work, e.g., "The beautiful schooner, 'Calthrop Neck', was in dry dock at South Boston in January of 1900." Also see ***stocks.***

dry goods: any merchandise, other than hardware, tools, fuel, food and spices, kept by a storekeeper or merchant, e.g., "As a dry goods merchant, among the many items of inventory, Eli stocked shoes, dresses, ***stuffs*** (q.v.), firearms, ammunition, sewing materials and equipment, and dyes."

dry run: See ***prong.***

dry sink: a small to medium sized cabinet, usually with a compartment or drawers and closeable doors beneath the top, with the well top divided into a work space and a shallow well, e.g., "She kept a walnut dry sink in the corner of the kitchen."

dryfatt: a barrel, cask, or other large container used to hold and ship dry goods, especially powders, e.g., "The powdered sulfur was shipped in a dryfatt of 525 lbs. capacity."

ducat: often mentioned in colonial writings, any of the silver or gold coins of various values issued at various times in Europe, e.g. "He paid three gold ducats for the colt."

duces tecum: an early writ or court order directing that a person appear before the court and bring certain mementos, papers, documents, or writings with him, e.g., "The Sussex order books revealed several subpoenas duces tecum." Also see ***subpoena.***

duchess: the lady of a duke, e.g., "Mrs. Simpson became the Duchess of Windsor upon her marriage to the abdicated King Edward."

duck: strong, heavy, plainly woven cotton or linen fabric, sometimes dipped in oil, wax, or tallow in order to render it waterproof, e.g., "During the Revolution, Mikaila made duck duffel bags for her sons to carry to war."

ducking stool, dunking stool, trebucket, tumbrel: a stool to which criminals, ***scolds*** (q.v.), those found guilty of crimes of morality, and other miscreants were tied for ducking under water as punishment, e.g., "Elizabeth Sherwood of Queen Ann County was sentenced to the dunking stool for witchcraft."

dudgeon: a small dagger, e.g., "His dudgeon and ***pepperbox*** (q.v.) probably revealed his need to carry weapons in his travels."

due bill: any written acknowledgment of a debt, often early used as money, e.g., "The entry noted that the defendant had given Bater a due bill in the amount of $6.00."

due honor: meaning that drafts or "checks" will be paid when due and presented, e.g., "The New York bank assured Georgia planter Bater that his drafts would 'enjoy due honor'."

duffel: coarse, napped woolen cloth, often used to make luggage bags, e.g., "His duffel bag served both to carry clothes and as a cover at night."

duffer: formerly a peddler, now usually an elderly man who does but little to provide more than his own keep, e.g., "While in 1850 a duffer might be travelling about selling wares of sorts, by 1950 that term would be used to describe a man who did but very little, e.g., "Mark spent most mornings on the courthouse benches visiting with the other old duffers who invariably were found there." Also see ***geezer***.

dugs: See ***digs***.

duke: a title of nobility that conferred no real estate or jurisdictional authority, yet ranked next below the Prince of Wales in deference and allegiance owed, e.g., "The Duke of Windsor would have been the King had he not abdicated."

dukes, duke it, duke it out: unknown to Johnson, one's hands; to fight, using only the hands as weapons, e.g., "When he offered to duke it out with the other boy, he was expressing an intention to fight yet employ no weapons other than his fists."

dulcimer: early, unlike now, a small stringed instrument played by striking the wires with small sticks, e.g., "The dulcimer of the early days was played differently from now."

dumb, deaf and dumb, deef and dumb: as today, deaf meant that the hearing was impaired; somewhat unlike today however, dumb meant unable to speak, e.g., "When he told that his daughter was deef and dumb, he meant that she was unable to hear or to make intelligible noises."

dumbwaiter: in ***furniture*** (q.v.), a small stand of stacked shelves that revolved independently, usually mounted on a pedestal and often placed in a parlor for holding small dishes of candies, sweetmeats, nuts etc.; a small shelf or series of small shelves mounted and moveable in a passage from the kitchen to the dining area, upon which food was placed for transport to those serving the people eating or preparing to eat, e.g., "When the men adjourned to the parlor, her mahogany dumbwaiter was placed there"; "The dumbwaiter was used to move the meal courses to the dining room and the empty serving dishes, etc., back to the kitchen."

dun: a color; brown and black; early used to describe animals, especially horses and dogs, e.g., "The horse was dun and the mare was ***brindle*** (q.v.)."

dung fork, dungfork: a manure fork; a large, tined fork used to scoop and move manure from one place to another, e.g., "His purchase of a dungfork and two 'scoops' revealed his ownership of horses or cattle, or both."

dung-hill fowl: See ***chickens***.

dungle fowl: See ***chickens***.

Dunmore's War, Lord: See ***Lord Dunmore's War***.

duplex: unlike now, a music box that was capable of containing and playing two cylinders or cones, e.g., "The duplex mentioned in the inventory was in no way related to housing."

Dupper's Beer: a beer made by the London brewer Dupper, believed to have caused the death of more than 200 colonists in the 17th century, e.g., "George Sandys cheered the prosecution of Dupper for his poisonous beer."

durant: probably now forgotten, but perhaps a fabric (stuff, q.v.) or a quilting design or pattern, e.g., "In the 1790s the well-known Philadelphia merchants, Kuhn & Risberg, advertised for sale 'Black, pink, white, green, pearl, and light blue sattin (sic?), persian, and durant quilted petticoats'."

duroy: a fabric with lengthwise cords or ridges, and if corded, called corduroy, e.g., "In 1798 Kuhn & Risberg of Market St., Philadelphia advertised assorted newly arrived cotton 'corded and plain duroys' for sale at their place of business."

Duryea Zouaves: See ***military combat units, famous.***

dust devil, dirt devil, hay devil: a small whirlwind or small tornado type movement of air, usually on a clear day, that draws weeds, dust and dirt from a small area up into the air, e.g., "Mikaila and Drake told Mrs. Bater that they had gotten dirt and hay in their hair and clothes as a result of a dust devil in the yard."

duster: similar or identical to a ***salt box*** (q.v.) and used for salt, pepper, or other powdered or granulated table seasonings; a light outer garment extending to below the knees and thought necessary and fashionable in early travel in order to prevent soiling of the clothes by dust and rain, e.g., "As a duster for cinnamon or pepper, she used her salt cellars"; "Ladies of fashion or affluence quite usually wore dusters when travelling in early automobiles or open carriages."

Dutch auction: an auction at which a price is called out in excess of the value of the property, and then is gradually reduced until someone places a bid, then the bidding moves upward in value, e.g., "Dutch auctions occasionally were held in early Ohio and Pennsylvania."

Dutch cupboard: a cupboard with closeable doors and shelves above and below, so called by reason of their popularity with German settlers, sometimes imprecisely called a ***pantry*** (q.v.), e.g., "Her Dutch cupboard was decorated by hand and was white."

Dutch metal, Dutch gold: a foil of copper and zinc alloy used as a substitute for gold foil, e.g., "If the patina is cleaned away, early inlays of Dutch gold are easily mistaken for true gold." Also see ***gold.***

Dutch oven: unlike now, a footed, shallow iron pot with a recessed, rimmed lid, e.g., "Dutch ovens were placed in the hot coals, and when the cook needed more heat for the dish being prepared, hot coals were placed in the recessed top."

Dutch, Deutsch, Pennsylvania Dutch: persons of German, Austrian, and central European descent or origin, and those of the Germanic tongue, usually not including persons from Holland, Belgium, Luxembourg, Denmark, or France, e.g., "Brittany's ancestors came from Mulheim to Bucks County and were thereafter referred to as 'Dutch' farmers."

Dutchware: See ***spatterware.***

duties: usually, fees or taxes levied upon goods moving from one country to another; sometimes, any tax or burden on the movement of goods levied by any governmental agency, e.g., "The Virginians considered the ***Crown*** (q.v.) duties on tea, sugar, and wine to be without justification."

duty, to stand: See ***watch***.

duvanto: a now unknown fabric; perhaps duvetyn, a cotton, wool, or silk napped material made in twill or plain weave, e.g., "The 1761 account of William Hunt with Belsches Brothers reveals the purchase of '2 ells of duvanto'."

dyed-in-the-wool, dyed in the wool: a superlative, referring to one whose ideas, customs or beliefs are staunchly and firmly held or considered, or one who has firmly assumed the views of another person or group, and derived from the fact that wool firmly holds the color of any dye, e.g., "Beautiful Allison Haskins was a dyed-in-the-wool Republican, if ever there was one!"

dying declaration: those statements of a dying person (who is fully aware that death is imminent) concerning the nature of his injuries and the party or parties responsible for the injuries, e.g., "The court minutes revealed that Mills was named as the perpetrator by the dying declaration of the badly beaten O'Neil."

dysentery, flux, bloody flux: severe diarrhea, often accompanied with blood; an intestinal disorder very often fatal in early times, e.g., "Despite his enormous wealth, Sir Francis Drake could not be cured of dysentery, and so, raving and delirious, he died in the Caribbean in 1596."

dysmenorrhea: as now, pain and cramping during the menstrual period, e.g., "For severe dysmenorrhea, Dr. Cheryl administered aconite, arsenic salts, amyl nitrate, and belladonna."

dyspepsia: early, any difficulty with digestion, e.g., "He was dyspeptic, and so chewed mint and hops and took cod-liver oil regularly."

dyspnoea, dyspnea: early, any difficulty in breathing, e.g., "The shortness of breath experienced by Cornice was said to have been dyspnoea, but may have been angina."

E

e'toffe du pays: (Fr., pronounced "a-toff-dew-pay") thick, woolen, homespun cloth, typical of the French colonies, e.g., "The ***Cajun*** (q.v.) mother often made children's coats of e'toffe du pays."

Eagle: a ten dollar U.S. gold coin; that American gold coin from which arose Double Eagles ($20.00), Half-Eagles ($5.00); and Quarter-Eagles ($2.50), e.g., "To the regret of many Americans, Eagles and all other gold coins were taken out of circulation in 1935."

earbobs, eardrops: earrings that dangle from the lobes. Also see ***bobs***.

earl: once the highest inheritable degree of nobility, now the third, ranking between a marquis and a viscount; corresponds to the French 'comte' and the German 'graf', e.g., "While the title of earl was not honored on this continent, some, such as the Thomas R. Roberts family of Ohio, could have been so indentified had they remained in the Old Country."

Here from a Chicago tintype of 1880 is a young lady who doubtless is wearing her favorite ear bobs.

earmark: a mark or brand, often recorded at early clerks' offices and then placed on an ear of animals, usually sheep, thereby revealing and placing the public on notice of ownership, e.g., "Fencing had not become reliable, so Paul entered his earmark into the records of the Clerk of Courts."

earthboard: the part of the plow that peels the dirt off the blade, e.g., "His reference to making an earthboard revealed his planting activity." Also see ***moldboard.***

earthenware: any utensil or dish made of fired clay, very common early, e.g., "The inventory revealed that Mrs. Haskins had two earthenware water jugs."

easement: a right of a person to use land of another for some special and specific purpose, e.g., "Evan sold a portion of his land to Mr. Bater, but retained a roadway easement across it."

Eastern Shore: usually, those counties of Delaware, Maryland and Virginia that border the eastern shore of Chesapeake Bay, e.g., "The Eastern Shore has been so-called in the records since considerably before 1700."

ebb tide: See ***tides.***

ebony, ebon, eben: very hard, beautiful, naturally black wood, early and until now imported to the colonies from South America, e.g., "The Haskins very much prized their ebony ***deed box*** (q.v.)."

ecchymosis: red or black and blue inflamed areas on the skin, e.g., "While ***apothecaries*** (q.v.) made up a mercurial ointment for the treatment of ecchymosis, early housewives often used a piece of raw red meat for the same purpose."

ecclesiastical councils, ecclesiastical law: judicial/advisory tribunals formerly (and still occasionally) held in New England and other jurisdictions for determining disputes between clergy and between clerk and church concerning orthodoxy, etc., e.g., "His view of the ritual of ***baptism*** (q.v.) was upheld after hearing and consideration by the ecclesiastical council."

eccoprotics: mild ***purges*** (q.v.), e.g., "As eccoprotics, Dr. Bater prescribed poke root and flax-seed oil, and housewives made ***poke sallet*** (q.v.)."

eclectic practice: a medical methodology often characterized by conventionally educated practitioners as dangerous and even sometimes harmful; the practice of healing by methods not accepted by many persons of the medical profession, e.g., "His views concerning healing with electricity were considered eclectic by some, and pure quackery by others."

ecphractics, ecphracticks: early, ***concoctions*** (q.v.) supposed to thin the liquids—***humours*** (q.v.)—of the body, e.g., "Most ecphracticks contained alcohol, some, a very high percentage (to the pleasure of many of those who pretended to be non-drinkers)."

ectype: a reproduction copy, e.g., "Early court orders often required that parties be handed ectypes of ***writs*** (q.v.) or orders."

Edwardian: pertaining to the years of the reign of England's King Edward VII (1901-1910), e.g., "The American manners and morals viewed by many as 'proper' and acceptable throughout the first half of the 20th century are called 'Edwardian' or ***'Victorian-Edwardian'*** (q.v.)."

-ee, (a suffix): from the Latin; a person or persons upon or against whom some legal effect or result has been or may to be brought about by another, e.g., "Having had a lien filed against him for his failure to pay, he was a lienee." (see also ***-or, a suffix***.)

effects: tangible ***property*** (q.v.) of a personal nature and always meaning other than interests in land or intangible ***assets*** (q.v.), e.g., "In addition to the other personalty, his effects, including three ***weskits*** (q.v.), were listed in the inventory."

effluxion (of time): the expiration of the term of years established in a lease or land rental agreement, e.g., "The old court record spoke of the effluxion of term, meaning that the lease had expired by its own terms."

eigne: (Fr.) the first born, e.g., "Early Louisiana records often refer to someone who was the first born of a family as the eigne."

ejectment: (writ of, or action in) a legal action by which one is ordered to vacate land or premises illegally held after expiration of an agreed term, e.g., "Mills would not leave after his lease expired so Miss Ferguson sought a writ of ejectment."

elaterium: an extract of wild cucumbers that acted as a powerful purge, e.g., "He prescribed elaterium only as a last resort."

elbowchair: an early term for any ordinary chair with arms that usually were padded or upholstered, e.g., "There was an elbowchair and a ***settee*** (q.v.) in the ***inventory and appraisement*** (q.v.)."

elder: usually, a senior member of a church congregation; in the New Testament, ecclesiastics; to many denominations, laymen selected for the governing of the church or congregation, e.g., "Because of his leadership and many years as a member, Paul was an elder in a Baptist congregation in Columbia."

elder title: the state of having ***perfected*** (q.v.) ownership prior to some other person, e.g., "In the dispute between Hines and Gross, the court found Hines to have the elder title."

electric belts: belts, worn at the waist, made of fiber and containing small current-carrying wires that were plugged into a wall outlet or powered by a battery; gadgets of the late nineteenth and early twentieth centuries, said to have great curative powers, e.g., "Many were the ignorant who bought electric belts, thinking that cures to many ailments might thereby be brought about."

electuaries: a paste-like lump or mass of medicines in a vehicle such as syrup, molasses or honey, and early used for humans and animals by placing it on the teeth and gums or between the same and a cheek, e.g., "Mr. Bater bought 14 pounds of tobacco in 1660 to be made into purging electuaries."

elisors: an early term for persons appointed by a court to select citizens as potential jurors or, in some jurisdictions, to execute ***writs*** (q.v.), e.g., "Some early Maryland writs of ***venire*** (q.v.) were carried out by selected elisors."

elixir(s): any strong medicine; a medicine or concoction having wide application, e.g., "His elixir of fruit juice, horehound, and grain alcohol was very popular, more for the alcohol than for any curative effects."

ell: a very widely used early measure of cloth equaling approximately one and one quarter sq. yards (36" X 45"), e.g., "Virtually every account of early dry goods merchants refers to ells of this or that fabric (stuff, q.v.)."

Ellis Island (NY): a former arrival, examination and inspection point for immigrants to the U.S., e.g., "Ellis Island was well known to virtually every early 20th-century immigrant bound for the eastern U.S."

eloped: unlike now, the word often bore a negative connotation, and meant to escape some bounds or to run away from legal or familial restraint, e.g., "When Drue and Ida ran away to be married even though her father had denied permission, since she was the person who had no permission, it was written that Ida eloped with Drue, rather than that he eloped with her."

elvelock: a woman's hairdo in the form of a knot of hair at the back of the head, e.g., "Elvelocks were very popular at the time of the Civil War."

emancipation: a release from the bonds arising by reason of age, contract, or servitude, e.g., "Bethany was emancipated from her term of servitude at the age of fifteen"; "An emancipated child is one over whom all measure of parental control has been relinquished." ***Emancipation Proclamation:*** that Presidential order of Abraham Lincoln, dated July 1, 1863, that declared all persons previously held in slavery in the States or territories of the United States, should thereafter be and remain freemen and women, e.g., "Since Lincoln had no jurisdiction in the Confederacy, the Emancipation Proclamation could not be enforced until the defeat of the South and the re-establishment of the U.S. government there."

Ember Week, Ember Days: any week in which an Ember Day falls; ancient English holidays observed widely in the early colonies, e.g., "The Book of Common Prayer established Ember Days as the Wednesday, Friday, and Sunday after the first Sunday of Lent, the day of the Feast of the Pentecost, September 14th, and December 13."

emblazoned: anything decorated or adorned with a symbol of heraldry; an enameled or inlaid surface, e.g., "The shield was emblazoned with the Parker arms"; "The jewelry box was emblazoned in red and yellow stained woods."

emblements: early crops and other growing harvestables produced by labor of the owner, e.g., "Upon one's death, his emblements often passed to his administrator or executor as personalty."

embrocate: to rub an injured or diseased part of the body with lotions containing alcohol, e.g., "Dr. Drake gave him 'pink lotion' with which to embrocate the rash."

emeroids: See ***hemorrhoids***.

emetic, emetick: as now and very common, early concoctions used to bring about vomiting, e.g., "The old doctor consistently used ipecac as an emetic."

emigrants: those who leave one place or region intending to remain in or take up permanent residence in another, e.g., "He was among those emigrants who after 1740 left the Palatinate for the colonies."

eminent domain: the taking of private property for public use, for which property the owner is compensated, e.g., "The government exercised its power of eminent domain when it took land from Haskins for use as a road and took cattle to feed the Revolutionary army." Also see ***condemnation***.

emmenagogues: early, medications thought to induce menstrual flow or abortion, e.g., "Being unmarried and pregnant, the old women advised Miss Wiley to take a half cup of ***coal oil*** (q.v.) and quinine as an emmenagogue."

empasm: any powder or substance used to rid the body of odors, e.g., "Common folks of the sixteenth century thought empasms were neither often necessary nor particularly desirable."

emphysema: as now, yet not early understood, e.g., "For emphysema, Dr. Bater sometimes prescribed arsenic, cod-liver oil, and prussic acid."

empiric: a medical practitioner who acts without science or training, e.g., "He was called an empiric by the polite and a charlatan by other of his neighbors."

empyema: any congestion or gathering of mucus in the chest cavity, e.g., "Black snakeroot and ***asafetida*** (q.v.) were popular as remedies for any empyema."

en ventre sa mere: (Lat.) early, common legal expression for "in the mother's womb"; the unborn, e.g., "He ***devised*** (q.v.) the land to the children jointly, and included any child en ventre sa mere at his death."

enamel: early, unlike now, any material to be inlaid, quite usually in wood, e.g., "The antique ***press*** (q.v.) was said to have been enameled with gold and rosewood."

encomienda: a feudal grant of land within a Spanish territory, e.g., "The Mexican records concerning encomiendas often are significant to Southwestern genealogists."

endite: See ***indict***.

enfeoff, enfeoffment: See ***feoff***.

engine: unlike now, any large mechanical device with parts that usually moved to some mechanical advantage, e.g., "The engine for the mill was a turnstile."

engineer, pilot: early, unlike now, the operator of a locomotive, engine, or other heavy propelled or internally powered equipment or machine; an elected office concerned with the equipment used for and surveys, platting, and boundaries of a county, e.g., "He was a railroad engineer"; "He was the elected County Engineer."

English Case Drink: See ***case drink***.

English kings and queens, years of: See ***regnal years***.

English lock: a type of firearm; a ***flintlock*** (q.v.), e.g., "He carried an English lock of .60 caliber."

engrain: to decoratively stain the graining in wood, thereby achieving variations in coloring and shading, e.g., "The mahogany was engrained with a black stain."

enlisted man, enlisted woman: See ***private, private soldier***.

enneatical days or years: the ninth day of a disease, after which it was early thought that a change was sure to follow; every ninth year of life, signifying a change or cycle, e.g., "They anxiously awaited the enneatical day, hoping that his condition would then improve."

ensign: a flag or standard of a regiment or other military unit; that person designated to carry the flag of a military unit; the lowest rank of commissioned officer in the U.S. Navy, e.g., "In Henry VI, Shakespeare said "...hang up your ensigns, let your drums be still," "Upon graduation from Navy flight school, he was commissioned ensign."

entailment, fee tail, fee tail male, fee tail female, etc.: a common (now legally ineffective) estate in land limited to a person and to the "heirs of the body" of that person—his or her ***issue*** (q.v.); an early estate in land wherein the ***descent*** (q.v.) is settled and determined, and by which ***grantors*** (q.v.) or ***devisors*** (q.v.) restricted all future transfers to the lineal descendants of a ***grantee*** (q.v.) or ***devisee*** (q.v.), e.g., "By making the 1747 deed '...to Sarah Drake and the heirs of her body', William Hines sought to entail the land." Also see ***dock, dock an entailment.***

Enterprise, U.S.S: See ***warships, American.***

entertain: sometimes unlike now, to provide shelter or housing for someone; to take another into one's home for little or no charge or compensation; to provide food and drink for patrons, as in an ***ordinary*** (q.v.), e.g., "Where an early New England citizen gave shelter to someone who had not been accepted into the town, it was written that the former had entertained that guest"; "In 1674, in Salem, Capt. More, being ***reduced*** (q.v.), was licensed '...to keep a publick howse of entertaynment for the selling of beer, wine and cyder'."

entertainment, private: See ***private entertainment.***

entranceway: See ***entry (architectural).***

entrements: (Fr.) small plates of food served between main dishes, e.g., "The banquet menu revealed seven entrements, including ***curds*** (q.v.) in cream."

entry: in law, a notation in a journal or record of some legal activity or decision; in land, the initial action taken in acquiring title to land that is to be settled. In the latter, an entry was followed by a warrant for survey, a plat and a deed, and a ***caveat*** (q.v.) could be filed by one who claimed any portion of the land within that entry, e.g., "The judge ordered that an entry be submitted detailing the agreement"; "He filed an entry for 100 acres lying along Chowan River." Also see ***land entry.***

entry (architectural), entranceway: unlike now, in the North, a small room at the front entrance; in the South, a hallway extending from the front entrance through the house and doored at the rear, e.g., "In the South, the entry (or entranceway) sometimes was called a ***dogtrot*** (q.v.)."

enumeration: in genealogy, usually, and somewhat imprecisely, any census or numbering of people in a given area, e.g., "Since only the heads of households were named, the ***Decennial Censuses*** (q.v.) from 1790 through 1840 are properly called enumerations, not censuses." Also see ***censuses*** and see ***enumerator.***

enumerator: one who makes lists of numbers of people, generally for tax or census purposes; properly, one who counts and records that enumeration, i.e., a count of persons, e.g., "Sarah was employed as an enumerator for the southern half of York County, Virginia."

epergne: (Fr., pronounced "a-pairn") two or more small serving dishes grouped together and mounted in a decorative metal frame, usually placed in the center of a table, e.g., "She served several ***sweetmeats*** (q.v.) and jellies in the silver epergne."

ephemera: unlike now, a fever that subsided in one day, e.g., "The old doctor waited until the second day to treat the fever, thinking it might be only an ephemera."

ephemeris: a journal or day book, e.g., "He referred to his writings in the ephemeris as his 'day notes'."

epidemic: a widespread infectious disease, e.g., "Of the many seventeenth and eighteenth centuries epidemics, conspicuous were beriberi, very early; calenture (yellow fever), 1609(?), 1624(?), 1649, 1668, 1691, 1699, 1793; dysentery and 'fluxes', 1607-08, 1618-19, 1684-86; influenza ('flu') in 1623, 1627, 1635, 1647, 1688 (perhaps the worst), 1697-99 (perhaps the worst of New England); malaria, 1657-59 and 1677-95; and measles in 1693-1700, and 1713, scurvy and common diseases (when 'seasoning' was inadequate), very early; and smallpox, 1667 (perhaps the worst), 1696, 1731."

epigraph: a quotation at the beginning of a writing, intended by the writer to be thought provoking, e.g., "The epigraph was a quote from Churchill concerning the strength and will of the American people."

epilepsy: as now, but not at all understood, e.g., "Having no understanding of epilepsy, Dr. Lockhart often administered arsenic, bromides, copper, zinc and silver chloride, and even musk."

Epiphany: an ancient holiday (still observed), celebrated in the colonies on the twelfth day after Christmas (January 6th), e.g., "The Book of Common Prayer prescribed Epiphany as a day for celebrating the coming of Christ as foretold by the appearance of the Star of the East."

epistaxis: a nosebleed, e.g., "For severe epistaxis, Dr. Haskins plugged the nares and administered digitalis and ***turpentine*** (q.v.)."

epistler: an early term for one who wrote letters and correspondence for others, e.g., "He served the local folks as an epistler, however, they called him a 'scribbler'." Also see ***scribe***.

epitaph: a statement, quotation, or verse on a monument or headstone, usually as a memorial to the deceased, e.g., "There are some humorous and particularly poignant epitaphs to be found in New England."

epitherm: any liquid medication applied to the outside of the body, e.g., "Mercurial ointments were popular epitherms of the nineteenth century."

epulotic: a medication thought to cause a wound to heal, e.g., "Powdered sassafras and 'slippery elm' bark, also used by the Indians, were widely used as epulotics."

equinoxes: either of the two times each year when the sun crosses the equator, and day and night are everywhere of equal length, occurring on very near March 21 and September 23.

equity, courts of: cases that sought remedies unavailable at ***common law*** (q.v.), in which fairness or the balancing of interests was decided by church officers, became known as cases 'in equity', and the church officers making such decisions were known as chancellors. In some states chancellors still sit, e.g., "The courts of equity provided remedies based upon fairness in cases often said to be beyond the 'letter of the law'"; "He sought equal use of the property in Tennessee, hence the case was in equity and heard by the chancellor." Also see ***court***.

Era of Good Feelings: that decade following the ***War of 1812*** (q.v.), during which war was over, the United States began to consider itself a power to be reckoned with, the westward movement into the Great Plains and beyond was underway, ***King Cotton*** (q.v.) reigned supreme, canals were undertaken, manufacturing—albeit primitive—was everywhere, the Indians were perceived as yet posing problems only in the distant west, and society appeared to be opening its doors upward, e.g., "As Mrs. Drake looked about, it seemed that all of life was better; the Era of Good Feelings dominated central Ohio."

error, writ of: that statement (of a person appealing a decision of a lower court) setting forth the errors alleged to have been made by that court, e.g., "The writ of error stated that the lower court refused to permit the ***defendant*** (q.v.) to adequately examine the witnesses."

erysipelas: any early rash of red, dark or yellow hue, sometimes accompanied by swelling, e.g., "***Belladonna*** (q.v.) and aconite were widely prescribed for erysipelas."

escheat: to revert to a prior owner, usually a government, through some failure of conditions, e.g., "Without legal reason, he neglected to clear the land or improve the property in any way whatever, so it escheated to the Virginia colony."

escritoir (Fr.): See ***box, writing.***

escritura (Sp.): any written instrument or document, e.g., "Early records of the Southwest reveal many references to escritura."

escutcheon: an ornament, usually of metal, surrounding a keyhole; early and now, also a family shield; an armorial ensign, e.g., "The escutcheons on the ***armoire*** (q.v.) were of solid gold"; "The family escutcheon was inscribed on a plaque of ***ebony*** (q.v.) and mahogany."

esquire, squire: a title now largely reserved to attorneys in the United States; in 1802 Johnson said, "an armour bearer or attendant on a knight", and a title of dignity next below a knight, e.g., "Just as had her ancestors, Allison referred to her family attorney as 'Evan Haskins, Esq.', reflecting her view that he was above a yeoman and even a "***mister***" (q.v.) in dignity and respect due."

estate: at ancient law, any interest in real property; generally and in genealogy, the totality of legal proceedings having to do with the death of any person; a valuable tract of land, usually including a large dwelling, e.g., "His estate in the land was one of ***fee determinable***" (q.v.); "Her estate was not settled until four years after her death"; "Their estate in the mountains was magnificent."

estate by the entirety (or entireties): early, a husband and wife were viewed as but one person (the man), and it followed that a ***conveyance*** (q.v.) to them could create but one estate in the man, yet neither could dispose of it without the consent of the other, and at the death of either the entire interest was vested in the survivor, e.g., "By reason of the fiction that husband and wife were one person, estates by the entirety could exist only in married couples." See ***joint tenancy.***

estate for years: that less-than-freehold interest in land for a fixed or determinable period of years, e.g., "When Luke leased the land to Griffith for twenty years, Griffith was said to have had an estate for years."

estreat(e), excript: early term for an exact copy of a document or writing, e.g., "The Surry court ordered that either the writing itself or an estreate be presented." Also see ***escritura.***

estrepement, writ of: an early ***common law*** (q.v.) ***action*** (q.v.) by which the remainder interest holder could prevent the owner of a life estate from "wasting" (acting to the harm of) that remainder, e.g., "The Pennsylvania court ruled that a writ of estrepement should issue against the lake to be created on the land by the life tenant."

et: past perfect tense of the verb to eat; a very common Appalachian expression, e.g., "Even Winston Churchill was known to say he had et, meaning he had eaten."

et al.: (Lat.) literally, "and others", e.g., "Genealogists should remember that ancestors may be revealed in the files of lawsuits wherein the caption lists known relatives followed by the expression 'et al'."

et ux., et uxor: (Lat.) and wife; and husband; e.g., "The deed was to Jean Mills, et uxor, hence, even though the husband's name did not appear, the researcher knew that Jean was married at the date of that document."

evensong: prayers or worship offered at sunset or in the evening, e.g., "The priest referred to their evening prayers as evensongs."

evidence: in genealogy, any writing, relic, memento, state of being, or remembrance that in any way tends to establish ***lineage*** (q.v.); facts, writings and states of being offered as proof of lineage or relationship, e.g., "Even though genealogists are not bound by courtroom rules of admissibility, hearsay evidence is not thereby rendered more reliable." Also see ***evidentiary***.

evidentiary: facts or states of being that in any way tend to establish other facts; facts tending to prove some proposition or hypothesis, e.g., "The inscription on the headstone was evidentiary as to the spelling of the name of the deceased. Also see ***evidence.***

evil: a three-tined manure fork, e.g., "He used an evil to spread manure." Also see ***dungfork.***

ewe: a female sheep, e.g., "The inventory listed both rams and ewes."

ewer: a bowl or container usually brought to the table for the washing of hands; large "finger bowls"; sometimes, wide-mouthed pitchers, e.g., "Though the precise utensil could not be determined, the inventory reference to '2 silver ewers' revealed a measure of family wealth."

ex facto, de facto: refers to some state of being resulting from some act that often was or may have been unlawful, incomplte, or improper; a state of being that must be accepted as a fact, though in fact the acts from which it resulted may have been improper or inadequate, e.g., "Ownership ex facto resulted when he found and took up stray cattle that bore the illegible brand of another person"; "Having lived together for years and having a daughter, Anne and Eli were de facto married, though there was no legal or religious recognition of that relationship." Also see ***de jure.***

ex tempore: the passage of time; in consequence of a passage of time, e.g., "The order revealing that his leasehold had died ex tempore told the researcher that the term of the lease had expired."

ex testamento: by the action of a will; e.g., "The court described Bethany's ownership of the land as ex testamento, meaning that she had gained it through the will of another." Also see ***ab intestato.***

examined away: See ***separate examination.***

except: in court records, to take exception to a ruling usually as to the admission or exclusion of evidence, writings, or demonstrative evidence, e.g., "The record revealed showed that when the court read the document to the jury, the lawyer objected, was overruled, and said 'Please note my exception'."

excepting, excepted: reserving, e.g., "Drake's ***conveyance*** (q.v.) of the land excepted the portion used as the family cemetery."

exchange, medium of: See ***medium of exchange.***

excise tax: a tax on goods, merchandise, or commodities being sold at retail (usually), e.g., "The excise taxes levied on rum and tobacco by the British served only to aggravate the colonials."

excommunication: censure of a person, church or discipline by a governing religious authority, e.g., "Excommunication was a most feared punishment in the days of deep religious convictions."

exec: See ***executed writ.***

execute, execution: the signing or making formal a document or writing that requires such an act; those common actions taken, usually by a ***constable*** (q.v.), ***sheriff*** (q.v.), or a deputy of those officers, to enforce a judgment or other court order; the actions of an ***executor*** (q.v.) in carrying out the provisions of a will, e.g., "The contract was executed by the parties on the 5th of July, 1786"; "The sheriff having been ordered to execute on the judgment, he took into custody the slaves of the defendant"; "In executing the provisions of the will, the executor had to have several tracts of land surveyed."

executed writ: the accomplishment of the purpose of any ***writ*** (q.v.); a writ or order endorsed to the effect that it has been accomplished, e.g., "The writ, carrying the endorsement 'exec.', revealed that its purpose had been accomplished by the ***sheriff*** (q.v.)."

executor, executrix: a person, male or female, appointed by a ***testator*** (q.v.) or ***testatrix*** (q.v.) in a will and approved by the court to carry out the terms of that will, e.g., "He was appointed executor and she executrix, and they were issued letters ***testamentary*** (q.v.), in the estate of William Midlam, deceased."

executory: that which is yet to be done or executed; incomplete; that which depends for its fulfillment upon the happening of future events, e.g., "The genealogist should be aware that executory deeds and contracts often have effects similar to wills"; "An executory interest in land is created when a deed provides for a transfer of title upon death of the owner."

exemption: a freedom from some duty incumbent upon others of the same class or group, e.g., "Occasionally, exemptions from tithes were granted by reason of poverty, prior military service, or disability."

exempts: those who, for one reason or another who were exempt from service or some other duty owed to government or some person or group of persons, often military, e.g., "The York County records listed Ferguson among the 'old exempts,' meaning he was too old or infirm to serve in the militia."

exequies: graveside burial rites, occasionally a funeral, e.g., "The exequies took place at the grave site."

exit certificate: an issuance of a certificate, usually by a clerk of a court or administrative official of government, e.g., "The Surry court noted 'exit certificate 100 ac. Clerk', meaning the Clerk of the Court had issued a ***certificate*** (q.v.) for 100 acres of land."

exit: a notation common in court reports meaning the court issued some order or process, e.g., "The entry revealed 'exit fi. fa.' meaning that an order (or ***writ***, q.v.) of ***fieri facias*** (q.v.) had been issued in that case."

expectancy: that which is expected, but for which there is no certainty or obligation upon others, e.g., "Even though it could be changed at any time, Bethany had an expectancy by reason of the bequest to her in her yet living grandfather's will."

extinct: usually in genealogy, a statement that a political subdivision has been abolished, or that a claim in heraldry or nobility has been lost beyond reprieve, e.g., "The Tennessee county of Franklin is extinct"; "The earldom which might have been his is extinct."

extinguishment of legacy: where specific property is the subject of a ***devise*** (q.v.) or ***bequest*** (q.v.) and at death of the ***testator*** (q.v.) the property no longer exists, e.g., "The order stated that the bequest of cattle failed by reason of extinguishment."

extract: in genealogy, a portion of a document, letter, book or writing, usually taken whole and verbatim from the original, in contrast to an ***abstract*** (q.v.), which condenses the information cited, e.g., "He extracted the last four paragraphs of the Gettysburg Address for use in his class."

exudation, exsudation: a sweating or perspiring, e.g., "Causing exudation was one of the ways thought helpful to bring the ***'humours'*** (q.v.) into balance."

F

f. feci: See ***fieri feci***.

facias: (lat.) an order from a court or a ***writ*** (q.v.) to a ***sheriff*** (q.v.), ***constable*** (q.v.), officer of the court, or a deputy thereof, "that you do cause", e.g., "The early writs of scire facias ('cause him to know hereof') are familiar to all genealogists who have worked with courts' records"; "Fieri facias ('cause it to be made') was frequently used to order a constable or sheriff to collect the amount of a judgment from such of defendant's assets as were available."

factor: one who, using his own name, sells something tangible for another person, usually an owner, e.g., "Factors in England were commonly used by Virginia planters and colonial manufacturers."

fagathy (-ies): probably now unknown, but perhaps fabrics containing fagoting, i.e., decorative criss-cross stitching across an open seam, e.g., "Vanuxem & Lombaert of 1800 Philadelphia advertised 'assorted fagathies' for sale at their store on Water St."

fagend: slang for a person who is disheveled or a person of little worth; the unusable end or raveling left at the end of the piece of fabric as a result of the weaving process, e.g., "Her reference to the young man as a fagend had nothing to do with his sexual preferences."

fagot, faggot: a bundle of sticks bound together, usually for burning; a freshly cut pine knot; now, a vulgar term for a homosexual, e.g., "He had provided the fagots for the outdoor lamps at the Governor's mansion"; "Burning faggots were their only source of illumination"; "He referred to all homosexuals as 'gays' or as faggots'."

fagot fork, faggot fork: a tined fork used to move or place faggots within a fireplace or other receptacle for burning, e.g., "She used the fagot fork to so place the wood as to cause an even fire."

faience: (Fr., pron. fay-e-ens) delicately decorated French ***earthenware*** (q.v.), e.g., "Brittany's faience bowl was made in New England, even though the name would not so suggest."

Fair Use: "...relates to the extent to which copyrightable writings or materials may be used without express license...." or permission. Loews Inc., v Columbia, etc. (1955 DC CA) 131 F. Supp. 165, 175; 105 U.S.P.Q. 302; aff'd', etc., 356 U.S. 934, generally, e.g., "Her use of his writings was for non-profit classroom comparison and analysis, hence probably was Fair Use."

Fair-play men: an irregular tribunal brought into existence in Pennsylvania about the year 1769, e.g., "The actions and decisions of the Fair-play men were not authorized by any government."

fairy lamp: a lamp using a short squatty candle, often with 2 wicks, and commonly used during pre-Victorian times before ***coal oil*** (q.v.) was widely available, e.g., "She had a fairy lamp made of china and one of metal."

fake: a coil of rope, e.g., "The inventory included a fake of hemp."

fall shoes: See ***French fall shoes.***

fall, saw, and maul: an early expression used in granting to a tenant or ***lessee*** (q.v.) the privilege of cutting and using the timber on a tract of land, e.g., "Luke granted Griffith the right to fall, saw, and maul the trees on the leased property."

fall-front desk, drop-front desk, drop-leaf desk: a free standing desk, usually with drawers below and a hinged writing surface folding upwards when not in use and thereby concealing small inside compartments and drawers, e.g., "The walnut fall-front was the finest ***desk*** (q.v.) in the estate." Also see ***desk, etc.***

falling sickness: epilepsy (q.v.), e.g., "Falling sickness was not early understood, and musk was one of the medications thought efficacious."

fallow: at rest; usually, to permit a field to lie unplowed and uncultivated for some extended period or for a season or more; pale red or pale yellow color, e.g., "He let the forty acres lay fallow for years"; "The cloth was fallow and brown."

Family History Centers: See ***Mormons.***

family name: See ***surname.***

family name files, vertical files: those alphabetical files maintained by libraries and genealogical societies that contain unbound correspondence, obituaries, research notes, sources, and miscellaneous materials having to do with a specific family or surname, e.g., "In the Family Name Files under 'Haskins' Allison found a short biography of her missing ancestor."

family tale, family tradition: a story, tale or recollection passed down through a family for a number of years or generations, usually not written, e.g., "According to an unproved family tale, he was descended from a brother of Sir Francis Drake."

family unit chart, family group sheet: a widely used genealogical form used to record pertinent information concerning births, marriages, deaths, parents, and ***issue*** (q.v.) of a single husband and wife unit. Quite usually a researcher maintains one family unit chart for each marriage encountered, e.g., "She kept a family group sheet for every marriage uncovered during her research."

famous military units: See ***military units, famous***.

fancy: unlike now, at various times, of the highest quality or designed to suit the most discerning taste; interestingly, if referring to a young male, it also meant one's lover, however a "fancy woman" was a prostitute, e.g., "To say she had a fancy gown revealed that it likely was expensive"; "He was her fancy man, and she was with him whenever possible"; "To say in public that she was a 'fancy woman' was an insult of the highest order."

fangot: a small quantity of wares, usually available to purchase, e.g., "The peddler was described as having carried with him '...a fangot of pots and pans, poorly made'."

fantasie (fantasy): early, occasionally a very unusual, catastrophic or devastating event, e.g., "In the song written about the Johnstown flood of 1889, the event was referred to as a fantasie." Also see ***waterspout***.

Farina, farina: sometimes now unremembered, quite usually meal, made from wheat or other cereal grains and served cooked, with milk, molasses, or honey used as sweeteners, etc., e.g., "In an 1862 ad for cigar cases, perfumery, and cologne stands, Charles Merrill of Exeter (NH) offered 'genuine Farina'"; "Cooked farina with maple syrup and milk has long been a favorite breakfast food of the Vermont Brown family."

farm table, country table: a plain, wide, longer than ordinary, often roughly finished utility table, sometimes with a single drop leaf, e.g., "She used the farm table for many purposes, and always sorted and cleaned her fruits and vegetables there." Also see ***harvest table.***

farm: before about 1825, ground or land under lease to or being "share cropped" by another person; similarly a farmer was one who farmed leased or rented land, e.g., "A person described in 1740 as a farmer very probably did not own the land."

farmstead: See ***stead.***

faro: early and now, a popular gambling game played with cards, where betting is done as to the order in which cards will fall, e.g., "The early mining towns had more than their share of faro tents."

farrier: very early, one who doctored animals; early, the same, or a ***blacksmith*** (q.v.) whose business was horseshoes and nails; later, one who for hire made horseshoes, shoed horses, and was knowledgeable in cutting and trimming horses feet, e.g., "The farrier came by once a month to check the horses' hooves."

farrow: a litter of pigs, e.g., "The inventory revealed three sows, two farrows, a boar, and ten shoats." Also see ***swine, hogs.***

farthing: a British coin taken from circulation in 1961, having had a value of 1/4 of a pence (p or d) or 1/40th of a Shilling (S or s), e.g., "A farthing of 1850 had the purchasing power of about twenty cents ($0.20) in 2000."

farthingale: a hoop over which was worn a dress, petticoats, or a skirt, the same used to cause the garments to flare out; a flared or hooped dress, skirt, or petticoat, e.g., "Scarlett wore a whalebone farthingale under a deep green velvet dress."

fast boards: those steps permanently attached to the side of a train car, caboose or locomotive, upon which one could step to gain access to an entrance or stand upon while the train moved short distances, e.g., "The Brakeman stood on the fast board as the caboose was moved to a position to be coupled to the train."

fat back: commonly used fat portion of meat from the ribs and back bones of hogs, often used frequently by the poor and frugal, e.g., "Pam will knew the difference between bacon and fat back."

fat lamp: any lamp that used animal fat or suet as fuel, e.g., "Even though her betty lamps were, in fact, fat lamps, Bethany did not refer to them by that name."

fat, fatt, vat: a vat into which anything liquid is placed for storage, particularly if it is intended that it ferment, e.g., "Bethany referred to the barrel in which apple juice was stored for winter use as 'the cider fat'." Also see ***dryfatt***.

fathom: a measure of depth equaling six feet, e.g., "In 1785, at its deepest the channel in New York harbor was twelve fathoms."

fatling: a young animal, usually a calf or steer, thought fat enough for market, e.g., "The ***husbandman*** (q.v.) was anxious to take the three Holstein fatlings to market."

fealty: in feudal law, a duty owed a feudal lord, e.g., "In 1740, William Cole was to deliver 'two fatt capons' and do a day's labor as tokens of fealty to the owner of the 'Mannor of Gunnpowder'."

feasance, feasor: a deed or act; a doing of something, e.g., "Malfeasance is an act done by one called a 'feasor' with evil or unlawful intent, nonfeasance indicates a result brought about through innocent inaction, and misfeasance denotes an undesirable result which followed an otherwise appropriate action having a different purpose and intent, e.g., "His malfeasance was evident in his breaking down the kennel door when he led his neighbors hunting dog away"; "Allison's accidental destruction of the neighbor's mower which had been left behind her car was held to be misfeasance"; "When the strong wind blew the neighbor's sign into Brittany's window, the neighbor was viewed as a non-feasor, though liable."

feather tick: a large, heavy cloth bag filled with feathers and down and used as a mattress; by reason of softness and warmth, feathers were the most desirable of ticking, e.g., "She had three ***ticks*** (q.v.), and one was a feather tick." Also see ***ticking bag.***

febrifuge: any medication thought to aid with fevers, e.g., "Eucalyptus and quinine were popular febrifuges."

Federal Courts: those courts, including the U.S. tax courts, U.S. District courts, Courts of Appeals for the Circuits, and the U.S. Supreme Court, generally having jurisdiction in appeals, jurisdiction in Federal crimes and Constitutional matters, and in civil matters between citizens of different states where the amount in dispute is in excess of a set amount, e.g., "The only appeal from the highest court of South Carolina was to the Federal courts, quite usually the U.S. Supreme Court."

Federalist Papers, The: a series of eighty-five discussion essays by Alexander Hamilton, John Jay, and James Madison concerning the ramifications of an adoption of the Constitution, e.g., "The Federalist

Papers have long been held most reliable concerning the motivations and thoughts of the framers of the Constitution."

fee: all lands and ***tenements*** (q.v.) held through recognition by a higher governmental or religious authority, e.g., "The fees of the bishopric were established by the mother church." Also see ***fee simple,*** see ***fee conditional***, see ***fee determinable***, and see ***entailment***.

fee conditional: any estate that is restricted to certain heirs; all fees conditional are "base fees", yet the converse is not true, e.g., "Since the land was conveyed to one of his daughters with the condition that she could transfer it only to her daughters, it was a fee conditional." Also see ***entailment***.

fee determinable: an ancient legal term signifying that the transferred rights in land would be varied or extinguished upon the happening of certain events or the passage of a certain amount of time, e.g., "The transfer of the land was in fee determinable, the condition being that, should Jean remarry, the title to the land would at that marriage be transferred as a matter of law to her eldest surviving daughter."

fee simple: (Lat., feodum simplex) an ancient legal term signifying that total measure of ownership in land which one might own under all the laws in effect at that place at the date of transfer, e.g., "He gained the land in fee simple from his father, even though he had been told that it would be ***entailed*** (q.v.)."

fee tail: a ***fee conditional*** (q.v.). Also see ***entailment***.

feed sack: See ***tote sack***.

fellmonger, fell monger: a dealer in skins and hides; one who earns a livelihood by selling, processing, or by scraping and removing hair from skins that are to be tanned and made into leather, e.g., "Most of Bater's fellmongers hoped to learn the art of tanning."

felly (fellies): See ***wainwrights*** and ***coachmakers, tools of.***

felt: cloth (fabric) of wool, made without weaving but instead by pressing the fibers together under heat, e.g., "Felt was inexpensive, and yet served the cabinetmaker well." Also see ***cabinetmaker***.

felts: See ***paper making***.

female trouble: as now, any of several general complaints concerning the female reproductive system, e.g., "For female trouble, the American Indians employed teas of Geranium, currants, cedar berries, milkweed, and black haw." Also see ***dysmenorrhea***.

feme, feme covert, feme sole, feme sole trader: (Fr., femme) a female; e.g., "A feme covert was a married woman and a feme sole was a widowed, unmarried, divorced, legally separated or presently unmarried woman, or a married woman who, through prenuptial agreement or other action at law, could act and contract—'be a free trader'—in her own right." A feme sole trader was a woman who traded on her own account, either by custom or because she had no husband, e.g., "Early South Carolina and Pennsylvania legally recognized feme sole traders, however many jurisdictions did not."

fence, fence laws, fence county: those terms describing measures taken or in effect within a county or state establishing whether livestock had to be "fenced out" or "fenced in," e.g., "Since very early, it has been necessary for political subdivisions to establish liability for animal mischief by determining whether animals must be kept in by their owners or kept out by non-owners; early Georgia, Oklahoma, Texas, and New Mexico provide examples of such legislative considerations."

fence county: See ***fence, fence laws***, etc.

fence rows, fencerows: lines of fence and the ground in and upon which the fence posts stood, e.g., "The fencerows always were a likely place to find small game." Also see **perambulators**.

fence viewer: See **perambulator**.

fence viewers: after about 1750, persons elected in each county of many New England colonies and of PA whose duty it was to inspect all fences and see that they were being kept in good repair, e.g., "If the fence viewers found fences in disrepair, that owner could not recover for trespass by the animals of others." Also see **perambulator**.

fencibles, fensibles: See ***sea fencibles***.

fender, fireplace fender: a usually decorative, low metal shield with curved ends, placed in front of a fire to prevent ashes and coals from spilling out into the room, e.g., "Sarah's fender was of highly polished brass."

feof, enfeoff, enfeoffment: possession; an ancient legal term meaning to give over or place in possession, e.g., "The term enfeoff in a deed meant that possession was being granted along with ownership."

ferae naturae: (Lat.) wild animals, e.g., "Unlike in old England, ferae naturae were free for the taking to all early colonials."

ferret, ferit, ferreting: thin, narrow, decorative cloth, early made of silk or cotton; a narrow woolen tape used to decorate clothing, e.g., The ledger of Parham's store revealed several purchases of ***yards*** (q.v.) of ferit"; "She sewed ferreting around the edges of the shawl."

ferrotype: See **tintype**.

ferry, ferries: as now, a boat used to transport people, animals and goods across a body of water for pay; (verb) to move people, animals and goods across water for hire at rates very often set by the county court or other county authority, e.g., "By 1750, there were 150 ferries licensed on James River"; "For his livelihood, Drake ferried folks across the Chickahominy at Richmond."

fetch: as now, a very common early expression meaning to bring or to go and retrieve, e.g., "Paul often said that a horse is worth only what it will fetch on the day of the sale."

feudalism, feudal system: that economic system of England and Europe during the middle ages, where lords owned land and vassals tended such; pertaining to interests held by a superior or a "lord"; the feudal system (introduced to England by William I) prevailed in Europe and the British Isles throughout the eleventh, twelfth, and thirteenth centuries and only very gradually disappeared, e.g., "To the casual observer, Maryland of the 17th and early 18th centuries, and the area of the Hudson River until well into the 19th century, appeared near feudal in the prevailing institutions"; "The earliest colonial immigrants left behind what yet was quite nearly a feudal society."

feuterer: a keeper of or one who boards dogs, e.g., "While early records of what is now the United Kingdom frequently spoke of feuterers, that term was apparently not in common use in Colonial America."

fiddleback chair, fiddleback wood grain: a chair with a back built in the shape of a violin; ornate and rare graining or configuration in fine wood, e.g., "The fiddle back dining chairs had upholstered seats and were of mahogany"; "The Empire table was of fiddleback walnut and was extraordinarily beautiful."

fiduciary: one who, by his own choice, acts principally in behalf of another person and is duty-bound to act to the benefit of that person to the exclusion of others, e.g., "The duties of an administrator and ***executor*** (q.v.) are of a fiduciary nature; to preserve and properly handle the assets of the deceased to the benefit of the heirs."

field: any land that has been cleared or cultivated, e.g., "The fields used for animal drives near Upper Sandusky were created by Wyandot Indians who annually burned off the vegetation."

Field bed: a four-posted, canopied bed, e.g., "The posts of a Field bed typically were not more than four feet high."

field commission: See ***commissioned officers, etc.***

field stone, field rock: See ***headstone.***

field tree: See ***plow tree.***

fieri facias, fieri feci, f. feci: See ***facias*** and see ***writs.***

fighting chicken: See ***dominicker.***

fighting rooster: See ***dominicker.***

figure, figuring: to dance, e.g., "There are many references to persons 'figuring' waltzes, Virginia reels, and other dances." Also see ***boards.***

filius: a son, e.g., "In his order, the Louisiana judge referred to the son of the family as filius familius, meaning that the child was an unemancipated male offspring."

fillets: See ***bookbinders and printers.***

filly: a young, female horse (and occasionally a newborn female mule) that has lived beyond a few days and has yet to be bred, after which it would be referred to as a ***mare*** (q.v.), e.g., "The filly resembled her ***dam*** (q.v.) and was chestnut." Also see ***horse.***

fine (to), fined: as now, a fine, a pecuniary punishment; early, to refine, purify, embellish or decorate; e.g., "He wrote in 1886 that the ore had been fined"; "The inventory spoke of fined bronze, meaning it had been embellished or decorated, probably with a different or more expensive metal"; "Richard Parker was fined 12S for his failure to attend church." Also ***see*** mulct.

fire clay: See ***glass making.***

fire devil: as with a ***dust devil*** (q.v.), a small cyclonic pattern of fire that may result from a large fire such as in brush or on prairie land.

fire dogs: See ***andirons.***

fire screen: a light, movable shield, usually three to 5 feet in height, and of any of many styles and materials, designed to be moved about and placed between the fire and a person sitting or sleeping in the room, thus preventing discomfort from the direct heat, e.g., "Her two fire screens were elegant and of brocade in walnut frames."

fire tongs: as now, long-handled iron pincers or grabs used to adjust, move, or position burning wood in a fireplace or stove, e.g., "The fire tongs always were near the fireplace in case burning wood fell out into the room." Also see ***fender.***

firearms, expressions based upon: as now, e.g., "Among many common expressions relating to firearms, our ancestors said 'long shot', meaning not likely to succeed; 'hot shot', describing one who has recently and quickly come to considerable power; 'big shot', for an employer, boss, supervisor or business leader; 'lock, stock, and barrel', meaning complete; 'go off half cocked', meaning to commence before preparation is complete; 'aim high', to have lofty and difficult goals; 'set one's sights on something', meaning to have a definite objective or goal; and 'straight as a ramrod', meaning to have erect posture or be scrupulously honest." Also see ***shooting irons,*** and see ***flash in the pan.***

fireback, fire plate: a heavy metal plate placed in the back of the fireplace to prevent the masonry from deteriorating and to retain heat and deflect it back into the room, e.g., "Most unusually, the iron fireback had ornate decoration."

fire-chunk: a thick or rather heavy piece of wood that has been set ablaze, e.g., "He wrote that they frightened the wolves away by throwing fire-chunks in their direction."

firecracker: See ***cracker.***

fire-eater, fire brand, fire breather: 19th-century term for those who were viewed as spokesmen for their views and were powerfully outspoken, particularly as to States' Rights and in support of or against slavery, e.g., "John C. Calhoun and Daniel Webster were widely known as fire-eaters and firebrands."

firelock: See ***flintlock*** and ***matchlock.***

fireplace fender: See ***fender.***

fireslice, fire peel: a small, shallow shovel used to move ashes and coals, e.g., "She used the fireslice to move coals to the ***trivets*** (q.v.)."

firkin, sugar firkin: a tightly lidded, handled container, made of wood early, and later of tin or other metal, and used to store granulated or lump sugar; one quarter barrel, about 8 gallons, usually of cheese, e.g.; "There were thirty firkins of cheese listed in the manifest." "Her sugar firkin was of tin."

first cousins: persons who share one or more common grandparents, e.g., "Her mother's sisters' children, were her first cousins."

first mate: See ***mate.***

first quarter of the moon: See ***waxing*** and ***waning.***

fish kettle: an oblong, iron kettle used for and often shaped like a fish, e.g., "She poached whole fish in the fish kettle."

fish their corn: a 17th- and 18th-century expression, describing the practice of fertilizing corn with pieces of ***junk fish*** (q.v.), e.g., "By reason of the cruelty of the Pequod Indians, the citizenry of old Salem felt that Indian 'carcases' might be used to fish their corn."

fishhooks in your pocket, have you: an expression intended to reveal that the speaker believes that another person is not paying his or her share of some, usually, immediate purchase or of a small debt, e.g., "When Gary again avoided paying his share of the luncheon check, Richard said, 'Hey Gary, you got fishhooks in your pocket?'"

fishmonger: a merchant or dealer in fish and seafood, e.g., "Before emigrating, Richard Roberts was a Welsh fishmonger." Also ***see*** monger.

fistes: fists, e.g., "His mention of using his fistes when needed meant that he was ready to fight if called upon."

fistula: a canal, opening or passage resulting from injury or disease that allows drainage to the surface, e.g., "Fistulas, especially in the abdomen, were not understood by early physicians, and but few undertook to disturb or treat them or their cause."

fit, have a: See ***fits and bad spells*** and see ***conniption.***

fitchew: See ***skunk.***

fits and bad spells, have a fit, have a fit and fall back in it: common superlatives not used in anger, and having to do with the attitudes or reactions of one to the actions of another, e.g., "Clarisa told the boys that their mother would have fits and bad spells if they took the toads into the house." Also see ***conniption.***

fixed, fixt, unfixed, unfixt: refers to the state of repair or readiness for use of metal mechanical devices, e.g., "The 1679 inventory lists two 'pistolls, 1 fixt, 1 unfixt'."

flagellet(e): a small flute, e.g., "Curiously, the 1740 inventory revealed the presence of a 'recorder, flute, and flagellet'."

flagon: an ancient term for a large mug or flask with a narrow mouth from which alcoholic beverages—typically rum, mead, or beer—were drunk, e.g., "The earliest records of some New England ***inns*** (q.v.) reveal drinks being served in flagons."

flail: an implement used to separate grain from husks and other chaff, e.g., "She had a hickory flail which she had used for years."

flame grain, crotch grain: the beautiful, highly desirable wood grain naturally created in the crotch of a tree, e.g., "Flame grain walnut and mahogany were prized by all cabinetmakers." Also see ***burl grain,*** and see ***cabinetmaker.***

Flandersware: stoneware (q.v.), originally from Holland and France, e.g., "Her Flandersware platters were most unusual."

flank companies: those military units posted on the extreme right or left or at the rear of an army or larger military unit., e.g., "Company "K" was one of the flank companies for the 55th Ohio at Chancellorsville." Also see ***skirmishers,*** and see ***armies, organization of.***

flapdoodle, flap doodle: nonsense or silly thoughts, e.g., "Many early writings describe speech and exchanges at dances and revelry as flapdoodle."

flapdragon: an early drinkers' game in which raisins were plucked from burning rum with the fingers, e.g., "Flapdragon was a popular pastime of drinkers and revelers during the long New England winter nights.

flash in the pan: derived from the action of a ***flintlock*** (q.v.) weapon when the ***pan powder*** (q.v.) ignites but yet fails to ignite the main charge; not lasting, of little permanent effect; giving the appearance of the capability of accomplishment, yet achieving little, e.g., "When he said that the new lawyer was but a flash in the pan, he meant that the lawyer probably would not accomplish anything of lasting value or would not be in business long." Also see ***firearms, expressions based upon.***

flask: early, a bottle or powder horn; later a small bottle with a lid, screw top, or stopper, e.g., "The flasks used now to carry alcoholic beverages on the person derive from small, early vessels used for any liquid or finely powdered substance such as gunpowder."

flat: as now, a shallow wooden box, usually holding ten or a dozen smaller containers for berries, small fruits, or vegetables; a flat bottomed boat used to transport freight; a superlative meaning very much so, absolutely, without doubt, total, etc., e.g., "She took two flats of berries to market to trade for other produce"; "He had a flat that he used to ferry goods to Charles City"; "Lee flat whipped Hooker at Chancellorsville"; "To a little boy holding a $10.00 bill with a smile, he said, 'You flat have that money, don't you'."

flatbread: thin, rounded, and flattened bread introduced here by Norwegian immigrants, e.g., "Sketches of 17th-century kitchens occasionally depict flatbreads stored so as to be available for immediate use."

flatiron, flat iron, sad iron: early, a heavy, black iron tool with a flat, polished—"smooth"—bottom that was heated on a stove or ***trivet*** (q.v.) and used for smoothing or "ironing" clothes or fabrics; later, any smoothing tool made of iron or steel, whether the heat source was self-contained or not, e.g., "She had three flatirons, each of which was used alternately while the others were heating."

flax wheel: a small, treadle-driven spinning wheel, usually used to make thread from flax (linen), e.g., "Virtually every home of the nineteenth century had at least one flax wheel." See also ***spinning wheel.***

fleam, fleem: an instrument used to pierce a vein or artery and bleed people or animals, e.g., "A 'small fleem' was listed along with other household items in the Hines inventory."

fleet, task force, task group: ships grouped for some task, usually combat; a fleet is made up of the ships and equipment needed for war on a large scale over a large area of ocean; a task force is a portion of that fleet selected for a specific military task; and a task group is a portion of a task force designated to perform certain aspects of the task, e.g., "During World War II Task Force 58 was a portion of the Pacific Fleet, and Task Group Bravo was a portion of Task Force 58."

fleeter, fleeting dish: a shallow, handled bowl or dish used to skim cream from the surface of fresh milk, e.g., "After each milking, she used the fleeter to skim the cream from the milk."

flesh fork, fleshhook: a handled, hooked, metal fork, usually pointed or with two tines, and used to remove meat from a boiling kettle or pot, e.g., "Diane used a flesh fork to remove the large pieces of boiled meat, which she then cut up and served."

flesh monger: a pimp; one who deals in the services of whores or prostitutes, e.g., "Shakespeare, in *Measure For Measure*, asks, 'Was the duke a flesh monger, a fool, a coward...?'"

fleshing knife: a common, curved-bladed, heavy knife used to strip the tissue refuse from the inner side of animal skins preparatory to curing, e.g., "There was a flesh knife and two large crock ***jugs*** (q.v.) in the inventory of Judith Parker's belongings." Also see ***tanners' and curriers' tools.***

flint glass: See ***leaded glass.***

flintlock, snaplock: a very common, early, hand-held ***firearm*** (q.v.) discharged through the action of a piece of flint striking a small, rough, metal plate (steel), thereby creating a spark that ignited the pan powder, the fire from which traveled through a small opening to the gunpowder in the chamber, e.g., "Before 1840, the flintlock was the most common of American firearms." Also see ***lock***, and see ***firearms, expressions based upon.***

flip: a highly favored, intoxicating drink consisting of sweetened rum combined with cider, beer, or ale, and usually heavily seasoned with cinnamon and nutmeg, quite usually served warm, e.g., "Many were the flips enjoyed in old Raleigh Tavern."

flipdog: a poker-like iron rod, heated to red heat in the fire and then thrust into drinks, especially a ***flip*** (q.v.) for the purpose of warming the drinks, e.g., "A large mug filled with rum, water, sugar, and butter, into which a red-hot flipdog had been thrust, became the much enjoyed ***hot buttered rum*** (q.v.)."

flivver: an early term meaning an old or barely operable automobile; thought by some to have derived from the words Henry Ford and livery, meaning a cheap or low quality automobile, e.g., "Winnie always referred to Ray's old cars as flivvers." Also see ***tin lizzie.***

flock: old rags, scraps of wool, or pieces of cloth, often used to stuff ***ticking bags*** (q.v.) or weave into rugs, when e.g., "Being a poor widow, her flock rug was the best she could afford."

flood tide: See ***tides.***

florin: a coin (first silver, then copper) equaling one tenth a ***Pound*** (q.v.), two shillings, or $12.00 to $15.00 in 1999), and equal to a Netherlands gulden, e.g., "The silver florin was quite usually accepted as payment by colonial American merchants."

floss: unlike now, soft, shiny silk thread of wide utility, e.g., "She often used floss in her embroidery work."

flow blue: occasionally called "flowing blue", china ware, usually ironstone, imprinted with designs of cobalt blue coloring of many shades that flowed or "bled" into the dish or bowl producing a smeared look, now highly prized, it was made after about 1830, e.g., "The flow blue ***pitcher and bowl*** (q.v.) kept in the master bedroom were made in Holland."

flowers: menstruation, from the Biblical description of that event as it appears in the original King James version, e.g., "As recently as 1953 Mrs. Powers still referred to her regular menstrual period as 'being in her flowers'." Also see ***menstrual rags.***

flub-dubs: extravagances; unneeded and unwarranted decorations or finery, e.g., "Lincoln referred to the pretentious White House decorations bought by Mary as mere flub-dubs."

flue cover: that metal or heavy fabric cover placed over the flue hole during the months when a free standing stove was not needed or used, e.g., "Each spring Will and the boys would take the iron stove to the barn and put the flue cover in place."

flummeries: See ***desserts.***

flutes: unknown as other than musical instruments, however, perhaps sometimes a gathering or group of men who were inebriated, e.g., "Sarah

Ferguson wrote that she had become disgusted with 'his gang of flutes in the parlor'."

flutter wheel: See ***millers' tools.***

flux, bloody flux: See ***dysentery.***

fly: as now, an opening in the lower front of any wearing apparel, especially pants of a man, e.g., "The word fly used to describe the opening in the front of a pair of pants is very old." Also see ***codpiece.***

flyboat: a light, shallow-draft, fast sailboat, popular on inland bays and wide waterways, e.g., "On windy days, Hunt used his flyboat to ferry men to and from James City."

Flying Tigers: See ***military combat units, famous.***

foal: to give birth to a horse or mule; a newborn horse or mule, male or female, e.g., "The jenny was ready to foal"; "The foal, being female, would be called a ***filly*** (q.v.) after but a few days and until she matured and been bred, whereupon she would be known as a mare."

fodder house: See ***baled hay house.***

folio: occasionally, any very large book; early and now, a dimension or measure of documentary material, usually of about thirty inches on a side; sometimes, pages printed on both sides, yet numbered on the first side only, e.g., "The volume was in folio and was quite unwieldy"; "The record was paginated in folio, so the researcher had to exercise care in citing it."

font: a letter or symbol with which to print; an often permanent, open container, bowl or basin usually made of stone or marble, within which baptismal water is kept, e.g., "The font Margaret used was 'Courier New' and the font size was 10"; "The font at St. Paul's was made of beautiful pink marble."

fontanage: a knot of ribbons on the top of the hat, e.g., "By 1800, the fontanage was no longer considered stylish in the American colonies."

fonzytish: from the German "pflantzentisch," meaning plant stand; a slice of a tree, usually walnut, butternut, or cherry, cut at right angles to the trunk, highly polished on one surface, and used as a stand for plants, thus keeping drippings from the carpets, e.g., "Her ***Dutch*** (q.v.) husband had sanded and polished her butternut fonzytish until the finish was like a ***looking glass*** (q.v.)."

foo-foo: an early slang term meaning to wash and clean one's self and to use colognes, perfumes, powders, hair oils and other products having a pleasant odor with the intention of pleasing others, e.g., "Drake smiled and said that he surely did foo-foo before his date the evening before."

fool: unlike now, often a jester or paid buffoon, e.g., "While now the word fool is a term of derision, in early times it often described the calling of the court jester."

foolscap: writing paper; a size of paper, usually 13 1/2 X 17, e.g., "The writing paper of early students often was a sheet of foolscap cut into quarters and fastened together at one corner or edge with a piece of thread."

foot stool, footstool, foot-stool, cricket: a low seat or stool, used for sitting or placed in front of a chair as a resting place for the feet, e.g., "The inventory revealed a bench and a foot stool."

foot warmer: usually, a small box, sometimes free standing, but often made to attach to the stretchers of a work table or desk, and usually having a metal liner into which hot ashes or coals were placed in order that the person there working might be able to warm their feet by placing them on the box, e.g., "Bookkeepers and office workers found foot warmers a cold weather necessity by reason of the inefficiency of fireplaces."

foot, men, horse: the infantry consisted of units of armed men who fought on foot and were known as "foot" or "men", and the cavalry consisted of units of armed men who fought on horseback and were known as "horse," e.g., "'All the King's horse and all the King's men couldn't put Humpty Dumpty back together again' becomes meaningful only if we know how our ancestors used those words"; "American Revolutionary War records are replete with references to regiments of British 'foot' and 'horse'."

footman: unlike now, a ***trivet*** (q.v.), e.g., "There were 2 footmans in the inventory."

Forbes Road: See ***roads, early.***

forced heirs: in ***Civil Law*** (q.v.), any persons who a ***testator*** (q.v.) may not arbitrarily deprive of a share of that ***estate*** (q.v.) without formally disinheriting them, e.g., "Those researching in early jurisdictions that applied the Civil Law, such as Louisiana, should be aware of forced heirs."

forcemeat: stuffing, as in a turkey, e.g., "The forcemeat contained, in part, soft sweet sausage, eggs, bread, seasoning and oysters."

forcible entry and detainer: an action to recover possession of land when the rightful owner has been wrongfully kept from the premises, e.g., "Forcible entry and detainer was the proper action when the neighbor fenced in a plaintiff's land, undertook to graze cattle on it, and refused to leave."

forcible trespass: a North Carolina action corresponding to forcible entry and ***detainer*** (q.v.) but applicable only to personal property, possession of which had been taken through an exercise of force or giving an appearance of force, e.g., "Even though he was not physically afraid of the taker, the owner of the hounds sought possession of them through an action alleging forcible trespass."

ford: a place where a river or stream may be crossed on foot or (occasionally) on horseback or in wagons, e.g., "Chattanooga and Atlanta still have major highways called Shallowford Road named for the early shallow fords to which those roads once led."

foreign judgment: a judgment from a court in a county or state other than that in which it is being executed upon, e.g., "Her discovery of a foreign judgment filed by her ancestor in the Marion County court records led her to his home county." Also see ***execute.***

forge: as a verb, to beat or hammer into shape; as a noun, a place where iron is made and shaped, usually for sale, e.g., "The iron he forged into decorative shapes was known as wrought iron"; "As with Catherine Forge after the battle of Chancellorsville, the original purpose of the Valley Forge was forever forgotten after Washington's army wintered there."

forks: contrary to popular belief, even though seldom seen in the 17th century, three- and four-tined forks for eating were in rather common use in this country by the years of the American Revolution, e.g., "Her silver forks had three tines and were made in England." Also see ***dibble*** and see ***dung fork.***

forms: record-keeping aids necessary to the family researcher and usually available in libraries, genealogical bookstores, and on the Internet, e.g., "James had preserved all his information on various ***lineage*** (q.v.) forms copied from Internet sources."

Forrest's Cavalry: See ***military combat units, famous.***

forsworn: an untrue oath in which the person making the oath knows of the falsity, e.g., "He was said to have forsworn the affidavit, meaning that he knew the statement to be untrue at the time."

fortnight: two weeks; fourteen days; one half a month or half the period of the moon, e.g., "Expressions using fortnight, such as 'He will be gone a fortnight' were very common in the early days."

forts: See ***stockades.***

forty and eight, 40 and 8, 40 et 8: an expression of World War I veterans and the American Legion, the term arose from the very simply furnished train cars called forty and eights by reason of the capacity of such to carry 40 soldiers with their back packs and 8 horses with their harnessing, e.g., "The term 40 and 8 was known to all veterans of World War I and became an early symbol of the American Legion posts."

Forty-niners, The: those 125,000 or so prospectors and opportunists who came from all over the world to California after the discovery of gold at Sutter's Mill in January of 1848, e.g., "Tens of thousands of descendants of the Tennessee Forty-niners now live in the west."

fossil: unlike now, any mineral dug from the ground, e.g., "His reference to mica as a fossil did not mean that it was made up of remains of prior life."

fostered, fostered out, foster parent: an ancient Irish custom carried to the Americas, and here modified to an arrangement whereby a child is given into the custody of another and, in exchange for care and keeping, is expected to perform the duties of a natural child; the condition of a person not of age, who, by agreement of his or her parents, was living with a family other than his or her own, and who is expected to perform services and otherwise conduct himself or herself as would any other child of the foster family; one who carries out the duties of raising a child without legally claiming that child as his or her own, e.g., "At the age of twelve, Bethany was fostered out to the Rev. Pinney home, there to remain until she married." See ***adoption and apprentice.***

foulard: an early, commonly used, usually lightweight printed silk fabric, e.g., "His ***cravat*** (q.v.) was of lavender foulard."

founder, foundry, caster: the art of casting molten metals in various forms and shapes through the use of molds or otherwise, e.g., "Typically, the founder received his raw product from the owner of a ***furnace*** (q.v.), after which he melted the metals and cast it in his molds or forms"; "Lowell and Jack Midlam had a most prosperous foundry."

foundling: an abandoned child which the natural parents have no intention of reclaiming, e.g., "Since James was a foundling at the church door, his lineage was almost impossible to ascertain."

fountain head: See ***springhead.***

four-plated stove, two-plated, six-plated, etc.: referred to the number of "plates"—cooking spots, 'burners'—on a wood or coal burning metal cookstove, thus revealing to the researcher its size and that it was for cooking and not heating, e.g., "The Rev. Cole inventory listed a '6 plate' stove, revealing a very large cooking stove." Also see ***cookstove.***

four-poster, poster bed: a bed with posts designed to hold a ***valance*** (q.v.) and canopy, e.g., "The canopy frame for Sarah's four-poster had been lost for many years." Also see ***pencil-post bed.***

fowling piece, birding piece: early term for a common, long-barreled, usually large-bored shotgun used for bird and small game hunting, e.g., "The stock of his fowling piece was of fine burl walnut." Also see ***shotgun*** and see ***cap and ball.***

fox chase: See ***chase, animal.***

fox, foxed: unlike now, one material decorated with another, usually leather or cloth, the prime or better material being that which is worked and the secondary substance being that adorned or decorated, e.g., "Her best shoes were cow-hide foxed with beaver"

fox-hole: See ***rifle-pit.***

foxing: yellow or brown stains that appear on old paper, e.g., "The paper showed foxing, yet was still very supple and strong."

foyer table: usually a long, rather narrow, well finished table made of better wood, sometimes of stand-up height, and used in foyers and entrance halls as places for guests' hats, gloves and calling cards might be placed, and usually maintained with a doily, lamp, and floral arrangements, e.g., "Mikaila's foyer table was of inlaid mahogany, and was decorated with fresh flower arrangements daily."

fractional currency: See ***shin-plaster.***

frail: a measure of raisins, about 75 pounds, e.g., "He wrote that he had '...shipped 2 frails of whites...' meaning about 150 lbs. of white raisins."

frail a banjo: unknown, but probably the picking of a banjo by one not knowledgeable in that art, e.g., "He wrote that while the group of musicians played the dance tunes, Evan had remained to one side '...frailing his banjo'."

fraktur: originally, a German style, early PA, colorful, often fully handmade (sometimes partly printed) painting, usually depicting birds, flowers, decorative calligraphy and scroll work, and bearing the names of those who are the subject, e.g., "The fraktur birth certificate of Diane's ancestor was her most prized memento."

frambisia: See ***yaws.***

frankincense and myrrh: early, very valuable resins from trees grown in Ethiopia and used in the making of incense and perfumes, e.g., "The story of the Wise Men and their frankincense and myrrh is well known to all Christians."

Franklin (State of): that proposed State of the Union, the constitution of which was adopted at Jonesboro, TN, in 1784, which state arose from the need of settlers to protect themselves from the Cherokees, and which eventually became a portion of east Tennessee, e.g., "Many descendants of the residents of Franklin now live in Texas, having left genealogical records in Tennessee."

Franklin, U.S.S: See ***warships, American.***

fraternities, sororities, and societies: as now; in genealogy, a valuable source of vital records concerning ancestors, as many early Americans belonged, e.g., "Of the many societies, the Colonial Dames, Masons (F. & A.M.), Knights of Columbus (K. of C.), United Order Of African Ladies and Gentlemen (U.O.A.L.G.), Rebekah Lodge, Order of Red Men (O.R.M.), Woodmen of the World, Shrine, Order of Odd Fellows (I.O.O.F.), Moose (L.S.M.), Sons of Italy, and the Elks (B.P.O.E.), are but a few, and all kept records valuable to the researcher where yet extant."

free blacks, free Negroes: those Negroes who were free men, whether by having purchased from or been granted freedom by their masters or by becoming citizens of, or being born in, one of the non-slave states or colonies, e.g., "The early records are replete with references to free Negroes or free blacks."

free range: See ***stock law*** and see ***fence***.

free school: an early term meaning a school supported by taxes, private sources, or churches, where no charge was assessed for the participation of a student, e.g., "She attended the first free school in the county."

free woman of color: a pre-***Civil War*** (q.v.) term for any woman, other than those of the white race, who was not bound to servitude, e.g., "Being half Cherokee, she was carried on the records as a free woman of color."

freedman, freedmen: early, any person previously bound to servitude and then freed; a manumitted or freed slave, e.g., "The formation of the Freedman's Bureau in 1865 brought consternation to the old South."

Freedman's Bureau: the result of Congressional action that sought to preserve the civil rights of the Negro, required by reason of the ***Southern Black Codes*** (q.v.) and other continued efforts of the South to subjugate the Negro, e.g., "The authority of the Freedman's Bureau of 1865 was enlarged in 1866."

freedom paper, freedom document: See ***manumission***.

freehold, freeholder: a ***fee*** (q.v.), ***fee tail*** (q.v.), or a life ***estate*** (q.v.) in real property; the holder of one of those estates, e.g., "While most land in the manor was leased for the life of the holder, Dimmitt was a freeholder; the owner in fee of his tract." See also ***fee simple***, and ***entailment***.

freeload, freeloaders: to openly benefit oneself at the expense of another, e.g., "Of the many expressions that arose from our early widespread use of firearms, freeload was but one; to load one's rifle or shotgun from the gunpowder, shot, etc., of another person without paying or offering to pay that other person." Also see ***firearms, expressions based upon***.

freeman, freemen: men emancipated from bound service to others, e.g., "In theory, all Negro slaves were freemen after the ***Emancipation Proclamation***" (q.v.).; "Evan had arrived as an ***indentured servant*** (q.v.) for 6 years, after which he was a freeman." Also see ***freedman***.

freeman's bath: unknown, e.g., "Sherwood wrote in 1836 that he knew of a '...freeman's bath in New Hampshire'."

freeman's roll: in the early colonies, a list of burgesses and freemen maintained by the county, precinct, or town, e.g., "The early freeman's rolls are very helpful to the family historian."

freewillers: See ***Redemptioners***.

French and Indian War: that armed conflict that occurred 1754/5-1763 between England and the American colonies on the one side, and the French and allied American Indian forces on the other, e.g., "Though many records exist, there were few formal discharges from military service at the time of the French and Indian War."

French fall shoes: apparently, low, better quality dress shoes for either men or women, e.g., "Some 17th-century references speak of French fall shoes." See ***shoes.***

French influence: many words arose from our experiences with the French who settled or maintained commerce with the colonies, e.g., "Bayou, toboggan, caribou, crevasse, levee, depot, cents, dimes, chowder, beaucoup, and the many Creole dishes and names are but a few."

French polish: a fine furniture finish, consisting of ***shellac*** (q.v.) mixed with spirits, and applied in several coats with great care, e.g., "Because of the experience required and the difficulty of application, French polish was used on only the finest of ***furniture*** (q.v.)."

French Wine: in early times, any better wine, but usually from France, e.g., "The manifest revealed two bbls. of French Wine from the Canary Islands."

freshet: annual or regular periods of high water in rivers and streams, e.g., "Grant knew that when the spring freshets came, the fords would not be passable."

fret: as commonly used, and the bands of metal or wood set perpendicular to the strings on a stringed instrument, e.g., "Cheryl was quick to learn upon which frets to place her fingers to create the desired sounds."

Friars: religious orders of men; a) Franciscans, Gray Friars and Minors, b) Augustines, c) Dominicans (Black Friars), d) Carmelites (White Friars), e.g., "The records of the Orders of Friars often are helpful in research." See also ***orders of nuns.***

Friends: See ***Quakers.***

frig, frig around: unknown to Johnson, to waste time or be unproductive, e.g., "He wrote in 1886 that his friend had been discharged from his employment for frigging around."

frigate: very early, a light vessel of both sails and oars; later, a light, square-rigged, sailing vessel; since the mid-nineteenth century, a man o' war larger than a destroyer and smaller than a cruiser, e.g., "The frigate *Golden Eagle* was noted for its extraordinary speed."

fringe loom: a common, small loom used to make fringing, e.g., "Fringe looms often appear in early inventories." Also see ***belt loom.***

Frisian: that Germanic tongue most like English and spoken by those called Frisians from the areas bordering the Netherlands province of Friesland, from Denmark, Western Germany and from the Frisian islands in the North Sea, e.g. "Of those who spoke German, the colonials most quickly came to know the meanings of the West Frisians."

frizzen: See ***gunsmiths' tools.***

frock, frockcoat: early, a tight-fitting coat for men; later, a dress or coat; today, any outer garment for a woman, e.g., "His frockcoat was of Irish linen and wool."

froe, frow: a common, large, thick-bladed tool with the handle at right angles to the blade, used to make shingles or cut wood into thin pieces, e.g., "He made the cedar ***shakes*** (q.v.) with a frow and much physical labor."

frog drownder: see ***drownder.***

frog gig: See ***gig,*** and see ***giggs.***

frog: a sheath hung from the belt to hold a sword or knife; a piece of heavy indented or pierced glass used to hold buds or flower stems, e.g., "Her frog was of pink ***milk glass*** (q.v.)."

froise: (Fr., froissier) bacon or ham enclosed in a pancake, e.g., "Froises have always been a favorite in old Louisiana."

fromp: unknown, perhaps frump, e.g., "The letter stated that the 18 year old woman was 'frompy'." Also see ***frump.***

frontal: quite unlike now, any medication or curative material to be applied to the forehead or temples, e.g., "Dr. Drake wrote of applying a pepper frontal."

fruitery: a place for storing fruits or other such produce, e.g., "Maggie called her ***cold cellar*** (q.v.) a fruitery." Also see ***buttery.***

frump: perhaps fromp; early, as per Johnson (1802), to mock another, to brow-beat; later and now, dowdy, drab, common in appearance, e.g., "Sarah said that at 52 she did not want to appear as a frumpy housewife." Also see ***fromp.***

fuero: (Sp.) a code of laws, e.g., "References to the fuero in the early Southwest refer to codes, either civil or criminal."

Fugitive Slave Law (and Acts): those enactments of Congress (1793 and 1850) and of several states having to do with and requiring the return of slaves who had unlawfully fled from their owners to "free" states, e.g., "The ***Dred Scott Decision*** (q.v.) was said to have confirmed the validity of the Fugitive Slave Laws."

Fulhamware: ceramic ware, particularly popular for tankards, mugs, drinking glasses, etc., "Fulhamware mugs occasionally were listed in the inventories of affluent New Englanders."

full (to), fulled cloth, fulling mill, fuller: usually, to clean wool; woolen and occasionally other fabric (***stuff,*** q.v.) made of thread that has been cleaned and from which the grease and oil have been removed; a factory in which, particularly, wool is cleaned and made ready for spinning; one who cleans or works with wool, e.g., "The surname Fuller is derived from those who make a living from fulling or operating a fulling mill." Also see ***occupations as surnames.***

full bore: a superlative, meaning at as rapid a rate or with as much force and effect as an instrumentality is capable, e.g., "A shotgun with a modified or no-choke barrel has less killing power at long distances than does one that is bored full, hence expressions such as 'he went at it full bore.'"

full moon: See ***waxing*** and ***waning.***

full sea: See ***tides, etc.***

fullers' tools: "Revealing of the likelihood that an ancestor may have worked as a fuller were tools such as a teasel (teazel), fullers' shears, a fulling mill, and large quantities of dyes." Also see ***full (to).***

fulling mill: See ***full, to.***

fulsome: usually, offensive or profane words, e.g., "A Northern newspaper referred to a speech extolling the virtues of slave holding Georgia as a 'fulsome and false praise of the least deserving of the states.'"

fungibles: movable, usually specifically unidentifiable, tangible personal property that may be interchangeable with another equal number, weight, or measure of the same product, e.g., "His wheat in the elevator called into play the law of fungibles."

fur: a furrow; synonym for far, e.g., "Furrows created in the course of planting crops were widely known in the Southern Highlands as furs"; "Martha wrote that her Civil War soldier son was 'fur away over in Alabama'."

furlong: ten (10) chains or forty (40) ***poles*** (q.v.) or ***rods*** (q.v.) equal one (1) furlong; there are eight furlongs in a mile, e.g., "The race was ten furlongs or 1.25 miles in length."

furnace: unlike now, any smelting installation, but usually for iron, e.g., "Catherine Furnace was to forever be associated with Lee and Stonewall Jackson."

furnishings: unlike now, one's personal items of dress or appearance, e.g., "Among the furnishings in Cheryl's inventory were several items of jewelry, a hand mirror and 2 combs, and a pair of gloves."

furniture: unlike now, those furnishings customarily found in the space or with the object being considered and necessary to make it complete and usable as designed, e.g., "The furniture of her ***bedstead*** (q.v.) included ***curtains*** (q.v.), a ***valance*** (q.v.), comforters, a ***rug*** (q.v.), and a ***ticking bag*** (q.v.)."

fusee, fusilier: one who is armed with a firelock or ***flintlock*** (q.v.), e.g., "The 16th Fusiliers, true to their name, were foot soldiers armed with English-made flintlocks."

fustian: a strong cloth made of linen or wool and cotton, e.g., "Fustian was an early favorite for better work clothes."

fuhthisis: See ***phthisis***.

G

G.I. Bill: those congressional enactments that provided relief, medical attention, funds for education, and guaranteed loans to the veterans of World War II and other conflicts since then, e.g., "Since 1945, the G.I. Bill has provided educational opportunities for (and genealogical records of) millions of veterans."

gabb, gab, gabbler: from the ancient noun, gabbler, meaning one who prattles, prats, or chatters incessantly, e.g., "When the teen age girls chatted seemingly without end, their grandmother said 'Girls, do your work now, and quit gabbing'."

gabbler: See ***gabb***.

gabions: early, a wicker or woven basket filled with earth, many of which often were piled together to form an entrenchment or military barricade; later, any woven basket, e.g., "He described the fort as having a north wall of gabions."

gaffer: early, a term of respect; later and now, an old man of little financial worth or estate.

gages: plums and apricots, e.g., "For 'plums in brandy', she directed that green gages (apricots) or blue gages (plums) be cooked in water with sugar equal to 1/2 the wt. of the fruit, to which brandy was added when the mixture was bottled." For other fruits, see ***shrubs.***

gaggle: very early, the noise made by a goose; to imitate the noise of a goose (Johnson, 1755); later 19th century and now, a group or family of geese, e.g., "Evan noted in the Day Book that he had sold a gaggle of geese to Bethany."

gaits, horse: as now, e.g., "A walk is as now; the pace, where both legs on a side are moved forward almost simultaneously, is used in cart racing; the trot, also used in cart racing, is a rough saddle ride between a walk and a run where the diagonal legs move forward almost simultaneously; at a rack, a rapid smooth pace is gained, and the diagonal legs move together but not simultaneously; in a canter, an easy comfortable run or gallop is provided; and at gallop, the animal may be brought to its most rapid speed, however it is exhausting for the beast." See ***dead run.***

gallatines: probably an early rendering of the word galantine, which was white meat, boiled, seasoned, and shaped into a mold in its own jelly, e.g., "Mikaila was taught how to prepare gallatines while attending the culinary institute." Also see ***dobes.***

gallop: See ***gaits.***

galvanize: as now in metal work; early, unknown to Johnson, and apparently derived from a 19th-century use meaning unusual or surprising; to dress in a costume of a different and often antagonistic nationality, religion or armed service, e.g., "When asked why the Confederate reenactors had dressed in Union uniforms for purposes of the parade, he said that they had 'agreed to galvanize.'"

games (of children): as now, e.g., "Among the myriad early children's games were whizzer, spin the button, gray wooley, bull pen, King's Cross, corner ball, cat ball, and town ball." Also see ***King's X, bowls, break the Pope's neck, pallmall.***

game pouch: an early, medium-sized, usually waterproof, heavy cloth bag with a shoulder strap, the same worn while hunting and serving as a carrier for dead small game, e.g., "She had lined his game pouch with ***oil cloth*** (q.v.) to prevent the blood from leeching through to his clothes."

game table: early, any of many styles of wooden tables used for playing chess, cards, or other games, often large with a rotating and folding top and made of better woods—cherry, rosewood, mahogany, or walnut, e.g., "Her Empire-style game table was of cherry with a walnut top that folded and rotated."

game worth the candle: See ***worth the candle, is the game.***

gangrene: death and decomposition (putrefaction) of soft tissues of the body from any number of causes, disease, trauma, loss of circulation, etc., e.g., "For gangrene of a large area, acids and maggots were used to remove the dead flesh; failing that, amputation was the only remedy."

gaol: a jail, e.g., "Early records frequently speak of gaoling the defendant." This spelling is still often used in the United Kingdom.

gaoler, turnkey: a jailer or one who tends to the cells in a jail or prison, e.g., "Many are the stories of early gaolers who were seriously injured by inmates in their charge."

gargles: as now, medications for sore and dry throats and coughs, e.g., "As gargles, among others, frontier women made teas of water lilies, sage with honey and vinegar, slippery elm, yellow root, quince seeds, mint and thyme, flaxseed and catnip."

gargoyle: carved, usually stone figures of creatures, often demonic or grotesque, originally hollow and designed to act as spouts carrying roof run-off water outward and away from the foundation of a building, particularly churches, e.g., "Designers of great buildings have understood the need to move water away from the foundations for millennia, and have done so decoratively through spouts carved in the form of gargoyles."

garlix: a fabric of unknown nature, e.g., "The 1761 account of Berry Smith revealed the purchase of a 1½ ***ells*** (q.v.) of garlix."

garret: any space under the roof and above some other room, e.g., "He kept the old ***joiner***'s ***tools*** (q.v.) in the garret."

Garter, Knights of the, Knights of the Order of St. George: the highest order of English knighthood; a symbol reflecting that order ranking next after nobility, e.g., "The garter of the Knights of the Garter is of blue leather, and the badge is an image of St. George."

gastralgia: almost any severe stomach pain; neuralgia of the stomach, e.g., "For gastralgia, remedies such as alum, atropia, Arsenic, Bismuth, and ether were prescribed." Also see ***gastric catarhh.***

gastric catarrh: inflammation of the lining of the stomach, e.g., "There being little difference usually, most of the remedies for gastralgia were employed for gastric catarrh." Also see ***gastralgia.***

gastric ulcers: See ***ulcers.***

gateleg table, swing-leg table: often simply "gateleg"; a popular variation, in many sizes and woods, of a ***drop leaf table*** (q.v.), having hinged legs on one or two sides that fold inward until flush with the table frame, permitting a lowering of the leaves, thus conserving space; generally the more legs, the older the table, e.g., "The ***cabinetmaker*** (q.v.) made gatelegs of any good wood at hand, but preferred walnut, mahogany, cherry, or butternut."

gauge block: any standard of length or other dimension, quite commonly made of metal, and used in virtually all early manufactories, e.g., "Jimmy's round gauge block was made of steel and was precisely the diameter required for the piston."

gauze: similar to now, a silk or cotton fabric woven so thinly as to be nearly transparent, e.g., "Gauze, especially silk, was so expensive in early times that any purchase of it in quantities for home use reveals wealth in that family."

Gay Nineties: the name given the decade of the 1890s, e.g., "The Gay Nineties were so called by reason of the prevailing feelings of peace and security, the invention of new conveniences including electric lights, the telephone, telegraph, and record player, rapid inexpensive transportation, dominance on the World scene, manufacturing and inexpensive products for everyday and everyone, expanding cities and employment, ever advancing education and, perhaps most of all, the growth and relative prosperity of the middle class."

gazetteer: a publication telling of towns (existing and extinct), the locations of county seats, waterways, roads, and places of interest within a certain area, e.g., "The Virginia Gazetteer revealed the location of Calthrop Neck."

gear: as now; the clothing and other necessities kept or carried by military personnel, e.g., "They were directed to gather their gear and fall in ***on the double*** (q.v.)."

gee, haw: commands given to a horse or team by early ***teamsters*** (q.v.) and drivers, gee meaning go ahead and haw meaning halt, e.g., "Every boy of the 19th century knew what gee and haw meant." Also see ***near and off.***

geedunk: a very early slang term of the military, especially the U.S. Navy and the U.S. Marine Corps, meaning candies, ice cream, ***confections*** (q.v.), or other sweets available to those aboard ship, e.g., "Every early U.S. Navy ship had its geedunk stand."

geezer: a pleasantly eccentric or somewhat childlike, yet friendly, old man, e.g., "She wrote that her 80-year-old uncle was a 'white-haired old geezer'." Also see ***duffer.***

geld: money, or a compensation or value, e.g., "The word geld indicating compensation for some loss is occasionally seen in American colonial records." Also see ***horse.***

gelding: See ***horse.***

genealogy: the study of lineage and family history through the gathering of data concerning those to whom one is related by affinity, consanguinity, or through historical interest, e.g., "Evan spent years doing genealogical research on the family of his daughter-in-law."

general assumpsit: See ***assumpsit.***

General Land Office: See ***land grants.***

general reference section: that portion of the library where works such as indices to periodicals, dictionaries, encyclopedias, reference works, maps, and gazetteers are usually located, e.g., "The Encyclopedia Britannica is located in the general reference section."

genesis (of counties): in genealogy, the origins or political lineage or parentage of counties, e.g., "From the county history, Diane learned that the genesis of Blair and Huntingdon Counties, PA, included Bedford and Cumberland Counties."

gentleborn: See ***gentleman*** and see ***base begotten.***

gentleman, gentlewoman: a person of affluence and gentility, or born to those of high station in the community, usually with a greater than average level of education, the so-called gentle-born, e.g., "In the 18th century, to be called a gentleman or gentlewoman was a high compliment."

gentlewoman: See ***gentleman, gentlewoman.***

Geologic Survey, U.S.; U.S.G.S: to genealogists, that government agency that creates and supplies maps of many areas of the U.S., e.g., "The U.S.G.S. maps (***topos, quadrangles,*** q.v.) are invaluable in gaining knowledge of places where ancestors lived."

Georgia, all over hell and half of: See ***hell and half of Georgia.***

Georgian: pertaining to the years of the reigns of the Kings George of England (1714-1830), e.g., "The chalice of St. Paul's is very early Georgian in age."

German influence: many words arose from our German ancestry, e.g., "Hex, sauerkraut, bummer, check, delicatessen, ecology, hoodlum, kindergarten, nix, phooey, scram, spiel, and frankfurters are but a very few examples."

get a livelihood (livelyhood): to gain a means of earning a living, from which in later years came the expression, "get a life", e.g., "The mother pleaded that her son should not be ***indentured*** (q.v.) as 'he could get a livelyhood through working for his uncle'."

gift horse, looking a ___ in the mouth: derives from the fact that the general health of a horse may be partially determined by an examination within its mouth of the teeth, gums, etc., e.g., "To look a gift horse in the mouth would be to insult the giver."

gig, captain's gig, frog gig: a small toy, usually on a string, that is whirled around the holder; a small, usually well cared for and appointed boat used to take a captain or high officers from a ship to shore or to another ship; a light, two-wheeled carriage pulled by one horse; a small, pointed, long-handled, 2- or 3-tined spear used to spear and catch frogs, fish, and small animals, e.g., "***Boats*** (q.v.) Stevens, being drunk at the time, steered the captain's gig into the side of the *USS Coral Sea*"; "As now we are eager to own our first automobile, sons of wealthy early families looked forward to their first gig"; "They went frog gigging." Also see ***chaise.***

giggs, jigs: an early rapid, lively and animated dance done with exuberance, e.g., "The expression 'When Sarah arrived home she danced a jig' meant simply that she was happy, delighted or joyous at the occasion."

gilded, to gild: gold covered, usually with gold foil, e.g., "The church was said to have a magnificent gilded main altar."

gill: a measure of liquid, often whiskey or brandy, equal to one half cup, e.g., "He told the ***barkeep*** (q.v.) he would have a gill of Scotch whiskey."

gimcrack, jimcreek: per Johnson, a small or unimportant mechanism; now, anything inexpensive that has no function other than decoration, e.g., "While in the early 18th century a gimcrack usually was an inexpensive decoration of the person, by the 19th century the word meant an object that was decorative but had no function."

gimp beaded: See ***gimp.***

gimp, gimp-beaded: fringing, often twisted silk and used for permanent decorations or edgings of garments, ladies' hats, etc., as in decorations used by a milliner; also, a limp, e.g., "By 1844, J. Ewing was selling a wide variety of ***stuffs*** (q.v.), including gimps"; "By reason of an old injury to his right leg, Todd was said to have a gimp."

gin men, ginmen: employees of a coal mine who do general labor about the operations, e.g., "Where occupations are listed, gin men often appear in early Kentucky and Ohio records."

ginny: See ***guinea.***

ginseng: as now, a root supposed to have medicinal value, e.g., "He made up tonics of ginseng and other plants."

girdle, girdled: an early method of killing trees in order that they might be easier cut and burned and the land cleared, it was done by cutting the bark completely through all around the trunk and so preventing sap flow, e.g., "After harvesting the walnut, butternut, and cherry, he girdled the balance of the stand of trees."

girth, girt: a strap attached to a saddle that stretches under the belly of a horse or mule and serves to hold the saddle firmly in place, e.g., "The girth is too tight."

Gist's Road: See ***roads, early.***

give out: a country term, used for any tense, to be exhausted, usually temporarily, e.g., "When told to pick another four bushels, he declared that he was give out"; "My legs give out on me."

give the miller his tithe: derived from the fact that early mills took a percentage of the grain being ground as pay for the grinding for others, and meaning that one quite usually must pay in some way for a service given over by another, e.g., "When Evan asked if he should pay for the kindness to his children by the toy maker, Todd told him that one must always '...give the miller his tithe'."

given name: those names other than surnames assigned to children, e.g., "Their given names were Biblical; Sarah, Joshua, Daniel, Absolom, Rebecca, and Ruth."

glaize, glaise, glaze: to put glass in a frame; to cause an object to appear to be covered in a thin transparent covering such as glass, e.g., "He was ordered to glaize the courthouse windows;" "The pottery had been glazed."

glass blowers: as now, e.g., "Jamestown had a glass factory and several glass blowers as early as 1609, two years after the arrival of the English colonists."

glass house: a manufactory of glass; a place where glass ovens are worked, e.g., "A glass house was built in Jamestown very shortly after the first settlement." Also see ***glass blowers.***

glass making: as with the glass blowers, flat glass manufactory, as in window panes, was underway before 1800, e.g., "An inventory or tax list reference to a servitor, blower, or wetter off, or to equipment such as marvers, fire clay, stirrers, skimmers, blowing horns, tweezers, or punties, likely reveal that the person was engaged in glass making." Also see ***glass house***, and see ***glass blowers.***

glebe, glebe land, glebe house: land or land and building owned by the church, the income from which goes to the church, e.g., "The National

Genealogical Society owns real estate and a house that originally was glebe land."

gleet: See ***gonorrhea.***

glyster: See ***clyster.***

go a'waltzing, to: the travels of a tramp, e.g., "After his wife died, he buried her, sold their little cabin and went a'waltzing." Also see ***billy.***

go haywire: a term meaning to become irrational upon the happening of a trying or disarming event. Wire for baling hay, being purchased bound into a coil and held in that shape by heavy cord, if not contained, will rapidly expand or open up in all directions when the cord was cut, e.g., "He said that when his sister was abandoned by her boyfriend, she went completely haywire."

go on the account: See ***account, to go on the.***

go without day: refers to a dismissal by a court of a party or his claim, e.g., "After his filing of a frivolous claim, the court ordered that Mills go without day, meaning without further day (time) and remedy in court."

God's plenty: See ***lord's plenty.***

godparent, godfather, godmother: a person, very often unrelated by blood, who has pledged himself or herself (usually with religious overtones, yet without financial responsibility) to the care, well-being, and upbringing of a child, especially in the event of death or misfortune of the parents, and considered an honor to both the child and the godparent, e.g., "His father's life-long friend was asked to serve as godfather to the boy."

Goering Division: See ***military combat units, famous.***

goin' jesse, a-goin' jesse, goin-jessie: source unknown; a superlative for excellent or for fine performance in a duty or purpose, e.g., "The old letter mentioned that the grist mill was really a goin' jesse"; "When asked if Allison would get the work done properly and in a timely fashion, Mikaila said, 'Hey, she is a goin' jessie'."

goiter, goitre: as now, an enlargement of the thyroid gland, e.g., "By 1885 goiter was being treated with iodides, particularly of potassium and mercury."

Gold Star Mothers, Gold Star Mothers' Day: a patriotic and service oriented organization of ladies whose sons were killed during American wars, e.g., "The Gold Star Mothers' Day was established during World War II."

Golden Spike Ceremony: See ***woodburner,*** and see ***Promontory Point.***

goldsmiths' tools: See ***silversmiths' tools.***

goloeshoes: See ***shoes.***

gone by the board, by the board: derived from shipboard slang, some object or opportunity irretrievably gone, as though having been thrown or lost over the side—the board—of a ship, e.g., "As had so many other opportunities, that chance for him to make a profit was gone by the board."

gonorrhea, gleet, clap: a venereal disease or sexually transmitted disease; however gleet sometimes also meant any seeping wound, e.g., "The social disease gleet often was treated with cod-liver oil or ***turpentine*** (q.v.), all to no effect." Also see ***syphilis.***

good graces, stay in someone's: from the ancient meaning of grace, which was to be "in the favor of", e.g., "While now the word grace quite usually is used in religious contexts, it once also meant favor, hence we sometimes strive to stay in the good graces of another person."

good price, good measure: an early and complimentary term, reflecting that not only were a storekeeper's prices as they should be, but also his or her measures were generous, e.g., "Mikaila was sure to compare prices and watch the measure carefully, and her statement that Drake gave 'good price, good measure' was high praise of that merchant.

Good Queen Bess: Elizabeth I, e.g., "Because of widespread feelings of security, "good times" and pride during her reign, Elizabeth I was often referred to as Good Queen Bess, even long after her death."

goodman, goodwife: a title of respect for those men and women who were of lower social status than gentlemen and ladies; when the word ***yeoman*** (q.v.) was used to refer to another or added as a suffix to a man's name, his wife became "goodwife," e.g., "Goodmen and goodwives were almost never referred to as Mr. or Mrs., and were addressed, for example, as Yeoman and Goodwife Bater." Also see ***Mr. and Mrs.***

goods: a common term referring to personal property, excluding animals and intangible assets, often used to refer to stock in trade or merchandise, especially fabric (***stuff***, q.v.) or clothing, e.g., "The goods named included articles of clothing, shoes, and cloth."

goodwife: See ***goodman, goodwife.***

goose drownder: See ***drownder.***

goosewing: See ***broadaxe.***

gorget: as now, a decorative large pendant, often of some symbolism or religious meaning; a crescent shaped gold or silver pendant worn by a colonial officer, e.g., "Allison wore a small Indian gorget that Evan had found"; "George Washington is often pictured wearing an officer's gorget."

got up: prepared, usually for presentation in some form, or ready for consumption or use, as with pre-cooked food, ***sweetmeats*** (q.v.), desserts or confections, e.g., "In 1859, in New Orleans, R. A. Howard advertised that his turkeys, hams, ***dobes*** (q.v.) and ***gallatines*** (q. v.), 'all would be got up with great care'."

gout: a painful inflammation and swelling of the joints, often in the feet (the big toe particularly), hands, and ankles, caused by excessive uric acid in the system, e.g., "Gout, as with so many other ailments, was not understood and often was treated with black snakeroot." Also see ***dropsy.***

graces, good: See ***good graces, etc.***

Graf Zeppelin, the: See ***lighter than air craft.***

grain: the smallest measure of dry weight in most systems, and originally equal to the weight of a "plump" grain of wheat.

grain hoist: See ***millers' tools.***

grain scoops: a shovel for grain, and see ***millers' tools.***

Grand Army of the Republic, G.A.R.: the counterpart of the United Confederate Veterans; a fraternal organization of Union Veterans of the Civil War, including those who served in the Navy, Marine Corps and nearly all others who made military contributions to the Union cause, it was a powerful political force in the late 19th century, e.g., "If one hoped to be elected to office in the 1880s, he sought the aid of the G.A.R." Also see ***United Confederate Veterans.***

Here, in full uniform and fifty years after the Battle of Gettysburg (1913) is Oscar W. Midlam, a Civil War veteran from Ohio and member of the G.A.R. Notice his gold-handled G.A.R. cane (lower right), his veteran's medal (above) and G.A.R medallion (below) and his G.A.R. lapel pin.

grand aunt, grand uncle: synonymous with "great aunt" or "great uncle"; a sister or brother of a grandparent, e.g., "Her grand aunt, Jean, was a sister of her maternal grandmother, Anne." See ***great aunt and great uncle.***

grand jury: See ***jury.***

grandam, grandame: now obsolete, usually meaning grandmother, e.g., "Shakespeare used 'grandam' for grandmother, yet interestingly, Johnson (1755) defined it to mean 'an old withered woman'."

grandfather clock, grandmother clock: tall clocks, the grandfather about 8 feet tall, and the grandmother about 5 feet in height, e.g., "Very few of our ancestors could afford such as the grandfather or grandmother clocks." Also see ***wag clock.***

grandparent: a parent of a parent of the subject person, e.g., "His mother's mother was his favorite grandparent."

Grange, Grangers, Granger Movement, Granger Laws: very early, a grange was a farm having all the buildings and conveniences needed for husbandry; those mid-west and Plains states farmers and planters who organized the movement for the purpose of securing reasonable railroad and freight rates for their products, the prevention of monopolies of dealers in grains, etc., a reduction in the number of middlemen who gained profits from their products, and colleges of agriculture, e.g., "The Granger Movement, at first a secret society of farmers, was largely responsible for the Granger Laws."

granny, granny woman: sometimes, a midwife; a woman of the community often called upon by reason of her knowledge of cures and medicinal herbs, by reason of her experience as a midwife, and occasionally because she had knowledge of the killing of and no fear of snakes, e.g., "Because of her knowledge of ***poultices*** (q.v.) and medicinal plants, Cally Roberts was often referred to as a granny woman."

grant (of land): often imprecisely called a ***patent*** (q.v.); usually, a transfer of title to land by government, through which settlement was brought about in consideration, variously, of a minimal measure of improvement or the payment of money, or both, e.g., "Drake was granted 160 acres by the Crown, and was required only to construct a small habitation and commence cultivation of a small portion of the land."

grantee: one to whom something is transferred by deed, quite usually land, e.g., "The deed for 100 acres named as grantees both Evan and his wife." Also see ***grantor.***

granting clause: that clause or wording in a deed which declares the parties who thereby are gaining ownership of (usually) land, e.g., "The granting clause named Evan, Drake, and Todd as the ***grantees*** (q.v.) of the land."

grantor indexes, grantee indexes: indexes (indices) to deeds, now usually computerized, compiled alphabetically in the surnames of the sellers (***grantors***, q.v.) or in the names of buyers or transferees (***grantees***, q.v.), e.g., "He found that grantee indices served the same purposes as did reverse indices in other states." See also ***direct and reverse indexes.***

grantor: See ***granting clause.***

grass widow: early, a woman whose husband has been absent from her for a long period or has abandoned her; 20th century, sometimes a divorcee, e.g., "Since he had boarded a boat going down Tar River and never again was heard of, Mikaila was called a grass widow."

Grasshopper Plague, the Great: See ***Plague of 1874.***

grasshopper: as now, and early a small legged pot or vessel used in cooking in a fireplace, e.g., "Martha called her small, footed cooker a grasshopper.

grate: as now, a frame or iron rack to hold burning wood or coal, so perforated as to allow ashes to fall through to the floor of the fireplace, e.g., "Every summer the ***blacksmith*** (q.v.) would make up several grates for sale later."

grave marker: See ***headstone.***

grave rock: See ***headstone.***

graver, scauper: any of several shapes of tools used by one to engrave or ***chase*** (q.v.), e.g., "The inventory listed three gravers, suggesting his work as an engraver or fine metal worker."

gray wooley (meaning lost): See ***games (of children).***

grays: a term used to refer to a team of two or more gray horses, e.g., "He used only his grays on the ***pleasure wagon*** (q.v.)."

grease and grits: a mixture of hot pork fat, bacon, or salt pork and ***hominy grits*** (q.v.); an early staple among Southern poor, e.g., "To many poor early Southern children, grease and grits often was all they could expect to eat for days on end." Also see ***mush.***

great aunt or great uncle, grand aunt or grand uncle: a sister or brother of a grandparent; the relationship of one to the brothers and sisters of any ancestor are determined by taking the number of greats in the title of that ancestor and adding one (1) more great before the word "aunt" or "uncle", e.g., "The sisters of his great-great grandmother (two greats) were his triple great aunts (three greats)."

great boots: leather boots that extended to the upper legs and hips, reminiscent of pirates, e.g., "Unless it was because they appeared pirate-like, it is difficult to understand why Jonas Fairbanks and others were charged in early Sussex with the misdemeanor of wearing great boots."

great god from Vicksburg: a friendly exclamation of unknown origin used by some early Southern Mississippi women, e.g., "Bob's grandmother, when told that the boys had brought frogs into the kitchen, exclaimed 'great god from Vicksburg, what next!'"

great grandparent: any ancestor prior to one's grandparents; a grandparent of a parent of the subject person; each additional "great" designates an additional past generation, e.g., "His grandfather's great grandmother was the most interesting of his great-great-great grandparents."

great guns and little pistols: an exclamation of surprise not attended by fear or trepidation, quite usually early used by Southern women, e.g., "When the little boys had spilled the basket of strawberries, Mrs. LeMay smiled and said 'great guns and little pistols, look what you have done!'"

Great Law: that Pennsylvania law of 1682 by which corn fields were to be fenced to five feet in height; unlike now, in Pennsylvania then cattle had to be fenced out, not fenced in, e.g., "If one had complied with the Great Law, he could recover damages from an owner of any animals or cattle that trespassed on the land." Also see ***fence, fence laws.***

great men: early American Indian leaders or those highly respected by their own people, e.g., "In Sept. of 1686, the court ordered 'four great men of the Nottoway tribe' to appear and answer for the killing of Mr. Jordan's cattle."

great pox: See ***syphilis.***

great wheel: See ***spinning wheel.***

greatcoat, great coat: a large, heavy coat designed to be worn over other clothes in extreme weather, e.g., "The children liked to play by wearing Paul's old greatcoat."

greciannett: unknown, probably a fabric (***stuff,*** q.v.), e.g., "In 1844, Ewing and Co. of Findlay, Ohio, advertised Greciannett for sale, together with 'almost every kind of Staple Dry-Goods'."

Green Mountain Boys: that small force recruited by Ethan Allen from the area of Castleton, VT (in the Green Mts.) that captured Fort Ticonderoga and Crown Point on 10 and 12 May, 1775, e.g., "Daniel Brown and Stephen Sherwood were proud of their service with the Green Mountain Boys." Also see ***military combat units, famous.***

Greenville Treaty: that treaty of July 22, 1814 that required the Delaware, Miami, Seneca, Shawnee, and Wyandot tribes to declare war on the British and, in exchange for western lands, those tribes ceded to the U.S. most of the tribal lands lying within the ***Northwest Territory*** (q.v.), e.g., "Prior to the Greenville Treaty, all Ohio land lying north of present-day Ohio Rt. 47 was held by American Indians."

Gregorian Calendar: See ***Julian Calendar.***

Gregorian period: those years of the Gregorian Calendar, e.g., "The Gregorian period or epoch began in 1582 and extends to the present day." See ***Julian Calendar.***

grenadiers: See ***armed men.***

griddle: unknown in to Johnson 18th-century England, apparently a grill or perforated iron cooking surface, "He wrote that he had griddled the lamb."

gridiron: unlike now, a large rack upon which to place pans, ***skillets*** (q.v.), etc. while cooking, usually having iron rods both front to back and left to right, e.g., "The ***blacksmith*** (q.v.) charged him 2 ***shillings*** (q.v.) to make a gridiron."

griff: a word of early Louisiana meaning the offspring of a Negro and a mulatto, e.g., "He wrote that the woman was 'too light to be a Negro, and too dark to be a mulatto, hence (she) must be a griff'."

grip: a single piece of handled luggage, usually what we now know as a "suitcase", "Because it was heavy and the sidewalk was slippery, Sarah asked Paul if he would mind carrying her grip to her room."

grippes, grippe, gripes: cramps in the stomach, abdomen, or bowels, usually the last named; sometimes labor pains; occasionally severe menstrual cramps, e.g., "In the seventeenth century it was thought that passing clouds might sometimes intensify the grippes of labor."

grist, gristmill, mill: early, food supplies, particularly grains; a mill in which grain is ground, early powered by animals or water; later and now, any grain to be ground; e.g., "Along with their churches, and even before schools, pioneer farmers built gristmills in order that they have meal and flour, then the most important of the staples."

grits: finely ground ***hominy*** (q.v.), usually served either as cereal with milk and a sweetener, or with butter as a side dish with eggs and meat, e.g., "A winter breakfast in old North Carolina quite usually included grits and butter." Also see ***hominy.***

grocery up: to supply the family with staples and food sufficient for several days or weeks, e.g., "They went to town every Saturday and socialized, bought sewing supplies, and groceried up." Also see ***-up.***

grog: an inexpensive drink of rum diluted with water, e.g., "He could only afford an occasional grog."

grossers: an early term meaning grocer, probably at first referring to wholesalers only, e.g., "Unlike now, early grossers stocked almost exclusively those items that would not spoil."

grubbing hoe: a heavy hoe used to break ground, e.g., "Grubbing hoe work was too heavy for her, so her son opened the garden every spring."

grunts: See ***desserts, early.***

guard, national guard: See ***militia.***

guardian: a person (judicially or by agreement) who is charged with the care and responsibility of the person, or property, or both, of another, e.g., "He was appointed guardian of his 90-year-old mother"; "Being over fourteen years old, he selected, and the court approved of his uncle as guardian"; "A ***testamentary guardian*** (q.v.) is one appointed by a provision of a will."

guardian ad litem: a guardian of an ***infant*** (q.v.) or other person legally incompetent to transact his own business or maintain his own well-being by authority of law, statute or court; guardians ad litem are required to prosecute in behalf of the protected or defend them from others, e.g., "When Jones sued the heirs, the court appointed guardians ad litem for those who were not yet of age."

gudgeon and pintle: a complete early door lock, usually of iron, the pintle being the pin placed in the eye of the gudgeon; also the mechanism of a ship's rudder, e.g., "The 1727 inventory revealed a gudgeon and pintle and an additional hasp."

guinea, ginny: a gold coin of Britain, having a value of about a ***Pound*** (£) (q.v.) and minted from the 1660s until well into the 19th century, e.g., "The guinea was very common in the American colonies."

gullbat: a nighthawk or whippoorwill, a common, rather large bird usually seen at dusk and early in the morning as it flies about 20 to 50 feet over the trees catching insects, e.g., "Nighthawks and whippoorwills were quite frequently referred to as gull-bats, especially along the eastern coast."

gum copal: resin, usually for caulking of ships or casks, e.g., "The listing in the Newport estate inventory of two ***hogsheads*** (q.v.) of gum copal likely indicates that the decedent was engaged in the shipping or associated businesses."

gun lock: See ***lock.***

gunny sack, gunny, burlap sack, tote sack: a heavy sack or bag used to carry feed, grain, sugar, and similar materials and made of jute, hemp, or similar natural material, e.g., "Very poor children very often had clothes made from old gunny sacks." Also see ***sack cloth.***

gunsmith: one who makes or repairs hand-held firearms, e.g., "The ***long rifle*** (q.v.) was the crowning achievement of the early Kentucky gunsmiths."

gunsmiths' tools: as now, e.g., "The presence of inventory entries such as locks, frizzens, barrels, barrel swages, rifling broaches, and reamers reveal that the deceased may have worked as a gunsmith."

gussy up, gussied: unknown to Johnson, it may in the distant past derive from the word gusset, meaning to apply a patch to reinforce cloth; now, lightly overdressed, usually used in referring to a young woman, e.g., "Anne gussied up before Hank arrived."

gust: early, any hurricane, tornado, or very heavy storm; later and now, a moderately strong wind of short duration, e.g., "Those Tidewater settlers who survived the immense and devastating hurricane of 1667 Virginia usually referred to it as 'The Great Gust'."

gutterman: a specially trained person who works in iron smelting, e.g., "Though hardly known for its production, the owner of Catherine Furnace served as his own gutterman."

guttie: a term of the 19th century meaning a golf ball, e.g., "Very early golf balls were called gutties because such were made of leather, hair and sometimes feathers, all tightly wound with thin rubber."

H

habendum clause: the clause or wording in a deed that describes the nature of the interest conveyed, e.g., "The habendum clause provided 'should the ***grantee*** (q.v.) die without ***issue*** (q.v.), then the land shall revert equally to all other grandchildren of the ***grantor*** (q.v.) then living'."

habeus corpus, writ of: any of a number of ancient ***writs*** (q.v.) directing a sheriff or other officer of government to bring a person forth for hearing or trial, e.g., "Often, one of the early acts of a President in wartime is to suspend the rights of aliens to writs of habeus corpus."

hacherd, ragged as a: unknown, but perhaps a jagged cut from a rough heavy tool such as a hatchet or tobacco knife, e.g., "He wrote that the saber blade was ragged as a hacherd'."

hack, hack lines: early, horses kept for hire; later, a business having for hire horses and wagons for pleasure or work, e.g., "A driver for *Peoples Hack Line* took Bill and Ida to the train." Also see ***livery***.

hackle, hackling: to dress and sort flax fibers preparatory to making cloth, e.g., "The hackling had removed the ***tow*** (q.v.), and only the long fibers suitable for better quality linen remained."

hagioscope: See ***squint***.

hair picture: a framed depiction of a person, design, or scene made of woven human hair, very popular during Victorian times, especially as mementos from a woman to her lover; the craft is known to have been practiced even before 1700, e.g., "As a birthday gift to her fiancé, Brittany made a tiny hair picture of her silhouette."

hairbines: See ***dorseteens***.

haircloth: any cloth into which hair has been woven, usually cotton and horse hair, e.g., "The chair was of haircloth." Also see ***horsehair upholstery***, and see ***harrateen***.

half boots: See ***shoes***.

half chest: See ***chest.***

half Eagle: See ***Eagle.***

half mast, half staff, half pole; flag at: meaning that a flag or banner is being flown at a distance half way up the height of a pole or flag staff, as is customary at the death of a person or persons determined to be deserving of that honor, e.g., "At the death of any President, it is ordered that the American flag be at half staff at all government owned cemeteries, buildings, and parks."

half section: See ***section.***

half table: See ***console table.***

half-crown: a common early British coin having a value of 2S, 6p, e.g., "In 1825, a half-crown would pay a common laborer for a full day of work."

half-flood: See ***tides.***

hall: unlike now, the living section (main room and kitchen) of an early home, e.g., "The hall mentioned in the 1680 inventory referred to the living quarters of the small house."

hall tree: unlike now, a very high-backed, armed, foyer or hall chair, without upholstery, and usually with a mirror mounted in the back at chin level, and with a coat and often an umbrella rack on either side, and sometimes a compartment beneath the raisable seat, e.g., "The hall tree was of the American Empire Style and was beautiful."

hame, hames: part of the harnessing of horses, mules, and other draft animals; the quite usually wooden, curved, upright struts attached to the collars and to which ***traces*** (q.v.) were attached, e.g., "The hames seen on many early draft horses often were polished and decorated with brass."

hammock chair, swing chair: a swinging chair for adults, having arms, back, and a foot rest, and usually hung from a rafter or a tree, e.g., "Cheryl very much enjoyed the hammock chair on hot summer evenings."

hammock: as now, a cloth or web bed, designed to be hung between posts (or trees) and rolled up when not in use, e.g., "In addition to her ***bedsteads*** (q.v.), the 1725 inventory listed two hammocks."

hand, hired hands: usually, a paid laborer or farm worker, a hired hand is one who assists in physical work or labor in exchange for compensation; a measure equaling four (4) inches, e.g., "The early censuses often revealed the presence of hired hands within the household." "In the U.S., the height of horses is always measured in hands; a fourteen-hand horse being a medium size animal."

hand adz: See ***cooper's tools.***

hand in the till: See ***till.***

hand irons: See ***dog irons.***

hand mill: small grist mill powered by a crank and not by water or animals, e.g., "Occasionally an inventory will reveal the presence of a hand mill."

handgun: See ***revolver*** and ***derringer.***

handguns: a small firearm designed to be held in one hand when firing, e.g., "Handguns have been made for centuries, the earliest having been ***matchlocks*** (q.v.) or ***flintlocks*** (q.v.), followed by ***cap and ball*** (q.v.), and were single shot and later double or multi-barreled revolvers (19th century), and finally (20th century) semi-automatic and automatic weapons." Also see ***revolver*** and see ***single action.***

hands down winner; winner, hands down: a superlative, one who is the undisputed victor or winner or who has succeeded in the final analysis; from any card game wherein at the end of the game, the cards of those remaining in the game are revealed and a winner is declared, e.g., "He said that in the spelling contest 'Drake was the winner hands down'."

handsaw: as now, and see ***housewright's tools.***

handspike: any bar or rod, usually long and of metal, used as a lever or to gain leverage or mechanical advantage, e.g., "With a handspike powered by three men, they could lift the corner of the building."

hang out a shingle: derived from the practice of painting one's name and trade on a flat board—a shingle—and so placing it as to be an advertisement or sign; to undertake a trade or profession and to display a sign revealing to the public that one has done so, e.g., "Dr. Drake entered the medical profession by working for another physician for a year and then hanging out a shingle."

hants: unknown, e.g., "She very clearly wrote that the dry goods store had 'hants a'plenty'."

hard money: coinage, money made of metal, e.g., "The requirement that hard money be paid for goods received was particularly troublesome to those with Confederate currency."

hard times coffee: an inexpensive substitute for coffee, e.g., "During the Civil War, by reason of the high price and scarcity of coffee, H. B. Newhall of Boston advertised and sold herbal substitutes called 'hard times coffee'."

harmonica, mouth organ, armonica: from harmonical, meaning musical; a small musical instrument of metal over holes, played by inhaling and exhaling, while gaining various tones by covering certain of the holes, e.g., "Before we were able to artificially reproduce sound, many of us created our own music, often through the use of an harmonica."

harness, harnessing, traces: refers to the total equipment by which a horse (or other animal) is equipped to pull a load, e.g., "Typically, a complete harness could consist of the crown piece, front, blinkers, cheek strap, noseband, bit, sidecheek, throatlatch, reins, hames, collars, martingale, hame tug, bellyband, breeching, crupper, hipstraps, and a terret."

harnessmaker: one who makes harnessing; one having knowledge of leather, metal fittings, and the needs of those who use animals to pull vehicles, e.g., "The local harnessmaker replaced the leather sleigh bell straps."

harpsichord: early, a common keyboard instrument, the strings being mechanically plucked, e.g., "The Mason harpsichord may yet be seen in their ancestral home." Also see ***spinet.***

harrateen: a warm, tough, long wearing fabric (***stuff,*** q.v.) made of wool and other animal hair, usually that of a horse, e.g., "Cheryl crafted a cotton flannel lined, harrateen work coat for her husband."

harrow: an implement for working soil preparatory to planting, having either several tines (early) or discs mounted side by side and parallel, e.g., "Drake's old harrow was designed to be used with either horses or a tractor."

Hartshorn, Hartshorn cookies: perhaps ammonium chloride in some form, used by ***Pennsylvania Dutch*** (q.v.) and German women as a flavoring for cookies called "springerles", e.g., "The reasons for using Hartshorn in springerle cookies are now perhaps lost." Also see ***springerles.***

harvest mite: See ***chigger.***

harvest table: a long, narrow table, usually without finish and sometimes with a drop leaf on one side, used to dress, clean and prepare fruits and vegetables for canning or preserving, e.g., "The old harvest table was made of but two boards and was quite valuable as an antique."

Harvey Girls: those early waitresses and barmaids who were contracted by the Harvey Company first to serve on passenger trains of the Santa Fe (A.T. & S.F.) Railroad, e.g., "The neatly dressed and pretty Harvey Girls were a welcome sight to weary train travelers of the late 19th and early 20th centuries."

hasted: hurried, hastened, e.g., "The records of old Salem reveal that a man, having been lost at sea for twelve hours, was washed ashore and, having 'hasted homeward' was welcomed by his distraught family."

hat box: See ***bonnet box.***

Hat in the Ring: See ***military combat units, famous.***

hat pin: a necessity in the days when women regularly wore hats, often beaded and, for the rich, jeweled or of silver or gold, e.g., "Sarah had more hat pins than she had hats."

hatchel, hatchelled flax: a tool with which to beat flax, thereby separating the fibers from the brittle parts, e.g., "Quality linen could not be made without first hatcheling the flax."

hatchet: a very common, short-handled, sharp-edged tool of many uses, including trimming felled timber, chopping brush and small trees, and killing poultry and small animals, e.g., "His hatchet always was at hand, especially when ***fencerows*** (q.v.) had to be cleared."

hatter: one who makes hats, e.g., "Throughout the first 300 years of our history the trade of the hatter was vital to our economy and dress." Also see ***hatters' tools.***

hatters' basket: See ***hatters' tools.***

hatters' tools: as the name would imply, e.g., "The trade of the hatter might be suggested where an inventory mentioned a hurl, stang or bow, bowpin, hatters' baskets, or a tolliker."

hautbois: See ***hautboy.***

hautboy, hoodboy: from the German, an early word for oboe; a musical instrument, e.g., "At her death in 1679, Judith Parker owned two flutes, a recorder, and a hautboy."

have a fit and fall back in it: See ***fits and bad spells***, and see ***conniption.***

haversack, habersack, knapsack: large canvas or leather bags used by military personnel and such as scouts to carry clothes and necessaries, in the case of a haversack, carried over the shoulder by one strap, and in the case of a knapsack, worn on the back and held in place by two straps, e.g., "Virtually every World War II veteran had carried a haversack and every Boy Scout, a knapsack."

having the stone: See ***stone.***

haw: See ***gee, haw.***

hawker: a peddler, a travelling salesman who carried his merchandise with him for sale, e.g., "The early newspapers often speak of hawkers."

hay devil: See ***dust devil.***

hay fever: as now, an allergy, e.g., "Hay fever, like all allergies, was not understood and often was treated with quinine or by the inhalation of carbolic acid."

hayfork: See ***pitchfork.***

haying time: that late summer period when hay was and is cut, dried, baled or stacked, and prepared for winter, e.g., "At haying time, every able-bodied man and boy was put to the task of 'making hay'."

haymarket: an everyday light outer coat of businessmen and gentlemen, usually made of better linen or light woolen fabric and named for the famous market street in London, e.g., "Haymarket St., London, known in the late 18th and first half of the 19th centuries for its fine markets and many shops, served to provided the name of the light outer coat worn by businessmen throughout the English-speaking world."

haymonger: See ***monger.***

head of household: that person who is or appears to be in control and charge of the other members of a family unit; usually, an owner, lessee, or tenant of property, if he or she also resides there; early, usually the father/husband or grown son, and if that member was dead or gone, then the mother or a ***feme sole*** (q.v.), e.g., "Her husband having been dead and her sons not grown, Great Aunt Jean appeared as the head of household in the 1880 census."

head rock: See ***headstone.***

head tax: a ***poll tax*** (q.v.); a tax levied on all persons of a certain age and class, and having no requirement or qualification except one's existence within that class, e.g., "The head tax of 1684 was deeply resented by the poor."

headaches: as now, e.g., "In the early days, headaches were viewed as ailments rather than as symptoms, hence were treated with everything from strong coffee to arsenic."

headrights: early, those rights and privileges, often including grants of land, partial relief from certain taxes, and bounties paid by governments, afforded those who paid for or otherwise provided transportation for emigrants to the colonies, e.g., "As the owner of sixteen (16) headrights in 1653, William Huntt was eligible for 800 acres of Virginia land." Also see ***land grants.***

heads: See ***coppersmiths' tools.***

headstone, field stone, field rock, head rock, grave marker, tombstone, monument: a marker designating the place of interment of one or more individuals, usually inscribed, and sometimes crudely made from wood or native stone without inscription, or with initials only, e.g., "At his gravesite, Martha found only a rough field stone bearing his initials"; "Since the headstone was nearly illegible, Trip used paper and chalk to make a rubbing of it."

hearsay: from hear and say; present statements repeating prior words of a third person not now present or available for questioning to test the truthfulness of those statements, such words being offered as proof of the matter that was stated by that third person, e.g., "Even though Allison told her mother that Jane took the family dishes, mother may not now repeat those hearsay statements in court to show who has the dishes because Allison is dead and she may have been mistaken, joking, exaggerating, or lying concerning the dishes."

heart disease: as now, vastly differing symptoms and pathologies, e.g., "As stimulants for heart disease, the Cherokees made a holly tea, the Dakotas and Winnebagos administered horsemint, the Delawares prescribed Virginia pokeweed, and the Pawnees thought morning glory was the best medication for those ailments."

hearth: as now, the dirt, stone, brick, or masonry floor of a fireplace, including that portion extending forward from the fire into the room, e.g., "Most early cooking was done on the hearth."

heaves: a disease, usually of horses or mules, similar to asthma in man; early, any substantial difficulty in breathing in man or animals, usually used in reference to the latter, e.g., "The Amish recognize the heaves in horses, even in the earliest stages."

Heck Day: See ***Hock-day.***

hectic fever: phthisis; a wasting disease of the lungs that probably often was emphysema, e.g., "Hectic fever was treated with calcium phosphate, quinine, and various ***tonics*** (q.v.), none of which gave permanent relief."

heel balls: See ***macheen.***

heel hound: a term of friendly derision for a dog that stays close to its master, and does not hunt, yet is not a lap dog. e.g., "He laughed and called his friend's old dog a heel hound."

heifer, heffer: a cow that has not been bred, usually under 3 years old, e.g., "The inventory listed 3 cows and 2 heifers."

heir: one who inherits property, real or personal, by virtue of the death of another, e.g., "He was an equal heir with his sister." Also see ***devise and bequeath.***

heirloom: any artifact, memento, or writing having value by reason of its family or ***lineage*** (q.v.) related origins, e.g., "Evan's most treasured heirloom was his great-great grandfather's pocket watch."

heirs and assigns: a common legal expression in deeds, wills, and instruments of transfer that confirmed that the asset was being transferred without restriction to further transfer by the recipient, e.g., "In early times, if a deed was made 'to John Smith', instead of 'to John Smith and his heirs and assigns', at John's death the title would have reverted to the ***grantor*** (q.v.)."

heirs of the body: lineal descendants only; natural offspring; an ancient phrase signaling an ***entailment*** (q.v.), e.g., "The bequest by William Hines was to Sarah 'and the heirs of her body', hence his son-in-law received nothing"; "The conveyance was unlawful and held to be in ***fee simple*** (q.v.) since 'to Sarah and the heirs of her body' created a ***fee tail*** (q.v.), which by statute had been ***docked*** (q.v.)."

hell and half of Georgia, all over: a superlative, presumed to reflect the desolate condition of eastern Georgia after Sherman's March, e.g., "Paul said that in order to have her as his wife, he would pursue Judith all over hell and half of Georgia."

helpmates: See ***helpmeets.***

helpmeets: helpmates; wives; "Early New England records often refer to wives as helpmeets or helpmates."

helve: as now, a handle for a tool such as an axe, hatchet, pick, mattock, sledge, hammer, etc., "In order to make the axe more efficient in the vast forest, Americans widened, lengthened, and added curves to the helves." Also see ***helved and ground.***

helved and ground: a handled and sharpened heavy tool, e.g., "He advertised that his axes and hatchets were '...well helved and sharpened'." Also see ***helve.***

hematuria, haematuria: blood in the urine from any cause, e.g., "Often not realizing it was but a symptom, for hematuria the old doctor administered potassium citrate, ***turpentine*** (q.v.), ergot, and lead acetate."

hemoptysis, haemoptysis: any expectoration of blood, e.g., "Not recognizing it as but a symptom of another problem, early physicians often prescribed ipecac or lead acetate for hemoptysis."

hemorrhoids, emero(i)ds: as now, e.g., "The doctor concocted a salve for emeroids."

hepatic diseases: now, hepatitis; pertaining to liver and liver functions, e.g., "Hepatic diseases often were treated with ***tonics*** (q.v.) of ammonium chloride or iodide, ipecac and rhubarb."

heraldry: the research and activities involved in the settling of the rights of persons and families to bear arms, of tracing genealogies, of determining of precedence, and of setting forth or recording honors, e.g., "The business of heraldry is the peculiar province of the ***Heralds' College*** (q.v.)."

Heralds' College: an English corporation, est. 1483 by royal authority, engaged in setting forth ***heraldry*** (q.v.), e.g., "Questions of one's rights to particular armorial bearings may be decided by the Heralds' College." Also see ***heraldry.***

hereditament: any right, asset, or object connected or associated with land that may be inherited, usually not including buildings, e.g., "Since the deed included all hereditaments, John was confident that he owned the flag pole, water well pump, and the fencing and posts."

hereinafter, hereinbefore: legal jargon used to refer to another term or provision within the same document, e.g., "...being the tract hereinafter described" or "...being the persons hereinbefore mentioned."

herpes: unlike now, any spreading, inflammatory condition of the skin or mucous membranes, e.g., "In early days, herpes often was treated with silver oxide, ***belladonna*** (q.v.) taken internally, ***calomel*** (q.v.) ointment, or electricity!"

Hessians: usually, those mercenaries from Hesse, Germany, who fought with the British in the American Revolution, many of whom defected, e.g., "While more than 900 Hessians were captured at Trenton, Washington suffered but 5 casualties."

hewed log house: a house made of de-barked, squared, hewn logs, e.g., "Their hewed log house took much more effort and time to construct than did a plain (or round) log house." Also see ***rough log cabin.***

hiccoughs: See ***hiccups.***

hiccups, hiccoughs: as now, e.g., "Myriad cures were prescribed for the hiccoughs, including ***camphor*** (q.v.) and chloroform."

hide: an ancient term for approximately 120 acres, e.g., "The word hide as a measure of land only rarely appeared in colonial records." Also see ***virgate.***

hide and seek and ***tag*** (as now): See ***games (of children).***

hides and skins: as now, e.g., "Hides are the skins of bulls, cows, horses, and (early) from oxen, moose, and bison, while skins were from small fur animals and calves, deer, antelopes, goats, pigs, or sheep, etc."

high horse, on a: See ***on a high horse.***

High Sheriff, high sheriff: See ***sheriff.***

high stepper: from the gait of a Tennessee Walking Horse or other well-trained horses; a superlative; a man, usually young, who is stylish, successful, proud, or of fine family, e.g., "Anne smiled and mentioned to Sarah that she thought that Eli was '...truly a high stepper'."

high wheel cycle, high wheel bicycle, high wheeler, wheel: an early bicycle having a very large front wheel (as much as 5 feet) and a much smaller rear wheel, so designed to ride over the rough streets and roads of the early years, e.g., "After removing the rubber ***tires*** (q.v.), Billy Drake rode his high wheel cycle on a tightrope."

high-ball: from early railroad signals whereby an 8" to 12" white ball was placed at the top of a rod or pole when all was clear ahead or there was no reason for the ***engineer*** (q.v.) to slow or stop his train at that point along the right-of-way; to have or be given permission in an enthusiastic manner, e.g., "Paul told Evan, 'Hey, my man, you have the high ball, go ahead with the plans'."

highboy: a popular, early chest of ***drawers*** (q.v.) on 8 to 12 inch legs, usually with 3 to 5 drawers, and occasionally with one or two doored compartments below the drawers, "The highboy listed in Selma's estate was of bird's eye maple and of the Queen Anne period."

high-tail: See ***skedaddle.***

hike: a rather recent term, apparently unknown to Johnson; during the 19th century the word apparently usually meant to walk long distances for military or work purposes; more often later and now, usually a long walk for pleasure, e.g., "The Civil War era references to hikes usually had to do with travelling long distances on foot for the purpose of battle." Also see ***tramp.***

hind: a male deer, particularly the English red deer, e.g., "Drake's ship, *Golden Hind*, was named for the fleet and powerful male red deer, the hind."

Hindenburg, the: See ***lighter than air craft.***

hinny: very early, to whinny; later and now, the young of a stallion and a donkey, e.g., "All laughed when the cowhand rode in on a scraggly little hinny."

hip flask: as now, a small-mouthed, thin, lidded, glass or metal container for spirituous liquors, carried on the person, usually under the coat and hidden from view, e.g., "Many early hip flasks were of blown, colored glass."

hitch, hitched: refers to a team of horses or other draft animals in place and the ***harnessing*** (q.v.) for such, e.g., "His hitch was well groomed and powerful"; "They are hitched and ready."

hither, thither, and yon: See ***yonder.***

hoarseness: as now, e.g., "Hoarseness often was treated with horseradish, borax, sulfurous acid spray, or tannin."

hobble, hopple: a tie between the legs of a horse or mule to control the length, and so the speed, of its ***gait*** (q.v.), e.g. "He always hobbled the horse to prevent it from ***cantering*** (q.v.) or running."

hobby horse: a stick with a depiction of a horse's head mounted on one end, the same straddled by children who then ran, pretending to be riding a horse, e.g., "Every little boy of the 17th, 18th and 19th century rode a hobby horse at one time or another." Also see ***shoo fly rocker.***

hobnail glass: glassware having small, rounded, smooth bumps on the surface, e.g., "Her favorite candy dish was of hobnail ***milk glass*** (q.v.)."

hock, hockheimer: usually, any white wine, originally a Rhine wine, e.g., "The ***Pennsylvania Dutch*** (q.v.) often spoke of a 'glass of hock'."

Hock-day, Heck Day: the 2nd Tuesday following the week of Easter, e.g., "Such ancient holidays as Hock-day, Hock-tide, etc., were largely abandoned by the American Colonials."

hockheimer: See ***hock.***

hoecake: See ***pone.***

hog cholera: See ***cholera.***

hog ranch: in the early West, often a house of prostitution, e.g., "When the hired hand laughed about his trip to the hog ranch, he was not speaking of a place where swine were kept."

hog sty: See ***sty.***

Hogmanay, hogmanays: the last day of the Scottish year, now December 31, but formerly March 24; small cookies made for the Hogmanay holiday, e.g., "Many early Scots settlers celebrated Hogmanay by permitting their children to go door to door for treats"; "Hogmanay cookies were sweet, light, short cookies made for the holiday of the same name."

hogs: See ***paper making.***

hogshead: an early measure of volume equaling 63 gallons, a ***barrel-cask*** (q.v.), used most frequently for the shipment of tobacco, e.g., "In 1728 Evan and Todd transported thirty hogsheads of tobacco on the ship *Charming Nancy*."

hold one harmless, hold harmless: to guarantee that if another suffers monetary damage, that person would be compensated equal to the loss, e.g., "It was common practice to require the father of a bastard child to hold the parish harmless from the expense of keeping that child."

hole: as now; early, a cove or inlet shielded from the tides and the winds, e.g., "Teach's Hole and Teach's Channel, named after William Teach—the infamous 'Blackbeard'—appear yet on nautical maps of Ocracoke Inlet and Pamlico Sound."

Holland china: See ***delftware.***

holland, chect holland: a fine linen cloth, at first imported from the Netherlands, e.g., "Early merchants' inventories almost always reveal a stock of holland."

Holland, influence of: many words arose from our Hollander ancestry and their food, e.g., "Waffle, coleslaw, cookie, landscape, caboose, sleigh, snooping, Yankee, and poppycock (dung) are but a few."

Hollanders: See ***Dutch.***

hollanders: See ***paper making.***

holler: from the ancient Saxon word "thaler"; a Scots-Irish mountain term for a cove or long and wide ravine or area between 2 hills or mountains, e.g., "Little Sally wondered if there were really woolly mammoths in the hollers of Tennessee Appalachia." Also see ***hollow.***

hollow shave: See ***shave.***

hollow, holler, cove: a hollow is a small narrow valley, usually closed in, or nearly so, by mountains or hilly terrain, as distinguished from a cove, which usually was a strip of land or an inlet open at one end, e.g., "While Conatser Cove was broad and open at one end, Ferguson Hollow—called Ferguson Holler, by the locals—was a rather deep, long depression surrounded by hills with no easy egress or ingress."

holographic will, olographic testament: a document intended by the deceased to be his or her will, hand written, signed, and kept by the deceased in such a fashion or place that its importance is apparent, e.g., "The handwritten document was submitted, ***parity of hands*** (q.v.) was accomplished, the evidence revealed that he intended the writing to be his will, so the court admitted it as his holographic will."

home place: one's principal residence; the word is nearly synonymous with ***domicile*** (q.v.), e.g., "She owned several tracts of land, but she considered the one on Snake Creek to be her home place."

homeopathic medicine: that frequently encountered early practice in which cures were undertaken by prescribing herbs and drugs thought to create the same condition as that from which the patient was suffering, e.g., "Homeopathic physicians fell into wide disrepute early in the twentieth century."

homespun: a plain fabric made of yarn spun in the home, e.g., "Very plain homespun clothing was the mark of the early rural working family."

Homestead Acts: the several legislative acts of Federal and states' governments by which land was granted in exchange for settlement and (or) improvement thereon, e.g., "He built a cabin, and undertook to clear the land that he had gained under the Homestead Act." Also see ***seating.***

homestead: See ***stead***, and see ***Homestead Acts,*** .

hominy block: unknown to Johnson because there was no hominy (or ***maize,*** q.v.) in Britain; a block of wood, 24 or so inches square, upon which hominy was ground into meal, from which grits were made, and note that pounded hominy and hominy meal were hominy that had been pounded or ground into meal in order to make porridge, gruel and grits, e.g., "Allison had a small hominy block that had belonged to her mother."

hominy, hominy grits: a common food, especially in the South; corn stripped of the hull by lye, and served either whole kernel or dried ground as hominy grits, e.g., "Fried hominy was a favorite food when served with ham or bacon, and grits with butter are enjoyed by nearly all Southerners." Also see ***grist mill.***

homolgate: in civil law, meaning to approve, e.g., "Early Louisiana records occasionally speak of a court homolgating an agreement."

hooch: See ***corn whiskey.***

hood boy: See ***hautboy.***

Hood's Texas Brigade: See ***military combat units, famous.***

hooker: a prostitute, e.g., "Contrary to popular belief, prostitutes were not first called hookers by reason of their presence in General Hooker's Army camps during the Civil War, but from the very early definition, to "hook" or to ensnare by guile or trick or otherwise." See also ***trick***.

hoop, hoop skirt: a light weight device worn under the dress and hung from the waist of a lady, designed to cause the outer skirt to be very full and bell shaped; very popular in other than household dress during much of the 19th century, and having from 4 to 10 flexible hoops of wire or whale-bone connected by cloth tape, e.g., "Virtually all photos of well dressed ladies of the Civil War years reveal a hoop skirt."

hooping cough: See ***whooping cough.***

Hoosier cabinet: See ***pantry.***

hopple: See ***hobble.***

horn smith, hornsmith: one who understood and worked animal horns or turtle shells into thin sheets to be used in the making of combs and ***hornbooks*** (q.v.) or to be sold to other craftsmen who made such items, e.g., "Among those who needed the services of the horn smith were the gold and silver smiths who made decorative use of the material, comb makers, knife and utensil makers (for their handles), the makers of eyeglasses who made frames from it, and surely the makers of buttons and inexpensive jewelry."

hornbook: an early teaching device for children; usually, the alphabet, numbers and tens of numbers, and simple fractions were printed on a board, over which a very thin piece of horn (later celluloid) could be folded down to protect the printing, e.g., "Hornbooks now are very rarely seen outside museums."

horse: now, any adult of the equine family; early, the word referred only to a male equine, including mules; a colt was a young male, a gelding was a neutered horse; a ridgling was a horse with one testicle removed, a stallion was a horse not neutered and used for breeding; a female, if bred once or more, was a mare, a filly was a young, unbred female, and a foal was a newborn of either sex, e.g., "Mikaila had a mare with a foal at her side, a horse, and a young colt." Also see ***foot, men, horse***.

horse collar: See ***collar.***

horse hair upholstery or cloth: a popular, strong and durable thick fabric used for upholstering from the earliest times until the early 20th century, it was made from woven horses tail and mane hair and usually dyed black, e.g., "She had a ***settee*** (q.v.) and two ***side chairs*** (q.v.) upholstered in horse hair." Also see ***harrateen*** and see ***hair cloth.***

horse harness: See ***harness.***

horse mill: a gristmill powered by a horse or other draft animal, e.g., "Where there were no streams suitable for damming, horse mills, while more expensive especially in the winter, served very nicely."

horse pistol: any large handgun; originally, a handgun carried in a saddle holster, e.g., "He referred to his old '.44' as a horse pistol."

horse tree, field tree, plow tree, stone tree: that large old tree left standing in the middle of a field upon clearing, used to provide shade and an occasional resting place for horses (and men) being worked in the hot summer sun or the rain, and also used as a central location and place to pile stones found in the field, e.g., "Many of the old horse trees yet stand in Ohio and Indiana."

horsecars: See ***streetcars.***

horses, famous: as now, e.g., "A listing of famous horses of American history surely would include Johnson's 'Messenger', Cobb's 'Terpsichor', Andrew Jackson's 'Truxton', Cody's 'Star', Endecott's 'Bill', Grant's 'Cincinnati', Jeb Stuart's 'Highfly', Sheridan's 'Rienzi', Lee's 'Traveler', Stonewall Jackson's 'Old Sorrel', Keogh's 'Comanche', and the great racehorse, 'Man O' War'."

horseshoe box: a small, usually ***primitive*** (q.v.), wooden box designed to hold 1 or 2 pairs of horseshoes to be carried to horseshoes ***games*** (q.v.), e.g., "The family still has Bill Midlam's horseshoe box."

horseshoes, horseshoe game: a game, usually played by men and boys, in which the iron shoes of horses are thrown at standing iron posts with the intention of catching the posts with the open end of the shoes, e.g., "Virtually every early picnic of rural families included men playing horseshoes."

hosepipe: early, any flexible, rubber tubing used to move liquids; our present garden hose, e.g., "The general store stocked hosepipe on a roll, and cut off the length desired by the customer."

hot buttered rum: an early and highly favored drink, especially in cold weather, consisting of a mugged mixture of rum, water, butter, and sugar, the drink then heated by plunging a red hot ***flipdog*** (q.v.) into the mug, e.g., "Many were the cold night visitors to early New England inns who were refreshed by a warm fire, friendly ***barkeeps*** (q.v.), ***flips*** (q.v.), and hot buttered rum."

hough: a hoof of any animal, e.g., "Early, the word hoof was consistently spelled hough, including by Johnson."

hour glass, sand glass: as now, a device to measure the passage of time, e.g., "The inventory revealed a 'large sand glass'."

house girl: usually a young slave woman assigned household tasks; early, sometimes a young indentured servant similarly engaged, e.g., "Some early Virginia comments concerning house girls seem to refer to young, indentured white women."

house raising: See ***raisings, etc.***

housewright, house wright, housewright's tools: one who builds residential structures, e.g., "John Midlam was a well known housewright in old Marion"; "Inventories that reveal broadaxes, chalk-lines and chalk-line reels, multiple adzes, levels, several augers and large handsaws may reveal the owner to have been a housewright."

hubbub: early, a near riot, "wild commotion" says Johnson (1802); later and now, mischievous, undesirable actions of several or more people, e.g., "When the planter saw the hands gathered together and shouting at each other, he demanded, 'Hey, what is all the hubbub?'"

huckster: early, a peddler of small wares, quite often for the kitchen; later and now, one who deals questionably in wares and goods of often little worth or of poor quality, e.g., "He was branded a huckster because of his prior practice of selling poorly made tin and ironware, nonetheless his clocks were presentable and of reasonable quality."

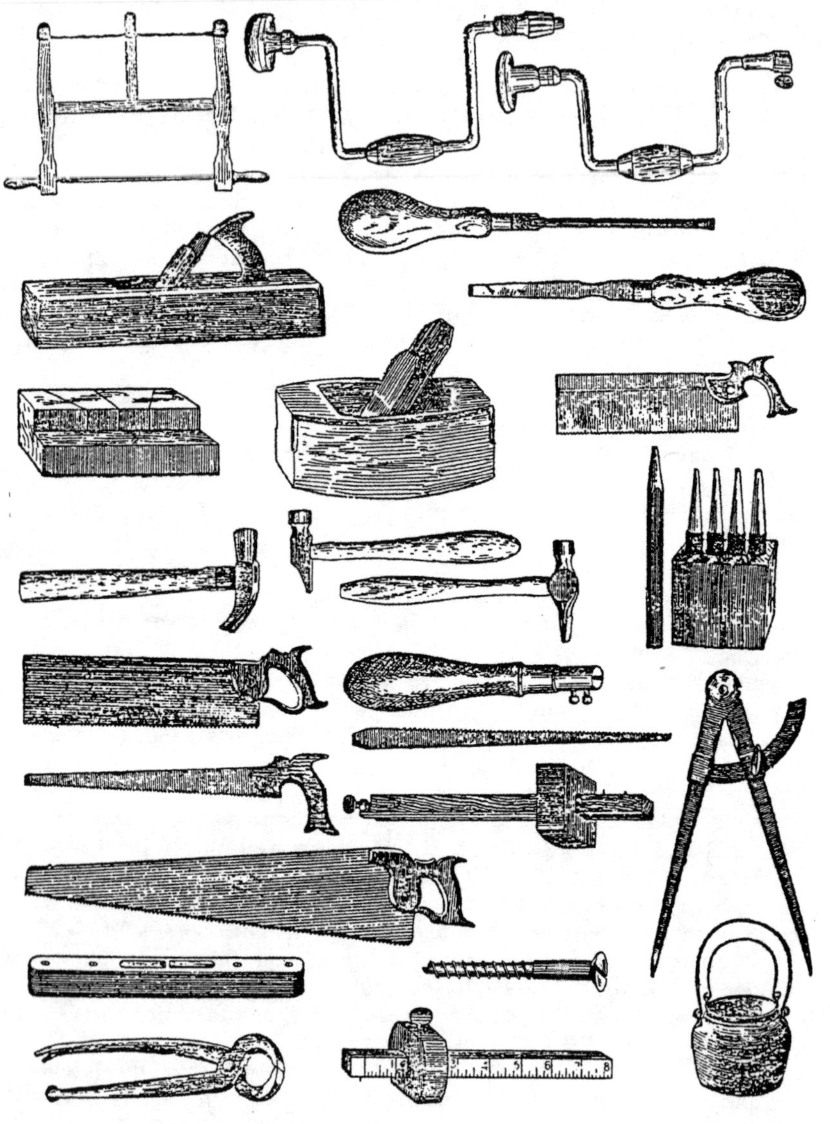

Housewright's tools. *(See p. 155.)*

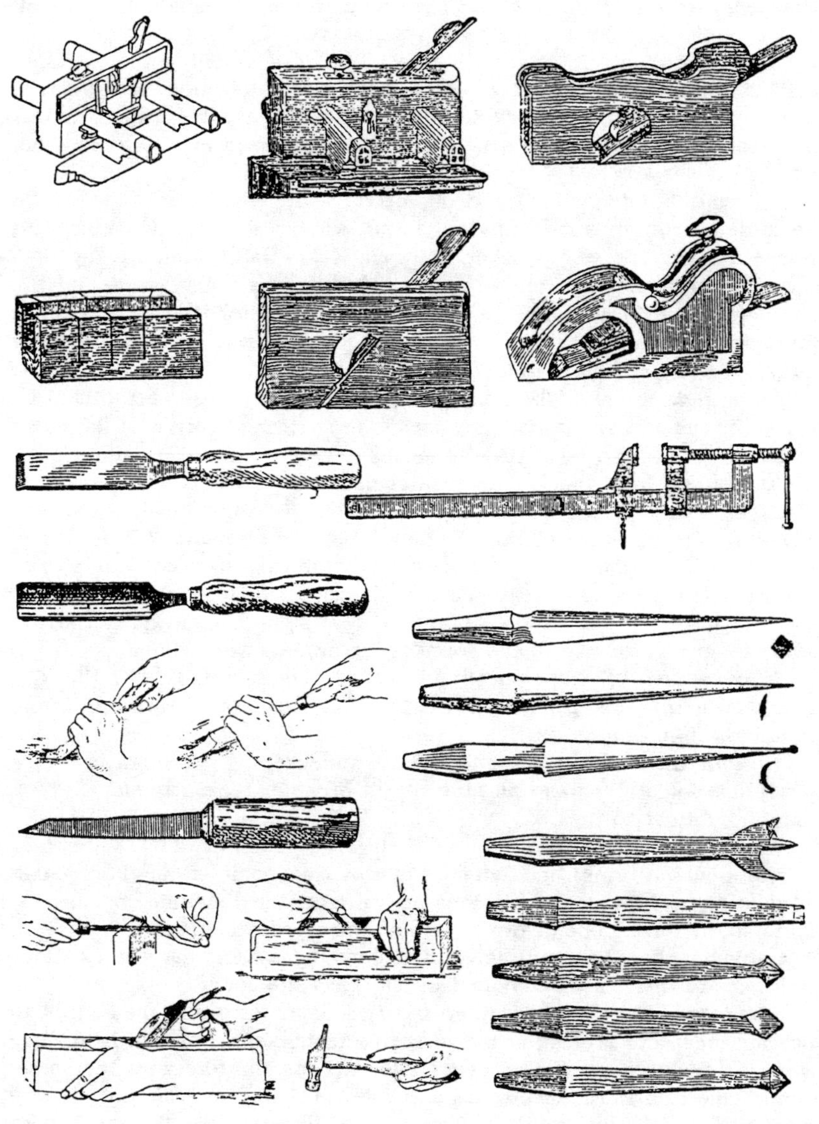

Joiner's tools. (See. p. 169.)

hue and cry, hues and cryes (to put out or call out): a message shouted to anyone within hearing that a criminal was fleeing, and all persons who heard were required to take up the chase to the extent of their capacity to do so, e.g., "Upon being asked how the criminal had escaped, the ***Sheriff*** (q.v.) related that the man was young and 'fleet afoot' and, though futile, he had 'put out hues and cryes all the while'."

hullabaloo: a disturbance, early, an exaggerated and extended discussion or animated notice given to some matter not meriting that degree of attention, e.g., "When he told of the large group loudly discussing the new councilman, Malinda asked, 'Why all the hullabaloo, for Heaven's sake?'"

humbug: not defined in Johnson, a term of the 19th century meaning a hoax, deception, or something that is not what it seems; one who is not what he pretends, e.g., "When Scrooge said 'Bah, humbug,' he was revealing his belief that the story of Christmas was a deception, and the characters and traditions associated with that holiday were without foundation in fact"; "Mikaila wrote that her fiancé was a '...real humbug, but she loved him dearly all the same.'"

hummuck: a small island in a marsh, a hill with trees surrounded by marsh or wetland—a ***sluice*** (q.v.), e.g., "The northwest corner of the Bater tract was said in the description to be '...a large pin oak on a hummuck.'"

humours: early, the four elemental bodily fluids, i.e., blood, phlegm, black bile, and yellow bile, e.g., "It was thought that imbalance of the humours was the cause of most disease." Also see ***bleeding***, and see ***bile***.

hundred: a subdivision of a ***shire*** (q.v.), governed by a ***constable*** (q.v.) and with its own court; a term occasionally appearing in American records, e.g., "In large part, hundreds no longer were significant in governmental affairs after our ***town*** (q.v.) and county governments were established."

hundredweight, cwt.: one hundred and twelve pounds, the 12 extra pounds being the ***tare*** (q.v.), e.g., "The inventory revealed three hundredweight of bronze."

Hungarian water: a ***cologne*** (q.v.) or incense, e.g., "Bethany's recipe for Hungarian water was one pint spirits of wine, 1 oz. rosemary, and 2 drachms ***ambergris*** (q.v.)."

huntboard: a sideboard on tall legs; a free standing server for refreshments during and after a hunt, reachable from horseback, consisting of a rather narrow, long top surface (the "board"), on tall legs, and usually having one or two doored compartments beneath the top, e.g., "Sarah's huntboard was of finely finished mahogany, and had cherry inlays in the board." Also see ***sideboard*** and ***butler's sideboard***.

Hunters, Long Hunters: when used as a proper noun, men hired to provide meat and protection for surveying teams; often paid in land, they were invaluable in such wilderness efforts; Long Hunters were the same, "long" referring to the length of the barrels of their ***flintlock*** (q.v.) or ***cap and ball*** (q.v.) rifles, e.g., "In Byrd's expedition of 1728 the meat most often provided by the Hunters was deer and cub bear."

hunting pouch: See ***shot pouch***.

hurl: See ***hatters' tools***.

husbandman: very early, one who bred and raised livestock; later, any farmer who kept animals, e.g., "Since the 1660 record reveals that he worked as a husbandman, Evan Haskins likely bred and raised cattle."

hussars: See ***armed men.***

hussy: Johnson (1802) says "a sorry or bad woman"; later and now, a woman whose flirtations are devious and purposeful, e.g., "Sarah felt that Jennifer's flirtatious words and actions revealed her to be nothing less than a hussy."

hutch: formerly, as in ***hutch chair*** (q.v.); recently, a cabinet with legs, usually tall, often with glassed doors above and exposed shelves, and drawers or doored compartments below, e.g., "She used her hutch as a linen storage and curio cabinet."

hutch chair, hutch table: a chair and table combined, where the table top is hinged so as to raise to the perpendicular and provide a back for the chair thereby uncovered, e.g., "Her hutch chair saved much space."

huzz, huzza, huzzah, huzzas: a very early term meaning a shout or loud exclamation, quite usually of approval, e.g., "It was written that the soldiers greeted Lee with 'many huzzas'."

hydrocele: a collection of fluid within the scrotum, at times accompanied with a tumorous growth, e.g., "Excision, electric puncture, and injection of iodine all were thought helpful for the hydrocele."

hydromel: See ***mead.***

hydrothorax: as now, a distended belly; an accumulation of fluid in the abdominal cavity, e.g., "Hydrothorax was treated by a near fluidless diet, iodine injections, or by the often fatal act of puncturing the belly to bring about drainage."

hypochondria: as now, e.g., "For hypochondria, ***asafetida*** (q.v.), caffeine, and opium were administered."

hypotheque: a ***Civil Law*** (q.v.) ***mortgage*** (q.v.), "Early Louisiana records occasionally refer to an hypotheque, meaning the same as mortgage."

hysteria: any "fits" or baseless fears, screaming, crying out, or unusual conduct thought to emanate from the mind, e.g., "Hysteria, not being understood, often was treated with cold compresses to the extremities, ***asafetida*** (q.v.), musk, quinine, vaporous oils, and alcoholic ***cordials*** (q.v.)."

I

ice box: before refrigeration, a usually cork-insulated, metal lined, large chest, often made of oak, and with a compartment in the top designed to hold blocks of ice weighing 50 to 100 lbs. and occasionally more, with one or two additional doors opening to shelves or compartments used to store perishable foods, e.g., "The 'ice man' delivered on Tuesdays and Fridays, and placed the ice purchased directly into the ice boxes of his customers."

icterus: See ***jaundice.***

ideal: in the upland South frequently, an idea, e.g., "The police chief remarked that he had no ideal what had happened at the crime scene"; "Allison said, 'Give me some ideal of your meaning'."

Ides, ides: the 15th day of March, May, June, and October, and the 13th day of the other months, e.g., "Early judges occasionally referred to future court or hearing days as commencing on the Ides of May, or the ides of one of the other months."

illiterate: in genealogy, a person unable to read or write sufficiently to correspond with others, e.g., "While able to take care of his daily business and financial affairs, he was illiterate."

immigrant: one who comes into a nation with an intention to remain, e.g., "He was one of the many German immigrants who arrived in America after 1709."

immigrations: some significant immigrations of other than those who left England and Wales were:

1624-1664, the Dutch and Walloons;
1637-1655, Swedish;
1683-1685, Palatines and Rhinelanders;
1685, French Huguenots;
1689, Scottish;
1710, Palatines;
1714-1725, Scots-Irish;
1725-1775, Germans and Swiss;
1735-1755, Moravians;
1827-1830, the great German and Irish movements;
1843-1885, Scandinavian;
1854-1870, Chinese (often railroad workers);
1885-1914, eastern and southern Europeans, Russians, Poles, Estonians, Latvians, Lithuanians, and Greeks.

imparlance: an extension or granting of time for a party to a lawsuit to further plead his or her cause, e.g., "Notation in a lawsuit of an imparlance should alert the researcher that a record of the case may also appear in the records of a succeeding term of court."

impetigo: as now, a contagious skin disease, often accompanied by sores on the face, feet, and legs, particularly among children, e.g., "Impetigo was treated with lead acetate, zinc oxide lotion, and quinine."

impotence: as now, e.g., "Impotence—a 'secret ailment'—was treated with gold chloride, lead arsenate, and (later) with electric shock."

impressment: the ancient British government privilege of forcing (drafting) persons or equipment into the service (usually, the navy) in time of war, e.g., "The impressment of merchant seamen into the Royal Navy very much aroused and angered the colonials, who felt that they had no dog in most of Britain's fights." See ***no dog in that fight.***

imprimis, imps.: in the first place; first of all; a legal term meaning the first of those listed, e.g., "The ***appraisal*** (q.v.) mentioned the kettle imps., referring to the first of several kettles and containers mentioned in the inventory."

in contemplation of death, contemplation of death: an expectation that death will surely follow by reason of some obvious sickness, injury, or impending danger, e.g., "The transfer of the land to his sons was in contemplation of death, hence was said to be a ***testamentary disposition*** (q.v.)." Also see ***nuncupative will.***

in diem, i.d.: for one day, e.g., "Some early records refer to an ***imparlance*** (q.v.) in diem."

in esse: literally, in being; in wills, administrations and agreements, usually a new born infant, e.g., "He left the land equally to his two children and a child in esse." Also see ***in posse.***

in gremio legis: protected by law, e.g., "Early Massachusetts records occasionally referred to livestock as having been 'in gremio legis until ownership' was established."

in loco parentis: in the place of parents; acting as a parent, e.g., "Early records often refer to older children, other relatives (aunts, uncles, etc.), or strangers appointed by a court as 'in loco parentis', meaning that such persons assumed the duties and responsibilities of a parent to usually younger siblings or to children other than their own."

in mora: a borrower, usually of property, who has failed to return it, e.g., "Louisiana records sometimes refer to a person in mora."

in perpetuam rei memoriam: literally, in perpetual memory of the matter; often referred to sworn statements or ***depositions*** (q.v.) taken to preserve a record of testimony, e.g., "He was asked to take Jones' testimony in perpetuam rei memoriam."

in personam, in rem: a legal action against a person; a legal action by virtue of or against some property, e.g., "If a record refers to a ***sheriff*** (q.v.) serving a writ in personam, that sheriff found the person, but if the service was in rem, the researcher knows that the party sued may not have been in that county but some property of his yet was located there."

in posse: unborn, a living fetus, e.g., "A child before birth is in posse, or in ventre sa mere, and after birth is ***in esse*** (q.v.)."

in rem: See ***in personam.***

in the bed: a common Southern expression used to relate that another has gone to bed or is resting or asleep in a bed, e.g., "The expression in the bed derives from the very early times when many beds were surrounded by gauze in order to keep insects from the sleeper, thus requiring that the person retiring actually get into the bed and inside the curtains."

in the room of: in place of; instead of, e.g., "A 1780 North Carolina roadwork record listed Nathaniel Drake as in the room of another man."

in ventre sa mere: See ***in posse.***

incense burner: See ***censer.***

inch: early, a measure of length equal to three (3) grains of barley laid end to end; one twelfth part of a foot, e.g., "An inch was described by Shakespeare as 'a nice point of time' and still in Johnson's time as three grains of barley."

inchoate rights: any interest in real estate which has not yet been realized or vested in the owner; in ***genealogy*** (q.v.), usually those rights of a wife during her husband's life that may ripen into ***dower*** (q.v.) rights at his death, e.g., "Their land having been in her husband's name, when he died her inchoate rights ripened into a one-third interest in the income from that land."

incontinence: as now, e.g., "***Belladonna*** (q.v.), bromides, and ergot were administered for urinary incontinence, all to no avail."

incontinent: early, unlike now, unchaste or self-indulgent, e.g., "His early reference to her being incontinent had nothing to do with bodily functions."

incorporeal property: See ***corporeal property.***

increase: usually referred to the issue of animals or slaves, e.g., "The will provided that Sarah inherited the slaves Jammy and Sal and their increase."

incunabula: very early (1450 to 1500) books printed with movable type, e.g., "In addition to the Library of Congress, the Pierpont Morgan Library of New York City and the Huntington Library of San Marino, CA, have substantial collections of German incunabula."

indenture: early, a covenant or agreement, so named because the counterparts were indented or had been cut (or torn) in an unusual pattern to prevent alteration; early, a document stating a debt in time and (or) service owed by one person to another, quite usually executed where transportation or training was to be exchanged for labor and time; recently, a deed or agreement, e.g., "His obligation to serve Captain Smith as a servant for four years was set forth in the indenture."

indentured servant: one who entered upon an agreement by the terms of which he or she exchanged time and labor for land, transportation, or (and) training, e.g., "In exchange for being transported to the Virginia Colony, she had agreed to serve as an indentured servant until her twenty-fifth birthday." Also see ***indenture.***

indexes, indices: plural forms of "index" e.g., "The indexes were contained in four volumes and also were computerized."

India rubbers: See ***shoes.***

Indian old fields: land cleared by American Indians, originally used as places of encampment, for animal drives, or to raise crops, e.g., "The locations of any local Indian old fields were well known to early settlers and were often used as designated meeting places, e.g., "The school was to be held each Monday morning throughout June in the Indian old field near Drake's Corner." Also see ***old field schools.***

Indian Title: those rights to land said to result from treaties between the white settlers and the American Indians; an unwritten legal presumption that the Indians had rights in land by virtue of their ages-old occupancy or use thereof, e.g., "The Indian title to the land north of 'Boundary Road' derived from the Greenville Treaty"; "The earliest settlers of Cumberland County believed that the Indian Title had been extinguished by the French and Indian War."

Indian Wars: refers to the many military conflicts with the Native Americans which took place during the last half of the nineteenth century, generally in the western states and territories, e.g., "Before leaving for the Indian Wars, he made a deed conditioned upon his return from such."

Indianapolis, U.S.S: See ***warships, American.***

Indians, American, influence of; Native Americans: many presently used words arose from our experiences with the native Americans, including the Eskimos, e.g., "Pemmican, wigwam, hickory, pecan, chipmunk, moose, terrapin, ***hominy*** (q.v.), totem, papoose, moccasin, tomahawk, raccoon, opossum, skunk (segankem), squash (askutasquash), smoke a peace pipe, Indian summer, Indian file, play possum, bury the hatchet, war path, igloo and kayak are but a few of such words."

indices: See ***indexes.***

indict, endite: a written accusation addressed to a court by a grand jury that one has acted or failed to act in such a way as to violate the criminal law, e.g., "The notation that he had been endited revealed that the grand jury had determined that he should be charged with a specific crime."

indigo: a plant originally cultivated in the Southern colonies, and from which blue dye was made, e.g., "The indigo trade was early thought to be a future mainstay of the Virginia colony."

induction: See ***private, private soldier.***

indulgence: a remission of punishment for sins, e.g., "The sale of indulgences caused many differences among early Catholic clergy."

infant: a child through the seventh year; at law, anyone under twenty-one years of age, e.g., "In early law a person was in "childhood" until the eighth birthday, and was a minor—a legal infant—until 'one and twenty'."

infantia: in ***Civil Law*** (q.v.), one under seven years, e.g., "The researcher of Louisiana should not confuse legal 'infantia' with ***'infant'*** (q.v.), the former referring to those under 7 years of age, the latter, usually, early, anyone under 21."

inficiato: in ***Civil Law*** (q.v.), a denial of a debt or obligation, e.g., "As to the money owing, the old parish record showed him to have declared himself 'inficiato'."

infirmary: See ***county home.***

ingross, ingrossing: early term meaning the creation of a perfect copy of a draft or other complete preliminary draft, e.g., "The clerk of the ***land office*** (q.v.) was ordered to ingross the grant to be made to Hughes."

injunction, enjoined: usually, an order by a court prohibiting or requiring specific actions, e.g., "The file revealed that he was enjoined from being anywhere near her house"; "The 1704 injunction required that he fence out the neighbor's cattle."

inkhorn, ink bottle, ink vial: a small container, often carried on the person, originally made of the closed end of a small horn and used to hold liquid ink; occasionally, a small carrying case for the quill pens, inks and drying powders or blotting materials to be used when writing,, e.g., "His inkhorn was made of the tip of a goat horn with a cork stopper"; "William Bradshaw had a small leather case of pens, inks and writing materials which he often referred to as his 'inkhorn'."

in-law: early, those who were related through affinity, adoption, or any other legal action that resulted in one being considered a part of the family unit; presently, those who are related through marriage only, e.g., "The boy spoken of in the record as his son-in-law was, in fact, an adopted child"; "Jane's husband is Jack's only in-law yet living." Also see ***affinity.***

in-lot, inlot: a lot or parcel of land lying within a village or municipality, e.g., "Drake owned In-lot 6 and also ***Out-lot*** (q.v.) 8 which adjoined #6."

inlot: See ***in-lot***

inmate: unlike now, one who dwells in the house of another, often in eschange for money or work; a prostitute who frequents ahouse of prostitution in order to engage in her trade, e.g., "The tax records revealing that he was an inmate in Martin's house had nothing to do with crime."

inn: early and now, a facility offering food, drink, and rest for overnight, e.g., "The inn at Salisbury was there before 1790." See also the entries for ***ordinary, tavern***, and ***pub***.

innocent woman: one who has never had illicit intercourse with a man, e.g., "The term innocent woman was not synonymous with virgin, since one could be a widow and yet be innocent."

inoficiocidad: anything done contrary to a duty or obligation, e.g., "Early records of Texas and Florida sometimes speak of one being inoficiocidad as to contractual obligations or taxes."

insinuacion: presentation of a legal document to a judge or magistrate with the intention of gaining legal approval of that instrument, e.g., "In very early Texas and Florida records one occasionally will be said to have gained insinuacion of a contract or of other legal document." But also see ***insinuation***.

insinuation: in ***Civil Law*** (q.v.), a legal instrument declaring one's intention to transfer title to property as a gift, e.g., "Unlike ***insinuacion*** (q.v.) in Texas and Florida, insinuation in Louisiana means to record an instrument of gift." Also see ***insinuacion***.

insomnia: as now, e.g., "Alcohol, ***belladonna*** (q.v.), opiates, and phosphorus all were prescribed for insomnia."

instant, inst.: meaning that a writing was being done or written during the same month as some prior writing, e.g., "When responding on March 25th to a letter written anytime previous to that date, yet within that same month, it is appropriate to write, 'I received your letter of the 10th instant'." Also see ***ultimo***.

instanter: immediately, at once, e.g., "Many early records tell of courts ordering persons to perform some act instanter."

institor: a clerk in a store, e.g., "Occasionally, in Louisiana court records, genealogists will find persons being referred to as institors for another person or business."

instrument: as now in law; a formal document of any kind, e.g., "The instrument of transfer was a deed."

intended wife: an engaged or betrothed woman, e.g., "Many early records reveal matters concerning intended wives."

intent to be naturalized: See ***naturalization***.

inter alia: literally, among other matters, e.g., "The court stated that Evan had complained of a trespass inter alia, meaning that he also had described other matters or activities integral to the actions comprising the trespass."

inter vivos: from one to another when both are living, e.g., "The entry revealing an inter vivos gift told the researcher that both parties to that transaction were alive at that date."

intercourse: See ***cover***.

interdiction, interdit: in Louisiana, a suit seeking a ***curator*** (q.v.) of one who is no longer capable of caring for his affairs and property, e.g., "The order stating that Jessie had gained interdiction for Leonard meant that there had been a legal action seeking a curator for Leonard's property, and that such action had succeeded."

inter-library loan: that service provided by most libraries by which, through loan, materials in one library are made available to the patrons of another, e.g., "While the local library was small, through the inter-library loan service she could gain use of many of the historical materials of the metropolitan library."

Interregnum, (1649-1660): literally, between sovereigns; refers to that government of the British Isles that ruled between the execution of Charles I and the recognition of Charles II as King, e.g., "Many of the followers of Charles I fled to the American colonies after he was beheaded." See ***Commonwealth.***

intertrigo: an early medical term, the meaning now unknown, e.g., "Dr. Bater's notes revealed that zinc oxide, calcium carbonate, glycerinate of tannin, and bismuth were administered for intertrigo."

intestate succession: gaining ownership or rights in property by reason of the effect of laws concerning assets of those who die without a will, e.g., "His father having died ***intestate*** (q.v.), he and his siblings took the property by intestate succession." Also see ***descent and distribution.***

intestate, intestacy: death without a valid will, e.g., "She left no will, so it was said that she died intestate and that an administrator had been appointed." Also see ***intestate succession.***

intestato: See ***intestate.***

introduction: that writing at the beginning of a literary work that states the parameters of the work and the approach of the author to the subject matter. It often reveals what periods, subjects or persons are not included, e.g., "The Introduction related that the material was set forth by family units in chronological order, commencing with an immigrant ancestor who was born in 1704."

intussusception: a term of varying meanings, usually an intestinal restriction or blockage, e.g., "***Belladonna*** (q.v.), effervescent ***enema*** (q.v.), tobacco enema, and 'irrigation of the bowels' were often prescribed for an intussusception."

invalid's chair: an early, high-backed, sturdy, potty chair with arms, designed for the elderly or infirm and needed by reason of the inability of such persons to go to the existing facilities, e.g., "In 1890 a better quality invalid's chair could be purchased for about the same sum as a pair of high quality ladies' shoes."

inventory: an itemization of assets; in genealogy, usually that list of the personal property owned by a person at the moment of death, e.g., "Paul's inventory included two slaves and his father's watch." Also see ***appraisal.***

Irish influence: many words arose from our Irish ancestry, e.g., "Shenanigan, buddy (bodach), shebang, shanty, and biddy are but a few."

Irish whiskey, Irish: a barley-based whiskey from Ireland, e.g., "Irish became a favorite here after the immigrations following the ***Potato Famine*** (q.v.) of the mid-19th century."

iritis: as now, any inflammation of the iris of the eye, e.g., "Incredibly, Dr. Lockhart administered blisters behind the ears, leeches, and occasionally mercuric arsenate in advanced iritis."

iron (to), irons, smoothers: the expression "to iron" was unknown early, and only in the late 19th and early 20th centuries have we "ironed" clothes; throughout history, we have "smoothed" fabrics and clothing with "clothes smoothers" made of iron (usually) or brass, e.g., "The 'smoothers' of the 17th, 18th, and 19th centuries have become the 'irons' of the 20th"; " Her smoothing irons were also known as ***sad irons*** (q.v.), ***flat irons*** (q.v.) and ***polishing irons*** (q.v.)."

Iron Brigade: See ***military combat units, famous.***

iron gibbet: a device of horrendous torture, composed of an iron frame cage shaped like a person into which a criminal might be placed and hung or put in public view, and from which there was no escape, e.g., "The iron gibbet was so designed that, when placed in it, a man could not bend at the waist or move his head, arms or legs more than an inch or two in any direction."

iron hands: usually large forceps or tongs, e.g., "He frequently referred to his tongs and long forceps used to bring pottery from the oven as iron hands."

iron master: one who was in the business of making iron; an owner of a smelter or iron furnace; an ironworks operator, e.g., "Iron masters utilized many services, including those of the woodcutter or axmen, colliers (diggers of coal), haulers, and ordinary laborers, e.g., "The father of George Washington was an iron master on the Rappahannock River south of Fredericksburg." Also see ***ironmonger***.

ironmonger: one who sold or dealt in hardware, iron, and metal products; one who operated an iron ***furnace*** (q.v.), e.g., "He was an ironmonger in early Shenandoah County"; "The ironmonger and owner at Catherine Furnace had no idea that his little place of business would be remembered so long as men speak of war." Also see ***monger.***

ironstone: originally, better white pottery from England; later, any heavy, white pottery or dish ware, e.g., "Bethany was proud of her grandmother's ironstone."

ISBN (International Standard Book Number): a unique 10-digit number assigned to and identifying books for the purpose of cataloging and for copyright searches, etc., e.g., "Publishers in the United States must apply to the Library of Congress to be issued ISBNs for their books."

isinglass, isingglass: usually, the crystalline, transparent form of the mineral mica, early used to cover the viewing aperture in a stove, e.g., "***Pot-bellies*** (q.v.) with isinglass were familiar to virtually all of the period 1765-1945."

issue: in genealogy, children or sometimes descendants of a specific person, e.g., "The issue of Paul and Martha all had blonde to brown hair as did their parents."

Italian influence: many words arose from our Italian ancestry and their food, e.g., "Pizza, spaghetti, lasagna, espresso, parmesan, macaroni, and broccoli are but a few."

item: as now; a term or word often found in wills, especially early, which served to separate ***devises*** (q.v.), ***bequests*** (q.v.), or paragraphs, e.g., "The third, fourth, and fifth items of the will were bequests to Selma's daughter and two sons."

iule, yule: pertaining to Christmas, e.g., "Occasionally one finds the word iule in early Virginia records."

iulebs: a medication now unknown; perhaps juleps, e.g., "York County, VA, Records; Vol. 3, p. 66, reveals the consumption of iulebs as cures for diseases."

J

jack: as now; also a flask; early, a small, often decorated container, carried about on the person and containing alcoholic beverages, e.g. "A 1679 Surry County inventory listed a 'jack and yt with silver', meaning a pocket flask ***chased*** (q.v.) with silver."

jack knife, jackknife: a large utility knife with one or more, usually three, folding blades intended to be carried on the person, e.g., "Most men of the 19th century carried a jack knife." Also see ***pen knife***.

jackboots: See ***shoes***.

jaconet, jacanet: a light weight fabric or cloth, first woven in India, usually of cotton and used for book spines, bandages, and widely in the manufacture of clothing. Also see ***leno***.

jag: a small, usually unmeasured quantity of firewood considerably less than a ***rick*** (q.v.), or a small, usually also unmeasured, quantity of a common dry substance such as lumber, nails, shingles, animal feed, etc., e.g., "He asked the neighbor if he might borrow a little jag of wood."

jailer: See ***gaoler***.

jailing for debt: See ***debtors' prisons***.

jake: an intoxicating liquor made by mixing Jamaica ginger with other intoxicants such as wine or cider, e.g., "Early Georgia and Alabama reports sometimes refer to barrels or bottles of jake."

jam cupboard: See ***jelly cupboard***.

Jamaica spirits: See ***rum***.

Jamestown colony: the first (May 24, 1607) successful English settlement on the American continent consisted of 105 men (73 of whom died in the first 7 months), which succeeded in no small part because of the arrival of supply ships (Jan. and April, 1608); those, the efforts of the famous Capt. John Smith and by reason of the settlers' efforts to raise food crops, e.g., "The 1609 charter of the Jamestown colony granted it land 400 miles wide, from 'sea to sea'."

japanned: finely lacquered and finished wood, very often black, and originally from the Orient, e.g., "Her japanned jewelry box was beautiful."

jardinière: a large, quite usually porcelain vase or pot for decoration, plants or to hold cut flowers, e.g., "Diane had a beautiful Nippon jardinière."

jardiniere stand: usually, an ornate, wooden flower or plant stand, often placed in a parlor or hall, e.g., "The affluent of Pennsylvania had jardinière stands; the poor had ***fonzytishes*** (q.v.)."

jaundice, icterus: a condition brought about by excessive bile in the system and characterized by a yellow color in the skin and whites of the eyes, e.g., "In early times, arsenic, ammonium chloride, iodine, nitro-muriatic acid, and rhubarb were administered for jaundice."

jean: a strong, twilled fabric, usually of cotton and sometimes of linen, e.g., "The jeans often advertised by fabric merchants of the 18th and 19th century had little to do with the usually blue so-called denim pants of today."

jelly: unlike now, referred to flavored, usually clear gelatin made from hog's feet or the amber colored jelly resulting from cooking down sheeps' feet, e.g., "She made the best jelly by adding sugar, cinnamon, mace, lemon juice, and white wine to the gelatin resulting from boiling down hogs' feet."

jelly cupboard: a short-legged cabinet, with a doored compartment of 3 or 4 shelves, used for storing canned foods, jellies, preserves, etc., e.g., "As were most in the North, Bethany's jelly cupboard was made of yellow poplar."

Jenkins Ear, War of: 1739-1742; that conflict between Spain and Great Britain, the result of which, in the American colonies, was the British siege of and retreat from St. Augustine in May, June, and July of 1740, e.g., "Unfortunately, the few records of the battles at St. Augustine during the War of Jenkins Ear yield little of value to the genealogist."

jenny: a female donkey, e.g., "He had a jenny for the children's ***cart*** (q.v.)."

jerkin: a doublet-like, tight-fitting, sleeveless garment, often made of leather or other heavy material, e.g., "Many drawings of 17th-century colonial men depict them wearing ***doublets*** (q.v.) or jerkins."

jersey wagon: a wagon pulled by a steer, e.g., "The Virginian wrote that many common Northerners moved about in jersey wagons or on foot."

jersy-man: a New World settler, usually from the island of Jersey, and sometimes from other of the English Channel Islands, e.g., "Early records occasionally refer to immigrants from the Channel Island of Jersey as jersy-men."

jesse: a large chandelier, usually hung in a great hall, church, or meeting house, e.g., "The parish record referred to a silver candle jesse." Also see ***goin' jesse.***

Jesus tarries, if the creek don't rise and: a superlative derived from the facts that in earliest American colonial times, there were but few bridges and all streams and rivers had to be forded in moving from place to place and also the ages old belief of certainty that Christ would return; assuredly so; an event almost sure to come about, e.g., "Sarah smiled and assured Anne and Jean that she would surely be at their weddings 'if the creeks don't rise and Jesus tarries'."

jewelers lamp: See ***shoemakers lamp.***

jewels: as medicines, gemstones early were thought to have value as remedies and medicines, e.g., "It was believed that ***tinctures*** (q.v.) of jewels such as coral and pearls were good tonics, ground emeralds controlled passions, ingested diamonds brought courage, rubies removed idle fancies, and amethysts prevented drunkenness and excessive sleeping."

jig: See ***giggs.***

jigger: See ***shave.***

jigs and stomps: dances of several undefined sorts, e.g., "He wrote that they had gone to the home of Mrs. Mills and had enjoyed an evening of jigs and stomps."

jigs, giggs: See ***dances.***

Jim Crow laws and institutions: laws enforcing segregation; after a black-faced minstrel of the ***ante-bellum*** (q.v.) South, the expression "jim crow" came to be a label somewhere in measure of derision between the belittling "colored" or "darkey" and the now distasteful epithet "nigger," e.g., "To list but a few, there were jim crow sections on streetcars, jim crow drinking fountains, jim crow rest rooms, and jim crow benches in the park."

jimcreek, jimcrack: See ***gimcreek***.

jink, jig: a prank or trick, e.g., "When Miss Brittany laughingly said the jig was up, she was saying that a trick had been played on someone and it had been discovered."

jinx: a symbol or sign, usually meaning bad luck or misfortune, e.g., "When the chickens died at the appearance of the white horse, Diane believed that the animal was a jinx on her fowl."

jitney: a vehicle, other than animal-powered and not on tracks, operating on a more or less repetitive schedule and used to move people, e.g., "Newspapers of the early 20th century often refer to gasoline jitneys."

joe: See ***Dobra***.

jog, jogger: unlike now, a push, or one who pushes dully and slowly; a light shake or jerk, e.g., "His reference to a man who jogged the load had nothing to do with running."

john house, johnny house: See ***privy***.

johnny cake board, as flat as a: a superlative, e.g., "An early Southern visitor to New England described the bosoms of the women there as 'as flat as a johnny cake boards'."

johnny cakes: probably derived from journey cakes; small, hard-crusted loaves of bread or large biscuits provided as refreshment to those about to travel some distance, e.g., "He put the johnny cakes in his ***pocket*** (q.v.)."

Johnson's Kentucky Cavalry: See ***military combat units, famous***.

joiner: one who makes a livelihood by knowing of and joining wood by glue, different joints, etc.; a now nearly forgotten trade, once very important to the cabinet and furniture makers, requiring knowledge of characteristics of expansion, contraction, warping, etc., in various woods, e.g., "He was known widely for his near perfect joining."

joiners' tools: as now, e.g., "A decedent who was a joiner may be identified by the appearance in an inventory of molding and rabbet planes, jack planes, smoothing planes, long jointer planes, trying planes, short jointers' planes, marking gauges, joiners' clamps, and bow drills." Also see ***joiner***.

joint tenancy: a legal term describing joint ownership where the interests were acquired by the owners through the same ***instrument*** (q.v.) and the interest of all owners are in all ways identical and equal, e.g., "The deed transferred the property 'to Diane and her daughters, jointly', and so created a joint tenancy."

jointist: See ***bootlegger***.

jointure: referred to the gaining of an estate for life by a widow as a result of the death of her husband, e.g., "The court spoke of the jointure of the ***relict*** (q.v.), revealing to the researcher that she had gained assets or income as a result of her husband's death."

jot and tittle, every jot and tittle: a superlative derived from the definition of jots and tittles, those being small marks such as accents and the dots over the letters "i" and "j"; to be exact and precise; a description of a task, usually intellectual, that is precisely and totally completed or finished, e.g., "Anne could have written that Shakespeare would have understood every jot and tittle of her writings'."

journals, journal entries: See ***minutes, minute books.***

journey: a day's travel, e.g., "From the French 'jour' meaning a day, we have journal for day book, 'tout jour' for forever, and 'journeyman' meaning one who works by the day." Also see ***journeyman.***

journey cakes: See ***johnny cakes.***

journeyman: early, one who had completed training or an apprenticeship, was no longer bound to any master, was said to be knowledgeable in his trade or craft, and usually worked by the day, e.g., "Even though the guilds never were rooted in the Americas, the term journeyman, meaning one who had mastered a trade and worked by the day, was in common use, even to now."

journey proud: said to be the reason one can not sleep during the night prior to an expected or anticipated journey, e.g., "Sarah wrote that she had been journey proud for two nights before her trip to meet her lover."

jowler: a hunting dog, e.g., "The 1711 inventory reference to a '***jowler slut*** (q.v.) and three dogs' revealed the presence of four hunting dogs, three of which were male."

judex: a judge, e.g., "***civil law*** (q.v.) systems such as Louisiana often refer to a judge as judex."

judges' minutes: See ***minutes, minute books and courts orders.***

judgment by peers: early, a trial by twelve persons, now occasionally six or some other number of jurors, e.g., "The order revealing that it was the judgment of his peers that he pay money simply meant that a jury so decided."

jujubs, jujubes: small plums, e.g., "She mentioned making wine from jujubs."

julap, julep: unlike now, water, usually sweetened with ***sorghum*** (q.v.) honey, maple or cane sugar, and used as the vehicle for medicine, e.g., "She ground the herbs to a fine powder and made a julap for the children.

Julian calendar: that yearly calendar authorized by Julius Caesar in 46 B.C. that was shown by Bede (in 732) to be 11 minutes, 14 seconds longer than one complete rotation of the Earth, thereby gaining a day approximately every 128 years, the same abandoned in favor of Pope Gregory's (Gregorian) calendar by the western nations commencing with France in 1582 and ending with the British Empire and the American colonies in 1752, e.g., "In abandoning the Julian calendar, the day following 2 September, 1752, became September 14, 1752, and March 25 was replaced by January 1 as the first day of any new year.

jumbals: See ***desserts, early.***

jumbuck, jumbah: a large male sheep, e.g., "Ferguson's York county 1747 inventory revealed three ewes and a jumbuck."

Junior: See ***Senior*** and ***Junior***.

junk fish: fish having little or no commercial value, e.g., "Early New Englanders ***fished their corn*** (q.v.) with the junk fish brought home by the fishermen."

jurat, jur.: literally, it was proven; early, a magistrate; that subscribing witness who swore to or affirmed the validity of any writing; often mistakenly read as "Junior", e.g., "The jurat was his brother."

jury: a group of people (in early times, men) sworn to ascertain the truth upon such evidence as was presented to them concerning some matters of fact; juries varied in number from six to twenty-four persons, e.g., "Twenty-four was the number of persons seated for a grand jury"; "The petit jury consisted of twelve men, all said to be 'tried and true'." See also ***venire*** and see ***juror*** and see ***judgment by peers.***

jury of matrons: See ***matrons, jury of.***

jury, trial by: See ***pais, per.***

jus: a right under the ***civil law*** (q.v.), as in Louisiana, e.g., "Early reports often speak of rights such as 'jus legitum', 'jus disponendi' or 'jus futurum', meaning a legal right, right to dispose of some property, or a future right."

jus ad rem: a contractual right to some personal property, e.g., "The Louisiana court order stated that the question concerned Ebert's jus ad rem." Also see ***jus.***

jus deliberandi: right to examine property before accepting it as one's share of some inheritance, e.g., "Before accepting the horse as his share of the Louisiana estate, he exercised jus deliberandi." Also see ***jus.***

justice of the peace: an elected officer (appointed in some jurisdictions) to maintain the peace in the county, and qualified to administer oaths and perform marriages; a judicial officer having quite limited authority and only as to minor crimes, misdemeanors, and matters of the peace; early, an officer of considerable importance before modern transportation facilitated trips about the county by a ***sheriff*** (q.v.) or his deputies, e.g., "As a justice of the peace in 1835, Cole was highly respected."

K

kas: a word of Hollanders and ***Pennsylvania Dutch*** (q.v.), meaning a painted ***wardrobe*** (q.v.), e.g., "Bethany's Dutch kas had two drawers in the bottom and was very ornately painted."

kay: See ***key.***

keck: a very early term, to vomit, to retch, e.g., "The 17th century entry related that the child had '...died of a keck fit'."

kedge, kedge boat, kedge-boat: a small boat used to guide and assist a large boat in a narrow channel or river, e.g., "The Civil War records have many references to kedge-boats, some of which had oars." Also see ***kedger.***

kedger: a small anchor for use with small boats—kedges—in rivers, backwaters and in slow moving currents, e.g., "The York County store inventory included four sets of oars and three iron kedgers." Also see ***kedge.***

keelboat: usually, a large, shallow-draft, flat-bottomed river boat, e.g., "Keelboats were common on the river at Plattsmouth."

keep your powder dry: be prepared; from the days when men carried gunpowder in pocket containers in order that it might be protected from the weather and so be usable when needed; a word of caution from commanders of men carrying ***matchlocks*** (q.v.) or ***flintlocks*** (q.v.) in combat, in which firearms the powder in the pan was likely to be ruined if exposed to the weather and so would not fire when the trigger was pulled, e.g., "While the Revolutionary War witnessed many admonitions to keep the powder dry, the expression now is but a suggestion that one should be prepared."

kelderkin: a small barrel, e.g., "The inventory of the old Hollander listed three kelderkins."

kell: a vegetable greens stew; that net-like system of muscles and ligaments that surround the intestines of most animals that early was fed to other animals such as hogs, e.g., "When she wrote that they had gathered the kells that morning, she probably was speaking of the greens to be used for a boiled meal."

kenting, kentings: an unknown cloth or fabric, not mentioned by Johnson (1755 or 1802), e.g., "In the 1790s Philadelphia merchants Kuhn & Risberg advertised for sale '7 8, 4 4, and 11 8 plain, striped and spotted kentings and needle worked kenting aprons'."

Kentucky Cavalry, Johnson's: See ***military combat units, famous.***

Kentucky rifle, long rifle, Pennsylvania rifle: a long, rifled barreled, ***flintlock*** (q.v.) musket developed simultaneously in Pennsylvania and Kentucky, noted for accuracy, and carried by many pioneers, hunters, and fighters, e.g., "Daniel Boone's favorite Kentucky or long rifle has been lost over the years." Also see ***flintlock*** and ***musket*** and see ***long hunters.***

kerchief, kercheef, handkerchief: spelled kercheif by him in 1802, Johnson defined kerchief as a cover of the head, thus a handkerchief, as now, is a kerchief used for another purpose, e.g., "When Moore wrote '...Maw in her kerchief and I in my cap....', he was describing his wife's head covering for sleeping on a cold night."

kerfing saw: See ***cooper's tools.***

kerosene: See ***coal oil.***

kersey: a heavy wool or wool and cotton fabric used for outer coats, e.g., "She needed 4 ***ells*** (q.v.) of kersey to make winter coats for the children."

ketch: a small sailing ship with 2 masts, the forward being the larger of the two, e.g., "Many ketches operated between the colonial South and the Caribbean Islands."

key, quay, kay: a wharf or point of loading and unloading of ships and boats, e.g., "John Cotton had an early trading post at South Quay."

kibble: early, a large metal bucket used to lift ore and debris from mines; later, occasionally a metal bucket used in a water well, e.g., "The old Welsh miner found it humorous that the well bucket was called a kibble."

kick the can: ("tag" of sorts, timed by reaching a kicked can.) See ***games (of children).***

kid: a young goat, e.g., "Not until the late 19th century did we refer to children as kids."

Kidd, Capt.: See ***pirates.***

kidney disease: as now, but not understood early, e.g., "For what were then thought to be kidney diseases, spinal ice bags, eucalyptus, and pipsissewa were administered."

killing time: that time of the year, quite usually late autumn, when swine and cattle were slaughtered and the meat prepared or preserved for the winter, e.g., "They made two hundred pounds of sausage and smoked 14 hams at killing time."

kilometer: See ***meter***.

kin, kinship: a loosely defined term referring to any and all of one's relations, whether by affinity, consanguinity, or by law, e.g., "As to her, his kinship was that of first cousin."

kindly: early, and now, especially in the Appalachian Mts., and distinct from the more common usage, a friendly request that something be done after a fashion or in a manner somewhat less exacting than that usually demanded for that task, e.g., "Jean told Evan that if he would kindly repair the upholstered chair, she would be ***much obliged*** (q.v.)."

king of the mountain, king of the hill: a contest of strength, usually of little boys, wherein one stood on top a small knoll or little hill and attempted to physically maintain that position while other players attempted to remove him from there by force of hands, e.g., "King of the hill quite usually was considered won when none were able to physically dislodge one of the players."

King's Attorney: a prosecutor or attorney representing the government, colony, or county, e.g., "As do our District Attorneys and Prosecutors, the King's Attorneys or their assistants prosecuted most of the criminal cases."

King's X, King's Cross: a very ancient expression by which children declare themselves temporarily exempt from game rules, e.g., "When Bethany's father called her to come from the game briefly, she shouted 'King's X', thereby invoking the ancient authority of the King as witnessed by his mark—his 'X'—and so preserved her status in the game." Also see ***games (of children)***.

kings and queens, reigns of: See ***regnal years***.

King's English: usually, the "proper" English spoken by the upper class and the educated of Great Britain, as opposed to dialects such as ***cockney*** (q.v.), Scottish, Irish, and other local or regional variations of the language, e.g., "In speaking, he was said to 'murder the King's English'."

kip: leather made of ***kid*** (q.v.) or goat skin, e.g., "Along with sole and ***upper leather*** (q.v.), kip and calf skins were being offered for sale in the advertisements in Ohio newspapers of the 1850s."

kippacks: shoes homemade by the poor or rural settlers and fashioned of three pieces of leather, one upper, one for the sole, and one for the heel, e.g., "Paul was known in the neighborhood for his kippacks made for his children, even though he had no training." Also see ***shoes***.

kitchen garden: that small garden kept by a housewife in which were planted medicinal herbs and plants, spices, vegetables, and fruits to be used by the family and not for barter or trade, e.g., "Mrs. Judy was proud of the kitchen garden and saw to its care on a daily basis."

kitchen table: a medium sized, sturdy, drawered table, occasionally with one of more small bins mounted below the drawers, e.g., "The kitchen table served as her work area for the cooking chores."

kitchen, roasting kitchen: sometimes unlike now, a container for cooking, e.g., "Medium to large metal, lidded and footed utensils placed before the fireplace and within which foods were baked or cooked sometimes were called kitchens."

kiver: unknown, perhaps a "cover" or quilt, e.g., "A 1714 York County inventory revealed a kiver, a ***rug*** (q.v.), and a ***bedstead and cord*** (q.v.)."

Klondike gold rush, Klondike: that rush of gold prospectors and speculators to the area on the Alaska border near Dawson, Canada, which took place beginning in August, 1896, e.g., "The Klondike yielded an estimated $175,000,000.00 in gold."

knapsack: See ***haversack***.

knee buckle: buckles used to fasten ***breeches*** (q.v.) below the knee, e.g., "Thomas Drake had a pair of ***Dutch gold*** (q.v.) knee buckles."

kneehole desk: a table with a flat top used as a writing and work surface, having adequate space in the center beneath the top to place a chair, and having 1 to 3 drawers or doored compartments on each side of the knee opening, e.g., "Evan's kneehole desk was of solid mahogany."

knell (knel), birth knell, death knell: early, knel(l) was the sound of a bell rung at a funeral; now, any sound signaling a birth, marriage or death, e.g., "Our ancestors used the term birth knell to describe the first cry of an infant as often as they employed the term death knell to describe the sound of the funeral bell."

knife drums: See ***paper making.***

knight: that rank of British honor next below a ***baronet*** (q.v.); since mediaeval times, a person who has been accorded that non-hereditary dignity by a sovereign of Britain or another nation, e.g., "Among the many famous knights were Francis Drake, knighted by Elizabeth I, and Winston Churchill, so honored by Elizabeth II."

Knights of the Garter: See ***Garter***.

Knights of the Order of St. George: See ***Garter***.

knob: a hill, wooded or not, and usually small; any high point of land surrounded by lower terrain or flatter terrain, e.g., "Because of the wild turkeys that wintered there, Evan spoke of the little hill of trees as 'turkey knob'."

knock down at auction: the accomplishment of a sale at auction, signaled by the banging of a small wooden hammer by the auctioneer e.g., "The ***armoire*** (q.v.) was knocked down to Mrs. Haskins."

knot: a measure of speed at sea; as commonly known in wood, or as in a rope wound back upon itself. See ***nautical mile.***

Korean Conflict, Korean War: that armed conflict between North Korea (and allied Communist forces) and the United States and its allies that took place from early 1950 to mid-1953, e.g., "Public Law 550 provided the ***G.I. Bill*** (q.v.) for veterans of the Korean War."

kraut cutter: See ***cabbage plane***.

Ku Klux Klan: that secret organization formed during the post-Civil War years, having as its purpose the subversion of the newly acquired rights of Blacks as citizens of the U.S., e.g., "After 1867, the Ku Klux Klan and its Ku Kluxers or Knights were responsible for all manner of lawlessness and violence."

L

lac: a resin from insects, the base for shellac, the vehicle usually being alcohol; a commonly used wood finish, e.g., "Few were the furniture makers who did not know of orange, brown, and white lac." Also see ***shellac***, and see ***lacquer***.

lacquer: that ***lac*** (q.v.) based finish found on most 20th century furniture, e.g., "Average quality furniture of the period 1910 to 1980 almost always was finished in sprayed lacquer."

lactation, lactate: the secretion or production of milk by a female animal, e.g., "For excessive or unneeded lactation in women, Dr. W. K. Drake administered quinine, ***belladonna*** (q.v.), and camphorated oil."

lacus: See ***alloy.***

ladderback chair, ladder-back: any of the several styles of chairs having horizontal slats in the back mounted so as to appear like a ladder; if not a reproduction, the more slats, usually the earlier the chair, e.g., "Her ladderback had nicely turned posts holding four slats, and she suspected it was of the 18th century."

ladies' hat box: See ***bonnet box.***

ladies' saddle: See ***side saddle.***

Lady Day: the feast of the annunciation of the Virgin Mary; usually March 25th; anciently, that date upon which many land rents for the growing season following were due, however it was observed on August 15th in early Ireland, e.g., "Lady Day was often celebrated in the early colonies. "As land rent, Owen Griffith was to 'pay 1 hogshead of tobacco and 1 fatt capon on each Lady Day following'."

laid paper: See ***paper making.***

lair and headstone: an expression of the upland South meaning a grave and marker, e.g., "Audie told her granddaughter that she knew the location of the 'lair and headstone' of her great grandfather Wright."

lam, lamming: early term for having taken flight or having escaped, usually from punishment; running away and hiding oneself from some work or legal service owed, e.g., "He was on the lam from the county jail, having escaped two months earlier."

lamb: a sheep, male or female, under one year old, e.g., "The inventory revealed '1 ewe, 2 rams and 4 lambs'."

lamp oil: See ***coal oil.***

lamps: any illuminating device, including those that contained candles, e.g., "He had whale oil, coal oil, and candle lamps in his collection." Also see ***betty lamp.***

lana: in ***civil law*** (q.v.), wool, e.g., The old Louisiana reports sometimes refer to lana cloth or ***stuff*** (q.v.)."

lancet, lance: a small pointed instrument used to open boils, blisters, and in ***bleeding*** (q.v.), e.g., "Old Ben Rodecker had a lancet that had belonged to his grandfather."

land certificate: See ***land grants***.

land descriptions: See ***metes and bounds*** and see ***courses and distances.***

land entry: as now; a claim for land under any of the many enactments by which land was granted to settlers or as a reward for military duty or assistance to the government, e.g., "After location and marking by a surveyor and payment of a fee, the act of recording by the land office of his claim for land was known as an entry or land entry." Also see ***entry.***

land grants, land certificates, land warrants, general land office: grants of land from the public domain; usually used synonymously with ***land patent*** (q.v.); that document or the act by which government conveys an interest in public lands to an individual, corporation, or institution; usually a transfer of government land that had not previously been titled to anyone or, if previously titled, had reverted to or been re-purchased by the government, e.g., "His land grant was for 200 acres that had reverted to the colony when the prior ***grantee*** (q.v.) had died without known heirs." Also see ***certificate land.***

land patents: See ***land grants***, and see ***patents.***

land warrant: See ***land grants***, and see ***patents.***

landau: a 4-wheeled carriage of the wealthy, with a top divided so that the back and front halves could be opened or closed independently, e.g., "The gold decorated landau of Marshall Field was well known in old Chicago."

landholder: generally now, synonymous with ***freeholder*** (q.v.); one who owns or holds land for himself or in trust for another, e.g., "He purchased the tract in fee ***simple*** (q.v.), and so became one of the forty landholders owning more than 300 acres in the county."

landmark: early, a monument establishing a boundary between two tracts of land, e.g., "It was illegal to move or remove early landmarks."

Langley, U.S.S: See ***warships, American.***

lantern clock: a shelf clock, so called by reason of the bell mounted on the top giving the whole the appearance of a lantern, e.g., "Lantern clocks date from the earliest colonial times and are now very rare."

lap desk: See ***deskbox.***

lap robe: a large, heavy blanket for use in a carriage or sleigh, often of animal fur, e.g., "Dr. Drake had a bearskin lap robe."

lappage: an overlapping of boundaries of real property, e.g., "The court determined that the lappage of their grants amounted to two ***rods*** (q.v.) along the west boundary."

larboard: synonym for ***starboard*** (q.v.).

larder: a ***pantry*** (q.v.), now, a storage room or closet for any cache of food; early and through the 19th century, that room or place where meat was salted or kept, e.g., "When the early homemaker spoke of her larder, she was referring to a cellar or other specific place where meat was prepared or kept."

lardner, lardener: though seldom seen in the colonies, the title of one who had charge of the larder and pantries of a very large estate, home, mansion, castle, etc., e.g., "When Evan arrived in Virginia, though well trained, he found no employment opportunities as a lardner."

Lares and Penates: usually, the spirits or saints that protected the household, e.g., "She wrote to her friend that her diligence as to her home apparently had 'pleased my Lares and Penates.'"

Larkin desk: an early 20th-century cabinet known for quality and usually made of oak, with a fall-front writing surface revealing small compartments within, a doored ***curio*** (q.v.) or book compartment above the fall front, and a paned, doored area containing book shelves, usually on the left, "While the desk perhaps is best known, Larkin made other items of ***furniture*** (q.v.) as well."

lascivious, lascivious carriage: as now, e.g., "The old Connecticut court branded indecent sexual acts by one against the will of another as lascivious carriage."

lasses: See ***molasses.***

last ditch, last ditch effort: probably derived from the order sometimes issued that armed men must hold their position even to the last trench (ditch), e.g., "Jackson's order was that the men make a last ditch effort before retreating."

last quarter of the moon: See ***waxing and waning.***

last, last maker: a mold over which shoes were made, someone who made wooden or iron molds for shoemaking, e.g., "The local blacksmith often served as the town last maker."

latch: usually referred to the wooden latch bar inside a door, the same lifted by a string or a handle, e.g., "The wooden beam used as a latch on the heavy door rendered the house quite safe from burglars and others not wanted." Also see ***latch string.***

latch string: that small rope or heavy string that extended through a hole to the outside of a door, which, when pulled, lifted the ***latch bar*** (q.v.) inside, e.g., "The expression 'the latch string is always out for you' meant that the person was always welcome at that home." Also see ***latch.***

late, late of, of late: one who has died or, occasionally, has departed a county or area, usually in the not distant past, e.g., "The deed revealed that he had received the land from his late father"; "The deed was from John Martin, late of Surry County."

lath, lathier: small, long pieces of semi-finished wood placed horizontally across joists or rafters to which tile or plaster is applied; though not mentioned by Johnson, one who makes, prepares, and installs lath, e.g., "Without lath and the lathiers who made and applied it, the early plastering or tiling of walls or other surfaces would have been at best unsatisfactory."

laundress: as now, a woman who does laundry for hire, e.g., "Civil War officers were permitted one laundress for each eight men."

laundry bat: See ***bat.***

laundry stove: usually a small, low, wood or coal burning stove with a flat-topped heating surface and no oven or other compartment, designed for use in the laundry room to heat water and soaps and boil dyes, bleaches, clothes, etc., e.g., "Only the affluent had laundry stoves or, for that matter, laundry rooms."

laurels: gold coins minted in England in 1619, e.g., "Reports of the early colonies occasionally refer to laurels, meaning money."

lavender water: a cologne or incense, e.g., "Brittany's recipe for lavender water was '2 cups spirits of wine (alcohol), 1 oz. concentrated lavender oil, and 2 ***drachms*** (q.v.) ***ambergris*** (q.v.)'."

laver: early, any bowl used for washing; later, the font or holder of baptismal water, e.g., "The porcelain laver revealed by the inventory almost surely was a washing bowl used with a pitcher."

law court of appeals: See ***appeals, courts of.***

lawn: a sheer cloth made usually of linen, or sometimes very fine cotton, e.g., "The ledger of William Parham's store revealed sales of ***ells*** (q.v.) of expensive lawn."

Lawrence, U.S.S: See ***warships, American.***

lay: a share of the catch on whaling and fishing boats, e.g., "It was said that Bates' lay of the whaling venture was 8%."

lay out, lay by: to fail to appear as directed, usually for work; to stand idly by while another does your share of assigned work, e.g., "When the man did not appear at 7:00 as ordered, Mark said 'I suppose he has laid out once again'"; "Jones was known to lay by while the others worked."

layabouts, louts: loiterers, and those who should do otherwise yet stand idly by and observe while others work, e.g., "Col. Thompson referred to some of his Continental soldiers as layabouts." Also see ***lay out.***

layd to, laid to (another): a designation of a perpetrator or other person who has denied some matter of fact or has not come forth as would have been expected; sometimes and early, the naming of the father of a bastard child by the birth mother, e.g., "The court record stated that 'she layd a bastard child to Carpinder'."

leach, lye barrel: a wooden container or barrel in which ashes and water were placed to make lye, e.g., "He had a tap in the bottom of the leach, from which she drew off lye to make soap."

leaded glass, lead glass, flint glass: heavy, brilliant, extremely clear glass containing lead oxide and early used in the finest of glassware, e.g., "The cut, leaded glass bowl was exquisite." Also see ***crystal.***

leaders, lead horses: that horse or horses placed in front in a multi-horse team, particularly trained to obey slight commands and to commence movement when so signaled, e.g., "The leaders in Lew's team of six were a pair of beautiful, near-white ***Belgians*** (q.v.)."

Leaghorn hat, leghorn hat: a high quality straw hat with a soft brim, e.g., "The 1761 account of John Daws revealed the purchase of a Leaghorn Hat."

league, leuca: a measure of distance, varying but usually 18,225 ft., about 3½ miles; in Spanish law, a league was 2.63 statute miles; in French law 1,500 paces; in early English law, 1,000 paces, e.g., "The distance the English ship traveled was stated in nautical miles, three of which equaled a league"; "In researching early Texas land grants, the researcher should remember that a square league was 4,428 acres, or a bit less than seven sq. miles."

lease: a possessory right in land; a relationship between a ***freeholder*** (q.v.) and a ***tenant*** (q.v.) by which the tenant pays something of value for possession and use of land for a specific or determinable period of time, e.g., "His lease was of fifty acres for twenty years at 500 pounds of tobacco per year." Also see ***lessee***, and see ***lessor***.

lease and release: an ancient method of conveyancing by which a lease was entered upon, immediately following which (often the next day) a release of ***seisen*** (q.v.) was given over by the seller to the buyer, the legal result being a ***conveyance*** (q.v.) in ***fee simple*** (q.v.), e.g., "The researcher must carefully examine all very early 'leases', as they may represent sales by lease and release." Also see ***lease***.

leather chip: perhaps now unknown; as to chip, Johnson (1755) says "in the names of places, imply a market," e.g., "The old Connecticut record speaks of a merchant and 'his leather chips'."

Leather Sealers: early elected officials in Pennsylvania whose duty it was to inspect the making and tanning of leather and goods of leather and to approve and apply a governmental stamp to that found acceptable, e.g.,

"Leather Sealers such as 'R. Skeels' were well known to early Philadelphia."

leatherdresser: the calling of one who cured and prepared hides for use as leather, e.g., "The leatherdresser supplied the raw materials for the ***harnessmaker*** (q.v.)."

leeching, bleeding: the use of leeches to heal or to draw off blood; by the 18th century, occasionally, the use of any medicines or other materials that were thought to have value in healing, e.g., "He used only brown leeches for bleeding"; "She wrote that to assist in the healing, the physician had '...leeched with green salve and ointments'."

left out: a Southern and western expression meaning that one has gone from some place, e.g., "Brittany told her friends that her father had recently 'left out for Nashville'."

lega: See ***alloy.***

legacy: a transfer of personal property by will or by order of a court in a proceedings involving an estate, e.g., "As his legacy, he received $6,000.00 and some corporate shares of stock."

lemner, limner: very early, one who drew or painted ***pictures*** (q.v.) for hire, e.g., "The 17th-century description of the man as a lemner referred to his calling as an artist."

leno, leno weave: a fabric, usually muslin; a manner of weaving that produces a sturdy, firm and open mesh as in muslin, e.g., "In the 1790s Philadelphia merchants Kuhn & Risberg advertised for sale ***gauze*** (q.v.), leno, millionet and jacanet muslin for handkerchiefs'."

lessee: one who, in exchange for payment or other thing or act considered of value, has specific possessory rights in the use and benefits of land without having ownership in the same, e.g., "Drake was the lessee of one hundred acres for three years."

lessor: one who gives over to another rights of use and possession in land for a certain term in exchange for something considered of value, e.g., "The lessor provided that the lessee might use such timber as was needed to build a house, provided that the resulting construction became the property of the owner."

letter of attorney: See ***power of attorney.***

letters of administration: the documents confirming that a person has been vested by a court with authority to control and direct actions having to do usually with the ***intestate*** (q.v.) estate of another; the court entry by which one is named ***administrator*** (q.v.) or ***administratrix*** (q.v.), e.g., "Her letters of administration also were filed in the adjoining county, since the decedent owned property there." Also see ***bond.***

letters patent: See ***patent.***

letters testamentary: those documents confirming that, pursuant to a will, a person has been vested by the court with the authority to control and direct actions having to do with an estate where the decedent died ***testate*** (q.v.); a court order or entry by which one is confirmed as ***executor*** (q.v.) or ***executrix*** (q.v.), e.g., "Having qualified as executrix of the will of her husband, Cheryl was issued letters testamentary empowering her to execute the provisions of his will." Also see ***letters of administration.***

leuca: See ***league.***

levels: See ***housewright's tools.***

levy: in genealogy, to levy a tax means to impose it, e.g., "The colony levied a tax of 1 ***shilling*** (q.v.) on each horse used in farming, the same payable yearly to the circuit court clerk."

lex loci: the law of the place, e.g., "The researcher often encounters the expression lex loci when a court spoke of the law of some other state where a contract had been entered upon."

lex scripta: written or codified law, as opposed to common law, e.g., "The Surry court stated that lex scripta had superseded the common law in the matter at hand."

Lexington, U.S.S: See ***warships, American.***

liability: an obligation, debt, or duty owed to or in favor of another person, firm, corporation, or government, e.g., "Among the liabilities of the estate was the money due the undertaker."

liber: unlike now, open and accessible; the state of a freeman, e.g., "The judge's use of the word liber in speaking of Mark's indentured servitude had nothing to do with books."

liber niger: literally, black book; the title of a book of accounts of Edward IV, wherein were listed his musicians and entertainers, household expenditures, etc., e.g., "From the Liber Niger Domus Regis we derive the expression 'putting her in his black book'."

Liberty Island, Bedloe's Island: the location of the Statue Of Liberty, e.g., "Until the early 1870s, Bedloe's Island was privately owned, after which it was purchased by the U.S. government for placement of the Statue Of Liberty and renamed Liberty Island."

library: most have collections dedicated to family history and genealogy; probably, the three largest in the U.S. are the Family History Library in Salt Lake City, the Allen County Public Library in Indiana, and the New York Public Library, e.g., "He often went to Fort Wayne to work with the genealogy collection of the Allen County Library.

library table: a sturdily built, medium to large table, often of a height sufficient to work standing up, and usually having a drawer and open book shelves on both ends below the writing and work surface, e.g., "Their library table was of inlaid walnut."

licenciado: an attorney or advocate, e.g., "Early Texas reports and writings often speak of licenciados, usually meaning lawyers."

lichen: early, any skin disease with eruptions or having a scaly or lichen-like appearance, e.g., "Dr. Lockhart used alkalies, arsenic, cyanide ointment, and mercurial ointments for the lichen."

licitacion: See ***auction.***

lick, animal lick: places where animals congregated in order to lick, usually salt, but also sometimes sweet sap from a tree or group of trees, e.g., "When large animals congregated at a salt lick, they often trod down the grass and vegetation over a large area, those areas becoming landmarks; such was Buffalo Lick which became Buffalo, Kentucky."

lick my calf, don't: See ***don't lick my calf.***

lien: when one fails to pay as agreed for services or materials, the supplier usually has a lien right enforceable against those assets or property to which the services and materials contributed or improved; a lien usually must be in writing and recorded, e.g., "Lien records often reveal the occupations and whereabouts of ancestors."

life estate: a possessory interest in land, once a part of ***dower*** (q.v.); a ***freehold estate*** (q.v.) for the remainder of the life of the person owning it, which could not be mortgaged or encumbered to an extent greater than the interest, and could only be conveyed away through the joinder of the remaining interests-the 'reversion', e.g., "Her life estate was provided for in her husband's will, and the land became the property of their son at her death." Also see ***remainder***.

life interest: See ***life estate.***

life tenant: See ***life estate.***

life, get a: See ***get a livelihood.***

lifts: See ***rigging.***

light: unlike now, a window or a hole cut in a wall in order that light and air might be admitted, e.g., "When the 17th-century court spoke of the burglar entering through the light, he was not speaking of illumination." Also see ***oiled paper.***

light infantry: riflemen having no packs or burdens to carry other than their own ammunition and usually a snack and a flask of water, e.g., "Being light infantrymen, their packs, cooking gear, and tents were brought up by the ***teamsters*** (q.v.)."

Light Infantry Corps: See ***military combat units, famous.***

light of the moon: See ***waxing and waning.***

light wood: fine, dry kindling, e.g., "He filled the basket with light wood for her to have near the stove while he was gone."

lighter: a small vessel used to transport goods to and from a larger ship anchored offshore, e.g., "Because the large ship drew too much water to dock at most places in Chowan River, lighters were used to load the tobacco and pitch and to offload the wine and other goods and commodities."

lighter than air craft: those helium or hydrogen filled non-rigid, semi-rigid and rigid craft designed and used for passenger carriage between 1895 and 1940 and used militarily from 1861 until now, e.g., "Those gas filled, non-rigid craft known as blimps saw widespread use during World War II, while rigid and semi-rigid craft designed to be used for passenger service were never perfected and were gone by 1940; some of such were *Deutschland* (the first of the great rigid ships), *Schwaben* (1st true passenger liner), *Akron* (crashed in 1939), *ZR-3* (a.k.a. *Los Angeles*), *Shenandoah* (1923-1925), *Graf Zeppelin 1* and *2* (1928-1940), *Macon* (crashed in 1935) and the famous *Hindenburg* which burned in New Jersey in 1937 with a loss of 36 passengers and 61 crewmen."

likely: while now it is used as a synonym for probable, early, it meant likable or a usually living thing or person who or which might be contemplated or viewed with pleasure, e.g., "Until the 20th-century, the complimentary expression 'she was a likely girl' was very common."

likely to crank: See ***cranky.***

limner: see ***lemner.***

limoges, Limoges, limogia: a French city, fine painted porcelain named for the French city of the same name paint, e.g., "The inventory of painted porcelain included some very early Limoges."

linch pin: the iron or steel pin, rod, or keeper that prevents a wheel from coming off an axle, e.g., "When now we speak of someone being a linch pin, we mean that he or she is capable of, necessary to, or is central to some effort." Also see ***wainwrights*** and ***coachmakers***, tools of.

line bees, lining bees: an early and present-day skill possessed by but few; the ability to watch a honeybee in flight and thereby locate the bee or honey tree, e.g., "Cane sugar being scarce and expensive, his skill at lining bees was appreciated by the entire family."

lineage: usually, the sum total or entirety of one's known ancestry through a particular person or ancestor, e.g., "His Roberts lineage was most interesting and was known across 6 generations."

lineal: in line of direct ascent or descent; relationship of parent to child through one or more generations, e.g., "He was lineally descended from Miles Standish."

linen draper: a merchant of linen, e.g., "John Griffin was an early linen draper of Cheapside, London."

linsey-silk: a homespun ***stuff*** (q.v.) made of wool and silk or linen and silk, e.g., "She wrote that, while most of the children's school coats were of linsey-woolsey, her better coat was made of linsey silk.'" Also see ***linsey-woolsey.***

linsey-woolsey: a heavy duty inexpensive fabric (***stuff***, q.v.) of cotton and wool and used for cold weather clothes and heavy duty work pants and shirts for men, e.g., "Jean enjoyed her linsey-woolsey clothes during the cold Vermont winters."

linsey-woolsey coat, crazy quilt: usually, clothing or a quilt made of patches of different colored wool cloth and stuffed with wool for warmth; occasionally, a heavy, homemade, linen and woolen coat, especially for men and boys, and often of quilt appearance, e.g., "She kept all the woolen and linen scraps for use in quilts and linsey-woolsey coats."

Lion dollar: See ***dog dollar.***

liquor shop: a place or business where intoxicating liquors are sold, e.g., "The Court referred to the business as a liquor shop, thereby revealing that liquor was sold but not consumed on the premises." Also see ***liquors.***

liquors: alcoholic beverages, e.g., "Spirituous liquors are those distilled and made from other than berries and fruit, malt liquors are beer, stouts, porter, and ales, and vinous liquors are made by the fermentation of fruit or fruit juices, usually grapes."

list, listed: early, often and unlike now, to enroll—enlist—men for military service, e.g., "Hines was said to have listed 18 Sussex Countians for service."

listed for foot, listed for horse: an indication that the person named, either through personal capacity or financial standing, was in a position to supply to the commonwealth or local militia a man to do duty as a foot soldier or able to supply a man and a horse for cavalry duty, e.g., "William Hunt was listed for horse, and James Griffen for foot."

listed for horse: See ***listed for foot.***

listen up: a command; an instruction that one give careful attention to what is about to follow; a superlative having to do with the degree of attention, e.g., "When Brittany told her students to listen up, they knew she expected their undivided attention."

liter: a unit of measure of volume, equaling about 2.1 pints, e.g., "His ***flagon*** (q.v.) of ½ liter held a drink of about a pint (two cups)."

literary property: writings or intellectual products protectable by law, e.g., "The Constitution provides specific rights to protection in literary property."

litigation: the submission of disputes for decisions and settlement by a court or other tribunal or adjudicating panel, e.g., "The litigation was heard in the circuit court of Sussex County, VA."

litigious right: a right that may not be exercised except through a lawsuit, e.g., "Old Louisiana reports sometimes refer to litigious rights."

live-ins: persons residing in a household other than that of their immediate family; unlike boarders, live-ins usually so acted and were considered almost as members of the family, e.g., "The census revealed his friend John to be one of the live-ins." Also see ***board***, etc.

livelihood, get a: See ***get a livelihood.***

liver and lights: unknown, e.g., "Mrs. Hines wrote that her husband was 'pleased with the liver and lights'."

liveried: a uniform in a particular color or design, often with emblems, arms, etc., supplied by one of high station to his employees for display on apparel, etc., e.g., "His drivers, liveried in dark blue and gold, were known to all of Savannah." Also see ***livery.***

livery of seisen (delivery of seisen): the ***common law*** (q.v.) symbolic ceremony by which possession was delivered over to a purchaser, e.g., "In livery of seisen, the parties went to the land, and the seller handed over a twig, piece of dirt, or other symbol of possession to the buyer."

livery, livery stable: the business of publicly renting out wheeled vehicles and (or) horses; an establishment for the rental of, and care and keeping of horses for hire, e.g., "Turner operated a livery stable at Salisbury for more than forty-five years." Also see ***hack***, and see ***locatio.***

loaf bread: ordinary bread in loaf form, to be distinguished from pan bread, e.g., "Marty often asked guests if they would like loaf bread with their meal." Also see ***sliced bread.***

loaf sugar: cakes or loaves of sugar, usually weighing 5, 7, or 9 pounds; the form in which sugar was sold before granulated sugar and cardboard packaging were known, e.g., "The price of loaf sugar in Sussex, VA, in 1760 was equal to $15.00 to $17.50 per pound in the money of 2000"; "Judith bought loaf sugar, and grated or cut it as needed." Also see ***sugar grater.***

lobster shift: See ***dog watch.***

lobster watch: See ***dog watch.***

Lobster-back: See ***Redcoat***.

locatio: letting for hire, e.g., "The old Louisiana reports sometimes refer to a wagon, ***hack*** (q.v.), or carriage locatio, meaning those vehicles at or for hire." Also see ***livery.***

locator: that person whose task it was (usually for pay) to locate boundaries of land preparatory to preparing an ***entry*** (q.v.), e.g., "Survey in hand, Sheriff Skeels sought out Mathias Wright to act as locator."

lock: as now; the mechanism of a firearm by which a propellant is contained and ignited for firing, e.g., "The expression 'lock, stock, and barrel', meaning complete or entire, arose from the fact that those were the three components of a complete hand-held firearm."

lockjaw: See ***tetanus.***

locks: See ***gunsmiths' tools.***

Locust plague of 1874: See ***Plague of 1874.***

lode, load: as now, but the former spelling apparently was unknown to Johnson (1802), e.g., "In addition to its present meaning, the words load or lode, as in 'mother lode', early referred to a vein of a metallic mineral such as gold or silver."

lodeman, loadman: a calling; a pilot of a boat which is used to bring a larger vessel to wharf after others have brought it to that immediate area, e.g., "The lodeman found work in the harbor at Savannah."

Logan's Elm: that giant elm tree south and east of Columbus, Ohio, destroyed by the Elm blight in the 1960s, under which Chief Logan was said to have spoken his famous words concerning his loss of land, home, and family at the hands of the early settlers while he had sought only peace, e.g., "After it died, Logan's Elm was cut into pieces and sold as souvenirs."

logcats: a now unknown game, probably played with dice, e.g., "As did Shakespeare, some 16th-and 17th-century writers referred to logcats."

loggerheads: small, iron or steel, removable catches that connected the collars and hames to the ***traces*** (q.v.), and so transferred the power of animals to a load; occasionally, the post at the rear of a whaleboat around which the harpoon line was wound, e.g., "The expression 'at loggerheads', meaning a meeting of diametrically opposed beliefs, arose from the fact that a loggerhead is that point at which the total power of a draft animal meets the full resistance of the load."

log-rollings: a game, most often for men or boys; a contest by two or more persons balancing on a smoothed and floating or free lying log, the object being to remain balanced while using the feet to cause the log to turn and the others to lose their balance and fall off, e.g., "The boys enjoyed log rolling in the pasture, the first to touch the ground with either foot being the loser."

lolly-gag: very early and from "loll", said by Johnson (1802) to mean lazing about "leaning against something like a pillar or post" and "gag" which early also meant speech spoken so lazily as to be indiscernible or non-understandable as when one slightly chokes; now, meaning to frivolously stand aside or to engage in lazy or unproductive activity while others are at work, e.g., "Sarah smiled and gently told Jean and Anne to stop lolly-gagging about while the other women were busy at preparation of the meal."

long hunters: See ***Kentucky rifle.***

long johns: See ***drawers.***

long rifle: See ***Kentucky rifle.***

long ton, short ton: 2240 lbs. avoirdupois, as distinguished from a short metric ton of 2000 lbs., e.g., "Their legal conflict was over whether the order for a ton of lead meant a long or a short ton."

looking glass: a mirror, e.g., "The 1679 Judith Parker inventory revealed the presence of a large looking glass."

loose cannon: derived from the violent and unpredictable movements of cannons upon firing when the tie-downs or recoil absorbing mechanisms were not in place, e.g., "Many are the politicians who have been described as loose cannons on the decks of the ships of state."

Lord Dunmore's War: named for Virginia Governor John Murray, Lord Dunmore, who, in 1774, in order to gain control of the then Northwest, seized western PA, thereby bringing on conflict with the Ottawas and the Shawnee under Chief Cornstalk; it was ended with the defeat of the Indians at the Battle of Point Pleasant, WV, on Oct. 10, 1774, e.g., "The Treaty of Camp Charlotte was one of the results of Lord Dunmore's War."

lord's plenty, a lord's plenty, a god's plenty: non-profane superlatives; the number or amount of something present or available is more than sufficient to satisfy the needs of any reasonable person, even an English lord, the wealthiest of all people except for the king, e.g., "When Allison asked if there would be enough cinnamon for the cookies, Diane remarked that there was a lord's plenty."

lorgnette: eyeglasses without ear pieces and held to the eyes on a short handle, e.g., "Even though it is difficult to understand why, lorgnettes were common during Revolutionary times."

lorimer: one who makes, shapes and sells hardware for draft animals, e.g., "The village lorimer made and shaped a 100 pairs of harness buckles for sale to the local harness makers."

Los Angeles, the: See ***lighter than air craft.***

losset: See ***trencher.***

Lost Battalion: See ***military combat units, famous.***

lot: unlike now, groups of one or more similar or identical items, e.g., "He sold two lots of assorted ***ironstone*** (q.v.)."

louage: in civil law, a contract for hiring or letting, e.g., "The Louisiana reports sometimes refer to agreements louage."

Louisiana Tigers: See ***military combat units, famous.***

lounge: an upholstered, long couch with a low back and an elevated end designed to be used as a head rest, e.g., "The lounge was Victorian and was of tufted wool and walnut." Also see ***couch.***

louts: See ***layabouts.***

love seat, courting chair: an upholstered chair for two people, popular during the Victorian and Edwardian eras, sometimes so designed that those seated were close and side by side and facing in opposite directions, e.g., "Their love seat was of walnut with a brocaded upholstery."

lowboy: any of many shapes and styles of small, low, short-legged ***chests*** (q.v.), having one to three drawers beneath a flat-topped surface, and often with a mirror mounted above, e.g., "She considered her Victorian lowboy to be her best piece of ***furniture*** (q.v.)."

Loyalists: those whose political allegiance remained with the British during the American Revolution, e.g., "At the close of the Revolution, many Loyalists fled to Canada out of fear of retribution by their neighbors."

loyalty oaths: those oaths of allegiance required to be sworn from time to time by early colonists variously to the Crown or to individual colonies, e.g., "Many times during the unrest of the 1760s the residents of Sussex county were required to swear loyalty oaths to King George."

lucifer: a term of the 19th century meaning a wooden match that one might strike to create the fire and derived from the tales that the Devil—Lucifer—could create fire at will, e.g., "Even well into the 20th century, Paul referred to the matches in the kitchen as lucifers."

lug: unlike now, a measure of land (pole, perch, 16 ½ feet); very rarely and to the very early Scotch-Irish, a human ear, e.g., "The early Scottish immigrant's reference to his field being 10 lugs long revealed its length to be about 165 feet."

lumbago: often sciatica; as now, chronic pain in the upper legs and lower back, e.g., "For lumbago, it was common to be treated with electricity, morphine, pitch plasters, or potassium iodide."

lumber: as now; early, sometimes standing trees suitable to being cut into lumber, e.g., "His reference to 'three acres of lumber' revealed that the trees had not yet been cut."

luminary emanations: luminescence of either animals or humans, thought to be a wondrous event to be found in the New World, e.g., "Susannah, the wife of Major Nicholas Sewell, was said to give off luminary emanations; sparks and noises 'like unto bay leaves in a fire'."

luncheon: unlike now, that quantity of food that could be held in one hand, e.g., "His reference to a luncheon in his pack meant that he taken with him a small snack or perhaps a single sandwich."

luster, lustre: a decorated or elaborate small to medium sized fixture for illumination, often a small ***chandelier*** (q.v.) or candle holder, e.g., "The 1814 Orndorff inventory listed a brass luster, and 'yt with pendnt'."

lustre, lustres: perhaps shining ornaments or glass pendants, e.g., "In 1859, in New Orleans, Alfred Kearny advertised that he had for sale 40 cases of British lustre 'in small papers.'"

lustring(s): silk yard goods, made all the more shiny by treatment and chemicals, e.g., "Late 18th-century ads often mentioned '...lustrings and other silks...'"

lusty: occasionally, pregnancy, especially advanced, e.g., "Evan wrote that his wife was 'lusty and her time was near'."

luthier: one who repaired and often made stringed musical instruments, particularly violins, e.g., "Parker appeared in the records as a luthier as early as the end of the 17th century."

lye barrel: See ***leach***.

lynx: See ***wildcat***.

M

macheen: perhaps now unknown, e.g., "In the 1790s Philadelphia merchants Kuhn & Risberg advertised for sale 'macheen and heel balls'."

mackinaw, makinhaw: as now, a heavy woolen coat for utility wear, e.g., "The inventory of his clothes revealed a new coat and an 'old makinhaw'."

Macon, the: See ***lighter than air craft.***

madam: early, a compliment and means of addressing ladies; a keeper or matron of a house of ill repute, e.g., "The word Madam was reserved for ladies, and was not used in addressing women of lower social position"; "Belle Waltring was probably the best known madam of the 20th century"

madder, mader: a yellow flowering plant dried and used for the manufacture of a yellow dye, e.g., "In May of 1831, Linda's ancestor, Alabamian John Morgan, purchased 1 oz. of "mader" (madder) dye powder and paid 6 cents for it (about $2.00 in present money)."

maiden: a young adult woman, not necessarily a virgin, at least not in the eyes of the criminal law, e.g., "Anna's indictment in Vermont for adulterous conduct referred to her as a maiden."

mail: early, a postman's bag or satchel and not the contents or correspondence carried therein, e.g., "It is from the early meaning of the word mail that we derived mailman."

mail, chain mail: armor, usually of woven metal strands or light chain, e.g., "In the seventeenth century, mail still was occasionally found in estate inventories, such probably having been kept as heirlooms or mementos." Also see ***corset***.

main engines: as now and a term of early mariners referring to the canvas sails and rope, e.g., "The three-masted Schooner, *Ferguson*, could spread a main engine of nearly an acre."

Maine, U.S.S: See ***warships, American***.

mainsworn, malesworn, malsworn: See ***forsworn***.

maize: See ***corn***.

major annus: leap year, 366 days, e.g., "The statement that the bull was born 'spring last major annus' meant that the birth took place during the preceding leap year."

majority: See ***of age***.

make distress: See ***distress***.

make hay: See ***haying time***.

mala fides: See ***bona fides***.

Malaga, Malaga wine (Mallego, Malligo): a strong, sweet wine, originally from the province of Andalusia in southern Spain, e.g., "It was to be expected that early southern colonials would develop a taste for Malaga."

maleficia: magic that was harmful or caused hurt or bodily or spiritual harm, e.g., "The 1684 court found that Jane's actions constituted maleficia, and sentenced her to the ***stocks*** (q.v.)."

Mallego, Malligo wine: See ***Malaga***.

mallet: a hammer made of wood or leather, used to strike surfaces softer than those of metal, particularly in woodworking, e.g., "Drake, the ***cabinetmaker*** (q.v.), had several sizes of mallets."

malt: any grain, soaked or cooked in water, then fermented, and then dried, e.g., "The use of malt in making beer is of very ancient origin."

malt liquor: See ***liquors***.

maltster: one who was trained in the use and mixtures of raw materials for the manufacture of beers and ales, e.g., "Maltster Drake Bater was known as one whose secret mixtures of hops, grains and sugar were unsurpassed in the making of stout and beer." Also see ***malt*** and see ***liquors***.

mammy bench: a short settee, occasionally on rockers and usually with a small removable fence extending across one half the front to prevent an infant from rolling off, upon which one might sit while tending the child, e.g., "The primitive hickory and maple mammy bench was her most prized ***heirloom*** (q.v.)." Also see ***settee***, and see ***rocker bench***.

man o' war, man-o'-war: a large ship of war, after 1700 usually owned or under the control of a government and having heavy cannon and armament, e.g., "The British men-o'-war operating on the ***Spanish Main*** (q.v.) often called at Jamestown."

mandamus, writ of: an ancient and still used ***extraordinary writ*** (q.v.) by which a court orders a non-judicial officer of government to do or forbear from doing some act, e.g., "In 1867 a writ of mandamus issued in

Louisiana against a ***sheriff*** (q.v.) to prevent the unlawful arrest of a black judge."

mandilion: a cheaply made, sleeveless, thigh-length, cloak-like garment with slits down each side, often worn by servants during early colonial times, e.g., "Because such were inexpensively made and received heavy wear, but few mandilions appear in inventories."

mangle: a device to "press" or ***smooth*** (q.v.) cloth, usually with two plates that closed together, but sometimes with rollers, e.g., "Many better early homes had mangles."

mania: a form of mental imbalance characterized by extreme agitation or violence, often with delusions, e.g., "In 1876 Susan's treatment for mania included doses of morphine and bromides and applications of cold to the extremities."

Manifest Destiny: that phrase, apparently first coined in 1845, which reflected the American view that it was our "God-given" and certain destiny to settle this continent, the Indians, Spanish, Russians and other claimants notwithstanding, e.g., "The cry of those who would annex Texas and be rid of 'foreign' interference in Oregon was 'It is our Manifest Destiny'."

manikin, mannikin: unlike our "mannequin", a small man, e.g., "The old Hollander's reference to Peter Schmidt as a manikin revealed Schmidt's stature."

manor, mannor: settlements in early New York and Maryland resembling feudal grants and usually requiring a nominal annual ***quit-rent*** (q.v.); a house and the land upon which it was situated; now largely unused, except as an occasional label for large private land holdings; occasionally used to distinguish a ***home place*** (q.v.) from other residential properties owned by same person, e.g., "Before 1740 Cole and Dimmit leased and farmed land within the Maryland Mannor of Gunnpowder." Also see ***mansion house.***

mansion house: Johnson says "the lord's house" and "the abode of the master"; the dwelling structure of a large landholder, e.g., "Early records almost never refer to a dwelling as a mansion house unless the land or wealth of the owner was substantial." Also see ***manor.***

man-stealers: a term of derision, referring to masters seeking to gain the return of their fugitive slaves, e.g., "The abolitionists were constant in their criticism of what they labeled the man-stealers." Also see ***slave-stealers.***

mantelet: a light, usually short, high quality woman's cloak, e.g., "The inventory reference to a 'silken mantelet' provided the researcher with a clue to the relative affluence of the family."

mantle (mantua, mantau), mantua makers: usually, a negligee or strapless light gown; a dressmaker who held himself out as a maker of better ladies' apparel, e.g., "One of her mantles was of the finest yellow silk"; "Dressmakers who specialized in gowns for very wealthy women were sometimes called mantua-makers or mantau makers."

manumission, to manumit, a freedom paper: the act by a master or court of releasing a slave to freedom; "Southerners often manumitted their slaves by will, and the documents of manumission that resulted—their freedom papers—were perhaps the most valuable possession of such former slaves."

manure cart, muck cart: a two- or four-wheeled cart or wagon upon which manure was loaded for hauling or spreading, e.g., "The task of loading and unloading the muck cart was dreaded by all."

manure fork: See ***dung fork***.

manuring, manuring corn hills (q.v.): to fertilize plants with food scraps, ***junk fish*** (q.v.) or animal manure, e.g., "While in-landers fertilized their corn with manure or food scraps, it was common for those near the coast to manure corn hills with pieces of fish."

maple sugar, tree sugar, maple syrup: sweeteners made by boiling down the sap of maple trees, e.g., "Maple syrup and maple sugar, often called tree syrup and tree sugar by our ancestors, were very popular, especially in the Northern States." Also see ***molasses***, etc. Also see ***sugar house***.

marbles, nubs: as now, round balls, usually between .5 and 1.0 inches in diameter, usually made of glass or fired clay and ordinarily used in games of children, particularly boys of the early years, e.g., "Evan was the best of the neighborhood marble shooters."

marble-top tables: little-known in the American colonies before Victorian times, but very common during the last half of the 19th and early 20th centuries and made in many styles and shapes, e.g., "The 1887 inventory of her estate revealed two marble-tops, both ***parlor tables*** (q.v.)."

marca, mark: German or English money, early equal to about £.65, e.g., "Early immigrants occasionally used marcas in their purchases, thereby revealing their German contacts or origins."

mare: See ***horse***.

Maritime Provinces: the Canadian provinces of Nova Scotia, New Brunswick, and Prince Edward Island, e.g., "The Acadians were those of French extraction who lived in the Maritime Provinces, particularly Nova Scotia." Also see ***Cajuns***.

mark: a symbol intended to substitute for a signature of one's name, usually used by those who were ***illiterate*** (q.v.) or physically unable to write their names; in husbandry, that mark—brand—on animals revealing ownership by a certain person, e.g., "His mark—O—appeared on his will and all of his deeds"; "His brand or cattle mark—OG—was duly recorded." See also ***marca***.

market wagon: See ***pleasure wagon***.

marksman: unlike now, one who could not write and, instead, made a ***mark*** (q.v.) on writings, formal documents and legal ***instruments*** (q.v.), e.g., "The court's reference to Hines as a marksman had nothing to do with his shooting skills."

marlin spike, marline: a common hand tool used in splicing rope, e.g., "Virtually all early farmers owned one or more marlin spikes."

marriage bonds: the first step in marrying by permission—license—of government; pledges of security proving the intent to marry (not the actual marriage) and usually required by early law, these bonds revealed the names of the bride and groom, date of the bond, name of bondsmen and of the witnesses, and insured that there were no legal impediments to the marriage, e.g., "Their marriage bond was recorded in 1755, was in the amount of £500, and was recorded, even though the license was not."

marriage certificate: a document completed by a minister or other person empowered to perform marriages, the same signifying that a marriage ceremony had been accomplished, usually pursuant to a marriage license, e.g., "The marriage certificate of Paul and Sarah was signed two days after the date of their license."

marriage, age of consent to: See ***of age***.

married close: to marry a close cousin or other closely related person, e.g., "It usually was the law that one could not marry closer than with their second cousins (the sixth degree of consanguinity)." Also see ***consanguinity***.

marrow scoop, marrow spoon: over many centuries bone marrow commonly was picked and eaten at meals, and a small narrow spoon-like eating utensil was required to remove it from the bones, e.g., "Along with her other Sterling, Anne had 6 silver marrow scoops."

Martinmas: November 11; an ancient holiday celebrating St. Martin of Tours, e.g., "Martinmas terms of court are occasionally mentioned in early Louisiana."

marver: See ***glass making***.

mash, mash a button: a term of the South, meaning to press down or to press against with a finger, e.g., "When instructing in use of the computer, Alabama resident Kemper very often would say, 'Now mash on the enter key'."

mash, masher: now obsolete, one who made advances or suggestive remarks to a girl or woman not well known to him, e.g., "While today we might say he 'hit on every woman he met', 100 years ago we would refer to such a person as a masher."

Mason-Dixon Line, Mason and Dixon's Line: latitude 39 degrees, 43', 26"; that boundary line growing out of the dispute between Lord Baltimore and William Penn concerning their respective proprietorships, Pennsylvania and Maryland; ultimately, slavery was institutionalized south of the line and by the Ohio River, e.g., "By the 1850s, those living north of the Mason-Dixon Line were being widely spoken of as ***'Yankees'*** (q.v.)."

Massachusetts Bay Colony: that name given to the early Massachusetts settlements (c. 1624-1629), particularly the colonies of the Dorchester Company, New England Company, and Massachusetts Bay Company, e.g., "John Endecott was Governor of the Massachusetts Bay Colony from 1628 until mid-1630."

mast: as in common usage referring to that upright large and strong pole from which sails were hung; forage for cattle, e.g., "His note that there was '...but little mast about' referred to the shortage of forage for his cattle."

master: as now; a slave holder; one who operates and manages a business where craftsman and apprentices were employed; one who has apprentices, e.g., "Just as Hines was called the master of his slaves, Parker was called the master of his apprentices and journeymen."

mastiff, bandog: a very large dog, frequently used for protection by families of affluence or those in very large homes, e.g., "References to mastiffs being bred for castle guard purposes may be found as early as the 14th century."

matchlock: a design of ***lock*** (q.v.) in use before and contemporaneously with the earliest ***flintlocks*** (q.v.), whereby the trigger mechanism moved a previously ignited fire source—punk—to and against powder in a powder pan, that burning powder then led to ignite the main charge and so propel the projectile from the barrel, e.g., "The matchlock was notorious for failing to fire when moisture was present." Also see ***flintlock***.

mate, first mate: that officer subordinate only to the captain of a merchant vessel, e.g., "The 1760 passenger list of the *Elizabeth* referred to Bater as the mate, meaning next below the captain in order of rank and authority."

maternal lineage, maternal ancestry: those ancestors to whom one is related through his or her mother, as opposed to ***paternal lineage*** (q.v.), that term relating to the family of the father, e.g., "Proof of the ancestry of her mother's great grandmother was the most difficult of her maternal lineage."

matertera: a mother's sister; an aunt, e.g., "The old Louisiana reports sometimes refer to matertera, matertera magna for great aunt, matertera major for great-great aunt (sister of great grandmother), matertera maxima meaning triple-great aunt."

matertera magna: See ***matertera***.

matertera major: See ***matertera***.

matertera maxima: See ***matertera***.

matrix: unlike now, that edition of a document from which all copies must be made, e.g., "The Texas court found that the copy was not from the matrix, hence was inadmissible."

matron: a married woman, usually elderly, e.g., "The reference to Judith Parker as a 'proper matron' revealed her middle to elder years."

matrons, jury of: twelve women impaneled as a jury to determine the pregnancy of a woman sentenced to death or lengthy incarceration, e.g., "Before executing the sentence of hanging, the sheriff was ordered to convene a jury of matrons to determine whether or not Rebecca Hutchison was pregnant."

mattock, mattick: as now, a heavy, long-handled tool pointed on one side and with a transverse blade on the other side of the head, used to break hard ground, cement, etc., "Every farm home had a mattock." Also see ***pick axe***.

maul, mawl: a very large hammer used to drive wedges, pilings, or to split logs; to split logs into rails, e.g., "Luke permitted Griffith to 'fall, saw, and mawl' the timber on the land"; "Lincoln spoke of mauling rails in old Illinois."

Mc- or Mac-, as a prefix: an early Irish (and sometimes Scottish) prefix meaning "son of," e.g., "The McKenzie (MacKenzie) clan was and is found on the northeast coast of Ireland." Also see ***O'-***, ***ap-***, and ***van-***.

McGuffey Readers: of the many textbooks, McGuffey Readers represent those few that are well known today; printed after 1836, from the "First" through the "Sixth" Readers, such still appear in many estate inventories, e.g., "Her great grandmother's Third McGuffey Reader was printed in 1837."

mead, hydromel: a strong, ancient intoxicating drink made with fermented honey, e.g., "Mead and hydromel made of honey have been known in England and the Scandinavian countries since at least Saxon times." Also see ***metheglin***.

meal: any ground grain, most commonly corn, e.g., "Margaret always referred to milled wheat or barley as flour and to milled corn as meal."

meander, meanders, meanderings: the wandering and varying courses of creeks, streams, and sometimes rivers, e.g., "Evan stated that a portion of the east property line followed the meanderings of Horsepen branch."

measles, rubella: red spots turning into red blotches over the body, usually commencing at the forehead and temples, and early, often fatal, e.g., " During the epidemic of 1772, measles often were treated with a mustard bath, ***Dover's powder*** (q.v.), ***purges*** (q.v.), phosphorus, quinine, fat rubbed over the skin, and tea made of wild cherry bark."

meat tub: See ***powdering tub***, and see ***salt it away***, and see ***salt tub***.

mechanic: Johnson (1802) says "a low workman"; later, a laborer who was skilled and worked with his hands, e.g., "Bater and Skeels intended that mechanics such as blacksmiths and wagon-makers have home building sites in order that the neighborhood might attract such skilled settlers."

medallions: See ***medals, etc.***

medals, bar medals, ribbon medals, medallions: those small military of fraternal decorations of specified colors and shapes, worn in clusters and usually over the heart, and consisting of vari-colored small cloth and metal parts, e.g., "Bar medals and ribbon medals very often are worn as substitutes for the larger medals and medallions awarded or permitted by reason of civil, military or fraternal service."

mediocre, mediocrity: unlike now, moderation, temperance in conduct; to a moderate degree, e.g., "Her reference to his activities as mediocre meant he acted in moderation and did not refer to the quality of his efforts."

medium of exchange, medium of settlement: very important early when currency of many nations, colonies, states and even cities and merchants were in circulation; those expressions used to describe or designate the currency or specie by which debts were determined and to be paid, e.g., "If a deed or contract stated that the amount owed by the buyer to the seller was 300 dollars in 'New York gold coin' (medium of exchange), unless the seller agreed later to accept a different currency or specie, that total of precisely that coinage was required to be paid at settlement (medium of settlement).

medium of settlement: See ***medium of exchange***

meeting clothes: See ***meeting.***

meeting, meeting house, meeting clothes: early expressions meaning a facility used by the local citizenry for meetings, religious services, and local governmental activities, e.g., The old meeting house was located not far north and west of the 1775 home of Lazarus Drake"; "Diane always referred to her attendance at Sunday services as 'goin to meetin'," and the good clothes to be worn as 'Sunday-go-to-meetin' clothes'."

melancholia: as now, extreme depression, early thought to be a distinct mental disorder, e.g., "For melancholia, he administered arsenic, compounds of gold, ***camphor*** (q.v.), musk, or morphine."

melanders, melandered: blisters or harness scrapes on the neck, forelegs or otherwise of a horse, mule or draft animal, e.g., "She wrote that her son had been worried about the serious melanders on the neck of her ***chaise*** (q.v.) mare."

melts, pork melts: the dark red to blood-colored, small intestinal muscles of a hog, used (illegally now) to darken the color of fat ground meat, e.g., "Claude told the butchers to make sure no strangers were near when the melts were added the ground beef."

Melungeons: those people of the North Carolina Appalachians believed to be of mixed Negro, Caucasian, and Indian blood, e.g., "Many of the dark-skinned Melungeons carry surnames well known in early ***Tidewater Virginia*** (q.v.)."

memento: a relic or historical artifact usually having particular significance to one's ***lineage*** (q.v.) or to some significant historical event, e.g., "Her most treasured memento was her grandmother's wedding gown."

memoirs: one's memories, usually written, e.g., "Grant's memoirs concerned much of his life as a soldier."

memorial cards: See ***mourning cards.***

men: See ***foot, horse.***

mendation: thought to mean recommendation, e.g., "It was written that, at the mendation of her physician, Mrs. Sarah Drake spent the ***sickly season*** (q.v.) in Saratoga."

meningitis: as now, inflammation of the meninges (coverings of the nerves), e.g., "Meningitis was not understood and was treated, to no avail, with potassium iodide, morphine, ice, and aconite." Also see ***spinal meningitis.***

menorrhagia: as now, excessive menstrual discharge, e.g., "For menorrhagia, Dr. Gregg prescribed salts of arsenic, ipecac, iron compounds, and quinine, or his own alcohol laced 'Constitution Water'."

mens rea: guilty knowledge; wrongful purpose, e.g., "In criminal cases, early courts frequently speak of the existence or absence of mens rea."

menstrual rags: fabric used as sanitary napkins by women, e.g., "Before the days of manufactured sanitary devices for women, virtually all had a quantity of small pieces of usually cotton fabric, called menstrual rags, to be used for that purpose, the same washed and dried after use, with only the wealthy disposing of such materials after each use." Also see ***flowers.***

mente captus: a degree of insanity, e.g., "An early Louisiana court spoke of mente captus, meaning habitual insanity."

mercer: a fabric (***stuff***, q.v.)merchant, usually dealing in silk, e.g., "Drake was a mercer of Cheddar, Somerset."

merchantman: a ship used in commerce, usually unarmed, e.g., "Many early merchantmen carried servants and slaves in addition to other cargo."

mere: mother, e.g., "The common old expression ***en ventre sa mere*** (q.v.) meant 'in the mother's womb'."

merino: wool of very fine quality, e.g., "A listing in an inventory of apparel made of merino usually reveals affluence."

Merrimac (Virginia), C.S.S.: See ***warships, American.***

merry: somewhat unlike now, the word early meant laughing or loudly cheerful, e.g., "The holiday song lyrics referring to 'merry gentlemen' probably indicated that they were loudly happy, perhaps bordering on being overly boisterous."

messuage: a dwelling house; sometimes a dwelling and the attendant buildings, e.g., "Most early deeds and many early court records speak of the land 'and the messuages thereupon'."

mestizo: a person of mixed blood, e.g., "Early Texas reports often speak of mestizos." Also see ***octoroons.***

meter, metre: 39.37 inches, e.g., "Though adopted in France in 1795, the metric system with its meters, kilometers, etc., has not become popular in the U.S."

metes and bounds: land boundaries, monuments and distances; objects or monuments and measurements, as opposed to ***courses and distances*** (q.v.), e.g., "Described in metes and bounds, the boundary was from an ash in the creek bank to a pile of stones in Flemings line, thence to the oak post in the old road, to the west line of Drake and, finally, to the place of beginning."

metheglin: an intoxicating drink made of fermented honey, similar to ***mead*** (q.v.), e.g., "Metheglin was well known in Wales before the 15th century."

metric ton: See ***long ton, short ton.***

metritis: any inflammation of the uterus, e.g., "For the little understood metritis, Dr. Lockhart administered various ***blisters*** (q.v.), iodoform to the cervix, and compounds of gold."

Mexican War: that armed conflict during 1847-1848 between Mexico and the United States, e.g., "Capt. Findlay served in the 39th U.S. Infantry in the Mexican War."

mezzotint, mezzotint pictures: an early means of creating a ***picture*** (q.v.) by smoothing and polishing along design lines drawn onto a rough, usually copper surface, e.g., "Mezzotint pictures were appearing in inventories as early as 1820." Also see ***tintype***, and ***ambrotype***.

miasmas, miasm: odors and gases that arose from swamps, wetlands, and other areas containing rotting or putrefying materials, thought to cause disease and weakening of the body, e.g., "Malaria, yellow fever and typhus were but two of the diseases thought to be caused by miasmas." Also see ***damps***.

Michaelmas: early, a common holiday dedicated to the Archangel Michael and celebrated on September 29, e.g., "Since it was written that he died at the beginning of the 'Michaelmas term' of court, she knew the death took place very near October 1."

microfiche, microfilm: a space-saving method of storing copies of original documents, books, etc.; with microfilm—the older of the two processes—each page is photographed on rolled film with one page of the original document in each frame; in microfiche, a number of pages are reduced in size and placed on a single sheet of film, e.g., "She checked out the microfilm of local newspapers and a microfiche of the book."

middle passage, Middle Passage: that part of the Atlantic Ocean lying between the west coast of Africa and the West Indies, "Literally hundreds of ships' logs refer to the time consumed in making the middle passage." Also see ***passage***.

middlings: center cuts of meat, especially loins or bacon, e.g., "Because such usually were more meaty, she insisted on middlings when buying pork chops."

Mid-Sea: the Mediterranean Sea, e.g., "Many early ships logs refer to the Mediterranean as the Mid-Sea."

Mid-Summer: the summer solstice; the longest day of the calendar year; June 21, e.g., "Mid-Summer has been a time of celebrations and observances for now thousands of years." Also see ***Mid-Winter***.

Midsummer-day: summer solstice, e.g., "June 21—Midsummer-day—was a day upon which many early contracts and land transactions required a quarterly payment, and also was the day upon which some early English colonials celebrated the Feast of St. John the Baptist."

midwife: an ancient occupation; a woman who assists women in childbirth, often for pay, e.g., "There often being no physicians in the mountains, many women employed midwives to assist in their delivery." Also see ***granny woman.***

Mid-Winter: the winter solstice, December 21; the shortest day of the calendar year, e.g., "The Provincial Governor declared that the celebration would be held on the eve of Mid-Winter, meaning the evening of December 20." Also see ***Mid-Summer.***

migrants: See ***immigrations*** and ***immigrants.***

mile: 1760 yards, 5280 feet, "There are 40 poles in a furlong and 8 furlongs in a mile." Also see ***nautical mile.***

miliner: See ***milliner.***

military age: that age at which one is liable to ***conscription*** (q.v.) for military service, i.e., the ***draft*** (q.v.); usually, over seventeen or eighteen and less than forty years of age, but volunteers of lesser and greater ages have been common in all wars, e.g., "He was eighteen, hence was of military age."

military combat units, famous: as now, e.g., "A list of the many famous or well known combat units of American history through World War II might include, from the French and Indian War: the Royal Americans; from the American Revolution, the Canadian Regiment ("Congress' Own"), Green Mountain Boys, Thompson's Pennsylvania Rifle Battalion, British Legion, Light Infantry Corps, 14th Virginia Infantry, 23rd Royal Welsh Fusiliers; from the War of 1812: Johnson's Kentucky Cavalry and the Red Sticks (Red Clubs, Native Americans); from the Civil War: the Squirrel Hunters, Hood's Texas Brigade, Louisiana Tigers, Wheeler's Cavalry, Stonewall Brigade, Iron Brigade, Duryea Zouaves, Pennsylvania Bucktails, Forrest's Cavalry, and Washington Artillery; from 1876 and the "Indian Wars": the 7th U.S. Cavalry; from the Spanish-American War: the Rough Riders and the 14th Ohio Infantry; from World War I: the 1st Infantry Division, Doughboy Brigade, 38th Infantry (of 3rd Div.), 94th Pursuit Squadron ("Hat in the Ring"), Lost Battalion, and Rainbow Division; and from World War II: the 1st Marines, 82nd Airborne, Black Sheep Squadron, Flying Tigers, Goering Division, Afrika Korps, Seventh Army, 8th Air Force, and Big Red One.

Military Land Warrants: See ***land grants*** (and notice that in NC a lowly private often received as much as 640 acres.)

Military Line, Treaty Line: terms occasionally seen in land records, meaning a boundary line between a Congressional reservation or Indian treaty lands and other lands, e.g., "In deed descriptions for lands separated by the Greeneville Treaty Line (Ohio Rt. #47) that old boundary is sometimes referred to as the Military Line." Also see ***Continental Line.***

Military Reservation: See ***Military Line*** and also ***Compact of 1804.***

military units: See ***armies, organization of.***

militia: the basis for the state and National Guard units of today; an armed body of citizens, organized by a state or a colony, and (as opposed to a standing army) active only in cases of civil disobedience, local emergency, or danger to the public good, e.g., "The local militia was 'called up' to fend off the Indian threat."

milk fever: early, a disease thought to be caused by lactation, and only later discovered to be an infection, e.g., "Young mothers feared the often fatal milk fever (as distinguished from the so-called ***'milk sickness'***, q.v.) that frequently occurred shortly after the birth of a child."

milk glass: common early opaque glassware, having a milky, pale white appearance, e.g., "She enjoyed her ***hobnail*** (q.v.) milk glass."

milk leg, white leg: undefined by Johnson, a swelling of the legs, formerly common to and after childbirth; a clotting (thrombosis) of blood in a vessel in the leg, causing much pain, swelling and redness, e.g., "She wrote that with every child she had suffered terribly from the milk leg"; "Milk leg, not being understood, was treated with ***tonics*** (q.v.), ***turpentine*** (q.v.) blisters, and even opium."

milk paint: an early coating made with skimmed milk and a pigment, usually berries or stains, e.g., "Milk paint, especially in blues and reds, was commonly used to finish primitive ***furniture*** (q.v.)."

milk sickness: a dreaded, often fatal, and mysterious disease, particularly of the Mississippi Valley, e.g., "It is now believed that the devastating milk sickness was spread to man by cattle that had eaten snakeroot." Also see ***milk fever***.

milk skimmer: See ***skimmer***.

milked, to milk: as now, and see ***mulct***.

milking stool: a short, usually three-legged stool used for sitting while milking a cow, e.g., "The old milking stool had been around since his grandfather's time."

milksop, milktoast: an unusually mild-mannered, often effeminate man, e.g., "Her reference to her husband as a milksop was a grave insult."

milktoast: See ***milksop***.

mill: See ***grist mill***.

millbills: See ***millers' tools***.

milled dollar, piece of eight, dollar, peso: early, a Spanish coin called a "reale" physically cut into eight pieces, hence a "piece of eight"; later, a peso or silver coin equal in value to 1/8 real, e.g., "Seventeenth-century trade records have many references to milled dollars and pieces of eight."

miller his tithe, give the: See ***give the miller his tithe***.

millers' tools and equipment: as now, e.g., "Writings mentioning flutter wheels, tailraces, grain hoists, windlasses, headraces, flumes, undershot or overshot wheels and wheel pits, millstone dressers, millbills, and grain scoops may be speaking of the work of a mill or of millers."

millionet: now probably unknown. See ***leno, etc.***

millstone dresser: one who carves or dresses millstones, and see ***millers' tools***.

millstones: See ***millers' tools***.

millwright: one who designs and constructs mills and the machinery for the same, e.g., "If they were to have flour for all, they had to induce millwrights to come to the frontier communities."

Minnesota, blockade runner: See ***warships, American***.

Minute Men: the name given that group of American patriots, particularly of the Massachusetts militia, who could be called out for immediate service should the colony be threatened by the British, e.g., "Genealogists have identified many, if not most, of the Minute Men." Also see ***Green Mountain Boys***.

minutes, minute books, orders, order books, judges' minutes, journals, journal entries: early, the minutes were the written records of the happenings that took place in a courtroom, and usually were made by clerks of that court and preserved in minute books; later, the written record of the proceedings in any case, no matter where or when that record was made, e.g., "Unlike the old minute book entries, it now is said that courts speak only through their journals, and journal entries are often the only record of decisions."

miscegenation: living together as man and wife by persons of different races, particularly white and Negro, e.g., "The Virginia Black Code of 1705 forbade miscegenation, and severely restricted movement about the colony by Negroes."

Mission Church, Old: See ***Old Mission Church.***

Missouri Compromise: 1820, the name given the much debated actions of Congress by which Maine entered the Union as a "free state", Missouri came in as a slave state, and all other Louisiana Purchase territory lying north of 36 degrees, 30 minutes, was to be "free", e.g., "After the Missouri Compromise, Missouri sought to exclude ***mulattos*** (q.v.) and ***free blacks*** (q.v.), causing the debates of the so-called 2nd Missouri Compromise."

Missouri, U.S.S: See ***warships, American.***

mistery, mystery: knowledge of a trade or calling, e.g., "The word mistery was common, but later was spelled mystery, from whence came the expression '...teach him the art and mistery of...'." See ***art and mystery.***

mittens: early, any coarse heavy glove, with or without fingers; sometimes, gauntlets that did not cover the fingers or thumb, e.g., "The mittens she was said to have crocheted for the children may have had fingers."

mitts: mittens, e.g., "A. H. Hyatt, of Ohio, offered 'mitts and gloves' for sale as early as 1844."

moiety: from the French "moien, meaning middle; an equal part; one of two equal parts; one-half, e.g., "There being but one other child, he claimed a moiety of the property."

molasses, lasses, black strap molasses, tree lasses, maple syrup, sorghum molasses, beet sugar: sweeteners and sweet syrups derived from plants or trees; black strap molasses is a thick, heavy, strong tasting molasses remaining after sugar is boiled off sugar cane, often used to make grain more palatable to cattle; sorghum molasses, or "lasses," results from reducing the sap of the sorghum plant; and tree molasses or "lasses" is maple syrup, the same derived by reducing the sap of the "sugar maple" tree, e.g., "Our ancestors often used black strap molasses to make medicines more acceptable to children, and used beet sugar, sorghum molasses and maple syrup-tree lasses as sweeteners for cooking and as syrups for pancakes, waffles, pastries, and on cereals and occasionally grits." Also see ***maple sugar.***

moldboard, mouldboard: that part of a plow behind the point that turns the earth over, e.g., "In early times, a plow consisted of a wooden moldboard with a replaceable plow point."

moldman: one who is trained in foundry working or in paper making, e.g., "Since he was referred to as a moldman and the inventory revealed more paper than one would expect of a man of his station, he probably worked as a paper maker."

molly pitcher(s): perhaps derived from the Revolutionary wife, Molly Pitcher, who is said to have assisted her husband's and other cannoneers when he fell wounded; any man (or woman) who acts as an assistant to a gunner, e.g., "When old Captain Drake directed that all molly pitchers be shown how to use the new swabs, he was not referring to women and their housework."

monarchs: See ***regnal years.***

money changers: an ancient and Biblical term, meaning one who converts the currency of one nation or government into that of another, e.g., "The Biblical reference to money changers in the Tabernacle is well known."

money enough to burn a wet mule: See ***burn a wet mule.***

money scales: small accurate scales or balances used to weigh precious metals and sometimes gemstones, e.g., "The 1731 inventory of the merchant Drake revealed a money scale."

monger: one who deals in or sells some food, commodity or item of trade, e.g., "Evan loved selling and commerce and was adept at it; at various times he had been a fishmonger (fish), ironmonger (iron), pewtermonger (pewter), haymonger (hay and straw), and a costermonger (fruits and vegetables)."

Monitor, U.S.S: See ***warships, American.***

monkey wrench: an early, straight-handled and adjustable steel wrench made in many sizes, so called by reason of the handle appearing as a tail and the adjustable jaws appearing like a monkey's torso and head, e.g., "While the trade mark also was a monkey, the name monkey wrench arose from the shape of the wrench."

monogamy: restrained to a single wife, e.g., "The word monogamy is the opposite of ***bigamy*** (q.v.) and ***polygamy*** (q.v.)."

monstrum: a box wherein relics are kept, often of a religious nature, e.g., "The early 17th-century inventory revealed an ebony and silver monstrum."

monument: See ***headstone.***

moon, phases of: See ***waxing and waning.***

moonshine: See ***corn whiskey.***

moreen(s): a heavy fabric, usually made of wool and cotton, and often used for winter petticoats, e.g., "In 1798 Kuhn & Risberg of Market St., Philadelphia advertised 'olive, brown and black moreens'."

Mormon War: See ***Nauvoo War.***

Mormons, The Church of Jesus Christ of Latter Day Saints, LDS: in genealogy, noted for their very fine library in Salt Lake City and for their "Family History Centers" throughout the World, e.g., "Helen spent many hours both at the LDS Library and at the local Family History Center." Also see ***Family History Centers.***

morning dress, morning clothes: early and interestingly, the casual, daytime house wear of a woman or the very formal daytime dress of a gentleman, e.g., "His morning clothes consisted of a cutaway coat, fancy ***waistcoat*** (q.v.), and gray striped pants." Also see ***mourning coat.***

mortality tables, mortuary tables: statistics, based upon averages, by which one's life expectancy is estimated, e.g., "Our mortality tables vary widely from those of the early days largely by reason of the decreased death rate of children."

mortar and pestle: a common small, usually ceramic or earthen bowl (mortar) with a handled, hard, grinding head (pestle), for grinding spices and medicines, e.g., "She ground medicinal plants with her mortar and pestle." Also see ***muller.***

mortgage deed of trust: See ***trust deed***, and see ***mortgage deed.***

mortgage deed, mortgage, purchase money mortgage: a formal, signed, and acknowledged document by which a borrower (mortgagor) conveys legal title to his or her property to a lender (mortgagee) as security for a loan of money or other thing of value; when the mortgagor (borrower) has paid the debt as agreed, the mortgagee (lender) transfers the title back by ***release*** (q.v.); similar to a deed of trust, except that in trust deeds the title is transferred to a third party agreeable to both the lender and the borrower, which trustee releases the title back to the mortgagor upon being properly informed that the debt has been paid as agreed, e.g., "As security for his loan, the land was transferred to the lending bank by a mortgage deed." Also see ***trust deed.***

mortgage release: See ***mortgage.***

mortgagee: See ***mortgage deed.***

mortgagor: See ***mortgage deed.***

mortis causa: by reason of a death, or in anticipation of death, e.g., "The common early expression donatio mortis causa means literally a 'gift by reason of death'."

mortuary: unlike now, a bequest to the parish church, often in payment of previous tithes not paid or to ease the conscience of the donor, e.g., "The Newport parish reference to the payment of 6S for mortuary had nothing to do with a funeral home."

mortuary tables: See ***mortality tables.***

mother hubbard: a straight, loose, full length, sleeved dress usually worn during pregnancy, often modestly adorned or decorated, e.g., "Her mother hubbards concealed her pregnancy until the final days." Also see ***chemise.***

motorman: as now with subways, one whose occupation was driving a ***streetcar*** (q.v.), e.g., "Early New York motormen usually worked twelve hour shifts."

mouldboard: See ***moldboard.***

mountebank: a term of derision; often a physician who publicly, as at a courthouse or ***town common*** (q.v.), proclaimed the efficacy of his concoctions and medicines, e.g., "Mountebanks were often spoken of in the same vein as were keepers of brothels."

mourning cards: those usually rather heavy and thick paper memorials to the dead, given at funerals and ***wakes*** (q.v.), they often were nicely printed on black backgrounds, stated the name of the deceased, date of death, age, and often a poem or inspirational words thought appropriate, e.g., "The 1892 mourning cards for Mrs. Martha Midlam were black with her name in impressed gold leaf."

mourning coat, mourning cloak, mourning clothes: a black wrap worn at funerals and wakes; those usually black items of apparel worn when in mourning, e.g., "Mourning coats and dresses appear in 18th-and 19th-century inventories of affluent people." Also see ***morning dress.***

mourning jewelry, mourning gifts: often bore the name or initial of the deceased, the date of death, and sometimes the age of the dead person, such rings, bracelets, pins, gloves, scarves, and pendants were given to mourners as remembrances of the deceased, e.g., "She had mourning rings and gloves from the funerals of ancestors."

mouth organ: See ***harmonica.***

moxa, moxas: dried wormwood leaves and stems placed on areas of the skin that itched or were erupted, and then were ignited, e.g., "Acting as counter irritants, moxas were thought to have great curative value."

Mr. and Mrs.: titles; in early times, used only when referring to those who held public office or who had gained wealth or the high respect and admiration of the community; usually used to refer only to those above the status of yeoman and goodwife, e.g., "As a ***Burgess*** (q.v.), he was addressed as Mr. Hunt, even though he was but a ***wheelwright*** (q.v.)."

much oblige, much obliged, I am much obliged: a common early expression meaning thank you, e.g., "Paul consistently showed his gratitude for any favor by saying simply 'much oblige'."

muck cart: See ***manure cart.***

muck heaps, dung heap: a pile of animal—particularly cattle—droppings or manure gathered together for future use as fertilizer, e.g., "Unlike now, most early fertilizer came from the muck heap."

mucket: perhaps deriving from the British expression, meaning a mean, coarse or ***common*** (q.v.) person, e.g., "Cheryl's reference to the neighbor as a mucket apparently had to do with his being rude, rough, and of poor manners."

mud-tailed horse: a term of derision or reflective of a horse that had not had proper care, e.g., "Evan commented that the old man was as 'unkempt as his mud-tailed horse'."

muffineer, muffinier: a small glass container, often of better glass, having a perforated lid and used to sprinkle sugar or other decoration on cakes, muffins, toasted breads, etc., e.g., "Diane's muffineer was of ***milk glass*** (q.v.) and was kept full of maple sugar."

muffoon: the soft, fine underfur of fur animals such as beaver, mink, otter, muskrat, etc., e.g., "The muffoon of the beaver was widely used in the making of beaver hats."

muffs and tippits, handmuffs: items of soft, warm, cold weather apparel for women; muffs, into which the hands might be placed, and tippets, being warm, usually wool or fur scarves for the neck and upper chest, e.g., "The Philadelphia Enquirer of February 1, 1792 advertised ladies' 'muffs and tippets' for sale."

mulatto, mulattoe: early, a person with one white and one Negro parent; later, any person of mixed black and white ancestry, e.g., "Even though she was but one-quarter black—a quaterone—she was spoken of as a mulatto."

mulct, milked: a required or exacted fine or tribute which, though legal, was looked upon as excessive or unnecessary, e.g., "With contempt, he said that the judge had mulcted him of 10S"; "The country man told that he had been in court and had been milked of his money."

mule: a work animal, half ***horse*** (q.v.) and half donkey, usually bred for size and strength and almost always unable to reproduce, e.g., "He had a horse for riding and three mules to do the heavy farm work."

mule chest: usually a combination blanket and two-drawered ***chest*** (q.v.) on short legs with a hinged top that opened upward, e.g., "The mule chest dated to 1840 and was of pine."

muller: usually, a stone, metal, or glass pestle used with bowls, mortars, and other hollowed containers to crush or grind sugar, spices, medicines, dyes, etc., e.g., "The expression 'mull it over' arose from the frequent early use of mullers." Also see ***mortar and pestle.***

mumblety-peg, mumbly peg, baseball with a knife: early games of boys played with usually small to medium sized knives, e.g., "During school recesses, boys playing mumblety-peg were common everywhere in the colonies and early United States." Also see ***pocket knife,*** and see ***pen knife.***

mumbly peg: See ***mumblety-peg***

mumps: as now, e.g., "For the mumps, the old doctor often administered leeches and induced almost constant action of the bowels."

muniments: documents concerning or proving ownership and title, usually to land or an inheritance, e.g., "The many early comments concerning delivery of muniments arose because recording was not yet common here and unknown in England."

murder the King's English: See ***Kings' English.***

mush, corn meal mush: a common, early, predominantly Northern food prepared by cooking corn meal in hot water until it thickens, and serving the mixture as a cereal or fried, with honey, molasses (***sorghum,*** q.v.), or maple syrup, e.g., "Will Midlam said that being poor meant you ate a lot of mush."

musket: a smooth-bored, large-caliber, hand-held firearm, first seen in the 16th century, and made obsolete by the rifled-barrel firearms of the late 18th and early 19th centuries, e.g., "The appearance of the rifled barrel caused muskets to fall out of favor." Also see ***long rifle,*** and see ***cap and ball.***

musketry: the use of rifles and muskets—hand held weapons—in battle, e.g., "Musketry probably was never more intense than in the Cornfield at Antietam." Also see ***small arms.***

mussuck: an early word meaning low, damp, untillable land; a small swamp or bog, e.g., "Early Virginia land records occasionally refer to land bordering a mussuck."

mustache cup: a large, handled drinking cup having a perforated half cover molded across the top, thereby facilitating drinking liquids without wetting one's mustache, e.g., "Affluent men often had several mustache cups."

muster, public days: as now, to gather or collect together; early, a gathering of the local or area militia at an appointed time and place, e.g., "What they called their public days and muster were usually those days upon which there was a gathering and training exercise of the local militia." Also see ***court days.***

mustizo: an 18th-century South Carolina term for a person of Indian and Negro parentage, e.g., "The term mustizo likely arose by reason of the similar term ***mestizo*** (q.v.)."

muzzle loader: an early firearm loaded by inserting a measured charge of powder and a projectile (***ball,*** q.v.) made tight with a small piece of cloth (wadding), through the muzzle end of the barrel, e.g., "With the advent of breech-loading weapons, the muzzle loaders were doomed."

myelitis: early, any inflammation of the spinal cord, e.g., "For myelitis, Dr. Drake thought electricity, ***belladonna*** (q.v.), and strychnine could be helpful."

myrrh: See ***frankincense and myrrh.***

N

nabob: a usually somewhat derisive term for a person of wealth, e.g., "When she referred to Mills as a nabob, she was suggesting that other than the wealth he possessed, in her view he was of little merit, standing, regard, or character."

naif, neife, nativus, villein: one born a slave or a ***bond woman*** (q.v.), e.g., The old Louisiana and Texas reports sometimes refer to naifs, meaning slaves."

name is mud, your: arising from the harboring and treatment of John Wilkes Booth by Dr. Mudd and the consequent wide condemnation of Mudd by the North, the expression commonly was used in a lighter vein, even in a jocular sense, and meant that one is sure to be criticized; the issue as to a person is forgone or final; one's proverbial fate is sealed, e.g., "When Evan threw dirt on little Allison's new dress, Mikaila said 'your name sure is mud now!'"

naming patterns: See ***onomastics.***

nankeen: a high quality, yellow or buff colored, Chinese cotton fabric (***stuff***, q.v.), e.g., "Even well into the nineteenth century, New England militiamen often were dressed in the colors of Washington's Revolutionary uniform; a blue coat, white waistcoat, and pantaloons of twill dyed pale yellow to appear like true nankeen."

napkin: often, unlike now, a handkerchief, article of feminine hygiene, or a child's diaper, e.g., "The napkins in the inventory meant handkerchiefs, and the ***diaper*** (q.v.) there listed probably was ordinary cotton or linen cloth."

Napoleon chair: an armed, backless, wooden chair without upholstery, common at the turn of the 20th century, e.g., "In 1910 he bought a Napoleon chair from Montgomery and Wards for the price of a good pair of shoes."

nappery: tablecloths, table linen, e.g., "The nappery in the Mason inventory was Irish linen."

NARA: National Archives and Records Administration, e.g., "She gained her ***NATF***-80 (q.v.) forms from the NARA. See NATF forms. ***nary:*** See ***ary.***

Nat Turner Insurrection: that Southampton Co., Virginia, slave revolt of 13 to 23 August, 1831, wherein 57 white men, women, and children were killed, after which a manhunt was organized and perhaps 100 Negroes were killed, and subsequent to which Nat Turner and 19 of his followers were tried and executed, e.g., "Gary's grandmother played in the old hollow tree trunk where Turner had hidden after the Nat Turner Insurrection."

NATF-forms: government printed forms designated NATF-80, NATF-81, NATF-82, etc., the same required to gain information held by the U.S. government concerning veterans, immigrants, censuses, and vital statistics; available from the National Archives and Records Administration (NARA), genealogical bookstores, and libraries, e.g., "By sending her NATF-80, she located the Revolutionary military records of her ancestor."

national guard: See ***militia.***

Native Americans: See ***Indians, American, etc.***

Native American military combat units: See ***military combat units, famous.***

nativity: one's place of birth, e.g., "Salisbury North Carolina was her place of nativity."

naturalization: the action by which the government of one country grants citizenship to a citizen of another, e.g., "The Welshman, Richard Roberts, was naturalized in Delaware, Ohio in 1844."

nautical mile; knot: a measure of distance at sea equaling 6076.1033 (once 6080) feet or a bit over 1.1 miles, originally a measure of speed through the water by counting the movement through the hands of a number of equidistant knots in a rope in a set span of time when that rope was lowered into the water from a boat or ship; e.g., "The giant aircraft carrier *Forrestal* was capable of a speed of 26 knots (per hour), or almost 30 miles and hour." Also see ***mile***.

Nauvoo Legion: See ***Nauvoo War***.

Nauvoo War, Nauvoo Legion, Mormon War: that short conflict at Nauvoo, Illinois, in 1846, between the followers of Joseph Smith (the ***Mormons***, q.v.) and those—the so-called Nauvoo Legion—who undertook to force Smith and his followers away, e.g., "The Nauvoo War resulted in the lynching and death of Smith and the migration of his followers to the Great Salt Lake."

naval stores: early, usually pitch, tar and turpentine supplied to ship owners and ship builders, and used to caulk and make sailing vessels watertight; now, any supplies for ships, e.g., "He dug a tar pit in order that he might supply naval stores to the shipbuilders on Albemarle Sound."

nave: Johnson (1802) says the "main part of a church"; e.g., "The nave of little St. Andrews Church was about 60 feet long, and the ***transept*** (q.v.) extended 20 feet from each side."

navis bona: a sound ship, e.g., "Early New England court records occasionally refer to a 'vessel navis bona'."

ne exeat: may not leave, e.g., "When the court has ordered a person to not leave the jurisdiction, early Georgia reports labeled it a 'writ ne exeat'."

ne unques accouple: never married, e.g., "The old Louisiana reports sometimes refer to a person 'ne unques accouple ***en loiall matromonie***' (q.v.), meaning never joined in legal marriage."

near, off: command given usually to ***draft animals*** (q.v.), "near" meaning turn to the left and "off" meaning turn to the right, e.g., "As did many men of his time, Dick Skeels taught his horses to turn left upon the command 'near' and right upon the command 'off'."

neat cattle, neat: livestock, not including horses, sheep, goats, and swine; in the West the word 'neat' was dropped from neat cattle, otherwise the meaning remained the same; an unadulterated, alcoholic drink consumed at room temperature, usually whiskey, e.g., "Broad Cole was taxed for four head of neat cattle"; "Todd preferred his Scotch neat."

necessary, a: See ***privy***.

neckcloth: See ***cravat***.

necropsy: an autopsy, e.g., "Early references to necropsy simply mean an autopsy."

nepos, neptis: grandson and granddaughter, occasionally the 'great' of those relationships, e.g., "Old deep Southern and southwestern court records occasionally speak of nepos and neptis, when referring to grandchildren in an impersonal or theoretical context."

nest egg: early, the single egg left in a chicken nest, thereby encouraging the hen to lay additional eggs, e.g., "The expression 'my nest egg' derives from the increase likely through leaving an egg in the nest."

New Amsterdam: See ***New Netherlands.***

New Echota, Treaty of: 1835, that treaty that ceded all Cherokee lands to the United States and provided that the Cherokees be settled west of the Mississippi, e.g., "Even though thought quite appropriate at the time, the Treaty of New Echota is not something of which we may be proud." Also see ***Trail Of Tears.***

New England Freedom Association: See ***slaves, fugitive.***

New France: the name given those territories early claimed by France, including portions of modern Canada and the north-central United States, e.g., "Until Jefferson's purchase in 1803, the land that now is Iowa was a part of New France."

new land: land not before disturbed—broken to the plow—or planted or harvested; virgin land, e.g., "Mark wrote that he was 'utterly in awe at the soil quality' in the new land he had broken to the plow that year."

New Netherlands: that series of settlements by Hollanders and Swedes in Manhattan and along the Hudson and Delaware Rivers (the capital at New Amsterdam), the territory of which was assumed and claimed by England c1669, e.g., "To the pleasure of the genealogists, many records remain of the activities of the New Netherlands settlers."

New Spain: the Spanish colonies in the New World (western hemisphere), e.g., "Because of the oppressive heat and humidity, southern Florida was considered one of the least valuable colonies in New Spain."

New Sweden: See ***New Netherlands.***

New World influence: many new words arose from our experiences with the unfamiliar conditions, flora and fauna encountered in the American colonies, e.g., "Backwoodsman, bobsled, bullfrog, eggplant, garter snake, groundhog, popcorn, prairie, squatter, and sweet potato, are but a few."

New Year's Day: now January 1, but March 25th in the English colonies, including on this continent, until 1752, e.g., "Jan. 1, 1752 was declared New Year's Day for that year, and thus ended the 'old calendar'."

New York Committee On Vigilance: See ***slaves, fugitive.***

Newgate Prison: that incredibly deplorable London prison, e.g., "Many was the Newgate prisoner who sought transportation and servitude rather than remain there."

next friend: one who, though not a legal guardian, is authorized to act in behalf of an ***infant*** (q.v.), a married woman (early), a mental incompetent, or other person laboring under a legal disability, e.g., "In 1678, when the estate was sued for a debt of her deceased husband, Anne was required to have a next friend appear with her in court."

Nez Perce: a tribe of Northern Plateau Indians sometimes noted for fine beadwork and accomplishment in hunting, e.g., "Chief Joseph of the Nez Perce tribe was well known and respected by American military leaders of his day."

Nez Perce War: the name given those conflicts of Oct. 1877 in the Pacific Northwest in which the U.S. cavalry and settlers fought the Nez Perce Indians under Chief Joseph, the latter having been defeated, e.g., "The Nez Perce War resulted in the Nez Perce Nation being placed on a reservation." Also see ***Nez Perce.***

Number 1, Nez Perce & Ila R.R.

An old abandoned train engine in Washington State. (See ***Nez Perce.****)*

nib: the point of a quill and later steel pen; that portion of a quill pen that was dipped in ink and pressed against paper for writing, e.g., "Quill nibs were cut with a ***penknife*** (q.v.), and contained a slit from the point upwards and a very small hole at the upper end of the slit."

nicknames: those abbreviations and variations of given names used to address another, e.g., "Even though her given name was Veronica, since it sounded like Fronica, her nickname was Franny."

night: at common law, that period between sunset and sunrise during which there was insufficient light to discern a man's face, e.g., "Before standard times were adopted and clocks became common, the common law definition of night served well, and after that, night became 30 minutes after sunset until 30 minutes before sunrise."

night chair: See ***closestool.***

night horn: perhaps a horn used to arouse people and give signals in case of fire or other emergencies, e.g., "The town minutes revealed that a night horn had been furnished to the toll bridge keeper."

night jar: See ***chamber pot.***

night sweats: early thought to be an ailment and not a symptom, e.g., "For night sweats, he prescribed red wine and honey."

nighthawk: See ***gullbat.***

nil dicit: a legal claim sustained against one who failed to plead or answer a significant portion of a complaint, or after doing so abandoned or otherwise did not go forth with his or her defense, e.g., "Judgments were called nil dicit where the defendant left the jurisdiction after being served with summons, thereby revealing to the modern researcher that the person may have migrated at that time."

ninny: early, a ***fool*** (q.v.); now, one of little or reduced intellectual capacity, e.g., "When they made mistakes in their games, Winnie often laughed and called her sisters ninnies."

nisei: a person of Japanese parentage born in the United States, e.g., "Many of the Japanese now living in California are called nisei."

nisi prius: a general term meaning any court, no matter how otherwise named (common pleas, quarter sessions, etc.) where issues are tried before juries and a single judge, e.g., "Even though the court was known as the Common Pleas Court, it also could be called a court of nisi prius."

nit, nit-wit: a louse or flea egg, the same combed from the hair of our ancestors, e.g., "To call one a nit-wit meant that he was of very little intellect or intelligence."

nitre, niter, saltpeter: potassium nitrate from which were made gun powder and dynamite, e.g., "The appearance of nitre in the inventory almost surely revealed a need to make explosives as fireworks."

nit-wit: See ***nit.***

no count: See ***not any account.***

no dog in that fight, I have no: a difference or incident into which one does not enter because he or she has no involvement in or interest in the outcome; a statement by a person that the result of some difference is not his or her business or concern, e.g., "When asked why he did not join in the political debate, Drake smiled and said, 'I sure have no dog in that fight!'."

noblemen, nobility: peerage (q.v.); except as visitors and occasional residents, none were recognized in the United States; usually, those who were entitled to bear ***arms*** (q.v.), including dukes, marquises, earls, viscounts, and barons, e.g., "As an earl, he was of nobility and enjoyed the benefits of that station." Also see ***heraldry.***

nodden-head: anencephaly; describes that condition wherein a child is born with an intact brain stem, yet with either none or but little more of the brain developed; a term of humor, meaning that the person so-called was not understanding that which should be easy to understand, e.g., "In 17th century America it was often suggested that nodden-heads were an act of punishment by a higher power or the work of the Devil"; "When her daughter said she did not understand the joke, with a smile Brittany said 'What a nodden-head'."

nodes: usually, swollen lymph glands not understood early, e.g., "For nodes, then thought similar to ***goiters*** (q.v.), potassium iodide and mercuric oleate applied locally were said to be helpful."

noggin: a large wooden mug or pitcher for beer, ale, etc.; slang for one's head, e.g., "He had his favorite noggin, and no one else used it"; "Bethany got bumped on the noggin."

nolens volens, no. vo.: literally, whether a person consents to an order or does not; whether willing or unwilling; a frequent court notation to a sheriff or other officer meaning that such officer is to serve the order or take the prescribed action whether or not the person being served or taken consents or objects, e.g., "The ***writ*** (q.v.) ordering the ***sheriff*** (q.v.) to take Bater's hogs into custody was endorsed nolens volens by the circuit court."

non compos mentis: not sound of mind, e.g., "The common expression non compos mentis was often used in courts' findings to explain criminal or other misconduct."

non est inventus, nonestinventus, (abbr. non est inv.): meaning "not found" or "not found within the jurisdiction of the court"; this expression often also accompanied the return of a ***sheriff*** (q.v.) when the person sought was dead, e.g., "The court noted that Parker was non est inventus, and that the ***writ*** (q.v.) had been served on the representative of the estate instead."

non obstante: literally, notwithstanding, e.g., "Early courts frequently spoke of rendering a decision 'non obstante veredicto (n.o.v.)', meaning contrary to the verdict of the ***jury*** (q.v.)."

non-commissioned, non-commissioned officers: See ***private, private soldier.***

nonsopretties: a fabric or cloth less expensive or not as well made as another of the same category in a grouping, e.g., "In the 1790s Philadelphia merchants Kuhn & Risberg advertised for sale 'Haerlem lace and nonsopretties'."

nonsuit: dismissal of a law suit at the order of a court, a finding that the claim filed was not valid, legal, or legally appropriate under the facts of the case, e.g., "The order of nonsuit found in the records revealed that the claim was considered ill-founded."

noodling: hunting for turtles or small animals by putting ones hands into the den or hole and grasping the animal, e.g., "Every early spring, Howard and Paul would go noodling for big river turtles."

noody-noddy: an expression of mild disapproval used to affect the conduct of small children, e.g., "Because of her playfulness and occasional mischief, the Sister told little Betsy that she surely was a noody-noddy."

nook and cranny, crannies, cranny: a superlative, meaning a thorough search, e.g., "To look in every nook and cranny has meant a thorough search since early times, when small objects were stored in crannies—chinks or clefts in an interior wall—and larger objects were stored or stood in corners-nooks."

nook, nooks: See ***nook and cranny.***

normal school: meaning those two year courses which provided an education then thought sufficient for teachers of the early grades, very common the early 20th century, e.g., "In 1921 and 1922, Miss Elma attended normal school at Agosta, Ohio."

North Virginia: New England, e.g., "Seventeenth-century English records sometimes refer to the New England colonies or settlements as being 'North Virginia'."

Northwest Territory: that area of the present United States north and west of the Ohio River and Pennsylvania; it became Ohio, Indiana, Illinois, Michigan, Wisconsin and Minnesota, and was first governed by the ***Ordinance of 1787*** (q.v.), e.g., "In 1788, the Fridley family settled in the Northwest Territory near Marietta, which area later became part of the State of Ohio."

nosegay: a small lot or bouquet of flowers, or a ball of aromatic materials, carried or worn on the person, originally intended to be sniffed and so counteract the noxious odors of cities, e.g., "The stench of sewage, dead animals, and horse droppings induced many affluent ladies of old Boston to carry a nosegay." Also see ***pomander***.

nostrums: later called "***patent medicines***" (q.v.); early ***concoctions*** (q.v.) touted as cures for many ailments, e.g., "Among the nostrums of the early years were Daffy's Elixir, Drake's Bitters, Dutch Drops, Evan's Elixir,

Ferguson's Eye Cure, Gascoins Powder, Goddards's Drops, Scot's Pills, Seignettes Salts, Venice Treacle, and a host of others."

not any count, not any account, no count: a term concerning worth or value, as in whether or not an object should be considered in a count or tabulation of like others, e.g., "Her comment that John was no count reflected her view that he was not a person of merit or value to his society."

not worth a Continental: See ***Continental, not worth a.***

Notary Public, Notary: one who is authorized to administer oaths as to the truth of facts contained in deeds, affidavits, depositions, and other writings, "Mrs. Diane Haskins was commissioned a Notary Public by the state."

novus homo: a new man, "Early courts often referred to pardoned criminals as novus homo."

nozzle: variously, a tea, coffee, or chocolate pot spout, or the socket for a candle in a ***chandelier*** (q.v.), sconce, or candleholder, e.g., "Diane broke a nozzle on her crystal ***sconce*** (q.v.)."

nubilis: one who may legally be married, e.g., "Early Louisiana and Texas reports occasionally refer to a person, quite usually a woman, as nubilis; that is, marriageable."

nubs: See ***marbles.***

nulla bona: no goods, absence of assets, e.g., "A common early endorsement by a ***sheriff*** (q.v.) on a ***writ*** (q.v.) of attachment was nulla bona, meaning he had found no assets of the defendant."

nullius filius: son of no one; a bastard, e.g., "Even though now a bastard is considered a child of its mother, early records occasionally speak of a person with no known father as nullius filius."

nunc pro tunc: literally, now for then, e.g., "Even though by the contract he should have finished the work earlier, the Essex court ruled that he might perform the contractual duty 'nunc pro tunc and be so paid'."

nuncupative will: (Lat., to solemnly declare) an oral will, soon thereafter reduced to writing; to create a valid nuncupative will, the ***testator*** (q.v.) must: a) be aware that death is imminent, b) with that awareness and before witnesses, make statements declaring his intentions concerning the disposition of his personal property, c) die, d) whereupon and within a reasonable time, the last wishes must be reduced to writing, e.g., "On the frontier and in sparsely settled areas where death often came quickly, nuncupative wills were frequent."

Nuns, school records kept by: See ***Orders of Nuns.***

nurly, nur: early Appalachian Mountain spelling of nearly and near, e.g., "At dusk, he assured the children that they were nur home."

nursery chair: a small child's chair designed to be a potty chair and having a raisable play surface similar to that of a high chair, e.g., "The old nursery chair had served all of Maggie's nine children."

nurus: a daughter-in-law; a son's wife, e.g., "Texas or Louisiana reports sometimes spoke of a daughter-in-law by her name followed by 'nurus', such as 'Mrs. Drake, nurus Martha Alexander Drake', or 'Mrs. Drake, Martha Alexander Drake, nurus'."

nutmeg graters, nutmeggers, cinnamon graters, spice graters: small hand-held utensils used to grate cinnamon, nutmeg, pepper, and other spices, usually home made of a small piece of grooved wood with perforated tin rounded up over the groove and nailed to the wood, the spice then rubbed against the perforated surface to grate it, e.g., "Jean's husband had punched her name into the back of her little nutmeg grater."

nymphomania: early, thought to be a disease, e.g., "For nymphomania, ***camphor*** (q.v.) and bromides were administered."

O

O.S.: See ***Old Style.***

O'-, a prefix: a Scottish prefix, early meaning "son of," e.g., "In very early Scotland, the name O'Connor meant son of Connor." Also see ***ap-, Mc-,*** and ***van-.***

oarsman: in colonial times, one who for hire provided transportation or movement of goods for others by rowing or otherwise propelling small boats, e.g., "The oarsman Hunt transported the ***Burgesses*** (q.v.) across James River."

oat sieve: a usually wooden-framed sieve, ten to twenty inches in diameter, used to separate chaff and debris from oats and other whole grains to be used in cooking, e.g., "Whenever oatmeal was to be made for the children, she got out the oat sieve."

oath, oaths: deeds and wills usually are proven by the oaths of subscribing witnesses; a sworn statement that the person will comply with some requirement, or that he or she is telling the truth concerning some subject, usually made in the name of God, e.g., "They took oaths that each would uphold the laws of King George III." Also see ***loyalty oaths.***

oaths of loyalty: See ***oath,*** and ***see loyalty oaths.***

obit sine prole, o.s.p.: used interchangeably with decessit sin prole (***d.s.p.,*** q.v.); died without issue, e.g., "Early probate proceedings often refer to a person 'obit sine prole', i.e., he died without children."

obituary: a memoriam to one who has recently died, usually in a newspaper and containing dates, accomplishments, and names of family members, and place of burial, e.g., "She learned the names of the sons of the deceased from the obituary."

obstetric: early, a midwife; pertaining to midwifery, e.g., "The parish reference to a payment for obstetric usually meant that a midwife was paid for her services."

ocasion: an accident, e.g., "Texas and California records sometimes refer to events as ocasion—Spanish for accident."

occupant claim, occupancy right: possessory rights to land; a claim to rights in land as a result of occupancy rather than by other legal means such as warrant, grant, or deed, e.g., "In his ***caveat*** (q.v.), he stated that he had an occupancy claim, having built a cabin on the property in which he and his wife had resided before any other claim or ownership had been asserted."

occupations as surnames: See ***surnames from occupations.***

octoroon: early, (from octa—eight) a person of one-eighth Negro blood, i.e., one black and seven white great grandparents, e.g., "In some states, as late as 1880 an octoroon was considered a Negro for voting purposes."

octrol: a duty or tax on goods, e.g., "Some early Louisiana reports refer to sums assessed as duties on whiskey and other beverages as octrol."

of age, of majority: the age at which one became an adult, i.e., presumed able and entitled to manage his or her own affairs and enjoy the civic privileges and rights afforded by his or her government; early, 14 for males and 12 for females as the common law age of consent to marriage; now, the achievement of twenty-one or eighteen years; e.g., "Being twenty-one, he was of age." Also see ***emancipation.***

of counsel: an attorney employed in the case at hand, e.g., "The expression 'of counsel' appears with great frequency in early ***'loose papers'*** (q.v.)."

off: See ***near, off.***

officers (army): See ***armies, organization of.***

officers' training: See ***commissioned officers, etc.***

offspring: synonymous with natural children or ***issue*** (q.v.), e.g., "In early times the word 'offspring' was more commonly used than was 'issue'."

Ohio Company: an organization of speculators and entrepreneurs who, in 1747, undertook to gain a million acres, more or less, on both sides of the Ohio River in what was called the ***Northwest Territory*** (q.v.), and also sought to make settlement possible there by dealing with the Indian claims, all to the aggravation of the French, who claimed most of that geographical area, e.g., "The activities of the Ohio Company in part led to a building by the French of fortifications on the Allegheny and the Ohio Rivers and ultimately to the French and Indian War." Also see ***French and Indian War*** and see ***Northwest Territory.***

Ohio Country: the ***Northwest Territory*** (q.v.) subject to the ***Ordinance of 1787*** (q.v.) and subsequent provisions; that indeterminate area north and west of the Ohio River, including present-day Ohio, Indiana, Illinois, and parts of Michigan, Minnesota, and Wisconsin; any of the formerly French territories north and west of the Ohio River, e.g., "Little did the colonial Virginians know that what to them was the vast and wild Ohio Country would one day be an economic and industrial giant." Also see ***New France.***

oil cloth: a common, heavy fabric, made waterproof by soaking the material, usually cotton or linen, in oil, grease, or paint, e.g., "In the 19th century, the poor often covered their windows with oil cloth."

oil lamps: usually, lamps that may be found in American houses and businesses after about 1860, a great improvement over candles and ***betty lamps*** (q.v.), they were in virtually every home by the middle of the 1880s; having adjustable wicks, usually chimneyed, of many designs and degree of decoration, some with reflectors, and burning whale oil or, more often, kerosene (***coal oil,*** q.v.), e.g., "She had eight oil lamps, including two small ***night lamps*** (q.v.)."

oil torch: a lamp for outdoor use, consisting of a metal oil reservoir of 4 to 6 quarts mounted with an open burner, the whole suspended from a post or outside wall, e.g., "Oil torches were common in the 1890s, and cost the equivalent of a pair of better ladies' shoes."

oiled paper: as the words reveal, paper to which oil has been applied, the same early serving in the place of glass in windows, e.g., "Oiled paper covered the ***lights*** (q.v.) in early New England cottages."

ointment pot: a small, lidded, glass jar used for home made salves, lotions, etc., e.g., "She always saved old ***salve tins*** (q.v.) and small jars in order that she not have to buy ointment pots when she made up lotions and other skin medications."

Oklahoma Land Rush: the name given the opening of Oklahoma lands for settlement, e.g., "By nightfall of April 22, 1884—the day of the

Oklahoma Land Rush—Oklahoma City had a population of 10,000, and almost 2 million acres had been claimed."

old dugs: See ***digs.***

old field schools: early schooling or classes held in cleared fields lying fallow were central to the frontier and back country settlements, e.g., "It is thought that an old field school was held every summer in an old tobacco field near the Drake plantation south and east of present day Courtland, Virginia." See also ***Indian Old Fields.***

Old Goody: a common, jestful reference to St. Nicholas or Santa Claus, e.g., "She wrote that she hoped Old Goody would soon arrive."

Old Mission Church: that structure at Upper Sandusky, Ohio, that served as the site of Reverend Finlay's mission to the Wyandot Indians; commenced in 1819, the mission ended upon the Wyandots being ordered to remove to Oklahoma, e.g., "Services are held at the restored Old Mission Church on many summer Sunday mornings."

old of the moon: See ***waxing and waning.***

Old Style, old style, old series, O.S.: as now, e.g., "Early courts referred to dates set forth by the ***Julian Calendar*** (q.v.) as Old Style or Old Series."

oleo, oleomargarine: margarine; a product of the early 20th century costing much less than butter, e.g., "Early oleo was colored yellow to imitate butter, and later it came with a small packet of yellow coloring to be mixed with the oleo to achieve the same appearance."

olographic testament: See ***holographic will.***

ome bueno: literally, a good man; often, a substantial or affluent person, usually a man, e.g., "Early Southwest writings occasionally refer to persons of standing as ome bueno."

omnibus: as now with engines, and early, though apparently unknown to Johnson (1802), a horse drawn bus used to carry people about a community, e.g., "Many a ***Southron*** (q.v.) mentioned the numerous omnibuses moving about the busy New York City streets."

on a high horse: a term reflecting a haughty or demanding, sometimes arrogantly condescending attitude, as though the person were riding a taller horse than those ridden by others in the group, and thus could look down upon those people, e.g., "When Jerry was overbearing, Sarah would say, 'get off your high horse!'."

on bal., on ball.: against a debt or balance owed, e.g., "The court ordered that he be paid '52S monthly on bal.'."

on the account, go: See ***account, to go on the.***

on the double: See ***double time.***

on the other side: on an opposite page, e.g., "Many court records refer to matters set forth on the other side (of a record)."

on the throne: on the toilet, e.g., "The expression probably arose from the fact that while King George II of England died while seated on a toilet, the official announcements stated that he was, in fact, on the throne."

once removed: See ***cousins, once removed.***

onomastic(s): in law, the study and comparison of writing; in genealogy, naming patterns and customs, e.g., "In the study of onomastics, the researcher must be careful to distinguish between patterns that arise from custom and country of origin from those which grow out of a desire to name children after particular persons or ancestors."

opetide: the period between ***Epiphany*** (q.v.) and ***Ash Wednesday*** (q.v.), e.g., "In early times it was thought that the ideal period for weddings was during opetide."

-or, a suffix: from the Latin, that person who causes or brings about some legal effect or result upon another person, e.g., "Having filed the lien to secure his money, he was said to be a lienor." Also see the following definitions: ***mortgage, testator, grantor,*** and ***-ee, a suffix.***

Orangemen: a secret society of Irishmen having as their purpose the perpetuation of the Protestant views of William of Orange, e.g., "The Orangemen were organized in 1795 and have been active even to now."

Order of the Cincinnati, Order of Cincinnatus: a patriotic association of officers of the Revolution and their lineal male descendants, e.g., The Order of the Cincinnati, of which George Washington was the first President, was named for Cincinnatus, a great Roman general and statesman."

Orders of Nuns, Religious Institutes of Catholic Women: those disciplines and orders of women who have dedicated their lives to the Catholic Church and its service, a few of which would be the Benedictine, Carmelite, Dominican, Franciscan, Servite, and Xavier Sisters, Sisters of Charity, Sisters of the Immaculate Heart, Sisters of Mercy, School Sisters of Notre Dame, Sisters of Our Lady of Charity, Sisters of Providence, and Order of St. Clare, e.g., "Most researchers overlook the vast records kept by Orders of Nuns especially concerning schooling and care of children, Catholic and otherwise, which records may be located through many sources, including local parish priests."

orders, order books: See ***minutes, etc.***

Ordinance of 1787: those Congressional acts for the encouragement of settlement and development in the ***Northwest Territory*** (q.v.); it provided for religious and legal freedom, opportunities for education, abolishment of slavery, and division into smaller territories and ultimately states, e.g., "The Ordinance of 1787 was the first law of the United States intended to legislate activity in that territory."

ordinary: a tavern and restaurant, open to the general public and having no overnight accommodations; a place of eating and drinking, the rates of which were usually set by the county court and sometimes by the early legislature, e.g., "By 1730 Peter Keiter had been licensed to operate an ordinary on the Skippack Road in Bucks County, Pennsylvania." Also see ***roadhouse, inn, pub, tavern*** and ***entertain.***

Oregon Trail: the well known trail from Independence, Missouri, to its official terminus in Oregon City, Oregon, the principal route for Oregon and northwest bound settlers, e.g., "The ancestors of many Oregonians and Washingtonians came across the Oregon Trail from Ohio, Kentucky, and Missouri."

organization of armies: See ***armies, organization of.***

orgeat: a party punch, e.g., "Brittany's favorite orgeat contained milk, cinnamon, rosemary, and sugar."

original sources: in genealogy, research materials that exist as originally written or preserved, as distinguished from those that may have been copied, reproduced, abstracted or modified in some way, e.g., "Among the original of her pension papers was a document bearing her handwritten signature." Also see ***primary sources.***

ornaments, trophies: those decorations, medallions, ribbons, and other accouterments supplied to a soldier or cavalryman designating unit, sponsor, etc., e.g., "The court of 1687 received an offer from Effingham to supply the county 'with Trumpetts, Drumes, colours, and ornaments'."

orphan: early, one whose father was dead, yet whose mother might be alive; now, one whose natural father and mother are dead and no action yet has been taken by agreement or by the court to appoint substitutes therefor, e.g., "The courts appointed guardians for orphans under fourteen, however orphans of fourteen years or more could choose their own, subject to disapproval by a court."

osnaburg: See ***oznaburg***.

ottoman: early, an upholstered divan or sofa; later and now, a padded, upholstered footstool, e.g., "In that the inventory revealed no other ***furniture*** (q.v.) for sitting, the ottoman listed may well have been what we now call a sofa."

ounce: 1/12 of a lb. Troy; 1/16 of a lb. avoirdupois; a measure of dry weight equaling 8 drachms or ***drams*** (q.v.).e.g., "Early measures of gold and silver quite usually were set forth in Troy ounces."

ouster le mer: See ***beyond sea.***

out of sorts: to not feel well or to be temporarily slightly ill, e.g., "Betty's ***gout*** (q.v.) caused her to be out of sorts that evening."

outage: early Maryland taxes levied on quantities of tobacco, e.g., "Early taxes on tobacco exports by the state of Maryland were referred to as outage."

outcry, auction, public vendue: early, a sale often on the courthouse steps, held by shouting an offer to sell to all who might accept that offer and buy; now, a public sale by auction held at a place determined by the owners or a court, e.g., "Many written records remain of sales at outcry (auction)."

outhouse: early, any building used in daily life that was separate and distinct from the main dwelling or business of the property; now, usually, a ***privy*** (q.v.), e.g., "The outhouse mentioned in the 1740 estate was a summer kitchen"; "At Halloween Drake and Evan enjoyed tipping over outhouses."

out-lier, outlier: those Carolina Revolutionary Patriots who left home and hid in the mountains rather than submit to an oath of allegiance to the King; as sometimes used early, perhaps a reference to a residence that was on the same property, yet not attached to a business building of that residence owner located on that same property, e.g., "It is difficult for the genealogist to identify the Carolina outliers"; "He wrote that the business of his New York neighbor, who was a ***cordwainer*** (q.v.), was in an out-lier."

out-lot: land lying adjoining or very close outside the bounds of a political subdivision, yet platted and managed under the control of a town, city or municipality, e.g., "Out-lot 8 of the village of Arlington belonged to Dr. Drake."

outwrought: See ***overwrought***.

oven rake, fire rake, stove rake, rake: a light, long-handled, metal, small, hoe-shaped utensil used to pull ashes from a stove or coals from a fireplace for use under ***trivets*** (q.v.), e.g., "Every household had an oven rake."

Over Mountain Men: those early settlers, mostly Scotch-Irish, of present day East Tennessee and far western North Carolina, so called because they lived in the wilderness in the Smokies and on the western side of the Blue Ridge, e.g., "The Over Mountain Men contributed about 500 to the total Patriot force of 1800 men at the Battle of King's Mountain."

over sea: See ***beyond sea.***

overseer: as now, one who superintended a large farm or plantation, usually with slaves, e.g., "The overseer was hired for the next growing season."

overseers of the poor: persons provided with government funds and charged with the responsibilities of attending to the needs of the poor, e.g., "John R. Martin was an early Pennsylvania overseer of the poor."

overshoes: See ***shoes.***

overshot wheel: See ***millers' tools.***

overwrought: worked up, excited, or distressed; from the early outwrought (Johnson, 1755) and derived from the brittle and weak steel that resulted from excessive working of it by the blacksmith or blade maker; e.g., "Though its original meaning is almost lost, the word overwrought is common today as a description of a stressed or anxious person."

oxgang: a very early term meaning 20 acres of land, e.g., "Johnson's Dictionary (1755) is one of the very few sources for the definition of an oxgang."

oxymel: a mixture of vinegar and honey, thought to have medicinal value in stomach ailments, e.g., "Oxymel was administered when the old doctor thought the stomach was not acidic enough."

oyer and terminer (courts of): literally, hear and determine, an ancient term for courts having jurisdiction in criminal matters; early, and in Delaware and Pennsylvania, the criminal branch of the lowest court of general jurisdiction, e.g., "Many states still call their highest courts of criminal jurisdiction courts of oyer and terminer"; "In 1807 the assault and battery charges against Mills were tried in the court of oyer and terminer."

ozaena: probably now forgotten; a complaint or malady of the 18th and early 19th centuries for which creosote or bromide inhalants, carbolic acid, and potassium permanganate were variously prescribed.

oznaburg, osnaburg: a common, coarse linen cloth, used widely for work clothes and utility purposes, e.g., "Virtually every ***dry goods*** (q.v.) merchant and general store of the 18th and 19th centuries listed oznaburg in their inventory."

P

pace, pacers: See gaits.

pack of wool: 240 lbs., a horse load, e.g., "Early records sometimes speak of packs of wool when referring to that commodity by weight."

packet: any ship or large boat that carried passengers, mail, or goods on a regular schedule, e.g., "During and after the ***California Gold Rush*** (q.v.), it was common to speak of making a trip to there on a packet."

pactio, pactum: bargaining, an agreement, e.g., "Many early records of Louisiana and Texas refer to 'pactum' and the 'pactio'."

paddock: unlike now, a large toad or bull frog, e.g., "Her reference to the paddocks at the rear of the barn pond probably referred to the toads that lived there."

paint: a common reference to a pinto ("painted") horse, e.g., "The stranger rode a young paint."

painter: early, a panther or cougar (mountain lion), e.g., "The records of early Ohio reveal frequent encounters with painters."

pais, per (from the French); per pays, trial by the country: trial by those who are of the same country or nation and who are peers of the person charged; trial by the people of one's own nationality, e.g., "A trial per pais, per pays, or trial by the country all mean trial by ***jury*** (q.v.) made up of one's peers."

Palatinate, Palatines: early, any county, city, or territory which served as the seat of the chief officer of a prince, king or ruling authority; now, residents of S.W. Germany, e.g., "The emigrations of the Palatines of the 18th century are well known to all serious genealogists."

palfrey: a small horse, usually thought appropriate for use by children and women, e.g., "Bethany's reference to the bay palfrey meant a small, medium brown colored riding horse." Also see ***bay.***

pallet: as now; early, occasionally a small bed frame or ***bedstead*** (q.v.), e.g., "They had two pallets for use when children visited overnight."

pallmall: a popular 16th-and 17th-century game in which the players attempt to hit a wooden ball through an iron ring at the other end of a lane of play similar to a bowling lane, e.g., "Drake and his contemporaries frequently played both pallmall and ***bowls*** (q.v.).

palm hat: similar to a straw hat; an open mesh, summer hat made of thin leaves of such as palm-like trees, e.g., "J. Ewing of Findlay, Ohio, was offering palm hats for sale as early as 1844."

pan; pan powder: any shallow, open, iron cooking utensil; the open, concave, round or oblong metal pan, approximately 1 to 1½ inches in diameter, attached to the side of the ***lock*** (q.v.) of a ***flintlock*** (q.v.) or ***matchlock*** (q.v.) firearm at the point where a small hole leads into the chamber and the main powder charge, the same designed to hold a small quantity of powder which, when ignited by a spark or a flintlock or the "match" of a matchlock, caused the main charge to ignite and discharge the arm, e.g., "The expressions pan and pan powder refer to a part of the lock and a portion of the ignition charge of a firearm, yet the words "dead pan," meaning an expressionless face, seems to incorporate neither usage." Also see ***touch off.***

Panic: market or financial crises, if national or affecting a large area of the country, e.g., "The Panics of 1819, 1837, 1857, 1873, 1893, 1907, and 1929 are the best known of the American financial crises." Also see ***Roaring Twenties.***

pannier, panniers: a basket or pair of baskets, early of wicker, for use on a horse to carry fruits and vegetables, e.g., "He wrote that the panniers were all but worn out and it would be difficult to have two more made before a month had passed."

pantofles: See ***shoes.***

pantry, Hoosier pantry, Hoosier cupboard, Hoosier cabinet: early, a room in which provisions were stored; later, a doored cabinet with a flour bin and a shelf above, a drawer with metal bread bin and hinged doors concealing shelves below, and a retractable, often porcelain, work surface between, e.g., "Her pantry was but a small ***primitive*** (q.v.) cabinet with a bread board for a work space."

paper hangings: wallpaper, e.g., "From the earliest days of New England through all of the eighteenth century, wallpaper was usually called paper hangings."

paper making, early: paper having been made in the American colonies by the last quarter of the 17th century, the tools of paper makers sometimes appear in inventories, e.g., "A listing in an inventory of rag stampers, plating hammers, plating rollers, hollanders, knife drums, stuff chests, tub barrows, agitators (hogs), paper molds, laid paper, deckles, and felts likely reveals that the deceased was involved in paper making."

paper molds: See ***paper making.***

paper of needles: a small stiff paper package of needles as sold by stores, e.g., "The 1847 inventory revealed 8 papers of Scots needles."

paper pins: those headed, straight, very thin, pointed steel pins very common before the invention of the stapler and the paper clip, and used to attach together two or more pieces of paper, e.g., "The 1830 store inventory revealed '12 lots of paper pins'."

papist, popery: a word of reproach for a person of or beliefs in the Catholic faith; Roman Catholicism, e.g., "It was said that many New Englanders hated all papists"; "Those merely believing in and adhering to the tenets of popery were not called papists, except in reproach."

parakeets: See ***Carolina Parakeets.***

paraphernalia, parapherna, paraphenalia: unlike now, property belonging to a married woman other than her ***dowry*** (q.v.), e.g., "Among her paraphernalia was a beautiful bay mare."

parcel: early, a small group of small animals, e.g., "He bought a parcel of rabbits."

paregoric: as now, a mixture of ***camphor*** (q.v.) and opium dissolved in alcohol, e.g., "Paregoric was widely used as a cure for diarrhea in children."

parianware, parian ware: sometimes, unglazed earthenware; more often, white, hard-surfaced porcelain, e.g., "Introduced in the 1850s, by 1860 parianware was being widely advertised, even in the West."

parish: an ecclesiastical district, having its own church or churches and pastors, priests, or ministers, e.g., "The parishes of early times had very great influence on the lives, conduct, and property of the parishioners." Also see ***processioning.***

parity of hands: a comparison of handwriting samples for authentication of a document where there are no witnesses summonable or available to the court; a doctrine used by genealogists to show identity of signators of documents, e.g., "Since there was no one yet living who witnessed his signing of the will, a determination by parity of hands was ordered."

parlor stove: a small, usually somewhat ornate, iron heating stove, often situated offsetting one of the outside walls, having limited fuel capacity, and fired only when guests were expected, e.g., "The parlor stove was lit several hours before Allison's guests were to arrive."

parlor table, center table: better tables of many styles and designs, from simple to very ornate, 20" to 40" across, often square with an open shelf serving as a stretcher, placed about a parlor or room, quite usually beside a chair, and used for placement of a lamp, perhaps a photo or ink drawing, and a book or two, e.g., "Allison had two ***wingback chairs*** (q.v.) and a parlor table for each." Also see ***tea table.***

parlor, sitting room: the room where special events were held or guests were entertained, e.g., "Bethany's parlor contained her best ***furniture*** (q.v.), carpet, and lamps and went undisturbed until special occasions or honored guests were at hand."

parson: early, a high honor and distinguished title; now, any preacher, even if of little education or learning, e.g., "In the early colonies, the term parson was bestowed only upon those ministers or preachers of high regard."

parsonage: early, a portion of the tithes, church lands, and offerings set aside for the minister—the ***parson*** (q.v.); now, the house or dwelling owned by the church and occupied by the minister serving that congregation, e.g., "Pastor Drake Bater's parsonage included the house and 18% of the tithes and offerings received from the parishioners."

partition: a wall; a legal action by which assets, usually real property, are divided; commonly, a division of the assets of a decedent among heirs, e.g., "Freeburn's will directed that a partition was to be built through a bed chamber, meaning that the room was to be divided by a wall"; "Since the land was left to the widow and several children jointly, a partition was sought by the children."

partition, deed of: an instrument of conveyance by which co-owners divide land they own into smaller tracts; a deed resulting from the action of a court ordering the partition or separation of the interests of the parties or co-owners of property, e.g., "All having interests by reason of the death of their father ***intestate*** (q.v.), the children executed a deed of partition dividing the land into a smaller farm for each." Also see ***partition***.

partner's desk: a very large, sturdy, flat-topped desk, having knee holes and drawers on opposing sides of the writing and work surface, and designed for two people to work facing each other, e.g., "The old Calthrop Neck lawyers had used the oak partner's desk for sixty years."

Partridge Island: See ***South St. Wharf.***

parvis, parviz, parvise, occasionally paradise: early, a ***church porch*** (q.v., Johnson 1802); a roofed, sometimes enclosed, space at the front of a church and sometimes with a ***stoup*** (q.v.), e.g., "The parvis of St. John's was enclosed and occasionally used early as a small place of instruction."

pass the buck: to defer, decline, or fail to be candid when there is an obligation to do so, deriving from early card games where a token—a buck—was passed around the table to the next person to deal, and should that person decline to do so, he would then "pass the buck" to the person on his left, signifying that he had chosen not to take his turn, e.g., "Ms Colleen said that he had 'passed the buck' when the clerk stated that the warranty was not his responsibility."

passage: as today commonly; early and until well into the 20th century, any extended ocean voyage of a ship, e.g., "He referred to anchoring in Cuba after virtually 'every passage' and of there contracting with the firm of Bater and Haskins for supplies and cargo."

passage money: sums paid for transportation by sea, e.g., "Many early records show debts for passage money."

passenger lists: those listings of people who were transported, usually across the Atlantic Ocean, from specific places or aboard named ships, e.g., "The name Johann Knertzer was found in the passenger list of the ship *Charming Nancy* when it departed Bremerhaven in 1728."

Passenger Pigeons: See ***pigeons.***

passenger ships: as now, the great passenger carrying vessels that met the burgeoning need for transoceanic travel and emigration, e.g., "Any list of the great passenger ships of the 19th and early 20th centuries surely should include *America* (1940), *Aquitania* (1914), *Austral* (1881), *Baltic* (1850), *Canada* (1848), *City of Glasgow* (1850), *Hammonia* (1867), *Imperator* (1913), *Khersonese* (1857), *Lusitania* (1906), *Mauretania* (1907), *Michelangelo* (1965), *Nieuw Amsterdam* (1938), *Normandie* (1935), *Orcades* (1937), *Péreire* (1866), *Persia* (1856), *Queen Mary* (1936), *Titanic* (1912), and *Vicksburg* (1872)."

The magnificent liner "Mauretania," sister ship of "Lusitania."

Passion Week: the week preceding Easter, e.g., "While the term Passion Week was more common in old England, it occasionally is mentioned in early American colonial records."

patacoon: a Spanish coin of the 18th century, apparently having a value of about 4S.8p, e.g., "It was not remarkable that the early 18th-century merchant showed receipt of three patacoons."

paten: Johnson (1802) says 'a small shallow vessel of metal from which meat is eaten; any small, shallow open container, especially as used in churches for collection of offerings, e.g., "We now usually call a paten a plate, especially as in collection plate."

patent medicine: so-called, since in the 19th and early 20th centuries patents might be had upon ***concoctions*** (q.v.) or ***nostrums*** (q.v.) without regard to their merits or medicinal value; any of the myriad concoctions said to have medicinal value, and consisting mostly of alcohol, ***bitters*** (q.v.), plant or tar extracts, flavoring, and sweeteners, e.g., "Drake's Bitters was a very well known patent medicine of the late 19th century."

patents, letters patent: a conveyance of land from a government, either previously untitled or in which a prior title has been extinguished, e.g., "He received forty acres by deed and one hundred acres by patent from the colony." Also see ***grant, land grant.***

SPEER'S SAMBUCI WINE!

PURE, AND FOUR YEARS OLD,

OF CHOICE OPORTO GRAPE,

FOR PHYSICIANS' USE.

For Females, Weakly Persons & Invalids.

Sambuco Vine of Portugal, the Great Remedy for Kidney Affections, Rheumatism, and all Chronic Complaints.

Excellent Wines for Females.

Every family, at this season, should use the

SAMBUCI WINE,

Celebrated in Europe for its medicinal and beneficial qualities as a gentle Stimulant, Tonic, Diuretic and Sudorific, highly esteemed by eminent physicians, used in European and American Hospitals, and by some of the first families in Europe and America.

AS A TONIC

It has no equal, causing an appetite and building up the system, being entirely a pure wine of a most valuable grape.

AS A DIURETIC,

It imparts a healthy action to the Glands and Kidneys, and Urinary Organs, very beneficial in Dropsy, Gout, and Rheumatic affections.

A delightful 1864 newspaper ad comparing women to "weakly persons and invalids," and suggesting that the wine advertised was sure to have value for women suffering many debilities.

paternal lineage (or ancestry): those ancestors to whom one is related through his or her father, as distinguished from ***maternal lineage*** (q.v.) which relates to the mother, e.g., "Learning of the ancestry of her father's great grandmother was the most difficult of her paternal lineage."

patience of Xanthippe: See ***Xanthippe, patience of.***

patroon: proprietors of early Dutch New York and New Jersey manors, e.g., "The patroons often left detailed records of their tenants and ***lessees*** (q.v.)."

patruus, patruus magnus, patruus major, patruus maximus: father's brother, great uncle on father's side, great-great uncle on father's side, triple-great uncle on father's side, e.g., "Early Louisiana records occasionally refer to a person as patruus, etc.".

patroller: a minor county official, usually under the supervision of a sheriff or constable, whose task it was to observe over a protracted period a very limited area usually in the vicinity of his residence, and report illegalities such as failures to pay tithes or taxes on crops, livestock and such, e.g., "The Patrollers of the antebellum South often served to ascertain whether or not blacks wandering about or on the roads had 'passes' or permission to be there."

patten: a separate thick sole attachable to shoes of women, thus elevating the shoe above footpath water and mud, e.g., "Mikaila had several pairs of pattens for use on rainy days."

patties, patty: little pies, cakes, or sweet pastries, e.g., "The rhyme 'Patty cake, patty cake, baker's man...', for centuries used to entertain children, derives from the little pastries called patties." Also see ***patty pan.***

patty pan: a pan for baking ***patties*** (q.v.), e.g., "There were 2 patty pans in the inventory." Also see ***patty.***

patutie, patut: the buttocks, e.g., "Winnie often said, smilingly, that she would bet her patutie that something was so."

pauper schools: established in Maryland by 1723, along with apprenticeships they provided often the only educational opportunities there were for early Southern poor young people, e.g., "While children of the rich were tutored or attended private schools, the poor often had to do without or wait for pauper schools."

Paxton Boys: those men from the western fringe of Pennsylvania settlement who were ordered arrested after their attacks upon peaceful Conestoga Indians, following which (1763), at Franklin's urging, rather than attack the legislators they submitted a petition resulting in greater protection for their frontier families, e.g., "The Martin family was well represented among the Paxton Boys."

pays, per pays, pais, per pais: See ***pais, per.***

pear cider: See ***perry.***

pebble spectacles, pebble glasses, pebble specs: early, quite unlike now, spectacles made of the clear, transparent, often quartz crystals found in nature; later, eyeglasses made of any clear transparent, colorless glass, e.g., "Gregor and Co., Camp and Canal Sts., New Orleans, advertised a variety of pebble specs as early as April 1859."

peck: 2 gallons dry measure, e.g., "He had a peck basket."

pectoral, pectoral cross, pectoral pendant: items of decoration or jewelry worn at the bosom, e.g., "Jean's beautiful pectoral cross was of silver."

pedigree: one's ***lineage*** (q.v.); the lines of ancestry through which one descends; a chart, account, register, or drawing of ancestry, e.g., "Drake's pedigree included Henry VI."

pedigree charts: those genealogical forms used to depict one's ancestry over several generations, e.g., "The five-generation pedigree chart is one of the most commonly used forms."

peel, slice, fire slice, thible: a thin, flat, round or oblong, handled cooking utensil used to move bread, etc., about, to, and from a hot oven, e.g., "Peels are often listed in early inventories." Also see ***pey peel***.

peerage, peeress, peer: In England, Wales, Scotland, and Ireland, refers to the five (5) degrees of nobility, e.g., "The peerage—degrees of nobility—were and are (in descending order) duke and duchess, marquis and marquise, earl (very early, called count) and countess, viscount and viscountess, and baron and baroness"; "A woman might be a peeress either in her own right or by reason of marriage to a peer." Also see ***peers***, see ***baronage***, and see ***heraldry***.

peers: originally, the nobility; now more commonly, one's equals, e.g., "A trial by one's peers means by a jury of citizens (one's countrymen)." Also see ***pais, per***.

pellagra: See ***blacktongue***.

peltries, pelts: uncured animal skins, usually only salted for preservation till processing, e.g., "In 1803 Fridley traded 900 peltries of muskrats, raccoons, foxes, and wildcats for 360 acres of Ohio land."

pelts: See ***peltries***.

Pembroke table: a small, usually well-made table with short drop leaves forming a square top, e.g., "Pembroke tables were highly favored because of the space saved when not in use." Also see ***drop-leaf table***.

pence ("d" early, or "p" more recently): a British denomination of money used as a standard in colonial America and for many years thereafter in several of the states; early, there were twelve and more recently ten pence in a ***shilling*** ("S" or "s" q.v.), e.g., "Tobacco had an established value of two pence (2d) per pound during most of the latter half of the 17th century."

BOSTON, JAN. 4.—*Weights.*—We learn that an agreement is circulating among the merchants for signers, to substitute, after the first of February next, the decimal 100 pounds for the hundred and quarters of English weight. We are gratified that our merchants have taken this step: It is a great improvement in the old mode, and will facilitate calculations in mercantile transactions. We wish that the different sections of our country would abolish the use of local currency and substitute the federal. A man now starting from Boston with a plain four pence half penny, for the South, finds it changed to sixpence in New York, to a fi'penny-bit in Philadelphia, to an eight pence in North Carolina, and to three pence in Georgia!—*Statesman.*

An article about the differences in local currencies, from the "National Intelligencer," Washington (D.C.), Jan. 18, 1825.

pencil post bed: a canopied bed with graceful, thin, narrow, and often gently tapered corner posts, e.g., "Allison's only really fine antique was the cherry pencil post bed of her great grandmother."

penknife, pen knife: now, any small knife carried in the pocket; early, so called since the same were quite usually used to make ***nibs*** (q.v.) for writing pens by splitting the ends of goose quills, e.g., "Since the 1753 inventory revealed the presence of a penknife, perhaps someone in the family could write." Also see ***quill pens*** and see ***nib***.

Pennsylvania Bucktails: See ***military combat units, famous.***

Pennsylvania Dutch: See ***Dutch***.

Pennsylvania Dutch ware: See ***spatterware.***

Pennsylvania rifle: See ***long rifle.***

Pennsylvania Rifle Battalion, First: See ***military combat units, famous.***

penny: See ***pence***.

pension records: those documents and data having to do with the military movements, activities, compensation and pensions of veterans, and their statements relating to such activities and stipends, e.g., "The proof of Diane's ancestor's combat service was revealed in his Revolutionary War pension records."

peonage, peons: bondage for debt; being ordered to serve a creditor nearly as a slave until the labor was thought to have equaled the obligation or indebtedness, the practice continued in the South until post-Civil War, e.g., "The records of Alabama, Florida, and Georgia reveal many instances of peonage that should be examined by genealogists." Also see ***debtors' prisons.***

peonia: a plot of land 50' X 100', formerly the reward to a Spanish military man for service, e.g., "Early California records occasionally refer to a peonia of land, thus providing a clue to the military service of an earlier owner."

pepperbox: an early, small, common, usually ***single action*** (q.v.) pistol or ***handgun*** (q.v.), wherein an elongated, revolving cylinder served as chamber and barrel capable of shooting five to nine shots without reloading, e.g., "As a lady of the night, she carried a pepperbox in her ***muff*** (q.v.)."

peppercorn: a single pepper seed, e.g., "As now, black pepper could be purchased in the form of dried peppercorns in bulk and then ground as needed for use of the household."

per stirpes: (Lat., by the stalk of) where one inherits that property, real or personal, that an ancestor would have inherited had that ancestor survived the benefactor, e.g., "Since the fourth son was dead, the ***devise*** (q.v.) to him went to his two children, per stirpes."

perambulate, perambulator: to survey or to inspect by passing through and observing, e.g., :"The office of Perambulator held in 1700 by Richard Skeels was common in what is now United Kingdom and in New England, and officer Skeels was, from time to time, called upon to list and evaluate lands, crops, and such other property as was to be regulated, controlled, taxed or owned by the political subdivision served by him." Also see ***fence viewer.***

perca: See ***pole.***

perch, square perch: See ***pole***.

Percheron: a breed of powerful, heavy draft horses, originally bred in France, usually black or dark gray, e.g., "He had a team of black Percherons." Also see ***draft animals.***

perfect a title: to clear a title; to remove all encumbrance or charges against the title of or ownership in any property, e.g., "Because of the old ***lien*** (q.v.) that had never been removed from the record of the Haskins land, Drake Bater was asked to perfect the title.

perfumer, perfumier: the occupation of mixing, bottling, and selling perfumes and colognes, e.g., "Mr. In den Hoffen is thought to have been an early Philadelphia perfumier."

periapt: See ***amulet.***

periodicals: any publications issued at regular time intervals; in genealogy, those publications concerned with matters of interest to researchers or concerning particular families or geographical areas, or both, e.g., "The periodicals maintained by the library included *1880 Hotel Newsletter* and Mrs. Linn's *Rowan County Register*, and *Heritage Quest.*"

peritonitis: as now, any infection of the peritoneum, e.g., "Before modern drugs, peritonitis was almost always fatal."

periwigs: as now, a wig, e.g., "In colonial times, virtually all affluent ladies and gentlemen owned and wore periwigs."

perpetuities (rule against): those provisions of law, dating to Henry VIII, that limit restrictions upon the right to convey title to real estate; generally, one may not restrict transfers of title to real estate beyond a life (or lives) in being at the time of the conveyance, plus twenty-one additional years, e.g., "His deed conveying the land 'for so long as St. Peter's Church shall stand' and then to his son's descendants violated the rule against perpetuities."

perquisites: anything gained through work or purchased with personal sums, e.g., "Perquisites mentioned in court reports almost never include property gained through inheritance or purchased with inherited sums."

perry: pear cider or liquor made from pears, e.g., "Perry, once very popular in America and easily made, was seldom seen after 1900."

persian(s): very fine, usually gray, black or brown fabrics made from the wool of lambs of Karakul sheep, e.g., "The persians advertised by fabric merchants of the colonies had nothing to do with cats."

personalty: all property other than real estate, and including money, e.g., "North Carolina treated slaves as personalty, however Virginia often dealt with them as though they were real estate." See ***assets.***

personero: attorney, e.g., "Many records of early California, New Mexico, and Texas refer to personero, meaning the attorneys involved in the matter under discussion."

Peruvian bark: See ***cinchona.***

pesa: 256 lbs., e.g., "Early shipping and commerce records of Spanish-speaking states often refer to pesas of commodities."

petit: small, minor; in law, the designation of a ***jury*** (q.v.) convened for hearing and determining facts in open court, e.g., "Of the common juries, there are petit juries and grand juries."

petit four, petit fours, petits fours: small, frosted or sugared cakes, early usually taken with tea, e.g., "Her reference to having 'tea and petit fours' revealed that she likely was above the ***common*** (q.v.) folks in manners and background."

petition of vacation: See ***vacation, petition of.***

petticoat: early and occasionally, a ***waistcoat*** (q.v.); usually a decorated underskirt for a woman, e.g., "Sometimes she wore several petticoats, each designed and intended to be slightly visible at the bottom when she danced and turned."

pettifogger: a lawyer who engages in less than honorable legal activity, or who undertakes petty claims of questionable validity, e.g., "In the days when those of the legal profession were considered people of high honor and station, being branded a pettifogger was a gross insult."

pettitoes: hogs' feet pickled or otherwise prepared for eating; the feet of children, e.g., "Johnson's definition of pettitoes quotes Shakespeare as 'feet in contempt'."

pew: unlike now, an enclosed seat or group of seats, usually restricted to families of men of affluence who contributed substantially to that church, e.g., "The Washington family had a pew of eight seats."

pewter cupboard: any open shelved cupboard, e.g., "Having no ***china cabinet*** (q.v.), the pewter cupboard was used to store Bethany's better dishes."

pewter, pewterware: early, a metal considered more desirable for eating utensils than all others except platinum, gold and silver; precious metals, having always been expensive, some had, as a substitute, pewter—a mixture of tin and lead (and sometimes copper); was manufactured here before 1650 and common by 1675, and virtually every estate of any size listed one or more items of pewter, e.g., "Seventeenth and 18th-century inventories reveal many pewter plates."

pewterer: a smith of pewter; one who worked pewter, e.g., "Richard Parker was one of the earliest of the Virginia pewterers."

pewterers' tools: as now, e.g., "The presence of a pewterer may be revealed where an estate inventory includes burnishers, floats, hooks, plate, spoon, and buckle molds, and quantities of pewter and 'hollow pewter'."

pewtermonger: See ***monger***.

pey peel, pey slice: while ***peels*** (q.v.) and slices are familiar, "pey" peels are now unknown; may have meant pie peel or a greased peel, e.g., "The 1679 Surry county inventory of Judith Parker listed '1 pey peel'."

phaeton: a better made, light, four-wheeled carriage with a top that usually was removable, e.g., "A phaeton that belonged to Andrew Jackson is on display at his mansion near Nashville."

pharmaceutist: a pharmacist or sometimes an ***apothecary*** (q.v.), e.g., "In addition to gaining chemicals and supplies from the ***druggist*** (q.v.), the early pharmaceutist or apothecary often was called upon to gather and mix natural herbs, berries, roots, and plants." Also see ***druggist***.

phases of the moon: See ***waxing and waning.***

Philadelphia Wagon Road: See ***Wagon Road, Great.***

philly-mort: from the French but commonly used in the American colonies; a ***sadd color*** (q.v.), early described as the brown shade of a dead leaf; e.g., "Miss Anne Lindsay's shawl was philly-mort and of fine cashmere."

phlebitis: as now, e.g., "Early, phlebitis was not understood, and often was treated with ***blisters*** (q.v.)."

phlebotomy, phlebotomist: one who was knowledgeable in the methods of ***bleeding*** (q.v.) or ***cupping*** (q.v.), e.g., "The barber also served as the village phlebotomist."

phlegm: See ***humours.***

Phoebe lamps: See ***betty lamp.***

phonetic: the spelling of words by the spoken sound of the same, rather than through custom or rules of language, e.g., "Her phonetic spelling of the German "Koerner" was 'C a r n e r'."

phthisis, fuhthisis: See ***tuberculosis.***

physician, physition: those who through the use of medicines, herbs, and ***concoctions*** (q.v.) sought to cure or alleviate pains and illnesses; early, clearly distinguished from surgeons (***chirurgeons***, q.v.), e.g., "As a physician, Dr. Drake utilized many of the herbs used by the Indians."

pick up sticks: a game; moving small sticks without disturbing others; see ***games (of children).***

pick, pick-axe: pick—as now—a heavy, handled tool pointed on both ends of the head, and used to break hard ground, cement, etc.; a pick axe has an axe blade on one side of the head and a point on the other end, e.g., "Many inventories reveal the presence of a pick or pick-axe or both." Also see ***mattock.***

picture: early, any depiction of a person or scene, including paintings, etchings, prints, photos, charcoal sketches, etc., e.g., "The 'pictures' appearing in very early inventories were usually silhouettes, charcoal sketches or oil paintings."

pie safe: a small pantry; a short legged, doored cabinet, usually with 3 or 4 shelves, and with one or two drawers below, circulation of air being achieved through perforated tin or screen in the panels of the sides or doors, or both, e.g., "Mikaila's pie safe, as were most in the South, was made of pine."

piece of eight: See ***milled dollar.***

piecrust table: any of several popular styles of small tables, including ***tilt-tops*** (q.v.) that have a scalloped edge (like a pie crust) on the top surface, e.g., "Brittany's pie crust tea table was beautiful ***burl*** (q.v.) inlaid walnut."

pig in a poke: derived from the early practice of carrying young pigs that were for sale in a burlap sack or poke; to purchase something without first examining or inspecting it, e.g., "When Bethany bought the ring without first looking at it, her father told her she should have known better than 'to buy a pig in a poke'." Also see ***sight unseen.***

pig nut, pignut: hickory nuts; the nut from the American hickory tree, e.g., "Maggie spent hours each fall picking the meat from pignuts and walnuts for use in her winter cakes and holiday cookies."

pigeon holes, cubby holes, cubbies: small compartments without doors, typically found in desks, e.g., "The ***rolltop desk*** (q.v.) had a small drawer and eight pigeon holes beneath the tambour.

pigeons: unlike now, passenger pigeons (now extinct) or mourning doves, e.g., "The pigeons, once seen, killed, and eaten by the millions were almost gone by 1880, and were extinct by September of 1918."

piggin: a pail, usually with a handle; a small wooden cup or container from which to drink liquids, e.g., "At times one may find it difficult to understand the intended meaning of a particular usage of then common words, such as in 1747 when Sarah Ferguson's inventory included '4 piggins' listed immediately after her 'mares named Brenda, Doris and Candy'."

piggy bank: so called by reason of banks for early children made from pygg—a dense, orange clay that could be fired readily, e.g., "Little pygg containers with a slot for the deposit of pennies served Colleen's children as banks, those soon known as piggy banks, and for centuries thereafter such were made in the shape of a pig."

pight: from the Southern Appalachian Mountains, the past perfect tense of the verb "to pitch", e.g., "Evan told his brother that he had pight the horseshoe close to the pin."

pigs: See ***swine.***

pike: See ***turnpike.***

pikemen: See ***armed men.***

pilchard: probably any of several species of small, edible fish, known well to early immigrants, e.g., "While the pilchards of southern Europe were quite probably of a different species, many small, edible, sardine-like fish found along the West Coast were often called by that name."

Pilgrims: See ***Massachusetts Bay Colony.***

pillion, pilion: a thin seat cushion, attached to the rear of a saddle and usually used by a woman riding behind a man, e.g., "She often went with him on short trips, riding on a pillion."

pillory: See ***stocks and pillories.***

pilot: See ***engineer*** (q.v.).

pin-a-fore: an early, long apron, pinned at the top to the ***bodice*** (q.v.) of a dress to keep it in place, e.g. "The fact that the apron was pinned at the fore of the dress gave rise to the term pin-a-fore."

pincer mold: See ***bullet mold.***

pinch: a small amount of seasoning; an amount of ***snuff*** (q.v.) placed between the teeth and lip or cheek, e.g., "All cooks know what a pinch is"; "To one who dips snuff, a pinch is that indeterminate quantity he regularly uses."

pinch box: See ***snuff box.***

Pinchbeck gold: said to be named for an English watchmaker of the same name who worked early in the 18th century, a gold colored alloy of copper and zinc, sometimes used in jewelry of low quality, e.g., "The 1788 inventory listed a Pinchbeck gold locket." Also see ***tombac*** and see ***gold.***

pine tag: a pine needle, e.g., "Very proper Virginia lady Sarah Ferguson often smilingly referred to her brother as being as 'worthless as a pine tag'."

Pine Tree shilling: thought to be the first coinage on this continent, coined in Massachusetts from 1652 until 1684, e.g., "Coin collectors prize their Pine Tree shillings." Also see ***pound.***

pin-money: the allowance to a wife for her clothes and small necessities, e.g., "The term pin-money derives from the necessity that early wives buy ***stuff*** (q.v.), thread, buttons, pins, and needles in order that clothes might be made."

pinnace: a light, quick sailboat, usually with one sail, e.g., "Many pinnaces were seen on Chesapeake Bay, James and Potomac Rivers."

pip, pips: early, Johnson (1802) says a hard growth on the tongue of a fowl; later and now, an infectious secretion, particularly common in chickens, e.g., "Judith noted in her accounts ledger that several of her dung-hill fowl had the pips." Also see ***chickens.***

pipe: in some sources, a volume measure of wine, usually 110 gallons; a measure of liquid equal to two ***hogsheads*** (q.v.); 126 gallons, e.g., "The ship manifest showed 6 pipes of ***Madeira*** (q.v.)."

pipe staves: See ***staves.***

pipes, smoke: as now, e.g., "Early colonial pipes were usually made of clay or of corncobs"; "In addition to the churchwarden pipe with a long clay stem, among many there also were reed stem clay pipes, short clay pipes and pipes modeled after those made by the American Indians"; "Dr. Drake noted that the tailors were 'warming their noses with smokepipes'." Also see ***churchwardens' pipes.***

pipes of wood: See ***pipe.***

piracy, pirates, privateering, privateers: privateering (against enemy shipping) and piracy (against all or any vessels) were common in American waters during the 16th, 17th, and early 18th centuries, e.g., "Of the many pirates, probably the best known in the American colonies were Capt. (William) Kidd, tried and hung in England in 1701, Stede Bonnet (hung in South Carolina in 1718), Blackbeard (William Teach), who was captured, killed, and beheaded in 1718 by a command under Virginia Governor Spottswood, and the privateer Jean Lafitte (1780-1825)."

piragua, piraqua: a large canoe with one or two sails, e.g., "Piraguas were common on old Albemarle Sound."

piroque, rowboat: early, small, light open boat, usually with oars, e.g., "William Hunt earned money by rowing people to and from Jamestown in a piroque."

piscina: a church vessel or open container with a drain, used to hold water (usually) for religious purposes, e.g., "The piscina was early English and its origin remains unknown." Also see ***font.***

pistareen: a Spanish coin of small value, e.g., "Some early Texas and California references speak of pistareens."

pistole: a coin, variously of France, Spain, and Portugal, having different values at different times, e.g., "His reference to receipt of '12 pistoles' gives little clue as to the value of the goods."

pitapat: a flutter or palpitation, e.g., "The personality of Scarlett's Aunt Pitty Pat was perfectly described by her name."

pitch: thick resin, sap, or tar-like substance that oozes from the bark of pine trees; to erect a tent or other temporary habitation, says Johnson (1802), e.g., "In the 1720s, Thomas Drake sold pitch for ship caulking"; "Scoutmaster Skeels directed the boys to pitch their tents on the high ground."

pitcher and bowl: a pitcher, usually of 2 to 4 quart capacity, and a bowl of somewhat greater volume and from 10 to 16 inches across by 3 to 6 inches deep, used as a set; and usually placed within a ***bedchamber***, on a ***commode, basin stand,*** or ***washstand*** (all, q.v.) in order that the occupant of that room might wash, shave, or otherwise be refreshed, e.g., "The pitcher and bowl in Mikaila's bedchamber were of the finest quality ***flow blue*** (q.v.) porcelain."

pitchfork, hayfork: a large, wooden or metal tined, long-handled tool to move hay, straw, etc., e.g., "Every farmer had one or more pitchforks."

pitching pennies: See ***spanfarthing.***

pitkin: a small, ***earthenware*** (q.v.) container used for boiling liquids, e.g., "The pitkins in the inventory were noteworthy, since all other kettles and pots were of iron or ***pewter*** (q.v.)."

pitsaw: an early, very large saw with hand holds on both ends mounted perpendicular to the blade, used to saw large boards, e.g., "To cut large beams and boards, one ***sawyer*** (q.v.) stood in a pit and another stood above on a large timber or railing, while both alternately pulled the pitsaw between them."

pityriasis: any of a number of misunderstood skin diseases where there was a scaling or flaking of skin, e.g., "For pityriasis, he often administered acetic acid, borax, or dilute sulfuric acid."

place: as ordinarily used; also, one's home, home place, or residence, e.g., "Har wrote that he would not have a bull on the place."

placitum: an agreement, e.g., "Some early Southwestern records speak of placitum, meaning a bargain or agreement.

Plague of 1874, Locust: the worst grasshopper infestation in American history, ravaged the west from the Canadian border to Texas, e.g., "Virtually every crop on the Great Plains was destroyed by the devastating Plague of 1874."

plaid: See ***tartan, plaid.***

plaintiff, complainant: that person lodging or bringing an action seeking legal remedy or redress, e.g., "The plaintiffs were the ***siblings*** (q.v.) of the defendant." Also see ***defendant***.

plaited: braided or pleated, e.g., "She wrote that her new blouse was plaited at the waist."

plane: as now, a tool for working, shaping, smoothing, or thinning wood, e.g., "Virtually every flat board produced before 1820 was hand planed at great effort."

planes: of many varieties, including trying, smoothing, long jointer, short jointer, jack, and rabbet planes. See ***joiners' tools.***

planishing hammer: See ***coppersmiths' tools.***

plankbottom chair, plank bottom chair: a very common, armless, sturdy, simple utility chair, low and straight backed, with 3 or 4 round, flat, or arrow shaped vertical splats or spindles, and a thick seat often made of a single piece of wood rounded downward at the front, e.g., "During the 18th and 19th centuries, the men of the house commonly made the plankbottom chairs."

plantation house: the main house; the house of the master, e.g., "The servants for the plantation house often were literate and well dressed."

planter: very early, one who earned a livelihood through agriculture; later, a reference to one of affluence and standing in the rural community and having substantial agricultural land holdings, e.g., "As a planter, he was expected to support the church, provide men for the ***militia*** (q.v.), and serve in public office as needed."

plasters: cloth, or sometimes flour and water dough, containing medications and placed over a location of internal discomfort or wounds from any source, e.g., "He advised mustard plasters as a medication for ***pleurisy*** (q.v.)."

plat: a scale drawing of a tract of land, e.g., "The plat revealed that the Drake lot was 100 feet wide and 435.6 feet deep, for a total of one acre."

plate: as now; early and in ecclesiastical matters, any utensil made of gold or silver, especially those belonging to churches; those shallow bowls or utensils used for collecting church offerings, e.g., "The ancient plate of St. Paul's consisted of two ***chalices*** (q.v.), one of them ***Georgian*** (q.v.) and one with a cover, two ***patens*** (q.v.), a ***ciborium*** (q.v.), and a Georgian chalice." Also see ***flagon.***

plate die: See ***silversmiths' tools.***

plate warmer: early, a doored, metal box either placed on or attached to a shelf above the cooking surface of a cook stove and used to warm plates before serving, e.g., "Brittany's big iron cook stove had an attached plate warmer."

plate, plating: as now, plating varied in quality and thickness, e.g., "Until about 1840, most plating was done by chemical process; after that, it was accomplished through electrolysis, e.g., "Allison's silver plated Rogers dinnerware was of high quality."

platform rocker, spring rocker: any of several styles of rocking chairs mounted a few inches off the floor on a stationary base, said to have been designed to prevent wear of the carpet, movement across the floor while rocking, and the crushing of children's feet by conventional rockers, e.g., "Diane had a walnut platform rocker of great beauty."

plating hammer: See ***paper making.***

plating roller: See ***paper making.***

platoon: See ***armies, organization of.***

play horseshoes: See ***horseshoes.***

play pretties: See ***curios.***

plead clergy: See ***benefit of clergy.***

pleas and quarter sessions (courts of): courts of general jurisdiction and record; in North Carolina, the lowest courts of record, usually synonymous with the terms "circuit court" and "common pleas court", they met quarterly, e.g., "He was charged with hog stealing and was summoned to appear before the April Pleas and Quarter Sessions."

pleasure wagon, market wagon: the former term apparently unknown in the South; a four-wheeled, sturdy vehicle having substantial space for hauling freight, feed, etc., with one seat, usually for two, mounted at the front, the whole of it used for both pleasure and utility, e.g., "Most families had either a buckboard or a pleasure wagon, ***carriages*** (q.v.) being reserved for the more affluent."

plebeyos: farmers or ordinary tradesmen and merchants, e.g., "In the Spanish speaking states references to plebeyos are common."

plethora: unlike now, an excess of blood, e.g., "For the plethora, Dr. Cheryl advised ***cupping*** (q.v.)."

pleurisy: as now, an inflammation of or infection in the lining of the chest cavity, very often fatal in early times, e.g., "The symptoms of pleurisy having appeared, he was in great fear for his life."

pleurodynia, Devil's grip: sudden chest pain, probably usually angina pectoris, supposed to return on the third day after the initial attack, e.g., "For Devil's Grip, Evan prescribed ether spray and mustard ***plasters*** (q.v.)."

Plough Monday: the first Monday after the end of the Christmas season; the Monday after ***Twelfth-Day*** (q.v.), e.g., "Scarcely observed in the colonies, Plough Monday probably derived from the requirement that work again be undertaken after the holiday season had ended."

plow board, scoured as a: See ***scoured like a plow board*** and see ***moldboard.***

plow shares, plow sheers: the leading edge of a plow that cuts the ground, e.g., "Virtually every 17th and 18th century rural home had one or more plow shares."

plow tree: See ***horse tree.***

plug hat: a man's tall silk or beaver hat, e.g., "Twain wrote that the driver of his hearse was to be '...up on the box in a plug hat and a boiled shirt.'"

plumb: when not used to describe water pipes and attached fixtures, an object or line that is near perfectly parallel or perpendicular to another object or line; a superlative meaning complete, to a fine degree or complete extent; well put together, e.g., "While adjusting one joist to be parallel to the next, Tripp said to onlooker Jimmy, 'Is it plumb?'"; "Anne told Jean that she was plumb worn out after driving all night"; "Dean told Sarah that she was 'plumb purty.'"

plumber: as now: early, one who was learned in the working of lead; one who casted lead and made shot, pipe, roofing, decorative lead, and lead for windows, e.g., "During the era of the American Revolution, the principal task of the plumber was making rifle balls and shot"; "Drake was an apprentice plumber in Williamsburg as early as 1726." Also see ***plummet.***

plumcake: a sweet cake made with raisins, e.g., "The term 'raisins' meant the same in early days as it does today, and plumcakes were not made with plums."

plummet: a thin piece of lead, used by early schoolmasters to line paper for the use of their students, e.g., "Lead pencils, as we know them, were too expensive for common use in the 1840s, so the teacher usually had a plummet."

plunder: occasionally in the Appalachians, furniture, e.g., "Mrs. Castillo related that her early mountain family and their neighbors often had referred to their furniture as plunder."

pluries: a term used to describe a ***writ*** (q.v.), order, or declaration of a court issued for a third time, as in pluries capius or pluries attachment, e.g., "A pluries attachment issued for 'costs and £23/7/10'."

pluries attachment: See ***attachment.***

pluries capius: See ***capius.***

Plymouth colony: that settlement of 101 persons under the authority of the Plymouth Company (32 "Pilgrims" and 66 others, including Miles Standish and 14 indentured servants), intended to land at the Virginia Company holdings, but settled at Plymouth, now Massachusetts, in December/January, 1620/21, e.g., "As with the ***Jamestown Settlement*** (q.v.), fully half the first settlers of the Plymouth colony perished during the first year."

pneumonia: as now, but not understood early, e.g., "For pneumonia, Dr. Drake often administered ***blisters*** (q.v.), ammonium carbonate, morphine, or mercury salts."

pocket: unlike now, a small pouch or bag, usually with a drawstring and carried attached to the belt or tied around the waist, e.g., "It was said that the hunter always carried hard bread and dried meat in his pocket."

pocket book, pocketbook: now, a purse; early, a small record, note, diary, or day book intended to be carried in a ***pocket*** (q.v.), e.g., "Dr. Drake's Day Book originally was his pocket book."

pocket knife: a medium sized, utility knife with one or more (usually two) folding blades, carried on the person and serving to skin game, cut rope, leather, cloth and other material, whittle, etc., e.g., "He had a

penknife (q.v.) that remained in the desk, and a pocket knife that he carried at all times."

pocketglass: a small mirror carried on the person, e.g., "The inventory mentioned her items jewelry and a pocketglass."

podagra: See ***gout***.

Point Pleasant, War at: See ***Lord Dunmore's War.***

poison bottle: before widespread literacy and to prevent injury to children, many homemakers stored poisons in bottles having small unpolished bumps or protrusions on the surfaces, thereby warning anyone picking it up of the danger present, e.g., "The medicinal arsenic was always kept in a poison bottle."

poke: originally a Scottish word for sack or ***pocket*** (q.v.); a small ***sack*** (q.v.) e.g., "The child said she would share her poke of candy with her brother." Also see ***poke weed*** and see ***cigar case.***

poke sallet: See ***poke weed.***

poke weed, pokeweed, poke sallet: an Appalachian (and Scottish) expression meaning a salad made from tender young shoots of the pokeweed; it, a plant of the South having purple/blue berries and thought to have medicinal value, e.g., "She made poke sallet of fresh poke shoots, sugar, vinegar, and bacon grease."

pole, rod, perch: in surveying, a measure of length commonly found in early deeds and equaling 16-1/2 feet; equal to a rod or perch ; there are forty poles in a furlong and eight furlongs in a mile, e.g., "The town lot was five rods wide and nine rods deep."

polecat: See ***skunk***.

poledavy: a coarse durable fabric (***stuff***, q.v.), usually made of flax or wool, e.g., "Poledavy was similar to linsey-woolsey."

polishing iron: a small, light, iron smoothing tool (now, an "iron") used for finishing collars, cuffs, lace, etc., when smoothing clothes, e.g., "Where polishing irons are found, it is likely that the appearance of the family was important." Also see ***iron (to)***

political subdivision: a division or portion of a larger political and geographical area wherein separate laws and regulations and a separate administration having to do with that place are in place, e.g., "After the Revolution, the colonies gave up much of their authority in order to become political subdivisions of the United States"; "A county is a political subdivision, as is a city."

poll tax: a head tax; literally, a tax on a category of persons within a certain political jurisdiction, usually of a certain minimum age and usually men (or ***femme sole,*** q.v., in some jurisdictions), e.g., "There was a poll tax on all males over sixteen living within the colony."

poll, polls: originally meant "head"; people singly considered, as in a ***poll tax*** (q.v.) where a tax is levied on each individual (on each "head") of any class of people; a place where people cast ballots; a voting place, e.g., "The 1694 poll tax exempted only slaves under eight and white children under twelve"; "The polls open at 7:00 a.m." Also see ***head tax.***

pollock: an inexpensive variety of codfish, e.g., "Interestingly, 1860s ads for cod are few, yet notices that a ***fishmonger*** (q.v.) had pollock were frequent."

polyandry: See ***polygamy***, and see ***bigamy***.

polygamy, polyandry, polygyny: the practice of people of either sex having multiple living mates, where such is legally permissible, but most commonly referring to the status of a man who has more than one wife (***polygyny***, q.v.); e.g., "***Bigamy*** (q.v.) differs from polygamy, because in the latter no crime is intended or in place."

polygyny: See ***polygamy***, and see ***bigamy***.

pomade, pomatum: as now, a scented ointment, usually having cosmetic purposes, e.g., "Bethany's pomatum recipe was simply sweet lard (without salt), to which was added 'any agreeable perfume'."

pomander: unlike now, a ball or clump of scented weeds, spices, perfumes, etc., carried on the person and thought also to prevent disease, e.g., "Her pomander was of lilac, rose, and lily petals and ***Peruvian bark*** (q.v.)." Also see ***nosegay***.

pomatum: See ***pomade***.

pone, corn pone, ashcake, dodger, corn dodger, cornbread, hoecake: staple bread and biscuits, fried or baked and made from ground corn (cornmeal, meal) virtually everywhere in the colonies and United States where corn (maize) was grown or otherwise available, e.g., "Pone was a baked or fried cornbread, ashcakes were small pastries made of corn meal, wrapped in green corn husks or leaves, and baked in an open fire, dodgers and corn dodgers were similar but broiled or cooked in boiling fat or grease, and hoe-cakes, again of corn meal, were so named since they were cooked on any convenient handled metal surface—hoe, ax, shovel, etc."

pontons: pontoons, e.g., "The captain wrote that he had seen to the launching of the pontons."

pony sleigh: See ***sleigh***.

pony up: to settle or pay an account or debt owing, e.g., "He told his wife that the merchant had required him to pony up on his delinquent account."

pony, pony keg: derived from the physical size of ponies when compared with horses, a small container from which to drink liquor; a small, often 5, 10, 15 or 20 gallon keg of beer, e.g., "His favorite pony hung on the back wall of the neighborhood tavern"; "Mark brought a pony keg of beer for the ball game."

pool checkers: a version of the game of checkers where the pieces may be moved in any direction, thought to have been adapted by early slaves from the French, e.g., "Pool checkers is yet a popular game with many Southerners."

poop, poop deck, poop lantern: the hindmost part of a sailing ship, the open, top-most deck at the rear of a ship, e.g., "When the great poop lantern of Drake's ship *Revenge* was extinguished, the captains of the other warships did not know what was expected of them"

poor farm: those early facilities for the care and keeping of those of little or no estate; a small farm, tended by poor residents where food was grown by them for their own use, e.g., "Martha was residing at the poor farm in Southampton County at the census of 1850."

poorhouse: See ***county home***, and see ***poor farm***.

popery: See ***papist***.

pop-robin: a batter of eggs and flour boiled in milk, e.g., "Many early New England breakfast consisted of pop-robin with sugar and fried salt pork."

porch, portico: unlike now, an entryway, later and somewhat unlike now, a roof supported by pillars and usually open on one or more sides; a covered walkway, e.g., "The porch of the church was converted to a vestry, and the portico leading to it was of flagstone."

porridge: early, unlike now, stew or thick broth made by boiling meat until it separated; later, cereal grains cooked in water until soft and thickened, e.g., "The porridge of the 17th century was the stew of the 19th."

porringer: a very common, short-handled, shallow pan or dish, usually of wood or metal (often ***pewter***, q.v.) from which was eaten all manner of foods, including liquids, stews, and cooked cereal grains (from whence, the word "porridge"), e.g., "As did virtually every inventory of the 17th and early 18th centuries, his estate included porringers." Also see ***trencher***.

Port, port: a sweet, red wine, originally from Portugal and very popular in the American colonies, especially with women; e.g., "Very often one would find port being sipped by women while the men were served ***sherry*** (q.v.). "

port, port side: See ***starboard***.

porter: a heavy, dark brown ale, probably from Ireland, e.g., "Until after the ***Potato Famine*** (q.v.), porter was not commonly found in the American colonies and states."

portico: See ***porch***.

portmonnaies, port mannaies: probably synonymous with the word portmanteau; a sea bag; a large bag or sack of canvas or other heavy material in which apparel was and is carried, e.g., "*The Exeter News-Letter* of April 7, 1862 carried ads by Charles Merrill offering for sale cigar cases, work boxes, and portmannaies."

posse, posses: an abbreviation of the Latin legal expression "posse commitatis"; any or all of the community that a sheriff might summon to his assistance to aid in capturing criminals or perform service for the public good, e.g. "Unlike the posses of early times, those of the American West often were volunteers actually deputized by oath."

posset: an intoxicating drink made from hot milk, sweetening, and spices, and curdled by adding wine or ale; probably French and a ***syllabub*** (q.v.), e.g., "The records of Southern taverns reveal the serving of possets."

post: the public mail service, e.g., "In the 18th century, the post was the only practical way to communicate over a distance."

post and plank fence: See ***post and rail fence***.

post and rail fence, post and plank fence, straight fence: a straight fence of split rails or rough lumber inserted in holes or slots cut into posts that have been driven into the ground at regular intervals, e.g., "Before wire fencing, post and rail fences were very common." Also see ***snake fence***, and ***barbed wire***.

post road: usually well defined roads with ***stands*** (q.v.) having refreshments for man and horse and designated and improved so as to facilitate the transportation of mail and government business and, incidentally, travel by the general public, e.g., "Tennessee Route #68 east of Crossville, Tennessee, was a post road from the early 19th until well into the 20th century."

posset: an intoxicating drink made from hot milk, sweetening, and spices, and curdled by adding wine or ale; probably French and a ***syllabub*** (q.v.), e.g., "The records of Southern taverns reveal the serving of possets."

post: the public mail service, e.g., "In the 18th century, the post was the only practical way to communicate over a distance."

Joseph Botner

BEGS leave to inform the Public in general, and his Friends in particular, that he has returned to this city, and has taken a Shop opposite the Coffee-House, in Front street, on the south side of Market street, where he carries on the SADLING BUSINESS in all its various Branches——Said BOTNER makes and sells the following Articles:

Ladies and gentlemens saddles, in the newest mode	Sword scabboards
All kinds of plated and polished bridles	Gentlemens boot garters
Portmanteaus and portmanteau trunks	Infantry, Horsemens and Jocky } Caps
Saddle bags	Coach, phæton & chaise harness
Valaises	Chairs trimmed in the neatest manner
Horse cloths	Waggon and cart gears
Fire buckets	Horse collars
Pistol holsters	Mane combs and sponges
Cartridge boxes	Curry combs and brushes
Sword belts	

He likewise has on hand, a general assortment of fashionable Whips.

Merchants or others, who want a quantity of Sadlery, may be supplied at a low rate—All Orders from Gentlemen in the city or country will be executed with fidelity and dispatch, 2aw f

†.† An APPRENTICE wanted.

Joseph Botner advertised portmanteaus and other leather goods, in the "National Intelligencer," Washington (D.C.), Jan. 18, 1825.

post and plank fence: See ***post and rail fence.***

post and rail fence, post and plank fence, straight fence: a straight fence of split rails or rough lumber inserted in holes or slots cut into posts that have been driven into the ground at regular intervals, e.g., "Before wire fencing, post and rail fences were very common." Also see ***snake fence***, and ***barbed wire.***

post road: usually well defined roads with ***stands*** (q.v.) having refreshments for man and horse and designated and improved so as to facilitate the transportation of mail and government business and, incidentally, travel by the general public, e.g., "Tennessee Route #68 east of Crossville, Tennessee, was a post road from the early 19th until well into the 20th century."

poster bed, four poster bed, canopy bed: beds having posts on each corner to support a framework from which hung the curtains used to keep insects and "drafts" away from those sleeping and to provide a measure of privacy, e.g., "With the invention of screening, she no longer needed the side ***curtains*** (q.v.), so he cut the posts off the poster bed." Also see ***pencil post bed.***

posterity: all of one's descendants, e.g., "We should all so conduct ourselves that our posterity need not be ashamed."

posy, posies: aromatic herbs, roots, or flowers, e.g., "Because they thought that certain plants had curative value in cases of Bubonic Plague, children were directed to dance in a circle around roses with posies in their pockets and sing "Ring around rosey, a pocket full of posies, ashes, ashes, we all fall down."

pot hook, pothook: simple, iron, "S" shaped hooks used to hang pots on a crane in a fireplace, e.g., "Every home had several pot hooks, usually made by the local ***blacksmith*** (q.v.). Also see ***crane.***

pot metal: an inexpensive, brittle, cast metal used for pots, pans, kettles, and similar containers, e.g., "While her pot metal kettles were inexpensive, they often were broken if accidentally dropped on the stone ***hearth*** (q.v.)."

pot rack: as now, a rack, either free-standing or designed to hang on a wall, intended to hold pots and pans when not in use, e.g., "Jean's pot rack hung on the wall near the ***bread box*** (q.v.)."

potash: the lye resulting from slowly pouring water through ashes, particularly hickory, e.g., "Potash and lard or other grease cooked together made soap." Also see ***leach.***

Potato Famine: that period of severe economic distress suffered by the Irish people during the period 1845-1855, during which many emigrated to the United States, e.g., "Helen's ancestors came to New York City at the time of the Potato Famine."

potato scoop: a long-handled tool with 10 to 16 tines placed side by side in the shape of a scoop shovel, e.g., "The potato scoop design made it possible to pick up potatoes as the dirt passed between the tines."

pot-belly, pot-bellied stove: a small, round, cast iron (later, steel) heating stove, vented through a wall, designed to burn coal or wood, and usually placed in a central room, e.g., "With the coming of the Franklin Stove and the iron pot-bellies and ***cook stoves*** (q.v.), the open fireplace as a source of heat for a room was doomed." Also see ***parlor stove***, and see ***laundry stove.***

pothecary: See ***apothecary.***

potichomanie: a hand craft practiced by women of the mid 19th century, wherein decorated paper was glued to the inside of a glass vase or other bottle-like container and the rest of the interior was painted, e.g., "Potichomanie—a craft practiced by women and girls that flourished for many years—probably was introduced by *Godey's Ladies' Book* in 1855."

potter: as now, those who made and fired pottery for utility and decoration, e.g., "Excavations of the earliest works at Jamestown reveal the efforts of the potters."

poultice, blister: a large patch, usually of cloth, and sometimes of dough, mush, or meal, into which has been placed medication, the whole then applied to a wound, swelling, inflamed or erupted area, e.g., "For the unknown swelling, she made a poultice of ***turpentine*** (q.v.) and tobacco juice."

Pound (£): a British denomination of money used as a standard in colonial America, the world, and in several of the United States even after the Revolution; generally, if a sum was stated in silver or by silver certificate, it was called Pound Sterling until very recently; there were and are 20 shillings in a Pound (£), and 10 (formerly 12) ***pence*** (p or d, q.v.) in a ***shilling*** (S, q.v.), and 4 ***farthings*** (q.v.) in a pence, e.g., "The deed related that the ***consideration*** (q.v.) was 'twenty Pounds Sterling'."

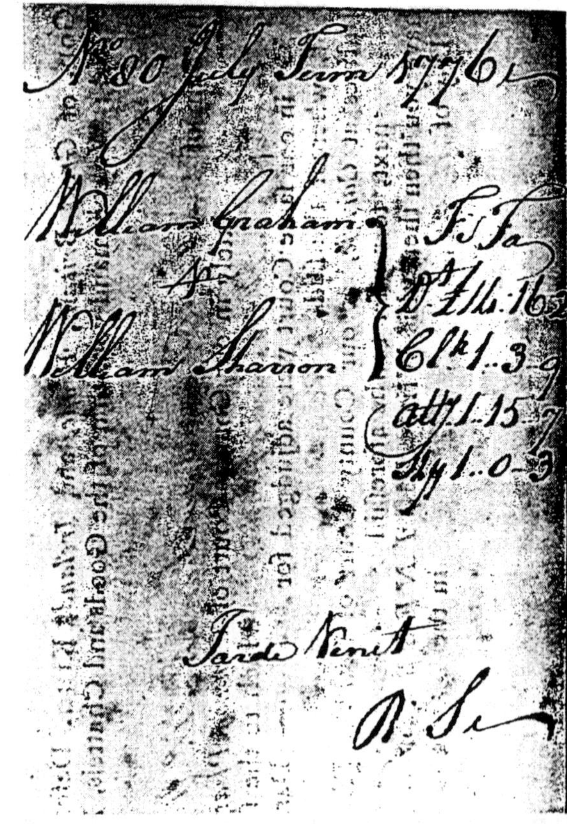
No 80 July Term 1776
William Graham
vs
William Shannon
Fi Fa
Clk 1..3..9
atty 1..15..7
Shff 1..0..3
Tarde Venit

Here in a 1776 "return" by a sheriff are seen the ordinary symbols for referring to our English money in Pounds, shillings and pence. Note that the sheriff was due 1 Pound, 3 pence while the lawyer was entitled to receive 1 Pound, 15 shillings, and 7 pence. At the bottom is a seldom seen endorsement, "Tarde Venit;" those words meaning that the sheriff did not receive the writ until after the date it was due to be returned to the court.

pound, lb.: a dry weight, e.g., "A pound (lb.) avoirdupois is 16 ounces, however a pound Troy is but 12 ounces." Also see ***Pound (£)***.

poverty: as now, meaning the state of being extremely poor; in genealogy, usually those legal conclusions concerning assets that were required before pensions were awarded to veterans and others who served, or provided services or material to, the U.S. government, e.g., "Carner's pension application set forth his infirmities as well as his condition of poverty."

powder box: usually, a small box for talcum or other powdered cosmetic, e.g., "Her powder box was inlaid with ivory and was ***japanned*** (q.v.)."

powder dry, keep your: See ***keep your powder dry.***

powder horn, powder flask: a small waterproof container, occasionally of metal, but more usually made from 6 to 9 inches of the pointed end of an animal horn, with a narrow stoppered opening or neck, used to carry the gunpowder needed for loading ***muzzle loaders*** (q.v.), ***muskets*** (q.v.), etc., e.g., "His steer powder horn had belonged to his great grandfather."

powder mill: a small usually cranked mill used to grind saltpeter (potassium nitrate), sulfur, and charcoal into powder form for the making of gunpowder, e.g., "As an enlisted man, John Salling, the last probable survivor of the Civil War, had dug saltpeter and helped to haul it to the powder mill."

powdering tub, powder tub, salting tub, salt tub: a long, deep, large, quite usually wooden tub or container in which large pieces of meat were placed for salting or otherwise applying preservatives, e.g., "Haskins's powdering tub was large enough to hold the meat from two hogs."

power of attorney: an instrument by which one has temporary legal authority to act in in a limited way in behalf of another, e.g., "Drake's power of attorney was for the purpose of handling the affairs of his cousin, Evan, who was going abroad."

prayer: as commonly now; in law and genealogy, that section of a legal pleading wherein the court is requested to grant some certain relief, money, etc., e.g., "The court's record stating that Sarah prayed for divorce had nothing to do with her religious attitudes."

precinct: early, in some places, political subdivisions often nearly the equivalent of counties; now, usually a small area within a town or city; often now not in use except for voting purposes, e.g., "Early North Carolina Precincts conducted their affairs as though they were counties, even before they were so declared"; "In 1870 Todd resided and voted in the 3rd precinct of Richmond."

precipe, praecipe: written instructions, usually from a litigant, to the clerk of the court, e.g., "The precipe directed the clerk to summon Mills, thereby providing a clue for the researcher that Mills likely was then known to be within that county."

preemption of occupiers, occupiers preemption: See ***occupant claims.***

preface: that writing appearing in the front of a literary work that often reveals the rules, discipline, and attitude of the writer as to the subject matter, e.g., "The preface revealed that of the genealogical evidence presented the author felt at liberty to include statements he believed, though the hearsay and material presented could not be substantiated by any other records."

prefect, prefet (Fr.): an officer of government charged with the administration of the law in his section or district, e.g., "While a prefect is often an administrative officer, in New Mexico prefects were and are probate judges."

preferment: to advance a person to higher social status or station, as in ***manumission*** (q.v.), e.g., "While freeing slaves was manumission, elevating citizens to rank was preferment."

prelacy, prelate: the or one of the highest officers of any organized church, usually Catholic, e.g., "The records of Salem mention that Governor Endicott hoped that the colony would provide rest for those upon whom the 'weight of the prelacy rested heavy'."

preponderance of evidence: a legal measure of proof; in genealogy, a measure of proof of lineage thought insufficient by most scholars, e.g., "When the evidence tending to prove one hypothesis outweighs, even minimally, the evidence tending to prove a contrary theory, the first hypothesis is said to prevail 'by a preponderance of evidence'." Also see ***clear and convincing*** and see ***beyond a reasonable doubt.***

Prerogative Court: in New Jersey, a court of appeals from decisions of the ***orphans' courts*** (q.v.), e.g., "While prerogative usually means a notable extra measure of power or authority, when that word appears in New Jersey as a name for the court in which some case was considered the researcher must also search out the records of the lower court from which the appeal to Prerogative was made."

press of men: See ***impressment, etc.***

press, in: early, presently in print, e.g., "The 1814 advertisement spoke of the new three volume set as being 'now in press'."

press, to press: See ***iron (to),*** and see ***clothes press.***

press, trimming press: See ***bookbinders*** and ***printers.***

pressbed: now, a hide-away bed; a bed designed to be folded up to form a seat or couch, e.g., "Pressbeds are commonly found in 19th-century inventories."

pressed, pressed to death, peine forte et dure: a crushing of the body by adding iron or stones until the chest cavity collapses, e.g., "One of those charged with witchcraft in old Salem was pressed to death." Also see ***pressed glass,*** and see ***prest.***

pressed glass: glass, some of very high quality (Sandwich, Northwoods, Indiana Tumbler, etc.), with designs impressed while near molten; early, sold as a substitute for the more expensive cut glass and occasionally then spoken of as "poor man's cut glass", e.g., "The Chrysler Museum has on display some elegant and very rare pressed glass." Also see ***prest,*** and see ***pressed.***

prest, pressed into service, were prest: summoned to service by some legal authority, e.g., "***Constable*** (q.v.) Smith prest John and his horse to service of a ***warrant*** (q.v.)." Also see ***pressed glass,*** and see ***pressed.***

pret, pret a interet (Fr.): a loan, e.g., "Early Southern records occasionally speak of 'pret a interet', meaning a loan upon which interest was charged."

pretermitted heir: a child who has been excluded from a will without mention or provision by a parent, e.g., "In some instances, pretermitted heirs have been provided for as though the parent had died ***intestate*** (q.v.)."

pretty, pretties: See ***curios.***

primary sources, primary materials: in genealogy, a term reflecting one's view concerning some source; usually refers to those writings thought to be unchanged since originally written; "original" materials are those written at or near the time of the event by one who had direct knowledge of the matter and apparently had no reason to be other than candid, truthful and complete; sometimes, any materials considered by the user to be more reliable than available ***secondary sources*** (q.v.), e.g., "In his research, he used the court's orders as primary sources."

primer, primmer: basic facts and numbers, usually used in early schools as a teaching aid; very early, a prayer book; 19th and early 20th centuries, a book of fundamental principles for children and usually their first or early lessons, e.g., "The ***McGuffey's First Reader*** (q.v.) was also called a primer."

primitive furniture, primitives: furniture made by other than those trained in the art of furniture or cabinet making, e.g., "Most furniture of early rural families was primitive, it having been made by the men of the family." Also see ***country furniture.***

primogeniture: the ancient and exclusive right of the first born male to succeed to the family property; a doctrine manifest in many early estates by which the eldest son, or his eldest son, etc., inherited family property to the exclusion of all other of that male's siblings, the widow, and any other relative without regard to need; an ancient principle, abolished in Georgia in 1777; North Carolina in 1784; Virginia in 1785; Maryland and New York, 1786; South Carolina, 1791; Rhode Island, 1798 (in RI, land was inherited equally with the eldest son receiving a double portion), e.g., "Even where outlawed in principle, the primogeniture in fact appeared in many early wills." Also see ***siblings.***

printers: See ***bookbinders and printers.***

prison ships: hulks of ships used as places of incarceration, e.g., "The filth, heat, cold, and hardships undergone by American soldiers placed in British prison ships defy description."

private entertainment: an ***ordinary*** (q.v.) that also provided food, drink and facilities for private parties, and thought by some also to occasionally refer to houses of prostitution, e.g., "In 1815 Virginian Nate Lipscomb was granted a license to sell wine, and on 25 June 1839 he was licensed to operate '...a house of private entertainment at Merry Oaks'."

private, private soldier, enlisted man, seaman: the lowest ranking of persons in the militia, army, navy, cavalry, air force or artillery who have finished ***recruit training*** (q.v.), the word "private" being a remnant from the days when soldiers were such by their choice, as opposed to those who owed a duty of arms to some lord or owner of their person, e.g., "After induction (by requirement of law, 'the draft') or enlistment (by voluntary action), all non-commissioned members of the armed forces, including those in the Navy and the Coast Guard are and were known as 'recruits' until completion of their basic (or 'recruit' or 'boot camp') training, after which they are and were known as privates or private soldiers, except in the Navy and Coast Guard, wherein they are known as seamen."

privateers: See ***piracy.***

privy, necessary: an outdoor toilet; a dug pit, over which a bench with holes and a small, doored shelter were built, used for personal relief, e.g., "Privies were known to all, rich and poor alike, until the advent here of indoor plumbing in the late 19th and first half of the 20th century."

prize, prizer, apprizer, appraiser: as now; early, one who evaluates; an appraiser, e.g., "Who we now call an appraiser was also known to Johnson (1802) as a prizer or one who prized."

probate, probate courts: as in "to probate a will," that legal process by which the terms of a will are executed (put into effect) or the procedures required for intestate deaths are undertaken; sometimes, those legal processes involving any estate, ***testate*** or ***intestate*** (q.v. as to all); relating to proof of wills; presently (in American law) a general term used to refer to any matter in which probate courts have jurisdiction, such as matters of death, orphans, adoption, children, lunacy, guardians' estates, etc.; often called orphans' courts or surrogate courts, e.g., "In most states, a judge of a probate court is elected for a term of years"; "The entry declaring the will to have been 'admitted to probate', meant that it had been ***proven*** (q.v.) and was subject to such proceedings as might be necessary to bring to fruition its purposes."

probative value: the weight or evidentiary worth of a bit of evidence as it relates to some matter in question or being proved, e.g., "The Bible entry had great probative value in determining his age at death."

procedendo (writ of): an ancient and still used ***writ*** (q.v.) by which a higher court orders a lower court to proceed in its duty, e.g., "The Supreme Court, by a writ of procedendo, ordered the lower court to proceed with the charge against the defendant."

processioning, processioners: under the ancient authority and guidance of the ***parish*** (q.v.), the walking (processioning) of the boundaries of private lands within the parish by appointed, knowledgeable, and responsible parishioners in order that boundaries be determined and boundary disputes be resolved, e.g., "The processioners of Newport Parish confirmed the Thomas and Richard Drake lines in late March of 1723."

Proclamation Money: late 18th-century currency, particularly of North Carolina, the value of the currency as a means of settlement said to be "established by proclamation," e.g., "He paid for the land with Proclamation Money."

professional researcher: those who do genealogical research for others for hire, e.g., "She hired a professional researcher to search in the ***D.A.R.*** (q.v.) Library for her veteran ancestor."

profit a prendre: a right to remove something such as minerals or crops from land, e.g., "One of the profits a prendre was the right to harvest the wheat."

progenitor, progeny: a common ancestor; the collective descendants of a common ancestor, e.g., "Her progeny at her death included thirty grandchildren and fifty-four great-grandchildren."

prohibition (writ of): an ancient and still used ***writ*** (q.v.) by which a court orders that another arm of government refrain from acting in a certain fashion, e.g., "The writ of prohibition ordered that the ***assessor*** (q.v.) discontinue with establishing increases in the assessed value."

Promontory Point, Promontory, Utah: that place in present-day Utah where the Central Pacific and the Union Pacific tracks met to complete the first transcontinental railroad, e.g., "It was at Promontory Point on 10 May,

1869, that the *Jupiter* and *Engine 19* met, ***cowcatcher*** (q.v.) to cowcatcher, signifying the completion of the great transcontinental railroad."

prones: prunes, e.g., "She regularly crushed and boiled prones especially for the small children and the senior members of the family."

prong, run, dry run, branch, rivulet: very small streams or branches that may or may not carry water year round, e.g., "He described as a prong that small run that was often dry in the summer and fed Horsepen Branch."

proof: in genealogy, that accumulation of evidence sufficient to establish some matter of lineage, e.g., "The proof of his death came from the death certificate, the family Bible, and the newspaper."

proper English: See ***King's English.***

propres, propriete propres: any property inherited from any blood relative, e.g., "Early Louisiana records sometimes speak of propriete propres, thereby providing clues as to relatives."

propriete: See ***propres.***

Proprietors, proprietors: meaning literally, those vested with some exclusive control, e.g., "The leader of the group of Proprietors to whom the King granted the right to control and govern in North Carolina was Anthony Ashley Cooper."

prostatitis: as now, e.g., "For prostatitis, he advised the use of hot enemas and suppositories of opium."

Protestants: any religious group that is other than Roman Catholic, e.g., "The word Protestant derives from protests against Catholic doctrine by Luther and others."

prothonotary: the principal ***clerk*** (q.v.) of courts in some jurisdictions, e.g., "In New York and Pennsylvania the Prothonotary is the counterpart to the Virginia Clerk to the Circuit Court."

proud flesh: swollen flesh, usually as a result of an injury, e.g., "Mikaila wrote that she had been thrown from her mare and her arm was bruised and proud."

prove: the accomplishment of gathering or collecting evidence sufficient to meet the requirements of some discipline as to a matter at issue; the act of confirming through witnesses that a writing is the valid and subsisting will of a ***decedent*** (q.v.), e.g., "She proved the ***lineage*** (q.v.) through Bible entries, censuses, and tax records"; "The witnesses to the will appeared and proved it." Also see ***proof.***

provender, carry provender: provisions, usually food—grain and hay—for burden animals; occasionally, foodstuffs for men on the move, as in a military operation, e.g., "It was said that Arnold's troops had to carry provender with them, as otherwise the horses would have starved in the winter wilderness of upstate New York."

province: in genealogy, a place or geographical area considered to have a measure of autonomy, government, or body of laws that differentiate it from other places or destinations, e.g., "He went out to the English provinces."

Psalm Book: See ***Bay Psalm Book.***

psalter: a psalm book; the Biblical book of Psalms, e.g., "The psalter of the inventory likely was an ordinary book containing psalms."

PT-109, U.S.S: See ***warships, American.***

pub: usually, sometimes now an ***ordinary*** (q.v.) in the U.S.; earlier, a small tavern dispensing alcoholic beverages and food, yet having no overnight accommodations, e.g., "Early 20th-century Boston was widely known for its neighborhood Irish pubs."

public days: See ***muster***.

public house: See ***tavern***.

public(k) times: a term almost exclusively of the very early South, especially in Jamestown and Williamsburg, it meant those days during which the general assembly (***House of Burgesses***, q.v.) was in session, e.g., "Publick times were always well attended, especially after Williamsburg became the capital of Virginia in 1699."

puddings: See ***desserts, early***.

puddler: an early term for one who knew the art of agitating molten iron in order that the air thus caught up in the iron might partially purify the same, e.g., "As with Catherine Furnace near Chancellorsville, virtually all furnaces where iron was smelted had one or two experienced puddlers."

puerperal fever, puerperal convulsions, purple fever, childbed fever: early, a seizure during labor or immediately thereafter, often fatal, and generally accompanied by loss of consciousness or mental aberration; a dreaded, usually fatal infection, early thought to be a disease peculiar to those giving birth and not understood as sometimes a result of unsanitary conditions, e.g., "Many a young woman was believed to have died of puerperal fever."

pulleys: See ***rigging***.

pulpiteer: now unknown, e.g., "In 1838 Mr. Bater mentioned in the diary entry that he '...had needed a pulpiteer, but none were at hand'."

pummy: apparently, anything left over from farm production that could be fed to livestock, e.g., "Some early writings speak of pummy in association with cattle."

pumps: See ***shoes***.

punch: intoxicating beverage; a flavored drink, usually containing fruit juices and, in early times, of high alcohol content, e.g., "Early punches often were made of wine or rum and fruit juices, hence the expression 'it has a punch'."

puncheon: heavy lumber, roughly dressed, for use as timbers or floors, e.g., "Puncheon floors occasionally were found in early schoolhouses, otherwise the floors were dirt."

punk, spunk: rotten wood taken from the inside of a maple tree and often used to ***carry fire*** (q.v.), e.g., "It was easier to ***borrow fire*** (q.v.) from a neighbor by carrying spunk rather than a shovel or container of hot ashes."

punt: a small, flat-bottomed, usually two-seated boat with oars or poles, e.g., "There was usually a punt or two waiting at the Jamestown landings on the James River."

punty, punties: See ***glass making***.

puny: a word of several meanings; in Johnson, "young, inferior, petty, of an under rate"; in the Southern Appalachians and the West, the state of being sickly or not well, where it is expected to be of short term or temporary; in the North, usually, one who is naturally and perhaps permanently thin, small, or weak, e.g., "Shakespeare in *Coriolanus*, wrote 'Lest that thy wives with spits, and boys with stones, in puny battle slay me'"; "Diane remarked that her husband had been puny with the flu three times in December"; "Allison mentioned that Diane's fiancé '...surely was a puny little fellow of but 120 pounds.'"

pupillus: in ***civil law*** (q.v.), one under the age of puberty, often an orphan or ward, e.g., "Early Louisiana records occasionally described the ages of orphans as pupillus."

pur autre vie: literally, during the life of another, e.g., "Interests in land given to one pur autre vie lapse when that other (autre) person dies."

purchase money mortgage: See ***mortgage deed.***

purge, purgatives, cathartics: early thought to be helpful in myriad ailments and complaints; causing the evacuation of the body, especially the bowels, e.g., "In their desperate efforts to affect cures, early physicians often administered violent purges, including mercuric chloride."

Puritans: those who insisted on strict conformity to the doctrines of the Anglican Church, e.g., "During the 17th century the Puritans became a powerful force in both England and the American colonies."

purser: that person charged with keeping the books and accounts of a ship, e.g., "Dan Boucher was once the purser of the 17th-century ***Quaker*** (q.v.) ship *Blessing*."

pursey: short of breath: occasionally, obese, e.g., "The doctor wrote that the senator was pursey, probably meaning that he was short of breath"; "Bethany wrote that her friend Jean 'was pursey of late and so was eating like a bird.'"

put some back: a very early expression meaning to save or protect by placing objects of value or money back in the rear of the cabin, away from the typically single door through which thieves might come, e.g., "When asked about her savings, Roxanne said she had put some back for a new bed for Winnie."

putting on airs: See ***airs, putting on.***

pygg: See ***piggy bank.***

Q

quadrangles, quads, topos, U.S.G.S. topographical maps: very fine and detailed maps of small geographical areas published by the U.S. Geological Survey and available for much of the U.S., e.g., "Sarah found 7½' quadrangles for the township at the Chamber of Commerce office." Also see ***Geological Survey, U.S.***

quadrille: a five-part square dance for eight people; a card game for four people, e.g., "They danced a quadrille and several Virginia ***reels*** (q.v.)." Also see ***cotillion.***

quadroon, quaterone: a person having one Negro and three white grandparents, e.g., "While he appeared to be of Caucasian background, he was, in fact, a quadroon."

quads: See ***quadrangles.***

Quakers: that religious discipline organized in England circa 1650 and best known on the American continent through William Penn and Pennsylvania, e.g., "While the colonies early witnessed widespread persecution of the Quakers, by 1685 that discipline was active and prospering in Pennsylvania and in eastern North Carolina and Tidewater Virginia among other places."

qualify: a recognition that one has met some requirement for admittance, office, or recognition, e.g., "As the widow and ***relict*** (q.v.) of the deceased, she qualified as ***administratrix*** (q.v.) of her husband's estate."

quantum meruit, quantum valebant: that unpaid amount or quantity to which someone was entitled or deserved; that amount which certain materials or goods were worth, e.g., "Early lawsuits were sometimes styled 'in quantum meruit', meaning that the complainant had not been paid for work or services, and 'in quantum valebant, meaning that he had not been paid for goods sold, in both cases often revealing the occupations and places of ancestors."

quarter chest: See ***chest, chest of tea.***

Quarter Eagle: See ***Eagle.***

quarter houses: slaves' quarters or cabins, e.g., "The ***overseer*** (q.v.) wrote that the quarter houses were much in need of repair."

quarter section: See ***section.***

quarter sessions, courts of: See ***common pleas, courts of,*** and see ***pleas and quarter sessions, courts of.***

quarter sessions, quarter sessions of the peace (courts of): Pennsylvania courts of misdemeanor criminal jurisdiction, usually acting at the time of or by the judges of courts of ***oyer and terminer*** (q.v.), e.g., "The Ohio county court had criminal jurisdiction identical to the Pennsylvania courts of quarter sessions of the peace."

quarterly courts: Kentucky courts that hear appeals from the ***justices of the peace*** (q.v.) and have original jurisdiction in most civil cases, e.g., "The records of the Kentucky Quarterly Courts remain and are excellent research sources."

quarto: usually, about 12" X 9½"; a 19" X 24" sheet folded twice resulting in 8 pages (4 leaves) for printing, e.g., "The book was bound in quarto." See also ***folio.***

quaterone: See ***mulatto*** and ***quadroon.***

quay: See ***key.***

quean: very early, a whore, e.g., "Our terms 'queenie' and 'queen', meaning a woman of the night, derive from the ancient term quean."

Queen Anne's War, War of Spanish Succession: 1702-1713, ended in the American colonies by the "Peace of Utrecht"; those conflicts between New Englanders and Minas, Beaubassin, and Fort Royal brought on by the Abenaki attacks on Deerfield, Massachusetts, and Winter Harbor, Maine, and between armed Carolinians and armed men at St. Augustine, all to prevent the alliance of France and Spain, e.g., "But very few records remain concerning those who took up arms in Queen Anne's War."

Queen Bess: See ***Good Queen Bess.***

queen's ware: a hard earthenware, cream or beige in color, and first developed by Wedgwood, e.g., "As early as 1845 queen's ware was being advertised for sale in Findlay, Ohio."

queens and kings, reigns of: See ***regnal years.***

query: in genealogy, a request for information, accompanied by a brief summary of a research problem, e.g., "Mikaila's query read 'Seek those researching the John Meachum family of 1810 Vermont'."

quick consumption: See ***consumption, etc.***

quick, quickening, quick with child, quick child: alive; first discernible movements of a fetus, e.g., "The expression quick with child meant that the fetus had moved."

quietus: acquitted, as in dismissal after completion of a task; the discharge of one after service, e.g., "The Maryland court ordered a quietus, Drake having met the obligations applicable to him."

quill pen: an early writing instrument; the unfeathered end of a tail feather of a bird, usually a goose, both cut in half and split lengthwise and with a nib to permit flow upon dipping the same in ink, e.g., "His quill pen writing was difficult to read, probably because of the pen, the quality of the ink, and the texture of the paper." Also see ***nib***.

quilt: as now, e.g., "In early times, all clothing scraps were saved in order that quilts might be made."

quilt frame: a large, usually collapsible wooden framework upon which is stretched fabric (usually of cotton) preparatory to making it into a ***quilt*** (q.v.), e.g., "The quilt frames were moved to wherever the ***quilting bee*** (q.v.) was to be held." Also see ***quilt***, and see ***quilting bee.***

quilting bee: a gathering of women for the purpose of making quilts, during which there was social exchange and instruction in the art for young girls, e.g., "Every neighborhood had its quilting bees."

quinsy, quinsey: any severe sore throat or "strep throat", e.g., "Just prior to the development of the pneumonia that is said to have led directly to his death, George Washington complained of quinsy."

quire: a merchant's measure of writing paper, usually 24 sheets, e.g., "In the mid 18th century writing paper was very expensive, often the present day equivalent of $30.00 for a quire, or more than $1.00 per sheet."

quit-claim, quitclaim: often imprecisely called "quit-claim deed"; an instrument by which is transferred whatever interest one may have in property (usually real estate) to someone else, and which contains no warranties or representations concerning the nature of the ownership being transferred, if any, e.g., "Even though he likely had no interest whatever, the court ordered him to quit-claim whatever he might possibly have."

quit-rents, quitrent: a rent or payment of an annual fee by a ***freeholder*** (q.v.) for the use of land; a tax, after which one had no further taxes due the state for that period, e.g., "The 1704 lists of those Virginians who were chargeable with quit-rents are very valuable genealogical sources."

quoddy boat: a New England fishing boat, usually pointed on both ends with one sail, e.g., "The lobstermen of old Maine often worked from quoddy boats."

R

rabbet, rabbet plane, rabbet saw: grooves in wood, and a plane with a sharp edge, used by ***joiners*** (q.v.), ***cabinetmakers*** (q.v.) and ***carpenters*** (q.v.) to make such grooves (rabbets) in wood, e.g., "His rabbet plane had a very sharp edge, facilitating the cutting of rabbets." Also see ***cabinetmaker.***

raccoon mill: See ***burr mill.***

rack: a device of punishment that slowly pulls the body apart; one of several ***gaits*** (q.v.) of horses, e.g., "Even though we occasionally ***pressed*** (q.v.) people to death, the rack apparently was not known in the American colonies"; "The rack is a comfortable ride."

raffia, raffia basket: palm leaves or the stems from such; a basket made of palm stems or leaves, e.g., "The Georgia 1811 inventory revealed 3 raffia baskets."

rag off a bush, that takes the: a superlative, referring to an unusual, remarkable or impressive event, usually of a small, local or personal nature, and probably derived from the early practice of hanging wet utility rags and small clothing across a bush to dry, the same sometimes carried away by a bird, e.g., "When Deane's dog, Sparky, had 9 pups, Anne exclaimed, 'Well, if that don't take the rag off the bush!', while at the same moment Jean said 'That really ***takes the cake***' (q.v.)." Also see ***menstrual rags.***

rag paper: See ***paper making.***

rag rug, ragrug: a rug, usually woven in the home from scraps of worn out clothing and other ***stuff*** (q.v.), e.g., "Ida wove 2 beautiful rag rugs made from scraps salvaged from worn-out and discarded clothes of her parents."

rag stamper: See ***paper making.***

ragged as a hacherd: See ***hacherd.***

railroad dick: See ***dick, railroad.***

Rainbow Division: See ***military combat units, famous.***

raisin gin tonic: a mixture of gin with dark raisins that has been allowed to set at room temperature for several weeks, the liquor of which is used as a tonic, e.g., "Throughout the winter months, Terry always kept handy a bottle of raisin gin tonic." (Editor's note: It is awful tasting!)

raisings, house-raising, barn raising: when the need arose, for whatever reason, for a family or church group to construct a house, church structure, school, or barn, pioneer settlers frequently gathered at the site of the proposed construction and together built whatever was needed, their wives and children assisting by cooking, carrying water, and running errands, e.g., "When the home of the old preacher and his wife burned to the ground, it was decided that a house raising would be held on the following Friday."

Raleigh's Colony: See ***Croatan Inscription.***

ram: a male sheep, e.g., "The inventory listed a ram and three ***ewes*** (q.v.)."

rammersman: a laborer of strength and endurance, as were those who drove pilings and posts, e.g., "Ads seeking rammersmen reflect construction work, and reveal the need for men of considerable size or strength who were practiced at work with tools such as heavy hammers and ***mattocks*** (q.v.)."

rancho: a small group of habitations or persons and their houses; a hamlet or small village, e.g., "The ranchos of early Texas and California writings were not individual houses."

range law: See ***fence, fence laws, etc.***

Range: See ***Section, Township, and Range.***

Ranger, U.S.S: See ***warships, American.***

rapine: the forcible taking of one's property, against his or her will, e.g., "Early comments about rapine had nothing to do with sex."

rasp: a large, heavy toothed wood file, e.g., "There were rasps of several sizes in his shop inventory."

rass: unknown 19th century Ohio expression; perhaps a fish (wrasse), e.g., "He wrote in 1880 that 'there were rasses a'plenty in the pond'."

rat cheese: a very sharp cheddar cheese enjoyed generally, and in the South particularly, which cheese was said to be the best to use as bait in a rat or mouse trap, e.g., "Sally seldom used the word cheddar, always referring to that product as 'rat cheese'."

ratine, rattinet: a loosely woven or coarsely meshed fabric made from finely knotted yarns, e.g., "Purple, brown, crimson and light blue rattinetts were advertised for sale in Philadelphia in the late 18th century."

rattan furniture: chairs, ***settees*** (q.v.), etc., made of woven rattan (the tough stems of palms), e.g., "The ***Gay Nineties*** (q.v.) brought to the market the popular rattan furniture."

rattlesnake root, black snakeroot: the common medication taken internally for snake bite, e.g., "The 17th-century colonials swore by black snakeroot for bites of any kind."

re, in re: as now, literally "in the matter of"; in regard to; e.g., "The case record titled 'In re Susannah Drake,' meant in the matter of certain legal action involving that woman."

reader (for microfilm or microfiche): that optical equipment or machine used to view ***microfilm*** or ***microfiche*** (both q.v.), e.g., "When she arrived at the library, all the readers were in use."

real estate, real property, realty: refers to land or interests or ownership in land; all other property is ***personalty*** (q.v.), e.g., "Her estate consisted of twenty acres of real property and personalty worth $3,000.00."

ream: a measure of paper, now quite usually 500 sheets, e.g., "The storekeeper had three reams of paper that he usually sold in single sheets or in ***quires*** (q.v.)."

reamer: See ***gunsmiths' tools.***

reasonable doubt, beyond a: See ***beyond a reasonable doubt.***

rebeck: a three-stringed fiddle, e.g., "Early French immigrants sometimes brought their rebecks, often the only musical instrument in the settlement."

Rebels, Rebs, Johnnys: usually referred to Southern soldiers, and occasionally to any Southerner during the Civil War, e.g., "Johnny Reb was the counterpart of ***Billy Yank*** (q.v.)"

receipt: a recipe, e.g., "Brittany wrote in 1884 that when she went west, her mother had given her many 'family receipts'."

reck: take heed, be mindful of, as in reckon, e.g., "A Texas court early recognized the word reck."

reclusion: incarceration, usually at hard labor, e.g., "A number of Louisiana records speak of imprisonment for crime as reclusion."

Reconstruction: the process by which those states that had seceded again became a part of the American Union, e.g., "The congressional acts between 1867 and 1878 by which the former Confederate states again gained representation and voice in the U.S. government were known as the Reconstruction Acts." Also see ***Civil War***.

recontre': from the French, a duel, e.g., "The New Orleans Picayune of September 5, 1842 spoke of a duel that had taken place as a 'recontre'."

record (to), registrar, office of: the act and office of entering documents or writings into the public records, whether by ***clerks*** (q.v.), ***recorders*** (q.v.), registers of deeds, registrars, or otherwise in accordance with "recording statutes"; an innovation and office peculiar to the American colonies and rarely then found in England, e.g., "Contrary to popular notion, a vast majority of early transfers of land here were recorded."

recorder: in genealogy, an early, common, wooden wind instrument, similar to a flute, e.g., "Among Judy's possessions were 2 flutes, an oboe, and a recorder." Also see ***record (to),*** and see ***hautboy***.

recruit training: See ***private, private soldier***.

recruit: See ***private, private soldier***.

rector: a parson or governor of a church, early quite usually of the Anglican Church, who received and managed the entirety of the income of that church (unimpropriated), e.g., "The rectors of the Church of St. Paul are known at least to 1685." Also see ***rectory***.

rectory, benefice: in England and the early colonies, the whole of the Episcopal church structures, ***glebes*** (q.v.), lands, ***tithes*** (q.v.), etc., of a ***parish*** (q.v.); the house, lands and all income or assets set aside for or dedicated to the support of a church and the rector and staff thereof; all the assets, real and otherwise of a church or parish, e.g., "The rectory of Upper Nansemond consisted of three churches"; "The rectory consisted of one acre of land, the house, furnishings, church and income amounting to about £28 per year." Also see ***rector***.

Red Clubs: See ***military combat units, famous***.

red rover come over (a tag-like game): See ***games (of children)***.

Red Sticks: See ***military combat units, famous***.

red-eye gravy: very common Southern gravy made from ham drippings and water and usually with but very little flour added, e.g., "He often asked for ***catheads*** (q.v.) and red eye gravy."

Redcoat, Lobster-back: nicknames and often terms of contempt for a British soldier, here, usually of the American Revolution, e.g., "The term Redcoat was not unique to the Revolution; it was as common in old England as in the colonies."

Redemptioners, free-willers: those who undertook to labor for some agreed or specified time period (average 4 years) in order to redeem themselves from the obligations owing to others for transportation to here or training provided for a calling, e.g., "As a Redemptioner, Brittany's ancestor had been required to work for four years to pay the cost of his transportation." Also see ***indentured servant*** (q.v.)

redeye: as now, a severe inflammation of the eyes, e.g., "Dr. Lockhart administered a boric acid ***collyrium*** (q.v.) for the redeye."

redgum: a disease of the newborn, usually characterized by an eruption or by dark coloration of the gums, e.g., "Even though sometimes treated as a symptom of some other ailment, redgum usually was short-lived and harmless."

redhibition: a suit to rescind a sale for the reason that the goods are worthless or so difficult of use that the buyer would not have purchased it had he known, e.g., "The Louisiana civil code permits suits of redhibition, often leading researchers to ancestors and merchants."

redoubt: Johnson (1802) says, the outwork of a fortification; an enclosed earthwork or position of war, generally constructed overlooking a likely path of attack and in sufficient numbers to protect some inner fort, works, or facilities, e.g., "The English Redoubts #9 and #10 at Yorktown are well known to all students of that Revolutionary War battle."

reduced: disabled or physically disadvantaged, usually by reason of accident or injury, rather than as a result of hereditary or genetic defects, e.g., "In 1674 'Capt. More' was adjudged reduced by the Salem court."

redware: inexpensive stoneware, red by reason of the iron oxides in the clay, e.g., "Diane had a pitcher and several other items of redware."

reek: unlike now, steam, smoke, vapor or odors, e.g., "The comments that the baker's shop reeked of bread did not mean that it had a foul odor."

reel, rele: a device (revolved by hand) upon which yarn or thread was wound usually as it was spun, e.g., "Early inventories showing spinning wheels also often listed a reel or rele."

reel, Virginia, See ***Virginia reel.***

regiment: See ***armies, organization of.***

Regina: See ***Rex.***

registrar: See ***record (to).***

regnal years: the years of the reign of a monarch; since the earliest times, used as a means of stating and establishing the dates of contracts, documents, legal writings, and events (also see ***Rex, Regina***), e.g., "The 16th of the regnal years of King George III was 1775." Regnal years of English monarchs since 1400 are as follows:

Henry IV, 1399-1413
Henry V, 1413-1422
Henry VI, 1422-1461
Edward IV, 1461-1483
Edward V, 1483
Richard III, 1483-1485
Henry VII, 1485-1509
Henry VIII, 1509-1547
Edward VI, 1547-1553
Mary, 1553-1558
Elizabeth I, 1558-1603
James I, 1603-1625
Charles I, 1625-1649
The Interregnum (Cromwell, etc.), 1649-1660
Charles II, 1660-1685
James II, 1685-1688
William III and Mary, 1688-1702
Anne, 1702-1714
George I, 1714-1727
George II, 1727-1760
George III, 1760-1820
George IV, 1820-1830

William IV, 1830-1837
Victoria, 1837-1901
Edward VII, 1901-1910
George V, 1910-1936
Edward VIII, 1936
George VI, 1936-1952
Elizabeth II, 1952-

regular army: that force of armed men and women maintained over a protracted period, usually better trained and not called, enlisted or assembled for any immediate purpose, e.g., "Units such as the 1st U.S. Sharpshooters, 7th U.S. Cavalry, etc., were regular army units, while volunteer and ***conscript*** (q.v.) units, such as the 55th Ohio Volunteer Infantry and the 43rd North Carolina of the Civil War were not 'regular' and did not carry the designator 'U.S.'"

Regulators, War of the Regulation: that association of western South Carolina settlers and farmers who (1769-1771) sought schools, roads, churches, courts—government—and refused to pay taxes to far off Charleston until they received those social features of life, e.g., "The Battle of Alamance between 2000-plus Regulators and the ***state militia*** (q.v.) resulted in the defeat and hanging of six Regulators and the end of their organization."

reigns of kings and queens: See ***regnal years.***

reinsman, rainsmen: usually, that person who drove an animal-drawn stagecoach or passenger vehicle team; sometimes, any driver of a team of multiple animals, e.g., "The reinsmen of the Columbus to Pomeroy stage were colorfully described."

relationship: in genealogy, the extent to which one is related to another, whether by ***affinity*** (q.v.), ***consanguinity*** (q.v.), legal action, or by choice, e.g., "Her relationship was unknown until the family Bible record was discovered."

relative reliability of source: See ***reliability of source, relative.***

relative: as now, a kinsman or kinswoman, e.g., "A relative may be by blood or ***affinity*** (q.v.)." Also see ***relationship.***

rele, Virginia: See ***Virginia reel.***

release, release of mortgage: See ***mortgage.***

reliability of source, relative: in genealogy, that measure of certainty or evidentiary weight to be accorded any bit of evidence as it relates to some issue to be proved, e.g., "Having found a headstone bearing one date and a column in a newspaper stating a different date, she had to consider the relative reliability of those sources."

relict: a widow or widower, e.g., "Parker married the relict of William Huntt in late 1669 or early 1670."

remainder: generally, an interest in land which will take effect upon the termination of some prior interest or interests, e.g., "Through his remainder interest, he gained possession at the death of his mother who had been a life tenant." Also see ***life estate.***

render, rendering: cooking down of any substance; usually, the boiling down of fat from hogs, thereby producing lard and ***cracklins*** (q.v.), e.g., "At ***killing time*** (q.v.) enough lard was rendered to last the winter."

repertory, repertories: the notes required to be kept by notaries public concerning all contracts acknowledged before them, e.g., "Early repertories yet remain in archives of Southern states, particularly Louisiana."

res: a thing, object or asset; the subject matter, particularly of a lawsuit, e.g., "Many courts' reports and writings refer to the res of the action, usually meaning the subject matter in dispute or under consideration, such as a tract of land, a cow, a portfolio of stock certificates, etc."

residence: See ***domicile.***

reticulate: net-like cloth (***stuff,*** q.v.); a fabric so openly woven as to have a high percentage of open space, as in a fish net, e.g., "The inventory spoke of both fish netting and 'reticulated stuff'."

reticule: a small bag or purse, e.g., "While, in earlier times, reticules were small bags made of mesh or web fabric, by the mid 19th century they were being offered in fine silks and linens for use by ladies in carrying their personals."

revenant: a ghost or spirit; one who returned from the dead, e.g., "Sally rather doubted the existence of revenants, and when others spoke of such she believed instead that perhaps ***ancestral memories*** (q.v.) were being experienced."

reverse indexes: indexes to deeds compiled alphabetically in the surnames of the grantees/transferees (usually, buyers), e.g., "Since he knew his ancestor had lived in the area, he searched the reverse index to see if that ancestor had bought land there." Also see ***direct indexes***, and see ***grantor/grantee indexes***.

Revolutionary War: See ***War of Independence.***

revolver: a repeating handgun (pistol), so designed as to mechanically move 4 to 9 (usually 6) pre-loaded rounds into firing position; first patented by Samuel Colt in 1835, e.g., "The Colt revolvers were said to have won the West."

Rex, Regina: monarchs, male and female, e.g., "Since monarchs are said to have no surnames, Elizabeth Regina means simply Elizabeth, Queen."

ribbon medals: See ***medals***, etc.

ribbon slide: a small, decorative, pendant-like contrivance, usually with two holes bored vertically, through which both ends of a neck scarf are pulled, e.g., "Decorated ribbon slides for ladies were being advertised before the Civil War. Also see ***bolo, bola.***

rick: a measure of firewood measuring 4' X 4' X 4'; one-half a ***cord*** (q.v.), e.g., "They burned nearly a rick of wood per week in their big fireplace."

rickety: derived from the disease rickets, wherein the joints are diseased and weak, especially the knees; usually referred to unsteady or unstable furniture, especially chairs, e.g., "Allison said that the chair had been rickety since the week after her husband made it."

riddle: a coarse sieve, e.g., "The inventory listed a colander and a riddle." Also see ***colander***, and see ***searce***, and see ***tea strainer***.

riddley spoon, ridly spoon: a spoon with perforations or slots cut into it in order that solids may be removed from liquid foods, e.g., "The Mikaila Bater inventory listed 2 small and 1 large riddley spoons."

ride: a horse, and later and now, an automobile or powered vehicle, e.g., "It was written in *Southern Odyssey* that the South '...was a land where the rides were handsome, the air pure, and the girls beautiful.'"

ridgling: a horse with one testicle removed, e.g., "Horses called ridglings had been half castrated, and thereby supposedly rendered more gentle."

riding chair: a two-wheeled, single-seated vehicle, much like the now-familiar Chinese rickshaw, often used in early cities, pulled by a person and usually for hire, e.g., "Rather than tie his horse in the sun for the day, Mr. Bater took a riding chair to the capitol building."

ridly spoon: See ***riddley spoon***.

rifle, rifling, rifled musket: a hand-held ***firearm*** (q.v.) with spiraled grooves in the barrel, thereby causing greater accuracy by reason of the spin imparted to the emerging projectile, e.g., "The invention of rifling soon brought the demise of the ***smoothbore musket*** (q.v.)."

rifle-pit, rifle pits: a hole, fox-hole, or trench dug by fighting men or women and by which some protection was offered to at least the lower part of the body, e.g., "Diane and Jean enjoyed contemplating the Civil War while walking through the long abandoned rifle-pits at Malvern Hill."

rifling broach: See ***gunsmiths' tools***.

rigging: the ropes, pulleys, clews, sheets, tacks, lifts, brails, blocks and other equipment used to support and spread sails on early sailing vessels, the "standing rigging" being that which supported the masts and, once in place, remained until replacement was required, and the "running rigging" being that constantly changed and adjusted during movement of the vessel, e.g., "Mr. Haskins often spoke of the extensive knowledge required by a seaman of the often more than 300 lines making up the rigging on a three-masted vessel."

right smart: a superlative, usually meaning that one has or has witnessed the presence or accumulation of a larger quantity or measure of people, material, commodity or objects than would usually be expected or needed in the immediate future, e.g., "Loreda commented that she and her friend had seen 'right smart' of Tennesseans during their cruise."

rindle, rindle of blood: unknown, yet probably a small amount of some fluid, e.g., "His diary revealed that his friend had been shot dead, '...yet there was but a bare rindle of blood'."

ring, ring of bells: as now and, unlike now, the totality of chimes and bells of a church, e.g., "Mr. Ferguson said that the Richmond church early had a ring of 6 bells weighing a total of 1600 lbs."

ring around rosy: See ***posy, posies***.

rising, rising of the lights: perhaps "boils" and the "***croup***" (q.v.), e.g., "Jim's Internet request for a definition of 'rising' grew out of the death report of a 19th century child in his family."

rising of the lights: See ***rising***.

rivulet: See ***prong***.

rixdollar: the German (reichsthaler), ***Dutch*** (rijksdaalder, q.v.), or Danish (rigsdaler) coins having a value equal to about 4S, 6p in the late

18th and early 19th centuries (about $25.00 in 2000), e.g., "Immigrants often arrived at Philadelphia and New York with rixdollars in their purses, only to be cheated by the ***money changers*** (q.v.)."

road, roads: as now; to seamen, early and now, a channel (sometimes canal) of a depth and sufficiently clear of obstructions to permit passage of larger boats and ships, e.g., "Perhaps the most well known use of the nautical term 'roads' is found in the name of the city, Hampton Roads, Virginia." Also see ***roadstead*** and ***stead.***

road cart: See ***sulky.***

road wagon: a usually inexpensive, topless passenger vehicle or carriage with four large wheels and one seat for 2 or 3 people, e.g., "The ordinary road wagon could be purchased for 25% to 40% less than a better quality one-seated, ***topless buggy*** (q.v.)."

roadhouse: a business offering food, drink, and entertainment for travelers and food and drink for their animals, and usually without overnight accommodations, e.g., "Settler's roadhouse on the Bucyrus pike near Waldo, Ohio, was well known to early Ohioans." Also see ***inn***, and see ***ordinary***.

roads, early: Zane's Trace from Wheeling, West Virginia, to Maysville, Kentucky, Braddock's Road from the Potomac to Fort Pitt, Forbes' Road from Fort Loudon to Fort Pitt, and Gist's Road from Fort Cumberland to the upper Monongahela River were 4 of the earliest roads that served western Pennsylvania and the ***'Ohio country'*** (q.v.). Shortly thereafter, other famous ways were Philadelphia-Lancaster Turnpike, then Knoxville Road that tied together Wilderness Road (through Cumberland Gap and north into Kentucky) and the Cumberland Mt. settlers, and Walton Road (west and south through Tennessee and beyond); the National Road (Cumberland Rd.) from Cumberland, Maryland, to Wheeling, now West Virginia; the Territorial Road that opened up southern Michigan, and the Chicago Road that opened up northern Indiana and Michigan.

roadstead: from the ancient ***"stead"*** (q.v.), meaning place, and ***road*** (q.v.), meaning a channel or way of passage, a very early term meaning a quiet backwater or bay of sufficient depth that ships or large boats could be safely anchored, e.g., "Early Virginian writings refer to ships riding at anchor in a roadstead near Jamestown." Also see ***farmstead***, and see ***homestead***, and see ***bedstead***, and see ***stead***.

roan: a color, usually reddish brown, brown or black, thickly sprinkled with whited hairs, especially of horses and dogs, e.g., "Dr. Drake gave Sarah Ferguson a beautiful roan mare."

Roaring Twenties: that period after World War I during which prosperity was at hand, the stock market seemed to have no upper limits, world dominance by the U.S. seemed at hand or imminent, and a measure of personal freedom was felt by reason of high wages, shorter work days and weeks, and inexpensive automobiles, e.g., "The Roaring Twenties came to an end with the collapse of the stock market in October and November of 1929, particularly marked by Black Thursday, 24 October of that year."

robe: See ***buffalo robe.***

rock fever: See ***Bang's disease.***

rock: as now; origin unknown; a hand-held reel with a ball hanging below, upon which ***hatcheled*** (q.v.) flax and wool were spun into thread, e.g., "Occasionally an inventory will mention a small or a large rock."

rockaway: a light, 4-wheeled carriage with a permanent top and lowerable, waterproofed side curtains, e.g., "The rockaway was a favorite of those of new affluence who yet thought a doored carriage to be pretentious or too expensive."

rockbait: See ***stickbait.***

rocker, rocking chair: early, a rocker had much shorter rocker boards (runners) than now, especially in front where they extended not much more than an inch or two; often primatively made by attaching short rockers to straight chairs, e.g., "The short bars on the family rocker revealed to her that it likely was very old."

rocker bench, rocker settee, rocking settee: a ***mammy bench*** (q.v.) with rockers, e.g., "She often sat on the rocker bench, entertaining and rocking the baby while chatting with her guests."

rod: See ***pole.***

Rogers' Rangers: named for Robert Rogers, a group of frontiersmen active during the ***French and Indian War*** (q.v.); Rogers, after a colorful career punctuated by Washington ordering his incarceration, died in England, e.g., "Dalyell, Putnam and Stark are known to have been Rogers' Rangers."

roles: now probably unknown, "On June 24,1845, in New Orleans, Ezekiel Brown bought 8 ***ells*** (q.v.) of roles."

roll wagon: a horse-drawn vehicle of commerce, having rollways and bars so mounted as to roll barrels forward and backward in the bed of the wagon and thereby facilitate loading and unloading, e.g., "Virtually every early brewer had a roll wagon, since beer was universally sold in round wooden barrels."

rolls: See ***bookbinders and printers.***

rolltop desk, rolltop, curtain top desk, tambour desk: a common, popular desk of the Victorian period to now, usually of oak or walnut, with a kneehole and drawers on both sides below, a retractable slatted top (tambour) that was either of quarter circle or "S" shape behind which were several small drawers and ***pigeon holes*** (q.v.), e.g., "Her 'S' curve rolltop desk was of walnut and had belonged to her grandfather." Also see ***tambour.***

romall: probably an inexpensive, thin cotton or linen cloth, e.g., "In 1798 Kuhn & Risberg of Philadelphia advertised 'low priced romall handkerchiefs'."

rood, rood loft, rood screen: ¼ acre; a crucifix or an image of a saint (Johnson, 1802); an alcove or section of a church in which relics, crucifixes, and other religiously significant items were and are kept and sometimes displayed; an often elaborately decorated partition separating the rood loft from the ***nave*** (q.v.) of a church, e.g., "The rood loft of St. Paul's was 12 feet above the floor of the nave"; "An early rood screen at St. Andrew's was donated by Mikaila Bater."

room: as now; in genealogy, in the place of, or instead of, e.g., "As overseer of the road, he served in the room of Peter Smith." Also see ***stead.***

room and board: See ***board.***

room freshener: See ***vinegar of the 4 thieves.***

rooster, fighting: See ***dominicker.***

rope bed: until the early years of the 19th century, most beds were made with ropes stretched within a frame (***bedstead***, q.v.) to support the

ticks (q.v.) or primitive mattresses; after rope beds came slatted beds, e.g., "Even though likely made earlier, some rope beds were still in use in the middle of the twentieth century."

ropes, know the: a commendation or compliment revealing considerable knowledge of one's business, field of endeavor, or assigned task; a term of mariners on sailing ships meaning that the seaman had learned much about the operation and what was required of him in his efforts with sails and rigging, e.g., "When Sarah said that Paul surely knew the ropes in his writing, she was relating that he was very knowledgeable in such efforts."

Rosenoble: a very early English coin having a value of ¾ Pound Sterling, e.g., "There is at least one 17th-century Virginia reference to a Rosenoble."

rotgut: early, distasteful, poorly made or low quality beer; now, slang for any alcoholic beverage, particularly cheap whisky, e.g., "Parker said that he had 'filled his belly with rotgut' during the preceding evening."

rough log cabin, round log cabin: a cabin or house made of logs with or without the bark yet in place and the logs yet round (not hewn), e.g., "It was much less work and quicker to construct a rough log cabin than one of hewn logs." Also see ***hewed log house***.

Rough Riders: that force of cavalry under Col. Theodore Roosevelt (later Pres.) that saw service in the ***Spanish American War*** (q.v.), e.g., "Contrary to popular belief, the Rough Riders were dismounted during the famous San Juan Hill attack." Also see ***military combat units, famous***.

rough shod: a superlative, derived from a horse which had shoes that were poorly and roughly made, and meaning that a person or group was meanly or heavily handled or treated, e.g., "When Daniel Drew used all economic advantage to bring the bankruptcy of other railroads, it was said that he ran 'rough-shod' over his competition."

round log cabin: See ***rough log cabin***.

Roundhead: very early, a ***Puritan*** (q.v.) or a follower of Cromwell, so named by reason of the practice of cutting their hair in a short and round style, e.g., "While in early Virginia many were said to be ***Cavaliers*** (q.v.), very few references to Roundheads are to be found."

routs: a disorganized assembly of the poor, rabble, or riff-raff, e.g., "The Governor ordered his ***foot*** (q.v.) to prohibit and put down the rout."

Royal Americans: See ***military combat units, famous***.

Royal Navy: the navy of Great Britain, e.g., "The Royal Navy has been so called since the 17th century."

rub doctor: early, and in some places yet, a chiropractor, osteopath, or any other persons holding themselves out as having curative powers through manipulations of the body, e.g., "Dr. Tripp, having been well educated in the art of chiropractic, rather resented being referred to as a rub doctor."

rubella: See ***measles***.

rubican: probably an early name for what we know as an the Appaloosa horse; a horse of dark color with a small spots of white or gray on the rump, e.g., "The few early New York writings mentioning rubicans likely were references to horses marked as are modern-day Appaloosas."

rubstone: See ***whetstone***.

ruche, ruch, ruching, ruke: material used to decorate, particularly, the collar or sleeves of a dress, e.g., "Diane noted that she had not enough ruching to finish Bethany's dress."

ruddle: red or pinkish colored dirt or earthen ware of the same colors, e.g., "Jean described the iron-rich soil around their Georgia home as ruddle"; "Anne told of her ruddle crocks."

ruff: a usually heavily starched, linen neckpiece commonly worn in the 16th and 17th centuries, e.g., "Queen Elizabeth I was commonly portrayed wearing a ruff."

ruffle one's feathers: to aggravate or slightly anger another person, e.g., "When he rudely spoke ill of her sister, Betty's feathers surely were ruffled."

rug: early, any bed or table cover or bedspread; coarse, nappy, thick woolen or other heavy fabric upholstery; later, as now, a floor covering, e.g., "His 1740 inventory included a bed and ***furniture*** (q.v.), a ticking bag and a rug." Also see ***counterpane.***

rule: a ruler, e.g., "The rule was like another thumb to the ***cabinetmaker*** (q.v.)."

rule against perpetuities: See ***perpetuities, (rule against).***

rule of three: an early measure of one's education; often, the "three Rs"; meaning that one could "read, write, and cast accounts" or "...and cypher," that is, do simple addition, subtraction, multiplication and division; occasionally, that specific knowledge of mathematics through algebra sufficient to determine an unknown 4th number where the other three were known, e.g., "The plantation owner had provided that his sons were to be educated to the 'rule of three'; that, likely meaning that they were to be taught to read, write, and understand the business accounts of the farm."

rum, Jamaica spirits: a high alcohol content liquor enjoyed by the American colonists and today, e.g., "The 1694 manifest listed three barrels of Jamaica spirits."

run: See ***prong.***

rundle: early, a step of a ladder, e.g., "He commented that the boy should be careful because a rundle had broken and another was loose."

runlet: an early term meaning a small barrel, e.g., "The 1749 inventory revealed 2 runlets."

runnel: an early term meaning a very small stream, e.g., "Mr. Drake suggested that the term 'run', often used to describe a small stream or rivulet, originated from the early term, 'runnel'."

running rigging: See ***rigging.***

rush bottom chair, cane bottom chair, cane chair, cane back chair: any chair with a woven bottom, back, or sides, usually of rush, cane, or thin wooden strips, e.g., "Cheryl and mark had three ***primitive chairs*** (q.v.), two rush bottom and one ***plank bottom*** (q.v.)."

Russia leather, Russian leather: a fine, highly polished leather, usually black, burgundy or deep red, and early considered a mark of substantial wealth, e.g., "In 1675, and revealing of her affluence, Mrs. Parker had four Russia leather chairs."

rusticate, to: to reside in the country, e.g., "Rich Southern urban families often were said to rusticate in the northern states during the hot summer months, particularly in upstate New York, Massachusetts, New Hampshire and Vermont."

rye coffee: a warm beverage made by boiling rye, either dried or as picked, e.g., "While coffee was oftentimes scarce on the frontier, rye was not, and so rye coffee often served as a substitute, albeit a poor one, for the real thing."

S

S.C.C.: sworn chain carrier, see ***chain, etc.***

sabbat, Sabbat: a usually secret gathering of witches or followers of the Devil, e.g., "Sabbats are held in many places, even today, by those who worship dark spirits, pray to the Devil, or pretend to possess or have a capacity to call upon the occult powers"; "An early New England record speaks of American Indians gathering '...as for a Sabbat'."

sabbed: unknown, perhaps a misspelling of stabbed, e.g., "Miss Bethany wrote in 1847 that while in Richmond, she had been told that '...Jonathan had been sabbed.'"

saber, sabre: the "sword" of a cavalryman; an early weapon with a long, slightly curved, heavy blade, e.g., "Griffith's will bequeathed to his son his 'sabre and ***Buckanear gun***' (q.v.)."

sachem: usually, a chief of a confederation, group of tribes, or league of Indians, e.g., "The Five Nations of the Iroquois had an elected sachem."

sack: a sweet wine, early from the Canary Islands, e.g., "Many slave traders also carried sack, particularly to the Southern colonies."

sackcloth: as suggested by the word, a coarse material (often hemp) used to make feed, grain, or ***tote sacks*** (q.v.), e.g., "The very poor often made clothes for children from sackcloth."

sacristy: a compartment or place where vestments and other items of religious significance are stored, e.g., "Virginia parson Nettles wrote that since he had 'no place for a sakerstee' (sacristy), he kept the vestments at home." (Also see ***rood loft.***)

sad, sad ware, sadware: made of iron; any iron cooking utensil or ware, e.g., "Among the items listed were two large sad kettles."

sad griddle: See ***griddle***.

sad iron: meaning a heavy smoothing iron (Johnson 1802); in the 18th century and after, a tool used to smooth (press) fabrics, having a detachable handle, usually weighing from 4 to 6 lbs, and large enough to retain heat longer than a flatiron, e.g., "She had three sizes of sad irons, 4 lbs, 5 1/8 lbs, and 5 3/8 lbs." Also see ***flatiron***, and see ***iron (to).***

sadd colors: dark and earth tones, e.g., "Diane's wardrobe was almost entirely of sadd colors and quite unlike that of Allison, who preferred clothes of bright and vivid shades."

saddler: one who made saddles, e.g., "Early records frequently speak of harness makers and of saddlers."

safe: unlike now, a pantry, e.g., "The safe mentioned in the early floor plan had nothing to do with money or jewelry." Also see ***pie safe***.

safeguard: a long, ladies' outer coat, worn over other apparel to protect the clothing beneath from water, mud, etc., "Her safeguards saw little use after she became too old to ride."

safety matches: an invention of the early 20th century eliminating the phosphorus head of a match, thus preventing ignition by friction on other than a match container scratching surface, making possible the safe storage and transportation of such without fear of accidental fire, e.g.,

"Because of her fear of fire, Maggie was happy to see the coming of the safety match."

sagathies: a now unknown ***stuff*** (q.v.), e.g., "The newspapers of Salem (Massachusetts) for 1770 reveal that 'woolen cloths, sagathies, swanskins, cotton, thread and worsted hose' were being sold in considerable quantities."

salading: probably, vegetables and herbs with which to make salads, e.g., "Sarah wrote that there was 'fruit and salading a'plenty in the garden'." Also see ***poke sallet***.

salamander: unlike now, a medium to long handled, flat piece of iron, heated to high temperature and held over any cooking food where the top is to be seared or browned, e.g., "The cook used the salamander to brown the top pie crust after the filling had cooked."

Salem Witch Trials: that series of charges made and trials held during and immediately before 1692 which culminated in some 14 women and 5 men being hanged, one man being ***pressed*** (q.v.) to death, and 4 dying in jail (none were burned), e.g., "The Trasks were among those caught up in the Salem Witch Trials." Also see ***witchcraft***.

saleratus: soda; sodium bicarbonate; as now, used in cooking, e.g., "The scarcity of 'soda' in early Pennsylvania led to the use of corn cobs burned to ashes and settled as a substitute for saleratus."

sallet: See ***poke sallet*** and see ***salading***.

salon: See ***saloon***.

saloon, salon: unknown to Johnson, and unlike now, from the 19th century, a large area for the convenience, comfort, lounging and leisure of ship or train passengers, e.g., "Even though he was a ***teetotaler*** (q.v.) and disapproved of alcoholic beverages other than as medicines, it was not remarkable that Tom Roberts wrote that he had spent the morning in the saloon of H.M.S. *Mauretania*."

saloon table: See ***tavern table***.

salt: See ***salt dish***, and see ***worth his salt***, etc.

salt box: a wooden container in which salt was stored in considerable quantities, e.g., "He noted in his account book that there were about 180 pounds of salt '...on hand in the salt box'." See ***salt dish***.

salt carriage: a very sturdy, medium size, wide-tired wagon, occasionally with a lid over the bed, used to haul salt and similar dry commodities, e.g., "On May 13, 1831, New Market Alabamian, W.F. Scott paid $900.00 for a '340 salt carriage'."

salt cellar: See ***salt dish***.

salt dish, salt, salt cellar, dredging box, duster: small, shallow, open dishes or containers for storing or serving salt; until granulated salt was widely marketed, there were no salt shakers, and salt was placed in open containers, either a larger one in the center of the table for the use of all or, in refined homes, in smaller dishes at each setting, e.g., "Mrs. Vanderbilt is said to have had leaded, cut glass salt dishes in their retreat in Asheville."

salt it away, salt some away, salt away: derived from the common practice of salting meat in order that it be available for future consumption, e.g., "Our ancestors usually spoke of salting away some of their money, meaning it was being kept for future use." Also see ***put some back***.

saltinet: perhaps a salt shaker or small salt box used to dispense salt in small quantities, e.g., "The 1828 inventory mentioned a quantity of salt and a saltinet."

salting tub: See ***powdering tub.***

salting: See ***salt it away,*** and see ***powdering tub,*** and see ***put some back.***

saltpeter, saltpetre: usually potassium nitrate; a nitrate used to make gunpowder and explosives; a compound thought to have medicinal value, e.g., "Saltpeter and other potassium salts were administered as diuretics, and were thought valuable in ***treating heart disease.***"

salve tins: a small lidded tin or metal container used to keep salves, lotions, etc., e.g., "She washed all old salve tins in order that they might be reused." Also see ***ointment pot.***

salver: early, Johnson described it as a dish used to carry leftovers from the table; a tray for serving finger foods; in the colonies, usually a pan to catch drippings, e.g., "She served hors d'oeuvres on a silver salver"; "There was a salver near the fireplace." Also see ***dripping pan.***

salvor: one who salvages sunken, damaged, or abandoned ships, "Many of the early salvors sought the iron and other metals from which wrecked ships, in part, were made."

sampler: fabric needlework ***pictures*** (q.v.) and samples of the sewing skills of the maker, usually a young girl or woman, they bore the name of the maker and also displayed numbers, letters, sayings, proverbs, Biblical verses, and decorations, e.g., "The beautiful little sampler was dated 1838 and was made by Mikaila Bater."

samson: See ***wainwrights*** and ***coachmakers, tools of.***

sanctuary: the innermost part of a church; now, like very early, any place of safety and comfort, e.g., "Not even the King's designated men could enter the sanctuary of a Catholic church in order to arrest or take someone away."

sand glass: See ***hour glass.***

sanded, sanding: as now; early, an application of sand to a house floor, e.g., "In 1777, when William Baker was being paid for sweeping and sanding the Council Chamber, he was not using sandpaper."

Santa Claus: See ***St. Nicholas.***

Santa Fe Trail: that trail that opened commerce and trade with the east and Missouri from the far southwest, e.g., "William Becknell must be given considerable credit for the opening of trade over the Santa Fe Trail."

saplin: a sapling or young tree, e.g., "As with other words ending in 'g' the use of the word saplin in place of sapling was common in American colonial writings."

sarsenet, sarcenet, sarsnet: a fine, high quality silk fabric, e.g., "Green, light blue, black and pink sarsenets were frequently advertised by fabric and stuff merchants during the 18th-century." Also see ***stuff.***

SASE: a self-addressed stamped envelope enclosed with requests made to others for genealogical assistance, e.g., "Good genealogical manners require that a SASE be included if response is expected."

sash: a raisable window, usually paned, e.g., "Moore revealed something of house construction when he wrote 'Away to the window I flew like a flash, tore open the shutters and threw up the sash'."

A lady in a fancy dress; see ***sarsenet.***

sash glass: window panes, e.g., "The sash glass was broken by the ***gust*** (q.v.)."

saucepan: as now, a small pan in which food was boiled or fried, e.g., "The many inventory references to ***skillets*** (q.v.) often meant saucepans."

saucered and blowed: a common expression meaning that preparation has been completed; derives from the early practice of pouring hot drinks from a cup or mug into a saucer, blowing across it to cool it, and then pouring the fluid back into the cup for consumption, e.g., "When he said that the little chest was saucered and blowed, he meant that it was completed and ready for use."

sausage gun, sausage stuffer: a rather long, metal tube with a piston in one end and a smaller tube (with an opening) in the other end, into which is loaded bulk sausage, the same forced through the small end aperture into the ***casing*** (q.v.) to make link sausages, e.g., "At ***killing time*** (q.v.), nearly all rural families made good use of a sausage gun."

saw set, saw jig: a small, hand-held, but often bench-mountable tool designed to hold a saw when sharpening it and to guide the user as to the angle at which the teeth should be reset, e.g., "Every early ***joiner, cooper, carpenter***, and ***cabinetmaker*** (all, q.v.) had saw sets."

saw the elephant, have seen the elephant: a superlative, it arose in the time of Barnum (mid 19th century) when the elephant was a principle reason for attending a circus. It meant that the speaker had experienced a highly significant, awesome, dreadful or horrific event, quite usually battle or combat, e.g., "When describing the horrors of Malvern Hill, Ferguson told his friends that he had seen the elephant and did not like it."

sawbuck table: a very sturdy, large table of the colonial era, usually unfinished, and with legs crossed in "x" shape on both ends secured by a beam between them, e.g., The sawbuck table often did duty as a ***harvest table*** (q.v.)."

sawyer: an occupation; one who has the tools and knowledge to accurately saw wood and, especially, to make veneers of all kinds for use by furniture makers and ***cabinetmakers*** (q.v.), e.g., "As a sawyer, he bought raw lumber from the sawmills and sold the finished products to the cabinetmakers."

say laws?: a superlative, usually spoken in interrogatory form, especially used by Appalachian Mountain people and meaning that the listener is surprised, shocked, dismayed, or at a loss for words as a result of (usually) vulgar or profane utterances or actions of another in the immediate presence of the listener, e.g., "When the stranger swore angrily in front of the women and children, Marty looked at her friend and exclaimed 'say laws?'."

scald head: a condition where the head of an infant or very small child is covered with scabs and lesions, e.g., "Old Dr. Lockhart applied ***turpentine*** (q.v.) or an ointment of sulfur and tar for the scald head."

scales: early, a balance or balance pans used for weighing; now, any device used to weigh anything, e.g., "In the inventory, the scales were distinguished from the ***steelyards*** (q.v.)"

scaps, skeps, gums: hives of bees, e.g., "Every early Pennsylvania farm had a scap or two of bees."

scarlatina: early, thought to be a mild form of the dreaded ***scarlet fever*** (q.v.), e.g., "At the first symptoms of scarlatina, Dr. Drake prescribed ***belladonna*** (q.v.) and ammonium carbonate."

scarlet fever: a common, greatly feared disease that often was fatal, e.g., "For scarlet fever, among other treatments thought then to be effective, Dr. Drake administered mercury, mustard bathes, phosphorus, and sharp ***purges*** (q.v.) followed by vapor baths."

scate: See ***skate***.

scattergun: See ***shotgun***.

scholars: though Johnson defined the word as we commonly do now—"a man of letters...a pedant...a man of books"—much of 19th-century America used the word as a synonym for student, e.g., "Dr. W. K. Drake wrote a boyhood teacher who assisted him in his studies '...while the other scholars were at their play'."

school land(s): land required by law to be used for school purposes, e.g., "It was early proposed that in every ***township*** (q.v.) of 36 square miles 640 acres (the equivalent of a full ***section,*** q.v.) was to be set aside in perpetuity as school lands."

school records, Catholic: See ***Orders of Nuns.***

schoolmaster's desk, master's desk, schoolteacher's desk, clerk's desk: any of several designs of tall, lightweight desks with a flat, large work surface, often with turned legs and stretchers and occasionally with a fold-down writing surface concealing ***pigeon holes*** (q.v.) and small drawers, or occasionally with a light roll top and drawers below the writing surface, e.g., "Her schoolmaster's desk was of white oak, with a lockable ***tambour*** (q.v.) and small compartments inside." Also see ***rolltop desk.***

schools, old field: See ***old field schools.***

schooner: a light, fast ship, rigged fore and aft, e.g., "Many were the schooners owned by the merchant princes of New York City."

Schwaben, the: See ***lighter than air craft.***

sciatica: See ***lumbago***.

scire facias, writ of: an early court order directing that some person or persons show cause why some matter of record should not be enforced or used to advantage, e.g., "Early land patents often were subject to writs of scire facias where one was occupying land patented or granted of record to another person." Also see ***scire feci.***

scire feci: the endorsement on a writ of ***scire facias*** (q.v.) revealing that the ***sheriff*** (q.v.) notified a person that he was to come forth and answer the ***writ*** (q.v.), e.g., "The words scire feci written on a document reveal to the researcher that the sheriff of that county found the party named as ***defendant*** (q.v.) and gave him notice."

scite: a not uncommon spelling of the word site, e.g., "It was written that Ann Sherwood was ducked at a 'scite on Lynhaven Bay'."

scold: a nagging wife; a woman known to make or encourage trouble or disagreement among neighbors, e.g., "An early court report quoted a husband as saying '...she was but a common scold'."

sconce: early, and often now, a wall-mounted candle holder, usually with a small mirror behind the candles for enhanced illumination or decoration.

scoops: unlike now, usually a large ladle or handled container, e.g., "The scoops in the inventory probably were ladles."

Scotch, Scotch whiskey, Scots whiskey : a highly favored blend of whiskeys made in Scotland from malted barley, e.g., "Scotch has been an American favorite since the mid-18th century."

scotch hands, scotch paddles: small, short-handled, wooden paddles, usually ribbed on one side, for working or handling butter or mixing color into ***oleo*** (q.v.), e.g., "Her scotch hands revealed the use of many years."

Scots-Irish immigrants: the majority of whom arrived between 1715 and 1775, particularly from the area of Ulster, who either were or were not ***descendants*** (q.v.) of those Scottish who had migrated from Scotland to Ireland during the preceding decades, e.g., "With the coming of the sturdy Scots-Irish, a certain wanderlust—'itchy feet'—was infused into the American personality."

Scots-Irish influence, Scotch-Irish influence: many words and expressions arose from our Scotch-Irish ancestry, including 'axe to grind', 'dumb as a wedge', 'dumb as a basket of rocks', 'set on the fence', and the words a-feared, a-fishing, a-going, a-doing, etc., damnedest, chaw, injin, picter, clabber, yous (as a plural of you), and the addition of 'all' as a suffix, such as you-all, where all did you go, what all did you do; e.g., "Bog, inch, and whiskey are but three other examples of the Scots-Irish influence in out language."

Scots whiskey: See ***Scotch.***

scoured as a plow board: See ***clean as a plow board and*** see ***moldboard.***

scours: a frequent or continuing stomach ache from any of many causes, e.g., "Bethany wrote that Evan had suffered from the scours for more than three weeks, and she was worried about him."

scrag, scraggly, scraggy: somewhat unlike now, a very thin or lean person or animal, e.g., "When Brittany wrote in 1845 that her horse had become scraggly over the winter, she likely meant that it was too thin, and not that it was unkempt or had not had good care."

scramble: somewhat unlike now, meaning to gather together in a rather disorganized, random or disorderly fashion, e.g., "The diary reveals that Will Ferguson had put ashore and scrambled 71 slaves."

scrape the bottom of the barrel: a superlative, meaning by analogy, to glean the last remnant or final bit or amount of any material, as in the early wooden sugar, salt, chemical, and dry commodities containers, e.g., "When the known philanderer was elected, it was said that the party 'sure scraped the bottom of the barrel' to find him."

scrapple: a very common, early Dutch food made of corn meal, pork, seasoning, and usually buckwheat flour, e.g., "Fried scrapple was a favorite at Dutch breakfasts." Also see ***Dutch.***

scribbler: See ***scribe.***

scribe, scribble, scribbler, scribner, scrivener: a writer; one trained in the art of writing; one whose occupation was writing for others for hire, e.g., "The surnames Scribner and Scrivner derive from the very early terms scribe and scribble."

scrip: early, a small writing, coupon, or paper redemptive of merchandise or stock in trade; later and now in the U.S., usually paper currency of fractions of dollars not printed by the United States, e.g., "After the Civil War, scrip was printed in many denominations less than a dollar."

scrub brushes: See ***clamps.***

scruple: a measure of dry weight equaling 20 ***grains*** (q.v.).

scurvy: a disease causing painful joints and mental apathy, peculiar to mariners, recognized and cured from the earliest times, it nevertheless likely affected as many as 30,000 men during the American Civil War, e.g., "In 1610 Dr. Buhun prescribed fresh oranges, limes and lemons for the scurvy of Lord Delaware."

scutch: See ***break and scutch flax***.

scythe: a long handled tool with a long and sharp blade set nearly perpendicular to the slightly curved handle, and used to cut wheat and other long stemmed grains or cereals, e.g., "Swinging a scythe under an August sun was incredibly tiring."

sea bag: a large bag used to carry clothes, usually made of canvas and long carried by seagoing men, e.g., "All veterans of the U.S. Navy since the Revolution would recognize a sea bag." Also see ***portmannaies***.

sea fencibles, sea fensibles: men enlisted for service as soldiers on board ship, e.g., "The U.S. Marines have many of the same shipboard duties as the sea fencibles enlisted by Sir Francis Drake."

seal: the act of placing a personal symbol on a document, widely used before literacy was common; an impression of one's seal or sign, usually made in a wax wafer or impressing or penetrating a document for the purpose of confirming the willing execution of the document by the person whose name appeared; the small metal device bearing the ***signet*** (q.v.), symbol, or sign of the owner, e.g., "Major Bond noted that the ***grantor*** (q.v.) had not used a seal because no wax was available at the time of the signing"; "His seal was carried in his ***weskit*** (q.v.) and was of gold."

seaman: See ***private, private soldier***.

searce, searcer, bolter: a small, fine sieve, e.g., "She had a little silver searce that she used to strain her tea." Also see ***tea strainer, colander***, and ***riddle***.

seasoning: unlike now, the acclimation by newly arrived slaves and indentured servants particularly, and immigrants in general, to the summer heat and little understood diseases of sub tropical Virginia and the South, e.g., "The need for new arrivals to be seasoned led those who had a choice to arrive in Virginia, the Carolinas, and Georgia in the autumn or early spring."

seat and mistery: See ***art and mystery***

seated land: See ***seating***.

seating, seat, seated land: those governmental requirements that land which was the subject of patents and grants should be inhabited for certain time periods before title could be perfected, implicit in which was a measure of improvement; to satisfy the seating requirement, inhabitation by either an "owner" or a tenant usually was adequate, e.g., "The seating requirement caused him to build a cabin for himself and his son's family."

secession: those acts by which the Southern states left the American Union to become the Confederacy, e.g., "Commencing with South Carolina on December 24, 1860, Mississippi, Florida, Alabama, Georgia, Louisiana, Texas, Virginia, Arkansas, North Carolina, and Tennessee seceded from the Union and formed the Confederate States Of America.

second cousins: (third, fourth, etc.) those persons who share a common great-grandparent; to each "great" in the title of the most recent common ancestor, one (1) is added to determine the degree of cousinhood, e.g., "Their great-grandmother was their most recent common ancestor, so they were 2nd cousins." (1 'great', plus one, so "2nd" cousins); "They shared common great-great-great grandparents, so were 4th cousins (3 'greats', plus one, equals '4th' cousins)."

second day dress: an expression of the middle and upper classes, quite usually of the Old South; a dress to be worn by the bride on the day following her wedding, e.g., "Anne's mother was careful to select a second day dress appropriate to their travel plans."

secondary sources, secondary materials: in genealogy, terms reflecting a subjective view of the user as to the reliability of some source; usually refers to those research materials that are not "original" and were abstracted or extracted from or are compilations of original sources; materials considered by the researcher to be less reliable than primary sources, e.g., "The abstracts of the original court's orders were secondary sources."

secret diseases: venereal diseases, e.g., "The chancres described in early medical records were caused by the 'secret diseases'."

secretary: any of several styles of drop- or fall-front desks with drawers below and doored bookshelves above or to one side, e.g., "Diane's secretary was of oak and belonged to her great-grandmother."

Section, Township and Range: divisions of land by which much of the United States is described, e.g., "Ranges are determined by north-south lines 6 miles apart, the same numbered from east to west, those in turn divided by east-west township lines, also 6 miles apart, the same numbered from north to south, resulting in squares of 36 square miles, those being called townships, which, in their turn, are equally divided into 36 sections of 640 acres each (1 square mile). Thus Section 9 of Township 3 South, Range 15 East (abbreviated Sec. 9, T3S, R15E) is easily located."

Section of land: a square mile; 640 acres, ½ Sections, ¼ Sections, and ⅛ Sections are also common measurements of parcels of land e.g., "There are 36 sections in a ***township*** (q.v.) a half Section is 160 acres, etc." Also see ***Section, Township*** and ***Range***.

seed drill: See ***drill***.

seedcake: a small, sweet pastry, containing aromatic seeds such as caraway, e.g., "Seedcakes are some of the many delicious pastries known since the earliest times."

seen a sight of: a superlative, reflecting long experience or practice in observing something, e.g., "When told that he was a good judge of horseflesh, Midlam responded, 'I seen a sight of 'em, sure enough.'"

seignior: from which is derived the Spanish señor, e.g., "As with 'Mr.' in the English language, the Spanish term 'Seignior' was reserved to gentlemen and men of affluence, political position or high station in the community."

seized and possessed: an expression meaning that one is legally in possession of a tract of land, e.g., "Bethany was legally seized and possessed of the tract, even though it was actually occupied by her tenant."

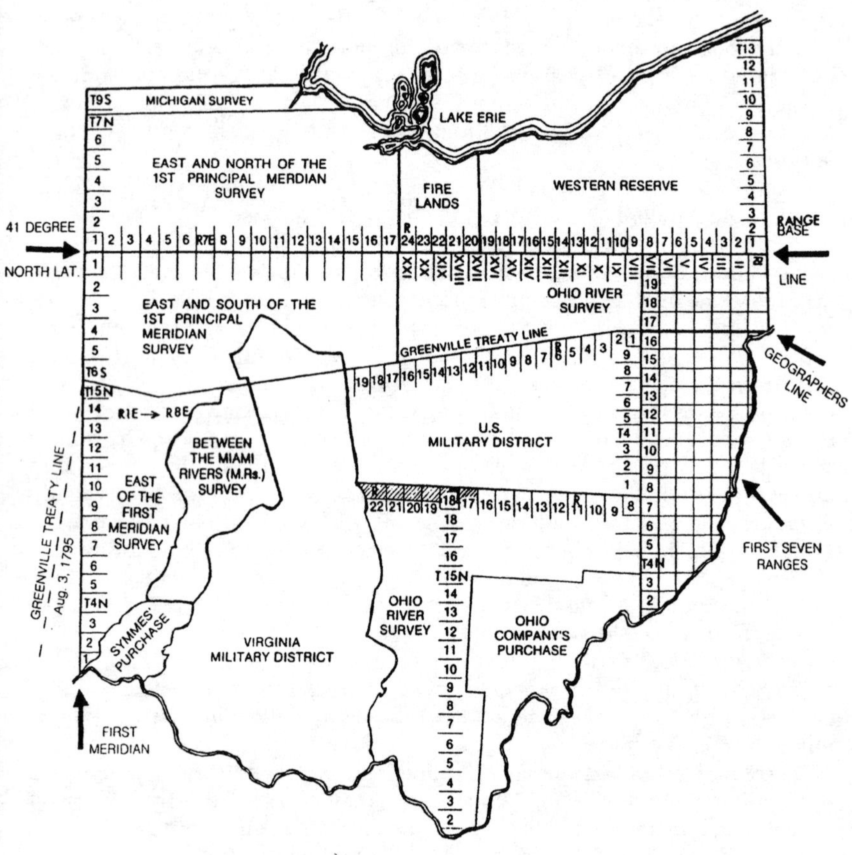

*Map of Ohio showing the several surveys from which most descriptions of land in **Ranges, Townships** and **Sections** were derived.*

SECTION OF LAND, 640 ACRES

A township is made up of 36 sections.

selectman, selectwoman: those municipal or town officers having executive powers and elected by New England towns to conduct the day-to-day business of that political subdivision, e.g., "The county administrators or executives of some states have their counterparts in New England selectmen."

Seminole Wars: those conflicts with Negroes and American Indians of east Florida that were viewed as a threat to the peace of Georgia and resulted in the capture of Pensacola and St. Marks, bringing U.S. dominance over all of north and east Florida, e.g., "Jackson's actions in the 1st Seminole War resulted in an improved position in foreign affairs for his administration."

send out of town: See ***warn out of town.***

Senior and Junior: abbreviated "Sr.," and "Jr."; terms that reveal the existence of another person of the same name; early, applied to either males or females, not necessarily related; now, usually father and son, e.g., "Elizabeth Jones, Sr., and Elizabeth Jones, Jr., acted as witnesses to Brittany's will."

senorio: usually real property, e.g., "Many early southwestern writings refer to senorio."

sense God gave a pine tag, the: See ***pine tag.***

separate examination, separately examined, examined away: questioning of a wife, privately and out of the presence of the husband by one appointed by a court or by law authorized to take oaths, concerning whether she acted of her own free will in executing a deed or other legal instrument, e.g., "Early law required separate examinations to assure that husbands did not coerce wives into legal actions contrary to their interests."

serge: a fine cloth, made of linen or wool, e.g., "The passenger lists revealed that Drake was a sergemaker from London."

Service Right, service right, Military Right, military right: any entitlement to land that was a reward by state or federal governments for military service in the early days of this country, e.g., "Revolutionary soldiers, as well as those of the War of 1812, quite usually were permitted to sell their Service Rights for whatever price they chose."

servitor: one trained in the art of ***glass making*** (q.v.), e.g., "The census revealed that Harruff was working as a servitor in 1824."

servitude: See ***indentured servants.***

set on fire, set them on fire, set him on fire, etc.: a superlative, used to describe the actions of another which, while not illegal, border upon illegality or take advantage of the bargain in a questionable or sharp way, e.g., "When told that Smith was granted the contract for the work, the lawyer with a frown emphatically said, 'He will set them on fire!'"

settee: any of the many styles of seats with backs, for two people, usually upholstered, with arms, and very widely used, e.g., "Many 19th-century inventories listed settees."

settle, settle bench, settle chair, settle bed: a long wooden seat or bench, with a high wooden back (sometimes spoked) and wooden arms; a chair for one, of "settle" styling; a bed with a tall hinged sideboard or a tall and hinged head or foot board that could be lowered for use as a table, e.g., "While most were plain and sturdy in appearance, Mikaila's settle bench appeared very much like Windsor furniture."

settlement, medium of: See ***medium of exchange.***

Seventh Army: See ***military combat units, famous.***

sewing frame: a tool of the ***bookbinder*** (q.v.), e.g., "Many inventories of estates of bookbinders list fillets, presses, rolls, trimming presses, and sewing frames."

sewing press: See ***bookbinders and printers.***

sewing table: somewhat of a luxury, a small table of a height appropriate for a seated woman, usually of better wood, often with a folding extension, and with a cloth bag beneath for scraps, pieces of thread and refuse of sewing, e.g., "Diane's sewing table was mahogany and had been a birthday gift."

sexton: the chief administrator of a cemetery, either church or secular; occasionally, a church handyman, e.g., "The records of sextons often provide genealogical information not available from any other source."

sexual intercourse: See ***cover***.

shake a stick at: a superlative deriving from the fact that one can quickly point at numerous objects, especially when out of doors, e.g., "Diane said that her Virginia mother and grandmother both had 'more boxwoods than you could shake a stick at'."

Shakers: that religious sect brought here in the 1770s that advocated common ownership of real estate, celibacy, and an austere life, e.g., "The simplicity of Shaker life was reflected in their magnificent, yet very simply designed ***furniture*** (q.v.)."

shakes, palsy: any of the several, little-understood nervous disorders, including Parkinson's syndrome, e.g., "He treated the palsy with ***tonics*** (q.v.), aconite and potassium bromide."

shallop: a small boat with one or two sails, used for near shore fishing and light hauling, e.g., "Many were the shallops on 18th-century Chesapeake Bay."

shaloon: a light woolen fabric, e.g., "It is likely that the shaloon Mr. Bater purchased of Mr. Parham was used for the linings in better cold weather clothing."

shanker: See ***chancre.***

share, plow share, sheers: the metal point of a plow, e.g., "'Beat their swords into plowshares' is intelligible only if one knows what a share was."

share cropper: See ***cropper***.

shave: a two-handled tool used to shape wood by drawing the sharpened edge toward the user, e.g., "A shave used to hollow wood as in making a ***porringer*** (q.v.) was called a hollow shave, and a hollow shave with a straight blade on the other end was called a jigger or jigger shave." Also see ***drawknife*** and see ***shave, animal.***

shave, animal: those, usually wooden, pole-like struts extending forward from the axle of a one horse ***buggy*** (q.v.) or ***wagon*** (q.v.) to the sides of the horse or other draft animal, and between which the animal is hitched for pulling, e.g., "Shaves were used for lighter loads than were ***tongues*** (q.v.) and ***trees*** (q.v.)." Also see ***swingletrees***, and see ***collars***.

shaving cup: a handled mug in which was placed shaving soap, the same wetted and agitated with a shaving brush, thereby creating a lather with which to shave, e.g., "Virtually every man of the 19th century who shaved had a shaving cup and a ***straight razor*** (q.v.)."

shaving mirror: a small, adjustable, free-standing mirror, of a size to be placed on a ***washstand, chest of drawers, commode,*** or ***bedside table***

(all, q.v.) e.g., "Whenever a male guest was in the home for overnight, Allison placed the shaving mirror in the guest ***bedchamber*** (q.v.)."

shawfowl: a decoy, usually to attract ducks or geese, e.g., "While very early commercial duck and goose hunters on Chesapeake Bay often spoke of shawfowls, the term decoy seems to have been preferred by early in the 19th century."

Shay's Rebellion: that Massachusetts uprising (mid-1786 to Mar. 1787) by destitute farmers seeking a paper money issue and other financial relief, which acts led to the raising of forces by both Massachusetts and Congress, the death of 5 "Shaysites," and the collapse of the insurgent force, e.g., "As in Bacon's Rebellion, in order that their families not suffer from knowledge of their participation, many of the men of Shays' Rebellion remained anonymous (to the chagrin of present-day genealogists)."

shay: See ***chaise***.

shebang, the whole: a superlative referring to the entirety of an organization, structure, or task to be built, done or gained; from the name given a shelter built of grass and brush to provide a measure of protection from the elements, particularly from the hot sun, e.g., "Civil War soldiers often threw up shebangs when they were required to be at one place and exposed to the hot summer sun for hours at a time, and when one soldier built the whole of it, he was said to have the done the whole shebang."

sheer, sheers: See ***share***.

shellac: a fine and ancient finish for furniture and other wooden objects, made of a resinous substance exuded by the insect ***lac*** (q.v.) dissolved in alcohol, e.g., "Most furniture made before 1880 was finished in shellac."

shemmy: See ***chemise***.

Shenandoah, the: See ***lighter than air craft***.

sheriff: very early, "shire reeve" or high sheriff; an ancient office, recorded in England before the 12th century; a "High Sheriff" had wide authority and jurisdiction within a county and spoke for the Crown, the courts, and government in general; later and now, the elected chief administrative and peace officer of a county, having duties in assisting all courts of general jurisdiction, summoning juries, serving writs and executing court orders, e.g., "The judge ordered the sheriff to take William West into custody and hold him until the next ***term*** (q.v.) of court."

sherry: originally, an amber colored wine with an added alcohol content and made in southern Spain, e.g., "Early colonials bought ordinary sherry and then added grain alcohol to fortify it."

Shetland wool: the wool made the fine undercoat of the Scottish Shetland sheep and pulled by hand from the animals, e.g., "The fabrics made from Shetland wool were among the finest available in colonial America."

shift: early, a woman's undergarment; now, a long, straight, unadorned woman's dress, e.g., "Susannah had three shifts when she died."

shilling (S or s): a British denomination of money used as a standard in Colonial America and for years thereafter in some of the states; there were 20 shillings in a pound (£), and 10 pence in a shilling (earlier, 12), but it was not everywhere of uniform value; e.g., "In Virginia, in 1755, the price of a pound of sugar for home use was one shilling, six pence (written: 1s,6p or /1/6)." Also see ***scrip***.

shimmey, shimmy: See ***chemise***.

shin-plaster: paper money of diminished worth; paper money having a value of less than a dollar; fractional currency, e.g., "The term shin-plaster arose when certain paper currency came to have so little value that it might have been used to dress cuts or bruises, as on the shin."

shindig: a party or gathering, usually for the purpose of dancing and frivolity, noteworthy for the lack of training in the art of dancing by some participants and the resultant bruising and injury to the legs and feet of their partners, e.g., "Tennessee country and mountain folks even yet commonly refer to parties as shindigs."

shingle: See ***hang out a shingle.***

shinney, shinny: homemade Louisiana whiskey, e.g., "A Louisiana court found McClinton guilty of making shinny."

ship breakers: See ***broken up ships.***

ship of the line: a large warship; an armed vessel of 74 or more guns, e.g., "Britain, with her great ships of the line, ruled the seas from the time of Francis Drake until early in the 20th century."

ships, passenger: See ***passenger ships.***

ships (famous): Of the best known ships moving to and from the American colonies and states, surely one would list Columbus' *Nina, Pinta,* and *Santa Maria*; Hudson's *Half Moon*; Drake's *Revenge* and *Golden Hind*; Jones' *Bon Homme Richard*; Perry's *Lawrence*; Jamestown's *Susan Constant, Godspeed* and *Discovery*; *Mayflower*; *Speedwell*; *Virginia* (first ship built in the American colonies); H.M.S. *Serapis*; U.S.S. *Constitution*; *Monitor* and *Merrimac* of the Civil War; and *Maine, Hornet,* and *Arizona.*

shipwright, ship carpenter: one whose trade or calling is that of designing or building large boats or ships, e.g., "The building of ships was a joint enterprise utilizing the skills of many, including those trained in the art and mystery of the shipwrights, keelers, ropers, ships' carpenters, and caulkers." Also see ***surnames from occupations*** and see ***art and mystery.***

Shire: an English breed of powerful, heavy draft horses, brown or bay with white markings, e.g., "The great Shires and ***Clydesdales*** (q.v.) both were predominantly a rich brown color."

shire: early, a political subdivision in England made up of an indefinite number of ***hundreds*** (q.v.); now, a county, e.g., "Somersetshire is now Somerset County."

shoddy: poorly made, of very low quality, e.g., "The shoes and uniforms of the early soldiers often were incredibly shoddy and unserviceable." Also see ***chintzy.***

shoemaker: one who made shoes and boots, distinguished from a ***cobbler*** (q.v.) or ***harnessmaker*** (q.v.), e.g., "Samuel Martin was a shoemaker in Holidaysburg in 1840." Also see ***cordwainer***, and see ***cobbler***, and see ***botcher***.

shoemakers lamp, jewelers lamp: by placing a candle behind a clear glass container or bulb of water, the light was diffused broadly and shadows on close work were reduced, hence the name, e.g., "He had a brass shoemakers lamp with two large candles and four bulbs mounted around them."

shoes: unlike now, e.g., "Milton called shoes shoons; early poor and rural dwellers tied pieces of leather or heavy cloth to their feet for out of doors and used lighter cloth for indoors; straight boots (jackboots) and half boots or demi-boots (both heavy and 'dress', and sometimes with very broad, draping tops as portrayed by the "Three Musketeers") were commonly worn by men, especially on horseback; by the time of Henry VIII shoes often had thick cork soles (2" plus) and were known as pantofles; for the wealthy, early fashion required very long toes pointed upwards (early, even tied to the knees with chains of tiny links); by 1715, wooden shoes (pattens), open at the back, with metal rings to keep the feet above mud and water, were common, and wooden heels were used on all leather shoes, especially among the French and Hollanders; clogs, open at the back (as now) were wooden and without the rings of pattens; goloeshoes (hence the term 'galoshes') were thick leather and, as were pattens, were open at the heel; knots of flowers or colored cloth decorated the buckled or stringed shoes of 18th century women of means (some strings were jeweled or made of gold and silver thread, and were valuable enough to appear in inventories); leather French fall shoes were low, of better quality, and worn by both men or women, and women of means also wore highly decorated silk and satin or half leather and silk; 1825 to 1850 saw shoes with square toes, and wooden high heels (cross cut heels) were common; by 1835, as now, India rubbers and overshoes were worn over shoes to prevent moisture; and not until the early 19th century were shoes made for the left and right foot.

shoo fly rocker: the source for the expression is lost, we think; a rocking toy for children, with a seat mounted between small silhouettes of small horses, the whole on double rocker bars, e.g., "The shoo fly rocker had belonged to Evan's father."

shoo-in: easy to accomplish, as in moving animals by simply uttering that sound—"shooo", e.g., "Sarah told the children that while they would have to herd the goats to the pen, the lambs could simply be shooed in."

shoons: See ***shoes***.

shoot the king, if you: See ***don't wing him***.

shooting iron: ***firearms***, (q.v.) usually of short barrel held in one hand, e.g., "The expression 'shooting irons' probably arose in the early days when firearms were made locally and of iron from the local blacksmith."

shooting match, shootin' match: contests of accuracy usually with ***rifles*** (q.v.), popular during the period 1750-1950, usually attended with prizes and gambling, e.g., "Sgt. York participated in neighborhood shootin' matches until well up in years."

shopboard: a wooden work bench, e.g., "In early times the word bench usually meant seat, and a shopboard was a work area at which one stood."

short ton: See ***long ton.***

shot pouch, powder pouch: a small bag of leather or waterproof cloth, tied to the belt or worn over the shoulder, and used to carry the ***shot*** (q.v.), ***caps*** (q.v.), ***balls*** (q.v.), wadding, etc., needed for the operation of firearms carried for hunting, e.g., "He had his father's old shot pouch."

shot: round lead pellets used in shotguns, made in various sizes from "00 buck" to "#9" and even smaller, selected based upon the size of the animal to be hunted, e.g., "He used 00 buck for deer, #2 for turkeys, #4 for ducks and geese, #6 for rabbits, grouse and pheasant, and #7 and #8 shot for quail." Also see ***shotgun.***

shotgun, scattergun, fowling piece, bird gun: of many makes and models and of various "gauges" (size of load and barrel diameter), a ***firearm*** (q.v.) firing multiple small lead pellets—shot, q.v.—quite usually used for ducks, geese, wild fowl, small game, and pests, e.g., "Every fall he took up the old 16 gauge shotgun and went hunting for grouse and quail."

Shrove Tuesday: the day before ***Ash Wednesday*** (q.v.), e.g., "Early Episcopal and early court records often speak of Shrove Tuesday."

shrubs: a cherry juice liqueur, e.g., "Her recipe for cherry shrub called for finely strained juice from ripe whole cherries cooked in a double boiler, to which sugar was added, the mixture placed in qt. ***bottles*** (q.v.) with 2 ounces of ***brandy*** (q.v.) in each, the bottles then sealed and stored until needed."

shutters: unlike now, hinged covers or shields for windows mounted inside the house behind the windows (***sashes,*** q.v.) and used to seal the house from intruders and severe weather, e.g., "Knowing what shutters and sashes were renders the "Night Before Christmas" intelligible, since there Moore wrote '...away to the window I flew like a flash, tore open the shutters and threw up the sash....'"

sibling: from the Saxon "sibb"; early, any relative or kinsman; later and now, brothers and sisters, e.g., "Having then but little interest in ***collateral lines*** (q.v.), she did not research the ***descendants*** (q.v.) of her grandfather's siblings."

sick time: the time immediately prior to and immediately after one's delivery of a child, e.g., "Maggie's sick time was not far off."

sickle mill: probably a place of business where sickles, scythes, chisels, saws, etc., were manufactured, repaired, or sharpened, e.g., "Roberts wrote that he had been faced with either repairing his own equipment or '...having that sorry Snyder's sickle mill do it'." See ***sorry*** and see ***sickle.***

sickle: a short-handled implement with a sharp, curved thin blade used to cut weeds, grasses and other stemmed vegetation, e.g., "The sickle was a necessity in cleaning ***fence rows*** (q.v.)."

sickly season: the Southern summer months (those without "R"s) when diseases, particularly malaria, were common, e.g., "Rich early Southerners went north during the sickly season to avoid the ***miasmas*** (q.v.) that they thought brought malaria and other disease."

side by side, bookcase: inexplicably, occasionally and early sometimes called a ***buffet*** (q.v.); usually, any of several styles of cabinets with a single, paned door and bookshelves on the left, a drop-down writing surface with compartments and ***pigeon holes*** (q.v.) within, often having a doored compartment above on the right, and often with a small mirror above the drop writing surface, e.g., "Allison's side by side, that she called a bookcase, was oak and had bookshelves and a small, paned compartment."

side chair: chairs of many designs and styles, straight-backed, usually without arms and either upholstered or with padded, woven, or leather seats and no other upholstered surfaces, designed to be placed against a wall and moved to a table or about the room as needed, e.g., "Mikaila had pressed-back, oak side chairs that were kept side by side against the ***parlor*** (q.v.) wall."

side saddle, ladies' saddle: a woman's saddle, having both stirrups on one side, and so made as to permit a woman to ride without being astride the animal, e.g., "The 1679 Judith Parker inventory revealed '1 old side-saddle'."

side table: any small to medium-sized table, occasionally with a revolving or folding top, so shaped as to set against a wall in hallways, foyers, etc., e.g., "Sally's side table was of mahogany with a folding top and also served as a ***game table*** (q.v.)."

sideboard: a long, usually rather narrow, waist high, serving piece, narrower and with fewer drawers than a ***buffet*** (q.v.), and usually made of high quality, highly finished wood, with a drawer or two and usually doored compartments below the work surface; used to serve refreshments or as a buffet, e.g., "Bethany's Queen Anne sideboard was nearly covered with cookies and every other imaginable dessert." Also see ***huntboard***, and see ***butler's sideboard.***

sidekick: a companion or friend, quite usually of a man, e.g., "Since two horses might protect each other by quartering, whereby one might kick to the rear and the other to one side, rural folks often referred to a close companion as a sidekick."

siege: war fought by cutting off ingress, egress, and supplies to an enemy position, e.g., "Sieges of significance during our Civil War include those of Ft. Sumter, Vicksburg and Atlanta."

sieve: early, and before inexpensive wire, sieves sometimes were strung with human hair; as now, a strainer, e.g., She had sieves, ***colanders*** (q.v.), and a ***riddle*** (q.v.)."

sight of: See ***seen a sight of.***

sight unseen: an adverb for a purchase, or object contracted, bargained for, or accepted without it having been examined or inspected it, e.g., "When Allison bought the horse without having examined it, Todd said she had bought it sight unseen." Also see ***pig in a poke.***

signatures (theory of): that early theory of medicine in which every illness had a natural cure, e.g., "Since walnut meats had a shape similar to the brain—its signature—those nuts were prescribed for headaches and any other ***distempers*** (q.v.) of the brain."

signed, sealed, and delivered: an early expression, once restricted to deeds, that stated the three requirements for a deed to be effective; later, and now, meaning that an action involving a writing has been accomplished, e.g., "In addition to being executed, very early deeds had to sealed and actually delivered—handed over—to the ***grantee*** (q.v.), hence the expression signed, sealed, and delivered."

signet ring, Jesuit ring: a ring bearing ones initials, used early to seal documents by pressing it into melted sealing wax, e.g., "The signet ring of Thomas Drake bore the initials 'TD'."

silk mercer: See ***mercer***.

sillibub: See ***syllabub***

sills: See ***thills.***

silver: the word silver often appears in inventories, even though the items were not silver or silverplate, e.g., "African silver was silverplate usually made in Birmingham, Eng., at about the time of our Civil War; Brazil silver was nickel plate; Waldo or Waldo silver was a gold colored ware made in Connecticut in the 1890s; Siberian Silver was silver plate on a copper base metal; Oregon silver was inexpensive plate made in England near the end of the 19th century; and German silver also was not silver, but an ***alloy*** (q.v.) of cheaper metals."

silver oar: that standard appearing in a court in admiralty; a miniature silvered oar carried by law enforcement officers as a symbol of authority when executing orders from a court of admiralty, e.g., "When a group of pirates were hung in Newport in 1723, the Marshall carried a small silver oar as a mark of his authority."

silversmiths' tools, goldsmiths' tools: as now, e.g., "Even though their devices were similar to those of the coppersmith and the pewterer, the occupation of the silversmith or goldsmith is sometimes revealed in writings or records that refer to such as spoon or plate dies, wire draw benches, blocks or machines, swage blocks, burins, small vises, and snarling pins."

simlins: white squash, a mainstay of many regions of the U.S., and especially from the South, mid-South and mid-West, e.g., "Major Puryear asked Betty to fry up some simlins and onions fresh from the ***kitchen garden*** (q.v.)."

simples: any herb, root, or plant used for medicinal purposes, e.g., "The New World and its native peoples provided many previously unknown 'simples' around which the ***Dutch*** (q.v.) built a substantial trade in Europe."

single action revolver, double action revolver: revolvers (q.v.), a hand-held weapon that may be cocked preparatory to firing by pulling back the hammer (single action) or by pulling back the trigger or the hammer (double action), e.g., "Colt revolvers were first made only in single action, followed later in double action." Also see ***revolver*** and see ***handgun***.

singletree: See ***swingletree***.

sink: a permanent wash basin with a drain in the bottom; any spot or area of land within which water drains off downward and into the underlying strata, e.g., "Maggie was delighted when Will installed in her kitchen a sink and a little hand pump to lift water from the cistern"; "The Skeels survey referred to the west property line as extending to a red oak tree in the sink." Also see ***dry sink.***

Sir and ***Madam:*** early, titles referring to noblemen and their ladies; until recently, reserved for gentlemen and their wives or ladies of great accomplishment and high standing, e.g., "Francis Drake became Sir Francis upon being knighted by Queen Elizabeth I"; "There being tithables residing there in 1677, the household of 'Madam Parker' was listed."

sire: a male parent animal, usually a ***stallion*** (q.v.), e.g., "The sire was a beautiful black ***thoroughbred*** (q.v.)."

sissers, scissors: as now, e.g., "In Virginia of the 1760s the value of a pint of good rum or a silk handkerchief was about equal to that of a pair of scissors."

sister: a ***sibling*** (q.v.); a nun; a term often used in the Biblical sense, e.g., "His siblings consisted of four brothers and three sisters"; "Care must be exercised since the records of the old church refer to unrelated members of the congregation as brothers and sisters." Also see ***brother.***

sitting, sitting of court: a time limit, the length of time of a session of court, e.g., "The court ordered that sometime during that sitting of the court the ***sheriff*** (q.v.) was to give her 21 lashes."

sitting room: See ***parlor.***

Six Mile Tree, six mile trees: very often the landmarks designating the corners of townships, e.g., "The southwest corner of Township 3S, Range 14E. was at the road intersection and was marked with a giant walnut called Six Mile Tree." Also see ***Section, etc.***

sixpence, su'pence: an English coin commonly found in the American colonies in the 17th, 18th, and 19th centuries, having a value of ½ shilling (6 pence), e.g., "Sixpence coins were common, particularly among seafaring men." Also see ***pence.***

skate, scate, ice skate: unlike now, early skates were shoes with metal plates tied to them, e.g., "Blades on ice skates were uncommon early in other than eastern Europe."

skedaddle, high-tail: to leave some place on foot at a rapid pace or with urgency, e.g., "While he spoke of skedaddling, his friend said that he had high-tailed it out of there."

skeer, skeer in them or him: fright (scare); one who is frightened, e.g., "George Drake assured the others in the regiment that he would do his share to 'keep the skeer in them Yankees.'"

skein: usually, a winding of some number of loops of yarn; to merchants, a measure of number (often 40) and length of loops of yarn, e.g., "If from her own ***wheel*** (q.v.) and for her own use, a skein was an indeterminate number of loops"; "He sold her three 200-foot skeins of woolen yarn."

skep: very early, a beehive shaped like an inverted basket and made of coiled rope tied together to prevent its collapse; early, usually a round ½ bushel wooden or reed basket, often with handles, e.g., "Early depictions of beehives almost always show them as skeps"; "The 1751 inventory revealed 'two oaken skeps'."

skewer: as now, a pointed metal utensil for moving pieces of food from one place to another, e.g., "So common were skewers that very few inventories even mention such."

skiff: a rowboat, nearly pointed on both ends, occasionally with a single sail, e.g., "Every early landing had skiffs moving to and fro."

skillet: unlike now, a small kettle used for boiling small quantities of food, e.g., "Early inventories have many references to skillets, meaning what we know as ***saucepans*** (q.v.) or small kettles."

skimmer: a long-handled, metal kitchen utensil, usually shallow and with or without a removable perforated top, used to skim grease, bones and undesirable materials from the surface of boiling or cooking stews and foods, e.g., "Skimmers were used in virtually every 18th-century kitchen." Also see ***glass making***.

skins in the limes, in the limes: apparently referred to animal skins being cured for making leather, e.g., "Harris was said to have no estate except for some 'skins in the limes'."

skins: See ***hides and skins.***

skirmishers: those armed men placed, usually at the front or flanks and sometimes at the rear of a body or larger unit of armed men or military resources and charged with the duty of detecting and holding off advances by an enemy until a larger force might be assembled or called to that battle scene, e.g., "At Chancellorsville, the right wing Union skirmishers sent many unheeded messages to headquarters telling that a large force was moving through the woods at their front." Also see ***flank companies.***

skiver, hides and skins skivers: See ***tanners' and curriers' tools.***

skunk, polecat, fitchew: as now, the common skunk, e.g., "Her reference to the 'dogs being sick from the polecat' meant that a skunk had sprayed them from short distance causing nausea and vomiting."

slant top desk: See ***desk***.

slave: one who is owned by and held as property of another, and who may gain personal freedom and liberty only through action by that owner or by law, e.g., "Having been purchased by that family, she was their slave, as were her children." Also see ***manumission***.

slave insurrections: as stated, e.g., "Any listing of the many slave uprisings or insurrections should include the ***Nat Turner Insurrection*** (q.v.); the 1687 planned revolt of Tidewater slave, Sam, who was captured and sentenced to wear an iron collar for life; the revolt at James City and Surry in 1710, resulting in the hanging of the 4 instigators; the Rappahannock revolt of 1722 wherein the master of 15 slaves found them and foiled their plan; Gabriel Prosser's Insurrection of 1800, which brought Prosser's hanging; the Norfolk incident of Easter morning 1802, which resulted in the hanging of 1 and a reprieve of another; and the John Brown affair of 1858, wherein Brown undertook to arouse and arm the blacks at Harper's Ferry, VA (WV), failed, and was hung for his actions."

slave-stealers, slave stealers: those who stole or harbored slaves, usually Northerners, e.g., "As did many, the old Savannah preacher was vehement in his condemnation of the 'Yankee slave stealers'." Also see ***man-stealers.***

slaver: an early ship used in the slave trade, e.g., "Many early American port and ships' records refer to slavers."

slaves, fugitive, assistance to: as written, e.g., "The New York Committee On Vigilance (1835), the New England Freedom Association (1845), and the Chicago Police Association (1850) were but three of the many groups that sought to assist fugitive slaves in their flights from their masters. Also see ***slave*** and see ***slave-stealers***.

slaw, coleslaw: unknown to Johnson, a salad made of cabbage, e.g., "The familiar American term, coleslaw, derives from kohl, meaning cabbage, and slaw meaning salad." Also see ***poke sallet***.

sleave: probably, to untwist or to separate a twist of yarn, e.g., "Allison wrote that the little girls had been given the task of 'sleaving the yarn'."

sleepers: ancient term meaning the large beams under the floor of a barn and other large buildings, apparently other than a residence, e.g.,

"Worrell wrote that the crop had been so great that the weight had 'broke the barn sleepers'."

sleigh: as now, a horsedrawn, winter vehicle on runners, e.g., "Of the many styles, types, and qualities of sleighs, some of the more recognizable were town sleighs and town runners, those light sleighs used as the names imply, about town and on short trips; the coal box sleigh, simple and often home made and appearing much like a large box on runners, and an Albany pony sleigh, which were well known, nicely painted, rather expensive and sleek."

sley: probably to ***sleave*** (q.v.); perhaps a weaver's shuttle, e.g., "She wrote that she had spent a day sleying silk"; "The Cole inventory mentioned a '...loom and sley'."

slice: See ***peel.***

sliced bread: as distinguished from bread that is served in loaves from which those eating it break pieces, e.g., "Marty often asked guests if they would like sliced bread with their meal." Also see ***loaf bread.***

slicer: very early, a large knife, and if serrated, used to slice bread, if not, used for meats, etc.; later, a mechanical utensil with a revolving blade used to slice meats and cheeses, e.g., "The 1679 Parker inventory included 2 slicers, a ***cleaver*** (q.v.), and a ***pey peel*** (q.v.)."

slicker: See ***tanners' and curriers' tools.***

slipper chair: a small, low, upholstered chair without arms, so designed that a woman wearing a bustle might sit and put on or remove slippers or shoes by reaching down to either side of her dress, e.g., "Sarah's Empire slipper chairs were upholstered in red velvet and were elegant."

slop, slops: early, a mixture of corn meal, bran and tailings from grain fed to hogs; also a navy term, meaning inexpensive clothing, sometimes a mariner's wide-legged cropped pants, a heavy shawl, loose jacket or tunic, or other outerwear for seamen, e.g., "While his farmer-brother spoke of slopping the hogs, Seamen Trip occasionally spoke of his slop chest, meaning that small wooden container wherein he stored his tobacco, personal effects, stockings and other items of apparel."

slop, slop bucket: usually, a container for table scraps, leftovers, and food remnants or by -products (sour milk, etc.) saved for feeding to hogs; that pail or bucket used to carry food to hogs; very rarely and early, a ***thundermug*** (q.v.), e.g., "Slopping the hogs was one of the first chores assigned to farm children."

slop bowl: a term apparently of the middle class meaning a small table bowl in which were placed tea dregs, seeds and peelings from fruits, etc., e.g., "She said she formerly placed a slop bowl on the table when big meals were being served."

slow fever: unknown, probably a symptom of one of the many diseases that gradually brought on an elevated body temperature for an extended period, e.g., "The *Chronicle* related that W. O. Kearley had died of slow fever."

slow poke: probably an early railroad term referring to one who moved too slowly in stirring or poking the fire in a locomotive, e.g., "When haste was needed and she dawdled in doing her part of the work, Sarah smiled and told Jean that she was a real slow poke."

sluice: a water gate or vent for flowing water; the water or watercourse surrounding an island or ***hummuck*** (q.v.), e.g., "The prospector had a long, horizontally grooved sluice that separated the gold from the water"; "He wrote that the sluice was nearly dry."

slumps: See ***desserts, early.***

slut: female dog; a ***bitch*** (q.v.); a very common, quite acceptable, early expression, not considered vulgar until the Victorian-Edwardian era, e.g., "Many were the classified ads of the 1850s that told of sluts for sale."

small arms, small arms fire: hand held weapons; a military situation in which the fire of hand held weapons is dominant, widespread, or intense, e.g., "The battle of Shiloh was decided by small arms fire." Also see ***musketry.***

smarty-pants: very early, and recently a jibe-like expression for an adolescent girl or young woman, usually, who is of brisk, acute, lively, or overly sharp wit or intellect, e.g., "When she insisted on always being the first to answer the questions and then was in error with many answers, the other children called her smarty-pants."

smelling salts: of many recipes, thought to revive those who were faint, e.g., "For smelling salts, to 1 oz. potassium acetate (called 'sal diureticus') in a ***sniffing bottle*** (q.v.), she added ½ oz. of sulfuric acid and a few drops of lavender oil."

smelter: See ***iron master.***

smith: one who works metal, i.e., tinsmiths, goldsmiths, silversmiths, coppersmiths, blacksmiths (***iron***, q.v.), etc., e.g., "His neighbor was Paul Revere, the silver and gold smith."

smiths work: iron work done for hire, e.g., "In 1687, the court approved payment to Haskins for 'smiths work on the jail door.'"

smock: a woman's undergarment; a ***shift*** (q.v.), e.g., "In early times, many women's garments worn under other clothing were called smocks."

smoke tongs: See ***smoking tongs.***

smoke-jack, chimney jack: a rather ingenious device designed to more or less slowly ratchet or turn a ***spit*** (q.v.) as the air and heat flow in a chimney increased or decreased, e.g., "The smoke-jack made it possible for her to be about other ***chores*** (q.v.) while the meat cooked."

smokepipe: See ***pipe.***

smokes: any form of tobacco that was to be lit and smoked, e.g., "Maggie always spoke of 'you men's smokes' when referring to pipes, cigars, and cigarettes."

smoking tongs, smoke tongs: a tool by which a hot coal from a fireplace might be picked up and used to light a pipe, cigar, or other tobacco form, a lamp or another stove, e.g., "There being no matches early, it was expected that tavern keepers would provide smoking tongs for their patrons."

smoothbore, smoothbore musket, smoothbore gun: a firearm firing a single shot, as in a ***rifle*** (q.v.), but without spiral grooves (***rifling***, q.v.) in the barrel, e.g., "The old inaccurate smoothbores were relegated to the gun rack when rifling was invented."

smoothers: See ***iron (to).***

snake fence, zigzag fence, waving fence: so called by reason of its appearance; a fence without posts made with split logs laid with the ends overlapping in a zigzag fashion, e.g., "Before wire fencing, snake fences were common where the soil was so rocky as to make driving posts difficult." Also see ***post and rail fences,*** and ***barbed wire.***

snakeroot: any of several roots or plant parts believed to have value in treating venomous snake and insect bites, e.g., "One physician's snakeroot might be different from that of another." Also see ***rattlesnake root***.

snarling pins: See ***silversmiths' tools***.

sneet: snow and sleet mixed; often found where there is much warm moisture in the upper air and yet the lower levels of air are below the freezing mark, e.g., "The word sneet has been known in the Southern mountains since early times."

sniffing bottle, sniff bottle, sniffer: occasionally known as a ***tickler bottle***, (q.v.); unlike now, a usually glass stoppered bottle for ***smelling salts*** (q.v.), e.g., "Bethany's sniffing bottles were of high quality glass."

snood: a loosely woven, net-like covering for the hair of a woman, said to derive from such coverings worn by Scottish women, e.g., "Judith wore a black snood with her mourning clothes."

snow roller: a horse-drawn vehicle having a huge roller instead of front wheels, used to flatten the snow on streets so as to facilitate the use of sleighs and cutters, e.g., "The purchase of a snow roller by the little town was a boon to those who had to move about during the winter."

snowbroth: a cold liquor or alcoholic drink, e.g., "As did Shakespeare, Mikaila referred to a barrel of apple jack that was kept outside in the cold as her '...husband's snowbroth...'"

snowdonets: perhaps a heavy fabric from which to make work clothes or pants, e.g., "In July of 1798 Kuhn & Risberg advertized for sale plain and spotted jeans and snowdonets."

snuff: powdered or finely chopped tobacco, used by placing a small amount (a ***pinch***, q.v.) between the teeth and lips or cheek, e.g., "Snuff has been widely used since early in the 17th century." See also ***dip***.

snuff box, snuff tin, pinch box: a metal box, often ***chased*** (q.v.), small enough to be placed in one's pocket, and in which is carried chopped smokeless tobacco—***snuff*** (q.v.), e.g., "She had a chased silver pinch box."

snuff miller: one who understood varieties of tobacco and ground it into snuff, e.g., "The ***tobacconist*** (q.v.) often was his own snuff miller."

snuff spoon: a small spoon used by ladies to pick up a small quantity of ***snuff*** (q.v.), e.g., "Snuff spoons were owned by very few women other than those of wealth." Also see ***snuff***, and also see ***snuff box***.

snuffer: as now, a small, long handled, triangular or round cup used to put out a candle by gently placing it down over the flame; also a cutting device to clip the charred portion of candle wicks, e.g., "Parker made her a brass snuffer"; "Since wax melted down more quickly than wicks, it occasionally was necessary to clip such wicks with a snuffer."

soap: as now; early, produced by adding lye (made by adding water slowly to fine ashes—hickory was preferred—and draining off the resulting liquid) to clear boiling lard (made by cooking down pork fat), and stirring and cooking until the mixture thickened, then cooling and slicing into blocks, e.g., "The grease resulting from skimming stews and ***rendering*** (q.v.) lard was used with lye to make soap."

soapstone, soap earth: a soft stone, similar to talc, used widely to smooth and polish table tops, hearths, etc., e.g., "By 1860, soapstone was widely advertised for sale as a cleaner and polishing powder."

socer: a father-in-law, e.g., "Early southwestern records occasionally speak of a socer."

societies: See ***fraternities, sororities and societies.***

Society Of The Cincinnati (The): See ***Order of the Cincinnati.***

sock darner, sock egg: a handled, glass or smooth wooden elongated ball used to insert in and shape stockings being repaired, e.g., "Allison's sock darner was porcelain and beautifully made."

sod house: in those portions of the Grteat Plains where few or no trees grew, the first settlers constructed houses of squares of sod with woven grass roofs, e.g., "Some Eastern-born wives of early Nebraska settlers broke into tears upon first entering the sod houses that they were to call home."

sofa bed, bed lounge: an upholstered ***couch*** (q.v.) with a slightly elevated end to be used as a shoulder and headrest and a usually straight, upholstered back shaped like a headboard or the back on a ***lounge*** (q.v.), e.g., "Sofa beds were common in late Victorian times."

sofa: any upholstered, armed seat for more than one person, e.g., "Johnson defined a sofa as a 'seat covered with ***rugs'*** (q.v.)."

softening of the brain: See ***brain.***

solar: land with a house, e.g., "Early Texas and California references to one's solar have nothing to do with the sun."

sole and upper leathers: leathers made for use by ***cobblers*** (q.v.), ***cordwainers*** (q.v.), and shoemakers, e.g., "In the early days, when every community had businesses where shoes were made or repaired, sole and upper leathers were purchased by those shoemakers and cobblers for making soles and upper shoe parts."

solicitor, solicitor in chancery: a lawyer knowledgeable in the workings of the courts of equity when law and chancery were considered to be separate court functions, e.g., "In 1844, in Findlay, Ohio, attorneys E. Girt, E. Thompson, J. Barnd, James Goodman, M. C. Whitely, D. Higgins and A. F. Parker advertised their services as Solicitors In Chancery." Also see ***chancery.***

solstice: that point on the vertical, above which the sun does not rise in summer, and below which it does not descend in winter, e.g., "The summer and winter solstices and the vernal and autumnal ***equinoxes*** (q.v.) were the means by which a precise calendar was drawn."

songs, popular: as now, e.g., "A list of popular and well known early rhymes and songs must include *Mother Goose* (c. 1715); *Beggar's Opera* (1752); *Messiah* (1770); *My Days Have Been So Wondrous Free* (c. 1760); *Yankee Doodle* (1767); *All Hail The Power Of Jesus' Name* (1793); *President's March* (1793); *Hail Columbia* (1798); *Old Oaken Bucket* (1813); *Star Spangled Banner* (1814); *Turkey In The Straw* (c. 1834); *We Won't Go Home Till Morning* (1842); *Old Dan Tucker* (1843); *Jimmy Crack Corn* (1846); *Oh, Susannah* (1848); *De Camptown Races* (1850); *Old Folks At Home* (1851); *Massa's In De Cold Cold Ground* (1852); *Frankie and Johnny* (1850); *Old Kentucky Home* (1853); *Darling Nelly Gray* (1856); *Jingle Bells* (1857); *Dixie* (1859); and *Old Black Joe* in 1860."

Sons of Confederate Veterans, The: a non-profit society of men whose ancestors or ancestral uncles or cousins were Confederate veterans of the Civil War, e.g., "His great-great grandfather, George A. Drake, was in the 43rd North Carolina, making Al eligible for The Sons of Confederate Veterans."

Sons of Liberty: 1765-1766, those groups of men, particularly under Samuel Adams, usually of port cities, who viewed themselves as Patriots and serving the public good, and who undertook to rebel against the Stamp and Townshend Acts, etc., by inciting others to join them in destroying 'stamped' documents, undermining the authority and public regard of servants of the British, and harassing other citizens who did not share their views, e.g., "The best remembered activity of the Sons of Liberty was the Boston Tea Party."

Sons of the American Revolution, The Society of, (S.A.R.): a hereditary and charitable organization of men descended from persons who served honorably in any military unit or performed other valuable service to the cause during the American Revolution, e.g., "Since his fifth-great grandfather was with the ***Green Mountain Boys*** (q.v.), he was eligible for membership in The Society Of Sons of the American Revolution."

Sons of the Revolution, Society of: a hereditary and charitable organization of men descended from persons who served honorably in any military unit or in any office of colonial government during the American Revolution, e.g., "It is said that those eligible for The Sons of the Revolution descend from patriots whose conduct would have been treasonous, had we lost that war."

Sons of Union Veterans of the Civil War, The: a non-profit society of men whose ancestors or ancestral uncles or cousins served the Union during the Civil War, e.g., "The service of their third-great grandfather Midlam in the 55th Ohio Volunteer Infantry during the Civil War render both Evan and Drake and their male descendants eligible for membership in The Sons of Union Veterans."

sop: See ***catheads*** and ***sop.***

sored: See ***soring.***

soreing: See ***soring.***

sorghum, sweet sorghum, sorghum molasses, sugar sorghum, sorgo, molasses: a sweetener made from the sorgo plant, very widely used across the mid-South and South, particularly where maple syrup was not easily or commonly produced, e.g., "Many of the old horse-drawn ***turnstiles*** (q.v.) used to crush sorgo for sorghum are still in use."

soring, soreing, sored: a method of training a horse, especially a ***Tennessee Walker*** (q.v.), to lift its front feet very high between steps by weighting those feet and shoeing them so as to bring pain when that foot touched the ground, e.g., "The cruelty of soring has caused it to no longer be tolerated nor practiced by horse lovers." Also see ***high stepper*** and see ***Walker.***

sororities: See ***fraternities, sororities, and societies.***

Sorosis, sorosis: a woman's club or organization dating from shortly after the Civil War; now, any woman's club or organization, e.g., "When she write that her 'sorosis provided relief from the housework', she was not referring to a skin disease."

sorrel: usually, a brownish, red to yellow color, particularly of horses or dogs; rarely, a seasoning, e.g., "Stonewall Jackson's horse was named 'Little Sorrel' by reason of its color."

sorry: as now; also meaning a person of little account; one who is on welfare rolls by reason of an unwillingness to help himself, does not work, is kept by another person not required to do so, or one who has no ambition to achieve even the most pitiable standing; Johnson (1802) says, "vile, worthless, vexatious", e.g., "Evan said of cousin Jerry, 'He is sorry as all get out and always has been'."

sorts, out of: See ***out of sorts.***

sot-weed: an early slang term for tobacco, due to its addictive or intoxicating effect upon users—they were "be-sotted"-e.g., "Henry's family made their fortune in the seventeenth century by exporting sot-weed to England from the Virginia Colony."

sounder: a group of hogs, e.g., "In 1847, Mark Bater wrote that he had come 'upon a sounder of young wild boars'."

Soundex: a specially-developed index system, particularly applicable to censuses after 1870, by which, through the assignment of numbers to vowels and first letters of names, one may search the census and other records, e.g., "The Soundex record for Marigold Ferguson is found through assigning numbers to the letter 'm' and then the letters 'f', 'r', 'g' and 's'."

South St. Wharf (New York City): a point of landing and inspection for Irish immigrants during the Potato Famine years and before Ellis Island was put into operation as the main immigration inspection place, e.g., "South St. Wharf was well known to Irish immigrants of 1847 and 1848."

Southern Confederacy: See ***secession.***

Southrons: an ante-bellum word for those, usually men, who declared the states of the South as their homes, "The owners of the spas and resorts at Saratoga always were happy to have the Southrons and their free spending wives and families."

sow: early, to plant by hand casting (***broadcasting***, q.v.) seed from side to side, and later by a crank operated device to similarly cast seed, e.g., "The old method of hand sowing was hard and time consuming." Also see ***drill.***

spadebone: early term meaning shoulder blade, e.g., "Dr. Henry Mills wrote that the arrow had penetrated the spadebone."

span, a: two or more draft animals to be used in ***harness*** (q.v.), not necessarily a matched team, e.g., "He wrote that he had purchased a span of mules at the sale and probably would use one of those in his best team."

spancel: to hobble; to prevent large animals, particularly horses, oxen and mules, from moving off by tying their front feet together, e.g., "Spancelling was common when pioneers stopped for the night."

spanfarthing, spanpenny: as now, a game, played by both adults and children, in which coins were tossed at a mark, circle or target, e.g., "In the colonies the terms 'penny pitch' and 'pitching pennies' seem to have taken the place of the English games named spanpenny and spanfarthing."

Spanish American War: that armed conflict that occurred during 1898 and 1899 between Spain and the United States, e.g., "Carl Midlam was with the 14th Ohio Volunteers during the Spanish American War."

Here, in full dress uniform except for his hat, is 1st Sgt James Messenger of the 14th Ohio, who served in the Spanish American War.

Spanish dollar: Spanish silver coins, often physically cut into halves or quarters, a half dollar being equal to 5 nine-pences, and a quarter dollar being equal to 5 fi-penny bits, e.g., "The Spanish dollar, either whole or cut into pieces, was a commonly circulated coin in the 18th-century American colonies." Also see ***dollar***.

Spanish Main: the Caribbean Sea; the coastal land bordering the Caribbean Sea, especially along south Florida and central America, e.g., "The Spanish Main was the haunt of pirates such as ***Blackbeard*** (q.v.)."

Spanish people, words gained from: many words arose from our experiences with the Spaniards who settled or maintained commerce with the colonies, especially those who lived in Florida, the Southwest and in California, e.g., "Conquistadores, barbecue, chocolate, tomato, enchilada, stilleto, marijuana, plaza, stampede, and tornado are but a few of the words which trace to the Spanish language."

Spanish Succession, War of: See ***Queen Anne's War.***

spanking, spanking team, brand spanking new: a superlative; smart, quick moving, handsome, shining, gleaming, showing no signs of use, e.g., "He had a spanking pair of blacks used only with the sleigh"; "Ida said the wagon was brand spanking new."

spark, sparking: to court; to engage in romantic activities, physical and otherwise, e.g., "Gazebos were favorite places for sparking."

spark (a): in the 17th century, usually a diamond, e.g., "Anne's inventory revealed that among her jewelry was a ring with 'two sparks'."

spark lamp: a small lamp of minimal illumination, first with a candle and later using ***lamp oil*** (q.v.) as fuel, commonly used as a night light, especially in hallways and in the rooms where small children slept, the name derived from their use during courting (***sparking***, q.v.) e.g., "She kept spark lamps in the foyer and in the nursery." Also see ***night lights.***

spatterware: common to 18th- and 19th-century estates and often called "***Dutch***" (q.v.) or "Pennsylvania Dutch" ware, it usually was earthen, with stippling, splashed, or dabbed colors over a differing base color, e.g., "Her spatterware was white with blue-green stippling."

spavins: a bony or very hard crust like growth that appears on the inside of the forelegs or above the hooves of horses, mules, donkeys, or burros."

specie: coin of precious metal, e.g., "Mention of consideration in specie means that the land was bought with coin money, quite usually silver or gold."

specifics: patent medicines and concoctions marketed by apothecaries, physicians, and promoters, the same widely advertised as having curative effects for specific ailments, e.g., "It is interesting that during the early 20th century, 'Humphreys Specifics Co.' marketed 35 such mixtures, all of which were priced at 25 cents for a small bottle, except for 'heart disease', 'epilepsy', and 'nervous debility'; those, priced at $1.00 for a bottle of the same size as the other remedies."

spect, I spect, I spect so, spected: a common Appalachian expression meaning, I anticipate, probably, or I expect, e.g., "She said her husband spected they'd arrive before nightfall."

spectral evidence: information said to be gained or learned from the supernatural, apparitions, spirits, ghosts, etc., e.g., "The judge branded as spectral evidence Marigold's statement that she had learned of the murder through a vision."

spell: Johnson (1802) gives as one definition "...a turn of work." There is the basis for the expressions, "come sit a spell", "she was gone for a spell", "he was sick for quite a spell"; e.g., "Drue would always invite passers-by to join him on the porch and 'just sit a spell'."

spermaceti, spermacoeti, whale candle wax: a white or nearly colorless wax obtained from the head of a sperm whale, early used to make high quality candles, salves, perfumes, and ointments, e.g., "While the poor used ***tallow*** (q.v.), the rich had spermaceti candles."

spice graters: See ***nutmeg graters.***

spice-wood: usually, wood or roots from the sassafras tree, e.g., "Strong spice-wood (sassafras) root tea was believed to have many medicinal qualities."

spider: a ***skillet*** (q.v.) or frying pan; usually a shallow, iron cooking pan with short legs, e.g., "She made a small pile of coals on the ***hearth*** (q.v.) and placed a spider over it."

spigot: a faucet or small valve for controlling a flow of liquid, usually, early, from a wooden cask or barrel, e.g., "Maggie called the faucet a spigot."

spin her cuts: See ***cuts.***

spin the button: See ***games (of children).***

spinal meningitis: a dreaded, early known, very often fatal disease of the nerve coverings of the spine (meninges), e.g., "For Helen's spinal meningitis, he administered compounds of mercury, aconite, opium, quinine, and prescribed cold baths, all to no avail."

spinet: early, a small ***harpsichord*** (q.v.); later and now, a small piano, e.g., "Early inventories of the rich often reveal spinets."

spinning wheel, walking wheel, wool wheel, wheel: a large wheel for spinning thread and yarn, common in nearly every home of the early years, and used to make yarn for fabrics of all sorts except linen, e.g., "In addition to a ***flax wheel*** (q.v.), they had a spinning wheel, which Mikaila referred to as a walking wheel because she rotated it with a short stick while standing beside it."

spinster: any woman considered by her peers as having passed the age at which she would be expected to first marry, and only occasionally used to refer to widows, e.g., "Being twenty-eight years old and unmarried, she was identified in the census as a spinster."

spintals: perhaps unknown, but such may be apples, e.g., "Allison wrote that after the apple harvest they made 'spintal butter'."

spirits of, spirituous: alcohol or alcohol based, e.g., "Spirits of wine was natural alcohol boiled off wine and retained for later use."

spirituous liquors: See ***liquors.***

spit and polish: a description of or a nickname given a military officer or command known for neatness, cleanliness and orderliness; military neatness and cleanliness generally, e.g., "Since soldiers, even now, spit upon boot wax (polish) after it is applied and before buffing, thus providing moisture needed for a bright shine, the term spit and polish came to describe neatness or officers or units known for such."

spit: as now, e.g., "Often the spits were very large, holding as much as an entire hog." Also see ***smoke-jack.***

splint lights: the earliest illumination used in the American colonies, and previously used by the Indians; a simple thin splint of fresh pine 6 or more inches long, which, when lit, burned brightly for 15 to 30 minutes, e.g., "Though early splint lights dripped ***pitch*** (q.v.), gave but little light, and brought the danger of fire, such often were the only light available other than a fire or fireplace."

spoke shave: a common, sharp edged tool of the ***cabinetmaker*** (q.v.), ***wagonmaker*** (q.v.), and ***wheelwright*** (q.v.), used to shape and trim round spokes, struts, chair stretchers, etc., e.g., "He had several sizes of spoke shaves."

sponge: bread dough, e.g., "By 1648 there were bakeries in New England and by the Revolution in virtually every colonial town, each making barm (yeast culture) and sponge, and selling the finished loaves of breads and sweet pastries."

sponsor: as now; and one who presents or stands in ceremonial behalf of another (usually a child) for religious purposes such as ***baptisms*** (q.v.) or dedications, e.g., "Mrs. Bater's sister and brother were sponsors at the baptism of Mikaila."

spontoon: a spear or halberd carried by 18-century infantry officers and which could be used as a weapon if necessary, with a metal tip that was engraved with an identifying symbol or insignia which assisted a soldier in locating his unit on a battlefield, e.g., "As the smoke cleared Private Midlam was relieved to see the spontoon of an officer of his infantry unit."

spoon die: See ***silversmiths' tools.***

spooning: light, amorous activities, especially by young couples; not mentioned by Johnson, yet believed to derive from the early Welsh practice of presenting a spoon to persons welcome in the household, especially fiancés and lovers of daughters of the family, e.g., "When asked where he and the teenage daughter had been, the boy responded, 'spooning on the porch.'" Also see ***spark.***

sporting house, whorehouse: a house of ill repute, a house of prostitution, e.g., "Rhett Butler frequented Belle Watling's sporting house."

sports (adult): of the many early pastimes and adult games, perhaps the best known were fox and raccoon hunting with hounds, quarter-horse racing, footraces, ***bowls*** (q.v.), and gambling; later, shooting (***shootin' matches,*** q.v.), ***thoroughbred*** (q.v.) and harness racing (see ***sulky***), fishing, and wrestling and boxing matches, and in the early 20th century, as now, baseball and hunting."

spouse: as now, one's wife or husband.

spring house: a shelter, usually of wood, built around and over a spring (or well) in order to keep animals and insects out of the water, e.g., "In 1957, on the Cold Harbor battlefield, there yet remained a spring and spring house that had quenched the thirst of the fighting men present there in 1864."

spring rocker: See ***platform rocker.***

spring wagon: a large wheeled, usually open, sturdy farm utility wagon, drawn usually by two animals and having a spring-mounted wooden seat in front for the driver and one or two passengers, e.g., "Ida was ever conscious that, even though her father owned a nice carriage, most families went to church in nothing more than a spring wagon."

springerles, springerle cookies, Hartshorn cookies: a hard, ***Pennsylvania Dutch*** (q.v.) cookie, seasoned with ***Hartshorn*** (q.v.), and often hung on and eaten from Christmas trees, e.g., "Vera made springerles every December."

springhead, fountain head, bold spring: that spring or fountain of water that acts or works as the head or original source of a river or stream, e.g., "He wrote that when he sold the land, he lost ownership of the springhead, yet retained the use of it throughout his life."

spruce: neat, yet without elegance; early, to be dressed in a manner over and above one's ordinary style; occasionally very early, to dress in an affected, unusual, or pretentious manner, e.g., "Our expression 'get spruced up' derives from the early definition of spruce."

spud, tanbark spud: See ***tanners' tools.***

spurtle: unknown, e.g., "Allison wrote that the family had been through many tedious times and that a few weeks before her husband had the spurtle."

spurway: a road for horses, yet too narrow for carts or wagons, e.g., "Mrs. Deane noted that a spurway had extended the length of Calthrop Neck."

squad: See ***armies, organization of.***

squadron: Johnson (1802) says "part of a fleet, a certain number of ships"; now, more likely, a group of combat aircraft, e.g., "The American Eagles, Flying Tigers, Black Sheep Squadron and Torpedo Bomber 1 were very famous American World War I and World War II squadrons of fighting aircraft."

square, all square, squared away, square built: other than the four-sided geometric figure, to settle an account; to set in order; strongly built, e.g., "He said that they were all square as to the debt"; "The ***bo'sun*** (q.v.) shouted that he expected the lifeboat lines to be squared away at once"; "She said he was square built and very strong."

square built: See ***square, etc.***

squared away: See ***square, etc.***

squeezer: See ***wringer.***

squibs and crackers: fireworks, usually of an exploding nature, e.g., "It was written that at the announcement in Findlay of the surrender of Lee there had been many 'squibs, crackers, and cannon volleys'."

squint, hagioscope: a very early English word; a slit or aperture in an inner wall through which the high altar of a church may be seen from the ***transept*** (q.v.), e.g., "The Church of St. Peter and St. Paul had a beautiful ***piscina*** (q.v.) and squint."

squire: See ***esquire.***

Squirrel Hunters: See ***military combat units, famous.***

sramstag: an animal horn, probably of a deer, and used for knife or utensil handles, e.g., "In the 1790s Philadelphia merchants Kuhn & Risberg advertised for sale 'buck, sramstag, splitbone, ebony and ivory handled knives and forks'."

St. Anthony's Fire: any serious skin condition that was eruptive or gangrenous, e.g., "For St. Anthony's Fire, Allison administered ***turpentine*** (q.v.), mustard ***plasters*** (q.v.), or clove oil."

St. Crispin, St. Crispianus: religious societies of Paris shoemakers, e.g., "St. Crispin (St. Crispianus) was an early French saint who honored the craft of shoemaking."

St. Nicholas, Santa Claus, Old Goody: the patron saint of children, early portrayed as a cleric, but by 1820 depicted as an elf covered with chimney dirt and soot, e.g., "The magic reindeer of St. Nicholas were first given names in Moore's 'The Night Before Christmas'."

St. Vitus' Dance: See ***chorea.***

stable: See ***livery.***

stack bookcase: enclosed bookshelves with glass paned, hinged doors that open upward into a recess, usually made in increments of one self-contained shelf, with a separate detachable bonnet for the entirety, and stacked three to six high, e.g., "The stack bookcase was four high and of oak."

stacks: shelves of books or other writings in a library, public or private; may be open to the public—open stacks—or closed to use except through an accountability system, e.g., "The Mormon library in Salt Lake City maintains generally closed stacks, however access to the books through the attendants is speedy and efficient."

Staffordshire: very popular, usually fine china, creamware, porcelain, and ***stoneware*** (q.v.) of all types and styles, made in Staffordshire, Eng., by a number of makers, and often seen in early inventories in the colonies and the U.S., e.g., "Her Staffordshire Toby Jug was Deane's most prized ***curio*** (q.v.)."

stage line, stagecoach, stage coach: usually, a business using horse-drawn vehicles—stagecoaches—between distant points at more or less frequent intervals, e.g., "The stage line operated between Columbus and Pomeroy, and the stagecoaches ran on Mondays and Thursdays."

Stage Road, stage road: usually a particular public or toll road designated for or generally used by horse drawn vehicles and stagecoaches, e.g., "The present day street in front of the Crossville Art Circle Public Library, which dates from 1800, was and remains known as the Old Stage Road."

stagecoach: See ***stage line.***

stallion: See ***horse.***

stancher: a tourniquet or any other mechanical device used to stop bleeding, e.g., "He wrote that he quickly made a stancher of strips of a shirt and tied it around the cut leg."

stand, stand for office: to be a candidate for some public office; an early way station, where food and drink for both travellers and their animals might be purchased, most having either the most sparce or no accommodation for overnight sleeping, e.g., "He stood for state senator that year"; "By 1795, Johnson's stand was in business on the ***Wilderness Road*** (q.v.) some twenty miles west of Crab Orchard Inn."

stand duty: See ***watch***.

stand the watch: See ***watch***.

stand-up bath: not until after 1870 were bathtubs anywhere in common use, and in rural areas even much later than that, resulting in a need by all to wash themselves from a bucket, basin, or ***pitcher and bowl*** (q.v.) while standing, giving rise to the expression, e.g., "Many was the mother who, having not been wet all over since childhood, maintained her cleanliness through stand-up baths."

standing off, standing out, etc.: See ***standing toward, etc.***

standing rigging: See ***rigging***.

standing toward, standing south (etc.), standing off, stood in, stood out, etc.: an expression reflecting the position or activity of a ship, particularly a sailing ship, e.g., "The lookout shouted to Captain Drake that an unidentified ***man-of-war*** (q.v.) was standing out from Teach's' Channel and that another was standing south from *that* one."

stang (bow): See ***hatters' tools.***

starboard (larboard) and port: usually pronounced star-bird and port; to one facing forward aboard ship, the right-hand side of a vessel is starboard and the left side is the port side, e.g., "As a vessel moves up the James River, Jamestown is on the starboard side, and Scotland and Hog Island are to port."

starch, starch factory, starcher: as now, a stiffener of cloth, originally made from potatoes and usually used to stiffen linen, now made from corn, wheat, beans and many other vegetables, e.g., "Starch was made in starch factories by men (and occasionally women) employed as starchers."

state(s), States of the Union: those political subdivisions, previously territories, that were admitted to the Union upon gaining legally sufficient population and approval of application to Congress, e.g., "Since, except for the original thirteen colonies, all other states were admitted by Congress after petition by their residents, the applications often provide valuable information concerning early settlements."

States' Rights: simply stated, that view that the thirteen colonies reserved to their future statehood any and all powers and privileges not specifically given over to the federal government at the ratification of the Constitution, e.g., "Contrary to the thinking of the States' Rightists, the Unionists took the view that the federal government had gained all powers and authority necessary to maintain itself and any institutions approved by a majority of its people through the Congress, President, and Supreme Court."

station: as now; early, a stop along a stagecoach route or a railroad, e.g., "The I-40 Campbell Station Road exit identifies the highway that once took travelers to the now long gone railroad stop and small depot known as Campbell Station."

stave, stave off: as in the plural of staff, Johnson (1802) says poles and to push off or fight with poles or large sticks, e.g., "While today the expression stave off applies to non-combative actions to prevent some effect on oneself, it was not so in early times." Also see ***staves***.

staves, pipe staves: slats of wood, slats used to make wooden barrels, e.g., "Kent Island was the site of one of the earliest pipe stave manufactories." Also see ***pipe***.

stays: strengthening of any of several parts of ladies' garments, as now, e.g., "Early high quality stays for ladies garments often were made of the cartilage from the mouths of whales." Also see ***whalebone***.

stead, instead: ancient, even to Johnson in 1755, an ancient word meaning place, e.g., "As we have for centuries, we yet say 'instead of', usually meaning in the place or position of another person or object"; "The terms bedstead meaning place of going to bed, homestead meaning place of the home, roadstead meaning place in a channel, farmstead meaning place of the farm, all are remnants of the use of the very ancient word 'stead' meaning place."

steel: as now, a metal; unlike commonly now, hardened steel rods having a lightly roughened surface and used for the sharpening of knives and other cutting edges, e.g., "The 1737 inventory revealed 'a ***slicer*** (q.v.) and the steel for it'."

steelyards, stillyards: a weighing device (scale) with an adjustable beam and weights, usually hung from a hook and used to weigh heavy objects, e.g., "The steelyards in the inventory had been used to weigh tobacco."

steep: See ***steeps and bottoms.***

steeps and bottoms, steep and bottom: refers to the high and low points on a tract of land, e.g., "He wrote that the 'steeps and bottoms on the home place are not well defined, but still there is good drainage'."

steer: a male bovine, castrated before sexual maturity, e.g., "The inventory revealed four steers, two calves, and a bull."

steerage: the least expensive class of shipboard travel, quite usually at the rear of the ship across which all odors flowed as the ship moved forward, e.g., "The fact that a family arrived here steerage class usually reveals that they were poor or very frugal, or both."

Stentorian shout: a term of literature and early newspapers, a very loud shout, e.g., "Homer's herald, Stentor, was said to have a shout as loud as might be produced by fifty men."

step-back cupboard: See ***cupboard***.

Sterling: a standard of value, silver content, and purity of English silver coin metal, e.g., "In colonial writings the mention of Pound Sterling (£) meant that the debt, obligation, or payment was to be made either in English silver coin or in other currency having an established exchange value equal to such a coin."

stick: probably a small measure or roll of cloth goods such as ribbon or heavy cord; sometimes a candleholder, e.g., "It was written that during 1763 Mr. Kitchen bought three sticks of ***twist*** (q.v.)"; "The term candlestick derives from the candle and the stick or holder."

stick, shake a: See ***shake a stick at.***

stick and mud chimney: See ***wattle and daub.***

stickbait, rockbait: unknown, e.g., "He wrote that while in the siege of Richmond he and his friends had 'gathered stickbait' and later referred to the same incident as having 'rockbait a-plenty'."

stiletto, stillettoe: a long, thin bladed, sharp knife sharpened on both sides and used as a weapon, e.g., "He had a stiletto hidden in his luggage."

stillyards: See ***steelyards.***

stinted: limited in amount, number, or size, e.g., "It was written that the wealthiest of our early New England ancestors sometimes brought a 'stinted store of carpets with them'."

stirpes: See ***per stirpes.***

stirrers: See ***glass making.***

stob: a term of the early mid-West and perhaps the South, and meaning a large club or piece of wood; sometimes a wooden post, e.g., "He testified that the Indiana man had '...hit him a heavy lick with a elm stob;'" "Will referred to his pile of fence posts as 'a jag of stobs'." Also see ***jag.***

stock: in genealogy, one's ancestry or lineage, from which arises the expression, "The family is from good stock." Also see ***lock, stock and barrel,*** and see ***firearms.***

stockade, stockade fort: an enclosed fort; an enclosure with walls of heavy timbers or tree trunks pointed at the top and placed in the ground side by side so as to be impenetrable by ordinary means, e.g., "Thirteen Unknown Soldiers of the War of 1812 were buried within the Fort Morrow stockade."

stocks and pillories: the former, a device having holes in which to secure the ankles and sometimes the wrists, and the latter, a device designed to firmly secure the hands and head of a person condemned to that punishment; both were usually placed in a public place for all citizens to see and ridicule the miscreants or criminals; a term often used to describe the supporting timbers for a ship, particularly a sailing vessel, while in dry dock for repair or maintenance, e.g., "Upon formation of that county, the Sussex court promptly ordered that stocks and a pillory be constructed and placed on the courthouse lawn"; "Will Ferguson ordered that his schooner be off the stocks, out of dry dock, and in the water by the 26th of January." Also see ***dry dock.***

stomacher: a highly decorated, often jewelled garment of the 15th, 16th and 17th centuries, worn over the chest, e.g., "***Good Queen Bess*** (q.v.) is almost always portrayed wearing a beautiful stomacher."

stone: a measure of weight; 14 pounds, e.g., "It was written that Drake Bater weighed '10 stone' (140 lbs) at age thirteen."

stone (the), having the stone, having the gravel: quite usually, kidney or gall bladder stones, which brought grievous suffering and for which, until surgery in the mid-18th century, there were no effective cures, e.g., "An Indian remedy for stone was a tea of hydrangeas."

stone tree: See ***horse tree.***

Stonewall Brigade: See ***military combat units, famous.***

stoneware: any ware made of ceramic, e.g., "Inexpensive stoneware was very common and widely used in 19th century America."

stoup: occasionally spelled stoop; brought from England, a permanent holder or basin for holy water and often placed at the main entrance to a church, e.g., "The stoup of St. Paul's was to the right of the doorway of the north ***porch*** (q.v.)."

stout: a dark, beer-like brew made from toasted malt and having a high hops content, e.g., "Stout was popular in Civil War New York City."

stove in: of unknown origin, a common country expression meaning to push or force inwards by a hard blow, e.g., "Evan said that the collision had stove in the front fender of his car."

straight fence: See ***post and rail fence.***

straight razor: a very sharp knife with a folding blade used for shaving, e.g., "Until well into the 20th century, there were no satisfactory shaving tools other than the straight razor."

strake: See ***wainwrights and coachmakers, tools of.***

strand: the shore of the sea or a large river, e.g., "A land description mentioning a boundary at a strand means at the edge of the high water mark of a river or the sea."

strangery, stranguary: stricture of the urethra; early, often prostatitis or cancer of the prostate; difficulty and pain in urination, not at all understood by early physicians, e.g., "Dr. Lockhart prescribed opium enemas and hot hip baths for strangery."

straw hat: as now, see ***palm hat.***

street washer: a horse- or mule-drawn vehicle that sprayed water on streets during the summer, thereby rinsing away refuse, manure, etc., and keeping down the dust, e.g., "The new street washer kept much of the dust out of the stores along the main streets of 1880 Yorktown."

streetcars, horsecars, trolleys: public conveyances, usually on tracks and designed to carry a considerable number of people; streetcars and trolleys usually were powered by electricity, and the earlier horsecars by horses, e.g., "Virtually every late 19th-century city of any size had, first, horsecars and, later, streetcars or trolleys."

stretcher: in ***furniture*** (q.v.), those struts or reinforcements between the legs of tables, chairs, and other furniture, so mounted as to add strength and stability to the whole, e.g., "In furniture of the William and Mary period, ***turners*** (q.v.) often made stretchers for better furniture with round ball shapes."

stroke: See ***apoplexy.***

stroking, stroking of a corpse, stroking the body: early judges, ***coroners*** (q.v.), and ***sheriffs*** (q.v.) frequently required a person suspected of murder through violence other than the obvious (by gunshot or stabbing) to touch or rub the corpse, it being supposed that it would show signs of life or lividity if the suspect was guilty, e.g., "No signs of life having been witnessed upon stroking, the Mills was released."

strong box: a movable, secure, safe-like and lockable container used to store and transport money or other valuables, e.g., "Paul insisted that for the duration of the trip Brittany have her jewelry remain in the stagecoach strong box."

strong waters: brandies, liquors, and spirits, e.g., "In 1662, in Salem (MA), William Woodcock, an apothecary, was granted a license to distill strong waters."

strop, strap, razor strop, razor strap: a very common strap of polished leather used to put a final edge on a very sharp knife or ***straight razor*** (q.v.) by rubbing the blade to and fro against it, e.g., "Every barber chair had a razor strop hanging at the barber's hand height."

stuff chests: See ***paper making.***

stuff: a very common early expression meaning any unfinished cloth or material, e.g., "The 'other stuffs' referred to in the inventory were pre-cut and finished fabrics."

sty, pig sty, hog sty: a shelter, or as Johnson (1802) says, "a cabin" for hogs, e.g., "Early hog stys were but triangular shelters made of bark and closed on one end."

subpoena: an order directing one to appear before a court or other body having the authority to summon, e.g., "Since she failed to answer the subpoena delivered by the ***sheriff*** (q.v.), the court found Drake in contempt."

subscribing witness: one who, in writing on a document, attests to the validity of a signature of another person on that same legal instrument, e.g., "Subscribing witnesses to a will were and are required to be present when the maker of that will executed it."

sucket: candy (q.v.), hard candy; sugar candy; any ***sweetmeat*** (q.v.) or confection to be dissolved in the mouth, e.g., "There are numerous instances of quantities of suckets being in merchants' inventories."

sudoritick: a ***purge*** (q.v.); any medication that induced sweating, e.g., "Sweating having been considered necessary to a balancing of the ***humours*** (q.v.), numerous plants were used as sudoriticks, especially very hot peppers."

suffrage, suffrages: a right or privilege to vote; the authority to participate, usually by vote, in elections, the plural meaning "votes" being now obsolete, e.g., "In the election of 1798 Allison and Mikaila sought to gain the suffrages of their husbands and sons"; "On August 25, 1920, when Elma was eighteen, the 19th Amendment provided suffrage for women."

sugar, a: a sugar bowl, usually without a lid, e.g., "The inventory revealed eight salts and a sugar." Also see ***sugar box,*** and see ***salt dish.***

sugar, loaf: See ***loaf sugar.***

sugar box, sugar pot: early, a box to store and keep cake or loaf sugar dry and free from insects; usually, a sugar bowl, e.g., "The sugar box was of cherry wood and her sugar pot was of ***pewter*** (q.v.)." Also see ***sugar***, and see ***loaf sugar.***

sugar camp, sugar house, sugary: a place or "camp" where maple syrup was boiled or reduced to sugar, usually within a grove of maple trees and near a road, e.g., "A part of the old Strine property had once been a sugar camp, said to have been so used since Indian times." ***sugar cutter:*** See ***sugar grater.***

sugar firkin: See ***firkin.***

sugar grater, sugar nippers, sugar hatchet, sugar shears, sugar cutter: household tools for dividing or breaking up ***loaf sugar*** (q.v.), e.g., "During the 17th and 18th centuries refined sugar was so expensive in the American colonies that every grain was carefully plucked from the sugar grater."

sugar nippers: See ***sugar grater.***

sugar tit: a piece of absorbent fabric either soaked in or wrapped around sugar or other sweetener, shaped like a nipple and very commonly given to infants to pacify them, e.g., "She regularly made sugar tits from maple sugar and cotton cloth."

sugary: See ***sugar house.***

Vanuxem & Lombaert

HAVE FOR SALE,

At their STORE in Water ſtreet below Market ſtreet,

SUPERFINE and ſecond broadcloths
Tammies, duroys & ſagathies
Chintzes and calicoes
Printed and ſtamped dimities
Sattin Marſeilles quilting
Mantuas, modes & ſattins
Luſtrings and other ſilks
Black Genoa velvet
Black & white ſilk gloves and mitts
Barcelona ſilk handkerchiefs
Black laces & thread ditto
Flanders linens from 20d to 6/8 a yard
Holland ditto from 6ſ. & upwards
Table linen and diaper
Aſſorted threads
Hatts of all kinds, from 3 4 of a dollar to five dollars
Fans and umbrellas
Feathers & artificial flowers
Pins by the pound
A few bales of cotton candle wick

Printing, writing, ſheathing and wrapping paper
Blank books of all ſizes
Paper hangings
Oil cloth for wrappings
Looking-glaſs plates of ſeveral dimenſions
Mahogany and gilt framed looking-glaſſes
Gilt and plain mouldings
Liquorice ball
Alicant anniſeed
Framed ſlates
Grind ſtones
Spaniſh whiting
Chalk
Pipes in cheſts
Claret in caſks
Ditto in boxes from 15d. to 3s. per bottle
Champaigne wine, firſt quality
Malaga wine in bottles
Arrack in bottles
French cordials
Gin and anniſeed in bottles

ALSO,

Freſh raiſins in boxes and caſks
Sherry wine in half pipes and quarter caſks
A large ſcale beam compleat, with weighing poſt
A ſmall ditto
Elegant marble chimney pieces

All perſons indebted to the eſtate of Lacaze and mallet are deſired to make payment to Vanuxem and Lombaert, being empowered by the aſſignees of ſaid houſe, to ſue for the ſame.

Likewiſe, all perſons indebted to the late houſe of De Heyder Veydt & Co. are deſired to make payment to the ſaid Vanuxem and Lombaert, who will ſatisfy all demands againſt ſaid houſe. 2awtf

A variety of goods and stuffs offered by Vanuxem & Lombaert in the "Pennsylvanina Packet and Daily Advertiser," July 20, 1789.

suit, suite: in furniture, as now, e.g., "A bedroom suit usually consisted of a ***wash stand*** or ***commode***, a ***chest of drawers*** or ***chiffonier***, and a ***bedstead*** (all, q.v.), while a parlor suit usually was a ***settee*** (q.v.) and two matching chairs."

suitcase: See ***grip***.

suite: See ***suit***.

sulky, road cart: a very light, single-seated vehicle for one or two people, having two high wheels and pulled by one horse, commonly upholstered and used for short trips about a city, or stripped down, made very light, and pulled by pacers and trotters in racing, e.g., "The famous Houghton Sulky Company of Marion was yet in the business of building sulkies in 1950." Also see ***gait***.

sullage: See ***swill and sullage.***

summary: in genealogy, a writing using different wording that abbreviates, summarizes, or paraphrases significant or important portions of another writing or source, e.g., "In writing summaries of the abstract works of others, one must be aware of the copyright laws as to such matters." Also see ***abstract***, see ***extract***, see ***copyright***, and see ***Fair Use***.

summer kitchen: prior to air conditioning and modern appliances, cast iron stoves created and retained heat in such quantities that for summer use such were moved to a place outside the main house kitchen (winter kitchen) or other rooms and usually into an open sided, roofed outside room, e.g., "The annual ***chore*** (q.v.) of moving the big stove to the summer kitchen fell to the men of the Midlam family."

summer soldiers, sunshine patriots: Revolutionary War expressions, disdainfully referring to those who were willing to serve in the warm months when campaigning was relatively easy, but held back from service in the winter season, e.g., "As so well stated by Thomas Paine, during the early days when there was no draft as we know it, men were at liberty to be summer soldiers if they so chose."

summons: a ***subpoena*** (q.v.); an order directing one to appear before a court or other body having the authority to summon; courts issue summons, and ***sheriffs*** (q.v.) serve them, e.g., "A summons issued ordering John Boortly to appear at the next court in the matter of the claim against him by Richard Parker."

sumptuary, sumptuary act: regulating spending aspects of life and what were viewed as extravagances, e.g., "Remarkably, in 1742 a sumptuary act was passed in Massachusetts regulating the numbers of mourning gloves, scarves, and rings that might be given away at funerals."

sun plane: See ***cooper's tools.***

sun time: before the railroad and the invention of the telegraph in the 19th century required an adoption of standard times and time zones, time usually was reckoned by the position of the sun at noon wherever one might be, especially on June 21 and December 21 (the summer and winter ***solstices*** (q.v.), resulting in many different times across the country and even between 2 cities close together, e.g., "Until rapid communication from area to area made standardized time keeping necessary, even the President found that sun time well served his needs."

Sunday best: See ***meeting.***

Sunday go to meeting clothes: See ***meeting.***

sunshine patriots: See ***summer soldiers.***

Superior Court: a term of varying definition; in some states the lowest court having appellate jurisdiction; elsewhere, a court of original jurisdiction; and in still other jurisdictions, an ordinary court of ***nisi prius*** (q.v.) jurisdiction, e.g., "The family researcher should know the meaning of the words 'superior court' in that state in which courthouse research is being done."

suppawn: a stew of sorts, made from ground parched corn and boiled with pork or other meat scraps, e.g., "John Daws of the 14th Virginia often had little but suppawn for his daily meal." Also see ***corn soup and fat back.***

supplate: unknown, yet probably a part of a grist mill, e.g., "The miller wrote in 1846 that at great effort he had replaced the supplate."

Supreme Court: a term of varying definition; our highest Federal court, maintaining ultimate appellate jurisdiction and original jurisdiction in matters of extraordinary ***writs*** (q.v.); in some states, the lowest court having appellate jurisdiction; in other states, the lowest court having original jurisdiction (of record), e.g., "The case was appealed from the Court of Appeals for the Sixth Circuit to the U.S. Supreme Court"; "The first appeal from decisions made in California is to the Supreme Court"; "He filed his original lawsuit for damages in the Supreme Court at Albany, New York."

surety: one who, through a pledge of money, real estate or other thing of value, guarantees the truth of some matter or the appearance or proper conduct of himself or another; nearly synonymous with ***bondsman*** (q.v.), e.g., "Evan acted as surety for the administrator of the Haskins estate."

surfeit: overindulgence in food or drink, e.g., "Surfeit was treated with caffeine and a diet of vegetables and fruit."

surgeon: See ***chirurgeon.***

surname: the family or "last name" of a person, quite usually that of the adoptive or natural father, e.g., "To the delight of their father, Cheryl gave her surname to her first son, Drake Charles Bater, and Diane named her first daughter Allison Drake Haskins."

surnames from occupations: as commonly known, e.g., "Over many centuries and for varying reasons, our ancestors often assumed an occupation or calling as a surname, several of the many examples of which are Archer, Boyer (a bow maker), Bowman, Brewer, Bridger, Butcher, Carpenter, Carter, Carver, Chandler or Candler (a candle maker), Cook, Cooper, Cordiner or Cordner (a cordwainer), Currier, Cutler, Draper (a drapery and hangings maker), Driver, Fuller, Horner (a horn smith), Hyder, Jester, Joyner or Joiner, Keeler (ship builder), Ledbetter (lead beater or lead wright), Mason, Miller, Munger (a peddler or salesman), Nadler (a needle maker), Nailor (a nail maker), Piper (a pipe maker), Porter, Potter, Proctor, Roper, Ryder, Sadler, Sawyer, Saylor, Scribner, Seigel (a brick or tile maker), Shepard or Sheperd, Shoemaker, Slater (a slate worker), Smith, Tanner, Taylor, Thatcher, Tiler or Tyler, Turner, Wagner, Wainwright (a wagon or coach maker), Warner (sometimes a keeper of rabbits), Weaver, Whistler, Wright, and Zimmerman (a carpenter).

surrey: a four-wheeled carriage with two forward-facing seats, usually with a removable top, e.g., "The musical *Oklahoma* accurately depicted a 'surrey with a fringe on top'."

surrogate's court: a court of probate jurisdiction, e.g., "The New York Surrogate's court has the same jurisdiction as do the ***Chancellors*** (q.v.) of Tennessee." Also see ***probate court.***

sutler: originally, to show; a person who sells ***gee-gaws*** (q.v.), food, drink, newspapers and necessaries usually to an army on the move, e.g., "Sutlers went everywhere that Lee's army went"; "The re-enactment brochure revealed that sutlers were permitted by invitation only."

Sutter's Mill: a mill being erected by J. W. Marshall for Johann A. Sutter on a branch of American River in Eldorado County, California, at which site Marshall discovered gold (24 January, 1848), the spread of the news of which sparked the California Gold Rush, e.g., "After his discovery at Sutter's Mill, Marshall waited for days before telling Mr. Sutter and others." Also see ***Forty-niners.***

swage, swag, swagged: a steel tool of the ***blacksmith*** (q.v) used to create bends in unheated iron, e.g., "He had the apprentice hold one end while he swagged the other end."

swage blocks: See ***silversmiths' tools.***

swagman: a tramp; one who repeatedly works a short while, then resigns the work and travels on, e.g., "Sarah quietly referred to her father-in-law as a swagman, but all knew that her words truly dignified his tramp and derelict lifestyle."

swanskin: a soft, usually cotton, flannel stuff, e.g., "A 1707 entry of old Salem (MA) reveals ongoing sales of swanskins." Also see ***stuff.***

sweet lard: lard without salt, e.g., "Fresh and sweet lard was often used for cooking pastries."

sweet oils: any edible oil, especially as in medications, e.g., "Needing a sweet oil, for toothaches Dr. Drake used clove oil mixed with chloroform."

sweetbreads: the pancreas of a calf or pig; a delicacy of kings, e.g., "Mrs. Randolph's recipe for 'oysters and sweetbreads casserole' is superb, albeit loaded with cholesterol."

sweetmeats: usually, candied fruits; sometimes, any confection or very sweet finger food, e.g., "She made sweetmeats of many varieties, including raspberries, cherries, peaches, plums and strawberries."

swift: See ***yarn swift.***

swill and sullage: waste from the home, swill being left over waste food and liquids from the table and kitchen and sullage being sewage, e.g., "The 1924 newspaper announced that the new sewer would handle 'swill and sullage alike'." Also see ***slop, slop bucket.***

swine, hogs: early and now, a pig or shoat is a young hog of either sex, shoats being the younger; a boar is a grown male; and a sow is a grown at least once-bred female, e.g., "The inventory listed the swine as '3 sows with ten shoats, 18 pigs, and a boar"; "Most early writings and inventories speak of swine generally, or of hogs, sows, and shoats and pigs particularly."

swine plague: See ***cholera.***

swing chair: See ***hammock chair.***

swing horses, swing team: lead horses or that horse or horses ahead of the wheelers and usually just behind the lead horses, usually younger, strong, and trained to turn as commanded; a toy, a small replica of a horse, saddle, and bridle mounted on springs and a stand, the same used by children in pretending to ride a horse, e.g., "If the family could not afford a swing horse, ***hobby horses*** (q.v.) were the next best thing"; "The swing horses were three-year-old black Percherons, just learning to work as commanded."

swingleg table: See ***gateleg table.***

swingletree, singletree, doubletree, whippletree, whiffletree, tree: a pivoted crossbar used with draft animals, usually of hickory or oak, to which ***traces*** (q.v.) are connected, thereby delivering the power of horses or other ***draft*** (q.v.) animals to the load; a doubletree is used when two animals are ***hitched*** (q.v.), e.g., "As the boy Paul pulled onto the scales, the team pulled the tree in two."

sworn statement: written or oral testimony to facts that involve some legal proceeding or is done in compliance with a requirement of government, the same usually invoking the name of God and done before an officer empowered to administer ***oaths*** (q.v.), e.g., "To gain a widow's pension, Mrs. Midlam had to submit a sworn statement that she and the veteran had married on January 26, 1847."

syllabub, sillibub: a favored early drink made of milk curdled by the addition of wine (or cider), usually with a sweetener added, e.g., "Syllabubs topped with sweet whipped cream were a favorite of many."

syndic: a ***burgess*** (q.v.) or ***recorder*** (q.v.); an agent of a corporation or university, e.g., "The courts' records reveal a finding that a syndic acted as an agent for Minnesota corporation though he did not so intend."

synod: any general meeting of ecclesiastical people concerning religion; a meeting of ecclesiastics within some specific district or area, e.g., "A synod was held in Pencader Hundred in the state of Delaware."

syphilis, great pox: as now, the dreaded, crippling venereal disease, e.g., "Though none was successful, early physicians strove desperately to cure syphilis." Also see ***chancre***, and ***clap***.

T

tabby: early, an older ***spinster*** (q.v.), a gossiping woman; later and now, a handsome, plainly woven silk fabric; a gray or tawny, often striped, house cat; in the seaboard South, a mixture of oyster shells, lime, sand, and water used as in building, e.g., "Colleen told Jess of her new dress of gray tabby, and he laughed, thinking of their cat and also of his construction business."

tack: in Scotland, a lease, e.g., "Early Scottish settlers in the colonies occasionally referred to leases as tacks."

tackle: See ***blocks and tackle.***

tacks: See ***rigging***.

tacky party: unlike now, probably forgotten and perhaps a gathering where taffy or candy was made and 'pulled', "Mikaila wrote, 'I very much enjoyed my evening with friends at the tacky party'."

taffeta: a thin, finely woven silk, e.g., "Taffeta appears in many early inventories."

taffy pull: See ***candy pull.***

tag, pine: See ***pine tag.***

tag: See ***games (of children).***

tailrace: See ***millers' tools.***

take against a will: an expression used widely, meaning that one dissents from the terms of a will and, instead, chooses to exercise his or her privilege to inherit through the laws of descent and ***distribution*** (q.v.) or by intestate ***succession*** (q.v.), e.g., "In 1804, the records reveal that Judith Matheny took against the will of her husband, Daniel."

take aholt: from to take a hold on something; to lay hands on preparatory to bringing muscular force to bear upon some object or machine, e.g., "The foremen ordered the four laborers to take aholt of the big turnstile."

take the waters: usually meaning to go to a facility or resort offering mineral baths for one's health, e.g., "Stonewall Jackson often took the waters in the resorts of Shenandoah Valley."

takes the cake, that: a superlative, meaning that an event is remarkable or unusual or impressive, and derived from the centuries-old practice of awarding cakes to winners of various contests at fairs and markets, e.g., "When Sarah saw Henry playing with the dogs of which he had been afraid she said, 'Well, if that doesn't take the cake!'."

talesman: a prospective juror summoned from among bystanders or folks about the halls and grounds of the courthouse, e.g., "Early references to talesmen are common, since on ***court days*** (q.v.) many of the citizenry were in and about the courthouse."

talisman: early and perhaps unlike now, a character, charm or amulet that was thought to invoke magical powers, e.g., "The inventory listed 'three talismans'; probably charms or amulets."

tallow: animal fat, usually beef, melted, poured into molds, and cooled and, as were whale ***spermaceti*** (q.v.), beeswax, and the wax extracted from bayberries, used to make candles or burn with a wick for illumination, e.g., "Her tallow candles were the best she had until bayberry season arrived."

tam-o'-shanter: a tasseled cap, originally from Scotland, usually made of wool and having a berm that falls slightly about the head, e.g., "Tam-o'-shanters were commonly worn by young men of the colonies."

tambour desk, tambour: See ***rolltop desk.***

taminy: a ***stuff*** (q.v.) made of wool, e.g., "The inventory listed a taminy ***weskit*** (q.v.)."

Tammany Hall: the meeting place of the Tammany Society, a powerful Democratic Party organization of the last years of the 18th and the 19th centuries, e.g., "The influence of members of the Tammany Society over now two hundred years has been so great that their meeting place—Tammany Hall—was and is synonymous with political power."

tammy (ies): a fabric made of any of several fibers, early used to make petticoats and undergarments; also, a loaf of bread, e.g., "Vanuxem & Lombaert of Philadelphia advertised assorted tammies for sale at their store on Water St."; "The farm hands asked for tammies with their mid-day meal."

tan-yard: a place where hides are tanned and leather is made for sale, e.g., "In 1846 the village of Williamstown, Ohio, was said to have a blacksmith, a joiner, a cabinetmaker, a dry goods store, two carpenters, a tan-yard, and three saloons."

tankard: a large, wooden or metal mug, with a lid and handle, e.g., "The old tavernkeeper still served ale in big tankards."

tanners and curriers: those who tan skins and make leather, e.g., "Leather for shoes and animal harnessing being a necessity of life, by the coming of the American Revolution virtually every village had tanners and curriers." Also see ***tanners and curriers, tools of.***

tanners and curriers, tools of: as now, e.g., "Revealing of occupations as tanners or curriers, among others, were bark mills, bloom pins and scrapers, dehairing knives, fleshing knives, skivers, slickers and spuds."

taper: a long slender candle, commonly used in sconces and tapered at the wick end nearly to a point; a string or wick coated with wax sufficient to stiffen it for use in lighting other candles or gas lamps, e.g., "Cheryl had a ***sconce*** (q.v.) that held three tapers."

tar pit: a large, dug hole in which pine trees were burned, resulting in tar pitch dripping to the bottom, from which it was collected and sold as naval ***stores*** (q.v.) and for other caulking purposes, e.g., "There was a tar pit on the 1760 Lazarus Drake land."

tares, tare: as now; also, a weed that grew in English wheat fields, e.g., "The early Virginia professor referred to a class of students as a 'nothing but a crop of tares'."

Tarleton's quarter: to give no quarter or show no mercy, e.g., "The cruelty toward prisoners and defeated colonials by British General Banastre Tarleton led to the expression 'Tarleton's quarter', meaning no mercy would be shown."

tartan, plaid: unlike now and unknown to Johnson, tartan referred to the pattern of a woven fabric, while plaid meant either the pattern or an item of clothing, e.g., "While we do not use the terms as originally, the words tartan and plaid, meaning a patterned, colored ***stuff*** (q.v.), are common today."

task force: See ***fleet.***

task group: See ***fleet.***

tavern, saloon, tippling house: a place where drinkers are entertained, usually with minimal or no food and without overnight accommodations, the rates of which were frequently set by a court having county-wide jurisdiction; a saloon usually was a lower class tavern, e.g., "To the dismay of the preachers, every small town had its share of taverns and saloons"; "The upper class might occasionally speak of having visited a tavern, but not admit to frequenting a saloon."

tavern table: a small, usually square or rectangular, very sturdy table, sometimes with one or two drawers, and occasionally of small drop leaf design, the slightly splayed legs providing stability, typically used by two, three or four people while imbibing, e.g., "Bethany's maple tavern table dated from about 1850."

taverner: a saloon or tavern owner or keeper, e.g., "In 1663, his good character established, John Ruck was granted permission to be a taverner."

tax lists: lists of taxable persons, sometimes by occupation, calling, or property owned, the ages of which varied at different time periods and places, e.g., "The 1846 Blair county tax lists revealed three men surnamed Martin."

tax office: usually, the office of the local or county tax ***assessor*** (q.v.) or tax collector; often, a state or federal office of similar purpose, e.g.,

"They sought the early county personal property tax records in the tax office and at the historical museum."

tea chest: a lidded, wooden box designed for the transportation of tea and usually holding 60 lbs., e.g., "The tea of the Boston Tea Party was in chests."

tea maker: a tea strainer or hinged, sieve like spoon used to hold tea for brewing, e.g., "The inventory listed two tea silver tea makers."

tea strainer: a very fine sieve, typically used to separate leaves or grounds from tea or coffee and to strain medications, e.g., "She had all sizes of sieves, a tea strainer, a ***searce***, a ***colander***, and a ***riddle*** (all, q.v.)."

tea table: a table of many designs and periods, small, rounded or square, light in weight, without drawers and used to serve teas, coffee, or chocolate, e.g. "Her tea table was cherry and Victorian in styling." Also see ***center table.***

teacher's desk: See ***schoolmaster's desk.***

teamster: unlike now, one who earned a livelihood by driving a team of animals, usually horses or mules, e.g., "Drake worked as a teamster for the Moores and Ross Milk Company." Also see ***wagoner***.

teetotaller: one who does not consume alcoholic beverages of any sort, e.g., "The statement that Paul was a teetotaller was not synonymous with saying 'he did not drink'; the former meaning that he disapproves of and does not participate in that practice, and the latter meaning that he chose not to do so though he may not object to others doing so."

Templars, Knights Templar: a religious order of knighthood organized in 1119, and having a modern counterpart in the form of a Masonic Order, e.g., "The original Knights Templar often undertook to protect travellers from harm and be charitable and helpful to poor Christians and pilgrims on journeys to religious sites."

temses: See ***cooper's tools.***

tenancy by the entirety: an interest based on the ancient legal fiction that husband and wife were one person; an equal ownership by a husband and wife in the whole of something by reason of a conveyance or transfer to them naming both; when the marriage ended by whatever means, the estate or interest went to the survivor, e.g., "Unlike a **joint tenancy** (q.v.), where either party may sell mortgage, devise, or otherwise dispose of his or her interest, in a tenancy by the entirety both husband and wife must join in any action affecting the interest."

tenants in common: those who own land together with another person, yet gained that ownership by varying means or at different times, e.g., "The tenants in common were John, who gained his 1/3 interest through the will of his father, and James, who purchased his 2/3 from the father before that parent died."

tender age: early, under fourteen years, e.g., "The court appointed a guardian for the son who yet was 'of tender age'." Also see ***of age***.

tenements: structures situated on a specific tract of land, usually habitable, e.g., "The lease included the tenements and the rentals to be received from such."

Tenerife: See ***Canary***.

tent; to pitch: See ***pitch***.

tenterhooks, tinterhooks, on tenterhooks: hooks, shaped as fish hooks, attached along the sides of a wooden frame, and over which cloth was tightly stretched in order that it could dry without wrinkles or bends, from whence is derived the expression, e.g., "Saying that 'she was on tenterhooks' meant that she was in a state of stress or anxiety." Also a now probably unknown meaning, e.g., "A 1707 entry in the records of Salem reads 'Nicholas Trask shall set up his tenter-hook as he desires'."

ter-tenants: from early New England; probably, lessees or renters of the town properties, e.g., "The Salem records mentions of ter-tenants apparently referred to those who farmed common town lands."

term, term of court: in genealogy, that period of time during which a court is regularly in session, e.g., "The Surry Michaelmas term of court began on June 1, 1674, and continued for twenty four days."

terminer: See ***oyer and terminer (courts of).***

territory: a political subdivision having the accomplishment of statehood as its ultimate purpose, e.g., "The Territory of Alaska became a State of the Union in 1959."

tessellated, tessellated street: a very early expression meaning a floor or pavement of squares varied in color and texture, e.g., "The entrance hall of the ancient church was said to have been 'tessellated'."

testamentary, letters testamentary, testamentary capacity, testamentary power, etc.: a common term pertaining to wills and the execution of the terms by the executor, and also pertaining to gifts, deeds, appointments, and documents in general that do not take effect until the moment of death, e.g., "Having qualified as ***executrix*** (q.v.), letters testamentary were issued to her"; "The deed having transferred land to a son in lieu of any devise under the will was said to be testamentary in nature." Also see other "testamentary" entries here.

testamentary disposition: a conveyance or transfer of property by deed or gift in such a way as to appear like a will, e.g., "His statement in the deed that his impending death was the reason for transferring the land to his daughter made it a testamentary disposition." Also see "testamentary" entries here, and see ***in contemplation of death.***

testamentary guardian: a guardian named in a will, e.g., "The court recognized the testamentary guardianship of John, who had been named in his brother's will as the person to care for the minor children." Also see other "testamentary" entries here.

testate: death with an operative (legally valid) will, e.g., "After her death testate, her executors undertook to execute the provisions of her will."

testator, testatrix: one who makes a will, e.g., "As testator and testratrix, Paul and Martha Drake each devised the land to their daughters."

teste, teste me, te.: witnessed or confirmed by me, the signer, e.g., "At the bottom of the copy was written, 'teste. G. Williams, Cl. Ct.' meaning that Gary Williams, Clerk to the Court, confirmed that the copy was a true one."

tester, tester bed: a posted bed with a framework for curtains or canopy, e.g, "The tester bed was listed, as were a ***rug, valance***, and ***curtains*** (all, q.v.)."

tetanus, lockjaw: a dreaded and much feared, quite usually fatal disease resulting from bacteria entering the body through wounds, bites, and other penetrations of the skin, and attended by violent spasms and rigidity of certain muscles, especially in the face, e.g., "Early physicians even tried tobacco juice in their futile attempts to cure tetanus."

tetter: any of several breakings out or eruptive diseases of the skin, such as impetigo, psoriasis, or eczema, e.g., "Many cures, including ground insects and tar, were used for tetter."

Texas, Republic of: 1836-1845, that short-lived republic (Sam Houston, Pres.) based on a constitution (adopted March 2, 1836) similar to that of the U.S., which after the battles of the Alamo (March 6) and San Jacinto (April 21) entered upon a treaty of peace with Mexico, 8 years after which Texas gained admission to the Union under Pres. Tyler, e.g., "The Republic of Texas was being formed during Santa Anna's siege of the Alamo."

that takes the cake: See ***takes the cake, that.***

that takes the rag off the bush: See ***rag off the bush, that takes the.***

thatcher: a very early term for one who had the training and knowledge needed to weave a roof from reeds and plants, and did so for others in exchange for pay, e.g., "Judy ordered her overseer to have a thatcher work on the roof of the slave cabins."

they'd, thaid: common Appalachian expression meaning they would or they had, e.g., "He said they'd better get a move on if they were to finish before dark."

thibet: unknown, probably a fabric, e.g., "In April of 1862 A. R. Wiggin, a New Hampshire merchant, advertised, 'Thibet, Muslin, and Cambric Robes'."

thible: See ***peel.***

thill, thills, sills: either of the shafts of a carriage, wagon or cart, between which an animal is hitched for pulling, occasionally, yet rarely, called sills, e.g., "He wrote that the left thill of the sleigh was cracked and he would replace it at once." Also see ***thiller***, and see ***shaft***, and see ***tongue.***

thiller: rare, the last animal in a team; that animal closest to the driver, e.g., "He noted that the thiller was a big Percheron."

thimble: recently, as now; early, a sleeve mounted in a wall or ceiling, through which the stack or exhaust from a stove could pass to the outside and designed to prevent fires in the walls or ceilings, e.g., "Without a thimble, the danger of fire was very great."

thirds: a rather imprecise manner of referring to that share of a deceased husband's estate to which a widow was entitled if there were living issue, e.g., "The court ordered the administrator to divide what would have been the 'widow Parker's thirds' between her two surviving sons."

Thompson's Pennsylvania Rifle Battalion: See ***military combat units, famous.***

thorn: (þ) or (y) an ancient Saxon symbol, common in early writings and, when written in longhand, similar to the small case letter "y", it represented the sound and letters "th", e.g., "The thorn (y) often is found preceding 'at' for the word 'that', preceding 'is' for 'this', and preceding 'e' meaning 'the'; our ancestors were not saying 'ye'."

thoroughbred: early, meaning of very fine bloodlines; now, those horses bred primarily for speed and stamina and ridden in contests of jumping, steeplechasing, and flat racing, e.g., "Triple Crown champions Citation and Man O' War were two of the most famous thoroughbreds."

thraldom: slavery; occasionally ***voluntary servitude*** (q.v.), e.g., "Descriptions of people as in a state of thraldom occasionally appear in 17th-century records of passengers of ships."

thrall: ancient term for servant, a ***slave*** (q.v.); bondman or serf, e.g., Some very early Virginia records speak of thralls."

thrave: a very early and now obsolete measure (24) of sheaves of grain, e.g., "In 1698, he wrote that he had traded '16 thraves' of straw for a sow."

threshing, threshing time: at harvest season, that labor-intensive task of harvesting grain, especially wheat, and loading it into the threshing machine that separated the stalks and chaff from the grain, e.g., "At threshing time, as the women prepared huge mid-day meals, the men of the neighborhood, all working together and assisting each other, undertook the harvesting and threshing of the crops, the following day moving on to the next farm."

throne, on the: See ***on the throne.***

throw away, throw away person, throw away animal: a person or animal of little worth, value, or desirability; a ***common*** (q.v.) person, e.g., "When told that her friendly cat, Marigold, was very pretty, Sarah said that she had been but 'a throw away kitten'."

throw down: an expression of the South and west, the derivation of which is now likely unknown, meaning to be critical of another person, usually when that person is out of the presence of the one so speaking; to humiliate, ridicule or chastise one or a group of persons, in or out of their presence, e.g., "Mrs. Mills felt very strongly that her friend should not throw down on their acquaintances after those persons had left the party."

thrush (the): an infection causing sores and white spots in the mouth, usually of infants, e.g., "For thrush, Dr. Drake prescribed potassium chlorate washes and eucalyptus."

thundermug: See ***chamber pot.***

tic-tac-toe: See ***ticktack.***

tick, go on the tick: a tally of debts; to be able to charge for services, as in a hotel or restaurant, e.g., "The rich young Southern wrote that unless his father sent him some money, he would have to 'go on the tick'." Also see ***ticking bag.***

ticking bag, tick: what we commonly know as a mattress; a bag made of heavy cloth, usually canvas or ***oznaburg*** (q.v.), and filled with straw, feathers, or rags (flock), e.g., She had three ticking bags that she referred to as her 'ticks'."

tickler bottle: See ***sniffing bottle.***

ticktack, tic-tac-toe, tit-tat-toe: all are synonyous, and as now, e.g., "Ticktack was a favorite game of our ancestors."

tides, ebb-, waxing-, waning-, high-, flood-, low-, full sea: the movements of the oceans as a result of the effects of the gravity of the moon, e.g., "When a tide is at its maximum height, it is at full sea or high tide; at the lowest point, it is at low tide; when 'coming in' it is waxing or at flood tide; when it is half way to flood tide, it is at half-flood, and when 'going out' it is waning or at ebb tide."

tidewater Virginia (or NC, GA, MD, etc.): any of the seaboard counties lying generally in the area below the fall lines of rivers affected by the tides, e.g., "The fishing in the estuaries of tidewater Virginia was and remains superb."

tierce: 1/3 of a ***pipe*** (q.v.); 42 gallons, e.g., "He ordered two tierces of ***Madeira*** (q.v.)."

tiffany, tifany: somewhat unlike now, very sheer, very high quality fabric made of silk, used for better dresses, veils, and occasionally by the wealthy for bed curtains, e.g., "References to tiffany are not uncommon in early inventories."

tighter than the wax on a wall: See ***wax on a wall, tighter than.***

tightwad: an overly frugal person; one who is a penny-pincher, derived from those who were very careful to load a ball—a projectile—so wrapped in cloth as to make it fit very tightly in the barrel of a musket and thus reduce the gunpowder required for effective discharge, e.g., "His habit of never tipping the waitress resulted in him being widely known as a tightwad."

till, hand in the: See ***till.***

till: Johnson (1802) says "a money box in a shop"; now, any cache of ready money frequently used and accessible, such as a cash register or change drawer, e.g., "Mark thought that Jerry had a tendency to thievery, and suggested that he probably had his hand in the till when he should not do so."

tillage: land that had been cleared and was suitable for agriculture, e.g., "Open, undeveloped land that was free of impediments to planting and sowing was advertised as tillage."

tilt-top table: any of the many styles and many sizes of tables with a top that tilted to the vertical position for storage or to conserve space, e.g., "Mikaila had a walnut, cloverleaf-shaped tilt-top table that had belonged to her grandmother."

tin lizzie: an early term for any small, cheaply made and inexpensive automobile, even if new, e.g., "While she referred to their little 1932 Chevrolet as a tin lizzie, Winnie referred to Ray's old Ford sedan as a ***flivver*** (q.v.)."

tincture: any medicinal mixture using alcohol as the solvent or vehicle, e.g., "Tincture of iodine has been a widely used antiseptic, even very early."

tinder box: a small box, usually wooden, designed to hold the materials needed to start a fire, i.e., flint, a piece of steel, and very fine, very dry, wood shavings (tinder), e.g., "Before matches, only the tinder box saved one from going to a neighbor to ***borrow fire*** (q.v.)."

tinker: now, one who does small jobs that require but little knowledge or expertise; early, Johnson defined such a person as a mender of old brass, e.g., "In early times brass wares, pots, pans, and utensils were of such a cost that many families found it necessary to have a tinker repair them." Also see ***tinker's damn.***

tinker's damn, not worth a: a superlative, meaning that some object or person was of very little or no value or worth, e.g., "Paul frequently said that his lazy brother-in-law was not worth a tinker's damn." Also see ***tinker.***

tinsmith: one who has knowledge of and makes utensils, toys, lamps, etc., from tin and associated metals, e.g., "The first tinsmith in town did very well financially."

tinsmith, whitesmith, tools of: as now, e.g., "The presence of several sizes of tin snips, tin dippers, flatting hammers, and soldering irons reveal the trade of the whitesmith (tinsmith).

tintype, ferrotype: a photograph made on a piece of sensitized metal, usually tin, e.g., "There are many tintypes yet in family collections." Also see ***ambrotype***, and see ***wet plate process.***

tinware: any of the many utensils and household items made of soldered tin; inexpensive and not very durable, tinware often was sold from door to door, and occasionally came painted, especially in New England, upstate New York, and Pennsylvania, e.g., "She had owned many pieces of tinware, however at her death but few of those remained." Also see ***tinsmith.***

tippet: See ***muffs and tippets.***

tippit: See ***muffs and tippets***

tippling house: See ***taverns***, and ***ordinaries***.

tire: unlike now, the metal band secured tightly around the circumference of a wheel, the same holding the rim tight against the spokes and hub, and upon which surface the wheel rolled, e.g., "Upon the loss of a tire, a spoked wooden wheel would not last long."

tithables, tithes: in the church, those portions of income allotted to religious causes; in genealogy, usually those persons subject to taxation by virtue of their age, property owned, or residency; one is tithable when required to pay tithes, e.g., "The total money received as tithes was £220"; "Richard Parker Jr. was first shown as tithable in the 1686 Surry County lists."

title: reflective of rights owned in some property, real or personal, e.g., "Title in land is said to vest in the devisees at the moment of death." Also see ***devise.***

title, to perfect a: See ***perfect a title.***

titled land: See ***land grants.***

tittle: See ***jot and tittle.***

toad in a hailstorm, move like a: a superlative, meaning to hasten away or quickly seek shelter from danger, just as a toad or frog would if pelted by hailstones, e.g., "Evan commented that when the fight started Allison left out like a toad in a hailstorm." Also see ***left out.***

toaster: a handled, wire or fine wrought iron holder used for toasting one or more slices of bread over an open fire, e.g., "The use of early toasters was a ***chore*** (q.v.) often assigned to little children."

tobacco knife, tobacco cutter: a large, heavy, wooden-handled, long-bladed knife with a sharp curved tip, used by swinging it to cut the heavy stems of tobacco for harvest, e.g., "Virtually every Southern farmer had one or more tobacco knives."

tobacconist: an occupation or calling; one who has knowledge of and sells or deals in tobaccos, pipes, cigars, etc., and the uses, care, and handling of such, e.g., "Every city of the 19th century had several tobacconists." Also see ***snuff*** and see ***snuff miller***.

toboggan: a small sled with a flat bottom that curves and extends upward and backward in the front; in the southern Appalachians, often a soft knit wool covering for the head and ears, e.g., "In early times, oak or hickory was planed thin, moistened, and shaped in a curve over a frame, thus making a toboggan for children"; "Marty insisted that the children wear their toboggans when going out in the cold."

tod: a measure of new wool; 28 lbs of wool, e.g., "The inventory revealed '2 tods of wool'."

toffee pull: See ***candy pull.***

togs, togged: very early, dressed in a gown or gowns; later and now, any clothes worn over undergarments, e.g., "When Mrs. Haskins said, 'Get into your togs, children, we are about to leave', she meant for them to dress completely for the planned trip."

toilette, toilet articles: as now, the acts of a lady in grooming herself, and the tools, powders, make-up, etc. for that grooming, e.g., "As were (and are) most fine Virginia ladies, Ms. Sarah was very modest and asked total privacy when at her toilette."

tole, took tole (as with toll): to be paid for some service, e.g., "The records of old Salem (MA) reveal that a miller was cited for having 'taken tole' that was excessive."

tolliker: See ***hatters' tools.***

tomato, tomatoes: Devil's Fruit, e.g., "Since some tomatoes grown in southern Europe were poisonous, early settlers here presumed that the American tomato had the same qualities, however the American Indians revealed that those grown here were quite edible."

tomb: early, somewhat unlike now, a monument containing a dead person, e.g., "There is an altar tomb in the Church of St. Peter and St. Paul."

tombac: a mixture of copper and zinc having the color of gold and used in inexpensive jewelry, e.g., "The difficulty with tombac jewelry was that the copper content left tell-tale green marks on the skin." Also see ***Pinchbeck gold,*** and see ***gold***.

tombstone: See ***headstone.***

tomfoolery: unknown to Johnson, innocent or silly games or behavior, said to have been derived from the silly actions of one Tom Shelton of the 19th century, e.g., "Maggie told the children to immediately quit the tomfoolery."

ton: See ***long ton, short ton.***

tongue: that wooden shaft extending forward between draft animals to which were attached ***whiffletrees*** (q.v.), through all of which animal power was brought to bear to move a load, e.g., "Tongues were usually oak, elm or hickory." Also see ***swingletree.***

tonics: as now, elixirs supposed to aid in general health, e.g., "Tonics were made from myriad substances, including alcoholic drinks and teas made of blackhaw root, brier hips, curled mint, dandelion root, gentian, goldenseal root, and St. John's wort."

tonneau: a rear seat, or sometimes, a closed compartment of seats in early automobiles, e.g., "Colleen's 1918 Cadillac was custom made with a closed tonneau of 4 seats behind the front seat."

toothdrawer: one who pulled teeth for hire, e.g., "Dental science (and, thus, dentists) having been virtually unknown, ***chirurgeons*** (q.v.), toothdrawers, and parents served in their stead."

top buggy: See ***buggy.***

top: See ***whirligig.***

toper, tosspot: an ancient term meaning a drunk; one who is frequently inebriated, e.g., "While Eugene occasionally overindulged, he was not known as a toper or tosspot."

topos: See ***quadrangles***, and ***Geological Survey, U.S.***

Tories: in the colonies (including the American), the 18th century political party made up of those who supported the British in their view that the established church, monarchy, and existing form of government and status of colonies should be maintained, e.g., "At every turn, the Tories were rebuked by those colonists who sought independence."

torrify, torrified: to roast or parch, usually fruits or grain, e.g., "Malinda's recipe called for torrified rhubarb, meaning rhubarb stalks that had been roasted until soft."

tosspot: See ***toper***.

tote sack: See ***gunny sack***, and ***sackcloth***.

touch coup: See ***coup, etc.***

touch off: to discharge a rifle or shotgun; derived from the early need to touch the powder in the ***pan*** (q.v.) with a piece of burning ***punk*** (q.v.) in order to discharge an early ***matchlock*** (q.v.), e.g., "When he laughed and said he had 'touched her off', he was revealing the ages-old custom of referring to a firearm of the 15th, 16th, and 17th centuries, and of the practice of referring to one's weapon in the female gender." Also see ***flintlock***.

touching the dead body: See ***stroking***.

tow, tow linen: linen made of the shorter, less workable and less desirable light-colored fibers present after flax has been scutched (see ***break and scutch***), e.g., "The tailor assured Allison that the coat was not of tow linen."

tow-head, tow-headed: a person, usually a child, with very light to blond hair, e.g., "As children, Ray and Anne Lindsay were tow-headed."

town: now, usually a small political subdivision without a court of general jurisdiction; in New England, early, a governing authority much like a county, that usually received grants of 36 sq. miles (now, also a ***township***, q.v.), e.g., "During the mid 19th century, small towns serving as agricultural centers were scattered throughout the Midwest"; "She went to the Salem town meeting in order to be heard on the tax issue."

town books: records of the New England towns, comparable to county records of many other colonies and states, including those of the South, e.g., "By 1635 it was ordered that every man's lands should be 'entered on the town books.'"

town crier: early, that person hired by governments of cities to shout or otherwise make public announcements; that calling and person paid for by a community to announce new laws, news, the hour of the day, and affairs of interest to the townspeople, e.g., "In the late 17th and early 18th centuries, before the advent of inexpensive newspapers and clocks, town criers were very common, especially in New England."

town meeting: a meeting, usually at regular intervals, of the qualified voters of a New England ***town*** (q.v.) in order that the affairs of that political subdivision might be determined and carried out, e.g., "In its 'town meeting' of 1987, Fentress County, TN, undertook to copy the Greenwich, CN, model."

town pay: payment of individuals from New England public funds, e.g., "In 1679 Salem ordered that ***bellmen*** (q.v.) were to have town funds 'or produce' in exchange for their services."

town runner: See ***sleigh***.

town sleigh: See ***sleigh***.

town square, square: that area, usually in the center of town and surrounding the courthouse or public buildings, set aside for public use, e.g., "Since all knew where it could be found, the square was often a designated meeting place."

town-ball: See ***games (of children).***

township: (abbr. "T") in some states—OK, UT, KS, IL—a political subdivision and part of a county or precinct, varying in size; in surveys of public lands of the U.S., 36 square miles (6 miles X 6 miles, 36 ***sections*** (q.v.) of 1 sq. mi. each), e.g., "In early times, Justices of the Peace and Constables represented the broader law and kept the peace within a township"; "Throughout Ohio and Illinois, most lands that once were public lands are divided into townships of 36 sq. miles."

Township: See ***Section, Township, and Range.***

trace, traces: See ***harness.***

trace: a marked path or trail, usually through the wilderness, e.g., "Zane's Trace was well known to all travelers heading west through what was to be Ohio." Also see ***harness, harnessing, etc.***

trade dollar: a silver coin of 420 grains of silver, ***Troy*** (q.v.), e.g., "The coinage of trade dollars resulted from a need for a uniform quantity and quality of silver to represent the U.S. dollar."

trade winds: those prevailing winds that flowed generally south from England to the Equator, thence westerly to South America and from there northerly along the eastern coast of the U.S., the same utilized by merchant sailing vessels to move goods and trade between countries, e.g., "By riding the trade winds, a ship from Spain or Portugal could quickly move from those countries to the West Indies, there unload and reload, and then return to Europe and England from north of Florida and the middle colonies."

tradesman, tradesmen: a shopkeeper; one who kept store of common dry and hardware necessities, e.g., "What later were keepers of general stores early were known as tradesmen."

Trail Of Tears: the migration from the east to Oklahoma of the Cherokee, Chickasaw, Choctow and Seminole Indians, which movement resulted from the purchase of the eastern Cherokee land in 1835 and the policies of the government and President Andrew Jackson during that period, e.g., "The Trail of Tears included their trek across the Sequatchie Valley of east central Tennessee." Also see ***New Echota, Treaty of.***

trains, great: as now, e.g., "A list of great passenger trains of the late 19th and early 20th centuries surely would include 'Royal Blue', 'Bluebird', 'Orange Blossom Special', 'City of San Francisco', '20th Century Limited', 'Wabash Cannonball', 'Zephyr', and 'Chief'."

trammel: a fireplace hanger for pots, kettles, etc, e.g., "A kettle hung on the trammel most of the winter." Also see ***crane.***

tramp: as now, though apparently unknown to Johnson (1755 and 1802); early, a rather long walk or voyage, usually in part on foot, and often without important or business purpose, e.g., "Tom Roberts referred to his trip to Wales in search of his ancestry as 'my tramp.'"

transcontinental railroad: See ***woodburner***, and also see ***Promontory Point.***

transcript: a verbatim record or exact reproduction of a portion or all of some proceedings, writings, or words, e.g., "A transcript was made of most of Mikaila's writings for use by researchers."

transept: substantial spaces, wings, or aisles constructed perpendicular to the main hall (***nave***, q.v.) of a church structure and often dedicated in purpose to a chapel, the choir, or an organ, e.g., "The transepts of St. Paul's were so designed as to create a ***cruciform*** (q.v.) shape to the church."

transfix: early, somewhat unlike now, to pierce through (Johnson (1802), e.g., "While now our reference to being transfixed means that a person's attention or gaze is fixed on some other person, action or object, formerly the meaning was quite different."

Transylvania ('State' of): that temporary state and government formed during the Revolution (1775) by Kentucky settlers, most of whom had Virginia and North Carolina roots, e.g., "As a monument to the efforts of the North Carolinians, Transylvania College thrives today at Lexington, Kentucky."

traslado: a copy, e.g., "Early Texas, New Mexico, Arizona and California reports often refer to trasladoes, meaning simply exact copies of some other document."

traveller: See ***wainwrights and coachmakers, tools of.***

trawl, trowl, troll: as now, to drag bait or lures behind or alongside a boat in order to attract and catch fish, e.g., "Drake wrote that he and his son made a living by 'trowling in Chispeak Bay'."

treacle: molasses, e.g., "Early retail grocers always stocked treacle."

Treaty Line: See ***Military Line.***

trebucket: See ***ducking stool.***

tree lasses: See ***molasses.***

tree sugar: See ***maple sugar, and see sugar.***

tree sugar: See ***sugar.***

tree syrup, tree sugar: See ***maple sugar.***

tree: See ***swingletree.***

trencher, losset: early, a common, small to medium-sized, flat and rarely slightly hollowed out plate, usually made of wood, upon which meat or other food to be cut or carved at the table was served, e.g., "Every home of the 17th and 18th centuries had one or more trenchers."

trepan: a surgeon's tool used to cut sections from the skull, e.g., "The trepan and the practice of trepanning were well known even before the Christian era and not uncommon in England in Elizabethan times."

trestle table, trestle bench: a common, usually roughly finished table or bench with two legs shaped like an inverted "T", e.g., "The old trestle table in his shop had served as a table in the house during harder times."

trial by jury: See ***pais, per.***

trial by the country: See ***pais, per.***

trick, turn tricks: as now; since it early often was thought that acts of prostitution were the fault of the woman and were brought about through provocative or sensuous actions or words that were thought irresistible to men, a single event or act of sex for pay, e.g., "Officer Haskins warned Linda that he would arrest her if he caught her turning tricks at the horse race." Also see ***hooker.***

tricorne: a three-pointed or triangular shaped colonial hat, usually of felt, e.g., "When men wore their tricornes, it often was to draw attention to their natural hair or their dislike for ***periwigs*** (q.v.); and more often than wearing such, they carried their hats."

trigger, tricker: a trigger of a firearm; that part of a gun by which the shooter starts the process of ignition of the charge, e.g., "In his 1802 edition Johnson apparently preferred tricker to trigger, when describing this operating part of a firearm."

trimmer: as now, and a wooden beam or joist in the top cover of a water well, e.g., "His comment that he had replaced a rotten trimmer at the well had nothing to do with the hedges."

trinkets: small, decorative, usually inexpensive items worn on the person, e.g., "Early listings of trinkets often included lesser jewelry."

trivet kettle: a lidded iron pot with three legs, used like a ***trivet*** (q.v.) and pot, e.g., "In addition to her trivet kettle, Margaret had two other kettles."

trivet: a usually small, perforated, flat, iron platform with 1 to 4 inch legs, used to support pots, frying pans, over hot coals at a fireplace, e.g., "She pulled coals out on the hearth with the ***oven rake*** (q.v.) and placed a trivet over them to heat the pot."

troll: See ***trawl***.

trolleys: See ***streetcars***.

trophies: See ***ornaments***.

trot: See ***gaits***.

Troy weights: that system of weights by which precious metals and bread were measured in early times, e.g., "Physicians and ***apothecaries*** (q.v.) from colonial times down to the mid-twentieth century used ***Troy*** (q.v.) weight equivalents.

truck: early and to now, to deal or trade in or exchange commodities for other goods, e.g., "His comment that he had a fine truck garden had nothing to do with vehicles."

truck-wheels: early, unlike now; a slice of oak, e.g., "Early carts used to haul ***truck*** (q.v.) produce often had as truck-wheels slices of oak cut at right angles to the tree trunks with holes in the center through which the axles passed."

truckelbed, truckle bed: See ***trundlebed***.

trumped up, trumpery: to cause an appearance of value where little is present, e.g., "The old cruet ***caster*** (q.v.) was painted and trumped up."

trumpery, trompery: early, usually of trifling or no value, e.g., "In describing miscellaneous items of old clothing and fabrics and another entry including such as saw teeth and small worn metal objects used in farming, entries in the 1667 inventory of Mrs. Jane Harty estate included '1 small case with trompery' and '1 hatchett and trumpery'."

truncheon: a short club or heavy short stick to be used as a weapon, e.g., "Evan wrote that he had witnessed a man beat another with a truncheon."

trundle bed, truckle bed: as now; a bed, sometimes on ***casters*** (q.v.) wheeled and low enough to be stored beneath another bed, e.g., "The need to move beds aside during the day resulted in many early inventories listing trucklebeds or trundlebeds."

trust deed: often imprecisely called a "mortgage deed of trust"; similar to a mortgage deed, however in trust deeds legal title is conveyed in trust from the borrower to a third party agreeable to both parties; as with mortgages, if the debt is paid as agreed, the land is reconveyed to the borrower by that trustee, e.g., "His brother-in-law served as the transferee in the trust deed." Also see ***mortgage deed***.

tryptych, triptych: a hinged holder, of usually three panels, for photos, drawings, or other works of art, e.g., "Tryptych photo holders that folded up into the width and height of but one of the sections have been common throughout our history."

tub: early, unlike now, usually a measure of 60 lbs. of tea, e.g., "As were other dry products, ***camphor*** (q.v.) often was measured in tubs, however the weight varied from 56 to 86 lbs., however with tea a tub seems to universally have been 60 lbs." Also see ***chest***.

tub barrows: See ***paper making***.

tuberculosis: See ***consumption, etc.***

tucker: a small piece of linen worn out of doors to cover and thus shade the breasts of women wearing low-cut gowns, e.g., "The fear of skin cancer, desirability of clear, pure white skin, and disdain for 'tans' led to the summer wearing of tuckers by most early women." Also see ***bib and tucker***.

tucker-bag: the food bag of a tramp, e.g., "Old William always had some dried beef in his tucker-bag."

tumbler: usually, as now; occasionally, an ornate or highly decorated, rather large earthen, porcelain, or ceramic, nearly cylindrical container without handles, e.g., "Her prize tumbler was cameo cut."

tumbrel: See ***ducking stool***.

tun: 4 hogsheads (256 gallons) of wine, oil, and other liquids, e.g., "The word ***'hogshead'*** (q.v.) appears more often than 'tun' in early mentions of wine and other liquids."

tureen: as now, a medium to large, ordinarily glass or porcelain container, usually with a lid, from which soup, gravy, consomme or other liquid was served, e.g., "Cheryl's soup tureen had been a part of Maggie's first set of dishes."

turf and twig: an ancient expression manifesting a transfer of possession and ownership of real property through the act of handing over to the grantee of a clod, piece of turf, bough or twig, e.g., "Some very early Virginia deeds carried the expression 'turf and twig' reflecting the symbolic physical delivery of possession of the land."

turkey pen, partridge pen, etc.: a large cage trap with an opening underneath and in the bottom, having sides and a top so openly slatted as to not appear to an animal to be enclosed or box-like, e.g., "He placed corn in a trail leading underneath and then into the bottom of the turkey pen, knowing that once in the cage the birds would not attempt to go downward to escape."

turnbench: a small lathe, e.g., "From the earliest times, turnbenches often were made of iron."

turner: an occupation or calling; those who have knowledge and experience in wood lathe and wood shaping operations and able to create turned parts for ***furniture*** (q.v.), e.g., "When called upon to make truly fine furniture containing round parts, the ***cabinetmakers*** (q.v.) relied on a local turner for such shaping."

Turner, Nat, Insurrection: See ***Nat Turner Insurrection***.

Turner Thesis: that hypothesis of Frederick Jackson Turner (and also Beard) that the American frontier, and not the influences of commerce and the 'old countries', was by far the greatest factor in the molding and shaping of the American personality, character, and government, e.g., "The Turner thesis was studied by virtually every history student of the 20th century."

turning Arnold: to become a traitor or give allegiance to an enemy, e.g., "Griffin, having taken up arms for the Crown in 1781, was said to have turned Arnold, referring to the Revolutionary War treason of Gen. Benedict Arnold."

turnkey: early, one who worked for a ***sheriff*** (q.v.), tended to the needs of prisoners, and had the responsibility of caring for the keys to the locks of a prison or jail; now, anyone working about the courthouse or jail who has a measure of authority over prisoners, e,. g., "The sheriff referred to the officer then on duty as the turnkey." Also see ***gaoler.***

turnpike, pike, corduroy road: very common, an early road constructed by laying down trimmed, small trees transverse to and across the roadbed; often a toll road with toll gates and toll bridges, e.g., "Even into the 20th century, turnpikes often retained the corduroy ***washboard*** (q.v.) appearance and feel."

turpentine: a derivative from the sap of pine trees, used very early for its supposed antiseptic properties and as the liquid vehicle for paint, e.g., "She lanced the boil and then put turpentine on it."

tutelary, tutor: as now; also a guardian or having the guardianship of a minor boy or girl, e.g., "The York County reference to the tutelary standing of Mr. Bater revealed his guardianship of some young person or persons."

tutor: See ***tutelary.***

tweezers: See ***glass making.***

Twelfth Day: January 6; the twelfth day of Christmas, upon which the festival of the Epiphany was celebrated; the traditional end of the Christmas season, e.g., "After the Revolution years the twelve days of Christmas and Twelfth Day celebration were but scarcely observed in the American colonies."

Twenty Negro Law, 20 Nigger Law: an 1861 Confederate legislative effort to keep enough men at home to prevent the escape of Negro slaves, e.g., "The 20 Negro Law (disparagingly called the '20 Nigger Law') provided that one white man in any family was exempt from military draft for every 20 slaves working on the premises."

twiffler: undetermined; perhaps a dish for hot puddings, e.g., "Twifflers apparently were known only in inventories of the American colonies."

twist: heavy string or cord, e.g., "The 1762 merchant's ledger reveals that Hines bought '3 sticks of twist'." Also see ***stick.***

two handed, two-handed: unlike now, large and bulky; too large to be lifted or handled by one man, e.g., "The chest was said to be 'two handed'."

tyke, tike: a small dog, e.g., "Sarah referred to her little dog, Doris, as a 'cute little tyke'."

tympany: flatulence, e.g., "Dr. Richardson administered an herb remedy for tympany"; "His comments concerning Richard's tympany had nothing to do with music."

U

U.C.V.: See ***United Confederate Veterans.***

U.S.G.S.: See ***Geological Survey, U.S.***

ulcers, gastric ulcers: as now, any draining or seeping sore or destruction of the inner wall or lining of the stomach, e.g., "His arm was ulcerated as a result of infection"; "Gastric ulcers not being understood, such harsh remedies as arsenic, silver oxide, and lead acetate were employed."

ultimo, ult.: a term used in writings and correspondence revealing that the writing at hand was being done during the month succeeding some prior act of writing, e.g., "If responding on March 10th to a letter written to you on February 20th, it would be appropriate to say, 'I received your note of the 20th ultimo'." Also see ***instant***.

ultramarine: a very deep blue dye, e.g., "She used ultramarine, called French blue, to dye his work clothes."

Uncle Tom's Cabin: an 1852 anti-slavery novel by Harriet Beecher Stowe that sold over 1.25 million copies, and gave rise to exaggerated anti-slavery sentiments across the North, e.g., "Margaret suggested that Uncle Tom's Cabin did more to bring war than did any other single writing."

under eaves bed: a short-legged, very low bed with little or no head or footboard, e.g., "There were two under eaves beds in the ***garret*** (q.v.)."

underground railway: that loose organization of over 3000 anti-slavery citizens which operated from about 1830 until the last days of the Civil War and provided hiding places and varying measures of transportation and sustenance for negroes making their way to the North, e.g., "What is now the Stengel-True Museum in Marion, Ohio is said to have been a 'station' on the underground railway."

undershot wheel: See ***millers' tools.***

undulant fever, brucellosis: an often fatal disease causing severe remittent fevers in humans and abortions in many animals, e.g., "The occurrence of spontaneous abortions in two cows caused Brittany to fear the presence of undulant fever." See also ***Bang's disease.***

unfixed, unfixt: See ***fixed***.

Union Army: the armed forces of the U.S. (the North) during the Civil War, e.g., "The Union Army often was referred to as 'the Boys in Blue'."

Union Veterans, Sons of: See ***Sons of Union Veterans, The.***

union: in genealogy, a marriage—ordained, licensed, or ***common law*** (q.v.)—or other legal association of man and woman, e.g., "They were married in 1850, and to that union were born six children."

United Confederate Veterans: (The, U.C.V.) a fraternal, non-profit organization of Confederate Veterans of the Civil War, including those who served in the Navy or government; as was the ***G.A.R.*** (q.v.), the U.C.V. was a powerful political force in the last years of the 19th century, e.g., "If one hoped to be elected to Southern office at the turn of the 20th century, he sought the aid of the U.C.V."

United Kingdom, United Kingdom of Great Britain and Ireland, U.K.: the official title of the kingdom of England, Scotland, Wales, and Ireland, and usually the colonies and possessions of that Kingdom, e.g., "The United Kingdom was an ally of the U.S. during World Wars I and II."

unnatural will: a will that disposes of an estate to strangers and largely or entirely excludes those who would have been expected to benefit therefrom, e.g., "A California court referred to Shay's will as unnatural."

up, -up, as a suffix or adverb: a very early expression, usually a superlative; to complete, to attain a maximum or gain a sufficient amount or number, e.g., "Shoot up the town, speak-up, close up, fix up, dress up, wash-up, eat up, set up, pile up, make up, grocery up, beat up, and blow up are typical uses of the suffix -up"; "When asked why she was making a trip to town, Diane replied that she had 'to grocery-up for the holiday'."

upper leather: See ***sole and upper leather.***

urban: being within a city, borough, village or concentrated settlement, as opposed to a rural location, e.g., "Records revealing urban lifestyle of the 19th century are common."

uremia, uremic poisoning: a fatal and early misunderstood retention of those wastes usually disposed of by the kidneys, e.g., "Diuretics, caffeine, crotan oil, and mustard ***plasters*** (q.v.) all were believed to give relief in cases of uremia."

ursicatories: medications used to cover wounds and prevent infection, e.g., "Glycerin was a base for many favorite ursicatories.

USGS topos: See ***quadrangles***.

uxor: See ***et ux.***

V

V.F.W., Veterans Of Foreign Wars: that fraternal organization of American veterans who have served during wartime and outside the continental limits of the U.S., e.g., "Unlike the ***American Legion*** (q.v.), to be a member of the V.F.W., one must have served beyond our borders."

vacation, petition of: as now, a legal request to set aside some order by a court, or seeking relief from some directive; also, a request that commissioners or other town or county officials consider vacating a road, e.g., "In 1844, a petition of vacation was presented to the Commissioners of Hancock County (OH) seeking the abandonment of a portion of the 'Ottawa and Sandusky State Road'."

valance bed, valence, valons: a bed, usually having a removable fabric top, and with draw curtains and at times a fringe surrounding the canopy; a decorative drapery that hangs from the canopy of a bed, e.g., "There was a valance bed and ***curtains*** (q.v.) in the inventory of Diane's estate"; "The presence of several valances in the inventory is an important clue to affluence."

vale: See ***dale***.

valid: legally sufficient; binding and of force and effect, e.g., "The deed was valid, it having been properly written, executed, and delivered to the proper person."

valons: See ***valance bed.***

van-: a prefix meaning from; originally used to refer to a town, village, or other area or political subdivision from which the subject person came, e.g., "The name van der Hoffen is revealing of an area in which that family may once have lived and called home."

vara: a Spanish-American measure of length equalling 33 inches, e.g., "While a meter is about three inches longer than a yard, a vara is about three inches shorter."

varmint, varmit: any animal, especially squirrels, foxes, wolves, hawks, owls, lynx, coyotes, prairie dogs, Carolina Parakeets, etc., early considered to be a nuisance to settlers or to their crops or livestock, and upon which bounties often were paid, e.g., "Bounties were being paid for the ears of wolves and other varmints as early as 1670." Also see ***bounty***.

varnish: a fine, very hard finish for use on wood, especially fine ***furniture*** (q.v.) and musical instruments, and made of natural resins dissolved in spirits, e.g., "The varnish on Stradivarius violins is of the finest natural resins and has lasted for hundreds of years." Also see ***shellac***, see ***lacquer***, and see ***lac***.

vat: See ***fat, fatt, etc.***

vatman: a person trained in the art of ***paper making*** (q.v.), e.g., "In 1775 Evan Haskins was referred to as a vatman in the tax lists for eastern Pennsylvania."

vaudevil: from which arose our vaudeville; Johnson said 'songs sung by the vulgar, a trivial strain', e.g., "The change from disdain for the vulgar called vaudevil to the classification of light and gay humor and dancing as vaudeville did not take place until the late 19th century."

vellum: very thin kid or lamb skin, finely finished and used for important documents, e.g, "Many early land grants were written on vellum."

vendee, vendor: a vendee is a buyer, and a vendor is a seller of personal property (***personalty,*** q.v.), e.g., "In vendor and vendee the suffixes -or and -ee are from the Latin."

vendue, public vendue: an auction, e.g., "Many early documents speak of matters sold at public vendue." Also see ***outcry.***

venereal diseases: See ***chancre***, see ***clap***, and see ***syphilis.***

venire facias, venire, venireman: usually that ***writ*** (q.v.) or list of citizens ordered to appear as prospective jurors, e.g., "A notation that an ancestor appeared on the venire or venire facias, or was a venireman, means that he or she was qualified and had been selected as a prospective juror during that ***term of court*** (q.v.)."

venter: any of the three cavities of the body, i.e., the head, chest, and abdomen, e.g., "Early writings of physicians and ***chirurgeons*** (q.v.) often speak of ***distempers*** (q.v.) within one of the venters."

venue: that county or place where an event is said to have taken place or where one may demand that a lawsuit be heard, e.g., "The property was in Rowan County, so venue for an action in detainer was also there."

vera, vera., ver., vera record: abbreviations for "verified" often found at the conclusion of early documents, and followed by the name of the clerk or other verifying officer, revealing that the document is a true copy or is exact when compared as against another copy or the original, e.g., "In the 1679 inventory, following the words Vera record, the clerk of Surry placed a ***"crossed p"*** (q.v.) and then his initials, meaning 'per himself'."

veranda: a covered portico or porch, e.g., "Verandas were a common feature of Victorian houses."

verify, verification: usually, an oath as to the truth or validity of some writing; occasionally, an oath as to an oral statement, e.g., "He verified the complaint of the lawsuit."

vertical files: See ***family name files.***

vest, to; vested: rights or title that has devolved or become established in some person, firm, accrued, absolute; an interest that may not be divested from the new owner without some voluntary action or inaction on his part, e.g., "When the land was conveyed 'to Sarah for life, and then to her daughter, Anne', at the death of Sarah the entire interest was said to have vested in Anne.

vesting: usually, better-to-fine fabrics (***stuffs***, q.v.) to be used for the making of vests (***waistcoats***, q.v.), e.g., "By 1844, A. H. Hyatt of Findlay, Ohio was advertising 'vestings' for sale."

vestry, vestrymen: in the American colonies, the entirety of the ministry, elders or church wardens and the parishioners; occasionally, a small room in a church; often, a committee or group of people (early, usually affluent men or women) appointed to tend to the physical condition and business affairs of a church, e.g., "The vestry register contained notes as to various activities of the church, congregation, and the minister, including some baptisms, deaths and repairs to the church"; "William Hunt was a 17th-century vestryman in Charles City County."

veteran: in genealogy, anyone who served in the military for any period of time (whether the service was by conscription—***draft***, q.v.—or voluntarily), in any ***militia*** (q.v.) unit or in the service of the federal, state, or territorial government or militia, and who was separated from that service unit by other than a dishonorable disharge, e.g., "Matheny was a veteran, having served during the Revolution in the militia from Shenandoah County."

Veterans of Foreign Wars: See ***V.F.W.***

veterinarians: early physicians and ***chirurgeons*** (q.v.) also cared for livestock and especially valuable horses and dogs, e.g., "As early as the 1640s, the records reveal that John Spilman recovered his fees for veterinary care of a horse belonging to Bater."

vicar: a priest, clergyman or parson of a church (impropriated) who receives a salary or some part of the tithes and total income of the church served by that person; one who assists a bishop, e.g., "Where there is a mother church, the vicars often are paid an amount determined without regard to how much further additional or increased income the church might gain."

Victorian, Victorian/Edwardian: pertaining to the years of the reign of England's Queen Victoria (1837-1901) and her son Edward VII (1901-1910), e.g., "Throughout the 100 years between 1850 and 1950, and even until now, Victorian and ***Edwardian*** (q.v.) rules of personal conduct have dominated the American scene."

Victorian period: that name given the period 1840-1900 (Queen Victoria's reign) during which dark colors, massive, often ostentatious, Baroque, Gothic, and geometrically elaborate designs in furniture and architecture dominated, e.g., "Of the 'antiques' marketed in the last quarter of the 20th century, Victorian pieces were the most common."

victualer: a grocer or seller, quite usually of unprepared food, e.g., "The ships' victualer made a handsome profit by supplying the ship with foodstuffs." Also see ***victuals, vittles.***

victualling house: a business that served food and drink, without dancing, entertainment or lodging; a restaurant, usually serving alcoholic beverages, e.g., "In 1679 John Clifford was granted leave to open a victualling house in Salem, Massachusetts."

victuals, vittles: often, any food; sometimes, ready-to-eat food, e.g., "He was the railroad's victualer"; "The many early references of seeing to or gaining the wherewithal for the family vittles referred to ordinary daily foods or nutritional necessities."

videlicet, viz.: "to-wit" and "that is" are videlicets; that symbol or term indicating that the words following are comments or itemizations elucidating the remark, e.g., "His comments that 'the livestock, viz., two cows, three horses, and a mule, were bequeathed to the eldest son' was an example of the use of the videlicet."

vinegar of the 4 thieves: a room freshener, especially for ***chambers*** (q.v.) of the sick, e.g., "Brittany wrote 'To make vinegar of the 4 thieves, to a gallon of strong vinegars (in an ***earthenware*** (q.v.) container) she added a handful each of leaves of lavender, sage, rosemary, wormwood, rue, and mint; the covered container then was left in the hottest sun for 2 weeks, after which it was carefully drained, and the fluid was bottled with a clove of garlic in each bottle'."

vinous liquors: See ***liquors***.

vintner: one who sells wine, e.g., "Wine shops are operated by vintners."

virgate: a very early term meaning ¼ ***hide*** (q.v.), about 30 acres, e.g., "The words hide and virgate are only very rarely seen, and then usually in the records of New England and the middle colonies."

virginal: a common, small, square or rectangular plucked stringed musical instrument held in the lap, e.g., "Virginals were perhaps the most common of the stringed instruments found in the early colonies."

Virginia (Merrimac), C.S.S.: See ***warships, American***.

Virginia cloth, Virginia plain: plain, unbleached, ***homespun*** (q.v.) fabric from which work and slaves' clothing were made, e.g., "Many early North Carolina inventories reveal quantities of Virginia cloth."

Virginia reel: from an early Scottish dance (reel, rele) brought to Virginia in the 17th century, modified, and very much enjoyed by colonials, e.g., "At the party, Jean and Evan danced several waltzes and as many Virginia reels."

Virginia rum: probably, rum made in Virginia or specifically for Virginia merchants, e.g., "The 1772 inventory revealed a 'half barrel of Virginia Rum'."

virtuous: as now, e.g., "A 19th-century Georgia court said that a woman is virtuous if '...she has never had sexual intercourse with another, though both her mind and heart be impure.'"

vital statistics: information important to the efficient operation of government; dates of births, deaths, marriages and divorces, number of children, mental disability, etc., e.g., "By the end of the first quarter of the 20th-century all states required the collection of the vital statistics of that state"; "The Ohio Bureau of Vital Statistics is located in Columbus."

vittal, vittals: a corruption of the word victual. See ***victuale***r and see ***victuals***.

vittles: See ***victuals***.

vixen: a female fox, early viewed as a ***varmint*** (q.v.) upon which bounties were paid, e.g., "The vixen had 4 ***cubs*** (q.v.)."

viz.: See ***videlicet***.

vizard: a mask or pretense, e.g., "The early court report said that the 'vizard would be taken off and his wickedness plainly demonstrated'."

void, voidable: for genealogical purposes, void meant that the intended result never took place or certain activity was ineffectual in accomplishing that which was intended; voidable meant that knowledge has been gained or acts done in the time period since the original acts, agreement or bargain were done or made, which acts permit or require rescission or change, e.g., "A marriage between 14-year-olds is void; a marriage between people who thought they were divorced but were not is voidable."

voider, dish basket: a deep basket, usually of wicker, into which the dishes and eating utensils were placed as they were cleared from a table, e.g., "Voiders were uncommon in poor households."

voyageur: Fr. for voyager; the name given early French explorers, traders and trappers of Canada and the American Northwest Territory (q.v.), e.g., "The French voyageurs were trading with the Indians in central Illinois before 1750."

W

waffle iron: as now, a small, hinged, iron griddle with long handles used to bake waffles in a fireplace, e.g., "The waffle irons saw much use on cold winter mornings."

wag: Johnson says, one who is "ludicrously mischievous"; one known for frequent humorous repartee or humorous quips, e.g., "Jeannie called him a wag when he said that Tennesseans were Virginians with bad grammar."

wag clock, wag on the wall clock: usually, only the works of a tall clock, so named because the pendulum appeared like a dog's tail and was designed as to hang on the wall until a cabinet might be made, e.g., "Maggie and Will hoped someday to have the village cabinetmaker make a 'grandfather' cabinet for their wag clock." Also see ***grandfather, grandmother clocks.***

Wagon Road, Great; Great Philadelphia: that heavily travelled route of immigration to the west and south that extended from Philadelphia west to Lancaster, thence through the Shenandoah Valley (the "Valley Road") and into the Carolinas, Georgia, etc., and especially to the area near present Salisbury and Rowan County, NC, e.g., "Many of the Germans of eastern Pennsylvania ended up in central Tennessee by travelling the Great Wagon Road and then the Walton Road."

wagon: a general term for any animal drawn vehicle used for general hauling and utility purposes, e.g., "Those of high station had carriages, while the bulk of society rode in wagons." Also see ***carriage.***

wagoner: a ***teamster*** (q.v.) not for hire, e.g., "Though Drake was hired principally for his knowledge and skill in the care and training of horses, he quite often served as the wagoner for the Fergusons of Malvern Hill."

wagonmaker: an ancient occupation or calling; one who had knowledge of the many parts of a wagon and the methods of best constructing and assembling such, e.g., "As a wagonmaker, he often needed the services of the ***blacksmith***, ***wheelwright***, and ***harnessmaker*** (all, q.v.)."

wainscot, wainscotting, wainscot chair: wooden paneling, especially in halls and doorways; a very early, heavy, usually oak, hickory, or chestnut chair with a solid back, e.g., "The wainscotting was walnut and butternut"; "The wainscot chair dated from the 1650s."

wainwrights and coachmakers, tools of: many tools were unique to wainwrights, e.g., "An inventory that includes compass planes, fellies, linchpins, samsons, strakes, tires, and travellers may reveal the occupation of a wainwright or a coachmaker."

wair: a measure of lumber, equaling two yards by one foot by one inch, or 6 board feet of lumber, e.g., "By the period of the American Revolution, the word wair seems to have been abandoned in favor of 'board feet'."

waistcoat, wescot, weskit: early, a man's vest, later a vest for either man or woman, e.g., "His weskit was of burgundy silk"; "She wore a red velvet waistcoat."

wake: a vigilance or 'watching over' of a corpse, especially throughout the nights before burial; in America, usually accompanied by celebration, drinking, and partying, e.g., "Wakes came into existence centuries ago to prevent the burial of those thought 'dead' who actually were but in a coma."

walk the dog: an early superlative among men operating heavy or large machinery, probably derived from the fact that in the early days only the very finest of dogs would be walked, and even then only by those of the upper class, all other such animals fending for themselves, e.g., "When the big steam engine performed beyond the expectations of everybody, Evan smiled broadly and announced that it 'flat out was walking the dog'." Also see ***flat***.

walk: See ***gaits***.

Walker, Walking Horse, Tennessee Walker: a smooth-gaited saddle horse, usually a mix of Morgan and Standardbred, noted for the exaggerated high step of the front feet, e.g., "The Walker had been ***sored*** (q.v.), hence had a very high step."

walking wheel: See ***spinning wheel.***

wall-eye, wall-eyed, wall eye, walleyed: usually, a horse with an unusual amount of white or light gray coloring in one or both its eyes, or one with near white or colorless irises, e.g., "Jesse rode a walleyed Morgan." Also see ***horses***.

wallet: unlike now, a small bag in which necessaries were carried for a trip of some distance; a bag or knapsack carried by travelers and used for their necessaries, e.g., "For the requirements of the average work day, a ***purse*** (q.v.) took the place of the wallet"; "The reference to placing his wallet in the barroom did not mean he left his billfold there." Also see ***pocketbook***.

wallop: unlike now, to boil, e.g., "When Bethany wrote in the recipe that one cup of walloped cider was required, she meant that one cup was to be measured after the cider had been boiled."

Walton Road: See ***roads, early.***

wampum: strung beads usually made from shell and used as currency by some American Indians; an early medium of settlement, e.g., "Wampum also occasionally served as currency for the white colonists."

wamus: a short coat of heavy, warm, homemade cloth, common to the rural areas of the north, e.g., "The Carners of early Centre County were known for their red or deep blue wamuses given as gifts at Christmas."

waning: See ***waxing and waning.***

War Between The States: See ***Civil War.***

War for Southern Independence: See ***Civil War.***

War of 1812: that armed conflict between the United States and England during the years 1812-1814, e.g., "The British burned Washington during the War of 1812, and destroyed some of the Decennial Census of 1790 and much of the North Carolina militia records."

War of Independence, American Revolution: that armed conflict of the period 1775-1783/5 between the American colonies (with the aid of the French late in the war) and the British, as a result of victory in which the colonies became the United States, e.g., "His service in the Revolution made his descendants eligible for the ***D.A.R.*** (q.v.) and the ***S.A.R.*** (q.v.)."

War of The Rebellion: See ***Civil War.***

War of the Regulation: See ***Regulators***.

ward: a political subdivision of a city or town having very limited jurisdiction in matters of voting and elections, sanitary regulations, fire and police protection, and enumerations, e.g., "The ward and ***precinct*** (q.v.) leaders of early 20th-century New York City had wide political influence, though very little authority."

wardrobe: a common, tall, wide, deep, often collapsible, usually two doored cabinet of the 19th and early 20th centuries, without legs, and having a divider, hooks, pegs, and often a shelf and drawers, used as a ***closet*** (q.v.) for the hanging of coats and clothing in general, especially in the winter; also, a room in which clothes were kept; a closet; e.g., "Her 7 foot wardrobe was of walnut and broke down into 6 pieces for moving or for summer storage." Also see ***armoire***.

warehouse receipt: a written document providing evidence of the existence of personal property belonging to one person in the hands of another for hire (warehouseman); often used as currency by early colonials especially where cotton and tobacco was being used as the medium of settlement, e.g., "He paid for his horse with a warehouse receipt for 2 ***hogsheads*** (q.v.) of tobacco." Also see ***medium of exchange.***

warming pan: a ***bed warmer*** (q.v.) or a shallow pan for warming food, e.g., "In association with several other kitchen utensils, the Parker estate of 1679 listed 'a warming pan'."

warn out, warn out of town, send out of town: an expression of New England (and before that, England) meaning that those not eligible for citizenship or a place in town or those thought undesirable were told by the authorities to leave town, e.g., "Failure to comply with an order warning out often brought harsh punishment."

warrants: in law, an order by a court directing that a person or property be taken into custody; in genealogy, likewise, and also those written documents issued to persons in exchange for military service or contributions of money, goods and services, enabling the recipient to gain lands or assets previously belonging to the U.S. Government, the states, or the colonies, e.g., "John Carner sold his warrant for land."

warranty deed: a formal written document transferring interests in land and containing specific warranties concerning the extent of the rights transferred; the most common deeds used, these contain a description of the property, names of the buyers and sellers, are acknowledged ("notarized", "sworn to"), almost always are now recorded and, especially early, contain a recital of the consideration given in exchange for the property, e.g., "Through the descriptions contained, warranty deeds often make it possible for the researcher to locate the precise land owned by an ancestor."

warren: a place for the keeping of rabbits or hutches for rabbits, e.g., "The English surnames Warren and Warner (warrener) sometimes derived from the occupations of keeping rabbits or building warrens for rabbits." Also see ***occupations as surnames.***

wars: those conflicts, whether declared by government as a war or not, that bring men and women to duty with weapons in the public cause, e.g., "The French and Indian War took place between 1754 and 1763, and the so-called Indian wars for the most part were during the 2nd half of the nineteenth century."

warships, American: ships bearing armament and weapons and men trained to fight them, e.g., "A list of the most famous American warships might include, from the Revolution: the *Bon Homme Richard* and *Ranger*; from the War of 1812: the U.S.S. *Constitution, Chesapeake*, and *Lawrence*; from the Civil War: the U.S.S. *Monitor*, C.S.S. *Merrimac* (Virginia), and blockade runners *Minnesota* and *Alabama*; from the Spanish-American War: the U.S.S. *Maine*; from World War I era: the U.S.S. *Langley*; and from World War II: U.S.S. *Arizona*, U.S.S. *Franklin*, U.S.S. *Lexington*, U.S.S. *Enterprise, PT-109*, U.S.S. *Indianapolis* and U.S.S. *North Carolina*." Also see ***ship of the line***, and see ***squadron***.

wart: a proturbance in the skin, usually of other than flesh color, e.g., "Virtually every person has warts occasionally, some lasting a lifetime." Also see ***wen***.

wartrace, warpath, Indian trail, Indian path: the trails, paths or routes used by American Indians for travel, war, trade or otherwise, e.g., "U.S. Route 127 extending between Chattanooga and Cincinnati and beyond follows an ancient Indian path by which Southern Indians, including Cherokees, traded with those of the North, including the Shawnee and Delaware people."

wash boiler, wash kettle: a large, oblong, rather deep, lidded, often copper (early) and later galvanized boiling pan or small tub, usually of 5 to 10 gallon capacity, and used to boil and wash clothes, e.g., "The old copper wash boilers often were called 'copper kettles'."

washboard: a common household tool consisting of a small board with a ridged surface, one end of which was placed in a ***tub*** (q.v.) of water, against which soap and clothes were rubbed together to clean or "wash" them, e.g., "Before the 20th century, almost every housewife owned and had used a washboard."

Washington Artillery: See ***military combat units, famous***.

washstand: a small chest used in ***bed chambers*** (q.v.), usually having 2 or 3 drawers and a doored compartment below, and a splash board and towel rack at the top back of and above the work surface, and upon which were placed a ***pitcher and bowl*** (q.v.), ***shaving mirror*** (q.v.), etc., to be used for ***stand-up baths*** (q.v.) and refreshment after sleeping, e.g., "Margaret's washstands were Victorian in style and made of oak."

wassail, wassailing: a liquor made of apple juice, sugar, and ale; the word "wassail" literally meaning "to be healthy"; this drink was and still is typically served in cold weather at Christmas time, often carried and consumed while singing carols from house to house, when the carolers traditionally drink to the health of their neighbors; "The old Christmas song that mentions wassailing was speaking of a favorite liquor of the early colonies and old England."

watch, stand the watch, stand watch, stand duty: military terms meaning the specified hours, usually 4, during which guards or lookouts are posted at specific places within warships, forts, camps, or bases, e.g., "Every old sailor knew that the mid-watch was either from 10:00 PM until

2:00 AM or from midnight to 4:00 AM"; "Virtually every enlisted man in the armed forces was required to stand duty from time to time."

water cures: See ***take the waters.***

water witch: See ***dowser, etc.***

watercourse: a running stream, e.g., "Often the use of the word watercourse in a description makes it possible to specifically locate a property that once belonged to an ancestor."

waters, taking the: See ***take the waters.***

watershed: usually in genealogical records, an area of land being drained; sometimes, a crest of a hill, e.g., "The area around Nashville is in the Cumberland River watershed."

waterspout: as now; sometimes early, a catastrophic event caused by great amounts of water, e.g., "The great wave of water that destroyed Johnstown, Pennsylvania in 1889 was spoken of as a waterspout by at least two newspapers." Also see ***fantasie.***

wattle and daub: materials of construction; sticks and mud or clay, e.g., "Wattle and daub chimneys were common, especially in those Southern tidewater colonies where native stone was in very scarce supply."

waving fence: See ***snake fence.***

wax on a wall, tighter than the: a superlative referring to the tiny drops of hot candle wax that are splattered on a wall when it has been blown out, rather than snuffed, and when the person has not placed his or her hand behind the candle to prevent such spray, e.g., "Sarah and Jean agreed that, 'Uncle Jack was as tight as the wax on the wall and still had the first dime he ever earned'."

waxing and waning: as now, but usually the movements and visibility of the moon, e.g., "Because of its effects on tides, shipping, and its supposed effects upon the human body, crops and planting, many descriptions of the comparative visibility of the moon's surface have been used over the centuries, a few of which are, when the moon is invisible by reason of the shadow of the earth, it is said to be in the dark of the moon; when it is fully visible, it is full, that period also described as the light of the moon, and in the phases in between, called quarter moons, if appearing from the dark (waxing) it is in first quarter, if disappearing after full (waning) it is in last quarter, and if all but disappeared, it was known as the 'old of the moon'." Also see ***tides, etc.***

weathercock, weathervane: as now, a device movable by even a slight breeze, usually placed atop a house or barn and shaped in the silhouette of a long-tailed rooster (or other animal), which will rotate and thereby show the direction of the wind, e.g., "Early weathercocks usually were made of brass, lead, or wood."

weavers, itinerant or traveling: weavers of often considerable talent who traveled the countryside weaving rugs and fancy and intricate patterned cloth (***stuff,*** q.v.), e.g., "As with the ***catwhipper*** (q.v.), itinerant weavers brought news and gossip of the day"; "Unlike now, many early homes and families had looms and did their own weaving of cloth, rugs, etc."

week, a week: refers to a day more than one week but less than two weeks in the future, e.g., "On Sunday, he said he would leave 'Tuesday week', meaning on the Tuesday following the Tuesday that was within the same week as that Sunday"; "In relating to him on Friday that she was leaving a week from that coming Sunday, she said 'I'll be going Sunday a week'."

weeper: anything worn as an indication that the wearer is in mourning, e.g., "As weepers, she wore a black veil and black gloves."

weir: a fence set in a flowing stream to catch fish, e.g., "They would set the weir, then go upstream and wade toward it."

well laid on: an expression found in court orders directing a ***sheriff*** (q.v.) to whip criminals or ***slaves*** (q.v.), meaning that the blows should not be softened or made gentle, e.g., "In 1686, for having an illegitimate 'mulatto' child, Mary Poore was sentenced to 'tenn lashes on her bare back well layd on'."

Well-born Men: a tribunal of early New York, e.g., "Early New Amsterdam records reveal activities of the Well-born Men.

Welsh cupboard: a full open cupboard with a shallow work space between shelves above and shelves below, e.g., "Mrs. Roberts' 1838 Welsh cupboard yet remains in the family."

wen, win: a small proturbance in the skin, usually a sebaceous cyst and usually of flesh color, e.g., "Paul commented that wens had appeared behind his ears since boyhood." Also see ***wart***.

wench: on this continent, a slave woman, usually young, e.g., "Unlike in the British Isles, early Virginia records seem to reveal the word wench only when the reference was to slave women."

wescot: See ***waistcoat***.

weskit: See ***waistcoat***.

West Florida Republic: land between the Perdido and the Mississippi, formerly claimed by Spain, was seized on 26 Sept., 1810, by a group of Southern businessmen/expansionists, following which Congress and President Monroe incorporated it within the territory of Mississippi, e.g., "The West Florida Republic legally ceased to exist on May 14, 1812."

Westward Movement: that mass immigration of families to the western frontier of the American colonies and states that took place throughout the 16th, 17th, 18th, and 19th centuries; the phenomenon resulting from the availability of opportunity and inexpensive land on the western edge of settlement, e.g., "One of the main routes of the Westward Movement was up the St. Lawrence River, thence through the Great Lakes to Minnesota, Wisconsin, and beyond."

wet nurse: a woman employed to nurse and provide breast milk to the child of another woman, e.g., "During the nineteenth century women whose infants had died often sought employment by advertising for positions as wet nurses."

wet plate photography, wet plate process: an early process by which plates coated with light sensitive materials were exposed and processed into "negatives," from which photographic prints were made, e.g., "The wet plate process so well known from Mathew Brady's work was still actively pursued by W. L. Midlam as late as 1915." Also see ***what's it wagon.***

wether: a castrated male sheep less than a year old, so sterilized to improve the quality of the meat, e.g., "The early Bater inventory listed a ram, three ewes, and a wether."

wetter off, wetter-off: usually, an apprentice or one new to the ***glass making*** (q.v.) trade, e.g., "His occupation, having been listed as a wetter-off, was most unusual, and reveals that he probably was learning or working in the art of glass making."

whale bone, whalebone: the elastic-like, tough, flexible thin strips of bony material that are the substitutes for teeth in some species of whale, long used as the stiffeners in some ***hoops*** (q.v.), ***bustles*** (q.v.) and early corsets, and replaced by celluloid early in the 20th century, e.g., "Misses Diane, Bethany and Brittany would have nothing but true whalebone in their **hoops** (q.v.)."

whang: other than the common usage, leather strapping or leather lacing and the leather used for making such items; perhaps slang for intoxicating liquor, whiskey, etc., e.g., "The inventory revealed a 'bundle of whang'"; "She wrote that the ranch hands probably would return from town full of whang."

what's it wagon: a storage, processing and laboratory wagon used by early travelling photographers and equipped to serve as a "dark room" and film developer, e.g., "Old West letters and newspapers often refer to the arrival of a photographer and his what's it wagon."

wheel barrow, wheelbarrow, wheelbarra: a single-wheeled, two-handled device to carry any heavy item, especially earth, stone, etc., e.g., "The fully loaded wheelbarrow was more than the boy could handle."

wheel lock: See ***flintlock***.

wheel pit: See ***millers' tools.***

wheel stick: a short, simple stick used to move the wheel on a ***spinning wheel*** (q.v.), e.g., "Any short dried piece of wood might serve as a wheel stick."

wheel: See ***high wheel cycle***. Also see ***spinning wheel.***

Wheeler's Cavalry: See ***military combat units, famous.***

wheelers, wheel horses: that horse or horses harnessed closest to the front wheels of the wagon or carriage, usually the most powerful of the animals in the hitch, e.g., "Old Lew Wickersham had a pair of blacks as the wheelers, a pair of grays as ***swing horses*** (q.v.), and a pair of whites as leaders. Also see ***leaders***.

wheelman: usually, a male bicycle rider, e.g., "It was said that to be a wheelman on a high-wheel bicycle required strong buttocks."

wheels: See ***millers' tools,*** and see ***tire***.

wheelwright, wheel maker: an ancient occupation or calling; one having the knowledge needed to make spokes, hubs, axles, ***tires*** (q.v.), etc., needed for spinning wheels, wagons, carriages, turnstiles, and the like, e.g., "Charles Carner was an early Pennsylvania wheelwright."

whelp: a recently weaned puppy; occasionally, a word of gentle reprimand for children, e.g., "Maggie often smiled and called the boys whelps as she corrected their little errant ways."

whetstone, rubstone: a stone, found in many grits and sizes, used to sharpen knives, edged instruments, and weapons, e.g., "He had two sharpening stones, one for his ***hatchet*** (q.v.) and axe, and another for his wife's ***scissors*** (q.v.) and his ***penknife*** (q.v.)."

whiffletree: see ***swingletree***.

Whigs: in the U.S., an early political party of Patriots favoring the ***War of Independence*** (q.v.); later, as opposed to the ***Democrats*** (q.v.), they sought high tariffs and liberal construction of the Constitution, e.g., "Jefferson, especially in light of his work in framing the Constitution, had little tolerance for the views of the early Whigs." Also see ***Tories***.

whip: as now; one who drove a stagecoach or other animal-drawn, passenger vehicle, including a trolley or horsecar, e.g., "When carrying valuable goods or money, in addition to the whip, an Overland Stage crew also included one or more men who 'rode shotgun'." Also see ***yahoo***.

whipping: a method of punishing by use of a whipping post and a harsh leather strap—a "whipping strap", e.g., "Whipping was not outlawed in the U.S. until February 28, 1839."

whippletree: See ***swingletree***.

whirligig, top: a "top"; a toy that could be spun with the hands, a movable screw mechanism or a string, e.g., "A many-colored whirligig was a highly favored toy to be given upon special occasions."

whish broom: See ***whisk***.

whisk, whisk broom, whish broom: as now, a small, hand-held broom used to sweep crumbs, small bits of debris, etc., e.g., "Because of the gentle sound it made, Maggie called the little broom a whish broom."

Whiskey Insurrection, Whiskey Rebellion: that 1794 revolt by western Pennsylvania citizens concerning taxes levied upon whiskey, which resulted in Washington calling up the ***militia*** (q.v.) to quell the uprising; two participants were convicted of treason and later were pardoned by Washington, e.g., "Many participants in the Whiskey Insurrection have descendants living today."

whisky, whiskey: surprisingly, the word apparently was unknown to Johnson; an alcoholic drink distilled from grains in Scotland, e.g., "While today we refer to many different alcoholic beverages made from several grains as whiskies, in very early times only that made in Scotland was so-called."

whistle stop: a regular or appointed place or station where trains stopped if passengers or people with freight appeared upon the sounding of the train whistle or some other recognized signal, e.g., "While Owen's Station was called a whistle stop, in fact trains stopped there only when a bright metal signal was raised at that ***station*** (q.v.)."

white lightning: See ***corn whiskey***.

white mule: See ***corn whiskey***.

White Russian: usually, a citizen or emigrant from the nation of Byelorussia, e.g., "The Kliewers were White Russians from Minsk, the capital of Byelorussia, and emigrated in 1899."

Whitecaps: an organization of racists first formed in Tennessee and outlawed in 1896, e.g., "In practice, the Whitecaps did not differ from the ***Ku Klux Klan*** (q.v.)."

whites, the: a term used to describe a matter of feminine health; leukorrhea, e.g., "Dr. Duponcas advertised that his 'Golden Monthly Pills' would surely cure the whites in all women."

whitesmith: See ***tinsmith.***

whiteware: any white pottery, e.g., "She had several whiteware bowls."

Whitsuntide: the feast of the Pentecost held the 5th day after Easter Sunday, e.g., "For the most part, Whitsuntide was observed by members of the Church of England."

whizzer: See ***games (of children).***

Whole Duty of Man, The: a book of duties and responsibilities of a Church of England Christian, first published in London in 1694 and thereafter in several editions, e.g., "Next to the Bible and the ***Book of Common Prayer*** (q.v.), The Whole Duty of Man perhaps was the most well known book in the early South."

whole shebang, the: See ***shebang, the whole.***

whooping cough, hooping cough: as now, a deep, racking cough, e.g., "Whooping cough often was treated with chloroform, cod liver oil, tannin, or musk."

whorehouse: See ***sporting house.***

wicker, wicker furniture: furniture, usually woven of pliant willow branches, e.g., "Rattan ***furniture*** (q.v.) is sometimes referred to as "wickerwork."

widow's peak: a point on the forehead formed by the hairline of a woman, early said to be a sign that the woman was sure to be widowed, e.g., "The young woman lived in fear for her children by reason of her prominent widow's peak."

widows' pensions: in genealogy, those sums of money and other benefits awarded widows and (later) widowers by reason of prior military service of or contributions of time, services, or supplies by their deceased spouses, e.g., "As a result of her husband's ***War of 1812*** (q.v.) service, Martha Midlam received $8.00 per month as a widow's pension.

wig block: as now, a rounded form upon which wigs are shaped and stored, e.g., "There are many wig blocks shown in early households."

wildcat, lynx: as now, e.g., "By reason of their depredations of chickens, ducks, and young and small farm animals, wildcats were perceived as perhaps the worst of the common predators."

Wilderness Road: that somewhat ill-defined and well used route of substantial westward movement extending westward from the area of Salisbury, North Carolina, through the several gaps in the Blue Ridge and the Smoky Mts., thence through Cumberland Gap to Kentucky and north or through Crab Orchard Gap to Nashville and beyond, e.g., "Part of the family moved from Tidewater Virginia to western Tennessee across the Wilderness Road." Also see ***roads, early.***

will, to take against a: See ***take against a will,*** and see ***dissent.***

will: that writing which sets forth the last wishes and intended ***devises*** (q.v.) (real estate) and ***bequests*** (q.v.) (personal property) of a person; to be a will, the document must precisely comply with the law of the jurisdiction or state, and all states require at least two witnesses, e.g., "His will named three persons as ***devisees*** (q.v.), and was executed on 2 December 1769." Also see ***holographic will,*** and see ***nuncupative will.***

wimple: a head scarf tied under the chin, similar to that worn by nuns, e.g., "Wimples were common in early times."

windgun: a very early term meaning a "B.B. gun" or air rifle, e.g., "Windguns as toys for affluent children were known well before 1800."

windlass: See ***millers' tools.***

window curtains: sometimes, as now; more often early, a drawable drapery or tapestry to be hung in front of windows (***lights***, q.v.), e.g., "Newspaper advertisements of the mid-19th century lead us to suspect that the term window curtains often referred to drawable draperies."

window lights: See ***light***, and see ***oiled paper.***

Windsor chair: a chair of original American styling (c1700-1825), simple in design, light, and very strong, with a back of 5 to 9 spindles (the more, the older, usually), often made of hickory, pine, maple, ash, or of other hard wood that was on hand, often with a very shallow, saddle-shaped seat, and almost always painted and decorated, e.g., "As was typical, her Windsor side chairs had seven spindles and were painted."

wingback chairs: a common design, first seen in the side pieces of colonial chairs and still popular, armed, upholstered, with 6 to 8 inch legs, the back wrapping around to the sides of one's head, thereby preventing ***drafts*** (q.v.), e.g., "Allison had two tufted wingback chairs, each with a ***center table*** (q.v.) to accompany it."

winner, hands down: See ***hands down winner.***

winnowing, winnow: to separate grain from chaff, e.g., "Early winnowing was done by hand by agitating a large, shallow, sieve-like basket full of the plant picked."

winter kitchen: See ***summer kitchen.***

wire draw bench: See ***silversmiths' tools.***

wire draw block: See ***silversmiths' tools.***

witch ball: an open glass ball, often with a nipple or hole in the side, containing potpourri, colored paper or string, or flowers, and hung in windows, supposedly to ward off evil spirits, e.g., "While most women of the nineteenth century used witch balls as decoration, a few still believed that they warded off evil."

witch trials: See ***Salem Witch Trials.***

witchcraft: in the common view, the practice of sorcery, magic, and the casting of spells, etc., e.g., "Charges of engaging in witchcraft in the American colonies ended for the most part with the ***Salem Witch Trials*** (q.v.) of 1691 and 1692."

withe: any long flexible and stout stem of a plant used to tie and wrap materials together or used as a whip, e.g., "Drake and Evan tied him to the wagon, then took willow withes and pretended to be driving old dog, Sparky."

withey basket, withy basket: A handled basket made of thin, flexible twigs or limbs, e.g., "Allison wrote that she had made a withey basket from thin willow limbs."

witness: attestation; one who gives testimony, e.g., "Since she was present when the event occurred, Anne was summoned to be a witness to the facts."

woodburner, diamond stack woodburner: an early railroad locomotive that burned wood as fuel instead of coal, the word diamond being descriptive of the shape of some smokestacks, e.g., "Union Pacific's '#19' and Central Pacific's 'Jupiter' were the woodburners at ***Promontory Point*** (q.v.)"; "The characteristic diamond shape of the stack on many early wood burning locomotives revealed that the stack contained a spark arrestor to prevent fires along the right-of-way."

wooden hammer: See ***mallet.***

wooden horse: a wooden beam, two or three inches in width, placed horizontally at such a height that a man strapped to it could not touch the ground with his feet; a cruel and terribly painful 17th- and 18th-century device for punishment of errant soldiers and sometimes citiaens by which a man's entire weight rested on the area of his prostate, e.g., "The use of the wooden horse, as in 17th-century Salem, was one of the 'cruel and unusual' punishments later prohibited by our Bill Of Rights."

woodsrider: a superintendent of cutting or lumbering of trees, or surveying timber in a woods, e.g., "An early Florida court recognized the title of woodsrider as an occupation or calling."

wool mercer: See ***mercer.***

wool wheel: See ***spinning wheel.***

words, colonial, derived from other sources: See ***Spanish people, influence of; New World influence; Scotch-Irish influence; Indians, American, influence of; French influence; German influence; Italian influence***; and ***Irish influence.***

work beast: any draft animal, e.g., "His work beasts were well harnessed." Also see ***draft animals.***

work horses: See ***draft animals.***

work table: unlike now, any of many styles of small to medium, square, usually singly or doubly drawered tables, either with or without knee space beneath, e.g., "Marty's fine cherry work table was of Hepplewhite styling."

World War I: that armed conflict that took place between 1914 and 1919 and involved nations from across the globe, with armed participation by the U.S. troops in 1918 and 1919, e.g., "Howard Carner was a part of the American Expeditionary Force (A.E.F.) in World War I."

World War II: that massive, worldwide, armed conflict that took place between 1938 and 1945 and involved nearly the entire world, armed participation by the U.S. having been from December 1941 till August 1945, e.g., "Leonard Cody drove a tank with Patton's great Third Army in World War II."

worsted: a fabric, usually of high quality, made entirely from wool or wool yarn, and probably originally made in the town of Worsted, England, e.g., "Griffith was said to be a maker of worsted"; "Worsted had gained a reputation for its fine woolen goods by the 16th century."

worth his salt, worth her salt: an expression concerning ambition or social worth and derived from the need for maintaining a quantity of salt for every member of a pioneer family in order that their meat and other food might be preserved; not worth one's salt meaning of little ambition, of little social worth, a lazy, shiftless person, e.g., "She said Jean's new boyfriend was really ***sorry*** (q.v.) and barely worth his salt."

worth the candle?, is the game: a very early expression questioning the measure of importance or enjoyment of a game suggested or being played, and deriving from the days when little else but candlelight was to be found in homes, e.g., "Sarah revealed her doubts when she smiled and asked the children if their game was worth the candle."

wrick, rick: as now, to strain or wrench a joint such as in the arm, ankle or back, e.g., "Diane wrote that her husband had 'wricked his back while helping to lift the ***sleepers*** (q.v.).'"

wringer, clothes wringer, clothes squeezer: with the coming of the Industrial Revolution, myriad new time savers were devised, including mechanical washing machines and cranked wringers for wet clothes, e.g., "The 1870s newspapers spoke glowingly of the newly available metal and rubber 'clothes squeezers'—wringers."

writ of estrepement: See ***estrepement, writ of.***

writ of scire facias: See ***scire facias.***

writ: in genealogy, any order by a court in the name of a government (federal, state or local) addressed to a ***sheriff*** (q.v.) or other law officer; a legal device used to direct an officer of the law to take some object, sum of money or person into custody or see to the accomplishment of some requirement of the court or law, e.g., "Writs ordering that action be taken against ancestors are often very revealing, and are commonly found in 'loose papers' and archival collections."

writing chair: any of many styles and shapes of chairs having a writing arm or surface mounted to one side, e.g., "Original Windsor writing chairs in passable condition are valued at several thousands of dollars."

writing desk: a small box with a hinged, raisable lid on which one might write, and beneath which paper and writing supplies were kept, often held in the lap, but sometimes on legs or a pedestal, e.g., "The Empire writing desk was of ***flame grain*** (q.v.) walnut and mounted on a pedestal." Also see ***desk.***

writs (extraordinary): See entries for ***certiorari, habeus corpus, procedendo, mandamus,*** and ***prohibition.***

writs of error: See ***error, writs of.***

written law: the law as set forth by legislatures, as opposed to the common law, i.e., case law, e.g., "The foundation of the present French legal system is the written law (Civil Law), and that system followed their people to Louisiana." Also see ***common law.***

wussy: unknown, e.g., "In 1894 Mikaila wrote that Mr. Echerd '...was no wussy lawyer'."

Wyoming Valley Massacre: See ***Cherry Valley and Wyoming Valley massacres.***

X, Y, Z

Xanthippe, patience of: derived from the ever-continuing patience shown by Xanthippe, the wife of Socrates, e.g., "Concerning his loss of job after job, Sally displayed the 'patience of Xanthippe'."

yahoo (pron. "yea-who"): an uncouth or vulgar person; one who drove a stagecoach or other animal-drawn passenger vehicle other than a trolley or horsecar, e.g., "Those who knew the driver well called him a 'real yahoo'." Also see ***whip.***

Yamassee War: 1715-c.1718; that series of conflicts pitting South Carolina settlers against the Yamassees and Creeks and resulting in the ouster of the whites from the area west of Savannah River, following which the settlers and the Cherokees drove the other Indians from the area and built forts at present Columbia and Port Royal, e.g., "The genealogist will yet find a few records of those Carolinians who took up arms in the Yamassee War."

Yankee cakes: doughnuts, e.g., "The Yankee cake cutters listed in the early 19th century likely were tin doughnut cutters."

Yankees: originally, a person from New England; after about 1855, those who declared allegiance to or lived in a Northern state, e.g., "Yankee Doodle was an expression well known in Revolutionary New England"; "The expression 'damn Yankees' stated a view of many in the ***Civil War*** (q.v.) and Reconstruction South."

yarn swift, yarn reel: a revolving reel for yarn, mounted on a pedestal, and usually either short to accommodate a sitting spinner or three to four feet in height for those who stood at a ***spinning wheel*** (q.v.), in the latter instance known as a standing yarn swift, e.g., "She had a yarn swift that had belonged to her great-grandmother." Also see ***reel.***

yaws, frambisia: severe, excreting lesions of the skin caused by a parasite, red to burgundy in color and peculiar to the South and the Caribbean Islands, e.g., "When yaws appeared, early physicians routinely applied ***turpentine*** (q.v.), quinine, and various Indian ointments."

yay big, yea-big: a common expression used with gestures to indicate comparative size of some object, e.g., "Drake held his arms out wide apart and indicated the fish he had seen was 'yay-big'."

yearling: any animal, but usually an equine or bovine, that has passed its first year of life, but not yet its second, e.g., "Since small imperfections were not yet apparent to most buyers, he always sold his colts as yearlings."

years allowance, yearly support, yearly provision: that sum in cash or assets set aside for or allowed at various early times (not until 1796 in North Carolina) to a widow for the support, food, and provisions needed by herself and her children during the year following her husband's death, e.g., "The Georgia court approved 630 pounds of tobacco as Mikaila's year's allowance."

yellow fever: See ***calenture.***

yeoman: early, quite usually one who owned or had previously owned land in small quantity, and also one who farmed his own land for his own benefit and profit, e.g., "He owned three acres and spoke of himself as a yeoman."

On the following page, from a 1776 Pennsylvania order to a sheriff, are seen the words "yeoman" describing Samuel Mann; "aforesaid" referring to the county already named in the first two words; "ten Pounds" describing the sum of money owed by Mann to another person; and "lawful money of Pennsylvania" describing the acceptable medium of settlement.

Cumberland County ss

April Term 1776.

Samuel Mann of Cumberland County Yeoman & John Mann of the
vere attached to answer David Moor of a Plea of Trespass on the
and Whereupon the said David complains that Whereas the said
the nineteenth Day of April in the Year of our Lord one tho
, twenty three at the County aforesaid made their certain Note
alled a promissory Note with their proper Hands subscribed b
ame Day & Year & delivered the same to the said David by
aid Samuel & John then & there promised to pay to the said D
the Sum of ten Pounds lawful Money of Pennsylvania at or upon
September in the Year of our Lord one thousand seven hundred
[illegible] whereof & by Force of the [illegible]

Yiddish: that language of Germanized Hebrew words, e.g., "As early as 1740 it was said that many New Yorkers spoke Yiddish."

yoke, yoake, yoke and irons: a sturdy contrivance used to link together for work purposes two ***draft animals*** (q.v.), and consisting of two padded wooden collars and a connecting wooden or iron arm, e.g., "The old yoke was retired when he got rid of the oxen."

Yom Kippur: the most solemn and sacred holiday of the Jewish calendar, celebrated on the 10th day of the first month of the Jewish calendar (Tishri), e.g., "In 1993, Yom Kippur was on September 25."

yonder, yon: an early Scotch-Irish and English expression carried to the South and indicative of distance relative to the speaker; a remnant of those references to distance expressed in the words "hither, thither and yon" (here, there, and beyond), e.g., "When she said 'look yonder', the listener knew to turn his eyes not to 'here' or 'there', but rather to look beyond those imaginary parameters."

zephyr: early and through the 19th century, a strong wind; now, usually a gentle breeze, e.g., "Mark Twain's description of the 'Washoe Zephyr' has brought laughter to millions of readers."

zeppelins: See ***lighter than air craft.***

Zouaves, Duryea: See ***military combat units, famous.***

ZR-3, the: See ***lighter than air craft.***